Mexican Watchdogs

Mexican Watchdogs

The Rise of a Critical Press since the 1980s

ANDREW PAXMAN

The University of North Carolina Press
Chapel Hill

© 2025 The University of North Carolina Press
All rights reserved

Set in Minion Pro by Westchester Publishing Services
Manufactured in the United States of America

Library of Congress Cataloging-in-Publication Data
Names: Paxman, Andrew, 1967–, author.
Title: Mexican watchdogs : the rise of a critical press since the 1980s /
    Andrew Paxman.
Description: Chapel Hill : The University of North Carolina Press, 2025. |
    Includes bibliographical references and index.
Identifiers: LCCN 2025015443 | ISBN 9781469684970 (cloth) | ISBN 9781469684987
    (paperback) | ISBN 9781469684994 (epub) | ISBN 9781469687414 (pdf)
Subjects: LCSH: Journalists—Mexico—History. | Journalists—Violence against—
    Mexico—History. | Public interest groups—Mexico—History. | Press and
    politics—Mexico—History—20th century. | Press and politics—Mexico—
    History—21st century. | BISAC: SOCIAL SCIENCE / Media Studies | POLITICAL
    SCIENCE / Political Process / Media & Internet
Classification: LCC PN4968 .P39 2025 | DDC 070.0972—dc23/eng/20250527
    LC record available at https://lccn.loc.gov/2025015443

Cover art: (*Top*) Ramón Alberto Garza Garcia interviews President Carlos Salinas for
El Norte in 1990, courtesy of Ramón Alberto Garza Garcia. (*Bottom*) Nayeli Roldán
asking a question of Andrés Manuel López Obrador, Mexico City, 2023, © Rogelio
Morales Ponce/Cuartoscuro.com.

This book will be made open access within three years of publication thanks to Path
to Open, a program developed in partnership between JSTOR, the American Council
of Learned Societies (ACLS), the University of Michigan Press, and the University of
North Carolina Press to bring about equitable access and impact for the entire
scholarly community, including authors, researchers, libraries, and university presses
around the world. Learn more at https://about.jstor.org/path-to-open/.

For product safety concerns under the European Union's General Product Safety
Regulation (EU GPSR), please contact gpsr@mare-nostrum.co.uk or write to the
University of North Carolina Press and Mare Nostrum Group B.V., Mauritskade 21D,
1091 GC Amsterdam, The Netherlands.

Contents

Illustrations

Map

Preface
A History of Violence and Resistance

Since 2006, when at least ten Mexican journalists were murdered, it has become a truism that Mexico is the most dangerous country in the Americas for reporters and one of the riskiest in the world. That year was a watershed in the country's recent history, marking the start of President Felipe Calderón's "war" against the so-called drug cartels, or more accurately, crime syndicates.[1] Calderón's policy sent the homicide rate spiraling past 20,000 per year; with it, the killing of journalists and other assaults on the press climbed too. "Narcos" were not solely to blame: Corrupt agents of the state, such as municipal politicians and police chiefs, were often the masterminds. Also to blame were state governors, by fostering through their inaction a culture of impunity, and by revictimizing the dead with claims that journalists had somehow courted their fate. Further to blame were Mexico's presidents, for failing to commit sufficient resources and political capital to solving the crimes, thereby signaling that a journalist could likely be killed without consequence. The general public bore some responsibility, with its tolerance of the aggression. Mexicans commonly assumed that since journalists are shady characters, living off bribes and consorting with the corrupt, their deaths reflected a mere occupational hazard. When reporters were killed, those who protested were usually other media workers and few else.

Explaining why Mexico's journalists are so often murdered and why they have an unfairly poor reputation are two of the main purposes of this book. Mexicans' trust in their media has never been high, partly because public intellectuals long repeated that journalists were "gangsters" and that newspapers were "factual deserts."[2] There was some truth behind the exaggerations. During the "golden age" of the Institutional Revolutionary Party (PRI), which held every presidency and governed every state from 1929 until 1989, many Mexicans rightly suspected that much of what passed for news was propaganda, paid for by politicians. In other words, Mexico's press—like that of other Latin American countries—was broadly, though by no means wholly, clientelist. It reflected the PRI's modus operandi of building mutually beneficial relations with social sectors (its "clients") by bestowing economic favors in exchange for political support.[3]

In the 1990s and early 2000s, the press became more pluralistic, investigative, critical, and financially autonomous. But after a "spring" of fifteen to twenty years, politically vested interests came again to the fore and new concerns arose about scandals shaped to sell papers. The sense never went away that many journalists were *chayoteros*—takers of government bribes (*chayote*)—or that they were otherwise unethical: blackmailers, shills for big business, agents for politicians. The coexistence of liberal values (private ownership, publishers' concern with press freedom) and persistent clientelism led scholars Manuel Guerrero and Mireya Márquez to define Mexico's media, again like those of most of Latin America, as having a "captured liberal model." In practical terms, by 2018 the editors of media that managed to defy "capture" were worried about the state of Mexican journalism. As Daniel Moreno, founder and editor of news site *Animal Político*, put it, "There is a reason why the media now faces a legitimacy crisis. The public . . . generally assumes that the media is 'playing politics.'"[4]

Distrust arguably peaked during the presidency of Andrés Manuel López Obrador (2018–24), with whom much of the media had an unprecedentedly prickly relationship. López Obrador liked to claim that no Mexican president had ever faced such hostility from the press as he did; what is certain is that no president so often criticized the press, for he did so routinely in his five-days-a-week press conferences, sometimes insulting the media in a manner evocative of Donald Trump.[5] When López Obrador cast aspersions on watchdog media—that is, media affording space to civic-minded reporters, investigative journalists, and well-informed critical commentators—and when YouTubers, influencers, and other loyalists amplified his complaints, hashtags such as #PrensaChayotera (venal press) and #PrensaSicaria (hitjob press) started trending. In fact, *chayotero* was lazily but contagiously adopted by many of his sympathizers as a tar with which to brush all who wrote critically of the government, no matter where they drew their paychecks. Thus the belief that a free press is key to a functioning democracy, a belief with fairly shallow roots in Mexico, was alarmingly eroded. Meanwhile, the appalling rate of journalist murders continued apace under López Obrador, at roughly eight per year. Other kinds of aggression, such as intimidation and threats of violence, substantially increased.[6]

The double tragedy for Mexico's press is that the vast majority of these frequent crimes go unpunished. The problem is partly institutional. Owing to police incompetence, judicial timidity or venality, and interference by politicians protecting their clientele, in 2021 only 10 percent of murders in Mexico resulted in any sort of conviction. Among murders of journalists, for the 105 cases recorded during the decade from 2012 to 2021, the conviction rate was around 20 percent for the perpetrators (usually paid hitmen) and just 4 percent for the masterminds.[7]

Yet this book is no mere tale of journalistic woe. Reaching further into the past, one can detect the rise of an increasingly bold and free press. Admittedly, it was a long time coming. During what has been labeled the Dictablanda, the era of unrivaled and relatively pacific rule by the PRI between 1938 and 1968, Mexico's press was broadly co-opted with financial incentives by federal and state governments; hence it functioned as a propaganda machine. As Paul Gillingham, Benjamin Smith, and others have shown, there were many exceptions, which illustrated cracks in the PRI's authoritarian edifice and often testified to a restlessness beneath the surface of the country's much-touted "economic miracle." However, by cherry-picking their case studies, these authors may have overstated the collective import of such exceptions, which consisted of fleeting publications (bought off or suppressed within a few years), politicized rags that echoed intraparty feuding, or periodicals founded by blackmail artists to press authorities into granting subsidies.[8]

The government's repression of the 1968 student movement, including the massacre of dozens of peaceful protesters at Tlatelolco in Mexico City, did not mark a freedom-of-speech watershed. But it did plant a seed of antiauthoritarian resistance among many activist men and women, thereafter known as the Generation of '68, some of whom would rise to positions of newsroom leadership a decade or two later.[9]

A more immediately influential event occurred in 1976, when President Luis Echeverría engineered an internal "coup" at *Excélsior*, the country's leading broadsheet, against its independent-minded editor in chief, Julio Scherer García. Two hundred loyalists departed with Scherer, and the paper turned progovernment. Yet the president's plot was soon seen to be politically stupid. At *Excélsior*, Scherer and his lieutenants had chosen their battles, serving up critical comment on inside pages but pablum on the cover. At *Proceso*, the magazine Scherer founded five months later, criticism of the soon-to-depart Echeverría was blistering—the announcement of a feistiness that has persisted at the magazine to the present. A year later, another team from the "*Excélsior* diaspora" founded the left-wing *Unomásuno*, the most critical daily that Mexico had yet seen.

Both *Proceso* and *Unomásuno* were anomalies, however. Neither they nor the more left-wing *La Jornada*, founded in 1984 by a breakaway faction from *Unomásuno*, produced much of a ripple effect. Other media, especially in the capital, remained submissive, only daring to be critical when some scandal—a devastating earthquake in 1985, massive electoral fraud in Chihuahua in 1986—became too great for the state to control the story. As historian Vanessa Freije has argued, media amplification of such scandals suffused the public sphere with greater skepticism of the capabilities of the PRI. It also boosted the organizing and resistance of civil society and hinted at the electoral democratization to come.[10]

Nonetheless, it was not until the presidency of Carlos Salinas de Gortari (1988–94) that a broad opening to critical and pluralistic perspectives took hold. The political priorities and image consciousness of the president, the economic boom that anticipated the North American Free Trade Agreement (NAFTA), a cultural shift at newsrooms led by the Generation of '68, and the vision of media entrepreneurs together fueled a period of unusual effervescence. Gutsy newspapers launched and older rivals raised their game. New generations of editors and reporters cut their teeth covering the era's crises; many of them hailed from the modest end of Mexico's middle class and, at last, many of them were women. During 1994, the tumultuous year that closed the Salinas presidency, Mexico's watchdog press came of age.[11]

While admitting the early advances made by *Proceso*, *Unomásuno*, *La Jornada*, and a few bold regional media, this book argues that the Salinas era—not 1976, as journalists and academics have traditionally claimed[12]—constitutes the true watershed in Mexican media history. Its narrative resumes the story of the press that Smith and Freije have ably examined from 1940 to 1987.[13] Like Smith's study, it takes the oft-marginalized story of regional media into account, arguing that the best journalistic practices, such as a shunning of government advertising and a close monitoring of elections, sometimes flourished in the provinces before being adopted in the capital.

After Salinas, the press matured further during the next two presidencies, as social scientists Chappell Lawson and Sallie Hughes and journalist Cecilia González have persuasively documented (although the conclusions of all three seem overly optimistic in hindsight).[14] The continued development of a watchdog press and a decline in knee-jerk servility were enabled by two presidents, Ernesto Zedillo (1994–2000) and Vicente Fox (2000–2006), who showed forbearance with the media. They often did not like what they read, and sometimes they said so, but the days of presidential aides and cabinet members pressing publishers to spike a story, drop a columnist, or fire a reporter were receding.

By 2006, therefore, the arc of Mexico's press since the 1980s broadly reflected that of much of Latin America, where most nations were emerging from one form or another of dictatorship. As Silvio Waisbord demonstrated for Argentina, Brazil, Colombia, and Peru, and as Rosenthal Alves argued for Guatemala, Panama, and Chile (as well as Argentina and Mexico), watchdog journalism bloomed across the region, facilitating the process of democratization and providing forums for debate.[15]

Then came Calderón (2006–12). A year or so after he unleashed the army to combat the crime syndicates, the homicide rate began to soar. Bloodshed dominated the headlines, and the state saw a need to gain control of the "war on drugs" narrative. To do so, Calderón initiated a massive year-by-year increase in government advertising. All told, he would spend the equivalent of $3 billion in making his government look good.[16] Few periodicals resisted the siren call of federal cash, for they were starting to feel the pinch as readers and advertisers migrated to the internet. At the same time, governors too were increasing their PR outlays, and also their rhetorical and judicial attacks, to the detriment of press in the states. These trends persisted under Calderón's successor, Enrique Peña Nieto (2012–18), whose officials also revived the PRI's custom of withholding advertising from publications that discomforted them. The years 2006 to 2018 in some respects saw a downward curve for press openness, at least in legacy media, as the physical violence wrought by crime syndicates and corrupt politicians and the structural violence wrought by the discretionary allotment or withholding of official advertising undermined hard-won freedoms. But there were countervailing trends. In the magazines that flourished in the Calderón years and at the online news sites that took root under Peña, investigative journalism and long-form narrative blossomed as never before, as did the genre of in-depth journalistic books.

It may be too soon to generalize about the López Obrador years, which is why the period is confined to an epilogue in this book. Tentatively, it seems that Mexico's press may have experienced another watershed. The new regime slashed three-quarters of federal advertising (i.e., de facto subsidy support) for media overall, while favoring those most friendly to it, notably *La Jornada*, and applying an ad-spend boycott of critical media, such as *Proceso*. Together with the market contraction caused by the COVID-19 pandemic, these cuts prompted wave after wave of layoffs between 2018 and 2021. Papers massively downsized and so did some digital media. Some print titles disappeared, although not as many as one might expect, for many Mexican media exist chiefly as tools of political or economic influence. Spaces for investigative and long-form journalism were much reduced. At the same time, the press was never so polarized, with many publications becoming enthusiastically pro- or anti-López Obrador—and very often anti–each other. Polarization was deepened by the rise of social media influencers as purveyors (in most cases) of progovernment opinion and exacerbators of López Obrador's attacks on critical journalists and media.[17]

Some of the problems facing Mexico's press typify established trends throughout the Americas and elsewhere. As a 2019 report from Freedom House put it, "Freedom of the media has been deteriorating around the world over the past decade. In some of the most influential democracies in the world, populist leaders have overseen concerted attempts to throttle the independence of the media sector." Journalists working wherever corrupt politicians collude with criminal gangs, notably Colombia and Brazil, are similarly threatened, attacked, and killed, if in lesser numbers. Latin American media in general depend much more on government subsidies than their US or European counterparts, and critical papers can face boycotts, as happened to leading Brazilian title *O Globo* under President Jair Bolsonaro (2019–22), another frequent insulter of the press. Bolsonaro's derision of the media echoed the intimidating discourse of fellow populists, not only López Obrador but also Narendra Modi in India, Viktor Orbán in Hungary, Aleksandar Vučić in Serbia, and Trump in the United States.[18]

The disdain of presidents, the cutting of subsidies, and the veiled threats of provincial politicians are everyday forms of "media capture" in the twenty-first century. Anya Schiffrin has written of this topic, "Instead of a censor . . . marking up advance copies of local newspapers, journalists receive more nuanced signals as to what should be covered."[19] This is true of Mexico to a point, but along with nuanced signals there are death threats and murders, which have made the country the riskiest of any outside a war zone.

Polarization has become a regional problem. Under authoritarian regimes, such as in Venezuela, El Salvador, and Nicaragua, critical media have all but disappeared, leaving propagandists in their wake. Even in the United States, *The New York Times* has come under fire, not so much for abandoning balance (the paper long skewed Democrat) but for shutting down debate on some topics altogether. Former *Times* columnist James Bennet complained, "The *Times's* problem has metastasized from liberal bias to illiberal bias." Public trust in the US media has declined since the 1990s.[20] In Mexico, where trust in media overall (including TV news) has never been high, confidence in the press improved markedly in the 1980s and 1990s. But by 2012 it had dropped to below the level of the early 1980s, and by 2018 it had receded further, with only 27 percent of respondents to a World Values Survey study expressing confidence.[21] Under López Obrador, that figure has likely declined again.

Readers in English-speaking countries will inevitably find themselves drawing comparisons and contrasts with their own media. This book indeed refers to newspapers elsewhere, where appropriate. This is not to imply that US or UK journalism is necessarily superior. There is, after all, a rich literature on the failings of anglophone media, from Edward Herman and Noam Chomsky's classic *Manufacturing Consent*, which revealed the Cold War "propaganda function" of US papers and newscasts in their promotion of Washington's view during engagements in Vietnam and Central America; to Dean Starkman's *The Watchdog That Didn't Bark*, on how the US business press failed to investigate major banks and mortgage lenders before the financial crisis of 2008; and Nick Davies's *Hack Attack*, on the culture of phone hacking by reporters at Rupert Murdoch's British tabloids.[22] Further, some

Mexican scholars have argued that the particulars of the Mexican experience, especially among left-leaning media, invalidate the normative assumption often made by foreign scholars that Mexico's press should strive to emulate the liberal model of the press in the United States, Canada, and Britain.[23]

Nonetheless, since at least the 1970s—when a publisher applied principles learned in Texas to a renewal of *El Norte* and the founders of *Unomásuno* took inspiration from Spain's newly launched *El País*—many Mexican journalists have looked abroad to see how they might improve their work. By the early 1990s, innovative publishers were encouraging promising reporters to take master's degrees at US journalism schools. In the late 1990s, *El Universal* underwent the biggest renovation in its eighty-year life with the help of consultants from *The Dallas Morning News* and the American Press Institute. Liberal-left news site *Animal Político* drew a degree of inspiration from *The Guardian*. The irony, of course, is that much of Mexico's press embraced the Western capitalist model only a short time before that model began to weaken, with English-language legacy media forced to close, downsize, or court philanthropic patrons as readers rushed to news freely available online.

Whether or not polarization, distrust, and newsroom layoffs will persist during the presidential term of Claudia Sheinbaum (2024–30), much damage to the reputation and civic role of Mexico's media has been done. Spaces for watchdog journalism have declined. In the provinces, critical reporting is much diminished, and there is little sign that the murder of journalists is substantially lessening.[24] One reason for optimism, however, is that even during the press's bleakest times of rampant submissiveness to the rule of the twentieth-century PRI, a valiant minority of publishers, editors, columnists, and reporters dared to resist, as this book's early chapters show. Now, with legacy media fading in influence and news sites struggling to find the resources to hold power consistently to account, it may be up to a new generation of visionaries and idealists to harness the digital beast and keep Mexicans well informed.

———

This book provides an analytical narrative history of the Mexican press—print media and their digital cousins—from the 1980s to the present. Since newspapers and digital papers would be nothing more than aggregators without the reporters who write for them, this narrative intertwines the stories of Mexico's principal media with those of some of their most remarkable men and women. It also profiles the publishers and editors in chief responsible for journalism's main innovations. It places the whole in a political context: Mexico's hesitant shuffle toward electoral democracy during the last two decades of single-party rule, a process within which an ever more critical press played a crucial role. This tectonic shift has been followed by two and a half decades of postauthoritarian experience, which showed substantial press freedom in the short term but soon a troubling if incomplete return to media co-option and deference.

The tale begins with a sketch of my experiences as a young, expatriate journalist in early 1990s Mexico City. Here I was firsthand witness to the propagandizing that passed for journalism at most papers, the signs of *apertura* (pluralistic opening) evident in some, and the media's reaction to the crises of 1994: an Indigenous rebellion in the South, the assassination of a presidential candidate, and a massive currency devaluation around Christmas. In this introduction I attempt to evoke both the excitement and the unease of a fast-moving time when Mexico wrestled with the growing pains of democratization and the advantages and disadvantages of free-market economics.

Chapter 1 offers a historical overview of what many Mexicans termed the *prensa vendida*—the "sell-out" or progovernment press—which dominated journalism between the late nineteenth century and the late twentieth, establishing journalists as a generally untrustworthy species. It offers the case study of Juan Francisco Ealy Ortiz, owner from around 1970 of the prominent broadsheet *El Universal*, to exhibit the cozy clientelism that persisted between most print media and the hegemonic PRI, the party that ruled Mexico between 1929 and 2000. It describes what I call an "excess of press," whereby many Mexican cities hosted one or two dozen daily newspapers, most designed to curry favor on behalf of political or business interests. It then turns to *Unomásuno*, a paper founded in 1977 with state support but a critical vision, a paradoxical arrangement that reflected the government's willingness to allow escape valves, for such mechanisms validated the rhetoric of democratization without threatening autocracy. Such flickers of press freedom could easily be snuffed out by the state, as indeed befell many a critical publication during the long presidentialist rule of the PRI.

The next three chapters show how the evolution of a more truly independent critical press in the 1980s and early 1990s took place in the provinces before it emerged among the "national" newspapers (in fact, such dailies circulated little outside the capital). Chapter 2 begins with the Tijuana newsweekly *Zeta* and its charismatic founder, Jesús Blancornelas. As well as navigating the threat levels of an increasingly violent city, *Zeta* helped to monitor the Baja California gubernatorial election of 1989, the first to see a non-PRI candidate win. That outcome owed much to recently installed president Salinas. Elected in a vote heavily marred by fraud, Salinas sought credibility by deepening the PRI's hitherto tepid commitment to democracy, in part by loosening ancient federal controls over the media, a process examined in the second half of the chapter.

Economics is an important part of the Salinas-era story, for the negotiation of NAFTA, along with a privatization program, created a boom in the advertising market that allowed periodicals to depend less on state subsidies. The ability of some publishers and the inability of others to cultivate financial autonomy for their newspapers and magazines remains an analytical thread throughout the book.

Chapter 3 travels to Mexico's second-largest city, Guadalajara, where in 1991 a young academic and a businessman launched *Siglo 21*. The paper struggled initially but shot to local prominence with its unparalleled and uncensored coverage of an industrial accident that killed more than a hundred people and prompted political resignations. The episode shows how the success of infant media often depends on their ability to respond to disasters or scandals with greater alacrity than their older peers, whose instincts may be dulled by political compromises. (*La Jornada*, launched in 1984, underwent a similar experience with its superior response to the Mexico City earthquake of 1985.) *Siglo 21* was not long lived, but it proved the launchpad for some of Mexico's most influential journalists, including its editor, Jorge Zepeda Patterson.

Mexico's third-largest city, Monterrey, looms large in Mexico's newspaper history as the birthplace of *El Norte*, a paper transformed in the 1970s by a young owner-publisher, Alejandro Junco, a recent graduate in journalism from the University of Texas at Austin. Chapter 4 relates how *El Norte* became the financially sound platform from which Junco launched the Mexico City daily *Reforma*, which quickly overshadowed some thirty rival papers in the capital with its full-color design, its political pluralism, and the professionalism of its editors and reporters. *Reforma* was just six weeks old when the Zapatista Indigenous rebellion broke out in Chiapas, and its coverage of the tumultuous events of 1994 both cemented its reputation and reflected a sense among journalists in general that the government could no longer tell them what or how to write.

Chapters 5 and 6 tell the parallel stories of Mexico's two most important left-wing media of the past half century: the magazine *Proceso* and the daily *La Jornada*. Although born as a forum for criticism in 1976, *Proceso* underwent a transformation in 1982 when President José López Portillo abruptly cut off most of its subsidies. Under its much-admired director, Julio Scherer, the magazine responded by growing its readership through more adventurous (some would say sensational) exposés of official corruption, including a report on the private mansion of López Portillo himself. Until the mid-1990s, *Proceso* went unequaled as a thorn in every president's side and as a forum for investigative journalism. But Scherer's retirement in 1996 prompted an ungainly and damaging transition to new leadership, which coincided with a loss of readers as *Reforma* and a revamped *El Universal* competed for scoops. Investigative journalism, which had much relied on the leaking of documents by disaffected functionaries or political rivals, became more proactive.

La Jornada presents the curious but not unique case of a critical Mexican daily that lived off government support. Founder-director Carlos Payán turned out to be a talented, though not infallible, practitioner of the tightrope walk that this arrangement implied. *La Jornada* offered peerless coverage of industrial accidents, natural disasters, and the Zapatista rebellion, with an accent on the ineptness of government responses. But when covering presidential elections and reporting on State of the Nation speeches, the paper more or less toed the PRI's line. Payán (like Scherer) retired in 1996, and while the transition to new leadership went fairly smoothly, new editor in chief Carmen Lira proved increasingly autocratic and dogmatic, and the paper lost readers. Moreover, a nation largely content with neoliberal leadership and closer relations with the United States made the leftist-nationalist *La Jornada* look like an anachronism.

The next two chapters show how press freedoms in Mexico arguably peaked under Fox and certainly began to recede under Calderón, both of the right-of-center National Action Party. Under Fox (chapter 7), when the ad market was still strong and subsidies were at a low point, Mexican papers and magazines found themselves able to hold the president to account with little fear of reprisal. The experience of the new daily *Milenio*—another Mexico City paper with roots in Monterrey—showed that criticism of the president's image-conscious and politically ambitious wife could still redound to the discomfort of the reporter responsible. Nonetheless, press freedom flourished, thanks to Fox's hands-off policies, a healthy ad market, and a first-ever freedom of information act.

Under Calderón (chapter 8), the tide of press freedom began to turn. First, the president's war on the crime syndicates produced a soaring homicide rate, which included a horrifying increase in the killing of journalists. Second, in an effort to control the story amid bloody headlines, the Calderón government tried to buy off the national media by tripling subsidy outlays. Third, a major contraction in the national ad market in 2009, from which print media never recovered, made newspapers vulnerable to such overtures. Some papers indeed toned down their coverage of the violence, as did the major broadcasters, which together help explain why Calderón was able to leave office with a 53 percent approval rating, despite having accelerated a conflict that claimed 120,000 lives on his watch. This chapter also explores the origins of the prickly relationship between the press and López Obrador, which emerged when he served as mayor of Mexico City, and examines attempts at media capture by the world's number one billionaire at the time, Carlos Slim.

Recent studies have shown that electoral democratization has paradoxically coincided in Mexico with increased attacks on journalists, especially in the provinces.[25] Chapter 9 fleshes out this point, first by offering a series of vignettes that exemplify the variety of pressures that regional media have faced since 2006. Such pressures have included intimidation by off-duty police; shootings in broad daylight; kidnappings, either to scold prying reporters or to "disappear" them; revictimization through allegations of links to criminal gangs; and a resultant climate of self-censorship that produces *zonas de silencio* (zones of silence), where organized crime goes unreported. Meanwhile, investigations into the harassment and killing of journalists have often been marked by confessions obtained under torture, murders of investigators, bungled collection of evidence, gubernatorial meddling or indifference, a refusal of federal authorities to get involved, and a startlingly high rate of impunity.

The chapter then argues that, whereas discussion of violence against the Mexican press has focused on organized crime and inadequate federal protections, the actions (or inaction) of state governors have historically done most to explain the trend. Since 2000, it is in many of Mexico's states that democracy has most obviously lapsed into autocracy.[26] The chapter closes with two cases of brave defiance, both involving female crime reporters: Lydia Cacho, who exposed the sexual exploitation of minors by businessmen and refused to be cowed by a governor's attempts to silence her; Anabel Hernández, who wrote a best-selling book on the corruption of federal authorities by drug traffickers, had to flee into exile, but eventually was able to report on the conviction of her most infamous suspect.

Chapter 10 resumes a focus on presidential eras with the brief return to power of the PRI under President Peña. While the forces that had assailed press freedoms under Calderón persisted, and while those legacy media holding power to account diminished in number, new hope arose for Mexican journalism in the form of digital media. Three sites in particular stood out for investigative work: *Aristegui Noticias*, a spin-off from the popular radio newscast of Carmen Aristegui; *Animal Político*, led by *Reforma* veteran Daniel Moreno; and *SinEmbargo*, founded by former *Siglo 21* editor in chief Zepeda. Together with reporting by independent legacy media and new journalist collectives, their exposés—some of them partially funded by nongovernmental organizations—showed the PRI to be as corrupt as ever. Peña would leave office in disgrace, but more importantly, watchdog work on Peña and his predecessors lent credence to the claims by the left-wing López Obrador, during his 2017–18 presidential campaign, that he was the only candidate who could put an end to Mexico's chronic corruption. He won in a landslide.

It was thus a bitter irony for much of Mexico's civic-minded media that López Obrador turned against them. Employing a dichotomizing discourse—the "good" press supported his government, the "filthy," "bribe-taking," or "criminal" press criticized it—López Obrador not only stigmatized *Reforma*, *Animal Político*, *Proceso*, and *Aristegui Noticias*, he also deprived them of subsidy support. These tactics were replicated by some state governors. *La Jornada*, by contrast, was rewarded for its new role as quasi-propagandist (*quasi* because, like the *prensa vendida* of the 1970s, it retained some critical columnists) with more than four times as much government advertising as any other paper. The Epilogue sketches these trends and asks what is next for Mexico's embattled press.

This study does not engage with *all* aspects of Mexican journalism. It is chiefly a political and business history, as well as a story of influential publishers and remarkable journalists, rather than a social history. There is little attention to the tabloid press, the so-called *nota roja*, of whose social importance in an earlier era Pablo Piccato has written. (Piccato himself admits that the tabloids' critical edge, especially their exposure of crime and corruption, declined in the 1960s, as they "mostly settled into a moralistic support for the police." Others have noted that the tabloids ceased to function as a journalists' training ground by the 1980s.)[27] Nor is there much discussion of cultural journalism, sports writing, political cartoons, photojournalism, bloggers and influencers, or the public sphere, though each of these topics crops up from time to time. They are all worthy of analysis, but their in-depth inclusion here would have made the undertaking unwieldy. Likewise, TV and radio journalism are treated only when they have complemented or contrasted with the written word.

Finally, a word on methodology. As the introduction relates, I formed my first impressions of Mexican journalism while practicing it for three years. Next, as a correspondent for a US magazine and coauthor of a book on Mexican television, then as a US-based graduate student and junior academic who returned to Mexico at least once a year for research, I retained friendships within the press and accumulated hundreds of hours in newspaper archives. Finally, at the Center for Research and Teaching in Economics (CIDE) in Mexico City, I taught for six years a class on press history in the graduate journalism program, where most students were professional reporters. These experiences undergird the book's hybrid approach: a narrative history that combines journalistic prose with an academic sensibility. For example, I interviewed some 180 current and former journalists, many of them several times; with very few exceptions, I tracked down each article they discussed that came to be included in the text and have cited them in the notes.

I hope that readers will forgive my somewhat impassioned tone. This book is the fruit of more than three decades of engagement in one form or another with Mexico's press: years of shared excitement at its advances, and of shared frustration at attempts by the powerful to censor it, silence its critical voices, or undermine its credibility through lawsuits or public derision. One might call this book a celebration of Mexico's valiant watchdog journalists.

Acknowledgments

I must start by thanking the 180 or so current and former journalists who agreed to be interviewed for this book over a span of six years. Most of their names appear in the endnotes, but special thanks are due to those who spoke with me on three or more occasions: Samuel García, Daniel Moreno, Humberto Musacchio, Daniela Pastrana, Lázaro Ríos, Raymundo Riva Palacio, Wilbert Torre, Alejandra Xanic von Bertrab, and Jorge Zepeda Patterson, along with Sergio Aguayo of the Colegio de México and Jan-Albert Hootsen of the Committee to Protect Journalists. A tiny minority opted to be interviewed off the record. Most interviews took place in Mexico City (these included conversations with journalists from the border cities of Juárez and Tijuana). Dozens more were conducted in Acapulco, Aguascalientes, Guadalajara, Monterrey, Puebla, and Villahermosa. Several took place in London and Paris.

I thank the Center for Research and Teaching in Economics (CIDE) for its financial support. However, this diminished as of 2021, after Mexico's federal government took the ill-advised step of abolishing *fideicomisos*, a mechanism that enabled public institutions to receive and share external funding. The government also cut the budgets of public research centers, including the CIDE, and deprived them of an effective advocate at the federal level. For this book, I therefore bore roughly half of the travel costs incurred during the latter three years of research. Along with most CIDE colleagues, I hope for a less parsimonious and conflictive relationship between the government and higher education under president Dr. Claudia Sheinbaum and her sciences czar, Dr. Rosaura Ruiz.

I gained help with the book proposal from my indefatigable friend Benjamin Smith—who generously suggested I write this history in the first place—and from Sallie Hughes, whose rigorous 2006 study, *Newsrooms in Conflict*, I probably plundered more than any other. I received further comments on the proposal from Vanessa Freije, Eduardo García, Paul Gillingham, Ioan Grillo, David Lida, Gabriel Martínez-Serna, and Grisel Salazar. Valuable feedback on chapters and sections came from Benjamin Smith and Juan Larrosa-Fuentes; Nico Medina-Mora of *Nexos*; veteran journalists Sara Lovera and Homero Campa; and CIDE colleagues Catherine Andrews, Clara García, Jean Meyer, Pablo Mijangos (now of Southern Methodist University), and Grisel

Salazar (now of the Universidad Iberoamericana). A special thank-you goes to my friend Michael Bess, a born encourager, who, like me, joined CIDE Región Centro in Aguascalientes a decade ago.

During my sabbatical year at the University of Oxford's Latin America Centre (2020–21), I was encouraged and advised by Eduardo Posada-Carbó and Alan Knight, despite restrictions due to COVID-19. Lockdown-bending walks with Thom Rath, Timo Schaefer, Benjamin Smith, Dinti Wakefield, and my old friend and first publisher Consuelo Sáizar provided further food for thought.

I also gained many insights from the students I taught in the CIDE's journalism program between 2015 and 2020, most of them practicing reporters; I hope for a future revival of the program, which was regrettably suspended against the wishes of its faculty in 2022. Through their participation in classroom debate, my students helped me understand the ethical dilemmas, everyday risks, and job precarity experienced by Mexico's journalists; through their research papers, I extended my knowledge of press history. Here I owe special thanks to Arturo Aguilar, Rafael Cabrera, Jessica Castillo Belmont, Edgar Cera, Yared de la Rosa, Alejandro Domínguez, Julio González, Julene Iriarte, Gabriela Jiménez, Alejandro Juárez, Carla León, Luis Mendoza Ovando, Reyna Mora, Concha Peralta, Beatriz Pereyra, Aidee Rivera, Abraham Rubio, César Ruiz, Andrea Saint Martin, Nadia Sanders, Dalila Sarabia, Mirna Servín, Martina Spataro, Nelly Toche, Claudia Villegas, and Luciana Wainer. I also thank the CIDE research assistants who helped me, chiefly by scouring newspaper archives: Fernanda Fraga, Paola Martínez, Ángeles Paredes, and since 2022, the spotlessly efficient Alexis Hernández Fabián.

On research trips to Mexico City, I received *posada* from Rosie Arroyo, Robbie Lear, David Lida, José Juan López Portillo, Elisabeth Malkin and Eduardo García, Pablo Mijangos, Leticia Neria and Mark Aspinwall, Helena Wygard and David Luhnow, and my *tíos politicos* Paty Romero and Jorge Redondo. Laura Márquez and Rafael Colás kindly hosted me in Monterrey. My thanks to all of them for their hospitality and their conversation.

At the University of North Carolina Press, this book was greenlit by Elaine Maisner and then supervised by Debbie Gershenowitz, with help from Alexis Dumain and Lindsay Starr, along with Michelle Witkowski and Ashley Moore of Westchester Publishing. They are an efficient team and my thanks goes to all of them, as to Noemí Morales Sánchez, who created the map.

This book is dedicated to all who practice watchdog journalism in Mexico and to my wife and partner in parenthood, Itzel Antuna Romero.

Mexican Watchdogs

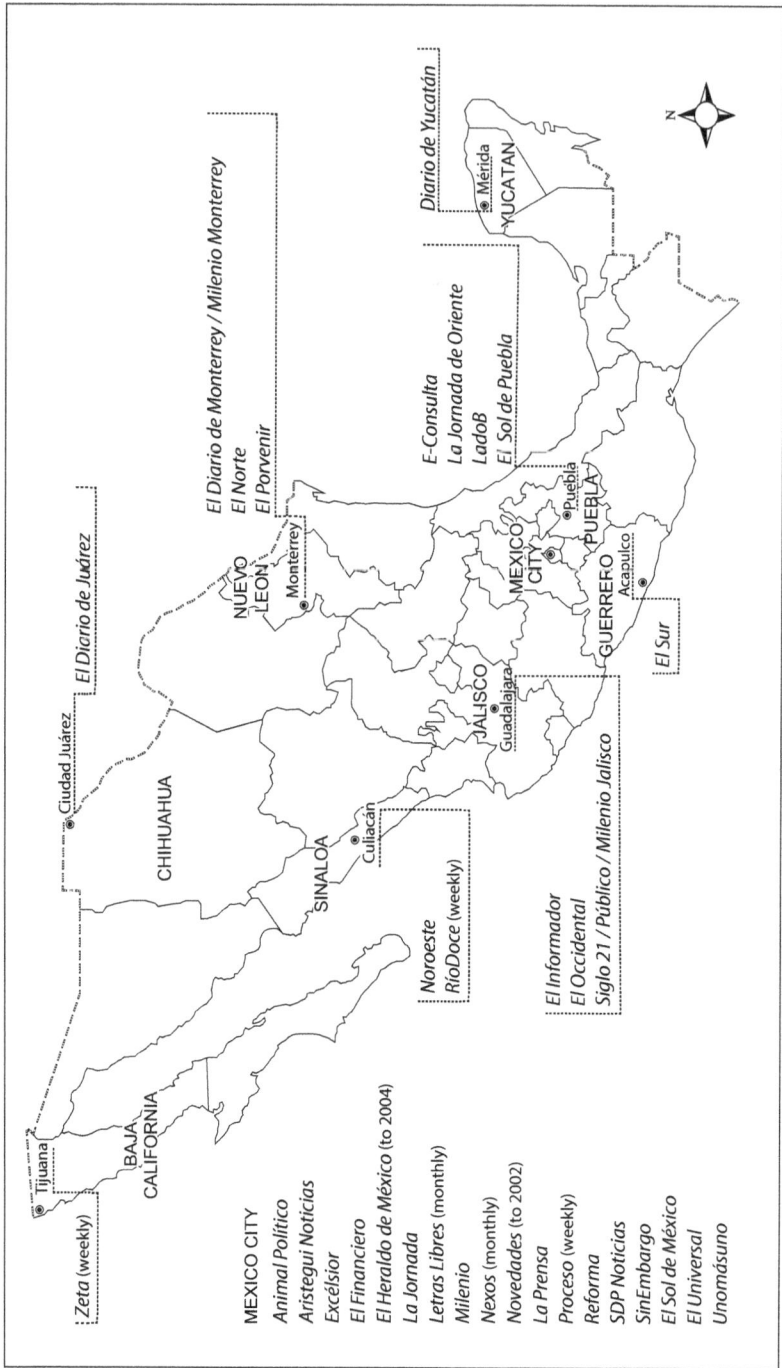

Mexico's principal news publications, as addressed in this book. Created by Noemí Morales Sánchez.

Introduction

An Expatriate Memoir

Mexico City, 1991

Clustered in the frantic heart of the Mexican capital, a dozen blocks west of where Aztecs once erected temples to insistent gods, stood the offices of the country's principal media. At the northern end of this huddle rose the oldest pillars of state propaganda, the broadsheets *Excélsior* and *El Universal*, along with the best-selling tabloid, *La Prensa*. At the southern end, occupying a four-acre lot, was the news operation of broadcast colossus Televisa; its owner declared himself and his employees to be "soldiers of the PRI [Institutional Revolutionary Party]." And in the middle were two smaller players: the spirited left-wing daily *La Jornada*, one of the very few periodicals that dared criticize the government, and the dull right-wing daily *Novedades*, whose sycophancy toward the ruling party would have been unalloyed were it not for its ownership of an English-language sister paper, *The News*. In September 1991, I started to write for the latter.[1]

The News was a community institution. Almost every American, Canadian, and Briton in Mexico City, and many in the rest of the country, seemed to have a subscription. Together with newsstand sales—the paper could be found in most major cities and tourism hotspots—this base gave it a respectable circulation of 15,000 or so. The paper had been founded in 1950 as an emblem and facilitator of US-Mexican friendship, which was then enjoying a postwar glow. As well as local news, it ran wire stories from *The New York Times*, Reuters, and the Associated Press. It published English-language event postings—school fairs, church services, amateur theater—and a busy letters page. Columnists included US agony aunt Ann Landers and veteran expats who dispensed advice to new arrivals. The paper was famed as a career launchpad; in the 1980s its staff included Alfonso Chardy, later a Pulitzer winner with the *Miami Herald* for reporting on the Iran-Contra Affair, and future war correspondents Judith Matloff and Anne-Marie O'Connor. *The News* appeared to be a viable business too, or close to it, carrying ads from the likes of American Airlines, British Airways, HBO, and American Express, which catered to the foreign personnel who were flocking to Mexico. Those firms and others were sensing a gold rush with the pending North American Free Trade Agreement (NAFTA), the signature policy of Mexico's dynamic,

The complete official English translation of the State-of-the-Nation Address/**Supplement**

1o. DE NOVIEMBRE DE 1992

The News

Monday, November 2, 1992　　　　　　　　　　　　　　　Mexico City Vol. XLIII No. 120

Salinas Promises Fairness And Sovereignty

Political Reform Debate Is Shifted To New Territory

By JIM SILVER
The News Staff Reporter

By proposing to regulate campaign financing, President Salinas on Sunday moved the political reform debate onto new ground — from the question of clean elections to the question of fair elections.

A year ago, political concerns hardly surfaced in the president's State-of-the-Nation Address. Salinas had won the approval of most of the opposition parties for his new electoral code in 1990, and his Institutional Revolutionary Party (PRI) had won a landslide victory under the new rules in the August 1991 midterm elections.

But a series of state elections since then — especially the July gubernatorial elections in Chihuahua and Michoacan — made clear that problems remained. Moreover, they related less to fraudulent vote counting — the traditional complaint of the opposition, and the focus of the 1990 law — and more to unequal conditions in the campaign.

Fourth *Informe* Includes Warning To United States

Special Report Pages 4,5
By STARR SPENCER
The News Staff Reporter

In his fourth State-of-the-Nation Address Sunday, President Carlos Salinas de Gortari pledged a more democratic multiparty political system that included fair elections and stressed his twin intentions to check inflation and boost small- and mid-size businesses.

He also issued a diplomatic but unmistakable message that he would fight future attempts by the United States to impose its laws on Mexico.

During the annual televised address, which this year took a little more than two and a half hours to deliver from the newly rehabilitated Legislative Palace, Salinas said the key concept governing his last two years in office would be the consolidation of existing programs, rather than forging new ones.

The address, also called the *informe*, held few surprises, as the president conveyed

The News of Mexico City at the height of its popularity in 1992. Courtesy of Jim Silver.

US-educated president, Carlos Salinas de Gortari. All these ingredients, mixed within an attractive full-color layout of over forty pages, gave assurances of a professional product.

Behind the scenes, however, we staffers were the most motley of twenty-something crews, accompanied by the odd old-timer. Though we were mainly Yanks and Brits, eight or nine nations were represented. How our jumble of occasional, junior, and would-be journalists produced so resilient a publication owed much to the paper's history of talented editors in chief. Each of them had to marshal what one observer termed the paper's "drifters, college dropouts, and aspiring Hemingways," who were hired for a pittance and prone to quickly moving on.[2]

As these editors were Americans, they had been schooled in a journalistic tradition somewhat different from the Mexican one, whose deference to officialdom exceeded that of US media. In the United States, an investigative impulse had flourished since the 1960s. The civil rights movement, the Vietnam War, the Pentagon Papers, and Watergate taught Americans that a chief purpose of the press was to hold the powerful to account.[3] But as these editors were also congenial types who had worked for years in Mexico before taking the paper's helm, they tempered their zeal for good reporting with acquiescence to the owners. These were the O'Farrill family, Mexicans of Irish descent and reactionary convictions. The family's conservatism made for a snug fit with both the semidictatorial comportment of the PRI and the Cold War outlook of the United States. At times, however, the editors found it tricky to balance their instincts with those of the O'Farrills.

Those tensions deepened in the winter of 1986–87, when Pete Hamill, a star columnist at *The New York Post* with prior experience in Mexico, spent three months at the helm. His coverage of a strike at the National Autonomous University of Mexico was not to the O'Farrills' liking, and he resigned under duress.[4] His exit heralded an era—the final fifteen years in the life of *The News*—in which no editor would last for long. This had much to do with the elderly Rómulo O'Farrill Jr., whose leadership became increasingly erratic and out of step with a society ever more insistent on a free press.

When I joined, Michael J. Zamba was at the helm. He had been tapped as editor at thirty, much younger than most predecessors, although he had worked for several papers and had a couple of books to his name. His manner was easygoing, and he read his adoptive country well. We liked him. After seventeen months in charge, he too would quit, exasperated at the owners' interference in editorial content.

Working for the O'Farrills: *Novedades* and *The News*

Novedades Editores, as the publishing company was called, inhabited a five-story edifice dating from 1910, at the corner of two downtown thoroughfares. Standing out amid the modesty of its neighbors, the building boasted façades of chiseled pale-gray stone, somewhat evocative of Paris. This was a style favored by the elite who governed before the Mexican Revolution—which would break out late in that year—in their awe of all things European. They had built this mansion to house Mexico's first branch of the YMCA, that club created for the physical, mental, and spiritual health of young Londoners in Victorian times. When "the Y" moved house, in 1953, *Novedades* moved in.[5]

The O'Farrills and their partners, the Alemán family, were not exactly newspaper people. In 1944, nine years after *Novedades* launched, company founder and fascist sympathizer Ignacio Herrerías had just faced down a newsroom strike when he was shot by a disgruntled employee. His widow took over for two years, before being encouraged (the word might be a euphemism) to sell out to a consortium led by a politician: Miguel Alemán Valdés. Since Alemán was about to become president of Mexico, he preferred that one or another of his friends be the face of the paper. Soon this fell to Rómulo O'Farrill (father of the man who paid my salary), who had made a fortune as an

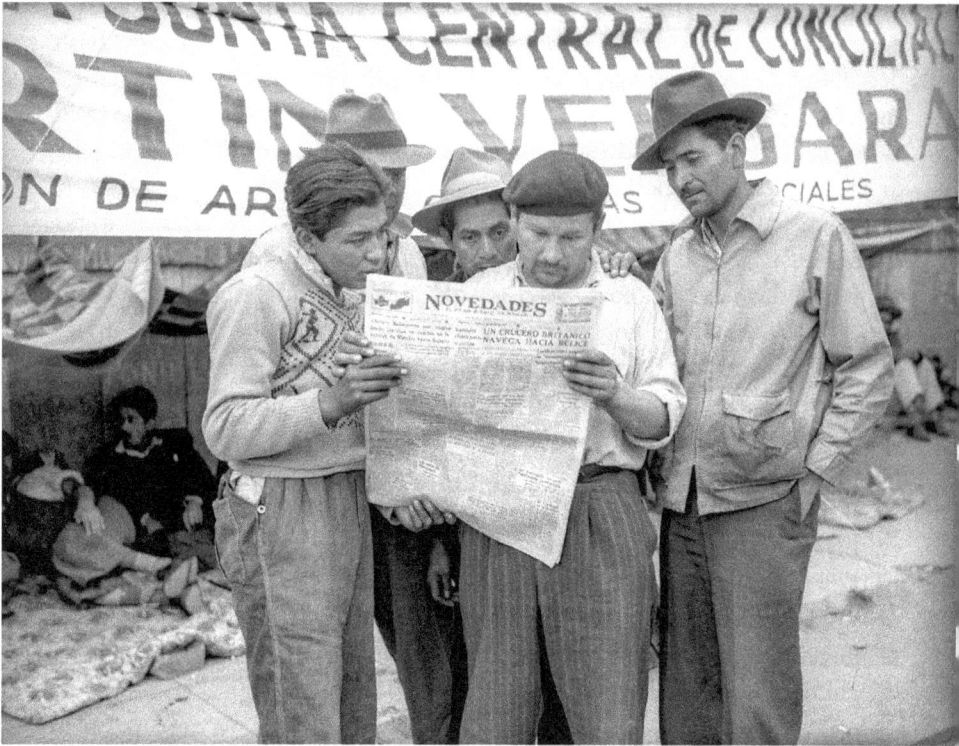

Striking workers reading *Novedades* in the 1940s. The paper's eight-column format and front page of fifteen or twenty stories remained typical of the major broadsheets until the mid-1990s. Reproduction authorized by the Instituto Nacional de Antropología e Historia.

automobile dealer. As president, Alemán would grant O'Farrill a major radio station license and then Mexico's first TV concession. In the latter case, Alemán was again a key investor. So O'Farrill became what Mexicans call a *prestanombres* (literally, lender of names), or front man, although he also held stakes of his own.[6]

As of the late 1940s, *Novedades* had two overriding purposes: to act as a propaganda organ for Alemán (a role it shared with most of the Mexican press, though perhaps more eagerly so) and to boost O'Farrill's business interests— his car dealerships, his radio station, his burgeoning TV network, and so on. The paper served President Alemán's investments too, which lay in tourism and real estate as well as television.[7]

For several decades, *Novedades* was probably a decent business. It was one of the capital's "big three" broadsheets, along with *Excélsior* and *El Universal*. Its presidential PR role was disguised in part by its respected columnists and in part by its hosting of Mexico's leading cultural supplement, the brainchild of public intellectual Fernando Benítez. Various kinds of government subsidy, likely extravagant while Alemán was in office and (as was typical for the Mexican press) still generous afterward, bolstered its balance sheet. So did the fact that its parent company was a market leader in adult comic books, or *historietas*. Luridly illustrated, these 100-page paperbacks featured square-jawed, muscular types coming to the aid of buxom damsels in distress, most of them blond. Such comic books sold by the truckload to the millions of poorer Mexicans whose substandard public schooling had left them semiliterate.[8]

By the early 1960s, according to one US observer, *Novedades* was "the nation's second-ranking quality newspaper."[9] But there were already signs of a weakening. Tensions between the right-wing O'Farrill and the left-wing Benítez, including over the latter's sympathies for the Cuban Revolution, had led to Benítez's ouster in 1961; he took the entire staff of his famed cultural supplement with him. Then, in 1965, the paper began to face competition for its core readership of middle-brow conservatives from *El Sol de México* (known as *El Sol*) and *El Heraldo de México* (known as *El Heraldo*), both of which improved on *Novedades* with color photos. Changes of editor at *Excélsior* and *El Universal* in the late 1960s gave those papers a qualitative boost. *Novedades* became remarkable for its unremarkability. O'Farrill and Alemán both died in the early 1980s; they left the business to their less impressive sons, Rómulo Jr. and Miguel Jr. These men preferred to involve themselves with a much more lucrative and influential medium that they inherited: Televisa, the world's biggest Spanish-language entertainment company. Here they were joint owners with Emilio Azcárraga, the voracious magnate known as "El Tigre." Televisa's TV channels and other promotional capabilities offered a route to reversing *Novedades*' fortunes. The paper was redesigned, with a simpler layout, color photographs, and glossy supplements. An intensive marketing campaign included star actors offering books and perfumes to new subscribers. But all this struggled to mask how *Novedades* was a desperately dull read. And then, in 1991, fed up with the capricious leadership of El Tigre, O'Farrill and Alemán opted to sell their stakes in Televisa, which meant the paper lost leverage with advertisers.[10]

The stately edifice of Novedades Editores housed an increasingly untenable business. The paper claimed sales of over 200,000.[11] But it was whispered inside the building that the real figure was close to 10,000, similar to that of *The News*, which had a much smaller staff. The parent company's comic book division was declining too. The only growth areas were some US magazines like *Vogue*, which the company had licensed for Mexico, and *The News*, thanks to the rising foreign business and retiree communities.

Entering that grand old building was like stepping into a retro rabbit warren. It was a place of low ceilings and linoleum-lined floors, interconnected by tiny elevators and higgledy-piggledy corridors. On reaching the third story, one came upon a neo-Dickensian layout. In the first office there was a row of telephones, three of them, for the twenty-five of us to share. Newsrooms the world over provided reporters with their own desks and phone lines, but not *The News* (nor *Novedades*, whose reporters shared a slightly less pathetic phone bank). Next along the corridor was the office of Miguel Alemán Jr.; he was never seen there, but it contained the one fax machine to which we had access, useful in those days before widespread email for when someone wanted to see our questions ahead of an interview. There followed the graphic design office, a managing editor's office (glass-encased, like mission control), and finally the newsroom, which we shared with *Novedades*. Closest to the entrance was the area allotted to *The News*. This consisted of rows of white desks, out of which arose white-cased Harris computers with green-text screens—the kind of late 1970s design that must have seemed futuristic when it was installed. By the time we arrived it looked quaint.

Every few months the building would shake. There was a terrific din. The first thought that came to mind for any novice reporter was: Earthquake! Mexico City had been struck by a big one six years before; some 10,000 people had died, and ruined tower blocks still dotted the downtown landscape. But the commotion merely signaled the arrival of the owner, on the rooftop helipad. Don Rómulo O'Farrill Jr., to use his formal address (the "Don" being an honorific), was said to be the twenty-fifth-richest man in Mexico. To us at *The News* he was "Don Rom." While we sometimes heard his helicopter, we almost never saw him. In my eighteen months at *The News* I met him just once, at a company Thanksgiving party. A septuagenarian of slender frame with salt-and-pepper hair and pale wrinkled features who sported a bowtie, he could have passed for a prep school Latin teacher.

Don Rom was nice but dim, with more of a gift for quiet diplomacy than for studying a balance sheet. (I once interviewed the celebrated author Elena Poniatowska, who had written for *Novedades* for three decades. She told me, "I always thought Rómulo was an idiot.") One day, Mike Zamba was called to Don Rom's spacious office, where he found that its accoutrements included a barber's chair. Helping out at the firm were several other O'Farrills. These included Don Rom's daughter Hilda, who ran the magazine division (almost into the ground); his son Víctor Hugo, who, as head of telenovela production at Televisa, was generally busy with his starlets, Salma Hayek among them; and his other son, Pepe Antonio, who acted as chief censor, nixing any story he felt too politically sensitive to run.

Pepe Antonio could be heavy-handed. This was a man rumored to enjoy rabbit hunting with an Uzi. It was also said that he showed up drunk at *Novedades* one night, insisting he needed to enter his office and very unhappy that a key for it could not be found. So he summoned the guard on duty at the entrance, borrowed his gun, and shot at the lock until the door opened. In 1987, Don Rom had named a Mexican to edit *The News*, an experienced business reporter named Roberto Mena. One evening Pepe Antonio decided to kill another story and Mena, already chafing at the son's impositions, visited his office to protest: "*I'm* the editor. *I'm* supposed to set editorial policy." At which point, Pepe Antonio opened his desk drawer, pulled out a .45 pistol, and laid it on the table. "It is I who set editorial policy."

In 1991, with Don Rom semiretired and Pepe Antonio absent for a while in rehab, it seemed that no one was minding the store. No one except Samuel Podolsky, the general manager. A former banking executive, Podolsky had been hired to try to make the company self-sustaining. Don Rom feared that President Salinas, neoliberal that he was, would cut government subsidies to the press. Podolsky had his work cut out for him. In short, *Novedades* was a sieve. Lulled into complacency by decades of the paper's living off handouts from the state, employees at all levels were on the make. The procurement department was making phantom purchases. The union reps were demanding large sums to keep employees in line. Human resources was overseen by a retired colonel who had married into the O'Farrill family and was said to be one of the most corrupt of all. Were these freeloaders being disloyal? Perhaps they felt they were not, since the company's chief source of income was not hard-earned sales but government subsidies.

Nor was *The News* a tight ship. Reporters only had to file one or two stories a day, and some of these entailed little more than writing up a press release. So we often put in half days. *The News* could have operated on two-thirds of its staff. Then there was the willingness of management to greenlight costly jaunts. My colleague Andrew Downie got to cover the Pan American Games in Cuba. David Luhnow scored a three-week trip to Rio de Janeiro for the Earth Summit of 1992. Within Mexico, many of us traveled on the company dollar. Andrew Cawthorne and Nicholas Petche were flown by commercial and then private plane to the remote highlands of northern Jalisco, to report on a famine among the Indigenous Huichol people. I flew to Cancún for a film festival, to the southernmost state of Chiapas to report on a religious conflict, and to Oaxaca to cover a visit by Prince Charles. These were all fantastic experiences for us, personally and professionally, but for so small a paper they made dubious sense.

The Government's Game

Shayne McGuire, son of the former *Newsweek* correspondent Stryker McGuire, joined *The News* shortly after I did. He would stay for less than a year, but as someone who had spent most of his youth in Mexico, he spoke fluent Spanish and, having grown up around reporters, he was quick to grasp the singularity of journalism *a la mexicana.*

Shayne's beat included Congress, and in May 1992 he was invited, along with two dozen other reporters on the congressional beat, to cover the Twenty-Third Mexico–United States Interparliamentary Conference in San Antonio.[12] The forum had taken on new importance given negotiations for NAFTA, and *The News* was happy for Shayne to go because Mexico's Senate was footing the bill. The day of the trip, the journalists convened at the Senate before being bused to the airport. Each was summoned in turn into the office of the press chief. When Shayne was called in, the man handed him an envelope. "This is for your expenses on the trip." Shayne glanced inside: The bills totaled at least $1,000.

"But the hotel, the meals, and the plane are all paid for, right?" he asked.

"Yes, yes, but this is for your *expenses,*" the man replied, adding a paternalistic smile.

Shayne shook his head and handed the envelope back. This earned him a "dumb gringo" look from the press chief.

The San Antonio conference lasted for three days and generated a moderate amount of news, but the reporters had plenty of time to themselves. The Senate continued to be a generous host. One night at the hotel bar, when he asked for the bill, Shayne was told that his tab was covered. He could not have spent $1,000 even if he'd tried, he thought . . . until the day of departure, when it all became clear.

As he waited on board the military plane that had flown them all to Texas, Shayne noticed that the flight kept getting delayed. Eventually the pilot announced that the crew was unable to fit everyone's baggage into the cargo hold. Could the passengers please vacate the eight rows in the rear, so the rest of the luggage could be placed there? Those seats were then filled up with the reporters' and the politicians' shopping: TV sets, boom boxes, computers, all manner of consumer electronics. And since it was a military flight, there would be no customs agents to hassle them on arrival in Mexico City.

Junkets were standard practice, and businesses were generous too. There was a mutual understanding between Mexico's private sector and its press that coverage required the offer of a freebie. Here *The News* conformed to the culture and our editors passed on the invitations. One December I was taken by minibus with several other reporters to cover a chamber music festival in San Miguel de Allende, where I was put up for several nights in a plush hotel in a colonial building. One spring I was flown to Los Cabos, and lodged at a spanking beachfront boutique, to interview Jack Nicklaus about a golf course he was designing.[13] Eduardo García went to Acapulco, courtesy of the high-end resort complex Las Brisas, where he tried to dignify the junket by writing on tourism in the city in general. Managing editor Kelly Garrett scored tourism junkets to Cuba (where he met Fidel Castro), Germany, and England, but since he was the hardest-working person at the paper, we didn't begrudge him his fortune.

Gifts were also standard, especially at Christmas. Shayne McGuire was at home in his downtown apartment one December evening in 1992 when the bell rang. There was a cargo van parked outside, and the driver was waiting to greet him. "We bring you a gift from the mayor, Manuel Camacho Solís," he said, sliding back the door. There were stacks of identical boxes inside. The driver hauled one out and offered it to Shayne.

"What is it?" the journalist asked.

"It's a fax machine," the functionary replied.

"No, I can't take that," said Shayne.

"You sure?"

"I'm sure."

State-fueled Christmas merriment took several forms. Many ministries threw parties for the reporters who covered them. David Luhnow, our environmental writer, was invited to a party at the Secretariat of Urban Development and Ecology (whose priorities were very much in that order). There his peers were excited to find that their Christmas presents consisted of large domestic appliances; in David's case, his was a full-size fridge. "I can't possibly accept that," David said. The host looked at him incredulously, as did the other reporters within earshot. So David made a joke about being a crazy gringo and said his editor had a no-gifts policy. Such generosity was not confined to the public sector. After I had penned a few freelance pieces about Mexican television, I received a call from the PR office at Televisa: They wanted to know my birthday. I told them I didn't celebrate it. After Elisabeth Malkin joined *The New York Times*, TV Azteca sent her an iPod, and when Eduardo García went on to Bloomberg, the Mexican stock market gifted him a microwave. Both of them returned these de facto bribes.

It was obvious to my peers on the national desk that most of their Mexican counterparts were coddled by the institutions they covered. Beat reporters were known as *reporteros de la fuente*, which translates literally as "reporters of the source," or possibly "reporters *belonging* to the source." Each source succored its lambs every two weeks, with cash-filled envelopes. These handouts were not usually given to novices, so *The News*'s beat reporters were excluded from ministry payrolls, but they sometimes witnessed the fortnightly ritual.

My colleagues gained many insights into how the press was viewed by officialdom. Government flacks expected their bulletins to appear in our pages, if not verbatim, then amply paraphrased. Additional information was handed out parsimoniously, either as a reward for past flattery or as a gift in the hope of the same. Interviews with bigwigs were meant to be undertaken with deference. Press conferences were calm affairs, journalists waiting to be spoon-fed and rarely challenging official claims, and in the provinces they included payments in cash. Andrew Cawthorne was offered an envelope by the staff of the governor of Chiapas; Starr Spencer had a similar experience in Veracruz.

Starr held the presidential beat, so several times a month she would be bused or flown to one of Mexico's thirty-one states to cover speeches and ribbon-cuttings by President Salinas. In a hotel press room in Veracruz, as she rushed to finish a story on the last day of a trip, Starr found herself pestered by one of the flacks of Governor Dante Delgado. "The governor would like you to have something," he told her several times, but she brushed him off as she typed. She was the last to file her story, so she sped down the hall to catch the press bus, her oversize shoulder bag flapping open. Suddenly the flack reappeared and stuffed a thick envelope into her pouch. "*Señorita*, the governor wants to give you this," he said, and span off. Starr fished it out and found inside a thick wad of bills. She was concerned about missing the bus but more concerned about being bribed. She raced after the flack, calling "Señor! Señor!" and when he turned around she thrust the envelope into his hand. She gasped, "I can't accept this!" He replied, "Yes, we were told you probably wouldn't."

For the professionally trained among us, the dynamic between press and politicians took some getting used to. Jim Silver went to cover a gubernatorial election in Chihuahua and gained a one-on-one with the PRI candidate, Jesús Macías Delgado. Finding the man evasive on the subject of his main opponent, Jim pressed him. Later, Jim heard that Macías had called *The News* to complain about his line of questioning. One day, Andrew Cawthorne returned to the newsroom livid that a secretary had asked, on his arrival to interview some bigwig, whether he was "the young man from *la prensita*." Not *la prensa*, the press, but *la prensita*. The diminutive form of the word denoted something fond, something unthreatening, something to be satisfied with a bagful of treats.

Not every periodical stroked the egos of those in power. One exception was *La Jornada*, the left-wing daily, which inhabited a shabby-elegant nineteenth-century building a short walk away. Even with my limited Spanish, I could tell it was less of a cheerleader for the Salinas regime. Its front-page leads were less complacent. Its cartoonists were more cutting, especially Magú, who contrived to make every politician look brutally ugly. His style fused *Hägar the Horrible* with Picasso's cubism and bathed the result in dirt. The other great holdout was *Proceso*, a weekly muckraking magazine, whose defiant covers promised juicy revelations of official incompetence and corruption. It usually delivered. But it asked a lot of work of its readers, who had to sift through lengthy excerpts of transcribed interviews—its favored reporting mode—to get the good stuff. Like *La Jornada*, *Proceso* was quite leftist and suffused with suspicion of the United States. And it forbade its reporters from taking bribes.

One day I entered our newsroom to find several colleagues huddled around a table, poring over the various sections of what I took to be a US paper: a full-color broadsheet, attractively designed, a bit like *USA Today*. Page 1 was limited to four or five stories, not the twenty headlines (followed by a paragraph and then a page jump) typical of Mexican broadsheets. An actress adorned the front of the showbiz section, her leggy photo stretching the length of the page. It was all unlike anything in a Mexico City daily. But no, the paper was in Spanish. "What's that?" I asked. "That," intoned Jim Silver, "is the best newspaper in Mexico." It was from Monterrey, a three-hour drive from the Texas border, and it was called *El Norte*.

Self-Censorship and Why Most of Us Quit

When Mike Zamba became editor of *The News* in December 1990, he had been encouraged to develop it as a US-style product; this was the same line that the O'Farrills had trotted out with his predecessors, but now the timing was propitious. The economy was looking up after a decade in the doldrums, and the business elite was confident that under President Salinas, the PRI's profound embrace of neoliberalism—mass privatization of state-run industry and services, free trade, financial deregulation, and a firm hand with the unions—heralded an era of profit. In keeping with the zeitgeist, Don Rom allowed Zamba to expand the reporting staff.

By spring 1992, *The News* was prospering. Since Zamba's arrival, circulation had nearly doubled to an average 27,000. This owed much to his hiring of more experienced reporters (fewer backpackers like me), along with a marketing executive. The paper also enjoyed a subscription bump with the 1991 Gulf War, and the new readers stayed with the paper. Some were part of the growing influx of foreign business executives; others belonged to Mexico's cosmopolitan elite, wanting to practice their English.

But Zamba was tiring of the inroads on his promised autonomy. *Novedades* had hired a manager to help supervise *The News*, a smiling rich kid from Peru with no hard news experience named Fernando Bambarén. Zamba increasingly found himself having to justify his editorial choices to the Peruvian. The constant "Why this? Why this?" from Bambarén wore him down. It was censorship by a thousand cuts. It was also the kind of daily aggravation designed to make a well-paid employee quit, for a firing would require a hefty severance. So Zamba told Don Rom that he did not wish to run a paper that purported to

US standards while betraying US ethics. His exit struck a blow to newsroom morale, and morale would sink further over the months to come.

It did not help that his replacement was Bambarén. The Peruvian did not last long, just enough to help propel the paper on a sad downward curve to oblivion. "Journalism is in my blood," he was once gauche enough to claim. When pressed as to what he meant, he said that some relative of his had been a reporter. We got an early taste of Bambarén's journalistic consanguinity when we found that stories that might embarrass the PRI were being withheld from the front page. Some of these involved murders of activists for the opposition Party of the Democratic Revolution, even though several Spanish-language papers gave the same stories prominence. Quizzed over this policy, Bambarén replied that he was "trying to run a family newspaper."[14]

Because we were young idealists, and because we disdained the political culture of paternalism and the media culture of deference, we did what we could to practice watchdog journalism. And because *The News* was a niche paper aimed at foreigners and published in a language that its owner barely read, we had some leeway to be critical.

We all knew, and mostly respected, the Mexican journalists' maxim: "You can criticize anything except the president, the army, and the Virgin of Guadalupe."[15] We also knew, but chafed against the fact, that these figures were metonyms: "the president" meant the whole regime; "the army" meant all security forces; "the Virgin" also meant the Catholic hierarchy. When we strayed across these lines, section editors with more years in Mexico would trim our copy and help preserve our editorial semi-independence. As in the days of Pete Hamill, however, they sometimes saw that a story needed to be told and opted to let us tell it like it was. Often, sooner or later, we would then feel the wrath of Don Rom.

Several gubernatorial elections were scheduled for November 1992, one of them in the state of Puebla, where the PRI's candidate was one of its most controversial politicians, Manuel Bartlett. Puebla was dyed-in-the-wool PRI territory, so Bartlett was a shoo-in, but he was also a "person of interest" to the Mexican and US public alike. This was the spirit of a profile by Jim Silver that appeared eight days before the election.[16] Acknowledging that Bartlett was de facto governor from the day he was unveiled as the candidate, Jim detailed his controversial past, when secretary of government.[17] First, Bartlett had worked to overturn gubernatorial and mayoral victories by the right-of-center National Action Party (PAN). Second, he was widely held to have engineered an election-night fraud in 1988, allowing Salinas to triumph over the leftist Cuauhtémoc Cárdenas. Third, and most damningly for *News* readers, he was allegedly under investigation by the US Drug Enforcement Administration (DEA) for having helped cover up the murder of DEA agent Kiki Camarena in 1985. Jim's piece was not an exposé. Though it included live quotes from half a dozen sources, the allegations had all appeared in print before, mostly in *Proceso*. But that *The News* should devote a full page to questioning the candidate's ethics was remarkable, not least because Don Rom, himself from Puebla, counted Bartlett as a friend.

The story might have ended there, for several days went by without a reaction from on high. Making sure that it did *not* end there was a fresh-off-the-plane Bostonian with a sly grin and a low tolerance for what he called (quite frequently) "bullshit." His name was Zach Margulis, and with Jim's article in hand he raced out to Puebla to dig up more dirt. He also called up US officials and lawyers investigating the Camarena murder. On November 3, five days before the vote, Zach filed a story that noted that the latest trial had been postponed, so any new details about Bartlett's involvement would not emerge until after the election.[18] On November 4, he filed a lengthier piece, tied to a DEA report that directly linked Bartlett to the murder of a Veracruz journalist in 1984. It also detailed the politician's likely knowledge, while secretary of government, of protections afforded to Miguel Ángel Félix Gallardo and other drug lords by secret service members whose agency reported to Bartlett.[19] This article never came out.

The next day, seeing his feature absent, Zach called up Bambarén from his Puebla hotel. The Peruvian told him his reporting was felt to be biased against the PRI and that he was barred from writing further about the election. Suspecting editorial spinelessness, David Luhnow asked Bambarén in private what was going on. The editor admitted that he had shared Zach's feature with Don Rom and been told that both he and Zach would be fired if it ran. By then, we later gathered, Bartlett himself had complained to O'Farrill, who in turn read Jim's and Zach's pieces (perhaps in translation) with mounting anger. "What kind of opposition rag am I running?" he was said to have asked Bambarén.

Don Rom then made his biggest mistake. His killing of Zach's feature, while an ethically dubious case of owner interference, was hardly surprising given his friendship with Bartlett. One could imagine US media magnate Rupert Murdoch or Canadian mogul Conrad Black making a similar call. But then he could have moved on, reestablished the *News*'s freedom to be franker than *Novedades*, and worked to restore morale, while remaining personally loyal to the PRI.

Instead, petulant and autocratic, Dom Rom doubled down, turning a drama into a crisis. The day after the elections, we found he had told Bambarén to halt *all* coverage of opposition parties, a ban that would stay in place for two months. Any political story written by a *News* reporter had to be vetted by Dom Rom's son Pepe Antonio. Those who tried to cover what was newsworthy, whether on politics, human rights, or even the environment, found their copy eviscerated before it ran or simply spiked. In effect, reporters assigned to any branch of government were more or less reduced to writing up press releases. On assignment in Tamaulipas, the site of a much testier campaign than Puebla's, Jeffrey Stoub was told to avoid covering opposition protests of electoral fraud.[20] One protest culminated in the burning down of an electoral office, an incident covered by all media, even Televisa, but Jeff's story was nixed.

Reporters on the national desk weighed their options. They protested by removing their bylines as long as the censorship persisted; all stories would be credited to *"The News* Staff." For a week or so, until Bambarén put a stop to the protest by threatening to dock pay, news reporters wrote parodies of the kind of nonstories appearing in *Novedades*, declarations by this official and that, and the subeditors entered into the spirit by crowning them with extra-dull titles. Shayne wrote one, about a chamber of commerce, headed "Canaco's Works Focus on the 'Common Good'"; Zach penned another, about city hall, that declared with delirious blandness, "D.F. Plans Positive New Projects."[21]

Zach called up *Newsweek* correspondent Tim Padgett and found a receptive ear. In the following week's edition, the magazine exposed the censorship at *The News*, naming Zach and summarizing his axed article about the DEA report. *Newsweek* added that Mexico's media in general had failed to raise questions about candidate Bartlett, "which flies in the face of President Carlos Salinas de Gortari's calls to make Mexico's election coverage more fair and open."[22]

Hot off the phone with Don Rom, Bambarén was furious. He called Zach to his office and yelled at him for fifteen minutes. Other media, starting with the Monterrey paper *El Norte*, picked up the *Newsweek* piece. My colleagues began talking to the news wires.[23]

As the story snowballed, Zach was invited to write an op-ed for *The New York Times*. "Blood and Ink in Mexico," boomed the title. The "blood" referred to Zach's attempt to connect censorship at *The News* with the recent killing of a reporter in Mexico City and the alleged deaths or disappearances of a further twenty-five media workers on President Salinas's watch. Of further embarrassment for Salinas—more sensitive to the foreign press than any of his predecessors—the column led by quoting a speech of his, in which he pledged "liberty of expression and respect for journalism," given just hours before the reporter's murder. Now, with the US Congress still to approve NAFTA, his regime had been made to look undemocratic and possibly homicidal in his main trading partner's newspaper of record.[24]

By criticizing his employer in so public a manner, Zach was begging to be fired. It would be both a badge of honor and further proof of censorship. Poor old Don Rom took the bait. He terminated Zach's employment four days later and had guards escort him out of fortress *Novedades*. The firing sparked yet another round of headlines, in both the United States and Mexico. As widely read columnist Sergio Sarmiento put it in *El Financiero*, "What is curious about this case . . . is that the firing in question was undertaken in a desire to protect the interests of the Mexican government, but if the deed achieved anything it was to affect them negatively." Referring to the whole Bartlett–Margulis saga, he added, "The persistent image abroad of Mexico as an undemocratic country was emphasized by this series of actions."[25] We later learned that Dom Rom lost some of the government subsidy for his papers over his bungling of the affair.[26]

Attempting damage control, the president's forward-thinking press chief, José Carreño Carlón, invited Zach to Los Pinos, the presidential palace. They spoke for two hours, Carreño voicing great concern. Then Zach had an audience with the chief executive himself. Salinas assured the reporter that the government had nothing to do with his firing. Then, to Zach's great entertainment, Salinas offered to find him a new job. Zach declined, flew back to the States, and landed a gig as a crime reporter with the New York *Daily News*.

Now almost all of us were looking to leave. By February, a reporting crew of twenty was down to seven.[27] In the spring, along with Elisabeth Malkin, Starr Spencer, and former *News* staffer Laurence "Lonnie" Iliff, I accepted an invitation from Mike Zamba to join *Mexico Insight*, a newsmagazine he was setting up at *Excélsior*. The switch felt like a step up the ladder. *Excélsior* was the second-oldest daily in Mexico City and the most famous. Its main building, overlooking a busy intersection on Reforma Boulevard, enjoyed a visibility higher than that of its rivals' headquarters. Its slogan proclaimed, "The newspaper of the life of the nation."

Excélsior: The Falling Giant

Excélsior was, by local standards, a legendary newspaper.[28] For most of its history since its founding in 1917 during the revolution, it had occupied first place in employee count, broadsheet circulation, and political influence. Traditionally, its ideology was conservative, sometimes very much so. In the 1930s, like various Mexican papers (and politicians) at the time, it sympathized with Hitler and Mussolini, admiring their bold nationalism and corporatist domination of the masses. More than most, it had to be cajoled to side with the Allies in World War II; the US, UK, and French embassies used the carrot of subsidies and the stick of advertiser boycotts by their nations' firms.[29]

Afterward, *Excélsior* became a stalwart cold warrior, US friendly and red-baiting. Its managing to do all this while supporting a regime that called itself "revolutionary"—ostensibly committed to state-led development and geopolitical nonalignment—was but one of the many peculiarities of Mexican politics. The ruling PRI was a broad church: All creeds were welcome, as long as one pledged allegiance to party and president.

Despite this tradition of conservatism and kowtowing, an eight-year interlude of leftism and independent-mindedness bolstered the reputation of *Excélsior*. Between 1968 and 1976, the paper had been edited by Julio Scherer, who had a gift for mixing with elites and for balancing deference to the regime with criticism of it. When that criticism grew too great for the comfort of Mexico's sitting president, Luis Echeverría, Scherer and his allies found themselves ousted in what was dubbed a state-engineered "coup." This had all occurred seventeen years before we expats climbed aboard to start *Mexico Insight*, but we found that the glamour of the Scherer era lingered in the collective memory of the press. Once inside, however, we found a culture of laxity and smugness.

Now a business reporter, I needed to scour the dailies for ideas for features. Yet as my Spanish improved, I realized that Mexican journalese was often inscrutable. Reporters rarely supplied context, so one usually had to know something about the matter beforehand to grasp a story's importance. There was often a flurry of superfluous detail, even in the lead: the digits of the license plate of a getaway car, the extra-precise job title of a source being quoted. In stories about officialdom, there was an awful lot of "he said," except that due to the idiosyncrasies of Mexican style this verb could not be repeated, so subsequent declarations were tagged "he emphasized . . . he underlined . . . he manifested . . . he elaborated." And since some reporters and columnists seemed to pride themselves on the length of their sentences, a reader sometimes needed stamina.

The prose reflected the tacit elitism of most Mexican dailies. Target readers were, above all, members of Mexico's political, economic, and cultural establishments; *la chusma* (the rabble) could get their news from television or the tabloids, and the high ratings and circulation of these media showed that this is just what the less well-off did. At *Excélsior*, only a smattering of readable correspondents and columnists, such as the political scientist Lorenzo Meyer, transcended the mediocrity. But the reporters themselves were hardly to blame. The few we got to know apparently spent their waking hours rushing from one press conference to another, as many as five in a day. They scarcely had time to develop much knowledge of the topics they covered. And their salaries were miserable. It was factory work.

If *Excélsior* journalism was lazily elitist, its business model was plain lazy. It relied on government advertising and subsidies and (it would later emerge) ran up huge debts with state agencies and development banks, which it got away with by incessantly pandering to the president and the PRI. It published a fairly popular afternoon edition, *Últimas Noticias*, but also carried the dead weight of two magazines, *Revista de Revistas* and *Jueves*, both of ancient origin. No one read them, but since *Excélsior* was a cooperative, axing them would have meant layoffs, which is hard for any cooperative to contemplate. Altogether the company employed some 2,000 personnel, and it seemed to tolerate all kinds of nepotistic abuse. Down the corridor from *Mexico Insight* was a spacious office called Informática. The word means "information technology," but there was little sign of either. The room was populated by several middle-aged women who spent their nine-to-five reading magazines and knitting.

Leading this enterprise was Regino Díaz Redondo, the slick, Spanish-born operator who had famously stabbed Scherer in the back to facilitate President Echeverría's coup. We reporters never saw him in the flesh, only on the front page of the paper. There he would self-importantly appear from time to time, interviewing some foreign dignitary while dressed in a shiny suit, the kind sported by mafiosi in *The Godfather Part II*. To his credit, Díaz Redondo gave us a freer rein at *Mexico Insight* than he allowed at *Excélsior*; perhaps Salinas, in his NAFTA-courting mode, had given him a green light. Mike Zamba would visit his preposterously large office every two weeks to go over our proposed feature stories, and during the two-year life of our magazine he never once said no. On one occasion he confided to Mike that, as a journalist, he felt restrained by *Excélsior* as an institution and he liked how we took on topics that he could not in the newspaper. Mike came to feel that Díaz Redondo had become ensnared by his own ambition. He liked the trappings and the glamour of his position, but he didn't like the job itself.

There was something altogether schizophrenic about *Excélsior*. It liked to think of itself as a *New York Times*–style gray lady, Mexico's somber newspaper of record, but it behaved like an impetuous *nouveau riche*. Even its building was bipolar. The older part, similar to the home of *Novedades*, was of gracious early 1920s vintage.[30] As the paper's employee count had bloated under Díaz Redondo, extra space was needed, so the director dreamed up an annex that would occupy the sharp corner between Reforma Boulevard and Bucareli Street. Inaugurated in 1987, the triangular annex was a marriage of concrete bunker and glass-paneled discotheque. The Spanish paper *El País* would list it as one of the five architectural monstrosities of Mexico City.[31] The base of the bunker was adorned with the pompous phrase "Information Corner," and the top of it sported a partial-wraparound board, to relay headlines in lights like the news ticker on the old Times Building in Manhattan. But this board was much shorter, so one had to stand infuriatingly still to read it, memorizing the first few words of a headline before these disappeared to make way for the rest.

Excélsior publisher Regino Díaz Redondo receives a prize from President Carlos Salinas. Courtesy of the Archivo General de la Nación (Fondo Hermanos Mayo, AG2/724).

A few weeks after joining, Elisabeth Malkin and I entered the elevator along with an elderly employee. "You two are with that new magazine in English, right?" "Yes," we replied, nodding. With gravitas, he said, "You should know, this newspaper, *Excélsior*, is one of the ten best newspapers in the world." Yet it was already obvious to us that *Excélsior* was doing less incisive work than *La Jornada* and *El Financiero*. Outside the capital, had we ventured to look, we would have found it qualitatively inferior to various papers that shunned conformity and served their cities with solid reporting: Monterrey's *Norte*, Guadalajara's *Siglo 21*, Hermosillo's *El Imparcial*, Mérida's *Diario de Yucatán*, and Tijuana's weekly *Zeta* were probably the best of them.[32]

The sorry fact was that *Excélsior* barely numbered among the ten best papers *in Mexico*. (I heard "one of the world's ten best" several times at *Excélsior*. Presumably some foreigner had paid the paper an ingratiating compliment during the glory days under Scherer, and old-timers had repeated the flattery until it became gospel.) Still, many *Excélsior* employees retained the complacent self-assurance that, in authoritarian societies, comes with proximity to power. *Excélsior* was still a mighty paper of a sort, not because of what it covered but because of what it left out. Through its calculated omissions it served the state, and the state protected its size, its bloated payroll, its benefits, and its access.

———

Each morning, an office boy would bring a stack of the day's papers up to our top-floor newsroom and deposit it inside the door: *Excélsior*, *El Universal*, *La Jornada*, the government-run *El Nacional*, and the financial dailies *El Financiero* and *El Economista*. We would comb them for leads that, investigated in depth, would make good features for our twice-monthly magazine. Elisabeth and I would peruse the business sections, which mostly offered slim pickings. *Excélsior*'s was full of international wire stories and said little about Mexico, so we gave up on it; *El Universal* was hardly better. *El Nacional* was dull to the point of self-parody. *La Jornada* was lively but unreliable on anything business related; it still used "capitalist" as a term of abuse. *El Financiero* and *El Economista* were less arduous than the broadsheets but full of soporific opinions by this bigwig and that; oddly, *El Financiero* was more interesting for its political and cultural coverage, while *El Economista* hosted Mexico's wittiest cartoonist, Nerilicón.

All this changed in November 1993, when *El Norte* of Monterrey launched a sister paper in the capital: *Reforma*. The concept was similar: attractive design, color photos, arresting charts, helpful graphics. Headlines that were direct, provocative, or both. Above all, inquiring stories that went beyond bulletins and declarations, told in clean prose. From that moment on, we all wanted to start the day with *Reforma*. Only then would we proceed to the other papers. By the afternoon, pieces of all of them would be strewn across the office—all except for sad *Excélsior*, lying untouched by the door.

Around the same time as *Reforma* debuted, there appeared in the bookshops a history of Mexican journalism's relations with the state. It had a yellow cover and a biting title: *Prensa vendida* (Sell-out press).[33] Its sardonic table of contents described each presidential period in terms of journalistic obeisance. For Miguel Alemán, consolidator of a dependent press in the early 1950s, "Thank you, Mr. President"; for Miguel de la Madrid, who ruled during the economic disaster of the 1980s, "We'll put up with it, Mr. President"; and for Carlos Salinas, "We'll modernize, Mr. President." As I flicked through the text, it seemed to me that scarcely any newspaper had been more of a sellout than *Excélsior*.

We wished we were housed at a better paper, but we were proud of our little fortnightly magazine, with its full-time staff of eight. We failed to gain distribution at Mexico's thousands of street kiosks, as the head of the vendors' union demanded a bribe too high for our budget. We hardly sold any ads. But through in-store sales and subscriptions we built up a circulation of 10,000.

Occasionally we made waves. Perhaps our finest moment was a scoop of sorts by Lonnie Iliff that all but forecast the armed uprising of Indigenous Zapatista rebels of January 1994. The previous August, after assiduously reading *La Jornada* and *Proceso* and gleaning tips from their reporters, Lonnie took himself off to Chiapas in search of guerrillas. And he really did take himself, as *Excélsior* would not pay expenses, so Lonnie hitched a ride with a freelancer. With his excellent, slangy Spanish and his California smile, Lonnie managed to get a lot of villagers to spill the beans. Even a spokesman for the Catholic bishop opened up to him. All in all, he was able to confirm: Yes, growing numbers of highland villagers were arming themselves, hoping to redress decades of abuse from white ranchers; yes, they dreamed of overthrowing the federal government; yes, their efforts were being coordinated, although it was unclear by whom. Díaz Redondo at first baulked at the story, but Mike convinced him that Lonnie's sources were solid. And so the feature ran: "Guerrillas in the Mist."[34]

About a month later, Mike got a letter from Mexico's central bank accusing the magazine of printing counterfeit money and warning that a repeat infringement would meet a lawsuit. Our crime was to have run a stock photo of a pile of Mexican currency alongside a business story. Mike took the letter to Díaz Redondo. The boss knew the drill: "This is the government's way of telling you they weren't happy with your 'Guerrillas in the Mist' story." A couple of months after that, all hell broke loose in Chiapas and *Mexico Insight* was vindicated. Dozens of foreign reporters parachuted in to cover the story, and Lonnie encountered several clutching copies of his feature.

Another exposé of ours introduced its author to the dark side of state-press relations in the provinces. Starr Spencer was covering the aftermath of the Chiapas uprising when she met Tomás Capistrán, a writer and cartoonist from Córdoba, Veracruz. Capistrán told her of a disaster in his hometown three years before, the explosion of a pesticide plant, which led to a surge of cancer and leukemia cases and of babies with birth defects. Starr traveled to Córdoba to investigate, and Capistrán introduced her to some of the victims, who had received little aid. She visited the plant and saw scant evidence of cleanup. When she called local authorities and said she was in Córdoba, a voice replied, "Yes, we know you're here." They refused her a face-to-face interview. After three days of reporting, Starr took the bus back to Mexico City, Capistrán dropping her off at the station. She later learned that, within half an hour, he had been abducted by federal police. For three days, he was detained and tortured in a clandestine cell. He was beaten naked. Solvent was forced down his nose, a plastic bag thrust over his head. He was plunged into water and pinned down until he blacked out. Since two colleagues from his newspaper had already been targeted—one murdered, the other disappeared—he did not expect to live. But then he was exhibited at a press conference as a guerrilla sympathizer and charged with resisting arrest and extortion. After two weeks in jail, he was allowed out pending trial, but the police continued to harass him. He fled to the United States. Three years later, by which time Starr had reunited with him and married him, Capistrán was granted political asylum.[35]

Excélsior's deficiencies were thrown into sharpest relief in 1994, when a decade's worth of crises crammed themselves into a twelve-month news slot. On January 1, NAFTA went into effect, and the glory of the Salinas era was marred at one simultaneous stroke when the Zapatista Army of National Liberation rose up against the government, the free trade agreement, and neoliberalism in general. On March 23, the PRI's presidential candidate, Luis Donaldo Colosio, was assassinated at a rally in Tijuana. On May 12, the PAN candidate humiliated the PRI's replacement candidate in the nation's first-ever televised presidential debate. On August 21, the election—which had been postponed due to the Colosio murder—went ahead, the PRI winning amid rumors of a sell-out by the PAN. On September 28, the second-in-command of the PRI was murdered in Mexico City. And on December 20, the newly inaugurated president, Ernesto Zedillo, was forced by a mounting trade deficit and currency speculation to devalue the peso, setting off a terrible recession.

At each new event, readers flocked—according to their politics—to *La Jornada*, *Proceso*, or *Reforma*. It had become fashionable to refer to old-guard members of the PRI, those most resistant to democracy and openness, as dinosaurs. *Excélsior* too was a dinosaur, outpaced by saber-toothed tigers on the left and the right.

Six days after the Colosio murder, I abandoned all loyalty to *Excélsior*. Everyone knew that Salinas would handpick a replacement; the mystery was who. On the morning of March 29, at PRI headquarters, Zedillo was unveiled to the public, so the first papers to carry the news were the afternoon editions. I was walking back to the office after lunch that day, and the display cases on the side of the building caught my eye. *Últimas Noticias* was already pinned up, the front page announcing the new candidate. What struck me was not so much the choosing of Zedillo as the way the news was packaged. There was no mention of the hand of Salinas, no mention of the surprising nature of the pick, no mention that the PRI's old guard had failed to influence the appointment. What the afternoon edition of *Excélsior* ran was effectively a press release, full of officialese that pretended that the PRI's selection process responded to the will of the party's constituent confederations and thus the will of the people.

I would leave *Excélsior* as soon as I could. I must have been doing something right at *Mexico Insight*, because in April I was courted for three jobs. The Reuters bureau chief suggested I apply for their Monterrey post, the

American chamber of commerce offered me the editorship of their magazine, and the Hollywood journal *Variety* called to discuss the new post of Latin America correspondent. A few weeks later, *Variety* flew me up to Los Angeles and put me up in a Beverly Hills hotel where the receptionist answered the phone in French. The editor said I could fly all over the region to interview TV executives and cover film festivals. There was little to debate. I went Hollywood.

That summer, having spent three years in Mexico and joined the ranks of the foreign correspondents, I felt I could start to hold my own amid the supremely confident cohort that dominated expat journalism: reporters for *The New York Times*, *The Wall Street Journal*, Reuters, the BBC. They would convene on Fridays at the Bar Nuevo León, a cantina in Mexico City's stylish Condesa neighborhood. Some nights twenty or thirty would show up, their ranks having swollen because Mexico was now a Major Story. There they would swap tales of Central American wars, trade tips about sources, and alternately advise and rib the newbies.

One correspondent, who joined the cohort in 1996, stood out as milder mannered, less of a talker than a listener. He worked for the *San Antonio Express-News* and his name was Philip True. Two years later, while hiking in the hilly remoteness of northern Jalisco, Philip was attacked and murdered and his body thrown into a ravine. Though two Huichol men were arrested, it was unclear whether they were guilty or scapegoats.[36] Until then, we foreigners assumed we were bulletproof. Sobering though the episode was, we continued to feel pretty much free to come and go as we pleased. The real threat was borne by Mexican journalists, especially those who worked in southern states with cultures of political impunity, like Veracruz and Guerrero, or in northern states with worsening rivalries between crime syndicates, like Baja California and Chihuahua. Before long, both kinds of problems and the violence they fueled would get much, much worse.

———

As for *The News*, the ground floor of my writing career and that of so many others, the paper expired on New Year's Eve 2002. By then, Don Rom was eighty-five. *Novedades*, with a swollen payroll of around 900, had neglected to modernize or embrace political pluralism as its rival broadsheets had done, and it had long been hemorrhaging cash. *The News*, with a payroll of 50, was in better shape, but its advertising business and its distribution outside the capital had been ineptly underdeveloped. Circulation had fallen back to 18,000, two-thirds of its peak of the early to mid-1990s, and ad sales had also fallen by a third.

Despite the paper's many failings, the passing of *The News* meant the loss of a connective hub for Mexico City's English-speaking community that would never be quite replaced. Closures of enclave-serving newspapers followed elsewhere, similar victims of the inexorable global shift away from print: *The Daily Journal* of Caracas in 2008; the ancient *Buenos Aires Herald* (founded in 1876) in 2023.

The romance of the expatriate newsroom, bustling with young people eager to share their newly gained knowledge of local politics, business, society, and arts, belongs to another era.

Chapter 1

Prensa vendida

The (Mostly) Sell-Out Press, 1896–1988

By assigning resources to the press, the government, quite modestly, only requests "a little reciprocity": excessive praise, the silencing of news, and the moral lynching of the opposition.

—Carlos Monsiváis, cultural critic

In Mexico, journalism is not considered a public service. From the dawn of Mexico's newspaper industry in 1896, the media has served those holding political power.

—Daniel Moreno, editor, *Animal Político*

El Universal: The President Is Our First Reader

Juan Francisco Ealy Ortiz took the helm of Mexico City's oldest newspaper at the age of twenty-seven.[1] A slender, handsome man and a dapper dresser, his wavy black hair greased back and his moustache clipped fashionably thin, Ealy resembled a younger version of Mauricio Garcés, a womanizing star of 1960s bedroom farces. Ealy did not have news in his blood. His father, Jack, the son of an Irish American immigrant to Mexico, was an engineer. While supervising a thermoelectrical plant in Durango, Jack Ealy had somehow allied himself with northern royalty, marrying the sister of Nazario Ortiz Garza, a former governor of Coahuila and now a senator. Juan Francisco loved his father, but his ambitions followed the model of his maternal uncle. As he grew up in Mexico City, where his father had come to own a factory, he dreamed of becoming a politician. As a first step, he started a degree in economics at the National Autonomous University of Mexico (UNAM).[2]

Ealy did follow his father in marrying up. The family of his wife María Dolores, the Lanz Duret clan, were politicos and eminent lawyers, with forebears among the nineteenth-century elite.[3] Moreover, they owned the respectable broadsheet *El Universal*, which dubbed itself "The great daily paper of Mexico."

As Ealy's luck would have it, the Lanz Durets were poor managers, and *El Universal* needed rescuing. Three generations of the family had failed to modernize their newspaper. Long-running intransigence among its six company unions (one for each department) had led to huge worker-benefits costs and obstructed the entry of talent. In sales and influence, *El Universal* lagged behind its broadsheet rivals, *Excélsior* and *Novedades*, and in the dreary gray-blue newsroom morale was low. So in 1968 the family invited the ambitious but likeable Ealy, who had held a series of jobs at the paper for eight years, to become general manager. This was not entirely the sign of a mother-in-law's benevolence. According to a secret service report, Doña Francisca Valdés de Lanz Duret, the paper's widowed owner, had accepted a bailout from Ealy's uncle Nazario, who, after leaving the Senate, had made a fortune in winemaking. The patriarch set his nephew's appointment as a condition.

As an astute outsider-insider, Ealy could gauge how much trouble the company was in. After a year or so on the job, he made the tactical move of letting on to a secret service agent that *El Universal* was experiencing "the most shocking bankruptcy"; this was a distress signal designed to reach the top of government. In October 1969, having fully charmed his way into the confidence of Doña Francisca, Ealy took advantage of his brother-in-law Miguel's absence (when the latter traveled to Germany to buy a new printing press), and convened a shareholder meeting in which he persuaded the rest of the family to name him president and CEO.[4] Journalism had not been his first choice of career, yet *El Universal* would allow Ealy a long life in politics, or at least in politicking. The relationship between Mexico's leading newspapers and its single-party state was one of ancient and cozy interdependence.

Whether assisted or merely inspired by Uncle Nazario, the energetic Ealy adapted quickly to the demands of his job. Within two years of becoming CEO, he had ingratiated himself sufficiently with his peers to become president of an association representing all the capital's major publishers.[5] He similarly ingratiated himself with the president, Gustavo Díaz Ordaz, and his right-hand man, Secretary of Government Luis Echeverría, whose brief included supervision of the media. Under Mexico's centralized political system, the favor of the president could mean for a newspaper the awarding of generous subsidies (in the form of "official advertising" and cash payments to employees), the granting of low-interest loans, the forgiveness or suspension of debts, and the help of the arbitration courts in solving labor troubles. His disfavor could mean the closure of the business, even by force. Favor was ordinarily gained by adulatory, banner-headline reports of the president's speeches and policies and fawning coverage of his ministers, along with a minimizing of bad news and policy errors. It could be augmented by direct lobbying and pledges of loyalty.[6]

Again as Ealy's luck would have it, as of 1968 the government found a special need for friends in the media. That July, a student-led civil rights movement surged onto the streets, protesting authoritarianism and police brutality and calling for the release of political prisoners. As the students marched, chanting their displeasure at the establishment, they popularized the cry

¡Prensa vendida! (Sell-out press!). Díaz Ordaz and Echeverría felt the movement a threat to Mexico's global image, for that October the country was to host the Olympic Games, the first "Third World" nation to do so. During the summer and autumn, Ealy and his brother-in-law Francisco Lanz Duret wrote letters to Echeverría, praising his firm hand with the students and seeking advertising from his ministry. Most of the press complied with the state's stigmatizing of the movement, calling the students terrorists, guerrillas, anarchists, mercenaries, or traitors. But *El Universal* ran some of the most consistently negative comments, with 79 percent of its opinion columns condemning the movement, against 59 percent in *Novedades* and just 9 percent in *Excélsior*. Ealy and Lanz Duret's letters continued after October 2, when several dozen student protesters were gunned down by the army in Tlatelolco Plaza, a massacre rumored (and widely believed today) to have been masterminded by Echeverría. Like almost all the press, *El Universal* reported the violence by peddling the lie that the students had been the aggressors, goaded by foreign agitators, and understating the number of dead. Its October 3 banner headline ran, "Tlatelolco: Battle Ground," and a subhead claimed, "For Several Hours, Terrorists and Soldiers Engaged in Heavy Fighting."[7]

Favor with the president could be further accrued in person, every June 7. Each year on that date since 1951, Mexico's publishers and editors had invited the head of state to a banquet, to pay homage to the great man and to thank him "for making possible the exercise of freedom of the press."[8] Taking place at one or another of the capital's fanciest restaurants, the occasion gathered several hundred journalists and featured speeches, first from a senior newspaperman, who would praise the chief executive in effusive language, then from the president himself, who would compliment the press for informing the public of the acts of his government, remind it that with great freedom came great responsibility, and sometimes chide elements within it for abusing their platforms through lies, distortions, insolence, or attempts to fuel readers' dissatisfaction.

Evocative of the court of Louis XIV, the annual ritual shimmered with symbolic gradations of proximity to power, which also reflected a courtier's ability to gain the favor of senior nobility: the banquet's organizers. These were veteran publishers like Martín Luis Guzmán, a once great novelist-turned-presidential toady, who ran *Tiempo*, a pale imitation of *Time* magazine; José García Valseca, owner of the nation's largest newspaper chain, branded *El Sol*; and Rómulo O'Farrill, publisher of *Novedades* and business partner of former president Miguel Alemán Valdés. In 1969, Ealy was named among a welcoming party of three who would greet President Díaz Ordaz at the door. In 1970, Ealy's role was raised a notch as Guzmán invited him, along with

President Miguel Alemán (*second from right*) converses with *El Sol* owner José García Valseca at the first annual banquet celebrating freedom of the press, June 7, 1951. Courtesy of the Archivo General de la Nación (Fondo Hermanos Mayo, CR1/5163).

O'Farrill's son Rómulo Jr., to collect the president from his official residence and accompany him by car to the event. Díaz Ordaz was no doubt happy to see him, for Ealy had been putting his paper to good sycophantic use ahead of that summer's election. Compared with Julio Scherer's *Excélsior*, *El Universal* had been giving the president's heir designate, Luis Echeverría, more than twice the front-page headlines, nine times the news space, and nine times as many photographs.[9]

By 1972, Ealy had gained sufficient recognition among his peers to be named the banquet's orator, speaking on behalf of the entire press.[10] It was a magnificent occasion, this time hosted by Mexico City's most avant-garde hotel, the Ricardo Legorreta–designed Camino Real. What had begun twenty-one years before as a luncheon for 128 senior publishers and editors had grown by degrees, and this year the guest list numbered more than 1,000, a record figure quite in keeping with the famed self-importance of President Echeverría. As Ealy addressed this multitude, on the eve of his thirtieth birthday, he showed himself an able artist of Mexican political discourse, with its interplay of hyperbole and subtle signals, assertiveness and deference. Such contradictory rhetoric had grown in prominence under Echeverría. Hoping to undermine rumors of his role in the 1968 massacre, he had taken office in December 1970 with a PR offensive. He freed political prisoners from the student movement. He backed the universities' autonomy from the interference of politicians and massively increased their budgets. His slogan was "democratic opening," and he expected the press to play a part.[11]

Having acknowledged the size of the day's gathering and given a special welcome to the lowlier employees present, Ealy began with calculated self-criticism: "Is it not timely that we leaders of Mexican journalism ask ourselves . . . whether our responsibility is always equal to our liberty?"[12] Here was an allusion to the repeated request of presidents past that the press act "responsibly," which was to imply that it should not rock the boat, that it should not weaken national unity by criticizing any politician without permission from the top to do so. Ealy continued, "Good information and good criticism make for correct orientation." Buzzword alert! "Orientation" was what the establishment offered to the masses, telling them what to think and how to vote. "No important person, no functionary, no institution escapes the critical signaling that journalism exercises daily." (This claim was purely Orwellian; daily, the press offered little but praise to each of these.) "Not even you, Mister President, because we have interpreted that criticism can and should be carried out beginning with the highest authority in the country."

Ealy was ostensibly taking at face value Echeverría's false magnanimity. The president had indeed called for criticism and he allowed it in small amounts, off the front page, in opinion columns. Covertly, his regime maneuvered to restrict or temper it: by upping the frequency of disguised propaganda insertions; by fomenting division between journalists; by letting a paramilitary goon squad beat up reporters and photographers covering a student protest in June 1971; and, two months after Ealy gave his speech, by orchestrating an advertiser boycott against *Excélsior*, whose editor Scherer had taken Echeverría's call for criticism more literally than he cared for.[13]

Ealy finished with a flourish: "This country is led by a clear intelligence, very broadly well-informed; by a firm hand, serene and tireless. We have a clean role model, a beneficial coordinator." Serene, clean, beneficial . . . How could such a man have had anything to do with the killing of student protesters?

————

In 1968, Ealy had begun to rescue his newspaper from economic crisis by aiding a state in political crisis. In the early 1970s, he helped Echeverría with his PR dilemma.[14] Not only did he praise him in print and in public, he opened *El Universal* to a permitted quantity of critical columnists, among them former members and allies of the student movement. Most notable was the celebrated engineer and leftist academic Heberto Castillo, whom Díaz Ordaz had jailed and Echeverría was about to free. Ealy's granting of a column to Castillo bolstered Echeverría's strategy of recasting himself as a democrat and his parallel strategy, common among Mexico's presidents, of permitting escape valves.[15] The majority of Mexicans, whose daily encounters with the press were limited to seeing the front pages exhibited at newsstands, only saw headlines lauding the regime.

Ealy reaped due reward. State development banks made his paper further loans, for much of its equipment dated from its 1916 founding. Despite, or perhaps because of, strikes called to protest his modernizing efforts, he was able to rein in most of the unions, subjugating one of them just three months before Echeverría left office. How he did so is unclear. Certainly he used scabs; certainly he kept the secret police informed of his progress; reportedly he bought off some of the unions, bribing their leaders. And he likely had help from the president, who, despite his avowed leftism, was not averse to reining in labor to the benefit of management. Ealy also drove up sales by improving content: the new columnists; a revamped front page that averaged fourteen headlines instead of twenty-seven, gave bylines to all stories, and included photos; and the expansion of its already unparalleled section of classified ads ("Aviso oportuno"), which was the paper's cash cow. *El Universal* overtook *Novedades*, regaining second place among broadsheets.

Then came a stroke of luck: In July 1976, Echeverría engineered his coup at *Excélsior*, whose critical columns had apparently become too much for the serene leader. Julio Scherer left under threat of violence, during a riotous assembly of the cooperative society that owned the paper, and 200 staffers quit in sympathy or solidarity. Ealy promptly hired several of the best of them, including the biting cartoonist Rogelio Naranjo. A local titan, albeit weakened by this exodus of talent, *Excélsior* would retain first place in political influence and circulation for another dozen years or so, but *El Universal* narrowed the gap.[16]

Ealy himself became very rich. In part this stemmed from the state-aided growth of *El Universal* as a business. In part it owed to infighting among the Lanz Durets, which allowed him to gain a majority shareholding (presumably aided by loans from Uncle Nazario). And in part it reflected the gratuities he collected as a staunch servant of the state. In the 1976 electoral campaign, *El Universal* backed Echeverría's handpicked successor, José López Portillo, with much greater obsequiousness than *Excélsior*. Under López Portillo, Ealy received a monthly retainer of 200,000 pesos, around $24,000 today.[17] Whether by coincidence or otherwise, when López Portillo made his most controversial call and decreed the nationalization of the banks in his final State of the Nation speech—angrily blaming them for a calamitous peso

El Universal owner Juan Francisco Ealy Ortiz (*at the microphone*) welcomes President Miguel de la Madrid (*on the left*) to the inauguration of his newspaper's new headquarters in 1986. Courtesy of the Archivo General de la Nación (Fondo Hermanos Mayo, AG2/1823).

devaluation that was partly of his own making—*El Universal* ran a supportive banner headline. The private sector's outrage at the move ran in eighth place, at the foot of the page.[18]

As Ealy became wealthier and more influential, and as he maintained his profile as high courtier to Mexico's presidents, he adopted the persona of a magnate. Or what he thought a magnate should look like. He built a luxury villa in rural Morelos on a 128-acre estate, complete with stables, a helipad, and a seven-car garage. He dressed in tailor-made suits that incorporated his four initials in gold thread; one design, in pinstripe, bore sequences of those initials down each stripe. He shunned wallets, preferring to carry in his pocket a thick wad of fifty-dollar bills, Tony Soprano–style. He bought a jet aircraft for the paper and used it to fly around the Americas and to Spain, giving talks about freedom of speech. First he would send an advance guard of fixers, whose job was to arrange parties as well as meetings with VIPs; the parties often included a cohort of pretty young women who were not known to be reporters. Ealy would fly in with an entourage that included several bodyguards. At home, in his mansion in swanky Las Lomas de Chapultepec, the Mexico City attorney general's office would sometimes lend him a detail of ten armed agents. He would travel in convoy through the capital, one security car in front of and one behind his Mercedes Benz. As his distinctive moustache started to gray, he dyed it black, along with the rest of his hair. And around the time he turned fifty—having divorced María Dolores Lanz Duret and married and divorced a second time—he took up with Perla Díaz, a former beauty queen twenty-four years his junior. His plastic surgery followed. One senior editor who worked under Ealy came to think of him as The Sheik.[19]

Within *El Universal*, Ealy developed his own personality cult. In the company's newly designed main building, his office occupied an entire upper floor and included an interior balcony from which he could look down on the newsroom. Portraits of him multiplied in offices and halls. His senior columnists lauded him on the front page. His image often appeared there too, celebrating milestones in the paper's history. On its seventy-fifth anniversary, the *El Universal* lobby received a bronze statue—not of the paper's founder but of Ealy. Julio Scherer observed that Ealy lived in a state of "permanent self-adulation."[20]

(Consciously or not, Ealy belonged to a global club of magnates for whom media control meant greatness. The parallels with Britain's Robert Maxwell are striking. When Maxwell bought the mass tabloid *Daily Mirror* in 1984, he had the office carpets changed to a design that interwove his initials. Maxwell liked to appear on the paper's front page, and when flying to meet foreign dignitaries he usually took a photographer. His emulation of a mogul's lifestyle included residence in a nineteenth-century Oxford mansion and travel by private jet. He had affairs with much younger women. Once a week, he would visit London's Savoy Hotel to have the chief barber dye his hair and his eyebrows.)[21]

"Attempt on the Life of Our Director, Mr. Ealy Ortiz," ran the banner headline on January 13, 1987. A close-up photograph showed two bullet holes puncturing a window at the rear of *El Universal*. The shots had been fired on the morning of the 10th, to "silence the defenders of freedom of speech." This was the work of "an expert marksman who, without doubt, used a high-precision rifle." (The article eventually admitted that Ealy had not entered the building that day.) Messages of support poured in, from politicians, business leaders, academics, and bishops. The next day's paper declared, "Repudiation and Condemnation of the Attack; Mexico Perturbed." Seven stories mined the episode. Similar pieces appeared for days. But an investigation by the city's attorney general undercut the claims of the Great Daily Paper of Mexico. The window that the shots penetrated belonged not to Ealy's office but to that of the photo layout department, where the owner never trod.[22]

And yet, for all his high and delicate opinion of himself, Ealy would prove to be Mexican journalism's great survivor, spending more than half a century at the helm of his paper. And he retained sufficient people skills to persuade many of the best editors and reporters to work for him. Journalists felt empowered by Ealy, thanks to his assurances, his dynamism, and his resources. That is, until their work upset his symbiosis with the state. Then he fired them.[23]

The State Is Our Financier

Like most of Mexico's newspapers and magazines, at least until the 1980s, *El Universal* had always been a political tool. Like many of them, it was born in a moment of political opportunity.[24] At the bloody height of the revolution, in April 1915, news had just reached Mexico City of the First Battle of Celaya, an unprecedented military defeat for Pancho Villa by forces loyal to Venustiano Carranza, when five foreigners convened to register a newspaper publishing company. They were a Briton, a Frenchman, a Belgian, a Spaniard, and the wealthy US merchant George W. Cook, who claimed, probably as legal sleight of hand, to be a Mexican. Little is known about their intentions, but circumstances suggest they had two aims for their paper: to back the Allies in the Great War, since the well-funded *El Demócrata*, launched the year before, was pro-German; and to back Carranza in the revolution. For almost eighteen months their project lay idle, likely because of wartime disruptions, but in summer 1916, Carranza's education minister, Félix Palavicini, left his post to take charge of it. Further wealthy businessmen and politicians put up capital, several of them beneficiaries, like Cook, of the *ancien régime* of Porfirio Díaz (1876–1911). These likely included the British construction and oil magnate Weetman Pearson, who had profited more than anyone from public works contracts under Díaz; certainly, Pearson's oil company El Águila leased office space to *El Universal* and advertised in its pages. The investors also included other senior allies of Carranza—by now the country's de facto president—such as his finance minister, Luis Cabrera, and future president Pascual Ortiz Rubio. The sums they invested in the paper may well have been "borrowed" from government coffers.[25]

El Universal debuted on October 1, just after Carranza issued a call for delegates to a constitutional convention. He then named Palavicini as one of those delegates, among a body of 190 who would spend two months forging the contents of the new magna carta; Palavicini headed the pro-Carranza faction. As both politician and press baron, Palavicini pushed for his born-again nation to become an electoral democracy, as distinct from the dictatorship of Díaz, but also for it to bear a good deal of social and economic continuity with the Díaz regime. His partners were of the same mind.

Pearson, for example, did not want to see Mexico's natural deposits national-ized, and for a secret fee Palavicini actively lobbied to protect his British partner's oil giant, El Águila. *El Universal* took a similar line.[26]

El Universal was not unusual in its politicized origins. *El Demócrata* was founded on Carranza's orders, and its director similarly became a constitu-tional delegate. *Excélsior,* born in 1917, was again pro-Carranza, and its back-ers included government officials who used public funds to buy shares. These three propaganda vehicles, along with many ephemeral publicity rags, were insufficient to prevent Carranza from being toppled in 1920 by the revolt of his leading general, Álvaro Obregón. But an important precedent had been set. The "revolutionary newspapers" would depend, directly or indirectly, on the financial support of the incumbent government.[27]

Thus the new press resembled the strongest example of the old. Founded in 1896, *El Imparcial* had marked the birth of mass-audience journalism in Mexico, with its technological sophistication (the first paper to use a rotary press), commercial savvy (the first with full-page ads), accessible cover price (one cent, against the five or six cents charged usually), and editorial advances (the hiring of a team of reporters, as opposed to reliance upon opinion col-umnists and literary writers). *El Imparcial* melded all this innovation with the tradition, dating from the 1830s, of accepting state subsidies in exchange for publishing propaganda. By contrast, the minority of papers that criti-cized the Díaz regime labored to withstand the penalties, also common since the 1830s, of heavy fines, beatings by hired thugs, and the jailing of recalci-trant editors. *El Imparcial,* whose attitude to regime opponents was to ig-nore them, counted Díaz's finance minister as its main investor. And when the *ancien régime*—briefly revived after a fashion by a military dictator—gave its final death rattle in 1914, so did the newspaper.[28]

In 1920, at the fall of Carranza, the new "big three" dailies pragmatically turned their backs on him and cast allegiance to Obregón. Palavicini him-self, however, was too much tarred by his closeness to Carranza to gain Ob-regón's trust. This and his defeat in a labor dispute—unions were empowered by the new constitution and would remain a force for publishers to reckon with for close to a century—compelled him to sell *El Universal* in 1923. The buyer was Miguel Lanz Duret, a loyal servant of the state, whose grand-daughter would marry Ealy.[29]

While *El Demócrata* closed in 1926, *Excélsior* evolved to become the na-tion's leading daily paper, with *El Universal* usually ranking second. How "na-tional" they ever were is debatable, even though they were often referred to as such.[30] Soon after launch, *El Universal* had begun deliveries by airplane to nearby cities, but neither it nor *Excélsior* would have great impact farther afield; at most, a quarter of their readership lived outside the capital.[31] Yet they became the essential reading matter of the country's political elite, its business leaders, its rapidly expanding federal bureaucracy, and much of the small but influential Mexico City middle class.

Like almost all newspapers and almost all news magazines—the latter emerging in the 1930s—these dailies persisted in their financial dependence on the government. Between the 1940s and the 1980s, when dependence was almost universal, the arrangement involved an array of supports. Most importantly there was official advertising (often in the guise of *gacetillas*, or prewritten stories) from federal and provincial regimes, together estimated at between 60 and 80 percent of a newspaper's revenues. Support also included monthly subsidies, sometimes delivered in cash-filled suitcases; low-interest loans from state-owned bank Nafinsa; reduced electricity bills; exemptions from workers' social security contributions; and a generous line of credit from state newsprint supplier PIPSA (Producer and Importer of Paper, S.A.). Then there were government payments to journalists, which allowed publishers to keep salaries low: handsome retainers paid to columnists, known as *igualas*; payoffs to reporters covering Los Pinos (the presidency), the Institutional Revolutionary Party (PRI), or federal ministries and agencies, in the form of fortnightly *embute* or ad hoc *chayote*; gifts of cars, houses, or even gas stations to those deemed most influential; trips to Acapulco; invitations to accompany a president to Europe or a police chief to a brothel. Electoral seasons were especially lucrative: From the campaign trail of Echeverría in 1970 to that of Salinas in 1988, assigned reporters could expect to pick up their regular *embute*, a campaign stipend, and a third envelope from the government of each state visited. Reporters also received a commission of between 8 and 15 percent of the value of advertising they sold to the ministries they covered. In the late 1970s, when state coffers were flush with petrodollars, a beat reporter earning a measly $5,000 a year might make $30,000 more under the table. Altogether, these supports created a disincentive for periodicals to grow their readership, for higher circulation implied greater printing and distribution costs in exchange for little extra revenue.[32]

This topsy-turvy arrangement turned Mexico's more prominent publishers into financial potentates, as the French essayist Jean-François Revel observed. They returned the favor with subservience. Or as Revel put it, "Thus the press is shackled in a hundred ways and besides it cheerfully puts up with its chains."[33]

"Cheerful enshacklement" is of course one way of defining clientelism. As Daniel Hallin and other scholars have argued, this reciprocal support mechanism between political powers (granting economic favors) and publishers (offering deference and enthusiasm in turn) long characterized most media in Mexico, as well as elsewhere in Latin America and in southern and eastern

Europe. In a classic study of the phenomenon, Hallin and Stylianos Papatha-nassopoulos noted that "the press for most of its history has been an advo-cacy press, created more for the purpose of making politics than making money." They also identified several commonalities particularly evident in the Mexican case: the centrality of clientelist relationships to the political system; the high degree of newspapers' dependence on state patronage; and how such clientelism "places a premium on public demonstrations of loyalty to the patron . . . [and especially] the President."[34]

In a few cases dependence was overt. When monopolistic ruling party the PRI was founded in 1929, it launched a daily paper, *El Nacional*. Soon after the cor-poratist Confederation of Mexican Workers was organized, it brought out a daily of its own, *El Popular*, in 1938.[35] More usually, dependence was hidden. From the mid-1940s, as José García Valseca created, or bought and refash-ioned, more than thirty newspapers across the country, each of his editors cultivated relationships with state and city governments that exchanged glow-ing coverage for subsidies. García Valseca was quite pushy in this regard, having his editors run negative stories and columns about uncooperative in-cumbents until they turned on the tap. "Blackmail journalism," as such prac-tices came to be known, endured for decades, especially in the provinces, where some say it persists to this day.[36]

A second kind of dependence involved periodicals funded not by the state but by individual politicians, such as had predominated in the nineteenth century.[37] Politicians ran papers as self-promotional investments for pursu-ing higher office, as propagandistic showcases for their deeds, or as vehicles for wielding a more subtle influence. Echeverría was believed by the secret service and others to have taken a significant shareholding in *El Universal*, which would help explain various anomalies: Ealy's fairly quick success in solving the paper's chronic labor problems; his being invited to join an inves-tor group that purchased the García Valseca chain after the Echeverría regime expropriated it on account of its massive debts; and the paper's publication of a monthlong multipart interview with Echeverría five years after he left office.[38]

More often, political investments in newspapers were carried out by state-level politicos. These ranged from *La Voz de la Frontera*, an influential Mexi-cali paper bought by Baja California governor Milton Castellanos and partners in 1973, to *El Periódico*, a capital-city daily funded in the 1980s by San Luis Potosí governor and national teachers' union leader Carlos Jonguitud.[39] In Tabasco, two recently departed governors acquired papers to help them pro-long their influence, with Mario Trujillo (1971–76) buying *Avance Tabasco* and

Leandro Rovirosa Wade (1977–82) cofounding *Novedades Tabasco*, while two-time gubernatorial candidate (and future president) Andrés Manuel López Obrador coordinated the founding of *La Verdad del Sureste* in 1991, when almost all other local media opposed him.[40] Furthering the notion that press and politics were interdependent—or twin playgrounds of the establishment—journalists sometimes became governors. These included Carlos Loret de Mola Mediz of Yucatán (1970–76), Guillermo Morales Blumenkron of Puebla (1973–75), and Oscar Flores Tapia of Coahuila (1975–81).[41]

Once Mexican industrialization accelerated in the 1940s, there arose a third kind of dependence: papers that relied on the core businesses of their founders, not only for start-up capital but for cash injections thereafter, naturally complemented by subsidies from the state. These media could promote their owners' businesses directly in their pages, via advertising and "news" stories, and indirectly, via positive coverage of those politicians well placed to favor such firms with contracts and concessions, tax exemptions, loans from state lenders, and so on.

Novedades was an early example. Its main propaganda function having been fulfilled once co-owner Alemán left the presidency in 1952, the paper's chief purpose was now to boost its owners' portfolios: Rómulo O'Farrill's auto dealerships, his Packard assembly plant in Puebla, and his Mexico City radio station; Alemán's real estate, construction, and tourism ventures; and the TV network that they owned together. Naturally, *Novedades* became a publicity organ for the singers and actors whom their broadcasters featured. In 1948, the same year that he took formal control of the paper, O'Farrill had become president of the Mexican Highway Association, so *Novedades* became a champion of all things automotive, including extensive coverage of roadbuilding and features on motor tourism. Editorially, it opposed tax increases on car ownership.[42]

In 1965, another industrialist from Puebla, Gabriel Alarcón Chargoy, launched *El Heraldo de México*, followed by *El Heraldo de Puebla*. Five years before, Alarcón had been divested by the state of a lucrative movie theater chain, which he co-owned with the expatriate US industrialist William Jenkins. His focus then turned to real estate. But Alarcón had an unsavory reputation. In 1954 he had been charged with plotting the murder of a union activist and convicted in absentia. The twin *El Heraldo* papers were therefore platforms for promoting his businesses, directly and by currying favor, and for cleaning up his image. These goals were clearly flagged when *El Heraldo de México* launched, its front page dominated by a grinning President Díaz Ordaz—described in a caption as the paper's "first reader"—holding an *Heraldo* dummy edition.[43]

Were *any* periodicals self-sustaining? Few, if any, in Mexico City appear to have been. Even magazines needed help, despite their lower overhead costs.

Until the launch of *Proceso* in 1976, newsweeklies seldom sold above 30,000 copies per issue.[44]

Mexico's best-selling daily was the tabloid, crime-heavy *La Prensa* (est. 1928). Structured as a cooperative, *La Prensa* lacked a single owner-publisher who might run his paper at a loss while he lined his pockets (although its editors in chief somewhat did so). As of the 1940s, the decade in which urban working-class population growth accelerated, it boasted sturdy revenues, and by 1967 it credibly claimed sales of 185,000, more than any other daily. Its size meant that it consumed less newsprint per copy than the broadsheets, and its capital-city focus dispensed with the need to spend much on regional coverage. And yet even *La Prensa* took generous subsidies, with 40 percent of its advertising estimated to come from the government.[45] If any Mexican paper were a legitimate business—apart from several low-cost, high-volume sports dailies and the notoriously sensationalist weekly *Alarma!*—it was not found in the capital.[46]

Owing to publishers' desire to peddle influence, to government willingness to fund friendly voices, and perhaps also to a state strategy of preventing any one paper from gaining too much influence, Mexico hosted a plethora of publications—an excess of press. Between 1950 and 1990, residents of the capital typically had around twenty-five daily papers to choose from, and as many as thirty-seven in 1982, after a five-year oil-exporting boom.[47] This excess of press and the factors that fed it were echoed at the state level. By 1988, the modest capital of Chiapas, Tuxtla Gutiérrez (pop. 250,000), had twenty-nine dailies.[48] Until bona fide critical and durable newspapers began to multiply in the 1970s (*Unomásuno* in the capital, *ABC* in Tijuana, a reinvented *El Norte* in Monterrey), the notion that quantity implied diversity was partly a sham. Some national papers were more left-wing (*El Popular, El Día*), others more probusiness (*Novedades, El Heraldo*). Some aimed for a middle- and upper-income readership (*Excélsior, El Universal*, and other broadsheets); others were down-market tabloids (*La Prensa*, the weekly *Alarma!*). Still others catered to sports fans (*La Afición, Esto, Ovaciones*). However, despite the intermittent critical column, all were *oficialista*, or loyal to officialdom. All praised the president. His speeches were "transcendental"; his policies "correct." All took from the public purse.

Mexico's media business model was evidently quite different from the Anglo-American one. As of the mid- to late nineteenth century, the viability of British and US print media was almost uniformly predicated on private advertising, sales at street corners and newsstands, and subscriptions. This is not to say that British and US newspapers and magazines were free from state influence. US periodicals, whose owners usually viewed themselves as part of the national or local establishment, tended to support government policy.

This was especially true of foreign policy, a compact that only began to erode in the late 1960s, once the horrors and inefficiencies of the Vietnam War became too hard for editors to ignore. British periodicals, more partisan than their US counterparts, tended to exhibit a higher degree of "political parallelism": support for the party in power if it matched the paper's ideology, antagonism otherwise.[49] But in neither the United States nor the United Kingdom did media depend for their economic survival on state largesse, even if the tendency of some press barons to hobnob with presidents and cabinet members at Washington dinner parties or invite prime ministers to meetings aboard their yachts sometimes suggested ethically questionable proximity.[50]

The economic independence of the Anglo-American press, along with the fact that most major owners were publishers first and foremost without other businesses to protect, generally freed their newspapers to pursue the ideals of democratic news media: keeping the populace well informed (albeit with an ideological spin) and holding the powerful to account. In Mexico, most publishers worked to keep the populace only partially informed, while protecting and flattering the powerful and defaming leftist dissidents. Their concern was not censorship, but the rich rewards that accrued by censoring themselves. And their complacency and complicity trickled down. Reporters sometimes called themselves *los chicos de la prensa* (the boys of the press), as though they were a gang of schoolkids running a cotton-candy racket. They competed for favors: bribes but also privileges. Established reporters often carried police-force badges, which they could whip out when they got into trouble. They parked their cars wherever they liked. Some senior personnel even carried badges—effectively get-out-of-jail-free cards—dispensed by the Federal Security Directorate, Mexico's principal secret service.[51]

"Journalism has been the refuge for tremendous social climbing," declared the veteran Monterrey columnist and educator Pedro Reyes Velázquez in 1977. "Young people come to it thinking they are going to earn a lot of money, that it's an easy means to a comfortable life. They know that 'coming to an agreement' with politicians, authorities, and functionaries, they can gain a very good income."[52]

Velázquez's views echoed conventional wisdom among the public: Journalists could not be trusted. A first-of-its-kind World Values Survey found in 1981 that just 36 percent of Mexicans held confidence in the press, against 64 percent who distrusted it. But this is not to say that all were bought off. Mexico's most prestigious journalism school, the Carlos Septién, had been founded in 1949 by members of the small National Action Party. An independent history of the school is lacking, but its teachers presumably imbued in the students an ethos that questioned the ruling PRI. Certainly, among its alumni emerged some of the most distinguished critical journalists of the

1970s and after: Vicente Leñero, Sara Lovera, Carlos Marín, Blanche Petrich, Raymundo Riva Palacio.[53]

As for old-school types, some might insist on a bigger handout or ridicule a small one. When the reporter Alejandro Manjarrez visited *Excélsior* in the 1980s, recently hired as its Puebla correspondent, he witnessed fellow employee Gastón García Cantú accept an envelope from an envoy of Joaquín "La Quina" Hernández, the powerful boss of the oil workers' union. García Cantú opened the envelope, thumbed the contents, and asked with a scowl, "How much is here?" "Twelve thousand," the envoy replied; that was about fifty dollars at the time. García Cantú raised the envelope in the air, waved it as though it were yesterday's taco, and yelled sarcastically across the newsroom, "Listen up, boys! Is there anyone here who wants twelve thousand pesos from La Quina?!"[54]

Venality and deference were the lament of the minority of journalists who swam against the current. As the antiestablishment columnist and cultural critic Carlos Monsiváis put it, "The relationship of [President] Alemán with the press produces a model acceptable to subsequent regimes: the abundance of concessions to newspaper owners, almost all of them captains of industry; the delivery . . . of government advertising; the institution of self-censorship, to save time and telephone calls."[55] Of course, it was relatively easy for well-paid writers like Monsiváis to hover unsullied above the cesspool. Run-of-the-mill journalists who tried to be ethical found themselves dragged into it. A female reporter at *Excélsior* once confessed that, after she resisted accepting the *embute*, her colleagues gossiped about her sex life and sabotaged her stories with false information until she caved in and accepted the cash-filled envelopes.[56]

On the other hand, a culture of acquiescence to the PRI combined with material self-interest to encourage journalists to self-censor too often. Preeminent historian Daniel Cosío Villegas called the capital's papers "a free press, which does not make use of its freedom." Cosío Villegas may have been exaggerating for effect (by no means was Mexico's press "free"), but the media resembled other institutions during the semiauthoritarian era. Of Mexico's midcentury Supreme Court (1940–82), historian Pablo Mijangos writes, "Formed in a hidebound and authoritarian legal culture, and with their gaze fixed on the perks of the system, the justices almost never exercised their independence."[57]

Milestones: 1968, 1976

When the army opened fire on demonstrators on October 2, 1968, one of the students running for cover was Humberto Musacchio.[58] Lofty, confident, and possessed of a frankness common to folk from the northern state of Sonora, Musacchio was in the latter stages of an economics degree at the UNAM. His origins were middle class—his father, son of an Italian immigrant, sold cashmere sweaters—and his politics hewed firmly to Marx. When the student movement erupted that summer, fueled by disdain of PRI potentates and their lackeys in the press, twenty-five-year-old Musacchio quit his part-time job as an office clerk and threw himself into activism. The events at Tlatelolco, which ended the lives of many of his peers and led to the arrest of more than a thousand, shocked him into a state of numbness.

When he came to, in early 1969, the young communist found himself with neither home, nor job, nor money, squatting with several comrades in the house of a friend. To earn a few pesos, they began to write book reviews for a government newspaper. Soon Musacchio switched to reviewing for the more acceptable *El Día*, whose Cold War sympathies lay with the Soviet Union. From there he jumped to *El Universal*, where he proposed to Ealy that he create and edit a cultural section; few papers carried them at the time. Ealy agreed, on the condition that he invite young people to collaborate. The publisher explained: President Echeverría is very interested that young people *express themselves*. Aware that Echeverría played a double game with Mexico's youth—crushing their protests with one hand, extending an olive branch and shiny gifts with the other—Musacchio nonetheless assented. It marked the beginning of a long career that would see him become one of Mexico's best-known editors and cultural critics, a career fraught with multiple changes of employer (as was typical of an arena notorious for backbiting and backstabbing), precarious finances, state interference, and tender egos.

Musacchio's experiences, shared directly or vicariously by thousands of urban students nationwide, would mark him as one of the Generation of '68. The term, as usually applied, encompasses not a whole generation but those young leftists who felt themselves both victimized and politically emboldened by the repression of Díaz Ordaz and Echeverría. Their story exemplifies how 1968, at least for Mexican journalism, was not a watershed but a seedbed. Or as historian Eugenia Allier has put it more generally, 1968 was "the movement that triumphed in the future."[59]

In the short run, while no viable political outlets existed, many of that generation would channel their energies into entry-level journalism, academia, and the cultural industries. In the long run, as limited political openings finally emerged, many of these men and women would mobilize. Their efforts as journalists and as activists would help usher Mexico toward electoral democracy. Politically, in the late 1980s, the Generation of '68 would splinter. Many backed the left-wing Party of the Democratic Revolution, founded in 1989; some aligned themselves with the PRI, being persuaded that it was at last serious about democratization; a few embraced the right-of-center National Action Party; others forswore party politics, convinced that no politico could be trusted. Yet all retained the article of faith that 1968 had *meant something*, broadly for the country, specifically for the press, and personally for their own coming-of-age as independent thinkers. Musacchio himself would later write that the student movement had demanded "new relations between the governing and the governed," so that citizens should no longer be "mere subjects"; in turn, among other things, that meant "the beginning of the end of that self-interested love between the press and political authorities."[60]

The road ahead was a roller coaster. Musacchio happily put out his twice-weekly cultural section, earning good money as editor. (His reporters earned the usual pittance.) But after three months or so, Ealy suspended him. It had occurred to Musacchio to devote an issue to critique of Martín Luis Guzmán. The elderly director of *Tiempo*, who fifty-five years before had ridden with Pancho Villa, and who had written the most celebrated novel of the revolution, glorifying its leaders, set his magazine to scorn the movement of 1968. One column jeered at "the illegitimate pretensions of a mob." At the Freedom of the Press banquet the following summer, Guzmán used his speech to congratulate Díaz Ordaz, to claim that journalists had been free to cover the movement, and to inquire whether the press had been loyal enough.[61] To Musacchio, Guzmán personified all that had grown rotten. But Guzmán, now a senator, held power. A senior editor raked the young man over the coals. Had he no idea that Guzmán organized the annual banquet? That he presided over the national textbook commission, which awarded juicy printing contracts each year to *El Universal*, to help it defray its operating costs? That he chaired the board of newsprint monopoly PIPSA, which provided subsidized paper on credit and often forgave its clients' debts? Musacchio would recall, "I was ignorant of how the prostitution of the press was a business so highly organized."[62]

A few months later, Ealy gave Musacchio a second chance: He could direct a page for younger readers. It was September 1971, and the first major event Musacchio covered was Avándaro. Conceived and later remembered as Mexico's Woodstock, Avándaro was a weekend rock festival held in an idyllic valley a two-hour drive west from the capital. More than 200,000 concertgoers converged.[63] Musacchio arrived with a photographer and was surprised to find a family atmosphere, for many parents had insisted on accompanying their sons and daughters. He was less surprised to find a gaggle of reporters hassling the organizers for free motel rooms, an open bar, and cash payoffs, all of which the organizers (perhaps naively) refused to provide. As the concert progressed, the booze flowed and marijuana fumes filled the air, but the crowd remained peaceful. As at Woodstock, the problems were organizational. Local vendors ran out of food after a few hours. The music did not start until ten o'clock the first evening, finishing at eight on Sunday morning. Narrow roads made for an immense traffic jam, so that Musacchio, having departed at one in the afternoon, only reached Mexico City after nightfall. And then he saw the first published reports: The headlines screamed "Orgy . . . ," "Satanic Festival . . ."; the stories gasped about mass nudity. Musacchio resolved to set the record straight. But that Tuesday, there was no sign of his write-up in the youth page. Nor was it held over for Wednesday. His report, photos and all, was spiked.

Musacchio had failed to toe the government line: Avándaro was a threat to the nation. Hordes of people, rich, middle class, and poor, had mixed together without state supervision; they had inhaled illicit substances and the culturally suspect intoxicant of US- and UK-inspired rock; their nudity and bad language were an affront to family values. Live rock would all but disappear from Mexico until 1990. Musacchio, opting to take a job in a university press office, decided never again to work for Ealy.

After 1968, the next milestone in the history of Mexico's press arose in 1976, with the famous coup wrought by Echeverría against Scherer at *Excélsior*. Musacchio was not involved in the episode, but he became a beneficiary. The ouster of Scherer and his senior editors prompted the resignation of most of the best writers. Together they came to be known as the "*Excélsior* diaspora," for the coup led to the creation of four periodicals; each was responsive to social concerns and keen to play a watchdog role, key ingredients of what Sallie Hughes calls a "first wave of civic journalism." The first was *Proceso*, the magazine that Scherer soon created with his closest allies. The second was *Vuelta*, a political-cultural monthly founded by poet and former diplomat Octavio Paz. The third was *Unomásuno*, a daily paper launched in 1977 by Manuel Becerra Acosta Jr., the son of Scherer's predecessor as *Excélsior* editor; and the fourth was *La Jornada*, another daily, founded in 1984 after a schism at *Unomásuno*.[64]

The success of these media showed the counterproductive folly of Echeverría's move, evidently born of autocratic impetuosity amid the strains of a worsening economy. The critical tone and cultural savvy of the new media made them highly influential, and their combined readership, including pass-around rates among students, likely fell not far short of *Excélsior's*.

Unomásuno: Rise and Fall of a Semi-Independent

As soon as *Unomásuno* hit the newsstands, Humberto Musacchio knew he wanted to work there. Everything about it seemed revolutionary, starting with its arresting title, which was stylized as **unomásuno**.[65] That name, literally "one-plus-one," implied a symbiosis between newspaper and reader. The format was neither a broadsheet nor a tabloid but something in between: a Berliner, a size favored in Europe. It was used by the new center-left daily *El País*, which was making waves in Spain following the death of right-wing dictator Francisco Franco and gaining admirers in Mexico. Another overseas source of inspiration was the current of narrative investigative journalism seen in parts of the US press.

The politics of *Unomásuno* were clearly left, but unlike *El Día*, which had been the choice reading of Mexico City lefties during the 1960s, it dared to be critical of the government. The payroll included several dozen Central and South Americans, mostly exiles from right-wing dictatorships, and unusual numbers of young university graduates and female reporters. Opinion columns were not confined to the usual pages but interwoven with news, and their writers ranged from liberals to avowed Marxists. For the first time, a major daily gave sustained attention to environmental and feminist issues. Pushing further a tradition of civic journalism tentatively begun at Scherer's *Excélsior*, it paid punctual attention to strikes and peasant mobilizations, as it gave greater voice to the marginalized. And it refused to censor their language: *carajo* (damn it), *cabrón* (bastard), and *chingada* (fuckup) now appeared in print. Photographs received more space, notably those by Pedro Valtierra, a brilliant young photojournalist with an eye for the plight of the poor.

Unomásuno's liberty to be critical owed in part to President López Portillo, who had taken office the previous December. Like Echeverría before him, but with greater sincerity, López Portillo began his term by encouraging a freer press. The paper's leeway also owed to the aid and protection of the secretary of government, Jesús Reyes Heroles, a liberal intellectual, who helped *Unomásuno* obtain a $350,000 start-up loan from the state bank Nafinsa. Reyes Heroles had an agenda, but a democratic one: *Unomásuno* would be his chief vehicle for promoting a package of reforms, passed in December 1977, designed to temper authoritarian government for the first time since the founding of the PRI. Far-left parties could gain legal registration, and opposition parties of all kinds could win congressional seats through proportional representation. A gradualist journey toward electoral democracy was set in motion, with mass media helping to push it along.[66]

During its first six years, Becerra's *Unomásuno* was unquestionably the best paper in Mexico.[67] Along with *Proceso* and the fearless columnist Manuel Buendía at *Excélsior*, it played a leading investigative role in holding the López Portillo regime to account and generating public outrage over the excesses of two of his cronies: Jorge Díaz Serrano, director of state oil monopoly Pemex, and Mexico City police chief Arturo "El Negro" Durazo. As Vanessa Freije has demonstrated, such scandals not only led to the professional demise and incarceration of both men but also fueled the public suspicion of the PRI, the culture of dissent, and an incipient clamor for electoral democracy.[68] In the long run, these reactions would boost support for opposition parties and contribute, in 1988, to the closest-run presidential election in half a century.

Musacchio took the *Unomásuno* entrance exam, got hired as a proofreader, and soon moved to the newsroom. Eager to learn, he volunteered as a subeditor when help was needed on any desk: regional news, international, the economy. He built a reputation for breadth of knowledge, which would bear fruit a decade later when he edited a respected encyclopedia.[69] He took an interest in the mechanics of production, often staying on at night to watch the preparation and operation of the presses. He also learned from the work of a colleague who was fast becoming famous for his independence of thought and clarity of prose: Miguel Ángel Granados Chapa.

Born in 1941 to a peasant farmer and a schoolteacher in Hidalgo state, Granados Chapa was a precocious talent who pored over the newspaper as a boy and studied the still novel subject of journalism at the UNAM.[70] In 1966, Granados Chapa applied to *Excélsior*. There he spent ten years, starting as a proofreader and working his way up to chief editorial writer. He became a member of Scherer's inner circle. Expelled with Scherer in 1976, Granados Chapa acted as his right-hand man in the founding of *Proceso*. But he quit after a year, worn down by the intensity of the work and rivalry with Scherer and wanting to do his own thing.

What Granados Chapa did best of all was write. In 1977, he started a column he would pen for the rest of his life: "Plaza pública" (Public square). With a name that evoked the concerns of ordinary people, "Plaza pública" offered well-informed analysis in precise and measured prose and delved into politics in a new way. It neither charged politicians for positive coverage, as was common, nor used the threat of negative exposure to squeeze them for a payoff, as was not uncommon. (Chiapas governor Absolón González once paid a newspaper $40,000 to kill a story.) Granados Chapa simply held politicians to account. So scrupulous was he in his shunning of corruption that when Musacchio first visited him at home he was taken aback to find him living in a small apartment with no TV set. "Plaza pública" came to the attention of a press agency, which took the novel step of syndicating the column, along with a couple of other op-eds that included "Red privada" (Private network), by Granados Chapa's mentor Manuel Buendía; soon the columns were appearing in dozens of papers across the country. "Plaza pública" was what Granados Chapa took to *Unomásuno*. It was there that the Catholic centrist (short, dark, sporting black-rimmed glasses, suit, vest, and tie) and the Italian Mexican communist (tall, fair, dressed in jeans and a cashmere sweater) became lifelong friends.

And it was there that Granados Chapa became a leading opinion writer. Media researcher Petra Secanella named him one of Mexico's four most-read columnists, along with *Excélsior*'s Buendía and two others. By the early 1980s, all four were syndicated to papers in the states, where local opinion leaders often quoted them. With their relentless focus on all forms of corruption, Secanella observed, "they exercise a political control that substitutes that of the inexistent [political] opposition."[71]

Granados Chapa dared even to hold the president to account. In August 1981, he got wind of a 200-acre ranch that the governor of the State of México, Jorge Jiménez Cantú, had presented to President López Portillo. Jiménez Cantú was about to leave office; perhaps he was angling for an ambassadorship. Granados Chapa heard that López Portillo was already making visits to the ranch with his family, to relax and ride the horses. In his Monday column, he deftly described the gift as a pending transaction. He closed by saying, "We are certain that, once the onerous present is offered, it will not be accepted." Everyone at *Unomásuno* held their breath. Few if any journalists at a major paper had accused a sitting president of corruption; this column perhaps came closest. Would state advertising be pulled, would a newsprint order go unfulfilled, would his boss Becerra get a *telefonazo*—a brusque phone call from a senior functionary— telling him to fire Granados Chapa? On Wednesday a handwritten letter arrived addressed to the columnist. The president informed him, "I have resolved not to fall into temptation." He detailed how enchanting he found the ranch, which made the temptation all the greater. But Granados Chapa was right. To accept was not illegal, but neither would it be seemly in the eyes of public opinion. *Unomásuno* printed the letter on its front page.[72]

Two years later, Granados Chapa quit the paper. So did Musacchio, who had risen to news editor, and three other senior editors: Carlos Payán, Becerra's second-in-command; Carmen Lira; and Héctor Aguilar Camín. There was an accumulation of grievances. The *Excélsior* exiles and others who founded *Unomásuno* had attempted a cooperative ownership, with shares distributed among thirty-two journalists. To secure the Nafinsa loan, given that a cooperative could not legally obtain one, they also set up a company. Even with the loan, they were far short of what they needed, so they found a book publisher, José Solís, to put up a printing press and office space in exchange for a 40 percent stake. Later, when relations with Solís soured, the newspaper board commissioned Becerra to sue for a buyout. But while ostensibly achieving this on behalf of the collective, he used a loan from his father-in-law to buy the shares for himself. These, added to the stake he already owned, gave him majority control. By the time Becerra admitted to this maneuver, many had grown doubtful of his leadership, which was visionary but increasingly imperious and, due to his alcoholism, erratic.[73]

The paper was fast losing money. A severe recession, which began in 1982, was one problem; another was mismanagement. The Unified Socialist Party of Mexico, for one, had been allowed to run up a large debt for display ads and *gacetillas*. The paper was politically vulnerable too, for the new president, Miguel de la Madrid, was more conservative than López Portillo. Under these circumstances and having reportedly taken a government loan to keep his paper running, Becerra took a hard line with the company union and laid off 100 employees. This struck many as a betrayal of the paper's ideals. Becerra also steered *Unomásuno* to the right; its coverage of De la Madrid's campaign was fairly generous. Perhaps the director had little choice, but his high-handed manner caused a loss of trust. After the senior editors quit, in November 1983, fifty staffers did likewise. Then forty-six contributors resigned in sympathy, including most of the leading columnists.[74]

"Another sad story of boss rule," Musacchio would later conclude.[75]

Those who quit *Unomásuno* soon launched a rival paper, with a more categorically left-wing identity: *La Jornada*. After the schism, *Unomásuno* soldiered on, its ranks decimated but not shorn of all talent, its ad revenues and subsidies depleted. It made new hires and continued for several years to do good, socially committed work.[76] Owing in large part to Becerra, the paper remained well connected with the Mexican left. This helped it score one of the scoops of the era when in 1986 it revealed a rupture within the PRI between Cuauhtémoc Cárdenas, a grandee of the institutional left, and the new neoliberal hierarchy. Cárdenas went on to leave the party and compete for the presidency in 1988, and when he lost that election, apparently due to fraud by the PRI, *Unomásuno* gave his protests its backing (as, to a lesser extent, did *La Jornada*). This was perhaps the first time since 1940 that a prominent Mexico City periodical had so overtly supported an opposition leader.[77] Would Becerra's valor return to haunt him?

The victor of that election, Carlos Salinas de Gortari, was said to be furious at the paper's breaking of ranks. Three months into the presidential term, on March 1, 1989, Becerra left the offices of *Unomásuno*, never to return. Months later, exiled in Europe, the publisher told *Proceso* that a representative of the sinister secretary of government, Fernando Gutiérrez Barrios, had pressured him to take $1 million in exchange for his majority stake and his pledge to leave the country. He said he had feared for his life.[78] But Salinas himself, speaking today, says that Becerra *voluntarily* reached an agreement with Gutiérrez Barrios, because his paper was bankrupt and deep in debt. Third-party accounts confirm the crisis: *Unomásuno* owed some $1.5 million in PIPSA payments, taxes, and social security dues. Then again, such obligations had gained deferrals for years, which gave the paper financial breathing space but let the state construct a vice that it could apply when it saw fit. Another problem was that Becerra's paper was fast losing readers to *La Jornada*. A reliable study claimed that circulation had fallen to 20,000, versus the 40,000 of its junior rival. If Gutiérrez Barrios did threaten Becerra, it was unlikely that he had to squeeze hard. A decade later, Becerra told his biographer that for some years he had wanted to retire to Spain; "I was fed up," he admitted, adding, "No one literally obliged me [to leave]." Two things are certain: Becerra would spend the rest of his life in Madrid, and *Unomásuno*, soon under new private ownership, became a government ally and slid into irrelevance.[79]

The episode reflected a political-elite obsession with the print media that seemed at odds with its popular reach. *New York Times* correspondent Alan Riding had noted the irony that while the country's combined daily newspaper circulation was less than 1 million, some 15 to 20 million people watched TV news every night, more than 90 percent of them viewing Televisa's *24 Horas*; this newscast slanted coverage to the right and toward Washington's worldview, subtly undermining many positions of the leftist-nationalist PRI. Riding claimed the obsession with newspapers reflected the state's "poor understanding of modern communications."[80] Yet both Echeverría in 1976 and Salinas in 1988 understood the written press very well. Unlike television, it held sway with politicians, bureaucrats, business leaders, union bosses, the professional classes, professors, and students: those whose loyalty was key to the stability of Mexico's top-heavy corporatist system. Hence, even a newspaper of marginal weight like *Novedades* could reap an extra $300,000 per week in cash gratuities from the PRI during the Salinas campaign; the party spared no expense to ensure that support for their candidate was solid.[81] Mexican presidentialism rested less on coercion than on perception, so sanctity of image was everything.

The fate of *Unomásuno* did not bode well for press freedoms. Presidents usually began their dealings with the media by being conciliatory, but the new regime seemed to signal that no threat to Salinas's kingly aura or the PRI's hegemony would be allowed. What followed was far more complex than that, and ultimately rather the opposite.

Chapter 2

Combative Regional Papers and the Salinas Watershed

> The greatest contribution to the transition to democracy in this country has come from the so-called "provincial press."
>
> —Javier Garza Ramos, former editor, *El Siglo de Torreón*

> The private sector felt empowered by Salinas to support a new, less ideological, more Anglo-Saxon form of journalism, with projects designed to rely on commercial advertising instead of government subsidies.
>
> —Jorge Zepeda Patterson, former editor, *Siglo 21*

Tijuana's *Zeta*

Adela Navarro was in elementary school when she knew she wanted to stand up for people.[1] It bothered her that some of her classmates picked on others. There was one bully who often tormented another boy, hitting him, stealing his lunch and his pocket money, making fun of his parents. One day, when the bully was about his business, Adela wedged herself between him and his prey and confronted him. He reached inside his backpack, grabbed a pair of compasses, and hit her in the face with the sharp end. (She still bears the scar.) The school called her father, and after Carlos Navarro had taken Adela for a tetanus shot, he called on the boy's parents to give them a piece of his mind.

Father and daughter shared a strong sense of justice. The moderately prosperous owner of a Tijuana carpet store, Carlos sometimes gave lodging to the less fortunate. Once he happened upon two Honduran teenagers crying outside the bus station. They had been abandoned by their *pollero*, the guide they had paid to smuggle them into the United States. He brought them home and hosted them for three months, while they earned enough to pay another *pollero* and make the crossing.

When Adela was small, her father would read to her from the newspapers. Carlos had quit school before junior high, as was common practice back in the 1930s, but he loved to be well informed. He would tell Adela it was important to know what was going on—in their city, in their home state of Baja California, in Mexico, and in the world. His breakfast consisted of coffee and two or three local papers. During the day he would consume a couple more, including *The San Diego Union-Tribune*, and on weekends he took *Proceso* and

Tijuana's near equivalent, a weekly paper called *Zeta*. Absorbing so much news, developing a civic conscience, and loving to write, Adela applied to study journalism. And when deciding where she wanted to work, she discarded all the dailies, which seemed in thrall to the authorities, and chose *Zeta*.

"*Zeta* is the only paper where I can *do* something," she told herself.[2]

Though several years from graduating, Navarro managed to get an appointment with *Zeta* cofounder and editor Jesús Blancornelas. After decades of practicing independent-minded journalism, Blancornelas was a local legend. She had buttonholed him after he gave a talk at her campus, the Autonomous University of Baja California. Now, in January 1990, they sat in his office: she, well dressed, oval-faced, bright-eyed, and eager; he, soft-spoken, bespectacled, bearded, and graying. They both spoke directly. What area did she want? he asked. The arts, entertainment? At most Mexican papers, women had yet to break into hard news. Navarro replied, "No, I want politics." Impressed by her directness, Blancornelas hired her on the spot. He told her she should ask Francisco Ortiz, another *Zeta* cofounder, for an assignment.

Navarro's parents were concerned about her choice of employer, and with good reason. Not two years before, a popular and provocative columnist for *Zeta*, Héctor Félix Miranda, had been executed in a professional hit. The murder fit a dismal history of local repression. In the 1940s and 1950s, Baja California's journalists had suffered more physical assaults—often at the hands of police—than those of any other state. A local lull in killings followed, but as of the early 1970s events in another northwestern state, Sinaloa, augured the shape of things to come, with journalists murdered at a rate of one every three years by *narcos* or their political protectors. One March morning in 1987, the office building of *Zeta* was raked with machine-gun bullets. Some journalists opted to carry guns, and many varied their routes between home and office.[3] Worse, in 1990, there was talk of a ruthless crime family taking root in Tijuana, led by the brothers Arellano Félix.

But Navarro was convinced that times were changing for the better. "When I started in journalism," she later wrote, "after learning . . . of the repression and persecution that journalists like Jesús Blancornelas and Julio Scherer lived through and survived, I thought that my generation had the path smoothened for them."[4] There seemed also to be a new openness emanating from Mexico City. President Carlos Salinas de Gortari was respectful of Blancornelas, despite his criticisms of the Institutional Revolutionary Party (PRI), and when cabinet ministers visited Tijuana they would come to *Zeta* for a sit-down interview.

Four years after Navarro started at *Zeta*, while she was still in her mid-twenties, Blancornelas was so impressed by her work that he invited her to join the editorial board. And twelve years after that, she would become publisher, the first woman to direct a major newspaper in the Mexican Northwest.

———

Zeta had launched in April 1980, with Blancornelas still in Californian exile following a hostile takeover at a previous paper of his, *ABC,* engineered by Governor Roberto de la Madrid. He took the precaution of having it printed in San Diego, so no Baja governor could interrupt its newsprint supply or send goons to smash its presses. With the lower fixed costs that came with being a weekly, it could more easily survive without government support; indeed, its sole investors were Blancornelas and Miranda. Once cover sales took off and advertising gained critical mass, it would also pay decent salaries. *Zeta* benefited from Blancornelas's skill as a business manager and was shielded from the worst kinds of aggression by his binational reputation. Already well known in California press circles, he spent much of spring 1980 giving talks about Mexico's press at US universities, the Organization of American States, and the United Nations.

"We who were dispossessed now know how to avoid another robbery," stated the front-page editorial of *Zeta*'s first issue.[5] The paper was sold by independent vendors, for regular hawkers belonged to a government-affiliated union, and its first edition's 5,000 copies sold out within hours.

Conceived of as a civic paper responsive to community interests rather than as an opposition organ, *Zeta* was buoyed by a demand for the uncompromised reporting that Tijuana had been missing for five months. Soon it added a slogan to its masthead: "Free as the wind." Freedom involved shunning official advertising and forbidding *embute*, and the paper's air of incorruptibility boosted its popularity. So did its willingness to take on risky topics for its cover feature, usually penned by Blancornelas. These included a 1985 scoop about a marijuana-filled warehouse; it was guarded by police in the pay of the brothers Arellano Félix, founders of what came to be labeled the Tijuana Cartel. Over the ensuing decade, circulation grew to around 30,000 and page count ballooned from 16 to 144, with an average 59 pages of ads. *Zeta* gave unusual space to readers' letters, eventually 10 pages per issue, making it a popular forum for complaint and even subversion ("Don't pay the property tax!"). It added columns; since Blancornelas was a devout Catholic, these included one from the bishop of Monterrey and another called "Seminarians Opine." It took others syndicated from the capital, like those of Miguel Ángel Granados Chapa and Héctor Aguilar Camín, along with the top cartoonists from *Proceso* and *La Jornada*.[6]

Félix Miranda, nicknamed "the Cat," was the biggest draw.[7] His fusillades melded rumor and critique with street slang and ribald jokes about *huevos*

Tijuana newsweekly *Zeta*, launched in 1980, first made the city's drug traffickers its cover story in 1985. Photograph by Ramón T. Blanco Villalón, courtesy of *Zeta*.

(i.e., testicles). His common touch made him the most beloved journalist in Baja. To the author Federico Campbell, he was "a journalist of the 'masses' . . . the bums, the poor, the marginalized, the humiliated, the victims of insults." His style was "sardonic, satirical, mocking, merciless, outspoken, incorruptible, foul-mouthed, and badly written."[8]

No politician or official was spared, not even Presidents José López Portillo and Miguel de la Madrid. He liked to ridicule *gringos* and *narcos* too. But his favorite targets were Baja California's new governor, Xicoténcatl Leyva, and Tijuana's mayor, Federico Valdés, whom he portrayed as drunken bribe-takers and profiteers. Nor did he spare politicians' wives, girlfriends, siblings, or offspring. When readers called him for help, he often relayed their concerns in print. So successful was the mix, the column came to run in national syndication. Some colleagues worried he took too many risks. Mexico's political elite were not used to being laughed at in the press. The satire of Mexico City's cartoonists barely offended, as it was mostly gentle or allusive. Sensitivity to public slights was pronounced in the provinces, perhaps because politicians outside the capital were less cosmopolitan and so less familiar with the biting satire practiced abroad, or perhaps because regional politics, unlike the increasingly technocratic federal variant, still involved displays of bravado and declarations of macho prowess.[9]

In another country—the United Kingdom, for example, where libel laws are notoriously strict—Félix Miranda would have faced multiple lawsuits. Mexican defamation law offered less protection to its public servants, who anyway preferred to avoid the publicity that a court case might bring, not least (so it was generally assumed) because a legal probe might well unearth evidence of what had been alleged, or worse. For those in authority who felt especially exposed or embarrassed, it was often more tempting to employ informal means of protest, involving armed thugs. But when friends ask Félix Miranda whether he feared for his safety, he would reply, "I have seven lives, like a cat."

On the rainy morning of April 20, 1988, Félix the Cat's seventh life abruptly ended. The forty-seven-year-old columnist was found slumped at the wheel of his Ford sedan. An autopsy retrieved thirteen shotgun bullets from his body. That evening, a crowd of several thousand protested in the city center. Unusually for a murder in Mexico, and most unusually for the murder of a journalist, the two killers were arrested and convicted. But this only accounted for the hitmen. What of the mastermind? During the trial of the first man to be caught, it emerged that both were security guards at Tijuana's Agua Caliente racetrack, operated by Jorge Hank Rhon. (The second, arrested in 1990, had also worked as Hank Rhon's bodyguard.) The son of a former Mexico City mayor, the fabulously wealthy Carlos Hank González, and a very rich man himself, Hank Rhon had become a frequent target of Félix Miranda's ridicule.

The potential case against Hank Rhon was complicated by the fact that Félix Miranda and he had once been friends. On the young man's arrival in Tijuana in 1985, Félix Miranda had praised him for creating jobs and supporting charities. They socialized together, and Hank Rhon confided in him. Little by little the relationship soured. By early 1988, Félix Miranda was trashing him in his column for poor investments and for breaking the law.

He used jocular slang to accuse him of serving cocaine at his parties. He laid into him as a know-it-all *chilango*, the common provincial term for arrogant folk from the capital, and nicknamed him "El Pirrurris," after a vain rich kid on a TV show.

Zeta covered the murder in fearless detail, zeroing in on Hank Rhon and four other principal suspects, and running a full page in each issue depicting the ghost of Félix Miranda calling for justice: "Hank, why did one of your bodyguards kill me?" In late May, in a 2,349-person opinion poll published in *Zeta*, 894 believed Hank Rhon to be the mastermind, with Governor Leyva way back in second. At the end of the year, Hank Rhon's father offered to pay for Blancornelas to live in exile with his family. This was one of several attempts that Hank González made to urge *Zeta* to lower its tone about Hank Rhon, each of which affirmed for Blancornelas the son's guilt.

As for his own safety, Blancornelas remained uncowed. "God gave me life. He will take my life when He wants, not when the politicians want," he told the *New Yorker*, a year after his friend's murder. "I feel like a torero. After I finish a story and it's being edited and printed, I'm afraid. But when it's out and many people have read it, the fear is gone."[10]

Zeta's detailed coverage of the investigation flagged inconsistencies and shoddy police work and helped secure the conviction of the hitmen. But it carried a sense of guilty-until-proven-innocent when it came to Hank Rhon. One cover image showed the logo of his racetrack transformed into a rifle dripping blood, with the legend, "As long as the opposite is not demonstrated . . . Hank."[11]

Perhaps Hank González simply wanted *Zeta* to stop besmirching his son, whose local prestige suffered. (Nonetheless, it would recover enough for him to be elected as Tijuana's mayor in 2004.) Besides, would Hank Rhon really have had his own employees carry out a hit? When veteran journalist Carlos Moncada traveled to Tijuana to interview Hank Rhon about the case, a senior employee of the businessman (and another of Blancornelas's five suspects), Alberto Murguía, let slip that he had run into Félix Miranda shortly before his death and tried to punch him; his columns had defamed his boss and assailed him and his family. Could Murguía have arranged the murder, to avenge various slights and curry favor?

Given state-level reticence in Mexico to let detectives investigate the powerful, victims' families and friends sometimes try to get federal agencies involved. After Félix Miranda was killed, a reporters' union compiled a study of colleagues murdered during the presidency of Miguel de la Madrid, now in its final year, and came up with twenty-nine. The government responded with a report of its own, likely the first of its kind, presented on Press Freedom Day in June. ("In Mexico, censorship does not exist," pronounced De la

Madrid at the banquet.)[12] This report, which studied twenty-four cases, not only smacked of a whitewash, it contained a catalog of disqualifiers, as though summing up the favored pretexts of state governors and offering a blueprint for future noninvestigations. It claimed all but five of the murders owed not to the practice of journalism but to random causes and added that some of those killed only pretended to be journalists. It found that three of the five exceptions involved reporters writing about drug traffickers (read: playing with fire). And taking the custom of blaming the victim one step further, it alleged that Félix Miranda was a heavy gambler and had twice participated in "scandals of passion."

In 1992, the newly formed and autonomous National Human Rights Commission briefly reopened the case but made no headway. As almost always occurred after the murder of a Mexican journalist, the mastermind went unconfirmed and unpunished.[13]

"Provincial" Journalism: Not Quite So Bland

In Mexico City, the literati long held that journalism outside the capital was a rickety arena of venal hacks singing their governors' praises. There was certainly a lot of *lambisconería* (brownnosing). The uniformly supine press of midcentury Puebla routinely called the governors "virile" and their speeches "transcendental." When Rafael Ávila Camacho opened his largest pet project, a 6,000-capacity school, on the day of his final gubernatorial address, one reporter warbled that the buildings' rooftop gardens were so beautiful "they render poorly made and lacking in splendor the Hanging Gardens of Babylon."[14]

Carlos Monsiváis wrote in 1980 that regional papers trafficked almost without exception in banality, political flattery, lurid crime stories, and "love for the causes of the Christian and capitalist West." Recent attempts at investigative journalism, he added, either never made it into print or were soon suppressed, allowing the powerful to live unperturbed.[15] In 1994, media scholar Raúl Trejo Delarbe claimed that, "with few exceptions," the regional press was "extremely improvised and weak," although he admitted a recent improvement in the northern states.[16]

The fundamental problem was that the brew of multiple papers and low readership that made Mexico City's press dependent on patronage was reproduced to an absurd degree in much of the interior. A state with a fifth or a tenth of the population of metropolitan Mexico City, like Puebla or Tabasco, might have half as many dailies, each one batting for some special interest. In Tabasco, as veteran journalist Erwin Macario puts it, "every governor has had a newspaper." Carlos Payán, founder and editor of *La Jornada*, used to comment ironically, "In the provinces, the journalist has a different relationship with the politician, because the sidewalks are narrower."[17] In other words, within smaller social spaces, collaboration was more common. So was the trend among publishers of placing their newsrooms within a block or two of the governor's palace or city hall. So was (and remains) the tendency for governors to hire reporters as their spokespeople, who sometimes returned to journalism at the end of the term.[18]

Nonetheless, as respected regional journalists told their own stories and as historians of the media looked beyond the capital, evidence emerged that provincial papers were—or under certain circumstances might be—more often critical than their Mexico City counterparts. One 1960 federal survey, unearthed a half century later, found that half of all editorial stances were either neutral or oppositional to local governments.[19]

Such relative autonomy had several explanations. Whereas the "national" press, as of the 1940s, was more or less controlled by a centralized federal strategy of carrot (subsidies and bribes) and stick (withdrawal of the same), provincial papers could exploit local political fissures. This might mean backing one faction of a state's PRI apparatus against another in exchange for financial support. Many states had at least three distinct nodes of power, between which rivalries could develop: the governor's office, the mayor's office in the biggest city, and the local public university, all with sizable budgets. During campaign seasons, it might mean backing the National Action Party (PAN) candidate for mayor (in Mexico City, by contrast, the mayor was not elected but appointed). Next, a lack of federal oversight allowed small-scale crusading media to exist unbothered by the secretary of government. Further, reliance on local subsidies freed ambitious editors to be more critical of the national regime, even (as in the case of Guadalajara's top paper, *El Informador*) the president and his cabinet. In border states, media looked as much to the United States as to Mexico City for inspiration. This proximity encouraged some publishers and editors to shun state dependence; it also allowed them a handy place of refuge—Texas or California—when threatened. Finally, as noted earlier of the García Valseca chain, the provinces hosted many a paper that drew much of its income from blackmail. Politicians and businesses would be hammered until they bought advertising, or hammered if they ceased to do so.[20]

What is less clear is how often provincial media were *consistently* critical, genuinely civic minded, and influential. Case studies of watchdog periodicals have tended to spotlight those that existed only for a few years, ceased their criticism after petty dictators reined them in, or had tiny print runs.[21] There were important exceptions. The most durable was the *Diario de Yucatán*, founded in 1925 as an elite-backed organ, which was openly critical of

Mexico's socialist-leaning regime and its local allies. It soon became and remains to this day the leading paper in Mérida. The right-wing Menéndez family that owned it persisted with an anti-PRI line all through the century, at times with remarkably forceful exposés of corruption and state violence.[22] On the other hand, while most large cities had broadsheets that represented the local business elite and disdained the PRI's more radical or statist policies, these papers generally resembled the broadsheet *gran prensa* of Mexico City: deferential news coverage, at least toward local authorities, along with a smattering of critical columns. As historian Paul Gillingham has put it, surveying the regional press of the 1940s to the 1960s, "political blandness" was "the default reporting position."[23]

In the 1970s the panorama changed somewhat. First, the leftist-populist rhetoric of President Luis Echeverría had business elites aghast. One way to organize a response was by founding an association, the Business Coordinating Council, which became a major lobbying body. Another was by founding probusiness newspapers. Then, in 1976, José López Portillo assumed the presidency, eager to set a more liberal tone. His government's initial tolerance of *Proceso*, support for *Unomásuno*, electoral reforms, and proposal (albeit fruitless) of a freedom-of-information act sent signals that journalists would be freer to write as they saw fit. And so, especially in the northern states, there arose a new wave of independent-minded papers, backed by business interests, some of which sympathized openly with the PAN: *Noroeste* in Culiacán, Sinaloa (1973); *Vanguardia* in Saltillo, Coahuila (1975); *El Diario de Juárez* in Chihuahua (1976); *A.M.* in León, Guanajuato (1978). Whether from start-up or within a few years, these papers gave approving coverage or at least a shared platform to opposition politicians. Given the marriage of monopolistic broadcaster Televisa with the PRI, these relatively daring alternative spaces proved crucial for Mexico's democratic opening, helping bring about victories for the PAN in several key mayoral races during the 1980s.[24]

In Baja California too the PAN was steadily gaining support, winning the mayorship of Mexicali in 1983 and Ensenada in 1986. July 1989 would see the next election for state governor, and the PAN was optimistic. It had a strong candidate in Ernesto Ruffo, the popular mayor of Ensenada. Tempering that optimism was the memory of Chihuahua in 1986, where a widely forecast gubernatorial victory for the PAN, which already ruled the state's biggest cities, was impeded by fraud by the PRI, with the aid of its allies in the media: Televisa and the *gran prensa*. Neither the massive public protests that ensued nor the sympathetic coverage of those protests and reports of ballot-rigging by international media and certain Mexican papers (*La Jornada*, *Proceso*, the Monterrey press) persuaded the federal government to step in. Nor did the election and its aftermath reflect well on the Chihuahua press: Though sympathetic to the PAN, *El Diario de Juárez*, the state's most influential daily, was induced or coerced by the PRI to downplay coverage of the protests. It claimed to be neutral, but even this was not enough for the newly elected PRI governor, Fernando Baeza, who pressed the paper's owners that autumn to fire eleven staffers.[25]

Blancornelas did all he could to support a fair election in Baja California and help prevent fraud. During the campaign, *Zeta* gave space to political debate and interviewed each of the candidates. But since most newspapers and Televisa backed the PRI, and since the PRI had governed poorly, Blancornelas favored Ruffo and the PAN. He also published regular opinion polls, which showed that Ruffo's prospects were strong; the polls thus served as a hedge against fraud by PRI officials. As it had done for previous elections, *Zeta* held a get-out-the-vote campaign, and for the July 2 ballot, it took the locally unprecedented step of placing observers at many polling stations (a tactic pioneered by *El Norte* of Monterrey). Ruffo won by a margin of more than 10 percent, and political insiders credited the long-term watchdog work of *Zeta*, along with the state's growing middle class, in having paved the way for the swing to the PAN. Ruffo's victory not only represented a personal triumph for Blancornelas, putting an end to rule by a party that had hounded him over his independence since the 1960s, it also heralded a new era for local state-press relations. Under Ruffo, government became more transparent, freedom of the press advanced, and subsidies and pay-offs were curtailed.[26]

All this affirmed the faith of the young Adela Navarro that the outlook for *Zeta* in 1990 was positive, despite the killing of Félix Miranda. (Or even because of it: Blancornelas would later admit that the murder had bolstered the paper's standing.) *Zeta* was now a solid enterprise, with twenty-two reporters and four photographers, most of them current or former students. There were also ten to fifteen college interns in its opinion polling department, of whom the better ones would be offered jobs. This hiring of students, mostly from Mexico's mushrooming communications programs (thirty-four in 1980, eighty-two by 1990), was now a nationwide trend. Few of them entered with much of a clue about journalism, for initially their teachers lacked experience in the field, but a university education at least marked a step toward the practical and ethical professionalization of the press.[27]

To many observers, the man who made the biggest difference between Chihuahua in 1986 and Baja California in 1989 was the president. In 1986, De la Madrid had taken the customary decision to approve of vote-rigging, or at least to turn a blind eye to it. (He did the same in the general election of 1988.) But in 1989, Salinas preempted any mischief by the Baja California PRI. Resisting pressures from party hard-liners in both Mexicali and Mexico City, he swiftly recognized the PAN's claim of victory.[28] This came only four months after his regime had ushered Manuel Becerra Acosta of *Unomásuno* into Spanish exile. So what was Salinas—autocrat, democrat, a mix of both?

Carlos Salinas: Seducing the Fourth Estate

The big-breasted doll stared at the balding politician with the prominent moustache as he took his seat among the intellectuals. The day was September 7, 1987, and the man was Carlos Salinas, minister of budget and planning. Salinas was soon to be unveiled as the PRI candidate for the following year's general election. His hosts were the elite among Mexico City's community of writers, or at least a substantial part of it. On either side of Salinas, as they all posed for a photograph, sat Miguel Ángel Granados Chapa, the columnist, and Gabriel García Márquez, the Colombian novelist and Nobel Prize winner, who had made Mexico his home. At a far end sat Carlos Monsiváis; his slight remove from the group was fitting, for ironic detachment was his mode. Behind them stood the newspaper editor Benjamín Wong; environmental activist Iván Restrepo, in whose home they were gathered; the chronicler and novelist Elena Poniatowska; the actress and producer Margo Su; and the editor and novelist Héctor Aguilar Camín. On a separate chair, near to García Márquez, sat the columnist León García Soler. In between the latter two men was the big-breasted doll herself, a mute witness to one of the most symbolic events in the intellectual history of a country that had always placed its writers on pedestals.

The doll, whose unusual presence would inspire the title of a documentary about the meeting (*La muñeca tetona*), belonged to Restrepo.[29] Restrepo's house, in the comfortable and central Condesa neighborhood, lent itself to such encounters: adorned with conversation-piece curios and a leafy patio— some of the foliage being marijuana plants—which functioned as an alternative dining area in fair weather. It was home to the Atheneum of Angangueo, jocularly named for a small town in Michoacán, with an ironic nod to the famous Atheneum of Youth that had arisen before the revolution. The new atheneum was a twice-monthly conclave of writers founded in the 1970s by Restrepo, Monsiváis, cultural maven Fernando Benítez, and star political columnist Manuel Buendía. As the group expanded, senior politicians sometimes asked if they could attend. A ritual evolved: Restrepo and his confreres would invite a cabinet member to join them each time they met, and once a year they would invite the president.

A second witness that day in 1987, at Restrepo's express invitation, was Mexico's leading photojournalist, Pedro Valtierra. He took the group photograph, which would remain largely unknown beyond its intimate circle for a generation. Valtierra had made his name at *Unomásuno* and *La Jornada*, and

UN DOCUMENTAL DE DIEGO ENRIQUE OSORNO
& ALEXANDRO ALDRETE

«Una vez que aceptas,
como la mafia, ya no te podías salir.»

DETECTIVE

Bengala. CUARTOSCURO

EDICIÓN Llora Spilk Bialostozky, FOTOGRAFÍA Marcelo Salén, INVESTIGACIÓN Diego Enrique Osorno, DISEÑO SONORO Gerardo Villarreal Guerra, PRODUCCIÓN EJECUTIVA Andrés Clariond Rangel, PRODUCCIÓN Teresa Blanco Gómez, Gabriel Nuncio, Diego Enrique Osorno, DIRECCIÓN Diego Enrique Osorno y Alexandro Aldrete

The documentary short *La muñeca tetona* (2017) explores the meeting of president-to-be Carlos Salinas with the Atheneum of Angangueo, a group of left-wing intellectuals linked to *La Jornada*, in 1987. Courtesy of Diego Enrique Osorno.

all those gathered that day had links to the latter paper; Granados Chapa and Aguilar Camín were founding directors, most held shares in it, and all contributed articles. So the Atheneum of Angangueo had a distinctly left-wing hue, and yet Salinas, whom Valtierra's group portrait showed grinning, was decidedly center-right.

With his Harvard PhD and his technocratic, austerity-enforcing, US-friendly role in the cabinet of De la Madrid, Salinas had nailed his colors to the conservative and cosmopolitan wing of the ostensibly leftist-nationalist PRI. He advocated neoliberalism. Whereas De la Madrid had begun a shift toward this free-market philosophy more or less out of obligation—Mexico's infirm economy and the hegemonic Washington Consensus left him little option—Salinas embraced it. Having watched two spendthrift populists end their presidencies by devaluing the peso, and disdainful of big-state inefficiencies and protectionism, he was bent on transforming Mexico much in the way that Margaret Thatcher was reshaping the United Kingdom. He would privatize state-run industry, deregulate the financial sector, weaken the unions, and draw closer to the United States. The dream was First World status.[30] He would need the press, and the widely respected public intellectuals who wrote in it, to help him sell his program to the people.

Salinas was a short and slightly built man, endowed with a very quick mind and boundless energy—as president he was dubbed "The Atomic Ant"—and the luncheon would be remembered fondly by its participants. Poniatowska recalled Salinas's curiosity about what each had to say. To a greater or lesser extent, the seduction was mutual. Most members of the Atheneum would vote for socialist candidate Cuauhtémoc Cárdenas the following year, but after the election they would return to Salinas's social orbit. Aguilar Camín, who deemed Cárdenas a retrograde, big-state populist, was the president's most enthusiastic supporter among the group.[31] He became a regular adviser; thirty years later, Salinas could still recite his telephone number. Salinas was apt to call out of the blue. Poniatowska once answered the phone to hear, "This is Carlos Salinas," and not believing that the president would ring without an intermediary, she answered, "Oh yes? And I'm the Virgin of Guadalupe," and hung up.[32]

When US president Bill Clinton feared his 1992 reelection prospects were being damaged by boat people arriving from Cuba and called Salinas to mediate with Fidel Castro, Salinas asked García Márquez to smooth the process; the novelist, a longtime friend of the Cuban dictator, happily complied. In May that same year, Salinas hosted a sixtieth birthday banquet for Poniatowska at the presidential palace of Los Pinos, and several of the Atheneum attended, along with other leading writers such as historian Enrique Krauze, who edited the influential political-cultural magazine *Vuelta*.[33]

With the international press, which was already used to being coddled, Salinas became yet more attentive than his forebears. The US papers needing little seducing, so content were they to see Mexico led by an English-speaking, pro-American, right-of-center reformer. In July 1988, *The Washington Post* minimized the recent electoral irregularities and rejoiced that "with Mr. Salinas, the PRI is moving in the right direction and moving fast." By early 1989, *The New Republic, Newsweek,* and the *National Review* had praised his character and resolve, and *The Dallas Morning News* feted him as "an individual who long ago ceased running for office and is now running for history." In April 1991, when Salinas returned to his alma mater Harvard to give a talk on free trade to the American Society of News Editors, 500 members showed up. The phrase "Harvard-educated Salinas" became a cliché in the US press; public intellectual Jorge Castañeda joked that the president's first name was in fact "Harvard-educated."[34]

Salinas's romancing of journalists and intellectuals proved more effective than that of most of his predecessors and all of his successors. Political scientist Chappell Lawson has called him "Mexico's undisputed master of image management." The scheme had multiple motives. By all accounts, including his own, Salinas genuinely enjoyed their company and the cut-and-thrust of well-informed exchange. He sought their counsel on social policy, in the field of diplomacy, and on cultural matters, especially regarding Mexico's image abroad. Recalls the former president today, "They gave opinions, rather than advice, and they were very frank. These served to calibrate my decisions."[35] A case in point: After Salinas promised in his inaugural address to reregulate the status of the Catholic Church, a *La Jornada* columnist, Roberto Blancarte, criticized the pledge and advocated for a firmer legal status for *all* religions. Years later, Salinas would admit in his memoir that Blancarte's column had prompted him to alter his religious reform accordingly.[36]

Octavio Paz, a poet, essayist, and founder of *Vuelta* magazine, won the Nobel Prize for Literature in 1990, and Salinas basked in the reflected glory, for Paz was a believer in his project. The septuagenarian writer even told *The New York Times,* "It's the first time in my lifetime when I feel there have been important changes in the country."[37]

Deepening a tradition practiced by all presidents with varying degrees of success, Salinas built a clientele among leading writers and editors: He would subsidize their periodicals and their books, invite them on presidential tours, award them grants, and create a television channel for cultural programming; they would be seen with him in public, polishing his aura as philosopher-king, and they would praise him, or at least pull their punches, in print. According to Jaime Abello, the Colombian director of the Gabriel

García Márquez Foundation for New Ibero-American Journalism, no country in the Americas budgeted as much state support for writers and artists as Mexico.[38]

Above all, after his election, Salinas's association with intellectuals would lend him credibility. He arrived at Los Pinos with a distinct lack of it, following a vote that was widely seen as riddled with fraud if not stolen outright. The public displeasure only heightened a general malaise, owing to rigged elections in Nuevo León, Chihuahua, and elsewhere and a sustained economic crisis dating from 1981—hence the common reference to "the lost decade"—which was forever to be associated with misrule by the PRI.[39]

Salinas's desire for credibility among Mexicans (and abroad, as a modernizer) would govern his relations with the entire press, propelling greater transparency and freedoms.[40] In sum, Salinas's six-year term was a watershed: It witnessed a more accelerated and far-reaching opening of Mexico's media than under any previous president; this would be true of television and radio as well as print. It was an incomplete opening, with contrary signals from the presidency and numerous setbacks. But the era's advances, driven also by editors professionalizing their newsrooms, a boom in private-sector advertising, and publishers launching committedly civic-minded papers, would prove more durable than those of the 1970s and 1980s. Independent periodicals became much more numerous, both in the capital and outside it. The consequences were not only a better-informed public but also, in the long run, a citizenry more inclined to vote for parties other than the PRI.[41]

Much of the sea change of the Salinas years owed to an evolution in newsroom culture: the assumption of senior posts by the Generation of '68; revulsion among many journalists at the PRI over the economic crash of 1982, the inept response to the earthquake of 1985, and rigged elections; and the hiring of idealistic graduates of the country's new communications and journalism programs. A small but influential number of journalists, both middle aged and young, visited the United States or Western Europe, where they witnessed or even studied a freer press; Spain's *El País* was a common source of inspiration.[42] Much of the change derived from a more general rejection of the PRI, especially among those journalists who saw themselves as part of Mexico's new civil society, pushing collectively for social improvements rather than waiting for the regime to offer them in exchange for votes. Over the past quarter century, urban readers had increasingly become "citizens of scandal," Vanessa Freije's term for a populace empowered by the print media's exposure of the failures and corruption of the state and their own collective organizing; these people demanded a more responsive and responsible press.[43]

And much of the change owed to publishers—especially outside the capital—embracing business models that did not depend on the state, or not nearly as much as before. Their confidence drew greatly on a booming economy and a host of new advertisers.[44]

The transformation also stemmed from the convictions and priorities of the president. Salinas had long been fascinated with the written word. Famous authors including Paz and Carlos Fuentes had luncheoned as guests of his father, Raúl Salinas Lozano, a cabinet minister in the 1960s. At high school he had founded two papers, both ephemeral but an instructive experience in the production of news. Soon after, he befriended the elderly Francisco Martínez de la Vega, a veteran of *El Día* and a political aide to presidents.[45] Salinas studied at Harvard during a time of rapid evolution in the US press. *The New York Times* and *Washington Post* were holding power to account as never before, above all by exposing the Watergate crimes of 1972–74—a story mined most effectively by Bob Woodward and Carl Bernstein of the *Post*—which induced the resignation of President Richard Nixon. The scandal surely showed the young Mexican how a free press might contribute to the checks and balances of a mature democracy.

In an off-the-record interview during the De la Madrid era, Salinas had remarked that he wanted to start each morning reading news that was credible. He said the press had lost its effectiveness as propaganda, because when the government wanted to persuade the people of something important, they tended not to believe what they read. He was right: In a 1991 poll, only 25 percent of Mexicans expressed a positive opinion of the press (69 percent of Americans did so in a slightly earlier poll). Speaking today, Salinas says the mechanisms used by previous presidents to orient the press and foster obeisance were self-defeating: "They were counterproductive, because they obstructed dialogue with the public. They were an anachronism." The claim may seem self-serving, but it reflects the man's famous self-confidence. Salinas welcomed dialogue, or at least the idea of it, because he believed that both his policies and his gifts of persuasion were infallible. As Scherer of *Proceso* put it, "He displayed the security of a high-flying academic."[46]

When Salinas took office as a self-described modernizer, he had a freer press in mind as part of his project. And as he had squeaked by at the ballot box, a freer press could be a signal to Mexicans that he was, despite initial appearances, a democrat. In his inaugural address of December 1, 1988, he vowed "to modernize" relations between the state and the press. At his first Freedom of the Press banquet, he adopted a conciliatory, flattering tone, proffering a relationship sustained by respect, constructive criticism, and clear rules to protect the lives and dignity of journalists. He fleshed out his ideas on modernization by proposing a public body to measure circulation and ratings and by offering to privatize the newsprint distributor PIPSA. This was a little too much modernity for some publishers, who preferred to keep their

President Carlos Salinas, at his first Freedom of the Press banquet in 1989, proposed to privatize the newsprint supplier PIPSA, thereby abolishing a tool of de facto censorship. Courtesy of the Archivo General de la Nación (Fondo Hermanos Mayo, CR2/2906).

dismal print runs secret and their subsidies and payoffs intact, no matter that state control of PIPSA had long been used to preempt or punish criticism.[47]

Heavy resistance from within the media was a key reason why change came slowly. As Sallie Hughes puts it, "Inertial newspapers such as Mexico City's *Excélsior, Novedades*, and *Unomásuno* maintained passive, subordinate, and monochromatic pro-regime approaches to journalism throughout the societal transformation of the 1990s."[48] Groomed and fed for decades as lapdogs of the state, many a publisher, editor, and reporter jealously guarded their juicy bone.

A Watershed Emerges

Salinas may have been the lead actor of the early 1990s, the architect of watersheds political, economic, and in the media, but he was also very much acted on. He was goaded toward a freer press by the implications of his neoliberal policy and the foreign response to it. In 1990, the president and his team opened talks with their US and Canadian counterparts about a trilateral trade deal, which would take effect during Salinas's final year of office as the North American Free Trade Agreement (NAFTA). As the deal took shape, it became ever more important to its partners that Mexico be a functioning democracy. Freedom of expression was universally considered a key ingredient. Testament to this concern was a convoy of overseas observers taking the pulse of Mexico's press and finding it weak. Already in 1989, UK human rights organization Article 19 and *The Dallas Morning News* had compiled surveys. In 1990, Americas Watch did so too, followed in 1992 by the Canadian Committee to Protect Journalists, and in 1994 by the US Committee to Protect Journalists. Common to the reports were concerns that Mexico's media labored under censorship, if mostly of the indirect, goaded-to-self-censor kind, and that its journalists, especially in the provinces, were being murdered in alarming numbers.[49]

The advent of NAFTA also prompted many international media to set up or expand their bureaus in Mexico City. While most of them afforded Salinas and his economic project flattering coverage, they intensified the spotlight on Mexican democratization. When heavy-handed censorship occurred (as at *The News* in 1992), they reported on it. And when their stories found the regime failing to fulfill its liberal billing, or quoted politicians expressing themselves with unusual frankness, Mexican papers felt emboldened to run such pieces in translation or pursue follow-up stories of their own.[50]

A free-market economy would stimulate a freer press in ways that largely escaped a president's influence. The privatization of state-controlled industry begun by De la Madrid was accelerated by Salinas, with the result that the telephone monopoly, the banks, both major airlines, and second-ranked broadcaster TV Azteca increased their ad spend and did so freer of government interference.[51] As of 1990, Mexico experienced a gold rush of foreign investors in anticipation of NAFTA's passage. After all, they now had 90 million Mexicans to sell to, 30 to 40 percent of whom could be classed as middle income. On an annual basis, foreign direct investment quadrupled during the Salinas years to $10 billion.[52] Together with greater spending by Mexican businesses, investment growth prompted a historic advertising boom as new businesses and franchises became advertisers. Broadcast quasi-monopoly Televisa fared especially well; in 1993, *Forbes* named its CEO, Emilio Azcárraga, the number one billionaire in all Latin America. Newspapers also benefited, the roughly $47 million they drew in 1990 soaring to some $105 million in 1994.[53] As the ad market escalated and as disposable income recovered from the slump of the 1980s, newspaper publishers found they needed to rely less on state handouts. An adventurous investor might—at long last—start up a daily newspaper that took no or negligible subsidies (from either federal or state governments), nor backing from political patrons.

Just as Salinas's motives were mixed, so were his impulses. For all his talk of modernization, there was a side of him that evoked the PRI autocrat of old.

His exile of Becerra of *Unomásuno* appeared to some as a settling of scores. In 1990, Puebla businessman Javier Moreno Valle had been spending a year preparing a national newspaper to be called *El Independiente*, hiring top talent and spending a million dollars in the process, when word reached him of a presidential veto. Salinas was said to consider the project "disturbing."[54]

There were other black marks on the president's record, which, although the doing of others, tended to redound to him; during these final years of what Enrique Krauze has called "the imperial presidency," dating from the consolidation of single-party rule in the 1940s, it was common for Mexicans to claim that no leaf dared tremble without Salinas's say-so.[55] One issue was the continued willingness, perhaps overeagerness, of servile publishers to silence writers who were taking too literally for their comfort the president's language on freedom of expression. In June 1991, popular *Excélsior* columnist Manú Dornbierer saw fit to publish a rumor that two brothers of the president, Raúl and Enrique Salinas, had taken a 50 percent stake in the company operating the Mexico City racetrack. Both the concession holder and the city's attorney general wrote denials, which the paper printed, but when Dornbierer defended herself in respective follow-up columns, each was spiked. Dornbierer then resigned from *Excélsior*, claiming she no longer felt herself either free or safe to practice journalism as long as Salinas remained in office.[56]

Another black mark was the persistence by Mexico's governors in seizing from local distribution points all copies of Mexico City publications that exposed their acts of repression or corruption. Most often affected was newsmagazine *Proceso*.[57]

Among independent-minded editors there was a special dislike of Otto Granados, the sharp, thirty-two-year-old presidential spokesman. Granados played bad cop to Salinas's congenial good cop, demanding more deference to the regime than editors betting on openness were willing to give, lest his cultivation of the president's credibility be set back. His calls to editors were frequent. When Salinas gave his second State of the Nation address, in 1990, reporters from *Proceso* and *El Financiero* were denied entry, while *Excélsior* and *El Universal* were allotted two seats each. And when the pope visited Monterrey that year, the long-running *El Porvenir*, which had taken a critical turn to the left, found its reporters denied credentials for events. Around the same time, that paper suffered a state-mandated audit and strikes apparently conjured by Mexico City. Granados also imposed a government ad boycott. After eighteen months, the paper's position was so grave that publisher-editor Jesús Cantú was forced by its majority shareholders—his own family, whom Granados's envoys had courted—to resign.[58]

Phone tapping persisted too. Its historic use against journalists is well attested in the archives of the secret police, and its prevalence in the Salinas years (and later) was affirmed by editors, reporters, and columnists—and the occasional mysterious delivery of transcripts or recordings of conversations with journalists to newspaper offices. As human rights activist and *La Jornada* contributor Sergio Aguayo put it at the time, "Of course they tap our telephones; those are the rules of the game."[59]

Worse, the killing of provincial reporters continued unabated. Journalists had been bumped off now and then for decades, often on the suspected orders of some political boss, such as Puebla's famously sociopathic governor, Maximino Ávila Camacho.[60] Hits ordered by drug lords, first documented in Sinaloa in the 1970s, spread to other states in the 1980s. Politicians, officials, and police officers—some in cahoots with crime syndicates, some corrupt in other ways—became more willing to settle scores with a bullet. Under President De la Madrid, at least twenty media workers were murdered, all but one outside Mexico City. Under Salinas, at least another eighteen would be killed. In 1992, the newly formed National Human Rights Commission (CNDH) released a report examining the De la Madrid–era cases, and while it could confirm that twenty-two journalists had indeed been murdered (not all of them necessarily due to their work), it was unable or unwilling to determine who was responsible in any single case.[61]

What happened to Víctor Manuel Oropeza, the victim of one of the most infamous murders of the era, typified the chasm between presidential pledges and local outcomes. At the Freedom of the Press banquet on June 7, 1991, Salinas declared, "There is no democracy without active and well-informed public opinion." Four weeks later, Oropeza, a doctor who wrote for *El Diario de Juárez*, was stabbed to death in his office. He had been one of the best-known political activists in Ciudad Juárez. After the stolen Chihuahua election of 1986, he joined in a high-profile hunger strike, in sympathy with the PAN. He penned columns criticizing electoral fraud and the Federal Judicial Police, an agency reputed for corruption. The initial investigation claimed that two men had entered Oropeza's office to steal psychoactive drugs and, on meeting resistance, killed him. It also claimed that bodies matching descriptions of the assailants had been found two days later, victims of a gangland-style execution. Oropeza's family rejected the findings and organized a protest rally, where the speakers included the PAN's defeated candidate from the 1986 election. The profile of the case climbed further when Oropeza's widow received condolences from the Vatican, she being the niece of Mexico's representative at the Holy See.

Unusually for a provincial case, the federal government stepped in. The attorney general, Ignacio Morales Lechuga, dispatched a special envoy—who soon claimed that Oropeza was "a homosexual and a drug dealer." With federal backing, the Chihuahua state attorney presented two detainees; one had confessed to the killing, the other to driving the getaway car, while a second killer was said to be on the run. The two were tried and convicted. Again, neither the family nor the PAN was satisfied. The forensic evidence of twenty stab wounds did not fit the claimed motive of stealing drugs, and $2,000 in cash had gone untouched. Morales Lechuga met with Oropeza's son and let family members and an assigned prosecutor review the case file. The CNDH got involved, and in February 1992 it released its report: The investigation had failed to consider Oropeza's articles criticizing the Federal Judicial Police; the supposed perpetrators were a couple of layabouts, well known to the police and arrested for convenience's sake; and they had been tortured into confessing. The CNDH demanded their release. Three local police chiefs were then fired for framing them. Under pressure from the CNDH, the Chihuahua attorney general would reopen the case in 1994. Two years later, state authorities claimed that they had lost some documents vital to the case, making further investigation impossible.[62]

The whole affair smelled of hit job and cover-up: an initial, ham-fisted explanation; a second, more detailed, again implausible explanation; an attempt to smear the victim; an attempt to link him to the illicit drug trade; the torture of random poor people to prompt confessions; bureaucratic inertia, incompetence, and likely sabotage. Together, the victim's profile and the details of the investigation suggest that Oropeza was likely murdered on the orders of a federal police commander. But Oropeza's family, like the vast majority of victims' relatives before and since, would never have the certainty of knowing, let alone the justice of a rightful conviction.[63]

Although violence against journalists persisted, Salinas and his spokesmen did take measures that directly or indirectly enhanced press freedoms. Otto Granados orchestrated several changes. In technocratic fashion, the press chief worked to standardize and professionalize the entire communications apparatus of the federal government. For too long, he felt, each ministry had issued whatever bulletins or leaked whatever information it cared to, sometimes at odds with the position of Los Pinos. (Like the "White House," "Los Pinos" could refer either to the presidential mansion or to the president and his inner circle.)[64] So he insisted on being permitted to name the press chiefs of each ministry—in most cases getting his way, with just a couple of party "dinosaurs," such as Tourism Minister Carlos Hank González, holding out— and the directors of the state-owned media. Here he made progressive appointments: the respected editor and columnist José Carreño Carlón to head government-owned newspaper *El Nacional* and Raymundo Riva Palacio, a star reporter at *Excélsior,* to head Notimex, the state-owned news agency. Coordination between all the press offices meant a more consistent message from the government and a lessening of the old culture of serving inside information to favored columnists at boozy lunches. Granados also profession-alized relations with the press more concretely by ending Los Pinos's monthly handout of cash to reporters.

"It was in bad taste, ethically speaking. It was not suitable for a modern presidency. It lacked elegance," Granados would reminisce. Salinas wanted to persuade reporters with what he was sure was the rightness of his policies, instead of buying them off with *embute*. "More importantly, it was completely useless. It didn't make for good reporting. It just allowed publishers to continue paying their reporters badly." Perhaps not wanting to strain relations with cabinet members, some of them twice his age, Granados refrained from directing ministry press offices to halt their own *embute* hoping that they would follow his lead. Some began to do so; others dragged their feet.[65]

Ignacio Rodríguez Reyna was a junior reporter at *El Financiero* when he was sent to Monterrey to cover one of the public forums held by Manuel Bartlett, the public education minister, to promote plans for increased spending. In his hotel room, Rodríguez Reyna found someone had slipped an envelope under the door. It contained cash and a note: "With the attentive greetings of the Minister." Roberto Zamarripa of *La Jornada* told him he had been similarly tipped. At breakfast they returned the envelopes to a flack and went to complain to the ministry spokesman, who denied he knew anything. Another day, at the Education Ministry, a functionary told Rodríguez Reyna she was surprised to see him. "You hardly ever come here. And look"—she pulled out a folder and opened it—"here are all your fortnightly payments." She added that Zamarripa had never collected his money either, nor had Homero Campa of *Proceso*. But there were another thirty or so reporters on the education beat who always did.[66]

As for Salinas himself, at the 1991 Freedom of the Press banquet he announced a professional minimum wage for Mexico's long-underpaid reporters. He also offered a program of state-backed mortgages for journalists and scholarships for their children. And when the US press cast a spotlight on Mexico's problems or electoral shenanigans, Salinas, quite unlike De la Madrid, was quick to act. In August 1991, a *Wall Street Journal* editorial opined that if Salinas wanted to banish the cloud that still hung over him from 1988, he should order that Guanajuato's recent gubernatorial election, in which the PAN's Vicente Fox had likely been cheated of victory, be reheld. The very next day, the PRI's governor-elect stepped aside, and nine weeks later the PAN took control of the state. That October, within two weeks of the Sunday *New York Times Magazine* running a five-page spread on rampant violence in Matamoros, federal police arrested local crime boss Juan N. Guerra. The capo, whose record of alleged murders included his own wife (he pleaded self-defense), would only spend a few weeks in jail, and for tax evasion at that. But the detention affirmed that Salinas could be moved, however incrementally, by bad press.[67]

Crucially, Salinas eliminated tariffs on imported newsprint, putting an end to PIPSA's near monopoly after more than fifty years of protection. This move, decreed in April 1990, was key on both a symbolic level and a practical one. PIPSA had served historically as a sword of Damocles over the heads of renegade publishers: It might either deny them newsprint or, more commonly, refuse to grant or extend purchases made on credit.[68] It had let a few periodicals accumulate huge debts, and these too could prove a weapon; the sum owed by *Unomásuno* had been one of the instruments used to persuade Becerra to accept a one-way ticket to Madrid.[69]

The PIPSA policy was enthusiastically reported on by the biggest newspapers: *El Universal, Excélsior, El Norte*. This reception, together with a growing public awareness of watchdog reporting and critical comment in *Proceso, El Financiero*, and *La Jornada*, likely explains why the second World Values Survey in Mexico, conducted in 1990, showed a growth in trust in the press. Now 48 percent of Mexicans expressed confidence in what they read, up from 36 percent nine years earlier.[70]

The liberalizing of the newsprint supply was the green light that publishers and editors yearning to practice critical journalism had been waiting for.[71] A few, like Blancornelas and Monterrey's Alejandro Junco, publisher of *El Norte*, were already doing so, but now their numbers would proliferate. During the rest of the Salinas era a second wave of civic-oriented media launched and gained traction. Taking the lead were publishers from the provinces.

Chapter 3

Siglo 21

Guadalajara Conceives a Prodigy

One of the youngest and most accomplished ventures in regional journalism . . .
Siglo 21 conquered in such a short time a place at the vanguard of the
Guadalajara press.

—Fernando de Ita, cultural critic

Guadalajara Explodes

At around eight o'clock on the morning of April 22, 1992, as pigeons pecked
at scraps in the plaza by the cathedral, Guadalajara's news vendors began to
display their wares. A pedestrian stopping to scan the front pages would
have found most of them offering the usual mix of global events and progovernment pablum. The staid market leader *El Informador* featured the swearing in of a provisional president in Peru. There was quite a different look on
page 1 of *Siglo 21*. This paper, a modest upstart, led with a hunger strike by
thirty women outside the governor's mansion, protesting a stolen municipal election. Below, an article warned of a dangerous fuel leak in the sewers
just south of the city's center. Turning inside, the reader would have seen
the warning starkly detailed: Firefighters who had inspected the sewers
were very worried; a map detailed the danger area; an explosion could be
imminent.

Two hours later, the explosion struck.

A five-mile stretch of Guadalajara streets, the very corridor mapped by
Siglo 21, literally blew up. Cars were tossed into the air. Buildings had their
façades ripped off. Stores were obliterated and buses tumbled into instant
ravines. According to eventual official reports, which may have undercounted,
206 people were killed, 600 were injured, and 3,000 homes across ninety-eight
city blocks were partially or completely destroyed.

Only *Siglo 21* had the story of pending disaster, because only *Siglo 21* reporter Alejandra Xanic had troubled to investigate the fuel leak. The day before, city officials had held a press conference to address the pervasive smell
reported by residents. They said the problem was under control, and this is
what the rest of the press ran with, accustomed as they were to printing official declarations as gospel—the dominant style of old-school journalism
known in Mexico as *declaracionismo*. But Xanic, a cub reporter, had been

CONTAMINACIÓN

Alarma por la descarga de solventes

La fábrica de aceites La Central, era, hasta anoche, la sospechosa de la descarga de solventes en el drenaje, que alarmó a vecinos del sector Reforma. La investigación del SIAPA, bomberos, Unidad de Protección Civil y Pemex prosiguió a lo largo del colector que conducía los gases explosivos

Trabajadores en la búsqueda de los gases explosivos

ALEJANDRA XANIC

La fábrica de aceites La Central era, hasta la diez de la noche de ayer, la principal sospechosa de la descarga de solventes que alarmó a los colonos de la calle Pedro de Gante, en el sector Reforma. Tal conjetura no ha sido confirmada, pero el rastreo que emprendieron desde la una de la tarde el SIAPA, los bomberos, la Unidad de Protección Civil y Pemex, por la red de drenaje, había llevado a los técnicos a traspasar las puertas de la fábrica y a considerar, en ese momento, que de sus ductos había salido la descarga y que podría tratarse de exano, hidrocarburo que utilizan en la producción las aceiteras y que es un contaminante explosivo.

Pudo deberse a un desperfecto de la fábrica, señalaban anoche, pues la presencia del solvente en el colector no fue constante y no parecía provenir de una fuga.

A las doce de la noche, seguían bajo la pista.

Pemex en mi cocina

En la mañana del martes, los vecinos reportaron que desde la madrugada salía "humo" y un olor a gasolina de las alcantarillas de sus casas. "Es de Pemex", aseguraban por la tarde. "Pasa esto cada año: como que lavan y dejan venir por el drenaje la gasolina".

La calle Pedro de Gante estaba en silencio y cerrada, desde la calzada Independencia hasta la calzada del Ejército. Muchos vecinos, sobre las aceras, miraban. "No nos han dicho nada, es lo que esperamos". "Que es gasolina de Pemex, dicen". "yo no sé; dicen que puede explotar pero todavía no nos informan".

tal energético.

La investigación dependía de los aparatos que portaban dos o tres sujetos y que medían la explosividad del gas.

Petróleos Mexicanos se empeñó en demostrar que los rastros no eran suyos. Juan Antonio Delgado, superintendente de la planta Pemex, insistió en que revisaron todas las subestaciones y que estaban en orden; la empresa no es la responsable aseguró.

Según otro funcionario, en cuanto supieron del reporte, salieron de la planta Pemex de La Nogalera y fueron a hacer pruebas a la empresa que, según ellos, era la causante; la fábrica aceitera. "A las seis de la tarde tomamos las primeras muestras", señaló.

Lo hicieron en las descargas de la empresa, y aseguró, reportaban la misma concentración de gas que llevaba el colector

Gasolina parece, Pemex no es

El gas que emanaba de las alcantarillas olía "a veces a gasolina y a veces a thinner", pero según los ingenieros de Pemex, el color del agua demostraba que no contenía

Poco tiempo después, la atención de los investigadores se desvió de la paraestatal. Encontraron una fuerte concentración de gases a la altura de la avenida Dr. R. Michel y Río Tototlán, en uno de los registros del colector. Los ojos voltearon sobre los muros de la aceitera.

Detrás de esa puerta

La comitiva, integrada por el Oficial Mayor del destacamento de bomberos, Mayor Trinidad López Rivas, el director del SIAPA, Gualberto Limón, el gerente técnico de este organismo, José Luis Macías, funcionarios de la Unidad de Protección Civil, de la policía municipal, y de Pemex, ingenieros y técnicos para toda clase de tareos, traspasó, bajo el asombro del vigilante, la puerta de la fábrica.

No había en ella alguna persona

que pudiera dar información. Todo el personal es sindicalizado, advirtió el guardia, luego de que solicitaran un guía para recorrer la planta; sólo trabajan bajo la orden de un memorándum, abundó.

El olfato, pues, debió ser instrumento elemental de la búsqueda, y acrecentó la sospecha.

En una zona de la planta, había un olor "igual" al que se expedía por el colector.

Comenzó la búsqueda en cada registro de la red interna de drenaje. Lecturas del "explosímetro": más o menos "explosividad", dos con trajes y cascos. Fue el olfato de los funcionarios del SIAPA que se acercó a lo que supusieron una prueba más cercana: al registro donde la concentración del gas era "total".

Había que buscar por dónde descargaba: abrir y cerrar registros, hasta que volvieron sobre los de la avenida R. Michel.

De nuevo sobre el asfalto, la comitiva decidió introducir una "sonda" por el registro que reportó mayor concentración del gas, para ver si llegaba al registro de la planta. Así podrían determinar si los solventes procedían de la planta.

Los vecinos de Pedro de Gante ya dormían; según los reportes, había descendido la presencia del gas en el área. Kilómetros después, continuaban tras la pista.

"Hemos tenido reportes semejantes, dijo el Mayor López Rivas, pero nunca tan complicados como éste.

A ocho horas de iniciada la averiguación, no había pruebas contundentes de responsabilidad.

A las doce de la noche, no había otro reporte que el antes mencionado. ●

Tras la pista: la primera clave

Its unique public warning of a dangerous gasoline leak, made a few hours before an explosion that killed more than 200, catapulted *Siglo 21* to fame as a Guadalajara news source in 1992. Courtesy of Juan Carlos Núñez.

trained by none other than Tomás Eloy Martínez, the famed Argentine novelist and journalist. At a workshop before her paper's launch, Martínez had insisted: Officials are not the only source of news! And so she had snooped around the area. At an entrance to the sewers, she happened on a crew of nervous-looking firefighters. She saw personnel from the state oil company Pemex wielding a so-called explosometer and overheard one of them say its reading was "100 percent." She followed the firefighters for hours as they inspected the main sewer and adjacent factories. By midnight, with *Siglo 21* holding the front page, she had quotes from the firefighters and enough detail of the leak's spread for a designer to produce the prescient map.[1]

Hers was a report that, together with rigorous follow-up coverage, would topple the mayor of Mexico's second city and prompt his incarceration. It would also help topple the governor of Jalisco, the state of which Guadalajara is the capital. It would make the twenty-five-year-old Xanic an unusually young recipient of the National Journalism Prize for reporting. It would establish *Siglo 21* as the most trusted news source in Guadalajara. It would contribute to the National Action Party (PAN) ousting the long-ruling Institutional Revolutionary Party (PRI) at both city and state levels in the elections of 1995. And it would set Xanic herself on a distinguished career in journalism that saw her, in 2013, become the only Mexican reporter ever to win a Pulitzer Prize.[2]

Jorge Zepeda Patterson: Professor of the Press

Three years before the explosion, at the beginning of the Salinas presidency, Jorge Zepeda Patterson was about to leave Guadalajara to start a doctorate at the Sorbonne when he took a phone call that would change his life.[3] At the time, the future founder-editor of *Siglo 21* and eventual overseer of numerous journalistic transformations was a late-thirties academic with no media experience. Slender, bearded, bookish, and possessing a warm smile, Zepeda Patterson was the grandson of a railroad engineer from Ohio who had settled in Sonora. His father was a railroad man too. This career and his mother's cancer made for a less than stable childhood. Jorge was born in Mazatlán, but when he was seven the family moved to Guadalajara. When he was nine his mother died. He spent his junior high years in private school because he won a scholarship, but then he returned to the public system.

While studying economics at university in the early 1970s, Zepeda met an unusual state official called Alfonso Dau. A Lebanese Mexican, Dau came from a wealthy textile family but had a passion for progressive politics. As director of the state government's economics department, he was politically ambitious, but he loved the arts and had an altruistic streak. At the suggestion of a colleague, Zepeda, already reputed to be handy with a pen, began to write speeches for him. After Dau left for Mexico City to work as an adviser in the López Portillo administration and Zepeda left for Michoacán to enter academia, they remained in touch over the next dozen years. Conversations ranged from the political legacy of President Lázaro Cárdenas, Zepeda's research topic, to Dau's obsession with Guadalajara's lack of a decent newspaper. On trips to Spain as a government envoy, Dau had become an admirer of *El País*, the journalistic guardian of that country's shift from dictatorship to democracy. He also respected *El Norte*. If Monterrey could have a modern, independent newspaper, why couldn't the bigger city of Guadalajara?

Zepeda's flight to Paris was just two weeks off when Dau called and told him it was urgent that they meet; he would drive to Michoacán to make it happen. "Jorge," Dau said, "we have to create what we always dreamt of. We need to make a newspaper like *El País* in Guadalajara."

This was rather more Dau's dream than Zepeda's. The academic replied, "Talk to me when I'm back in two years!" But Dau convinced him to take a few days from his Paris sojourn to visit Madrid and write a report. He handed him $1,000 for expenses.

Once based in Paris, Zepeda ended up visiting Madrid on half a dozen occasions, sometimes for a month at a time, and abandoning his doctorate. Dau's relentless enthusiasm made much of the difference—that autumn he paid a surprise visit to Paris and badgered him into accepting the editorship of the planned paper—and so did the reception he got at *El País*. Zepeda clicked with the editor in chief, Joaquín Estefanía, a fellow economist who loved the idea of *El País* having a Mexican godchild. Estefanía placed him under the wing of Miguel Ángel Bastenier, a respected editor who taught in the paper's in-house journalism school. Bastenier took him to editorial meetings and arranged for him to spend entire fortnights in each of the paper's main sections: national, international, the economy, and culture, along with the design and photography departments.

Dau's intentions with the paper were Zepeda's one source of doubt. *El País* was an attractive model because, while on the center-left, it had no party affiliation and its corporate structure was journalist owned (like Mexico's *La Jornada*). Dau, however, was a businessman with political aspirations. So during Dau's Paris visit, the two men debated at length how their paper might ensure an editorial autonomy that, while common at European and US newspapers, would set it apart from the typical periodical in Mexico and enhance its credibility from the get-go. They reached three agreements to ensure a firewall between the business and the newsroom: Zepeda would make all the hiring decisions; no journalist could talk to Dau unless Zepeda too were present; and Dau would pay for him to study journalism before start-up, as Zepeda needed first to be sure that he understood the profession—hence, his crash course at *El País*, which lasted six months. He also met frequently with a Paris-based designer, working on a look that combined the best of *El País* with the best of *Libération*, the left-wing French tabloid founded by the philosopher Jean-Paul Sartre.

Although Dau was in a hurry, it was important to both that they get it right. While Zepeda wrote up an eighty-page outline, Dau commissioned a market study, which affirmed a latent appetite for an independent daily, especially among students and young professionals. Almost eighteen months passed between Zepeda's return to Guadalajara and the paper's launch. Dau and several coinventors would invest more than $3 million in start-up. Meanwhile Zepeda planned a number of innovations for a paper that they opted to call—for its forward-looking ring—*Siglo 21* (21st century). First, equipment would be state-of-the-art. Eschewing the green-screened personal computers that were the industry norm, Zepeda bought Apple Macintoshes. Steve Jobs's latest gift to desktop computing, fondly known as "the Mac," enhanced the speed of composition and ease of subediting. Second, Zepeda would invest in feature-length journalism of the kind he had seen in Europe. At a minimum, this meant hiring enough reporters so that each had the time to do more than file news stories. He was impressed by how *Libération* would dedicate several pages each day to a section called "Evénements" (Events), comprising contiguous features, expert-opinion pieces, and timelines that would flesh out and contextualize the news lead. On days without a major story, the space was given over to investigative reports. Third, again like *El País* and *Libération*, the paper would have a reference center right next to the newsroom (not tucked away on another floor), replete with indexed clippings, annual reports, obituaries-in-waiting, and so forth, overseen by a designated journalist. It would be fully functioning before launch. And fourth, *Siglo 21* would have a weekly arts and entertainment listings section, inspired by London's *Time Out*. Called "Tentaciones" (Temptations), it would boost sales of the Friday edition.

Another idea Zepeda imported from Europe was to democratize the newsroom by doing away with the sharp Mexican distinction between the *jefe de información* (day editor), who would assign reporters their stories in the morning, and the *jefe de redacción* (news editor), who would enter each afternoon and take charge of editing reporters' copy and the page layout. Zepeda deemed this too hierarchical; it led to dueling fiefdoms. At *El País* he had seen how five or six section editors would each conduct story meetings in the mornings, reconvene around two o'clock in the afternoon to decide which items would likely lead their section, and then oversee the subediting; each step ensued in an atmosphere of collegial debate. And Zepeda wanted to lead likewise: not as a suspender-snapping son of a bitch who chewed out his underlings, but as an approachable boss who would mentor his staff.

Mentoring was vital because Zepeda wanted to populate his newsroom with sharp young writers who lacked professional experience. It was the centerpiece of his plan, as he later put it, to found a paper "totally uncontaminated by the history of Mexican journalism." Here Zepeda was tuning into an emerging zeitgeist; several other innovators had come to view hiring recent graduates as the key to obviating the graft commonly practiced by the old-school "boys of the press." In Monterrey, Alejandro Junco had pioneered the trend since the early 1970s at *El Norte*. In Mexico City, financial journalist Luis Enrique Mercado had launched the daily *El Economista* in December 1988 with a reporting staff entirely made up of recent journalism and communications graduates.[4]

This plan was why Zepeda compiled a style-cum-ethics manual, unusual if not unprecedented at a Mexican paper, which included rules about how reporters should and should not interact with their sources. Among other things, there would be no accepting of cash-filled envelopes or gifts and no seeking of commissions on ads; instead, Dau would pay them a living wage of $1,000 a month. This was why Zepeda contracted with syndicated columnists known for their integrity, like Granados Chapa, and the public intellectuals Carlos Monsiváis and Gabriel Zaid. And this was why Zepeda made hires like Xanic, who had no experience beyond student journalism and a little freelancing; starting in autumn 1990, he recruited from the public, left-leaning University of Guadalajara (UdeG) and the private, left-leaning Western Institute of Technology and Higher Education (ITESO), making presentations on campus and talking to communications professors, several of whom were so enthused that they asked to join too.

And this was why Zepeda brought in Tomás Eloy Martínez, a famous Argentine writer. That same autumn, Guadalajara hosted an international communications congress. Bastenier of *El País* was there, and he proposed to Martínez a meeting with Dau and Zepeda. Over breakfast the day before Martínez was to fly out, the two Mexicans persuaded the Argentine that they needed his help. Martínez was supremely cosmopolitan and experienced, having studied literature at the Sorbonne and cofounded periodicals in Buenos Aires and Caracas. Since he had toiled under dictatorship, he could offer real-world advice on how to report on unfriendly regimes. Martínez agreed to help give a workshop the following spring to Zepeda's prospective reporters. It would double as a filter, because, of sixty trainees, fewer than fifteen would be hired. These included Xanic, Luis Petersen Farah, and Salvador Camarena, from the ITESO, which had Guadalajara's only reputable journalism program, and Luis Miguel González and Rubén Martín from the UdeG.

"Tomás Eloy Martínez as my teacher!" Camarena recalls. "I didn't realize how fortunate I was." Says Xanic, "He sent us out into the street and gave us an hour to come back with a story. We had to learn what was novel and what was relevant."

Zepeda, Dau, and their team felt confident of *Siglo 21* because the landscape it was about to enter was desultory, dominated by eight-column broadsheets that trafficked in elite perspectives. Guadalajara's Gray Lady was *El Informador*, founded in 1917 by the Álvarez del Castillo family, which still owned and managed it. It was housed in an imperious city-center building opposite the state legislature. Dau's marketing study noted that *El Informador* avoided "all confrontation or critical analysis."[5] Ranking second was *El Occidental* (est. 1942), part of the vapidly progovernment chain Organización Editorial Mexicana, owned by furniture store magnate Mario Vázquez Raña. A selling point was the space it gave to crime. The only other daily to shift more than a few thousand copies was the far-right *Ocho Columnas*, founded in 1978 at the Autonomous University of Guadalajara, which had recently granted an honorary doctorate to right-wing Nicaraguan kleptocrat Anastasio Somoza. News-hungry UdeG and ITESO students, generally shunning local media apart from one or two radio stations, would snap up the limited copies of *La Jornada* and *Proceso* that arrived from the capital and share them over and over.[6]

Many students and recent graduates like those Zepeda hired found the Catholic-rooted conservatism of Guadalajara stultifying. But there were signs that change was afoot, a new pluralism and openness to outside ideas. At the UdeG, rector Raúl Padilla—as much a political boss as an educator—had in 1986 founded a Guadalajara film festival, La Muestra, soon famed as Mexico's best; in the first edition after *Siglo 21* launched, the winner would be the slow-burn vampire flick *Cronos*, directed by future hometown hero Guillermo del Toro. In 1987, Padilla had followed up with the Guadalajara International Book Fair, destined to become the largest in the whole of the Americas. Elsewhere, young people with a creative and antiestablishment bent were trying to commercialize their work. These included three irreverent cartoonists, Jis, Trino, and Manuel Falcón, who printed up their comic strips and satires in a magazine called *La Mamá del Abulón* (literally, "The scallop's mother," but also a risqué pun).[7]

Diego Petersen Farah, younger brother of trainee subeditor Luis, was another innovator. Born into a well-to-do family of German and Lebanese descent and son of a prominent member of the PAN, Diego opted to campaign for leftist candidate Cuauhtémoc Cárdenas in the election of 1988. For four years, with the support of his brothers and friends from the ITESO, Diego had been putting out a small weekly called *Paréntesis*. It was an artisanal answer to the drabness of the local press, and for Petersen the experience proved a good education, but the paper rarely sold more than 3,000 copies and it never made money. In the summer of 1991, engaged to be married, he had just decided to close the paper and seek work in academia when Zepeda invited him to lunch. Petersen told him he was done with journalism, but Zepeda insisted he visit his office. There he saw the *Siglo 21* mock-up and instantly loved it. He came aboard as news editor.

Unluckily for Petersen and his fiancée, the months to come were frantic. Dau and Zepeda fixed the launch for October 12, the locally festive Day of the Virgin of Zapopan, and Petersen's wedding was set for a week later, but inexperience killed the plan. On their first dry run, they produced a paltry two pages; at the second attempt they managed six. There were supposed to be forty! Academics on staff were taking days to write a single story. Petersen had to cut back his two-week honeymoon by half. Some days later, he arrived home at night to be quizzed by the condo's doorman: "Who are you?" "I live in that apartment over there," he replied, pointing. "No, sir, there's a woman living there and she's single." As for Zepeda, he had separated from his wife and was shacked up in a hotel.

On November 6 an exasperated Tomás Eloy Martínez raised his voice at Zepeda: "¡Cabrón, ya!" (It's time, you bastard!). The following morning, Zepeda announced that their ship would sail the very next day. But within hours, an iceberg came into view. They received a call inviting them to cover a press conference: Enrique Dau—Alfonso Dau's second cousin—was going to launch his long-anticipated campaign as PRI candidate for mayor. Zepeda and his editors had strained to tell everyone that *Siglo 21*, unlike almost every other daily in the history of Guadalajara, was *not* a political project. Who would believe them now?

"We *have* to lead with something else," Zepeda told his editors. All the other papers, feeding at the trough of the ruling party, would trumpet the Enrique Dau announcement. It was undoubtedly the news of the day, so they could hardly ignore it. But they needed to demonstrate how they were different. One of the few veterans on the paper was José Hernández-Claire, the head photographer, and he suggested they run a picture he had taken of La Minerva, a signature Guadalajara monument of the goddess of wisdom. But his was a faintly subversive take: The giant statue was foregrounded by a cowboy-hatted janitor walking past, cleaning pole in one hand and abandoned tire in the other, which together gave him the look of an adobe-born Don Quixote. Martínez came up with a cheekily arrogant phrase to superimpose on the picture: "From today, Jalisco is different." The banner headline claimed, "Guadalajara Demands More Public Security," alluding to rising crime and reflecting the project's commitment to civic journalism. The Dau announcement was dropped to the foot of the page. *Siglo 21*, at last, was born.[8]

And almost stillborn. For all the team's dedication, for all Zepeda's planning of what "different" might look like, Jalisco was underwhelmed. Containing only three or four journalists with professional experience, Zepeda's cadre of twenty was too callow. To some readers, the paper felt low on news content, coming over more like a weekly; part of the problem was that most reporters lacked their rivals' chummy relations with official sources, who might tip them off to stories. There was no crime page and, bizarrely for soccer-crazed Guadalajara, little attention to sport. To others, the daily pandered too much to the college crowd, with arts and music stories sometimes on page 1. To advertisers, the paper seemed like a tabloid and thus hard to disassociate from yellow journalism; the format was in fact a longer-than-tabloid Berliner, but that European design was little known. Worse, ad sales departments at *El Informador* and *El Occidental* seemed to be conspiring against *Siglo 21*, forbidding their clients to apportion it part of their spend. That problem forced the young daily to accept *gacetillas*, though unlike at most newspapers they were flagged as such ("paid insertion"). Circulation failed to rise above 4,000 copies, sales were often half that, and the planned 30,000 seemed a pipe dream. There was no Christmas bonus for staff, and in January even the paychecks stopped, because a bank loan that Dau had been counting on failed to materialize. Four or five staffers departed. Zepeda drafted a farewell editorial.

Siglo 21 was saved by two unlikely interventions. The first, in early 1992, was the magnanimous hand of Jorge Álvarez del Castillo, the veteran owner-director of *El Informador*. Serving on the local credit committee of Bancomer, one of the nation's largest banks, he recommended approval of the loan that Dau needed. He later explained that he did not view *Siglo 21* as a rival. This was a judicious claim, for when Dau's paper eventually took off, it was *El Occidental* that lost share. Perhaps Álvarez sympathized: Mexican banks were often reluctant to lend to the press, for fear the client would later blackmail its way into nonpayment ("Roll over the loan or we'll print *this* about you!").

The second intervention was the explosion that April.

As soon as his faith in Xanic's report was confirmed by the tragedy, Zepeda declared all hands on deck: Reporters, photographers, and editors were all to stop what they were doing, cover the disaster, and work on an afternoon special. "It exploded!" exclaimed the banner. Copies were handed out for free. And the next day they led with, "And the explanation?," a question directed at the state and city governments, which were being evasive and slow with rescue efforts, as well as at the Pemex oil company. Twenty-four pages covered the aftermath from all angles. An array of photographs gave preference to citizens' viewpoints and the plight of the afflicted, rather than to officials making statements. (Among papers outside Mexico City, *Siglo 21* was a photojournalism pioneer.)[9] For ten days, again in contrast to rival papers, *Siglo 21* demanded answers of Mayor Enrique Dau and Governor Guillermo Cosío, investigated the culpability of Pemex, and gave space to readers' letters, all of which added fuel to the public clamor.[10] After a week of official opacity and sustained protest, in which *The New York Times*, *El País*, and *Proceso* joined the local chorus against the autocratic governor, President Carlos Salinas de Gortari forced his resignation. Cosío was already unpopular and recently had been weakened further by a *Proceso* exposé of his nepotism and familial enrichment.[11]

Dau, who had only been mayor for a few weeks, was not only pushed out but jailed. His second cousin, Alfonso, had kept his word not to interfere in editorial at *Siglo 21*, despite pressures from the PRI to do so. But he surely wondered why Zepeda was eager to take part in what must have seemed to him like a scapegoating (Cosío successfully shifted much blame for the explosion to the mayor). To Zepeda and his reporters, the episode was a chance to hold all authorities to account, not just for the explosion but also for the underlying causes: an ossified culture of arrogance, negligence, and corruption. Still, between Dau and Zepeda, seeds of mistrust were sown.

Trust in *Siglo 21* itself, however, was soaring. The combination of Xanic's scoop, the same-day special, and the hard-hitting coverage that followed turned the paper from an also-ran into a major force in Guadalajara news. So did its credibility vis-à-vis other media. While several radio stations captured the outrage of the public, private TV stations privileged official sources and the state TV channel simply ceased to broadcast. *El Occidental* relegated the first news of the explosion to a graphic below the fold while leading with an interview by the newspaper's pompous owner, Mario Vázquez Raña, with the prime minister of Estonia. *El Informador* did better, giving the blast a banner headline, but it also surrendered much of page 1 to President Salinas's visit to the disaster zone and, in a photograph, it showed him holding the hand of a bedridden survivor.[12]

By popular demand, *Siglo 21* ramped up its print run to 25,000, before settling back to a postdisaster average of 12,000 or so. This was modest, but the daily's middle-income readership was politically influential and represented the consumer class that new advertisers sought to target. The paper was taking steps on the road to stability.

Democratizing Jalisco

As of April 1992, the city of Guadalajara and the state of Jalisco were reborn, socially and politically, in ways that recalled the impact of the 1985 earthquake on Mexico City.[13] To local media scholar Juan Larrosa-Fuentes, the conjuncture of the explosion, the authorities' inept response, and *Siglo 21*'s coverage of both "marked the initial collapse of a system of political communication that had operated in Jalisco for at least fifty years." Henceforth, the long co-opted media learned to seek explanations from their governments and investigate when answers did not come forth. The episode catapulted *Siglo 21* into the consciousness of the wider Guadalajara public and strengthened the paper's subsequent work. It also represented the first in a rapid series of events that undermined the local PRI and brought the state electoral democracy, fortified by a more engaged public sphere.[14]

Within *Siglo 21* itself, the aftermath brought the exhilaration of having arrived.[15] Coverage of local issues intensified, the rest of Jalisco received greater attention, the reporting staff eventually almost tripled from the twenty at launch. Zepeda started a political column, "La fuente" (The source), that was soon a must-read for elite gossip. Two local veterans were hired to cover crime, as Zepeda realized the need to balance innocence with experience. The cultural section made its mark by going beyond the standard fine arts coverage and taking in what was going on at street level. *La Mamá del Abulón*, the satirical revue of cartoonists Jis, Trino, and Falcón, became a supplement. Esprit de corps was high. Zepeda set the tone in shirtsleeves and jeans, debating over stories and not raising his voice. Diego Petersen brought his wit as a joker and raconteur. Dau too was well liked. Though his office was set apart, the sixty-two-year-old was friendly and gregarious. Petersen would jest that, with all its passionate, high-energy young men and women, "the newsroom reeked of hormones."[16]

"We were never as happy doing journalism as when we were there," recalls Luis Miguel González, who worked in the investigative unit. "Rather like at *La Jornada*, many people contributed ideas; there was a collectivist spirit. We all saw ourselves as equals."[17]

Its fame spreading quickly for its work on the explosion, *Siglo 21* drew admiring visitors. Within a day or two of the disaster, foreign correspondents covering the story showed up in the newsroom. In following months, publishers and editors seeking to improve or refresh their content asked Zepeda if they could come and observe: Jesús Blancornelas from *Zeta* in Tijuana, Jesús Cantú from *Noroeste* in Sinaloa, Enrique Gómez from *A.M.* in León; even *El Universal* sent personnel. Juan Angulo, a veteran of *La Jornada* who dreamed of founding a community-oriented paper in his home state of Guerrero, was another who made the trek, spending several days in the newsroom. The following year, in the Guerrero metropolis of Acapulco, he would launch the groundbreaking newspaper *El Sur*.[18]

The era brought *Siglo 21* further opportunities to practice cutting-edge journalism. On May 24, 1993, Guadalajara stumbled again into the global spotlight when, during a shoot-out between gunmen of the Sinaloa Cartel and the Arellano Félix Organization, Cardinal Juan Jesús Posadas Ocampo was shot to death in his Grand Marquis at the city airport. The next day, *El Occidental* trotted out the official version that the prelate was caught in the crossfire. *El Informador* mentioned that some of the bullets that struck the prelate had been fired at close range, raising the possibility of a deliberate hit. *Siglo 21* not only mentioned the close-range shots and the possibility of a targeted assassination but also floated the phrase "political motives." With a reader-friendly inventiveness rarely seen in papers other than Monterrey's *El Norte*, it displayed a large front-page graphic showing the exact location of the cardinal's car when he died. Over the following days, quizzical page 1 coverage in *Siglo 21*—and to some extent *El Informador*—undermined the official version. The Mexico City press then probed further, finding that the Tijuana gunmen had left the scene with police assistance. On the one hand, such coverage helped trigger conspiracy theories. On the other, it prompted public concern, which would grow year by year, that drug money was somehow corrupting Mexico's institutions.[19]

Giving *Siglo 21*'s work on the Posadas killing unparalleled immediacy were the talents of one of Zepeda's new hires, crime reporter Jorge Zamora, who had cut his teeth at another paper. Zamora had been surfing police radio when he heard about the shoot-out. He raced to the airport, where his pals on the force directed him to the crime scene. There he photographed the cardinal—slumped dead in his car with his face still uncovered, an image to be reproduced across the world—while rival photographers would arrive too late to get the same shot.[20]

Coverage of the Posadas killing took circulation up to 20,000, and *Siglo 21* got another boost the following spring, when PRI presidential candidate Luis Donaldo Colosio was shot. Since many Mexicans refused to believe that this was the work of a lone gunman, which was the theory Los Pinos pursued, the paper with a reputation for questioning official versions became Guadalajara's go-to source on the magnicide. By mid-1994, with circulation nearing 30,000, *Siglo 21* was generating a profit while sustaining a payroll that had grown—perhaps with an excess of confidence—to 200.[21] There was money to send reporters to other states on assignment. That summer, Nobel literature laureate Gabriel García Márquez set up his Foundation for New Ibero-American Journalism in Colombia, and several *Siglo 21* staffers would take courses there. Finally, and consolidating the paper's displacement of *El Occidental* as the city's number two daily, came the near coincidence the following winter of a massive devaluation of the peso, triggering an economic crisis, and the Jalisco gubernatorial election.

Such was the inertia of the Mexican electorate, following decades of clientelist shepherding of the vote, that the scandal of the 1992 explosion and the ouster of the governor had failed to cripple the PRI in Jalisco. In autumn 1994, as the gubernatorial contest got going, it was clear that the ruling party remained ahead in voter preferences. But it was weakened, the late December peso crash weakened it further, and President Salinas had been succeeded on December 1 by Ernesto Zedillo, whose commitment to electoral democracy was less ambivalent. Zepeda and Petersen were hardly PAN sympathizers, but they wanted to see the back of the PRI, believing that the center-right party (as opposed to the center-left Party of the Democratic Revolution) was best placed to unseat it. *Siglo 21* could raise confidence in an electoral process long rigged by supervising officials and their media allies. So when the national president of the PAN, Carlos Castillo Peraza, visited their offices for lunch, they were attentive to what he might have to say.

Castillo Peraza simply chose to charm them. Petersen found himself fascinated by the old soldier's tales of behind-the-scenes politicking. A follow-up call from a PAN spokesman went more to the point: Though the party was gaining ground—surveys by the UdeG showed as much—its prospects were hampered by the lack of a credibly neutral opinion poll; perhaps *Siglo 21* could commission one? The newspaper did not have the cash. But soon Castillo Peraza conveyed a solution: If they went ahead with a poll, he would drum up advertising from PAN-friendly businesses to cover the cost. So *Siglo 21* contracted with Harris, the venerable US polling firm, and a week before the vote it published the results: a clear victory for the PAN.[22] The PRI was furious, and the state government canceled its ad contracts with the paper. But in an echo of the Baja California election of 1989, in which vigilance by *Zeta* had played a key role, the Harris poll proved correct. On February 12, 1995, Alberto Cárdenas was elected, by a 15-point margin, as the first non-PRI governor of Jalisco.

The following day, *Siglo 21* accompanied the result with a large photograph, like a still from a film noir, of two nuns in a polling station. It was a clever double allusion to a constitutional amendment allowing priests and nuns at last to vote, and to victory by a party closely linked to the Catholic Church. Petersen wanted to place a punning header: "¡Feroz madriza!" (Mother of a beating!).[23]

The paper's role in the ouster of the PRI—from state government and from city halls in Guadalajara and elsewhere—marked a peak of attainment for Zepeda and his team. *Siglo 21* no longer faced threats from functionaries; leading local businesses at last bought ads. This is not to say that political relations were smooth, for the paper, true to its civic convictions, started applying its watchdog journalism to the PAN. Xanic and Rubén Martín revealed the inflation of budgets and use of shoddy materials in the building of a light railway line. Esperanza Romero exposed corrupt public works contracting by the PAN mayor of wealthy Zapopan, a scandal that forced the official to quit.[24] By now, Xanic, Martín, and Romero were part of a special investigations unit, the first at a Guadalajara paper and one of the first in Mexico. At a dinner meeting between Governor Cárdenas, his cabinet, and senior personnel from *Siglo 21*, Martín heard officials complain, "What's going on? We thought you were our friends!"[25]

Governor Cárdenas himself remained respectful of the paper's autonomy. The PAN's Ernesto Ruffo had been similarly hands-off toward Tijuana's *Zeta*. Later on, the PAN-affiliated successors of both men resorted to some of the coercive pressures that the PRI had once used.[26] The democratization of media in Jalisco and Baja California—not to mention other states, where autocratic customs ran deeper—would prove a slow work in progress.

A Public Divorce, New Frontiers

Once the PAN took power, relations between Zepeda and Dau began to fracture.[27] Eager to confirm its new direction, Guadalajara city hall made a show of revealing how much cash the PRI had showered on the press. At least sixty reporters had been on the municipal payroll (that is, picking up monthly *embute*), and ad buys had often been made in bulk and in advance, without oversight as to whether the inserts were published (in other words, ad spend had become a direct subsidy). One of the recipients of cash in advance, Zepeda was aghast to learn, was *Siglo 21*. Just before leaving city hall, the PRI had placed with Dau a one-year buy worth $50,000. Not only did the news damage the paper's name, it also made Zepeda doubly suspicious of Dau, as he could not find the sum in the company books.

More signs of misbehavior emerged. Zepeda found evidence suggesting that Dau was channeling some of the paper's revenue to a real estate venture in Puerto Vallarta. When his reporters investigated tax fraud involving local companies failing to make payments to the Mexican Social Security Institute (IMSS), they discovered the cheats included Dau. It transpired that Dau was also in arrears in contributions to the state-run employee housing fund (Infonavit) and pension plan; by 1997, in Zepeda's reckoning, the IMSS and Infonavit debts alone would total $1.7 million. Dau was under duress because the major loan he had taken in 1992 was fixed in dollars, which, following the devaluation of 1994, required twice as many pesos to pay off. Under the PAN, city hall and the state government had drastically reduced their advertising, posing a challenge to all local media; two small dailies closed immediately.[28]

Worse, the country was undergoing a deep recession. Was Dau cutting corners and fiddling the books to save the newspaper? Was his Vallarta investment a bet on easier profits that might in turn bolster the paper's finances? Or was he chiefly trying to save himself?

Reflecting years later, Luis Miguel González claims that *Siglo 21* "was not a project with very solid economic foundations" and that naivety about the paper as a business pervaded the newsroom. As reporters cared much more about editorial freedom, they were willing to tolerate modest salaries; besides, most still lived with their parents. After a few years, talented staff aspiring to better pay and greater responsibility began to leave.[29]

The question of Dau's priorities met a gut-wrenching answer in August 1996, when President Zedillo visited Guadalajara and met the city's media bosses. According to Zepeda, Dau was furious when it emerged that, in the case of *Siglo 21*, it was not the owner but the editor whom the president wanted to see. Zedillo revealed to Zepeda that when campaigning in Guadalajara two years or so before, he had met with Dau, who offered to place his newspaper at the service of his campaign for $1.5 million. Zedillo added, "No one ever proposed corruption to me as that man did."[30]

No longer able to trust his friend of more than twenty years, Zepeda planned his exit, finally resigning in April 1997. He went to Mexico City, ostensibly to start a new job, but actually to seek capital and buy his own printing press. Furtively working with senior allies at his old paper, he raised $1 million from Guadalajara industrialists. Equally furtively, one by one, he recruited most of his former colleagues; the evidence that Dau had defrauded them of social security and pensions payments aided his case. Then Zepeda gave the signal. Between August 8 and 11, just as creditors were closing in on Dau, around 90 percent of *Siglo 21*'s employees quit. Nearly 200 in number, the dissidents pledged their allegiance anew to Zepeda and just four weeks later launched a second start-up: *Público*. Dau, shocked by the exodus and feeling betrayed, was left to stagger on with a living-dead daily that was finally laid to rest at the end of the following year.

Público has been called an identical twin to *Siglo 21*, and in its Berliner format, bylines, and civic priorities it was a very close match. So was the defiant-cum-streetwise tone of its debut issue, which led with a leaked document showing local tensions within the PRI, above a large photo of fans at a farewell concert by Grupo Bronco.[31] Yet the fresh start allowed Zepeda to make some tweaks: The title ran in red, the photographs ran larger, a website was created, and investigative reporting was beefed up; Xanic and others paid greater attention to the presence of organized crime. The main innovation was out of sight: The paper was employee owned, with outside investment limited to just less than half the shares. After a few months of growing pains, *Público* was circulating 20,000 copies or so, below the average once attained by *Siglo 21* but enough to restore Zepeda and his team to second place in the market.

This time, the joys of a successful, independent project were short-lived. Six months after launch, Zepeda heard of the planned market entry of Monterrey-based Grupo Reforma, a publishing titan with successful broadsheets and tabloids in Monterrey and Mexico City. Its Guadalajara paper, *Mural*, would target almost the same middle-to-upper-class demographic as did *Público* and employ a similar watchdog ethic. Its start-up budget would prove enormous, up to fifteen times the $1.5 million that he had cobbled together.[32] Zepeda traveled to Saltillo, where Grupo Reforma had just launched the daily *Palabra*, and the city's established publishers told him to expect the worst: reporters and columnists lured away with double the salary; advertisers seduced with monthslong packages free of charge—as long as they stopped buying space in other papers.

Zepeda's success, in proving Guadalajara's appetite for civic-minded journalism, threatened to be his undoing. To protect *Público* and its employees, he needed a new sugar daddy. Failing to interest Spanish or US publishers, he approached another Monterrey media power, Grupo Multimedios. He hoped to part with just a one-third stake, but the Multimedios representative, an astute columnist turned executive called Federico Arreola, insisted on a majority. The deal was done in August 1998, and before the end of the year Multimedios modified the paper's name to reflect its media brand: *Público-Milenio*.[33]

Within months of the August sale, *Público-Milenio* lost two of its leading lights. Zepeda clashed with Arreola, finding him domineering and spoiling for a fight. "You know about journalism. I know about politics. Who do you think will win?" Arreola told him. For the good of the paper and its personnel, Zepeda moved to Mexico City in search of new challenges. After all, at the federal level, the PRI was still in charge and democratization an unfinished project. Just ahead of him, Xanic set out for the capital and a stellar career as a freelancer. Nonetheless, with Diego Petersen promoted to publisher—a popular call, for he continued Zepeda's collegial style—and Luis Miguel González to editor in chief, *Público-Milenio* remained a very good newspaper, for a decade.[34]

Despite its frictions, the Zepeda–Dau partnership left a far-reaching legacy. Guadalajara's media culture and the public sphere that it served were fortified, by the example that *Siglo 21* set during the coverage of the explosion, by the reduction in corrosive press subsidies from the party it helped bring to power, by the decline of the long-servile *El Occidental*, and by the generally progovernment market leader *El Informador* being prompted to raise its standards.[35] The design and format of *Público-Milenio*, adapted from *Siglo 21*, would in turn be adapted by Grupo Multimedios to create a new Mexico City paper, *Milenio Diario*, and to revamp or launch papers elsewhere.[36]

The *Siglo 21* legacy also persisted in human capital. Many journalists, like Xanic, took what they had learned in Guadalajara and went on to greater things. Luis Miguel González would rise to editor in chief of national financial paper *El Economista*. Salvador Camarena would direct the Mexico City lifestyle magazine *Chilango* and later lead the investigative team at the influential nongovernmental organization Mexicans Against Corruption and Impunity. Luis Petersen would serve for twenty years as editor in chief of *Milenio Monterrey*. The cartoonists Trino and Jis would make a national name for themselves at *La Jornada*. Head photographer Hernández-Claire would see his work published in *Le Monde*, *The Guardian*, and *The New York Times*.[37]

Zepeda would join and eventually direct *El Universal*, during an era of openness at the national daily. He would help forge the modernization of eight regional dailies and then create the successful news site *SinEmbargo*. He would also find the time to author several acclaimed novels and edit five remarkably frank books that profiled the powerful.[38]

Chapter 4

Reforma

Monterrey Conquers the Center

> The great difference between Junco and the other owners is that he understood that good journalism could be a business.
>
> —Daniel Moreno, editor, *Animal Político*

"Soldiers of Liberty"

It was the most expensive newspaper launch in Mexican history.[1] On the night of November 19, 1993, at a location in the south of Mexico City that was geographically and symbolically removed from the old huddle of downtown media edifices, more than 200 journalists gathered together. They stood in the spacious atrium of a classically lined, marble-floored building, a new headquarters so grandiose that some dubbed it a fortress and others a mausoleum. Alejandro Junco, the Monterrey publisher who had budgeted the project at $37 million, perhaps more, was presiding over a milestone moment: the birth of a capital-city newspaper designed as a self-sustaining business. But at the time, he later said, "it felt like jumping off a cliff without a safety net."[2]

Most of the people assembled before him were fresh out of university. Almost half were female. Round faced, bespectacled, and trimly bearded, Junco himself did not look much older, though he was forty-five. To an outsider, the scene in that sober space, framed by columns and the hacienda-style façade of the executive offices, might have resembled a Mormon convention. The men all wore ties, the women all wore dresses, and their faces all bore a happy look of pride and expectation. A corporate video played a specially written hymn: "All together, always united, soldiers of liberty . . ." A priest gave a blessing, quoting a passage from the book of Isaiah about the task of informing the people. Junco, who had described this project to *The New York Times* as a "national cathedral of journalism," gave a speech.[3] He reminded his employees of his company's values, as instilled during the months of training that most had undergone at the paper's elder sibling, *El Norte* of Monterrey. He told them that their first duty was to the community of readers. Then he proceeded to the printing hall, broke a bottle of champagne over the machinery, and switched it on. As he did so, a bell rang: "Let this bell be a call to attention about Mexico's problems," the magnate declared. The bright red rotary presses began churning out issue 1 of *Reforma*.

The newspaper looked like nothing else among the thirty-three dailies then available in the capital. Sporting a bold green title, with an image of the city's Angel of Independence superimposed over the *O*, its uncluttered broadsheet design evoked US dailies like the *Houston Chronicle*. Whereas most rivals were drably monotone, cover pages at *Reforma* ran in full color. Whereas most broadsheets began a dozen stories on page 1 to maximize revenue from government departments that paid for coverage, *Reforma*, which accepted no paid-for *gacetillas* and maintained a church-and-state separation between ad sales and the newsroom, ran three or four. Page 1 also featured a topical infographic, of which it was a local pioneer. As in other papers, the front page carried a list of its columnists, but over the first week these cumulatively offered an unequaled Who's Who of writers and a smorgasbord of ideological plurality: Miguel Ángel Granados Chapa, Carlos Castillo Peraza, Enrique Krauze, Humberto Musacchio, Lorenzo Meyer, Guadalupe Loaeza. The debut edition carried an op-ed by Nobel Peace Prize laureate and Indigenous rights activist Rigoberta Menchu.

Junco paid his columnists handsomely. While the Colegio de México historian Carlos Marichal was earning $50 a pop for his column in *La Jornada*, he was astounded to learn that his colleague Meyer was collecting $1,000 per piece in *Reforma*. The satirist and TV personality Germán Dehesa earned the most, some $40,000 per month for writing six times per week, or roughly $1,500 per column.[4]

Reforma also hosted two humorists who had been making waves for a decade at *El Norte*: Armando Fuentes Aguirre, who wrote a column that mixed jokes with political barbs under the pen name Catón (as in Cato, the Roman sage), and caricaturist Paco Calderón, whose brilliantly comic draftsmanship and willingness to satirize all comers would eventually, and rarely for a cartoonist, earn him a Moors Cabot Prize. Catón and Calderón encapsulated the breezy side of *Reforma*: It was a sincere, well-written paper, but it was also fun to read. Its bright colors and accessible graphics drew the eye. Its photos ran larger than in the other broadsheets. Features in the city section and the witty columns of Dehesa celebrated the metropolis in all its eccentricity. Other section titles used exclamation marks to suggest readers would be entertained as much as informed: Fashion!, In Shape!, the tourism section Time Off!, and for the weekend listings section, It's Friday!

Like the location of its offices, the paper's launch date was heavily symbolic: November 20. This was the Day of the Revolution, the civil war of 1910–20 that eroded an old order of hierarchical privilege and ushered in an era of wealth redistribution, public spending, mass education, and the expansion of the tiny middle class. It was also a day on which, by tradition, no other newspapers circulated and news vendors rested, so the *Reforma* staff would hand out copies

Deportes: Con su gol más reciente, Hugo Sánchez se convirtió en uno de los tres mayores anotadores en la historia española (1C)

Moda: GIANNI VERSACE LLEGA POR PRIMERA VEZ A MÉXICO (1D)

Sábado 20 de Noviembre de 1993
México, D.F.

80 Páginas
7 Secciones

REFORMA

CORAZON DE MEXICO

SECCIÓN A

Año 1, Número 00

CIUDAD

Pide Camacho respeto a la ley

Molesta a Vecinos edificio WTC

Nueve años de tensión

DEPORTES

Recibirá Cruz Azul a Pumas

Arrancan Panamericanos

OPINIÓN

Rigoberta Menchú

René Delgado

Jaime Sánchez Susarrey

Preparan partidos campañas presidenciales

Arrancan PAN y PRD

Inicia AN su convención; Comienza gira de Cárdenas

Por María Elena Medina, Rodolfo Montes y Miguel Pérez

Efervescencia política

Los tres principales partidos políticos enfilan un fin de semana de intensa actividad y proselitismo.

▶ **PAN:** Sus cuatro precandidatos 12A
▶ **PRI:** La gira de Ortiz Arana 12A
▶ **PRD:** El segundo intento de Cárdenas 10A

Condiciona Cárdenas debate

Promete responder a Serra

Candidato del PRD hará público su posición hoy

Por Miguel Pérez

Reducen dos puntos los intereses

Anuncia CSG baja en tasas

Facilitan crédito a pequeños empresarios a través de Nafin

Por Patricia Sotelo y Mayela Vázquez

Lanzan satélite

Por María Fernanda Medina

In contrast to most Mexico City papers, the debut edition of *Reforma* in 1993 led with a story not about the long-ruling Institutional Revolutionary Party (PRI) but about opposition parties the PAN and the PRD. Courtesy of Grupo Reforma.

for free. On this date, Junco was launching a newspaper meant to revolutionize journalism, educating the capital's citizens with greater frankness than ever as to what was really going on. The debut front page exhibited this intent. There was no banner headline exalting the president or a cabinet minister, as the first issues of *El Día*, *El Sol*, and even *La Jornada* had run. Rather, the main story announced "Arrancan PAN y PRD": The main opposition parties, the National Action Party and the Party of the Democratic Revolution, were starting up their campaigns for the presidency.[5]

"Pretentious," "sensationalistic," "provincial," "right-wing," "churchy," "pro-PAN," and even *oficialista* (progovernment) were all adjectives applied to *Reforma* by its critics. It was heavy on color and light on flavor. Its owners and senior editors were "the barbarians of the north." Since the daily bowed just before the Institutional Revolutionary Party (PRI) was to unveil its candidate, it was surely conceived as a PR vehicle, like a number of campaign-season papers in the past.[6] Many put-downs likely owed to professional envy, a guilty conscience born of taking bribes, or a metropolitan myopia that fixated on Junco and his managers as provincials.

The New York Times, however, was mostly impressed. "*Reforma* is not like other Mexican newspapers," it observed a month after the launch. The US paper noted that Junco's new daily was the sister of the "fiercely independent" *El Norte*; that it paid its junior reporters $1,500 a month, three times what most other cubs earned; that it offered a clean design with plenty of color and graphics, unlike most Mexico City papers, which were "a jumble of headlines and long passages of print"; and that it boasted a healthy haul of private-sector advertising. The *Times* commented that the paper's mostly young staff, having few contacts, had failed to produce many scoops and that the international section was thin. But it praised its efforts to include what US journalists were starting to term "news you can use," so as to lure people who rarely bought a paper: a full-page feature for office workers on how to find a good meal; a daily color-coded map showing the Mexico City IMECAs, or borough-by-borough air-pollution indices.[7]

In another singular trait, Junco's paper welcomed criticism and sought to learn from it. Five years earlier at *El Norte*, the Monterrey paper whose direction he had assumed twenty years before, Junco had instituted "editorial councils," each made up of a dozen well-informed citizens who met regularly with the section editors to discuss and criticize content and offer ideas. "The task of informing is so great and interaction with the community so complex," Junco wrote in an internal memo, there needs to be "organized work in which community and professional journalist team up." He brought the concept to *Reforma*. And on the paper's first anniversary, a special supplement included two pages of "judgments" by the paper's contributors and high-profile readers. Among the former, Gabriel Zaid flagged an abundance of typos, a TV-like treatment of high culture, and a deference to Los Pinos on economic issues; among the latter, business elite ideologue Juan Sánchez Navarro praised the paper's defense of journalistic freedom but found some of its opinions too leftist, while soccer star Hugo Sánchez called it easy to read and liked how the ink didn't stain his hands. The most common criticisms identified a dearth of world news and a tendency, in headlines, toward sensationalism. The most common compliments hailed *Reforma*'s pluralism and independence.[8]

Born in Monterrey: *El Norte*

The mix of strong opinions *Reforma* elicited, and the space it accorded them, said a lot about Junco himself. He was modest, by media owner standards, as was also evident in the rarity with which he appeared within his papers' pages (he later began a column but used a pseudonym). He shunned entourages and preferred taxis to limousines; another Juan Francisco Ealy Ortiz he was not. He sympathized with the economic project of Carlos Salinas, as was common within the US-friendly business culture of Monterrey, but he turned down the president's invitation to join a human rights committee, viewing the offer as a move to co-opt him. And he respected readers, something he had learned when studying journalism at the University of Texas at Austin and while directing *El Norte*.[9]

Monterrey's market leader had long been *El Porvenir* (est. 1919), which, like *El Informador* of Guadalajara, generally toed the government line, although it made an exception in the 1930s, when the socialist-nationalist policies of President Lázaro Cárdenas prompted a fierce reaction in Monterrey. At that time, local business leaders felt they could use another newspaper, one over which they had closer control, to champion their cause and advance capitalistic values. In 1938 they persuaded Rodolfo Junco Voigt, publisher of a popular evening broadcast, to set up a second paper, a more upscale product for morning readers: *El Norte*. A year later, the same businessmen helped found the PAN, the prochurch party of the Right. Junco Voigt's initial investor partner was the Cuauhtémoc Brewery (makers of Carta Blanca), while two other corporations, Vitro and Femsa, also took stakes. Each was part of the so-called Monterrey Group, a loose conglomeration controlled by the city's preeminent Garza and Sada families.

Within ten years, buoyed by the healthy ad market of Mexico's third-largest city, *El Norte* had the look of a going concern. In 1948 it could boast a page count of thirty-eight and a newsroom staff of twenty-four; by contrast, *El Sol de Puebla*, market leader in Mexico's fourth-largest city, printed a mere eight pages. This suggests that, like *El Porvenir* (and like the US newspapers from which both papers took inspiration), *El Norte* was able to turn a profit without a need for state handouts, beyond the generalized subsidy of cheap newsprint. This state of affairs was likely unique in Mexico. While financial data are hard to come by, available evidence indicates that, until the early 1990s, the only other daily paper with a long record of sustained financial autonomy was Mérida's similarly probusiness *Diario de Yucatán* (est. 1925). However, since the latter's main competitor, the progovernment *Diario de Sureste* (est. 1931), depended on various kinds of state support, the older paper was locally unusual.[10] So it seems reasonable to talk of a unique "Monterrey model" of self-reliant newspapers—the model that Alejandro Junco would export to Mexico City with *Reforma*.

Junco Voigt handed his paper over to his son Rodolfo Jr. in 1963, and the decade proved successful but turbulent for *El Norte*, as it pulled ahead of *El Porvenir* while gaining a reputation for sensationalism as well as independence. Rodolfo Jr. meanwhile plotted against the Monterrey Group, tired of its meddling in editorial content, as epitomized by the presence of a newsroom censor who nixed anything that might offend the Garzas and Sadas. By stealth, Rodolfo Jr. increased his family's shareholding until it had a majority. Conspicuously, he sold advertising space to rival brands like Corona beer. Such maneuvers prompted a Monterrey Group ad boycott. The outlook worsened in 1969, with the start of a lengthy intergenerational spat among the Juncos. Four years later, family patriarch Junco Voigt removed his son as publisher and handed control to his twenty-five-year-old grandson, Alejandro.[11]

Young Alejandro had already been making his mark. He had returned from Austin in 1969 full of ideas about what a modern newspaper should look like. To begin, it needed better-trained journalists, so the following year he invited one of his former professors, Mary Gardner, to conduct a summer workshop in Monterrey. Gardner, by now based at Michigan State University, would continue to teach summer school at *El Norte* for twenty years. As she became attuned to the vices of Mexico's press, she helped Junco cultivate a sense among *El Norte* staff that they were a class apart from other journalists—an aloofness later encouraged at *Reforma*. "You are not 'the boys from the press,'" she would tell them. "You should consider yourself professionals." For Gardner and Junco, journalism was a sacred mission. It also meant making the effort to dress well. Uniquely within the Monterrey press, Junco forbade *El Norte* reporters from taking bribes.

In 1973, the year that Alejandro Junco took the helm, the local elite was shaken by the killing of its most illustrious patriarch, Eugenio Garza Sada. One consequence was the Monterrey Group's scrapping of its ad boycott of *El Norte*. Both sides saw a greater enemy in President Luis Echeverría, whose leftist rhetoric the Monterrey elite blamed for giving license to the guerrilla group that had tried to kidnap Garza Sada, shooting him in the process. Junco himself felt Echeverría's wrath: In retaliation for *El Norte*'s criticisms, PIPSA cut off most of his paper supply, forcing him to reduce the page count and buy newsprint on the black market. The following year, PIPSA lavishly and cheaply supplied the upstart *Diario de Monterrey*, a "furiously pro-government" daily founded by a local radio and TV magnate, Dionisio González.

A quarter century later, the González and Junco families would go head-to-head in the creation of national chains of newspapers, but for now the main rival remained the more *oficialista* and staid *El Porvenir*. During the 1970s Alejandro Junco continued the work of his father in consolidating *El Norte* as Monterrey's leading paper, while using different tactics: the truce with the Monterrey Group; the first of several supplements targeting the wealthier suburbs, which included society pages that charged the rich to cover their weddings and baptisms; the creation in 1979, following a fraud-ridden gubernatorial election, of ad hoc teams of monitors, dispatched to polling stations on election days; and a more daring holding to account of governments. Echeverría was not the only president to take offense. When José López Portillo nationalized the banks in 1982, *El Norte* countered with ample space for private-sector hostility to the move and sharp criticism from commentators. The ensuing fury that redounded from Mexico City led Junco to temporarily relocate with his family to San Antonio. His flight to Texas represented an unusual loss of nerve, although the "de facto expulsion," as he would term it, also strengthened his resolve and that of his senior editors to remain autonomous.[12]

Aiding Junco in his quest for media supremacy was a young dynamo by the name of Ramón Alberto Garza.[13] Soon after Garza showed up in the newsroom in 1973, as a gangly, long-haired, but self-assured seventeen-year-old, Junco recognized his unusual nose for news and his ability to push readers' buttons. When he was twenty-one, Junco sent him to study journalism at the University of Texas at Austin; he later did likewise with a promising young woman, Martha Treviño. Once back at *El Norte*, Garza got involved in many of the paper's innovations, and in 1982 Junco named him editor in chief. Garza was just twenty-six. At *El Norte* and *Reforma*, Garza and Junco would collaborate for twenty-eight years, forging the most successful editor-publisher partnership in the history of Mexican journalism. Making all the difference was a simple, economic fact: Junco was able to give Garza free rein to edit as he saw fit because his company was financially solid. That is, Grupo Reforma, as it came to be called with the Mexico City launch, was strong enough as a business to withstand both the vengeful whims of governments and the vicissitudes of currency devaluations.

Under the Junco–Garza partnership, *El Norte* kept its critical attitude but enhanced its reader appeal. First it adopted a revamped, reader-friendly look, designed by a specialist brought in from the United States. Then it added an investigative reports unit, public opinion polls, a business section, and pullouts on food, health, and computing. Fittingly, in 1984–85, *El Norte* was probably the first Mexican paper to provide its reporters with computer terminals, as part of a $25 million hardware upgrade. Beginning in 1985, the paper won a series of international awards for design and content. Unusually for any Mexican daily, but foreshadowing policy at *Reforma*, it put women in multiple positions of responsibility; by 1988, eleven of its twenty-seven senior editors were female, including one of its three managing editors, the thirty-three-year-old Treviño. Again unusually, and again foreshadowing *Reforma*, it paid its reporters a living wage, so as to free them from the temptation of bribes. In July 1988, despite its favorable disposition toward Carlos Salinas, *El Norte* reported on fraud during the election; one of its reporters went undercover to reveal PRI activists stuffing ballot boxes. That month, the company moved into a palatial headquarters in downtown Monterrey, and *El Norte* was the subject of a flattering profile in *The New York Times*. Summarizing the paper's aggressive style and unusual willingness to challenge both the PRI and the PAN, the *Times* correspondent observed, "*El Norte* thrives on startling disclosures and takes on all comers."[14]

The Junco–Garza partnership pushed *El Norte* to new heights of popularity, but so did a spate of innovation at *El Porvenir*, which in 1982 had come under the editorship of a cofounder's grandson, Jesús Cantú.[15] A family black sheep for his leftist views, Cantú had joined as a young reporter six years earlier. Inspired by the Italian press during postgraduate study in Rome, he tried to pursue investigative journalism, which met resistance from the Monterrey establishment. He quit and set up a news agency. On his return, as editor, he steered the daily leftward and gave civil society a voice, including within the city's first letters page. His opinion section welcomed to Monterrey such Mexico City leftists as Carlos Monsiváis. His reporters—whom he hired from universities to replace the bribe-taking old guard—exposed electoral fraud in Nuevo León in 1985 and Chihuahua in 1986. Altogether, *El Porvenir*'s critical turn forced *El Norte* to try even harder.

Cantú had his differences with Junco; among other things, he accused the *El Norte* publisher of developing an aggressive team of news vendors who had muscled hawkers of rival papers off the most lucrative street corners.[16] But Cantú joined Junco in publicly assailing the culture of venality in the Mexican press and in forbidding his reporters to accept *embute*. Then, in 1988, *El Porvenir* supported Cuauhtémoc Cárdenas in his denunciations that Salinas had stolen the presidential election. Unfortunately for Cantú, his indie-lefty stamp did not sit well with Monterrey's more conservative leaders, readers, and advertisers, so the paper lost access to officials, market share, and revenue. An early misstep, in this very Catholic city, was to run a picture of the Virgin of Guadalupe in a miniskirt. The final straw, which brought the paper close to bankruptcy in 1991, was Otto Granados's lengthy federal ad boycott.[17] Cantú's fellow shareholders insisted he step down. *El Porvenir* then pivoted toward officialdom.

Well before then, *El Norte* had come to dominate the Monterrey broadsheet market, its print run more than doubling during the 1980s to around 100,000. Partly due to clients abandoning *El Porvenir*, its ad count—the basis for what Junco claimed to be the highest advertising revenue of any paper in the country—had swollen to the extent that one December 1990 edition reached 206 pages across ten sections. Junco told *The New York Times* that government spend amounted to less than 0.5 percent of revenues. And he ploughed much of his profit back into the paper, adding beats, sections, and local supplements and vastly expanding the staff. A newsroom of just 17 when he took over had ballooned to more than 300.[18]

While *The New York Times* was impressed with Junco's feats, others were less so, especially voices on the left. Media critic Florence Toussaint wrote that *El Norte* "seeks popularity on the basis of sensationalism, superficiality, and a supposed antigovernment posture that is only evident when some measure affects the interests of the wealthy classes of Nuevo León."[19]

Junco's outstanding concern, which he voiced frequently, was PIPSA. Although the ability of the state newsprint monopoly to cut off supply to critical media was a rarely used punishment, Junco had felt at least one president swing this sword, and he feared another might wield it again. Salinas seemed trustworthy: He praised Junco in public, paid a courtesy call at *El Norte* in 1989, and promised neoliberal reforms that matched Junco's inclinations. But had not López Portillo also wooed the business elite, only to nationalize the banks when his economic program fell apart? In the face of opposition from some publishers, Junco overtly lobbied for an end to PIPSA's monopoly. In April 1990, when Salinas cut tariffs on imported newsprint, Junco felt he had sufficient guarantee of the president's good intentions to be able to plan a sister paper for Mexico City. And the journalism gods were smiling on him: In 1991 he was awarded the prestigious Moors Cabot Prize from New York's Columbia University for his services to freedom of the press and panregional understanding.[20]

Junco had kept an eye on the capital for some time. In the early 1970s a few dozen copies of *El Norte* had been flown there each day, in response to demand from federal politicians and functionaries; by the early 1990s, the shipment had grown to 5,000. In 1983 the paper opened a small Mexico City bureau, which grew from two reporters to a dozen. And in 1990, Junco, Garza, financial journalist Enrique Quintana, and a Peruvian economist called Samuel García set up the first real-time Mexican financial news service, Infosel Financiero.

Similar in concept to the US service Bloomberg and launched on the back of a $10 million investment in a satellite uplink, radio capabilities, and dedicated phone lines, Infosel demonstrated Junco's ability to deal with the Salinas government. Federal functionaries had inherited the custom of divulging information that was supposed to be public only as a favor to preferred media and only in piecemeal fashion. As one analysis put it, "Basic economic statistics that are available to anyone in the United States are treated in Mexico as state secrets." To make Infosel feasible, Junco needed to convince the Treasury and the central bank to be consistently open and he needed to press the Mexican stock exchange to act likewise. He succeeded in each case, although the latter task took three years. By 1993, Infosel computer terminals could be found at most Mexican banks, brokerages, and major corporate offices and the company had hundreds of clients in New York. Revenues were $8 million that year, and Infosel would turn a profit in 1994.[21]

There in the Big Apple the Junco–Garza success story was drawing the attention of *The Wall Street Journal*. The esteemed financial daily was looking to take its brand into new markets, including Latin America. To the *Journal*, Junco might be the needed local partner. Junco himself had a different proposal: Why not partner on an *El Norte*–style daily for Mexico City? The executives at Dow Jones, parent company of the *Journal*, liked the idea. For eight months the talks proceeded, with the notion that Dow Jones put up capital for a 49 percent stake. In June 1993, however, the deal was called off. According to reports, the New Yorkers got cold feet over issues of control, but that was only half the story. The other half, so Garza later learned from an executive at the *Journal*, was that President Salinas had told them it would be a bad investment.

Some years later, Garza traveled to interview Salinas, who was by now living in exile in Ireland. At one point he asked, Why had he moved to block Junco's partnership with *The Wall Street Journal*? Garza suspected that Salinas had intervened because, with Americans co-owning *Reforma*, he would find it much harder to influence its coverage. The former president laughed and changed the subject.[22]

The Salinas Watershed, Continued

The mixed signals that Salinas at first emitted regarding a free press became more positive, including to publishers such as Junco, in the second half of his presidency. Yet they failed to communicate an outright commitment. It was as though the good angel on the president's one shoulder, singing hymns to liberty and democracy, was never quite able to drown out the bad angel on the other, whispering atavistic advice about corporatism and control.

A change of messenger certainly helped. Otto Granados had ended presidential payoffs, but his priority had been consistency of message and he blacklisted critical media. In April 1992 he stepped down to seek the slam-dunk post of governor of Aguascalientes, and his replacement was a bona fide journalist, José Carreño Carlón. Having written for a range of papers over several decades, including as a founder member of *La Jornada*, Carreño was widely known in the media, and with his diplomatic style he was widely liked. As he had also edited the state-owned daily *El Nacional* for three years before assuming his post as spokesman, he knew the official line. So Carreño was equipped to strike a balance between promoting Salinas's policies and fostering a more open press. Today, Salinas himself concedes that Carreño was much the engineer of change.[23]

In September, Carreño declared that the presidency would no longer pay the expenses of reporters accompanying Salinas on international trips; the media would have to pay their own airfares and hotel bills. The switch might seem minor, but it carried great symbolic weight: Change was afoot in the symbiotic relationship between Los Pinos and the press. Two months later, Carreño announced that federal ad spend on the media would be cut by half, with the remainder channeled only to higher-circulation media. By 1993, other reforms were initiated, further pushing the press toward a "First World" modus operandi: an extension of the pay-your-own-way directive to the president's domestic trips; a ban on *embute* from government ministries and dependencies; a minimum wage for reporters; the dropping of de facto subsidies such as tax deferrals and the waiving of electricity and water bills; and an end to the custom of *intercambio* with the Mexican Social Security Institute, whereby media would "exchange" their social security payments by giving the institute redundantly copious amounts of advertising.[24]

All in all, the government under Salinas would reduce its role as a life-support system for Mexico's press. Publishers would have to try harder to seek private advertisers, cut their extravagances, and pay their debts. Carreño's good intentions, however, were undermined by state actors who did not share his liberality. At many ministries, the exchange of favors and purchase of good publicity persisted, as they did in state governments.[25] Hardball persisted too, especially at the secretariat of government, whose bosses had often played bad cop to the president's good cop. In November 1992, Fernando Gutiérrez Barrios, secretary of government and a former director of the secret police, visited Julio Scherer to try to dissuade him from running an embarrassing piece on Salinas's chief aide, José Córdoba, pleading about the North American Free Trade Agreement (NAFTA) with aides to President-Elect Bill Clinton. Scherer bravely withstood the pressure and ran the report as a cover story. In 1993, Gutiérrez Barrios's successor, Patrocinio González Garrido, enacted an advertising boycott against a young but influential political magazine, *Este País*. Its editors felt sufficiently threatened by the minister that they took refuge for six months in the United States.[26]

The largely reconfigured state-press relations of the Salinas era had a leveling effect on the playing field, of the kind Junco had long advocated, and a liberating effect on freedom of expression. Even some of the party-line papers pricked up their ears. In the longest-lasting scandal of 1993, it was revealed that some twenty captains of industry had gathered for dinner at the home of a former finance minister and, at the urging of Salinas and the president of the PRI, each pledged $25 million for the ruling party's campaign coffers. The "collection-plate banquet," as the affair was dubbed, was a scoop not in *Proceso*—the traditional conduit for high-level leaks—but in the conservative financial daily *El Economista*.[27]

More broadly still, the new freedoms would be borne out in very frank coverage of the disaster-strewn final year of the Salinas presidency: 1994.

"A Breath of Fresh Air"

Junco and Garza hit the bull's-eye with *Reforma*. Its professionalism, breadth of content and viewpoints, and cutting-edge design put the rest of the capital's press in the shade. "A breath of fresh air" was a frequently paid compliment.

The old, established broadsheets, the so-called *gran prensa*, looked antiquated, even decrepit, by comparison. *Excélsior*'s long decline accelerated, the paper being hampered by its politically compromised front page, its excess of personnel, and the distracted management of Regino Díaz Redondo, who took many trips to interview world leaders.[28] *El Universal* remained fairly strong, thanks in great part to its unique plethora of classified ads, but it too lost readers. Among major papers, only *La Jornada* was unaffected little. Its left-leaning devotees would not be drawn to a paper for which Salinas's free trade agreement, coziness with the Vatican, and rapprochement with the United States were good things.[29]

The freshness of *Reforma* was soon accentuated with new columnists. Initially it had featured a raft of big names pilfered from other papers, but the roster soon included several striking new voices, cosmopolitan types with overseas graduate degrees who knew how to simplify complex topics for a broad audience: Carlos Elizondo Mayer-Serra (Oxford University), Denise

Dresser (Princeton), Jesús Silva-Herzog Márquez (Columbia). Their arrival reflected how opinion columns in general were becoming less baroque in style and more frank in content.

As often the case at newly founded media, such as *Siglo 21* in Guadalajara, team spirit kept everyone striving for excellence. Yet in contrast to most Mexican start-ups, Junco's news-gathering troops were hundreds in number. During its first four years, the *Reforma* newsroom probably boasted the greatest concentration of journalistic talent that Mexico has ever seen.[30]

Daniela Pastrana was one of the many novices.[31] In early 1992, senior staff from *El Norte* visited thirty campuses in Mexico City, including Pastrana's university, the Iberoamericana. Ramón Alberto Garza and María Luisa Díaz de León, assignments editor at the paper's Mexico City bureau, came to one of her communications classes and made a big impression as they described their project for the capital. Along with many of her peers, Pastrana filled out an application. Newspapers commonly held an entrance examination to sift through applicants, but Pastrana found that in this case the exam was just the first filter of several. Unlike at other Mexican papers, there would be no jobs handed out via friends pulling strings. Next came a personalized interview, followed by a six-week writing and editing course. Some of her friends withdrew, claiming these northerners were being too arrogant. At last, a year after her application, Pastrana was selected for several months of intensive preparation in Monterrey. In the end, Garza and his team received 800 applications, interviewed half of them, and gave jobs to a quarter.

Boot camp in Monterrey was as much a course in ethics and regimentation as it was in reporting. The recruits had to report to *El Norte* every morning at eight o'clock sharp. No jeans or sneakers were allowed. Men were expected to wear ties—and jackets when outside, even in July. Intimate relationships with sources were forbidden, and fraternizing with journalists from other media was discouraged. The prohibition on receiving gifts was so rigid (reporters attending a breakfast presser had to decline the meal), Pastrana would joke that you couldn't accept a glass of water from a source when the temperature was 100 degrees. Verification was crucial: Nothing in a press release could be taken for granted. You had to go and see for yourself.

As *Reforma* prepared to launch, Pastrana was assigned to the city desk, itself a US-inspired innovation, as Mexico City papers always rolled local news into the national pages—a symptom of how many *capitalinos* assumed that their metropolis *was* the country, or the better part of it. Under María Luisa Díaz de León, the desk was the paper's largest and as big as the entire newsroom of some of the capital's papers: four or five editors, three designers, and twenty-five reporters, all but three of whom were fresh out of college. They put out a daily section of eight to twelve pages, with space for innovative full-page features about urban culture. One of Pastrana's contributions explored the capital's bedroom-community trend; a photo essay profiled clowns who performed for coins at traffic lights.³² The team also paid unusual attention to faulty urban services, exercising so-called *periodismo de denuncia* (a form of watchdog journalism) on behalf of ordinary people.³³

Díaz de León was mother hen: looking after her charges, demanding excellence, scolding when necessary. Ramón Alberto Garza, as editor in chief, was the workaholic but hearty soul of the place, with a word to spare for each reporter, often accompanied by a tip-off for a good story. He was a great encourager and kept people's spirits up with his frank, sometimes scandalous, northern humor. Lázaro Ríos, the general manager, was *el buena onda*, easy to talk to and friendly with everyone.

In these early days, Junco himself would tour the newsroom as the paper was going to bed, discreetly monitoring what each reporter and editor was up to. He was formal but courteous. Early on, he gave the city desk a pep talk: "Just as *El Norte* smells of *cabrito* [roast kid, a Monterrey favorite], I want *Reforma* to smell of IMECAs [the air pollution index]." It was his tongue-in-cheek way of saying that the new paper had to feel *local*, and that was the city team's task. The collegial atmosphere made for very strong bonds. Pastrana would spend just four years at *Reforma*, followed by nine at *La Jornada* and then a distinguished career as a freelancer, but her strongest friendships dated from her years as one of Junco's "soldiers of liberty."

Daniel Moreno was one of the small number of experienced hires; at twenty-nine, he was three years older than the remarkably young newsroom average.³⁴ Like Pastrana, he found that *Reforma* reporters and editors shared a remarkable esprit de corps. Raised by a single mother who had to switch apartments several times because she struggled to make the rent, Moreno had grown up dreaming of become a historian or a musician. Leaving home at sixteen and picking up odd jobs, he took classes at the National Autonomous University of Mexico in both subjects but never finished. In 1988 he worked for the Cárdenas campaign. When his wife got pregnant the following year, he needed a fixed income, and a couple of friends at *Unomásuno* said he should apply. Manuel Becerra Acosta had just left, reporters had quit in sympathy, and there were openings. They got him an interview with Jorge Fernández Menéndez, an Argentinian who headed the Sunday political supplement. By luck, the editor mentioned that a reporter he had assigned to interview Pablo Gómez, of the left-wing PRD, was unable to do so. "I know Pablo Gómez," Moreno said, citing his political activism. Fernández Menéndez gave him the questions and Moreno debuted in print that weekend.

Unomásuno in 1989 was an odd place for a young leftist to cut his teeth, for with Becerra's exit the paper had U-turned and become *anti*-PRD. This made for a tough-love apprenticeship, as Moreno had to work twice as hard to get stories about opposition parties—the beat he was assigned—into the paper. Fernández Menéndez, who would later author respected books on political violence and criminal organizations, mentored Moreno as a writer. Still, the paper's general decline motivated Moreno to seek greener pastures. After two years or so he jumped to *El Economista*, which was starting to broaden its political coverage. He was there for a year, honing his craft by reporting on 1992's long slate of gubernatorial elections and so getting to know much of the country. Then he was invited to join the paper that many considered Mexico City's best: *El Financiero*.

The Brief Summer of *El Financiero*

The brainchild of Rogelio Cárdenas Sarmiento, a twenty-nine-year-old, British-educated economist, *El Financiero* had debuted in October 1981.[35] The date was a critical juncture: Mexico's economy was starting to topple into devaluation and depression. But the ensuing crisis aided Cárdenas Sarmiento, for the public demanded answers about the crash and subsequent bank nationalization. It wanted informed debate about the long-lasting consequences: inflation, unemployment, further devaluation, and the prosecution of some of the most corrupt. The capital's existing papers, with small and meek business sections, were ill-equipped to provide such answers. *El Financiero* strove to do so, and from a center-left perspective, which reflected its founder's convictions. The paper began modestly, with a start-up investment just shy of $500,000 and a staff of thirty-five, but thanks to lean operations and enthusiasm from readers and advertisers, it broke even after about five years.

In terms of political coverage, Cárdenas Sarmiento and his editor in chief, Alejandro Ramos Esquivel, planted their flag on July 7, 1988. While every other newspaper in the capital that day called the election for Salinas, *El Financiero*, sensing that fraud put the result into doubt, bravely led with "Aún nada para nadie"—effectively, "No one wins yet."[36] It was the first time in the sixty-year life of the PRI that a major periodical had snubbed its instant claims of presidential victory. The daily then gave ample space to mounting allegations of electoral fraud. The federal advertising and information boycotts that followed would last throughout the Salinas era, but these things bolstered the paper's credibility and at last gave Mexico City a daily paper that did not depend, or not very much, on subsidies.[37]

By the time Moreno came aboard, in late 1992, *El Financiero* harbored Mexico's strongest collection of journalists. These were ably led by Ramos Esquivel, who knew how to build team spirit and keep egos in check. In Granados Chapa, who had just switched from *La Jornada*, and Carlos Ramírez, who doubled as assignments editor, the paper arguably hosted the country's two most influential political columnists. It also had two of Mexico's leading satirists: Guadalupe Loaeza, whose musings on Mexico City's upper crust were collected into books that became durable bestsellers, and Germán Dehesa, a playwright who liked to skewer politicians.[38] There were seasoned reporters and editors such as Riva Palacio, Musacchio, and Rossana Fuentes Berain.

It was at *El Financiero* that investigative journalism was first concertedly practiced at a daily paper. Previously, it was only undertaken during major scandals. Even the muckraking magazine *Proceso* relied for many of its famous exposés on leaked information as opposed to active digging. After an army platoon ambushed Federal Judicial Police at an airstrip in Veracruz state in November 1991, killing seven of them, *El Financiero*'s Héctor González probed the official version that the shoot-out had been an accident. He revealed that army top brass taking bribes from the so-called Gulf Cartel had ordered the platoon to protect the narcos whose cocaine the cops were planning to intercept. The coverage successfully (and bravely) broached three taboo topics: drug trafficking, corruption among senior officials, and the army. The recently founded National Human Rights Commission swiftly launched an inquiry, its findings forcing Los Pinos to concede its initial explanation was false. In October 1992, six people were convicted, including two generals.[39]

At its 1992–93 peak of influence, *El Financiero* reportedly sold 70,000 daily copies, placing it third in the Mexico City market.[40] But it was vulnerable on two fronts. First, it remained a small operation, keeping its team together more through team spirit than with grand salaries and benefits. Second, while Cárdenas Sarmiento had largely severed the paper's economic connections with the state, he never purged the newsroom of old vices. Acceptance of bribes and gifts was discouraged, but not banned. A business editor mocked reporter Claudia Fernández for returning a videocassette recorder to Televisa, while keeping the one the broadcaster had sent to him. Investigative reporter José Martínez quit in the early 1990s, resentful of how some senior staff, such as news editor Javier Ibarrola, flaunted a degree of wealth out of scale with their salaries.

Reforma exploited both vulnerabilities, especially the first. Ramos Esquivel would lament that in some cases Junco offered triple the salary; that may be hyperbole, or merely true for the top columnists, but everyone was offered much more than was standard. And so, in the fall of 1993, a brain drain began from which *El Financiero* never recovered. Granados Chapa, Loaeza, and Dehesa departed, along with fellow columnist René Delgado, who had made his name covering the Central American wars for *Unomásuno*. Junco brought him in as opinion editor, and it was Delgado who ensured the paper's diversity of viewpoints: younger columnists as well as older; partisans of the left, right, and center. The backbone of the economics section defected to *Reforma* too. Riva Palacio and Fuentes Berain, top-notch editors, followed in 1994. Within this general exodus, thirty-five staff and columnists in total, were some of the paper's younger writers—among them Daniel Moreno.

Armed with its Monterrey money bags, *Reforma* sucked talent from many a paper. But none suffered as bad a hemorrhage as *El Financiero*.[41]

1994: Year of the Gun

On New Year's Day 1994, as word reached Mexico City of an uprising in the highlands of Chiapas, news organizations scrambled to get reporters and photographers to Mexico's southernmost state. The mostly Indigenous insurgents—who called themselves Zapatistas after Emiliano Zapata, a valiant peasant leader during the revolution—were said to have captured six or seven towns overnight, including the tourism hotspot of San Cristobal de las Casas. It was Mexico's first experience of a concerted rebellion since the late 1930s. The Zapatistas were calling for the overthrow of the government and the abandonment of NAFTA, which threatened to destroy the livelihoods of millions of farmers by flooding Mexico with cheap US corn. Dozens of foreign correspondents caught flights, most of the capital's papers dispatched staff, *La Jornada* sent a team that would eventually total fifteen, and the better regional papers joined the trek. Such was the public demand for news about the mysterious Zapatistas and their eloquent, fair-skinned, ski-masked leader, "Subcommander Marcos."

During more than half a century of semiauthoritarian rule by the PRI, abetted by a broadly submissive press, Mexico had avoided the militarization of government and sustained guerrilla warfare that had blighted the majority of countries to the south. This was the so-called *pax priista*. Now, the final year of the Salinas era, during which the president would pass his neoliberal baton to his handpicked successor, was starting with a crisis that undermined the promise of NAFTA from day one. In fact, it threatened to smear President Salinas's entire legacy. Would Mexico's press, flexing its muscles as never before but still not yet quite "free," be up to the task of covering the crisis?

After the high drama of January abated and the peace talks began—Salinas called an army ceasefire on the 12th, by which time between 100 and 200 people had been killed and thousands displaced—experienced observers of the national press evaluated the coverage. They were not entirely impressed.

"In the Chiapas war," wrote Raymundo Riva Palacio, "the Mexican press showed all its shortcomings." He found an inability to produce stories that went beyond spot news to explore the reasons for the uprising. The majority of Mexico City papers exhibited their loyalty to the state. Accustomed to relying on official declarations and press releases, such papers treated every bulletin as a news story. Given the sympathy of Bishop Samuel Ruiz of San Cristóbal for the Zapatistas, they often discredited the Catholic Church. The independent minority erred in the other direction: "They went too far in support of the guerrilla army, thus creating the impression that they were justifying the violence." Some of this skew, he admitted, owed to "the surprising press savvy of the Zapatistas." He singled out *La Jornada*, not only for pro-guerrilla bias but for excess: In January, it ran dozens of pages on the conflict every day, much of it repetitive. Readers could hardly see the wood for the trees. But Riva Palacio noted that systematic criticism of Los Pinos's military response by the independent press, which saw a massive increase in readership, helped sway public opinion. These media deserved recognition "for helping to stop the escalation of the war by adamantly insisting on a negotiated settlement."[42]

Sergio Sarmiento was more sympathetic, qualifying as "outstanding" some of the reporting of *La Jornada*, *El Financiero*, and *Reforma*; praising the work of the small San Cristóbal daily *Tiempo*; and finding good features in *Proceso* and a newish rival, *Época*. "This was not an easy time for reporters to embark on a crash course in war correspondence," he added. After the ceasefire, he found commendable analysis in *La Jornada*, especially a series on the complexities of land disputes by government agricultural adviser Arturo Warman; he also praised analysis in *Reforma*. Altogether, Sarmiento felt that the cause of press independence had been advanced. But he too considered most columnists shamelessly biased, especially in *La Jornada* and *Proceso*, with the Zapatistas cast as "modern Robin Hoods," while the "large landholders, the army, the government and neoliberalism were cast as the villains." Many reporters were little better, he felt; Sarmiento observed that when Subcommander Marcos had finished speaking at a peace talks press conference that February, the assembled correspondents burst into applause.[43]

While Mexico's press did not cover itself in glory in Chiapas, much of the blame, as Riva Palacio noted, owed to inadequate guidance from editors. Most of them were too addicted to government sources and the rewards that went with reproducing them. For reporters on the ground, however, the experience of Chiapas was often transformative, helping develop a conscience more attentive to the plight of the have-nots. Early summations of reporting on the Chiapas conflict understandably missed this trend.

Five years later, the scholar Sallie Hughes interviewed a reporter who had covered Chiapas for a magazine that "stayed alive" by batting for politicians and businessmen and drawing on federal advertising; it let its staff receive gifts of computers and the like for Christmas. This reporter "accepted the internal censorship and the gifts without question until he went to cover the Zapatista uprising." As editors censored his stories and as government flacks provided only token information, he questioned the relationship between the state and the press. The tipping point was an incident in which planes from the Mexican Air Force fired on a caravan of clearly marked press vehicles. No one was hurt, but four correspondents were badly shaken. A presidential spokesman failed to calm the ensuing disquiet among the press corps, some of whom yelled at him, "Murderers!" The episode prompted greater solidarity among reporters and made them more proactive in venturing to jungle towns to dig up their own stories.

"Chiapas changed everything. When Chiapas arrived, the press became uncontrollable," the reporter told Hughes. For many it was a time of epiphany, he added: "We knew who were the oppressed and who were the oppressors." The reporter soon quit his magazine and joined a "civic-oriented newspaper."[44]

César Romero Jacobo was another reporter for an *oficialista* organ, the magazine *Época*. This was property of Abraham Zabludovsky, son of chief Televisa anchor Jacobo; the president's brother Raúl was a coinvestor. Romero could not help but tell the Chiapas story the way he saw it. (It was his reporting that earned praise from Sarmiento.) Zabludovsky told him that President Salinas was upset with coverage of the conflict, even in the "loyal" press. The president had said, "Every reporter who sets foot in Chiapas suddenly considers himself a revolutionary." Two years later, Romero joined *Reforma*.[45]

Chiapas had a transformative effect on the foreign correspondents too. "Salinas fooled us into thinking he had modernized Mexico," wrote Tim Padgett of *Newsweek* in a personal reflection. For Padgett, the epiphany came as he entered the town of Ocosingo and saw dead and dying Indigenous guerrillas in the streets. "I realized there was something very wrong beneath the surface of the so-called 'Mexican miracle.' I felt deceived."[46]

Occasionally in the life of a country there occurs an event—usually a disaster—of such magnitude that even authoritarian regimes struggle to control how the media cover it. For Mexico, the Tlatelolco massacre of 1968 was one such event; the earthquake of 1985 another.[47] In 1994, Mexico was hit by three of them: the Zapatista rebellion; the broad-daylight assassination of PRI presidential candidate Luis Donaldo Colossio in March; and a massive devaluation of the peso in December. There were other scandals and controversies too, of the kind that the state apparatus would once have more easily contained: the March kidnapping of billionaire banker Alfredo Harp; another hard-fought presidential contest, which ended in August; the murder of the secretary-general of the PRI, again in broad daylight, in September; and revelations about the dubious wealth of President Salinas's brother Raúl in November.

For all these reasons, 1994 marked the apex of the Salinas watershed, when the gains in press freedom achieved since the president took office were definitively put to the test. The results, despite the media's frequent unprofessionalism, were positive. Los Pinos for the most part declined to clamp down, instead spinning each story as much as it could and weathering the bad publicity. Salinas surely realized that he could no longer hope to keep the press in line, whether by charm or by hardball. The year's crises were too big and too brutal; many Mexican journalists were now invested in press freedom; a swelling horde of foreign correspondents was watching, less susceptible to his persuasion after Chiapas; and there were foreign news channels now available on cable television, including CNN. So Salinas and the PRI placed their faith in Televisa for good PR, and the ever-loyal broadcaster, along with the recently privatized TV Azteca, helped see the party over the line in the summer's general election.

At first it seemed that the media winner of 1994 was *La Jornada*. The left-wing daily's coverage of Chiapas, peerless in depth and passionate conviction, brought great reward in new readership.[48] But as opinion polls showed, most Mexicans held only limited sympathy for the Zapatistas; they certainly rejected Subcommander Marcos's antipathy to capitalism and free trade. NAFTA had been well sold to the Mexican people (especially by Televisa), growth had picked up after a dip in 1993, and even through the year's second crisis, the Colosio assassination, most Mexicans stayed loyal to the PRI and expressed faith in its economic program, or in the similar program of the PAN. Between them, in that summer's election, the PRI and PAN collected 77 percent of the vote. The dismal 17 percent for *La Jornada*–backed Cárdenas of the PRD, running for the second time, owed to the candidate's focus on issues that mattered less to the majority (Chiapas and fair elections, as opposed to jobs and wages); his dull oratory and wooden performance in Mexico's first-ever TV debate; the PRD's weak finances; and marginalization by Televisa.[49]

Cárdenas's meager slice of the vote also exhibited the inability of *La Jornada* and regional papers like it (Puebla's *La Jornada de Oriente*, Acapulco's *El Sur*) to energize the vote beyond the true-believer base; this was especially true north of Mexico City, where leftist media were thin on the ground. But even in the capital, *La Jornada*'s overtly left-wing stance did not make the paper a go-to source for the average reader wanting to understand each candidate's positions. After the election, Zedillo's chief pollster opined that *La Jornada* readers represented a miniscule sector of the population, geographically centered in Coyoacán (the favored borough of middle-class leftists and seat of the National Autonomous University of Mexico), a sector "that is very politically active . . . but whose real impact on public opinion is small." PRD campaign spokesman Adolfo Aguilar Zinser averred that Cárdenas had focused too narrowly on the *La Jornada*–reading demographic, instead of luring the floating voter: "To him, *La Jornada* was the bible, thermometer, and mirror of his campaign."[50]

Appealing to the average reader and the politically undecided is where *Reforma* smartly stepped up. A detailed survey by Raúl Trejo found that Junco's paper supplied the most equitable campaign coverage among the capital's five leading papers in terms of column inches dedicated to each of the main parties (*Excélsior*, ever the lackey of the PRI, proved the least equitable). Such fairness boosted its credibility and thus its circulation, making it the biggest media beneficiary of the liberalizing trend under Salinas.[51]

Another boost came from a deepening of the paper's talent pool. Early on in the year—possibly spurred by slipups covering Chiapas—Junco and Garza realized their reporting staff was too green. Idealism and incorruptibility only took a journalist so far. So they beefed up the newsroom with older hands. Of course, they made sure to hold them to the same ethical standards; the human resources department sent representatives to the home of each potential hire to make sure that they were not living beyond a reporter's means. The recalibrated combination of vice-free innocence and street experience gave *Reforma* new momentum.[52]

With the influx, *Reforma*'s team looked unbeatable, but the concentration of talent proved a mixed blessing for Garza. As reporter Ernesto Núñez would reflect in hindsight, "The journalist is an egotistical being by nature. It cost [Garza] a lot of work to keep them all together."[53] For the time being, however, *Reforma* had unparalleled resources with which to handle the blizzard of news that came its way that year.

"We couldn't have chosen a better moment to be born," says Garza. Starting with one news event that could be anticipated—the official unveiling of Colosio as the PRI's candidate eight days after the paper's launch—the paper then covered a fast series of events that could not have been: the next-day resignation of Manuel Camacho Solís as mayor of Mexico City, upset at having been passed over for the nomination; the Chiapas uprising; Camacho's designation to head the peace talks and subsequent rumors he might replace Colosio as candidate; the Colosio assassination; the speculation and conspiracy theories that followed it; a three-horse presidential race; the August election itself; the killing of the PRI's secretary-general a month later—all this came within *Reforma*'s first ten months or so. By convincing many capital-city families that it was the most trustworthy voice during times of turbulence, the most reader friendly, and the most reliably distributed (Junco put unusual emphasis on home delivery), *Reforma* gained a circulation north of 50,000 by its first anniversary, more than twice its print run at launch. Counting its sister paper *El Norte*, whose circulation had climbed to 125,000, and its financial news service Infosel, the Junco operation was probably Mexico's most powerful newspaper organization.[54]

Junco had calculated that *Reforma* would reach operational break-even after two years or so; according to Garza, it met this target after thirteen months. And it did so while never taking more than 10 percent of its ad revenue from government sources. Here *Reforma* and *El Norte* were national leaders, but they were not alone in achieving a sustainably independent business model. Owing in great part to ad market growth driven by parastate privatizations and the advent of NAFTA, various regional papers seemed by 1994 to be viable without feeding at the fiscal trough. They were willing to demonstrate their independence with civic, or at least unsubmissive, news content: *Siglo 21*; the northern papers *El Imparcial* (Hermosillo), *Vanguardia* (Saltillo), *El Siglo de Torréon*, and *A.M.* (León); and in Mérida, *Diario de Yucatán* and *Por Esto*.[55]

Two episodes around the start of the paper's second year cemented *Reforma*'s reputation by underlining its autonomy. In autumn 1994, Junco picked a high-stakes fight with the News Vendors' Union (Unión de Voceadores). Murray Fromson, director of the Annenberg School of Journalism, described the union as "more . . . a cartel than a union."[56] Since its formation in 1923, it had all but monopolized newspaper distribution in Mexico City, and for most of that time it had done so as a servant of the PRI. This meant that a single call from a senior official could keep a paper or magazine with "uncomfortable" material from reaching the capital's 12,000 kiosks and portable newsstands. Junco suspected that old-guard members of the PRI, offended at the paper's critical line, were encouraging the union to suppress sales.

Junco found an excuse for a showdown in the union's historical insistence on days of rest for its workforce on five national holidays, on which all newspapers thus suspended publication; one of these was November 20, the birthday of *Reforma*. Junco insisted he would publish that day, the union refused to make an exception, and talks broke down. On October 31, the union began to boycott the paper.

Two days later, Junco launched a theatrical counterattack. Kitting out his reporters and columnists in white *Reforma* jackets and reminding them that they were "soldiers of liberty," he led them out into the streets to sell his product. Along Mexico City's busiest thoroughfares, drivers were astonished to see the likes of Granados Chapa, Guadalupe Loaeza, Lorenzo Meyer, and Germán Dehesa (the most often recognized, given his TV appearances) hawking papers at two pesos a pop. "Dehesa was key. He went out selling the paper for weeks, and we all wanted to sell alongside him," says Daniel Moreno.[57] And so the circus proliferated: Radio and TV personalities donned the white jackets and picked up bundles; so did actors and soccer stars. Politicians joined in, mostly from the PAN, including Mexico's future president Felipe Calderón. Talk radio's most influential voice, José Gutiérrez Vivó, championed the drive and encouraged his listeners to buy *Reforma*. Foreign media expressed their support, quite unlike most Mexican papers, for which Junco's daily was a commercial threat and the union a fellow client of the PRI.[58] The pages of *Reforma* itself bubbled with self-promoting headlines, combative op-eds, and photographs of celebrities waving the paper at motorists.

Then came stage two of Junco's campaign: On November 7, *Reforma* announced it was rolling out a street vendor recruitment drive, which would generate 4,000 jobs. The response was immediate, and salaried vendors in green overalls—women as well as men, as distinct from the overwhelmingly male News Vendors' Union—began to replace the white-jacketed vanguard. In turn, union members harassed and sometimes attacked the *Reforma* vendors, stealing their papers and sending some to the hospital. Attackers also targeted the paper's general manager, Lázaro Ríos, twice breaking into his home, calling his wife with death threats, and even attempting to kidnap his four-year-old son.

Los Pinos was ambivalent. Initially, Salinas had seemed to back the union, but on November 8 he weighed in and, surely mindful of posterity with just three weeks of his term remaining, declared that publishers were free to sell their wares as they saw fit. When Ríos told Los Pinos about the threats borne by his family, the incidents ceased. However, when the union filed two multimillion-dollar lawsuits against *Reforma*, for loss of income and reputational damage, the Salinas regime washed its hands of the matter by referring the dispute to the Federal Competition Commission.

By early 1995 it was clear that Junco had both scored a great propaganda victory and broken the back of the union monopoly. The green-suited army of *Reforma* vendors grew, becoming a Mexico City fixture and cementing the paper's autarchic image. Eventually the Federal Competition Commission ruled in the paper's favor. And the experience of battling a 20,000-member corporatist arm of the PRI left Junco's employees exhilarated.

"The Voceadores conflict was key in consolidating *Reforma*," recalls Núñez. "It generated a feeling of cohesion and belonging, especially for those of us in our early twenties." He adds, alluding to the mass resignation at *Excélsior* that led to the founding of *Proceso*, "It was like our 1976. We were telling the regime to go to hell. It wasn't just a job—we were part of a cause."[59]

The other indicative episode was *Reforma*'s first high-profile scoop. On December 9, with the Zedillo administration barely a week old, reporter Jessica Kreimerman, acting on a tip from Riva Palacio, published her discovery that the education secretary did not have the Harvard PhD that he claimed. Garza came up with the perfect needling headline: "He Calls Himself Doctor; He Isn't." Fausto Alzati had studied for his Harvard doctorate but failed to complete it. Further investigation, by *Reforma* and *La Jornada*, found that Alzati had also failed to complete his MA and even his BA, and that various other cabinet ministers had lied about finishing degrees in the United States or the United Kingdom, which had become calling cards for the politically ambitious since the Salinas years. In a final humiliation, Alzati felt moved to confess that he had been expelled from elementary school for misbehaving in the second grade.

"Falzati" (i.e., False Alzati), as he was now dubbed, resigned on January 22. The others who had embellished their CVs kept their jobs, but Alzati was especially vulnerable as minister for education. *Reforma*'s toppling of a cabinet minister, the first time a newspaper had done so in recent memory, was a severe blow to Zedillo. Alzati was one of his closest aides. For those who still doubted Junco's proclaimed distance from the PRI, here was evidence of his willingness to hold the regime to account in a fashion long spearheaded by *Proceso*.[60]

As the economy crashed, following the December 20 peso devaluation, Mexico's papers faced rising newsprint costs and falling ad spend. They were compelled to lay off staff and reduce page counts, *Reforma* included. But by now the paper had established itself, in the words of Fromson, as "the most talked-about daily in Mexico City." The US trade journal *Advertising Age*, echoing a sentiment already common among foreign correspondents, called it Mexico's "newspaper of record." And by summer 1995, boosted by its private army of vendors, circulation would climb above 80,000. Close to half that figure was accounted for by subscribers, an unprecedented feat in the capital.[61]

The Alzati scandal encapsulated how Mexico's press was much freer than six years earlier, when President Salinas took office. Crises under previous presidents had seen the press seize the opportunity for unfettered coverage, only to retreat into submissiveness after several weeks or months due to the obligations that went with state subsidies. But now, following Salinas's partial retreat from press co-optation, in the context of a much richer ad market, and with a growing number of newsrooms determined to offer more assertive coverage, a series of crises in 1994 combined to push wide open the door to press freedom. Such scandals not only received critical attention (albeit often partial or tarred by conspiracy theory), they also encouraged a more regular practice of investigative journalism and a newly standard questioning of authority.[62]

And it was *Reforma* that led the way. Antonio Ocaranza, who handled the foreign press for Zedillo, saw how his colleagues "operated" Mexico's news desks. Whenever a story was brewing that might embarrass Los Pinos, flacks would call each of the papers that evening and cajole them (or bribe them) into dropping or softening the piece: "Hey, give me a hand with this"; "I'm entrusting you with our version"; "I've got a couple of really cool photos I can send you." Says Ocaranza, "You couldn't shut *Reforma* up."[63]

Not all newspapers would cross the critical threshold. *Excélsior*, above all, remained resolutely, organically pro-PRI. For the time being, so did *El Universal*, partly because Ealy treasured and exaggerated his friendship with Salinas.[64] So did many lesser dailies, more dependent on state largesse, such as *Novedades*, *El Sol*, and *El Heraldo*. Indeed, by the end of 1994, much remained unchanged about Mexican journalism. Many publishers still ran their papers as vehicles for advancing their business interests or those of their political pals. Many editors still fielded calls from ministers or their flacks and duly toned down or killed certain stories. Many reporters carried on taking payoffs from their sources, especially at provincial papers. Among those who found that faucet shut off—as at the president's office—some gained deep-pocketed patrons within the chambers of Congress. And the PRI remained keen to bestow its favors on "the boys from the press."[65]

Moreover, most periodicals continued to revere the president, however they might expose his allies or question his policies. His words were still holy. Enrique Krauze once joked, "If a nuclear bomb had fallen on New York, many Mexican newspapers would have led the front page with: 'Nuke in New York; Salinas concerned.'"[66]

Despite such institutional inertia, *Reforma* joined *Proceso*, *La Jornada*, *El Financiero*, and multiplying regional papers such as *Siglo 21* and *El Sur*, along with provincial stalwarts such as *El Norte* and *Zeta*, in forming an unprecedented critical mass of media disposed to ask hard questions. Collectively, the press would never again be as submissive as when Salinas took office. Zedillo, who lacked Salinas's charm and authority, inherited the presidential sash under greater media scrutiny than any predecessor since Francisco Madero during the revolution. Journalists liberated by their experiences of calamitous 1994 felt empowered to pry. And they saw in Zedillo a novice politician who would likely not push back. Under regimes to come, when certain presidents tried to co-opt the press anew, their efforts to steer the national narrative would be undermined by the resistance of civic papers and by new and leaner media, publishing online.

Chapter 5

Challenges on the Left

Proceso

> Politicians and journalists seek each other out, shun each other, and
> meet up again only to disagree once more. They are species that repel
> each other yet need each other to survive.

—Julio Scherer, editor, *Proceso*

End of a Muckraking Era

Julio Scherer, the most influential journalist of his generation, reluctantly
stepped down as publisher-editor of *Proceso* in November 1996.[1] He had turned
seventy and had steered the watchdog magazine to its twentieth anniversary.
Along with his lieutenants, Vicente Leñero and Enrique Maza, he conceded
the time was right to hand Mexico's foremost excavator of corruption and
crime, impunity and despotism, to a younger team. Some of those who
had risen through the ranks had made names for themselves as reporters and
editors, and Scherer worried that they might leave if not given greater responsibility. When he hesitated, Leñero reminded him of the pact they had made in
1976: twenty years and then retire. Like Leñero, who was a playwright and novelist, and Maza, who had studied for the priesthood and remained interested
in theology, Scherer wanted to spend more time writing. He had penned four
books and he would go on to write or cowrite another nineteen.

His most recent, an impressionistic memoir of the Carlos Salinas de Gortari era (*Estos años*), suggested a further motive. For six years Scherer had
sparred with the president, holding his regime to account in print, while enjoying a personal rapport. It had been a fencing match between aristocrats:
two men of charm and poise, ideologically distinct, trying to get the better of
each other. Scherer, as he had been doing since Luis Echeverría held office,
drew as close as possible to the chief executive in constant search of the scoop;
Salinas, wary of the newsman's intent and loathing his magazine but aware
of his influence, let him draw near, trying to persuade him of the benefits of
his project. Scherer was one of a minority of journalists who were never se-
duced. *Proceso* consistently spun cover stories that were both revealing and
critical of the president's agenda—for example, on free trade talks with the
United States, Drug Enforcement Administration operations in Mexico, and
the country's leading industrialists, many of them helped to become billion-

The team that launched the left-wing magazine *Proceso* in 1976. Publisher-editor Julio Scherer (*center*) stands with his arm around his right-hand man, Miguel Ángel Granados Chapa. Courtesy of *Proceso*.

aires by the neoliberal policies of the Institutional Revolutionary Party (PRI).[2] Scherer had put Salinas on the cover a record twenty-three times during his presidency, and his doing so reflected equally his disdain for the regime's neoliberalism and a fascination with this singularly charismatic and transformative politician. As *Proceso* alumnus Carlos Puig later put it, "No one narrated the Salinas era as we did, no-one."[3]

Over the past two years, however, the straitlaced Ernesto Zedillo had been president. Believing himself fairly elected, and thus in no need of legitimization via the media, Zedillo cared little for the company of the press. "He always scorned journalists," says Daniel Moreno. "He considered us profoundly ignorant." So Zedillo would not fence with Scherer. This surely took much of the fun out of being editor of *Proceso*.[4]

The magazine itself was on a firm footing, more or less. It had endured, without softening its stance, longer than any critical publication since the revolution. Cover sales and subscriptions formed 80 percent of its revenues, largely liberating it from the pressures of state or private advertisers.[5] It had gained unprecedented popularity with its coverage of the Chiapas rebellion and the Luis Donaldo Colosio assassination, which had seen circulation spike above 300,000. During 1995 it landed fewer of the kinds of scoop that had made it famous, and its crew of reporters was aging, but it posed hard questions of Zedillo as he pulled Mexico out of recession while cosseting the country's poorly run banks and the magnates who owned them. Sales had tumbled during the crisis years, from an average of 194,000 in news-heavy 1994 to 82,000 in 1996, but economic recovery was well underway and the ad market was reviving too.[6]

If *Proceso* had a problem, it was the one Scherer identified: an excess of veteran talent. This implied an abundance of the egos that have often arisen in Mexican journalism, leading good writers to quit in search of higher rank or freedom from editors' instructions. Should this judgment sound parochial, consider that the most famous reporter in the United States, Bob Woodward, investigator of Watergate, has written for *The Washington Post* for more than fifty years. Helen Thomas, the celebrated White House correspondent, worked for United Press International for fifty-seven years. The Mexican press has no Woodward or Thomas. Veteran journalists typically have five or six media on their résumés; Raymundo Riva Palacio has fifteen. As editor, Scherer had been able to keep most egos in check by force of his own reputation, but he had not cultivated an heir apparent. His attempted solution, made at Leñero's suggestion, was to name not a single successor but a board of editors, soon known as "the Sextet."

Most of the six were members of the *Excélsior* diaspora. Rafael Rodríguez Castañeda had spent six years at that paper before Echeverría's coup. At *Proceso* he had become a shrewd and creative editor, and he had authored a celebrated compendium of media submissiveness, *Sell-Out Press*.[7] Froylán López Narváez was an admired writer who had defended the student movement in 1968 and had a side career as a journalism professor at the National Autonomous University of Mexico. Carlos Marín had emerged as the magazine's star investigative reporter and a convivial presence in the newsroom, with a knack for making his colleagues laugh. In 1986 he had coauthored with Leñero a journalist's manual that long remained the standard journalism school textbook.[8] Francisco Ortiz Pinchetti had become a senior political reporter, with a gift for campaign chronicles that exposed the electoral hocus-pocus of the PRI, and he got along well with directors and reporters alike. Then there were two younger talents who had joined *Proceso* after its founding, Gerardo Galarza and Carlos Puig.

The Sextet was a failure, riven with disagreement. Marín in particular was contemptuous of the arrangement. He and López Narváez both referred to Ortiz Pinchetti, Galarza, and Puig as "upstarts." "Traitor!" Marín whispered to Puig when he heard that he had accepted Leñero's invitation to join the board. After a few fractious months, Scherer removed half of its members, leaving Rodríguez Castañeda, López Narváez, and Marín. These became "the Triumvirate." This too was a failure, a running personality clash that gave mixed signals to reporters about what to prioritize and damaged the final product. Readers deserted *Proceso*, drawn away by new or improved rivals that offered a more readable and less ideological take. By early 1999, circulation had fallen by two-thirds from its peak. Scherer's creation looked like a magazine whose time had passed.

Julio Scherer: The Rare Bird

Proceso had never had it easy, beset by information embargoes and advertiser boycotts, the seizure of copies, and threats against personnel. The improbable story of its success owed greatly to Scherer.[9] Born in 1926 into a German Mexican family of bankers and lawyers, Scherer came from privilege, but not as much as most people supposed. When he was a young man, his father went bankrupt. The family had to sell their mansion; even the art on its walls and the antique books on its shelves were sold off. While Scherer entered *Excélsior* thanks to a family connection, that was par for the course in the profession and he started out as a scavenging reporter like almost everyone else. The most valuable gift that he took from his parents was instruction in being socially responsible and honest.

In an arena prone to brownnosing and profiteering, Scherer marched to a different tune. In 1956, he was relieved from covering a student strike at the National Polytechnic Institute when the paper's right-wing editor in chief, Rodrigo de Llano, felt his balanced reporting might jeopardize the government's position. In 1959, the Federal Security Directorate, Mexico's shady equivalent of the FBI, began to keep tabs on him as he reported on opposition politicians.[10] At a steel industry chamber of commerce dinner for the press, when the association's general manager personally handed out cash-filled envelopes to reporters from a tray, Scherer instinctively refused his, causing visible embarrassment to his host. Standing out physically with his fair complexion, long face, prominent nose, and wavy hair, he also stood out ethically. From a mix of admiration and teasing born of discomfort, or disdain (for, in shunning bribes, he was not a team player), his colleagues dubbed him El Mirlo Blanco (the Albino Blackbird; less literally, the Rare Bird).

In August 1968, Scherer was elected *Excélsior*'s editor in chief. He set about tackling the worst of the venal practices, such as the routine sale of page 1 stories (other than the lead) to whomever wished to pay for them and the "blackmail journalism" that veteran columnist Carlos Denegri had perfected to a science. Scherer hired young, uncorrupted reporters. Yet, contrary to some accounts, his eight years in charge were not an era of singular leftist critique and daring autonomy.[11] Rather, Scherer chose his political battles and walked an ethical tightrope; it was a strategy he would maintain, albeit less flagrantly, at *Proceso*. This meant tolerating the commissions earned by reporters on ads placed by their sources. It meant, in the words of Leñero, preferring "a reporter who was efficient but immoral to a reporter who was inefficient but honorable." It meant encouraging a critical take on the inside pages while keeping the front page party-line.[12]

Scherer's high-wire act was evident from the start in how he dealt with the year's biggest story: the student movement. The day after the Tlatelolco massacre, his banner headline claimed, "Fierce Combat as the Army Disperses a Rally of Strikers." *Combat*, as though between two armed sides; *strikers*, not students. But the inside pages showed defiance. Cartoonist Abel Quezada offered nothing but a large black rectangle, a slab of mourning, with a caption that simply said, "Why?" Photographs suggested the army was the aggressor. The editorial was critical. Columnists on the following day demanded answers. Yet had such resistance been enough, even under the strictures of a repressive state? At the following year's Freedom of the Press banquet, listening to Martín Luis Guzmán exalt President Gustavo Díaz Ordaz and receive lengthy applause for doing so, Scherer recalled with regret his paper's sins of omission: its cheating readers out of the full story, its failure to cover the plight of those imprisoned.[13]

Scherer fell off his tightrope on occasion. As he would admit in retirement, he made a point of befriending Carlos Hank González, the commanding and voracious governor of the State of México, a man soon famed for saying, "A politician who is poor is a poor politician." They dined in each other's homes. Their wives became fast friends. They exchanged gifts. But Hank González's gifts were more opulent than Scherer's, and when the governor presented him with a spacious car one Christmas Eve, Scherer did not turn it down. He only drew the line when the politician offered him a *second* car. Scherer would later come to think of Hank González as the epitome of corruption, but initially the politician's grace and the giddy effect of proximity to power had blurred the journalist's vision. Scherer would continue to befriend senior politicians—they fascinated him and there were no better sources of information—and he would continue to accept gifts, but less extravagant ones.[14]

Proceso was a different proposition from *Excélsior*. Enraged by their ouster at the hands of Echeverría and their betrayal by Regino Díaz Redondo, the trusted colleague who had seized the editorship, Scherer and his loyalists conceived of the magazine as a forum for *periodismo de denuncia*: denunciatory journalism that targets those in government. The term is sometimes translated as "investigative journalism," but with its frequent reliance on leaked information and acceptance of accusations at face value, it did not always involve much investigating. Sometimes, a disaffected *Proceso* veteran would record, the magazine paid inside sources to turn over revealing documents.[15]

The holding to account of the powerful that had increasingly characterized Scherer's *Excélsior* had been counterbalanced by a willingness to function much of the time as a mouthpiece for Los Pinos and its ministries—and to make money doing so. Now, in November 1976, the gloves came off. The perspective remained center-left, but the unifying motive was watchdog journalism and the guiding attitude was confrontation rather than ambivalence. As Raymundo Riva Palacio would put it, "*Proceso* became, for a decade, the only medium that hammered systematically against the walls of Mexican authoritarianism."[16] Being a smaller and more agile periodical, with a staff of sixty as opposed to many hundreds, *Proceso* faced much less economic pressure to pull its punches.

The magazine staked its watchdog turf with a debut issue, rushed out a month before Echeverría stepped down, that excoriated the president for big-spending populism, which had triggered the first peso devaluation in twenty-two years.[17] His successor, José López Portillo, having taken office at the start of the oil boom, proudly declared in 1977 that Mexico must learn how to "manage abundance." Five years later, his regime would flunk abundance management: A calamitous devaluation and suspension of foreign debt payments followed a plunge in the price of oil. All along, while accepting generous state ad buys, *Proceso* called out the government on its dubious planning. It had an especially effective analyst in Heberto Castillo, an engineer turned leftist ideologue, whose columns revealed how the state oil monopoly Pemex was massaging its figures, investing poorly, cozying up to union leaders, and overcommitting to the export market.[18]

Such vigilance caused growing irritation on high. This peaked in April 1982, with the magazine suffering its first federal ad boycott. The president famously and publicly justified the move by exclaiming, "I pay you so that you can hit me? Well no, gentlemen!"[19]

López Portillo's chief flack followed up with, "If you want to criticize the president, go ahead, but *not with our money.*" This phrase spoke even louder of the regime's self-entitlement, as though the public purse did not in fact belong to the public. The ad boycott nearly bankrupted *Proceso*. To survive, it raised its cover price from twenty-five pesos to forty, closed its news agency, and laid off thirty-five staff. But some veterans, years later, would admit to a silver lining. "Instead of harming us the boycott helped us greatly. It made us put our finances in order," said reporter Salvador Corro. Added Leñero, "The more the government hit us . . . the greater expectation *Proceso* generated." Circulation gradually rose by around 40 percent.[20]

In response to the boycott, *Proceso* fully embraced a line of journalism that would become a hallmark, drive up its readership, and cement its economic independence: exposés of corruption. That September, as the oil bonanza—

unchecked by transparency or accountability—turned into a bust, the magazine's reporters and photographers documented the newly erected palatial homes of three top officials. These were López Portillo himself, Hank González (now mayor of the capital), and Mexico City chief of police Arturo "El Negro" Durazo. The police chief was building a $15 million bayfront mansion in Zihuatanejo, which, with its Greek columns and statues, was dubbed "the Parthenon." In this case, reporter Ignacio Ramírez gained access by dressing up and getting hired as a construction worker. The government responded by seizing much of the magazine's print run, but public demand led *Proceso* to print more, the total marking a record of nearly 100,000 copies. Durazo faced more media scrutiny, then calls for a public inquiry. Further revelations about the police chief, in a sequel by Ramírez on Durazo's castle-like home in Mexico City, and in a memoir by a former bodyguard, heightened the public clamor for justice. Durazo fled, but in 1984 he was arrested in the United States and two years later extradited. In Mexico he was jailed and his properties confiscated, including the Parthenon.[21]

Proceso also dared to report human rights abuses and drug trafficking by the army and the police. From the mid-1980s, as organized opposition to the PRI increased and as the party responded with malice, *Proceso* exposed electoral "alchemy" and confirmed the strength of support for the National Action Party (PAN) and parties of the Left. These themes, discomforting to a state unused to such prying, help explain why the magazine continued to suffer partial ad boycotts from Presidents Miguel de la Madrid and Salinas.[22]

Under the guidance of Leñero, Scherer's right hand and closest friend, its front covers matured in late 1988 from an earnest text heaviness to a much bolder, single-topic format. A dramatic full-page photograph and a provocative title served to catch the eye from street newsstands, prompting Scherer to declare that the cover was "50 percent of the magazine." This art was perfected after Salinas entered office. One 1991 cover cheekily depicted the president from behind, the head and shoulders of the man the people often dubbed El Pelón (Baldy) facing an arena, with the legend, "Third State of the Nation Address: The Future That Salinas Wants." The overall effect was forlorn, as though the president were a peddler of pipe dreams. In late 1994, it was Salinas's sibling Raúl who featured. A story by Monterrey correspondent Antonio Jáquez, who spent three years investigating Raúl's self-enrichment, was crowned with the title, "El hermano incómodo" (The embarrassing brother)—and the phrase, coined by Scherer, entered the popular lexicon.[23]

Coverage of Mexico's interior was unparalleled. In the mid-1990s, at its peak of circulation and revenue, *Proceso* employed correspondents in at least half of Mexico's thirty-one states and fully half of its circulation reached outside the capital. Its exposés of abuses of power, often to the detriment of the

proceso

DIRECTOR GENERAL: JULIO SCHERER GARCÍA

El sexenio **LAS PALABRAS Y LOS HECHOS**

Cosío Villegas **MEMORIAS DE UN DISIDENTE**

Libre expresión **DE EXCELSIOR A PROCESO**

No. 1   NOVIEMBRE 6   1976 $10.⁰⁰

proceso
QUINCE ANIVERSARIO

DIRECTOR: JULIO SCHERER GARCÍA

TERCER INFORME
EL FUTURO QUE SALINAS QUIERE

SEMANARIO DE INFORMACIÓN Y ANÁLISIS   No. 783   4 de noviembre de 1991 $5000

While the covers of *Proceso*, as with its November 1976 debut (*left*), were text heavy, by the early 1990s they were provocative, in this case poking fun at President Salinas's dream of "first-world" status (*right*). Courtesy of *Proceso*.

poor, would prompt governors to have underlings buy up all copies before they hit the newsstands, a provincial practice that dated from the magazine's founding.²⁴

Proceso also had full-time correspondents in Washington, Havana, Santiago, Paris, and Madrid. The Washington correspondent during the Salinas years, Carlos Puig, found that his employer had the resources to pay for office space in the National Press Building, two blocks from the White House, and reporting trips that took him to forty of the fifty United States. Puig reflects today, "It was the golden age of *Proceso*, in all senses."²⁵

Scherer marshaled his contacts and engaged his charisma to prize tips and documents from officials so as to pass them on to his team. From the start, he forbade his reporters to accept government bribes, preferring to pay them better than most media did. Nor could they take commissions on ad sales; elsewhere, journalists sometimes hit up for ads the very officials they were interviewing. Unlike at most Mexican media, the advertising department was kept entirely separate from editorial. Scherer embodied the austere ethos at *Proceso* by living modestly. He did without a chauffeur and drove a Volkswagen Jetta. At *Excélsior* he had erred by losing contact with the rank and file, preferring the company of senior editors and big-name columnists and acting as an autocrat, an elitism that made it easier for Echeverría to oust him. He did not make that mistake twice. He cultivated esprit de corps, addressing each of his troops with *don* (sir) and summoning them for an effusive compliment when their stories pleased him. Quite likely, the desire for his approval inclined them to take risks, especially in reporting on corruption. When they failed to deliver, they got an explosive scolding, but this tended to build loyalty too, for his judgments were always frank and staffers remembered them as deserved.[26]

"*Proceso* was not a job, it was a cause," summed up author Federico Campbell, who spent a decade there. "It was defense of freedom of speech . . . [and] love for Scherer."[27]

It helped that Scherer was an experienced writer. This put him in a different category from Alejandro Junco, who limited himself to occasional opinion pieces for US media; Juan Francisco Ealy Ortiz, who seldom wrote anything but self-congratulatory speeches; and *La Jornada* editor Carlos Payán, whose legacy as a writer would consist of a single volume of pedestrian communist poems.[28] Scherer was an admired stylist. The doyenne of Mexican letters, Elena Poniatowska, described his prose as "rapid, incisive, lapidary, definitive"; when he reported on injustice, he did so "with notebook and heart in hand." During the magazine's first decade (though much less so in the second), he conducted high-profile interviews overseas, with subjects ranging from Fidel Castro to clandestine dissidents against the Argentine military dictatorship. In his early fifties he traveled to Central America to seek out a Salvadoran rebel leader. He was detained by Guatemalan border guards, accused of being a subversive, cuffed and blindfolded, and driven up a mountainside. There a junior officer probed his face with a pistol and told him, "I'm going to fuck you up, communist sonofabitch." He was held overnight before a senior officer intervened.[29]

Passionate and energetic, upright and dedicated, fearless to the point of naivety, Scherer drew admirers even among those who disagreed with him. The poet and Nobel laureate Octavio Paz, who leaned rightward in his later years, used to say, "He's a character out of Russian literature."[30]

Unsurprisingly, there grew around Scherer a personality cult, which some journalists found off-putting. But it was a cult quite different from that of the publicity-seeking Ealy of *El Universal*. Scherer became an icon almost in spite of himself, for he shied from giving interviews or making speeches. He never appeared on *Proceso*'s cover until after resigning. An obituary edition, full of testimonials from staffers, columnists, and fellow writers, would attest to a remarkable team spirit fortified by Scherer's presence. It continued after he retired, when he visited often.[31]

Scherer did not always get it right. First, *Proceso* usually omitted to approach the subjects of its exposés for their version of events. Right of reply was limited to the back-of-the-book letters pages, where protestations—which were frequent—might well go unread. (According to Riva Palacio and others, lack of right of reply was a persistent problem within Mexican journalism.)[32] Second, as was often the case in Mexico's press, the magazine's style was elitist, its features often lacking enough context for all but the initiated to quickly grasp their importance. Third, its role as Mexico's medium of choice for leaks of confidential information lent it to being used as a tool with which, as media analyst Raúl Trejo put it, "political cliques and personalities get their own back or try to beat up other cliques and personalities of the Mexican political elite."[33]

The most common criticism was that *Proceso* placed too much weight on shock value. José Reveles, who had joined the exodus from *Excélsior* and served as assignments editor, came to regard the magazine as too improvised and scandal driven, rather than systematic in delving into corruption, forced disappearances, and other critical issues. Reveles departed in 1984, retaining great respect for Scherer but tired of being overruled by him. Many found *Proceso* to be ominously dark, as though straining to counteract the sunshine narrative of *oficialista* media. "If you watched Televisa's news programs this country was wonderful to live in, but if you read *Proceso* on a weekly basis you would conclude it was about to explode," recalls journalist Eduardo García.[34]

Some felt the sensationalism worsened in Scherer's final years in charge. In the wake of the December 1994 peso crash, the nation was in crisis, and *Proceso* seemed to revel in fatalism: "The Collapse," announced the first cover of 1995, above the face of an uncertain-looking Zedillo; "The President Can't," opined the second; "The Government Gives In," adjudged the third, showing Zedillo with his arms wide, as though surrendering to a tsunami of troubles; "Humiliation before the United States," claimed the fourth, as Mexico requested a loan to cover its obligations and save its banks. And when US president Bill Clinton brokered a $50 billion bailout, the next *Proceso* cover, with a smiling close-up of Clinton, simply declared, "Chained."[35] Mexico had a long history of debt-related subjugation to foreign powers, but in this case Zedillo's government would succeed in paying off the loan ahead of schedule, in two years.

Reporting sometimes failed to live up to Scherer's insistence on depth. The editor himself was somewhat to blame, for he loved the interview format, and while he himself could elevate it to art, his employees often lacked that skill. Many features relied on a lengthy back-and-forth between the reporter and a single informant and left the reader to work out the important bits. Arrogantly, the magazine carried no table of contents, as though every article should be of equal concern to all readers. Business features were lazily negative, reporters quick to assume the worst about any firm.

Proceso was tardy among progressive organs in bringing more than a token number of women into the newsroom. Fellow havens of the *Excélsior* diaspora, *Unomásuno* and *La Jornada*, hired many female reporters, as did *El Financiero* and *El Economista*. Yet Scherer and Leñero believed few women could be of use other than as copyeditors or arts writers. Of the initial reporting crew of fifteen, just three were women, and they rarely wrote the cover story. Anne Marie Mergier, a Frenchwoman married to a Colombian, was an exception, as the magazine's correspondent first in Central America, covering the civil wars, and more lengthily in Paris, covering most of Europe and the Middle East. Mergier recalls than when she joined *Proceso* shortly after its launch, she found it to be "a group of unstoppable machos."[36]

Viétnika Batres entered *Proceso* in 1988 as a photo archivist. A daughter of left-wing activist parents who fumed at the distortions of Televisa newscasts and canceled their subscription to *Excélsior* when Scherer was ousted, Batres was raised as a *Proceso* devotee. Her first jobs came at *Unomásuno* and *La Jornada*, where Humberto Musacchio took her under his wing and female companionship was plentiful. At *Proceso*, by contrast, she found a newsroom culture that bordered on misogyny. The worst offender, she claims, was Carlos Marín. When alone in the photo archive, Batres several times looked up to see the celebrated reporter enter and shut the door behind him. He seemed to assume that his jovial persona and his fame gave him license. He would come close, making jokes and flirtatious remarks. Once he reached out a hand toward her neck and slid two fingers downward, starting to unbutton her blouse, before she was able to flee. Batres then took pains to avoid Marín, but she did not report the incident to Scherer, thinking he would do nothing; besides, she felt that complaining about a superior was unprofessional. Two or three years later, Marín pulled the same trick with her sister Lenia Batres, who worked as a part-time subeditor. Lenia (who in later life became a Supreme Court justice) was stronger and taller, and when the fingers reached her blouse she gave Marín a mighty smack. Those present in the newsroom saw Marín fleeing out the door, clutching his cheek in pain. Marín today says he has no memory of these episodes and considers them improbable.[37]

Despite its failings—many of them par for the era—no medium held the powerful to account as consistently and aggressively as *Proceso*. Since, as of 1982, it only received a small amount of federal advertising, and since Scherer was deft at parrying the thrusts of officials, *Proceso* was rarely bullied into spiking a story.[38]

For social and political impact, the Anglo world offered no equivalent to *Proceso*; elsewhere, Germany's probing but centrist *Der Spiegel* probably came

closest. An American might think of the magazine as combining the high profile of *Time*, the investigative ethos of *The Atlantic*, and the leftist slant of
The Nation. Summing up the magazine's achievement in 1989, Knight-Ridder
correspondent Patrick Oster called it "a thorn in every president's side," "the
most fearless, the most respected publication in Mexico," and "the best single source of what is really going on in the country." Julia Preston, a correspondent with the *New York Times* in the 1990s, spoke of her Sunday-morning
ritual: "With coffee in hand, studying each new issue of *Proceso* as if it were
a textbook and I a freshman student."[39]

To one-time staffer Campbell, the magazine's writers and cartoonists played
incremental but crucial roles in Mexico's democratization. He added, "We
were like a squadron of fighter pilots and Scherer was the captain of the military base that was *Proceso*." To young recruit Álvaro Delgado, "Scherer's office was always open. He was *eager* to talk to reporters. He'd come down to
the newsroom after story meetings and he'd say to you: 'Tell me something
new.'" And to Riva Palacio, "*Proceso*'s role in the democratic transition was
fundamental, especially during the '70s and '80s."[40]

Behind the scenes, however, the informality of Scherer's leadership—there
was no code of ethics beyond what the maestro saw fit—let strains of dysfunc-
tion fester. Much of this would emerge after a spate of staff departures a few
years hence. Disaffected veteran Ignacio Ramírez would pen a series in a low-
circulation magazine, alleging that Scherer ruled *Proceso* as an authoritarian, trampling on employee rights; that a celebrated Carlos Marín scoop on
the "Dirty War" against guerrillas in the 1970s owed to his purchase of documents from a secret service agent, who was then caught, tortured, and spent
ten years in jail; that the magazine had twice nixed reporters' attempts to
unionize; that a business manager had embezzled the company; and so on.
Even accounting for Ramírez's resentment at having been laid off, evident in
his visceral language, *Proceso* under Scherer appears to have operated with
the formality of a pirate ship.[41]

So, would the magazine continue to lead the democratic charge in the late
1990s, with rivals multiplying, internal frictions worsening, and Scherer no
longer at the helm?

Zedillo and the New Critical Landscape: (i) Scoops at *Reforma*

Ernesto Zedillo's ill-starred first year as president—buffeted by a 50 percent
currency devaluation, rising unemployment, soaring crime, and growing contempt for the PRI—was not yet complete when he was embarrassed to see a
private letter of his appear in the press. It was a confidential memo to Luis

Donaldo Colosio, whose campaign for president he had managed. Dated just days before Colosio's murder, the five-page missive seemed to affirm widespread rumors that Salinas had regretted his choice of successor; at the very least, Salinas was more interested in solving the Chiapas problem, to ensure his term ended successfully, than in helping Colosio win. To counter this dilemma—and to deter the ambitions of Manuel Camacho Solís, who seemed to be using his platform as Chiapas peace negotiator to position himself as Colosio's replacement—Zedillo recommended the candidate seek a pact of mutual support with the president. This memo was leaked not to *Proceso* but to *Reforma*.[42]

Junco's organ was starting to make a habit of beating Scherer's to the scoop. The week before, *Reforma* had caused a sensation by running a front-page photograph of Salinas's disgraced brother Raúl, perched on the prow of an Acapulco yacht, with his Spanish mistress sitting in his lap. They wore swimwear and broad smiles. Although taken three years earlier, the picture came over as a big "screw you" to Mexico's recession-battered public, from a man who now epitomized high-rolling graft.[43]

As for the Colosio murder, for eighteen months much of the press had fulminated at a lack of progress in the investigation and speculated as to who might have plotted it. The emergence of Zedillo's letter fueled the conspiracy theory that Salinas, or someone close to him, was the mastermind. To Zedillo, the leak was both a major distraction from solving the case—a frustrating business given that his attorney general's office was flip-flopping been "lone gunman" and "concerted action" hypotheses—and a galling invasion of privacy. The president wrote at once to Junco expressing his deep objection to the publication, which in his view violated elementary journalistic ethics. An intense public debate followed.[44]

Some in the media agreed with Zedillo. The head of state news agency Notimex accused *Reforma* of pioneering a "new yellow journalism" that sought to sell newspapers at any moral cost. Raúl Trejo decried the "drunken spree of freedom of speech" now evident in the press, which the "market-driven" scoop in *Reforma* typified; this story, he added, would only drive further gossip about Salinas, even though there was no shred of evidence of his complicity in the killing. Many newspapers echoed Trejo, terming Junco's decision to publish "sensationalistic," "immoral," "morbid," "mercantile," or even "destabilizing"—the last term being a traditional put-down by the submissive press for anyone who rocked the PRI's boat. Scherer dissented, making "The Leaked Letter" the next *Proceso* cover and dedicating ten stories to its significance. In one, Junco, who in the spirit of openness had published Zedillo's complaint, defended himself on the basis of news of public import.[45]

Ramón Alberto Garza later said he never doubted he should publish the memo: "A letter from the candidate's campaign chief telling him that he has problems with the sitting president is no mere private matter; he's not telling him 'Look, your wife is cheating on you.'"[46] Indeed, it is hard to imagine a US or European editor not making the same call.

A sense that the press was profiting from yellow journalism and failing to maintain standards would persist through the Zedillo era and beyond. A young colleague of Trejo's at his political magazine *Etcétera*, Marco Levario Turcott, regularly held the newspapers to account. He found them lacking journalistic rigor (favorite target: *Reforma*), excessive in their bias (usual suspect: *La Jornada*), and willing to host columnists who were—it could reasonably be deduced—on the take (example: *Novedades*, whose writer Juan Ruiz Healy glorified some public figures and insulted others).[47]

Levario raised important ethical questions. Wasn't *Reforma*, in its willingness to publish leaked documents and even telephone conversations, privileging unproven accusations over tested evidence and incentivizing illegal phone tapping?[48] In hindsight, however, deep-rooted cultural questions emerge. To what extent were *Reforma* and others abusing the freedom of speech that valiant journalists had long fought for, and to what extent were criticisms such as Levario's the unconscious legacy of decades of deference, during which the president, the army, and the Virgin of Guadalupe were off-limits? And again: How much was criticism of Junco a sincere objection to sensationalism, and how much was it motivated by envy of his commercial savvy or by anti-Northern prejudice? *Reforma* carried on regardless.

For Junco and Garza, a greater problem than the objections of critics was the challenge of retaining their team of star editors and reporters. There were tensions between the Monterrey veterans and the Mexico City hires; some of the former resented that *Reforma* soon eclipsed *El Norte* in influence, especially in politics; the latter found some Monterrey editors too idealistic, the gung-ho Garza excepted. Cliques competed, notably René Delgado's political news team and Riva Palacio's special reports squad. As *Reforma* grew in stature, politicians began planting stories, to send messages or gain advantage, and it seemed to staffers that they exploited the paper's internal fissures.

Riva Palacio and star reporter Ciro Gómez Leyva both quit in 1997. Riva Palacio felt that *Reforma* sometimes belied the ethics that Junco preached. There was the tabloid element: It would run photographs of dead children or sex workers without pixelating their faces; the famous image of Raúl Salinas on the yacht with his lover seemed to aid the attorney general's case against him by vilifying him—it amounted to state propaganda. The paper's directors had "adopted some of the worst vices of the U.S. press," Riva Palacio later wrote. They, and "particularly the editor-in-chief Ramón Alberto Garza, pushed rumors as major stories." He added, "The driving force of privileging scandal over precision was to sell copies of newspapers."[49]

Then there was the thorny matter of Junco's personal interests. During a scandalous saga known as Fobaproa, named for the state contingency fund that spent $43 billion bailing out the banking sector after the crash of December 1994, Riva Palacio found that Junco was a key investor in one of the banks that had gamed the system, Banco Confía. Its main shareholder, Jorge Lankenau, was jailed for fraud and tax evasion in 1997, and it struck Riva Palacio that Junco was partly responsible. Others worried that the paper sometimes defied its holy separation of business and editorial, which it had trumpeted at birth by locating the newsroom and the ad department on opposite sides of its atrium. Rodriguez Reyna, who would leave *Reforma* in 1998, found that his reporting on corruption met with redaction of the names of Junco's friends. Daniel Moreno similarly felt the paper too kind to fugitive banker Carlos Cabal Peniche, whose troubled bank was said to have loaned Junco part of his start-up capital. Editors were troubled by their suspicion that star business columnist Alberto Aguilar charged some of the business leaders he wrote about.[50]

On the other hand, Riva Palacio was ambitious. He was said to covet René Delgado's post as editorial subdirector. He tended to skip meetings and issue instructions at odds with Garza's. He refused to wear a tie. Former colleagues at both *El Financiero* and *Reforma* say he did not respect hierarchy.[51]

In the *Reforma* of the mid-1990s, sums up Gómez Leyva, "there were too many journalistic egos in conflict with each other."[52]

The exit of Riva Palacio and Gómez Leyva—along with the loss of other skilled writers, including city reporters Daniela Pastrana and Anabel Hernández, who both left the year before—marked the end of what was for some the golden era of *Reforma*. Pastrana, for one, felt her duties too rigidly confined. *La Jornada* lured her with greater responsibilities and the freedom to write narrative features.[53] Yet *Reforma* still drew top talent, most now lured from other papers, at what was still usually twice the going salary.

And from a public perspective, the paper continued to build a name for investigative journalism and arresting front pages, and thus as an alternative to *Proceso*. Much of this owed to its editor in chief. "Ramón Alberto Garza is one of the most astute editors I've ever known," says *SinEmbargo* director Alejandro Páez, who arrived at *Reforma* in 1996 for a four-year stint. "He could conceive of front-page designs in his head, complete with headline and picture. He kept the paper fresh with a constant flow of ideas."[54]

Now led by Rossana Fuentes Berain, the *Reforma* special reports team achieved some of the most remarkable coverage of the era when Mexico City was afflicted by a boom in kidnappings. One ringleader in particular was terrorizing the capital's wealthier neighborhoods: Daniel Arizmendi, popularly labeled "the Earcutter," after the physical proof he sent to his hostages' relatives along with his ransom demands.

Soon after he was assigned the story in November 1997, César Romero Jacobo obtained a copy of the police file on Arizmendi. It said the Earcutter had reaped nearly $5 million from twelve kidnappings. The file also suggested that senior police were shielding him. Romero then wrote a three-part series, "Kidnappings: Dying a Thousand Times," based on interviews with one of Arizmendi's victims. In a bizarre twist in May 1998, Arizmendi placed a call to *Reforma*—perhaps flattered by the paper's attentions—and delivered a rambling personal confession to Roberto Zamarripa, who was now assignments editor. Arizmendi said he had committed some twenty kidnappings; his wife and children helped launder the money; and yes, he cut off ears when wealthy relatives stalled on the payments. Following a manhunt ordered by Zedillo and involving hundreds of agents, and armed with further clues found in Zamarripa's interview, the secret service finally arrested Arizmendi that August. The headline in *Reforma*, quoting the captured criminal, reflected the paper's flair for striking phrases: "'I'm not sorry.'"[55]

Zedillo and the New Critical Landscape: (ii) Revival at *El Universal*

By 1999, *Reforma* had overtaken *El Universal* as the number one recipient of ad spend among Mexico City papers, according to a study by *La Jornada*. It was almost certainly the number one daily in sales and subscriptions too, although *El Universal*'s classified ads and *La Jornada*'s student following gave those papers higher pass-around rates and thus higher total readership.[56] By now, Junco's domain extended to four regions: *Reforma* in the capital and nearby cities like Toluca and Puebla; *El Norte* in and around Monterrey; *Palabra*, founded in 1997 in Saltillo; and *Mural*, launched in 1998 in Guadalajara. Said *The New York Times*, "Many now consider *Reforma* to be Mexico's most influential publication." Said *The Washington Post*, "Junco's four main newspapers . . . have transformed Mexican journalism, setting new standards for aggressive and—most agree—unbiased reporting." Their combined circulation approached 300,000, almost three times that of *El Universal*, whose regional editions were tiny.[57]

And so Juan Francisco Ealy Ortiz was no longer king of print media. What was the old fox going to do about it?

Ealy had begun to modify *El Universal* after the Colosio killing. Perceiving the PRI to be in decay, he distanced himself from it; opposition parties gained more space on page 1 and the Colosio case became a favorite topic. Then, in early 1995, Ealy distanced himself from Carlos Salinas, whose friendship he had long advertised. It was as though he were struck with guilt, after six years of bootlicking, or amnesia. His paper strained to flesh out conspiracy theories linking Salinas to Colosio's death.[58]

"All the papers did this, but *El Universal* was perverse about it," Salinas recalls. One banner headline, "Carlos Salinas, Mastermind in the Colosio Case," referred not to any dramatic revelation but to the finding of an opinion poll. The former president adds, "Only three months before, in my house, Ealy told me: 'I will be your friend for the rest of your life.' This was on December 1st, the day of Zedillo's inauguration."[59]

But *El Universal* was slow to react to *Reforma*. Ealy's editor in chief (or *subdirector general*, in the parlance of a paper that liked to remind employees who was boss) was an old-school operator called Luis Sevillano. This man's usual idea of front-page design was to include a story about the president, a story about the PRI, a story about the Catholic church, and so on, until most key members of the regime and its allies were accounted for. In editorial meetings, he would claim that Junco and his Monterrey rabble didn't understand Mexico City. "*Reforma* will only bloom for a day," he predicted.[60]

A greater change occurred in August 1996, when Ealy switched editors. Out went Sevillano, aged sixty. In came Roberto Rock, aged forty.[61] Rock would be better able to carry out Ealy's agenda of redeeming *El Universal* after more than six decades of pro-PRI passivity. Ealy could earn international prestige by doing so (he was envious of how Junco was respected), and he could counter the threat to his business posed by *Reforma*. But the younger editor was his own man, and as Sallie Hughes puts it in her analysis of *El Universal*'s rebirth, "Rock pushed for a more expansive transformation of the news pages than initially planned." Ealy conceded because of a relationship built on trust reciprocated by loyalty. Or as Riva Palacio claims, "For Ealy, Rock was his son."

Rock, who believes his unusual surname is Catalan, was both a born insider and a cosmopolitan. The son of an *El Universal* linotypist, he joined the paper as a cub reporter and, being a quick learner, was made head of national correspondents by age thirty-two. Three years later, in 1990, he won a Ford Foundation scholarship to spend six months at a US paper, landing at the Washington office of *The Baltimore Sun* and visited *The Washington Post* and *USA Today*. He sat in on story meetings. He visited Congress and studied its relations with the media. An amiable type, he visited Georgetown University and befriended leading academics. He had always dreamed of being editor one day. Now he might achieve it, armed with new ideas.

Rock next showed his skill with special projects, first by setting up an internal news agency to sell stories to provincial papers, next by creating regional editions of *El Universal* for Puebla, Morelos, and Toluca; the latter idea was inspired by the regional editions *The Washington Post* produced for Maryland and Virginia. For four years he served as one of editor Sevillano's lieutenants, and in the summer of 1996 he hired high-profile columnists, including the acerbically critical Carlos Ramírez of *El Financiero*. He also assembled an investigative unit to compete with *Reforma*'s. That August, Ealy named Rock editor. And five weeks later occurred one of the most bizarre episodes in Mexican media history.

On September 12, squad cars blocked the street outside *El Universal*, while dozens of police rushed with their rifles through the building, looking to apply an arrest warrant issued at the Treasury's request. They had come for Ealy, who was accused of evading some $5 million in taxes. Giving the theatrical operation an extra touch of the absurd, Ealy was not to be found; he had been tipped off and stayed at home. The next day he turned himself in, whereupon he was imprisoned for ten hours, before being released on bail. A year later, a judge sentenced Ealy, giving him a choice: He could spend three years in jail or pay a fine—of just $3,000.[62]

A financial slap on the wrist and daytrip to jail were a small price to pay for the massive PR boost the incident gave to *El Universal* as it remade itself as a critical paper—and to Ealy himself as he tried to reinvent himself as a paragon of free speech. Except for *La Jornada* and *Proceso*, the national and foreign press tended to buy Ealy's version of events: The arrest was "a witchhunt," "fiscal terrorism," "a decision by the government to suppress [our] critical and committed editorial policy." Rock maintains that stance today. He adds that a few months before, a columnist had relayed several demands from a senior cabinet minister, among them: Drop the conspiratorial Colosio coverage and fire Carlos Ramírez. Around the same time, Ealy hosted a meeting with foreign correspondents and told them, "We're on a collision course with Zedillo."

But precedents and comparisons suggest an alternative reading, or at least a complementary one. Ealy was viewed in political circles as a crook, using his paper for personal financial gain. A senior politician of that era opines, "He's an extortionist who sometimes practices journalism." A former editor claims he once saw a back room stacked with fifty labeled cell phones, each a hotline with a federal minister or senior politician, which Ealy's minions would answer whenever the subject of a pending story wished to negotiate. And it was likely no coincidence that Ealy's gradual conversion to critical journalism occurred amid further cuts in federal advertising spend; their lifelong subsidies dwindling, some publishers were pushing to compensate through improved circulation.[63] Might Zedillo or his finance minister, Guillermo Ortiz, have decided that the opportunistic Ealy deserved to be made an example of? Tax arrears were typical among newspaper publishers, but $5 million was a very large sum. And Ealy was not uniquely targeted, for the regime went after several high-profile tax dodgers, including boxer Julio César Chávez. Perhaps Ealy had made his "collision course" claim because he'd caught wind that the Treasury was after him and saw the chance to play the martyr.

If punishing tax evasion was indeed the state's motive, it does seem odd that it should settle a year later for so light a fine as $3,000. But a likely explanation is that Zedillo and Ortiz failed to anticipate the bad press that charging Ealy would cause them. Another possibility is secret negotiation: Suppose that Ealy—in the tradition of the extortionist Carlos Denegri of *Excélsior*—had a filing cabinet full of dirt on Zedillo and his ministers?

Ealy's pained contention that the state was suppressing his freedom of speech, if widely accepted at the time, looks weak in hindsight. One inconsistency is that Zedillo's treatment of the press was unprecedentedly benign. Although most media and most columnists remained deferential, a vocal minority were not, and they criticized Zedillo like no sitting president in memory. Zedillo reacted by either turning up his nose or chiding the press for sloppy standards. But he was not vindictive. In his complaints he did not mention names. Hardliners in the secretariat of government would sometimes call editors to have them tone down or nix a story, but rarely if ever did they press media owners to fire a reporter or drop a commentator.[64] By 1995, wrote Carlos Monsiváis, investigative reporting was fast growing and society was better informed. And in the gravest matter of violence against journalists in the provinces, the record was encouraging; fewer media workers were killed on Zedillo's watch than under any president since Echeverría.[65]

A second inconsistency is borne out on *El Universal*'s front pages. Over the five weeks between Rock's appointment and Ealy's arrest, page 1 stories, while frank in their coverage of cost-of-living woes, did not show a combative tone. On the contrary, treatment of Zedillo remained respectful.[66]

A third inconsistency in the state-repression theory is that *El Universal*, for all its digging into the Colosio case and hiring of critical writers, was not nearly as harsh on Zedillo as *Proceso*. In Scherer's magazine there had been the mean-spirited cover stories that had hammered him and his cabinet in early 1995. There had been further embarrassing covers since: "Zedillo Uninformed," "Nine Months of Nightmare," "The Day Zedillo Cried." Yet Zedillo left *Proceso* alone. Not only that, his administration bought advertising in the magazine—not a lot, but twice as much as the Salinas regime had placed.[67]

While *Proceso*'s sustained critique drew on its tradition of questioning presidents, the extra aggressive tone toward Zedillo reflected the zeitgeist: a new fearlessness in the press, born of the sea change under Salinas and furthered by his laissez-faire successor. One saw it at *Reforma* and *El Norte*, *La Jornada* and *El Financiero*, and at many papers in the provinces, and the public seemed appreciative. In 1996, the World Values Survey held its third Mexican poll and found trust in the press at an all-time high of 52 percent. Nevertheless, that 48 percent still distrusted the press showed that much professionalization was still needed and that deference too often remained a default mode.[68]

Undeterred by the arrest—surely recognizing that they could capitalize on it—Ealy and Rock continued to remake *El Universal* as a civic-minded forum. Political corruption, within each of Mexico's parties, became a major investigative theme, as did drug trafficking. Reporting by Claudia Fernández exposed bleak conditions in Mexico City jails for women; the local director of women's prisons was fired and the story became the basis for a TV documentary. Miguel Badillo bagged a scoop on Mario Villanueva, the PRI governor of Quintana Roo, with a leaked secret service report that accused him of drug trafficking and money laundering. Villanueva would be jailed twice, first in Mexico and then in the United States.[69]

And on September 30, 1999, *El Universal* completed its revamp with a new design. Like *Reforma*'s, the layout was based on US models, with large color photos, attractive graphics, blue separators, and a front-page story count reduced to four, plus a photo teasing a feature on the inside. On this day, the teaser was a large picture of a woman praying at an altar beneath an image of the Virgin of Guadalupe, the story being an exploration of Mexican immigrant culture in the United States. The page 1 lead was the first in a three-part series by Badillo and Marco Lara Klahr unearthing links between the Salinas family and organized crime: "A Capos' Summit with Raúl."[70]

Salinas bashing—which often involved mere speculation, or allegation reported as fact—had become a favorite media pastime.[71] It both catered to and fueled a popular belief that Salinas was the cause of most of Mexico's ills, a trope facilitated by a high-profile falling out between the former president and his successor. In other words, media still somewhat reliant on state handouts had an extra incentive to vilify Zedillo's enemy. Headlines about Salinas might look daring or exciting to the average reader, who remembered how effusively the press had praised him and how omnipotent he had once seemed, but politically and commercially they were a safe bet.

In 1999, *The New York Times* judged that *El Universal* had "reacted to *Reforma*'s success" and was "thoroughly invigorated." Analyzing the quality of reporting in March 2000, Sallie Hughes found that while *Reforma* was slightly ahead in helping readers interpret the news and running critical stories about political and business elites, *El Universal* held a slim lead in assertive reporting—as distinct from relying on press conferences and bulletins—and in average number of sources per story. In other words, *El Universal* was trying harder. As for *Excélsior*, whose reporting was stuck in single-source *declaracionismo*, the deferential recording of the declarations of officials, it lagged far behind in each category. Media observers agreed: The great Mexico City newspaper rivalry was now between Junco's paper and Ealy's.

But it was the collegial Rock who made the operation work. "He treated me as an equal, not a subordinate," says Claudia Fernández. She adds, "He knew how to reconcile the owner's needs with those of a paper trying to be independent, and also those of advertisers. He was very astute as to when to press and when not to. He was affable but prone to anger, a strong character. He had a contagious laugh."[72]

And so, despite its owner's idiosyncrasies, *El Universal* became another civic-oriented competitor, eating away at *Proceso*'s market.

Trials of the Triumvirate

By March 23, 1999, Julio Scherer was certain that his creation required invasive surgery.[73] *Proceso* had lost money in each of the previous three years, over $3 million in total, and what it had banked during the high-revenue Salinas era was all but used up. Weekly sales had dwindled to around 55,000, less than half the average for 1995. The previous week's issue, which led with the thoughts of novelist Carlos Fuentes on the next presidential election, had failed to sell 54 percent of its print run. Scherer fretted that the magazine had softened its critical tone and allowed progovernment voices into its opinion pages. Meanwhile some of its reporters were lobbying for a raise, even though auditors were recommending across-the-board cuts—including a third of personnel.

In September 1997 a respectable competitor had emerged: *Milenio Semanal*. A creation of Grupo Multimedios, owners of *El Diario de Monterrey*, this newsweekly was luring readers away with its more attractive design, color layout, centrist tone, and well-written, often investigative features. Inspired by the US politics and lifestyle magazine *George*, it counted former *Reforma* personnel Federico Arreola, Ciro Gómez Leyva, and Ignacio Rodríguez Reyna among its editors. The magazine announced its presence in striking covers, often with a tongue-in-cheek tone that distinguished it from *Proceso*. One showed likely presidential candidate Vicente Fox seated with his signature cowboy boots raised close to the camera.[74]

Milenio Semanal offered more humor than *Proceso*, which favored thudding political cartoons over anything that might make a reader laugh and whose columnists were uniformly serious. The new magazine ran satirical pieces by Jairo Calixto, who was rescued from the obscurity of a cultural supplement at *Excélsior* and would proceed to a stellar career as a radio and TV talk show host. It featured the comic genius of two young cartoonists, José Hernández and Antonio Helguera, whose biting collaborations relied on text as much as images. One 1998 double spread satirized the anglophone lapses of Rosario Green, secretary of foreign relations, with "Miss Green's English Lessons." These consisted of a series of racist slurs against Mexicans, ironically rendered harmless by the minister's "translations" (sample: "Wet back: Well-known song by The Beatles"). Green invited Arreola and Gómez Leyva to lunch, specifically to complain about the comic strip. Arreola insisted that no one had forced her to take a job that implies great costs as well as great satisfactions.[75]

Meanwhile the *Proceso* Triumvirate of Carlos Marín, Froylán López Narváez, and Rafael Rodríguez Castañeda was ever more at loggerheads, emitting confused signals about the magazine's priorities. Malaise in the newsroom had mounted. Since Scherer's exit, *Proceso* had witnessed an intensifying turf war between Marín and Rodríguez Castañeda. Both men were very sharp, both were very ambitious, and there the similarities ended.

Marín, endowed with a broad smile, plump cheeks, and a bushy moustache, was affable, a joker, an attention seeker, a holder of grudges, and an outrageous (sometimes outraging) flirt. He was responsible more than anyone for the most celebrated *Proceso* exposés. The best known was a 1980 report revealing the creation by President Echeverría and the Federal Security Directorate of the Brigada Blanca, a paramilitary group tasked with aiding the Dirty War against leftist dissidents; it killed or disappeared hundreds. Even during *Proceso*'s recent decline, Marín had impressed his colleagues and Scherer with his exclusives: on the will of the late media mogul Emilio Azcárraga and the disputes among family members for control of Televisa; on the involvement of senior army personnel in drug trafficking, as tracked by military intelligence; on the complicity of state police in a paramilitary massacre of forty-five Indigenous farmers in Acteal, Chiapas. Of the two rivals, Marín had the larger ego—he would later collaborate on a flattering biography of himself—but he kept the team in mind. His brief as codirector was as assignments editor, and he secured productivity bonuses and company cell phones for employees. Although he continued reporting, he generously shared story tips with junior colleagues.[76]

Rodríguez Castañeda was introverted and, but for a streak of black humor, serious. Some claimed he had a Napoleon complex, with his short stature and homely features, which drove him to be sly and calculating. Others felt he was brazen in his desire to be sole director, telling any who would listen that he was destined for the post and sucking up to Scherer ("Don

Julio, you remind me a lot of my dad"). His brief was news editor, which meant he had fewer daily dealings with reporters; this and his lack of charm handicapped him against Marín. But he had allies. One was Francisco Ortiz Pinchetti, who in 1998 founded the magazine's reporters' association, in part to cultivate support for Rodríguez Castañeda. Another was Scherer, who appreciated his steadfastness, his rectitude, his eye for cover design, and his commitment to keeping *Proceso* sustainable. It was Rodríguez Castañeda who had pitched the idea of a special edition on the thirtieth anniversary of the 1968 Tlatelolco massacre.[77] The issue sold very well and gave rise to other specials.

Scherer admired Marín's brilliance but, like some of his senior writers, found his ego grating. He would recall, "Marín moved around the newsroom and among management with clumsy airs of authority." Or, as Riva Palacio later averred, the old man chose Rodríguez Castañeda over Marín because Scherer "didn't like to be put in the shade."[78]

So Scherer intervened. Together with Leñero and Maza, he summoned the Triumvirate, ostensibly to discuss an auditors' report. Scherer summarized the report and the financial crisis it indicated. He added that part of the problem was a lack of uniform direction and consequent newsroom unease. No one interrupted him. After a pause, he said, "We have decided there ought to be named a single editor in chief."[79] After another pause, he said that the two natural candidates were Rodríguez Castañeda and Marín, and that the matter should be put to a newsroom vote. To Scherer, Leñero, and Maza, this was the democratic way of proceeding. To Marín and his ally López Narváez, this would make for a PRI-style election, the outcome preordained by those in power. They knew that Scherer favored Rodríguez Castañeda and they suspected that Ortiz Pinchetti, with his reporters' association, had already corralled most of the votes.

López Narváez was first to reply, announcing his resignation. Marín followed: Rising to his feet, he protested that the meeting had been convened under false pretenses and he refused to take part in an election. "I have to take an everlasting vacation," he declared.[80] Claiming he had a flight to Cancún to catch, he promptly marched out of the room. In fact, he at once defected to *Milenio Semanal*.

Rodríguez Castañeda won by default. When the directors descended to inform the newsroom, the mood was far from celebratory. Scherer made a matter-of-fact announcement. There was lukewarm applause. "I just hope this works," commented Leñero. Said the new editor in chief, "I'm sorry about Marín and Froylán, because although I also wanted to be editor of *Proceso*, I didn't want to climb over corpses."[81]

Was *Proceso* itself a corpse? Beyond the crises of egos, excessive costs, and diminished sales, there were weaknesses embedded in *Proceso*'s identity. As Riva Palacio observed at the time, the magazine's relentless negativity of tone was somewhat at odds with changes in Mexican society. A growing middle class and fast-rising university attendance, and thus a greater public engagement with news, were arguably better catered to by other, less pessimistic, civic media. Post-Scherer *Proceso* had lost its near monopoly over investigative exclusives and leak-based journalism, not only due to rivals but also because Mexico itself was becoming more open: its institutions more professional, its judiciary more independent, its opposition parties more vocal, and civil society better organized. The federal government itself was becoming more transparent. Even Televisa was attempting critical journalism. Among the very biggest scandals to erupt in recent years were the 1997 revelation that Mexico's drug czar, General Jesús Gutiérrez Rebollo, had been taking bribes from the Juárez Cartel, and the 1998 accusations that the Fobaproa fund, which had massively bailed out the banks, had persisted in doing so despite evidence of financial fraud. But neither scandal emerged from journalistic digging. The drug czar bombshell originated with an internal investigation, while the banking probe was spearheaded by the Party of the Democratic Revolution (especially Andrés Manuel López Obrador) and the PAN.[82]

There were further weaknesses. The magazine's design was archaic: Its inside pages all ran in black and white; there was still no table of contents; its presence online was weak. *Proceso* once possessed a mystique, embodied in its founder; this was a unifying force that smoothed differences between veteran employees, made junior ones go the extra mile for a story, and encouraged students to dream of working for him. The mystique had declined with Scherer's departure. Could anyone hope to revive it, let alone an editor who, to use Marín's unkind but not inaccurate put-down, was a deskbound journalist?

By Friday, three days after the Triumvirate was dismantled, some twenty employees had resigned in protest at the succession. Naturally, their resignation letter was made public. In an interview with *Milenio Semanal*, López Narváez sneered that Rodriguez Castañeda was a "small man" who was "brilliant at nothing." Marín dubbed his former colleagues "liars" and "traitors." For many years to come, his friends noted, Marín would seldom pass up a chance to badmouth *Proceso* and those who failed to quit in solidarity with him.[83]

In *Reforma*, columnist Germán Dehesa lamented, "Throughout many years, *Proceso* was for us a sort of Rock of Gibraltar . . . always marking a clear path amidst confusion and stolid official discourse." In its current crisis, he reasoned, "thousands of Mexicans end up morally damaged by this saddest of spectacles." Or as a headline in the *Los Angeles Times* put it, "A Beacon for Mexican Democracy Shines Less Brightly."[84]

There are two versions of how *Proceso* fared after the succession. One, popular among former employees, is that it never properly revived. No one could fill Scherer's shoes, and after his failed experiment with the Triumvirate, the old man had erred again by preferring the loyal Rodríguez Castañeda to the adventurous Marín. Thereafter, *Proceso* lived "from its past glories."[85]

The *Proceso*-never-recovered version owes much to a sanctification of Scherer and prejudice toward the less dashing and less convivial Rodríguez Castañeda. It surely underplays both the challenge of the decline in sales, and therefore revenues, by early 1999 and the strengths of the new editor—not as dynamic as Scherer, nor as well connected, but also less of an improviser.

A second version, attested to by the likes of Humberto Musacchio, Scherer's daughter María, and *Proceso* veterans who stayed on, holds that Rodríguez Castañeda brought an editorial and administrative professionalism to *Proceso*, along with well-defined direction after thirty months of infighting; such things were hailed by most employees.[86] He was praised for his skill as an editor of features and his knack for catchy covers. He showed a will to continue diversifying from the politics-heavy content of the Scherer era, a process begun in the early 1990s during the North American Free Trade Agreement debates and the Chiapas uprising, to embrace topics such as the Catholic Church, the army, drug trafficking, and the memory of the Dirty War. He proved honest, in refusing to profit from his privileged office. The magazine evolved too slowly for some, but what changes the new leader did emplace allowed it to regain some of its readers and consolidate its finances—a vital matter, as there were more federal boycotts to come, together with a growing reticence of businesses to buy ad space. Although its days as Mexico's peerless counterweight to power were behind it, *Proceso* would regain much of its relevance to the national conversation.

Another factor of the magazine's revival was a stroke of happy coincidence: The next race to Los Pinos was underway, and by late 1999 it was clear that the PAN had a viable contender in the ideologically vague but charismatic Vicente Fox, with his booming voice and his cowboy boots. Polling showed that Fox had a much better shot at defeating Francisco Labastida, candidate of the PRI, than Cuauhtémoc Cárdenas, running for the third time for the Party of the Democratic Revolution. This evidence, Ortiz Pinchetti's vast experience covering major elections, and his familiarity with Fox's career prompted Rodríguez Castañeda to assign his star chronicler to the Fox campaign. Public interest in the electoral race, and especially "the Fox phenomenon," helped lift sales—although not as much as it could have, for Rodríguez Castañeda's antipathy to Fox limited his appearance on the cover to a single issue during the eight-month season. Here arose a beef with Ortiz Pinchetti: The editor felt his coverage of Fox was too positive for the left-wing *Proceso* ("The bastard comes across as likeable!" he protested). He claimed the reporter was "entranced" by Fox. Ortiz Pinchetti found his stories subject to intrusive editing that eventually, he felt, constituted censorship.[87]

Scherer backed his successor. On one of his weekly visits to the newsroom he declared, "I prefer that mummy Labastida to that prostitute Fox!"[88]

A further lift came from Scherer's return to *Proceso*, not as an editor but as a contributor. In June 1999, he supplied the first of many scoops, which would grace the cover for more than a decade, with an exposé on the Tlatelolco massacre. Coauthored with Monsiváis, it drew from an unpublished account by a former defense minister, General Marcelino García Barragán. In sum, it confirmed what had long only been suspected: that the president at the time, Díaz Ordaz, had orchestrated the slaughter.[89]

Having averaged cover sales of 63,000 in 1999, *Proceso* would see a rebound in 2000 to an average of 75,000, not far shy of the figure for Scherer's last year in charge.[90] And fortunately for its bottom line, although *Proceso*'s natural sympathies lay with Cárdenas, Fox would win the election. Once the presidential palace was occupied by this rough-hewn man and his preening spokeswoman (soon to be his wife), a pair quite distinct from the sober mold of Mexican first couples, his missteps and her ambition would make for many a scandalizing cover story.

Chapter 6

Challenges on the Left

La Jornada

La Jornada is quintessentially a Mexican phenomenon: it is dogmatically anti-government, and it lives off the government.

—Raymundo Riva Palacio

Civil Society and the Conciliator: Carlos Payán

Between the mid-1980s and the mid-1990s, what *Proceso* was to magazines, *La Jornada* was to newspapers. Both channeled the Mexican left. Both were essential reading for the political set, artists and intellectuals, activist students, and foreigners trying to make sense of Mexico. Both defended human rights, giving voice to nongovernmental organizations and civil society more broadly. They led the way photographically: *Proceso* with its arresting covers (by the Salinas era), *La Jornada* with its street-level photojournalism. They featured some of Mexico's most provocative cartoonists. Both sold reasonably well, for a country in which less than 20 percent of the population were regular readers of periodicals. In the banner news year of 1994, when *Proceso* peaked, *La Jornada* averaged daily sales of around 100,000.[1]

Coincidentally or not, in 1996, the year that Julio Scherer retired, so did the sixty-seven-year-old editor in chief of *La Jornada*, Carlos Payán.

The origins of each periodical, though twelve years apart, had something in common too: They were born in a spirit of democratic participation, with ownership shared by multiple journalists and sympathizers, and in a mood of righteous anger. For the founders of *Proceso*, the target of their ire was President Luis Echeverría. At *La Jornada*, the passion was broader based: leveled not just, nor even principally, at Manuel Becerra Acosta, who had betrayed the collegial founding ideals of *Unomásuno*, but at the whole corrupt, incompetent, and repressive system of government.

When the self-exiles from *Unomásuno* were midway through designing *La Jornada* in May 1984, their world was rocked by a political murder. Manuel Buendía, Mexico's most influential columnist and one of the most credible, had long used his column—published in *Excélsior* and syndicated to dozens of regional papers—as a vehicle for investigation. By 1984 he was probing a range of sensitive topics: CIA operations in Mexico; corrupt politicians, labor leaders, and businessmen; embezzlement at state oil giant Pemex; and organized crime.

The so-called Guadalajara Cartel, led by Miguel Ángel Félix Gallardo, was at a peak of power and profitability, raking in somewhere around $4 billion per year. Its success owed in part (it later transpired) to the protection of secret police service the Federal Security Directorate. Buendía had been digging into the crime syndicate's connections to the directorate when he was shot, just after lunch, while walking in one of Mexico City's busiest shopping districts.[2]

Whenever leading journalists are murdered, especially in so brazen a fashion, it is common to talk of a "chilling effect" on the press and freedom of speech (in countries where journalists are *not* murdered, the term applies to libel suits). While media workers had been murdered at a rate of almost one per year since 1940, nearly all those crimes had taken place in the provinces, where rule of law was usually weaker. Except for the high-flying columnist Carlos Denegri—a serial philanderer who was shot by his wife—none of the victims had a profile to match Buendía's.[3] Some journalists fretted that if such a famous colleague could be gunned down in the capital, no one was safe.

Yet to others, including those planning *La Jornada*, Buendía's killing had a *galvanizing* effect. Héctor Aguilar Camín, one of the founding subdirectors, dedicated several pages of his political-cultural magazine *Nexos* to the significance of Buendía's "programmed execution" (he implied: by someone in authority). He also noted how Buendía's wake had united the often fractious press, with even Jacobo Zabludovsky, chief anchor at Televisa, coming to pay respects. At a demonstration, the cartoonist Bulmaro Castellanos, better known as Magú, gave a fiery speech that linked Buendía's killing to a history of state repression of journalists and social activists. In the words of Humberto Musacchio, another subeditor, "Manuel's death . . . raised our intent to be an anti-establishment paper."[4]

But it was typical of the ethical paradoxes of Mexico's combative media that in one respect the old ways would persist: financial dependence on the government. This was not the founders' intention. Carlos Payán and his team had kick-started the project with a fundraiser. At an event in February 1984 that drew 5,000 journalists and sympathizers, shares in the paper's publishing company were announced for sale to all comers. Artists including Rufino Tamayo, Francisco Toledo, and José Luis Cuevas donated works to be auctioned for the cause over the months that followed. By one account, 2,138 individuals bought shares, with voting rights limited to one vote per each of the 160 founder-journalists. But in a sign of their financial naivety, the founding directors had capped share purchases per person at 1 million pesos, which, given an ongoing devaluation, meant just $5,000.[5]

The founders' aims were first to democratize ownership and thus preempt a Becerra-style takeover—a goal that would be durably achieved—and second

La Jornada

MÉXICO, D. F. ● AÑO UNO ● NÚMERO: BAJO CERO
DIRECTOR GENERAL: CARLOS PAYÁN VELVER

En una reunión de iguales, se anuncia un nuevo diario

El financiamiento provendrá de diversos sectores de la sociedad civil

En una reunión de iguales fue lanzada esta noche la convocatoria pública para la fundación de un diario matutino, mismo que empezará a circular en los próximos meses y cuyo nombre será **La Jornada**.

En representación de más de setenta periodistas y escritores, Pablo González Casanova, Carlos Payán Velver —director del nuevo diario— y Héctor Aguilar Camín explicaron las razones de esta iniciativa, las características y principios del periódico y la estructura de la sociedad que lo editará.

Después de caracterizar el momento político que vive el país, los oradores del acto, celebrado en el Hotel de México de esta ciudad, señalaron la acusada derechización de los medios informativos a los que, con algunas excepciones, dominan "el conservadurismo ideológico y la estrecha lógica mercantil, cuando no la alianza extranacional". Dada esa situación, dijeron, es imprescindible un esfuerzo de información y crítica.

Dijo Pablo González Casanova: "No aceptamos el optimismo autoritario ni la esperanza sin pensamiento crítico. La voluntad nacional es necesaria y para ser efectiva tiene que ser lúcida. No aceptamos que con la claridad cunda el desánimo. Eso sólo lo sostienen quienes no quieren claridad."

Carlos Payán sintetizó la "vocación política" de **La Jornada**

como el ánimo de "estimular la participación de lector ciudadanos en favor de causas fundamentales de Méxic

El diario se propone, dijo, contribuir a la lucha "por la fensa de la soberanía y la independencia nacionales y la daridad con las luchas de otros pueblos por hacer reali esos principios; por el diario ejercicio y el respeto irrestric las garantías individuales y sociales que recogen las leyes damentales de México; por el compromiso con las neces des y demandas de los trabajadores del campo y de la ciu así como de las mayorías marginadas del país; por la de cratización de la vida pública, el ensanchamiento de la pl lidad política y el respeto a los derechos legítimos de las di sas minorías, y por la distribución igualitaria de la riqueza cialmente creada y la limitación de privilegios políticos y e nómicos de toda índole".

Aguilar Camín explicó la invitación a suscribir títulos accionistas diciendo que el grupo editor se propone consti "un instrumento de comunicación no subordinado a intere particulares, sean oficiales o partidarios, ni a las decisione mercantiles de un puñado de inversionistas". Se busca, d "una empresa nacida de la sociedad, pagada y financiada e aportaciones de sus individuos, comunidades y asociacione

Así será   La Jornada

Un diario tabloide, de 32 páginas, que ofrecerá abundante información breve, así como reportajes y entrevistas, documentos y crónicas de contexto. El diario combinará la información con la reflexión de fondo sobre los problemas de la hora. **La Jornada** consignará en sus páginas el movimiento de la sociedad, la realidad diaria y anónima de personas y sectores. Un diario que dé voz a quienes no la tienen. Un diario moderno y plural, abierto en lo ideológico y en lo político. Un diario que convoque a las nuevas corrientes de opinión que van surgiendo del medio político y periodístico, de las agrupaciones sociales, del mundo intelectual, de los centros de investigación especializados. Un diario crítico, ajeno al desahogo y al ataque personal, atento a los procesos que marcan la realidad diaria del país y las condiciones internacionales que lo determinan, en un espíritu profesional de intensa circulación de las noticias y las ideas.

El director general de **La Jornada** es Carlos Payán Velver. Son sus subdirectores Miguel Angel Granados Chapa, Héctor Aguilar Camín, Carmen Lira y Humberto Musacchio.

Actualmente se trabaja en busca de su identidad gráfica, Vicente Rojo será su autor, y él mismo se responsabilizará del diseño definitivo.

In early 1984, the future founders of *La Jornada* issued fundraising leaflets that doubled as personal share certificates. Courtesy of Héctor Aguilar Camín.

to place the start-up on a solid economic footing. The latter aim fell short. The million-peso investment cap limited the role of angel investors, who included several business and political leaders. Further, at a time when polarized Cold War rhetoric had yet to abate, many industrialists viewed the paper's social democratic identity as tantamount to communism, so advertiser interest was meager.[6] In the early months, the quarter- and half-page ads that were placed would total just two or three pages in each thirty-two-page edition.

Before launch, aware of their project's penury, *La Jornada*'s editors went cap in hand to Los Pinos to beg for subsidies: government advertising and guaranteed access to the cut-price newsprint supplied by PIPSA. Such approaches were standard practice. Carlos Monsiváis observed that President Miguel de la Madrid knew the value of escape valves—he tolerated most of the protest marches and rallies that multiplied during the long recession—and he likely saw *La Jornada* in similar terms. When his cabinet debated the matter, Manuel Bartlett, the hardline secretary of government, opposed the paper's mere existence. But *La Jornada* had a tentative advocate in Jesús Reyes Heroles, the education secretary, who seven years earlier had supported *Unomásuno*. Reyes Heroles did not argue for official advertising, deeming Payán and his team "dissidents" who had received sufficient aid at their former paper, but he saw the political utility of a new medium of the Left. So Reyes Heroles assuaged Bartlett's concerns with an appeal to his ruling party cynicism: "Look Manuel, it's really no big deal. The more there are [of these critical media], the lesser they are."[7]

Uncertain of its economic future but buoyed by quixotic zeal, *La Jornada* launched on September 19, 1984. Endowed with a bold "serious tabloid" design by artist Vicente Rojo and a name that meant "the workday" and telegraphed class sympathies, *La Jornada* had no equal as a critical high-profile daily. *Unomásuno* initially retained much of its audience, but having lost its best journalists to the leftist upstart, it could not resist a gradual desertion of readers; this decline would become pronounced after the Salinas regime coopted it. *El Financiero*, though independent minded, lacked the stylistic panache and daring cartoons that made *La Jornada* a favorite of students and creatives. *Excélsior*, which had clawed back some credibility after the ouster of Scherer with Buendía's famous column, now lacked both.[8]

La Jornada gained help in its efforts to get off the ground because an advertising boycott, coordinated throughout the government by Bartlett, did not prove absolute. There were ads from public universities and a state-run publishing house. There were *gacetillas* from a public health agency, which reportedly dared to buy a year's worth of ads in advance. However, the big-spending ministries stayed away, which appeared to doom the paper to a short life, like many a critical but shakily financed project before it. In late

1984, Aguilar Camín managed to obtain a meeting with the president and request that the boycott be lifted. "Count on it," De la Madrid replied. Soon, left-leaning officials like Governor Enrique González Pedrero of Tabasco and Finance Minister Jesús Silva-Herzog Flores were making purchases.[9]

There would be recurrent boycotts, designed not to sink the paper but to remind it to temper its criticism. It served the discourse of democratization of the Institutional Revolutionary Party (PRI) for there to exist moderately critical organs on the left, especially ones over which it exerted covert control. So here lay the original sin of the paper that aspired to be the most critical: dependence on federal largesse.

At its birth, *La Jornada* inherited much of what had once made *Unomásuno* avant-garde: solidarity with the have-nots, a commitment to democratic pluralism, a relatively large number of women on staff, provocatively critical cartoonists, a top-notch team of photojournalists led by Pedro Valtierra, and antiauthoritarian inspiration drawn from Spain's *El País* and France's *Libération*. Its professionalism showed in its hiring process. Juan Angulo, who would rise to become news editor, recalls taking an entrance exam for a proofreading position that lasted five hours and covered subjects from politics to great works of literature. The key difference with *Unomásuno*, at least at first, was a more collegial leadership. Carlos Payán was in charge, but he was limited to a four-year term, renewable for a second. Musacchio, Aguilar Camín, Carmen Lira, and Miguel Ángel Granados Chapa had equal status as subdirectors, and it could be assumed that employees would elect one of them to replace Payán, if not in 1988 then in 1992.[10]

Payán was a lawyer by training and a bureaucrat by background, but he seemed to many to be the right leader.[11] Blessed with charm and a romantic aspect—dark, wavy hair swept back, heavy eyebrows, haunted eyes, an impressive moustache—Payán could claim an affinity with workers, as he had been born and raised in Mexico City's old working-class district of La Merced. He had joined the Communist Party when it was risky to do so, during a national rail workers' strike in 1959, and later its local successor, the Unified Socialist Party of Mexico (PSUM). After making his first career as a mid-level bureaucrat, in 1977 Payán changed course. He ingratiated himself with Becerra and helped him found *Unomásuno*, as staff administrator and political liaison. Every Mexican media organization needed someone who knew how to flatter politicians and cajole officials; Payán mixed especially well with the PRI's left wing. A secret service report on *La Jornada*'s founding claimed Payán belonged to the PSUM's "Stalinist faction"; if that were ever true, he had clearly moved toward the center.

Some senior colleagues at *La Jornada* felt Payán's collegiality was self-interested, motivated by power: having it within the company, being close to it within the halls of government, promoting politicians of the Left. Even at the paper's founding, when voting rights were to be limited to the shareholding employees and contributors, Payán packed that number with friends and loyalists, so he would have more votes than the other four founder-directors. It was an unnecessary ploy, for even his peers recognized that his abilities as a conciliator—tempering newsroom egos and cajoling politicians—made him the obvious choice as editor in chief.

Payán initially made good on his commitment to a democratic, employee-owned newspaper by setting up an enviable working environment. The newsroom was arranged in "islands" of conjoined desks to foster collaboration. Reporters were given time to work on features as well as news, and the paper ran several multipage special reports each week. These often involved themes of social justice: underpaid seamstresses in Mexico City, a fishermen's cooperative in Sonora, factories closing as the PRI embraced neoliberalism, the strife of sisal growers in the Yucatán. Reporters, columnists, and editors, many of them members of the PSUM and hired directly by Payán, felt they were helping to build a better society. Reporter Sara Lovera recalls, "We threw ourselves *neurotically* into every topic!"[12]

Payán set a democratic tone by being a good listener. Reporters felt free to knock on his door. He backed them when officials complained that they were "misquoted." He and his subdirectors took care to explain when a story got spiked and gave staff time off when problems arose at home. Like Scherer at *Proceso*, Payán had gifts as a mixer that yielded not only political protection but also a slew of inside tips for stories.

Employees were better paid than at most Mexico City dailies, and before long they enjoyed better benefits, thanks to an unofficial, in-house union set up by cartoonist Magú. As at *El Financiero*, there was no prohibition on taking payments from sources, but the practice was frowned on and most employees resisted the bait. The custom of reporters earning commissions on advertising sold to the sources they covered was altered at *La Jornada*, so that these sums mostly fell into a kitty, to be shared equally. Though this reduced, rather than eliminated, conflict of interest, the step was innovative for the era. Similarly, while *La Jornada* accepted paid-for *gacetillas*, especially from state governments and during campaign seasons from the PRI, it identified them as such by running their headlines in italics. Although this signal was surely too subtle for the general public, dedicated readers came to understand it.[13]

The Earthquake and the Election

Having launched in September 1984 with a modest print run of 20,000, *La Jornada* soon had the chance to put its civic ideals into urgent practice when a series of gas tank explosions at a Pemex plant in the State of México killed at least 500 people and inflicted burns and wounds on another 7,000. The paper's coverage that November was both investigative and critical.[14] Its ability to combine empathetic reporting with arresting images was famously displayed in May 1985 when it covered a strike by 3,500 miners in Hidalgo state. Photographs by Pedro Valtierra showed how the protesting miners congregated naked but for their boots, belts, and helmets; their purpose was to call attention to the meager apparel their company provided, as well as to abnormally dangerous work conditions and proposed layoffs. Daring for a newspaper (in any country), a cluster of miners' bottoms greeted readers from the front page; a clutch of miners' penises was visible on page 9.[15]

Then, on the very day of its first anniversary, came an episode that would cement *La Jornada*'s reputation. An earthquake, Mexico's deadliest ever, killed at least 10,000.

The great natural disaster of September 19, 1985, pulverizing swaths of the capital and coming on top of three years of grueling national recession, was a massive social, economic, and political blow for an already weakened country. The scale of the destruction, with up to 800,000 rendered homeless and many midsize tower blocks collapsed, raised awkward questions about adherence to building codes. The reaction of Los Pinos began with a thirty-six-hour disappearing act by the president, followed by releases of conflicting information. Televisa's response, after several days of unusually candid reporting, was to minimize the damage.[16] Several of the mainstream papers, however, produced investigative pieces, and *Excélsior* dedicated a daily space for four weeks to the findings of experts who questioned official accounts of the devastation. These were signs that state control over the press had loosened since 1968, at least in moments of national trauma, when the government found it could no longer rely on *embute* to steer the narrative.[17] A watchdog trait emerged among more than a few of Mexico's daily papers, although another decade would pass before it became widespread and permanent.

La Jornada reported, photographed, investigated, and cited dissident experts too, but it also offered a unique platform to the public. The 1985 quake has been memorialized by Carlos Monsiváis and others as the event that gave birth to Mexican "civil society," or at least gave it an unprecedented boost, in that citizens united to help each other when their government seemed paralyzed. *La Jornada* had already described itself, in its debut editorial, as born of the efforts of "an important portion of civil society."[18] Now it was civil society's chief legitimizer and megaphone.[19]

Stories and opinion columns recorded how the common people formed rescue brigades and mutual aid groups. Photo essays showed teams at work in the debris and citizens handing out emergency supplies, with no uniformed officials in sight. Valtierra and his unit produced some of the most iconic images of the aftermath: dozens of young men standing atop the balconies of a housing block that lay almost horizontal, listening for survivors; a policeman, head bowed, walking past the wreck of the downtown Hotel Regis, its sign lying twisted in the rubble; an Indigenous woman, handkerchief clasped to her nose, passing by rows of coffins inside a baseball stadium, in search of dead relatives.[20]

The women of La Jornada stood out for their ability to show the disaster's impact on ordinary lives. Unomásuno had broken the news that hundreds of seamstresses were trapped in the rubble of some 200 clandestine sweatshops. Andrea Becerril followed up by reporting that it took officials more than a week to send heavy machinery to excavate one of the larger factories, by which time all but a fifth of the 125 women had died. She later revealed how a mill owner had gained special permission to enter his property and haul out safes and machinery, even as many of his employees remained stuck in the partly destroyed building; this story got picked up by many print and broadcast media. More explosive still was an exposé by Sara Lovera, reporting that city officials and manufacturers had contrived to keep the sweatshop conditions secret and that, in the wake of the temblor, the garment industry's top lawyer recommended factory owners suspend their 40,000 workers without pay. Lovera got the scoop by donning a silk dress and posing as a businesswoman, to gain entry to a chamber of commerce dinner.[21]

Elena Poniatowska initially wrote long-form chronicles about the aftermath for Novedades, where she had contributed since the 1950s. She relayed the testimony of volunteers and los damnificados, as the quake's displaced survivors were termed. But after a week or so, her editor said that her pieces undermined the president's desire for a "return to normal"; they also "depressed the readers." So Poniatowska took her talent for giving voice to the voiceless to La Jornada. A much fitter home for her empathetic work, the paper ran her chronicles on its back page for the rest of the year. Early entries were portraits of grief. In one, about a professor who volunteered at a makeshift morgue, the quotes evoked a deepening social consciousness: "It's not fair that in this country, hospitals, schools, government buildings, and public offices fall. It's not fair that it always hits those who are weakest." Increasingly, Poniatowska's accounts conveyed popular outrage at incompetent and corrupt officialdom and the inequality, classism, and racism that pervaded the city. "The state was surpassed on all fronts," one chronicle asserted. She would rework her witnessing into a book, Nothing, Nobody, that remains a classic of Mexican reportage.[22]

Over at El Universal, a new editorial team had quite a different experience. In March that year, the mercurial Juan Francisco Ealy Ortiz had chosen to elevate his paper's credibility by hiring, with fanfare in its pages, Benjamín Wong and José Carreño Carlón. Wong was a journeyman editor of creative reputation and leftist leanings, while Carreño was a respected columnist and one-time congressman. As they took a more independent tack, they had to field nightly calls from a presidential spokesman requesting some stories be highlighted and others buried. On one occasion, Secretary of Government Bartlett summoned Wong to chew him out. A week after the earthquake, *El Universal* reporters discovered that the ruins of the Mexico City attorney general's office contained the bodies of several Colombians. These detainees were found in the basement, with signs of torture and death from nonnatural causes. Wong ran the story on page 1, causing a sensation that rivaled that of the buried seamstresses. As reward for a scoop that embarrassed Los Pinos, as well as for publishing an estimated death toll that much exceeded the official count, Ealy instructed his editor to resign. Carreño and thirty-four other colleagues quit in solidarity.[23]

The press overall turned the earthquake into a multifaceted scandal, which weakened the popularity and legitimacy of the PRI, as historian Vanessa Freije has shown.[24] For decades the PRI had styled itself as the provider for every need and—aided by such lackeys as Televisa and the main broadsheets—the provider of all necessary information. But it was the antiestablishment *La Jornada* that emerged as the authority on the earthquake, a renown later boosted by anniversary editions and affirmed by praise for its coverage.[25] Journalists elsewhere, equally scandalized by federal incompetence, tried to do good work, but their efforts lacked the forum that Payán, balancing his leftist convictions with his skill as a political maneuverer, succeeded in preserving. Of course, it had long served the state to admit an escape valve for leftist activists; better they vent in public than channel their ardor into guerrilla combat, which is what the PRI had seen happening in much of South America since the 1960s. Yet the work of *La Jornada* in the final months of 1985 suggests the paper took a national tragedy as a chance to advance freedom of speech beyond the state's comfort level. Perhaps increased cover sales, driven to 30,000 by surging thirst for information, made up for reductions in official advertising.[26] But Payán could not do without those subsidies for long. Unfettered coverage had to alternate with restraint.

In 1988, during the next presidential election, the paper indeed reined in its socialist impulses. Although it sympathized with Cuauhtémoc Cárdenas of the National Democratic Front (FDN)—a sympathy at odds with most of the press, which was effusive toward Carlos Salinas de Gortari and ignored or maligned the leftist—*La Jornada* did less to back Cárdenas than might be supposed. Media analyst Raúl Trejo found that, during the height of the race, from late March until early July, *La Jornada* devoted just 14 percent of its campaign coverage to the FDN, less than the 17 percent it gave to another left-wing candidate, Heberto Castillo (who would withdraw a month before the vote in favor of Cárdenas), and far less than the 39 percent it afforded the PRI. The last figure was below the ruling-party support offered by *El Universal* (49 percent), *Excélsior* (59 percent), or the cringingly meek *Novedades* (89 percent), but it still implied an economic imperative. Privileging the candidacy of Salinas with the most column inches was the quid pro quo of subsidies, which by one estimate approached half of the paper's total revenues, and which in 1988 were boosted by massive PRI campaign spending.[27]

The paper then found itself in a pickle after commissioning a national opinion poll, a first for Mexico's press. Developed by former bureaucrat Miguel Basáñez, later a world-renowned pollster, the survey gave Salinas a mere 43 percent preference, 14 points above Cárdenas but substantially less than what the PRI—accustomed to outright majorities—was claiming. Before publication, the PRI got wind of the results and sent Basáñez a message urging him to "correct" his numbers. Facing a PRI threat to cancel payment on ads already placed, Payán was reluctant to make a stand. But a call between Basáñez and US political scientist Roderic Camp saved the day, for Camp offered to give the poll to *The New York Times*. Then the PRI suddenly relented, a switch that Basáñez put down to his phone being tapped. *La Jornada* ran the poll the day before the vote.[28]

On election night, however, with the result too close to call, *La Jornada* shied from matching the bravery of *El Financiero*, with its "Nobody Wins." *La Jornada*'s three-part header began with the PRI declaring a decisive victory, noted opponents' claims of fraud, but undercut them with Bartlett's demand for evidence.[29]

Only afterward, as public outrage swelled over the election's suspicious outcome, did *La Jornada* focus more attention on the FDN than on the PRI. During the six weeks following, with Cárdenas and others crying foul, the paper gave the FDN 46 percent of its postcampaign coverage, against 30 percent to the PRI. As had occurred after the earthquake, great public discontent gave *La Jornada* cover for channeling frank criticisms of the regime. So did the fact that other papers were paying attention, if less sympathetically, to Cárdenas's complaints.[30]

Here was the modus operandi of *La Jornada* and its editor in chief. Whereas Scherer took pride in *Proceso* being a constant critic, Payán chose his battles. It was a necessary strategy, especially during the precarious and recessionary years of the paper's 1984–88 start-up phase; even in the Salinas era, with the private market booming, some 70 percent of *La Jornada*'s ad take was public money. This dependent dynamic would persist until 2003 (and reappear later). Payán's ostensibly antiestablishment paper could be quite deferential, such as when reporting the president's State of the Nation address. The first time *La Jornada* did so, it devoted half the front page to a paraphrase of De la Madrid's call to unity in the face of economic crisis and a photographic triptych of the president, mid-speech, looking decisive. This annual flattery continued under Salinas.[31]

As though to compensate for its dissonance in national news, the paper adopted an aggressively partisan tone in international affairs. Leaders of the Latin American left received high praise, none more so than Cuba's Fidel Castro. The United States was vilified as an imperialist nation, a charge reiterated relentlessly by cartoonist Rafael Barajas, a.k.a. El Fisgón. In general, what the paper lacked in depth of reporting it made up for in stridency of tone. As Chappell Lawson wrote of *La Jornada* content of the 1990s, the paper's "criticisms of the regime tended to be ideological and reflexive, rather than investigative (and thus especially threatening)."[32]

Newsroom Ruptures and Indigenous Rebels

Having completed his first term as director, with sales at a new high thanks to the paper's relatively fair electoral coverage, Payán was reelected as director in 1988. It had been a rocky road. Though welcoming to young reporters and to women, *La Jornada* was an unusually conflictive workplace for senior personnel. Spats and resignations themselves became news.[33] First to quit, before even a year was up, was Musacchio. As the head of the news desk, Musacchio quickly tired of intrusions by Payán that he found nonsensical or heavy-handed. One was a brief and disastrous experiment with printing out every story to edit it rather than doing so on-screen, which pushed closing the edition so late that the printed copies sometimes failed to make deadline for distribution outside Mexico City. The final straw for Musacchio was Payán's order that he fire a recently hired and entirely competent reporter on account of his Trotskyist beliefs and his disagreements with the cartoonist Magú.[34] After two years Pedro Valtierra left, having fallen out with Aguilar Camín over the space accorded photographs, which the subdirector felt should usually yield precedence to text. Valtierra took four of the paper's photographers with him and set up the photo agency Cuartoscuro, which remains Mexico's most prestigious agency today.[35]

Aguilar Camín himself departed in May 1987, having joined the throng of public intellectuals from across the ideological spectrum drawing close to candidate Salinas. Though a center-leftist, Aguilar Camín deemed Cárdenas's brand of state-heavy socialism passé, a position that caused conflict with Payán and other senior personnel. They felt their cofounder had sold out; Aguilar Camín felt his colleagues had become too dogmatic. The distrust was epitomized after the election, when *La Jornada* ran a photo of Aguilar Camín at the PRI headquarters enjoying a cigar. He responded with a four-word letter to the editor—"Good photo, bad blood"—and sold his shares.[36]

These and other exits were eased by the abundance of options elsewhere. Whenever an editor, columnist, or senior reporter felt underappreciated, there was a score of Mexico City newspapers (twenty-five in 1990, by one count) and at least a dozen news or cultural magazines where he or she might land, or to which an owner might tempt them. The combination of excess of press, high salaries for senior personnel, and sensitive egos—notably such in a country where veteran writers are readily termed "intellectuals" and often develop circles of adherents—contributed to a journalistic culture in which changes of employ were frequent.

Some of the unrest among senior staffers had to do with Payán's balancing act. Knowing when the paper should be assertive and when it should pull its punches was of course fundamental to his job. When phone calls came from the office of the president or the secretariat of government, a director whose paper partly depended on subsidies had to tread carefully. In 1991, when it exposed vote rigging in gubernatorial elections in San Luis Potosí, *La Jornada* suffered another partial ad boycott. A year later, it was hit with a series of audits: Presumably some in the cabinet, perhaps Salinas himself, felt the paper too critical. So Payán toned down the coverage, which prompted several writers to resign.[37]

To some, Payán was too willing to be deferential. He would advocate placing the president more often on the front page. His paper rarely touched the prickly subjects of political corruption and the crime syndicates. Once, he was furious at a Magú cartoon that satirized the powerful labor leader Fidel Velázquez. The reason: Payán had dined with Velázquez the night before, so now his diplomacy was undercut. As late as 1993, *La Jornada*'s front page still gave far more play to "official agenda setting"—news and photographs of PRI politicians and functionaries—than to the voices of civil society and its concerns: corruption, electoral fraud, state repression, military excesses, drug trafficking.[38]

Concerns among some of the founding members about Payán's autocratic streak rose in 1992, when the director goaded the shareholders' assembly to rewrite the statutes, allowing him to stand as director a third time. This he did against Granados Chapa, in a testy campaign allegedly full of machinations, which helped prompt the latter's exit five months later. Thus, three of the five founder-editors were gone, leaving Payán and his loyal lieutenant, Carmen Lira. Nonetheless, a clear majority were with Payán. During the debate about the statutes, Granados Chapa had given an impassioned speech, warning against *La Jornada* becoming a fiefdom. Payán is not irreplaceable, he told the assembly. "No one is. Not Hubert Beuve-Méry at *Le Monde*, not

Juan Luis Cebrián at *El País*." But in Mexico, with its deep tradition of boss-ism, even in the cultural sphere, continuity of leadership held a compelling appeal. Publisher-editors accumulated political capital that was not easily transferrable, for it rested on carefully nurtured personal relations with elites. As Octavio Paz put it to *La Jornada* culture editor Braulio Peralta, "A newspaper *is* its director."[39]

Some felt Payán knew too little about news, and his interference in the newsroom raised hackles. Years after he quit, Granados Chapa would allege that Payán, lazy and often absent, left him to shoulder much of the work of directing the paper. Payán attended meetings at random, suggesting stories that *La Jornada* had already covered. "He was a politician," recalls Musacchio. "He was not a journalist, he didn't know how to write, he'd omit the accent from his own surname!"[40] Yet Payán used his political instincts and managerial skills to craft a distinctively polemical product and develop a loyal cadre of reporters.

———

By the second half of the Salinas administration, *La Jornada* had cemented its lead as the daily voice of the Left. *Unomásuno* had continued to shrivel, having suffered another flight of talent after the ouster of Becerra; its circulation was reliably estimated at 8,000, compared with 45,000 for *La Jornada*. On the other hand, with the precariousness of its business model, the paper's finances were still rocky. Discontent with Payán and an editorial line that was increasingly pro–Party of the Democratic Revolution (PRD) prompted talented writers to leave, especially for the more economically independent *El Financiero*.[41]

Then Chiapas blew up.

Subcommander Marcos proved himself a great seducer of the left-wing press, and *La Jornada* proved his most willing lover—to the benefit of both. It was not, however, love at first sight. On January 1, 1994, when word first reached the capital of the Zapatista rebellion, Payán assigned a front-page editorial that condemned it. (The next day, several veteran leftists convinced him that, despite the paper's pacifistic line, this position was plain wrong for *La Jornada*.) In his presidential memoir, Salinas recalls that he was visited at Los Pinos that January 1 by two senior media figures, who both advised him to crush the Zapatistas. According to a well-placed source, one of them was Emilio Azcárraga Milmo, the notoriously right-wing TV mogul. The other was Payán.[42]

Nonetheless, *La Jornada* became the first to profile Marcos at length and the prime outlet for his lengthy communiqués from the jungle (*Proceso* and *El Financiero* also received them but ran excerpts).[43] Payán assigned fifteen writers and photographers to cover the rebellion and its repercussions in Mexico

City. Suddenly the paper was essential reading for anyone, leftist or not, wanting to know what was going on in Mexico's southernmost state and to hear from the mysterious Marcos, who refused to speak to Televisa. Circulation roughly tripled; on the day it reported the government's ceasefire, January 13, the paper announced a print run of 164,000. By estimated readership, which depends not only on sales but also on how much each issue is passed around, *La Jornada* that year rose from being the capital's fifth most popular "serious" newspaper to occupying the number two spot, after *El Universal*.[44]

Blanche Petrich, another of the tough female reporters at *La Jornada*, was key to the paper's positioning as the go-to source on Chiapas. Of Czech and elite Yucatecan descent, Petrich was instantly recognizable among Mexican reporters: fair, slight, and petite, a pronounced limp (the result of childhood polio), and a no-nonsense demeanor. She had entered *Unomásuno* at the recommendation of Granados Chapa and impressed her editors with her reports on the civil war in El Salvador; she flew down at her own expense after requesting vacation leave. According to a secret service report, she then became a liaison with various Central American guerrilla groups.[45] Petrich went on to cover conflicts in Nicaragua and Guatemala, always with a passion for the views of the marginalized and oppressed. So when Subcommander Marcos first granted a full interview, he chose Petrich.

It was a tough assignment. "Getting to see Marcos was a painful exercise in journalistic tenacity," wrote Andrés Oppenheimer, who scored an interview after Petrich and noted that most reporters who sought Marcos failed. He added, "You had to spend days driving through the jungle, leaving messages for the guerrilla leader at various rebel checkpoints." Petrich's coup—datelined "Lacandón jungle, Chiapas," consisting of four days of interviews, and amounting to seven full pages of text—was widely hailed.[46]

The paper's peerless coverage of the Zapatistas—albeit one-sided to the point of reverence—benefited from a team of journalists committed to telling the rebels' story, many being experienced reporters in their thirties or forties.[47] Greatest enthusiast of all was Hermann Bellinghausen, a doctor and a poet as well as a Chiapas correspondent, who would continue to write about (some say propagandize for) the Zapatistas for many years. The following year Bellinghausen won the National Journalism Prize in the feature category, but he shunned it at the prospect of receiving the award from the hands of President Ernesto Zedillo, deeming him a repressor of Indigenous Chiapans.[48] The paper's team of photographers produced outstanding work, much of it dignifying Indigenous men and women by showing them armed and resolute, taking their destiny into their own hands.[49]

The tricky art of political juggling reached a zenith in that year's electoral season. Despite its sympathies for second-time presidential candidate Cárdenas, now of the PRD (a successor to the FDN), *La Jornada* took a reported $800,000 from the PRI. This paid for front-page *gacetillas* about candidate Zedillo at his campaigns stops (just as in *Excélsior* and *El Universal*). Payán next accepted a publicity buy from Roberto Madrazo, the infamously big-spending PRI candidate for the governorship of Tabasco that November, despite *La Jornada*'s loyalty to a rival candidate, Andrés Manuel López Obrador of the PRD. Payán then squared the circle by running a summer-long series of pro-Madrazo *gacetillas* in parallel with articles from the Tabasco correspondent that sympathized with López Obrador.[50]

Much as it was at *Reforma*, 1994 was a triumphant year at *La Jornada*. Here were two ideologically distinct media, united in their commitment to civic journalism, to holding the PRI to account, and to Mexico's democratization.[51] The difference was that for *Reforma* the year was a launchpad, from which it would climb past all other papers in reliability and fix itself as the nation's newspaper of record. For *La Jornada*, the year, or rather the first six months, was its peak. Never again would its influence be so strong.

Which is not to say that, as the excitement of 1994 abated, it lost ambition and vision. In February 1995, *La Jornada* became the first Mexican paper to enter the internet, with a website hosted by the National Autonomous University of Mexico (UNAM).[52] In February 1996, a group of current and former *La Jornada* cartoonists, led by the veteran Rius (Eduardo del Río) and backed by the publishing house Grijalbo, launched the satirical magazine *El Chamuco*. The Rius-drawn cover of issue 1 depicted President Zedillo as Frankenstein's Monster, robotically promising an end to Mexico's new economic crisis. *El Chamuco* became an instant and long-running success.[53]

And the biggest political scandal of 1996 owed much to Payán's support for civic journalism in the provinces. The story was the "Aguas Blancas affair": the fall of the hard-line governor Rubén Figueroa of Guerrero, likely instigator of a massacre of seventeen peasant farmers and proven accomplice in a cover-up. While it was Televisa's broadcast of footage of the crime—state police firing on peasant families crammed into two open-back trucks—that pushed Zedillo finally to oust his ally Figueroa in March, pressure had been mounting since the massacre the previous June. Crucial to that pressure was the investigative work of the husband-and-wife team of Juan Angulo and Maribel Gutiérrez, founders of the Acapulco daily *El Sur*. They had set it up in 1993 with backing from *La Jornada*.[54]

Amid the gray recession of 1995–96, with the country in the hands of a capable but gray technocrat who disdained the press, perhaps it was no surprise that Payán, like Scherer, decided to step down. Perhaps by then the PRI was sufficiently weakened that both felt their work was done. Certainly, the demand for *La Jornada* was shrinking, average sales tumbling by nearly half to 57,000.[55]

But for Payán there was another motive. In 1997, as a reward for loyalty to Cárdenas and the PRD, he was handed a seat in Mexico's senate. He did not even have to compete for it, because under a system of partly proportional representation, the PRD gained eight new seats that it could distribute among party veterans and pals.[56] It was a moment of triumph for Payán, political as well as personal, because the PRI lost control of the lower-house Chamber of Deputies for the first time, largely due to district victories by the PRD, and because Cárdenas gained election as Mexico City's first non-PRI mayor. As a popular tub-thumper for Cárdenas, *La Jornada* could claim to have played a role in the victory. However, much more influential—as audience analysis by Chappell Lawson has demonstrated—was the unprecedented decision of Televisa, under new CEO Emilio Azcárraga Jean, the son of El Tigre, to afford equal screen time and fair treatment to each candidate.[57]

The year marked a milestone for Mexican democratization, and so it did to a lesser extent for federal relations with the press. Once Salinas's spokesman Carreño had halted payoffs on the presidential beat and the federal ministries followed suit, some reporters found Congress and state governments more to their liking. At the Chamber of Deputies, *embute* and *chayote* were still to be had from parties and individual politicians. Using peer estimates, Lawson found that the portion of reporters still accepting bribes ranged from 8 percent at *Reforma* and 15 percent at *El Economista* to 90 percent at *El Día*, *Excélsior*, *El Heraldo*, *El Nacional*, *El Sol*, and *Unomásuno*. (The estimate for *La Jornada* was 28 percent.) When US freelancer Sam Quinones began to cover congressional debates, he was astounded at the chumminess with the press: Reporters and photographers mingled with lawmakers even when the chamber was in session. Some would sit in representatives' vacant seats. (Occasionally doing so himself, Quinones guessed that if he raised his hand during a vote, he might well be counted.) This free-for-all came to an end after the PRI lost its majority. Porfirio Muñoz Ledo of the PRD, as the chamber's new president, corralled the press into a "pen" at the rear. Following the austere tone set by Zedillo, cash for correspondents declined too, although never entirely.[58]

Carmen Lira and the Closing of the Ranks

Payán passed the baton in 1996 to his fifty-three-year-old adjutant, Carmen Lira Saade. Born to a Mexican father and Lebanese mother, she had cut her teeth at *Novedades* and then joined the fledgling *Unomásuno*, where she had drawn close to Payán. Already a respected reporter on worker and peasant activism, she burnished her a reputation as a social crusader with sympathetic coverage of the 1979 Sandinista revolution in Nicaragua. Like Payán, her leanings were communist and she believed in journalism that explicitly served left-wing causes. The secret service claimed she belonged to the "Maoist current" of the PSUM and—somewhat like her friend Blanche Petrich—helped channel money, arms, and intelligence to clandestine leftist groups in El Salvador, Honduras, and Guatemala. As of 1980, she had mostly held editing positions, although during the early years of La Jornada she did a brief stint as Washington correspondent (presumably a plum from Payán, for her English was rudimentary; she was said to follow events by watching Spanish-language newscasts). She was also a frequent and enthusiastic traveler to communist Cuba. As an editor, Lira earned respect, for she defended reporters and columnists when politicians called to complain.[59]

Lira's elevation to editor in chief might seem a progressive move, putting a woman in charge of a major national newspaper for the first time. In fact it was an old-school coronation. Thanks to Payán's machinations, there was no rival candidate. And just as the 1992 election had cost the paper one of its most respected cofounders, Granados Chapa, so departed another in 1996, Sergio Aguayo.

Mexico's long tradition of literary figures and leading professors (or "intellectuals") doubling as newspaper columnists had begun to evolve in the 1980s via an influx of academics with doctorates, often earned overseas. These included Enrique Krauze and Héctor Aguilar Camín, trained as historians at the prestigious Colegio de México; the Sorbonne-educated Jorge Castañeda; and Aguayo, who got his doctorate at Johns Hopkins University. Except for Krauze, who defined himself as a liberal, each embraced the Left; including Krauze (if only briefly), each wrote for La Jornada. But perhaps no academic at that newspaper or any other would so effectively use the press as a conduit for bringing research before the public as Aguayo.[60]

A member of the Generation of '68, Aguayo was nineteen when the Tlatelolco massacre occurred, and his activism in the Guadalajara student movement meant he twice had to flee the city under threat from paramilitaries or PRI thugs. His studies left him too little time for reporting, so he wrote columns. He went on to contribute to Aguilar Camín's Nexos and Unomásuno, but with the 1984 launch of La Jornada, of which he was a founder-member, and with seven years of teaching at the Colegio de México under his belt, he started a weekly column. That same year, he founded the citizen-led Mexican Academy for Human Rights (six years before the government set up the National Human Rights Commission); with writers Carlos Fuentes and Elena Poniatowska on its board, it probed violations and worked to educate the public about their rights.

For a dozen years at La Jornada, Aguayo used his column, and sometimes the news pages, to publicize his research into international affairs and his social activism. Like Granados Chapa, another inspiration, his aim was always to write so that anyone could understand his argument. His column was syndicated to regional papers (via an agency set up by his wife, Eugenia Mazzucato), which allowed him enough revenue to hire research assistants. The exposure turned him into one of Mexico's most prominent intellectuals, while his cutting-edge writings enriched *La Jornada*'s reputation as the main forum for civic concerns.

In 1991, he organized 330 observers for the gubernatorial election in San Luis Potosí. Their accounts of fraud by the PRI, reported in *La Jornada* and Aguayo's columns, kick-started a movement that pushed Salinas to force the victor to step down, just two weeks after his inauguration, and to arrange a fresh election. And in early 1994 he leveraged that experience into founding Civic Alliance, a network of electoral observer groups, again announced in the paper. In that summer's presidential election, 470 of them monitored polling stations all across the country.[61]

In championing effective suffrage, Aguayo sometimes found himself criticized for refusing to take sides—chiefly, that of the left-wing PRD, with which he sympathized and which most often met defeat by fraud. But he was convinced that his advocacy would only prosper by staying nonpartisan. A similar idealism would lead to his quitting *La Jornada*.

In August 1995, before leaving for a visiting-semester gig at the New School for Social Research in New York, Aguayo conferred with Carlos Payán. He admired Payán for protecting the paper from threats, such as from the PRI-affiliated news vendors' union and hard-liners like the former secretary of government Fernando Gutiérrez Barrios, and for backing him when he penned controversial pieces. He had voted for Payán, not Granados Chapa, in 1992. Now, he said, he was thinking of standing for the editorship. Payán said that was fine. On his return in January, however, when he told Payán he would declare his candidacy, the editor objected. He had already "consulted" the staff and there was "a consensus" that, when he was to retire, Carmen Lira should take over.

"I was surprised," Aguayo recalls, "because I thought that there'd be a democratic process, *La Jornada* being a leftwing paper. Perhaps I was naïve."[62]

The ironies were multiple. The daily that had done most to champion democracy was having difficulty practicing it. A writer who was emerging as one of Mexico's foremost clean-elections activists was the victim of a rigged vote. The editor who had wrought a platform for the PRD was lining up his successor like a bigwig from the PRI. Aguayo did not object to Lira per se, for they were friends, she had defended his work, and he thought she would make a good editor. But after several exchanges with Payán, he began to feel himself a persona non grata at the paper, and so he sought options elsewhere.

That September, he met with Lira and presented his resignation, along with a column detailing his reasons. To her credit, she published it.[63]

Aguayo then took his services to *Reforma*, and his star continued to rise. He would found another nongovernmental organization, a think-tank called Fundar, set up with aid from the Ford Foundation and dedicated to democratically strengthening Mexico's institutions, including the press.[64] He would write influential, book-length exposés of the state's historical use of the army and secret services to suppress dissent.[65] He would receive invitations for visiting professorships at the University of Chicago, Berkeley, and Harvard.

Lira, meanwhile, inherited the tricky task of halting the slide in *La Jornada* readership and revenues. The second of these problems was likely solved in part via the friendship of Mexico City's leftist mayors. It may be assumed that under Cárdenas of the PRD, who took office in December 1997, city hall spent more than it had previously on publicizing its work in the paper. That bump was likely modest at first, for Cárdenas had little interest in self-promotion. But his chosen successor, the showy Rosario Robles, who served from September 1999 to December 2000, spent lavishly on the media.[66]

Lira did innovate somewhat. Two months into her tenure, *La Jornada* launched a monthly supplement called "Letter S," after the Spanish words for "health," "sexuality," and "AIDS" (*salud, sexualidad, SIDA*). Its aim was to provide reliable advice about sexual health and to sensitize readers to nonjudgmental views and language, at a time when discussion of AIDS and other sexually transmitted diseases was governed by phobias and misinformation. The following year, in November 1997, the paper founded a Sunday political supplement called "Masiosare," jokingly named for an antiquated phrase in the national anthem. Carlos Monsiváis featured as a regular contributor, and its editor was Arturo Cano, whom Monsiváis had recruited from *Reforma*.[67]

"Masiosare" paid special attention to Chiapas, long after the rest of the capital's dailies lost interest: the festering sores left by the Zapatistas' uprising, the Zedillo government's attempts to marginalize their movement by channeling aid to non-Zapatista communities, and its alleged arming of paramilitaries. On December 14, Cano dedicated the magazine to the rising threat of bloodshed in the county of Chenhaló, a Zapatista bastion. It was a prescient call. Just eight days later, the Chenhaló village of Acteal witnessed the worst atrocity of the Zedillo era: a massacre by paramilitaries, reportedly backed by local members of the PRI, of forty-five Indigenous people attending a prayer meeting. The supplement's coverage of the massacre helped to preserve *La Jornada*'s status as the go-to source for discussion of Chiapas. So did Lira's promotion to opinion editor of Luis Hernández Navarro, a passionate defender of Indigenous causes.[68]

For Cano, the editorship of "Masiosare" was a personal vindication. During his four-year spell at *Reforma*, where he had arrived with a dozen years of experience, he had come to feel that opportunities for personal advancement were limited. He recalls that he chafed against the prejudices that some of the editors from Monterrey showed toward their Mexico City underlings, adding "and all the more so because of the color of my skin."[69]

Under Lira, *La Jornada* scrutinized the federal government more consistently. Reporters and cartoonists found that whereas Payán, anxious to protect his political friendships, had often encouraged them to tread softly, under Lira they were freer to do as they saw fit. Analyzing its reporting in March 2000, Sallie Hughes gave *La Jornada* an "autonomy score" equal to that of *Reforma* and well ahead of *El Universal*'s. Lira's innovations, which included replacing most of the section heads, succeeded during her first term in halting the paper's slide in cover sales. Its finances seemed healthy.[70]

After a modest election-year bump in 2000, however, the decline would resume, daily sales sloping to 43,000 in the first semester of 2002. Many moderate readers were switching to *Milenio*, a new paper with a pluralistic perspective. *La Jornada* founder-member Patricia Vega, aghast at what she felt to be worsening financial mismanagement and the high salaries of senior personnel, wrote a report (including the depressing sales figures), which some one leaked to *Etcétera*.[71]

La Jornada shared a major problem with *Proceso*. Readers could now find critical or civic-minded reporting at multiple alternatives: *Reforma*, *El Universal*, and then *Milenio*. Another issue, impinging on staff morale by her second term, was Lira's increasingly aloof and autocratic style, quite in contrast to Payán: a near-total absence from the newsroom, her insistence that reporters wishing to see her make an appointment, her refusal to meet with the employees' union, and a waiving of the journalist entrance exam to applicants favored by her clique. This inner circle of senior staff, prominent among them the Basque-born Josetxo Zaldua, was dubbed "the Court of Polanco"; the term referred to the ritzy neighborhood in which the paper was briefly based, but it also alluded to their high incomes.[72]

Still another problem was Lira's ideology, more dogmatic than Payán's and less tolerant of pluralism. Lira had set her tone in a speech during the 1996 handover, swearing to ensure that *La Jornada* supported social causes "from the trenches." Her paper lionized the student radicals who shut down the UNAM for about year as of February 1999, in an ever more unpopular dispute over tuition fees; that is, until near the end, when the daily turned against them, for its political and economic relationship with the rector was ultimately more important.[73] Egged on by senior editor Zaldua, the paper also championed the Basque separatist terrorist group ETA (Euskadi Ta Askatasuna).

La Jornada's commitment to ETA illustrated the paper's failure to move with the times—a failure also seen in its unflagging support for Cuba, even as an end to Russian subsidies laid bare its chronic economic mismanagement, and in its equally unflagging anti-Americanism. ETA's historic bombing and shooting campaign against Spanish government and civilian targets, which would take more than 800 lives and continue until 2010, was increasingly out of step with other separatist organizations. The Palestine Liberation Organization renounced violence in 1993, and the Irish Republican Army did so in 1997. The phenomenon of Islamist attacks, which reached a new level of transnational terror with the bombing of the US embassy in Nairobi in 1998, killing 200 Kenyans and 12 Americans, generated ever-greater revulsion toward terrorism among the global public—but not enough within the La Jornada editorial board for it to cease supporting ETA. As former staffer Ricardo Cayuela noted, this trend included the paper's refusal to call ETA a terrorist organization, its avoidance of reporting ETA attacks as the group's responsibility, and its sympathetic running of ETA pronouncements. One series of features, penned by Blanche Petrich on assignment in Spain, all but ignored Basque parties and civic groups that differed with ETA, said nothing of nonseparatist Basques, and forgot about the victims of ETA bombings.[74]

Lira's growing despotism—refusing to reveal accounts to stakeholders, firing people without telling them why—and leftist dogmatism contributed to a serious flight of talent during her first two terms. Centrist and center-left columnists departed, as did veteran staff. Ironically, much of the brain drain was female: veteran news editor Dolores Cordero ("For her, everything is black and white," she said of Lira); senior cultural reporter Adriana Malvido; South America expert Ximena Ortúzar; arts writer Patricia Vega; and Sara Lovera, the specialist in labor and women's rights.[75]

Carlos Monsiváis was arguably Mexico's most popular public intellectual and certainly La Jornada's premier regular contributor. His column, "A Toast to My Mother, Bohemians," synthesized current events and lampooned public figures with a signature ironic style. Without explanation, it disappeared in June 2001. Monsiváis told friends that he could no longer abide two things. One was Lira and Zaldua's backing of the terrorists of ETA, a motive that also prompted the exit of columnist Jean Meyer, a distinguished historian. The other was their unflagging support for Fidel Castro, in spite of Cuba's persecution of gay people. Monsiváis and Meyer both jumped ship to El Universal.[76]

Yet La Jornada remained a dream job for young leftists. A reporter hired in 1999 recalls being chosen from a hundred applicants. She adds, "I was treated as a star among my friends and welcomed with open arms when interviewing academics at the UNAM."[77]

The paper's traditions of support for the PRD and the Zapatistas afforded it a unique shine. So did its anti-Americanism. This trait gained renewed prominence after George W. Bush responded to the 9/11 attacks of 2001—which cartoonist El Fisgón sketched as payback for Hiroshima and Vietnam—by declaring a "war on terror" and invading Afghanistan and then Iraq. In 2002, a Pew poll found that 64 percent of Mexicans had a favorable opinion of the United States and just 25 percent held an unfavorable opinion. Still, the paper's displays of calculated gringophobia retained an appeal for a substantial leftist-nationalist minority.[78]

Rather like the Cuban dictator she admired, Lira became leader for life. When those whom she fired and other departed employees sold their shares in the holding company and thus surrendered their vote, she made sure they were bought by loyalists. Her mandate would be renewed every four years, without opposition, even as she became ever less visible to the rank and file. In 2020, in her late seventies, she would be renewed for a seventh term, but this time with a twist: The paper no longer even bothered to announce it.[79]

Adiós . . . ¡al PRI!

The midterm elections of 1997 proved a false dawn for Mexico's Left. In 2000, it was the right-of-center National Action Party (PAN), led by Vicente Fox, that succeeded in dislodging the PRI from the presidency after seventy-one uninterrupted years. As with the midterms, the stage had been set by President Zedillo's political reforms of 1996, which finally wrested elections from governmental interference by granting the Federal Electoral Institute (a creation of Salinas's) full autonomy.[80] And again, as in 1997, it was television rather than the press that made the most immediate difference.

Televisa, while still partial to the PRI, had never offered as fair a coverage of a general election, in both airtime per candidate and tone. "Democracy is a great client for television," said its young CEO, Azcárraga Jean. Of course, he was thinking mostly of ad spend, and indeed the parties committed an aggregate 54 percent of their campaign budgets to media, most of that on TV spots, as opposed to 25 percent in 1994. Mexico had never had as televisual a candidate as the PAN's tall and imposing, coarse and jocular, former Coca-Cola executive Fox. His media-savvy team—including advisers hired from Procter & Gamble and others flown in from Texas—knew exactly how to exploit Televisa's programming to the benefit of their "product"; that is, they knew how to market him, elicit positive coverage, and win TV debates. On the latter occasions, Fox got the better of the telegenic Francisco Labastida of the PRI and completely outshone the PRD's dour Cárdenas (running for the third and last time). The Fox team were also masters of memorable campaign slogans, built into provocative TV ads.[81]

Fox's victory also stemmed from a generational rightward shift, in which television, radio, and print media all played a role. In 1997, many voters had punished the PRI for two and a half years of economic turmoil by opting for the Left. Since then, the economy had recovered and many more were persuaded that free-market capitalism, the underlying ideology that the PRI and PAN shared, was on balance good for them and good for Mexico—while the PAN was better than the PRI, as it was felt to be less corrupt. (The free market had clearly *not* been good for the rural poor, but millions of them had responded to the North American Free Trade Agreement's damage to their communities by migrating to the United States, thus removing themselves from the electorate.) As in 1994, the PRI and PAN reaped an overwhelming majority of the vote, a combined 79 percent, against 17 percent for the PRD. There had recently been an economic crisis, but so had there been, more lengthily and fundamentally, a free trade–driven explosion of goods and services; an improvement in the quality of those goods and services; better-paid jobs, often with foreign firms, in manufacturing, retail, entertainment, and tourism; a 42 percent expansion of students in higher education; and a decline in the anti-Americanism that had long been a recruiting tool of the Left. As international reporters observed, Mexico—or at least the majority that lived in cities—seemed to be turning, albeit haltingly, into a middle-class nation.[82]

In tandem with the rise of neoliberalism on the economic plane, a delight in freedom to choose had grown in the public sphere. Take a trip to one of Mexico's new shopping malls and there were all kinds of US franchise restaurants and European clothing stores to visit. Turn on the television and Televisa's four networks were no longer the only option. Go to the movies and the movie palaces of yore had been replaced with multiplexes of up to ten screens. There the offerings were changing: Early 2000 saw the box-office success of the farce *Herod's Law*, the first film to criticize the PRI. Sacred cows were keeling over in bookstores as well. In 1999, former *El Financiero* reporter José Martínez published *The Lessons of the Teacher*, a bestselling critical biography of Carlos Hank González, the great plutocrat of the PRI. And in early 2000, former *El Universal* reporter Claudia Fernández released *El Tigre*, a coauthored portrait of media mogul and self-styled "soldier of the PRI" Emilio Azcárraga Milmo; this was Mexico's first warts-and-all business biography and another bestseller.[83] Altogether, the effervescence of choice, coupled with unprecedented defiance of the ruling party, had a synergistic impact on the July 2000 election. One no longer had to consume as one always consumed. One no longer had to vote for the PRI.

Despite the predominant role of television in the Fox campaign, over the previous six years it had been the print media, much more than Televisa, the PAN, or Fox himself, that had prepared the country for electoral democracy. It was civic-minded newspapers and magazines that had chipped away at the façade of the PRI, their exposés and spurring of public scandals showing it to be a party that too often failed to practice what it preached. It was civic media, along with allies in civil society, that ever more closely monitored elections and reported fraud. The independent press had proliferated during the 1990s.[84] What resulted was a quickening erosion of the PRI's aura of invincibility.

When Televisa aired footage of the Aguas Blancas massacre in February 1996, the scandal gained its context from the investigative work of *El Sur*. When, in the first presidential debate of 2000, Fox told Labastida, "I may be able to get rid of my rudeness. But you [of the PRI] will never be able to get rid of your sneakiness, your incompetence at governing, and your corruption," the charges resonated with the millions who tuned in, thanks to several decades of exposés in the gradually mushrooming watchdog press. Although the combined readership of such media remained small relative to Mexico's population, those exposés had gained a wider public via commentary on talk radio.[85]

Both reflecting the optimistic zeitgeist and stoking it, conservative and centrist media were ascendant. By the late 1990s, *Reforma*, pluralistic in its opinion pages but subtly sympathetic to the PAN, had become Mexico City's most influential paper, while its elder sister *El Norte* dominated Monterrey and younger siblings *Palabra* and *Mural* made inroads in Saltillo and Guadalajara. Alejandro Junco's company also launched an immediately successful capital city tabloid, *Metro*, in 1997. Number two paper *El Universal*, despite the hiring of leftist columnists, retained a center-right tone.

La Crónica de Hoy (usually referred to as *Crónica*) was launched in 1996 by real estate mogul and public contractor Jorge Kahwagi and represented the neoliberal wing of the PRI. It was rumored to count Carlos Salinas among its backers, although according to Raúl Trejo Delabre, a founding columnist, its business model largely relied on government advertising. Its editor, the Chilean-born Pablo Hiriart, had come under Salinas's spell when covering his presidential campaign, and its columnists included prominent Salinas sympathizers, such as his former press chief, José Carreño Carlón. The involvement of such personages, along with two board members close to the Salinas family, fueled the rumors about the former president, which Hiriart strenuously denied.[86]

The paper made a mission of scrutinizing the leftists who governed Mexico City as of 1997. *Crónica* revealed that Cuauhtémoc Cárdenas's senior investigative police chief had several times been persuasively accused of torture; he had to resign. It discovered that Leche Betty, a brand of low-cost milk devised by two PRD bigwigs for sale to poor constituents, was contaminated by feces.[87]

Milenio, which debuted with the new millennium and quickly became popular, also leaned center right. It preferred the PRI to the PAN, but it wholly rejected Cárdenas.[88]

On television, TV Azteca's nightly newscast *Hechos*, which was gaining ground on Televisa's, was harshly critical of Cárdenas as Mexico City mayor. During the 1997 campaign, monitors had detected quite an anti-PRD bias on *Hechos*. In 1999, TV Azteca relentlessly blamed "soft on crime" Cárdenas for the broad-daylight killing of a popular gameshow host, Paco Stanley, a gangland hit soon linked to Stanley's cocaine habit and role as dealer to Azteca colleagues.[89]

Meanwhile on the left, there remained few media to back Cárdenas beyond *Proceso*, *La Jornada*, and a few regional papers that *La Jornada* had helped to plant. Their consolation for losing the race to Los Pinos was that the PRD held on to the mayorship of Mexico City. Here, where voters overall leaned leftward and liberal compared with the rest of Mexico, interim mayor Rosario Robles had done well at the job and at touting the PRD's achievements. The victor was Andrés Manuel López Obrador, himself a skillful campaigner. This victory was especially good news for *La Jornada*: The paper had fully endorsed López Obrador. Carmen Lira was godmother to one of his children. Her newspaper, still lacking a self-sustaining business model, could now look forward to six more years of generous ad buys from the mayor's office.[90]

But another eighteen years would pass—including three electoral campaigns—before López Obrador could realize his ambition of reaching the presidency. In the meantime, *La Jornada* would lurch from crisis to crisis. Its axing of its supplements during the Fox era (even, in 2006, the lauded "Masiosare") would be but one early sign of this.[91] For those eighteen years, Lira's paper would largely be limited to a marginal role in the national conversation, until President López Obrador rescued it from its agony by buoying it with federal cash and making it his chief channel of written communication with his base.

Chapter 7

Under President Fox

The Promise and Problems of Openness

> Leaving aside Fox's good and bad points, it's undeniable that . . . Mexico's media and journalists could begin to do and tell with much greater liberty than during the years of the PRI's hegemony.
>
> —Adrián López, editor, *Noroeste*

"Towel-Gate" and the *Milenio* Dream

Anabel Hernández was on a mission. The target in her sights was the spokeswoman and fiancée of the recently sworn-in president, Vicente Fox. This woman was formally Martha María Sahagún Jiménez, but everyone called her Martha. During the previous year's electoral season, as one of Fox's senior aides and his press liaison, Martha had become a household name, for she was attractive and opinionated and clearly gunning to be First Lady.[1] She was also suspected of being a lavish spender who felt herself beyond account, which is why Hernández, a reporter at *Milenio*, was on her trail.[2]

Like many who had covered the 2000 election, Hernández found Martha overly protective of Fox's image and quick to blacklist those she considered unfair. Just like her forebears in the Institutional Revolutionary Party (PRI), Martha would call editors and ask for a troublesome reporter's transfer to another beat. After Hernández published a questioning feature on Martha's remodeling of part of the presidential mansion, Los Pinos, she found her access curtailed. At *Proceso*, María Scherer would have a similar experience later that year, when Martha contrived to exclude her from traveling on the presidential plane. One afternoon, Hernández returned to the *Milenio* newsroom with no Los Pinos story to report, on either the mansion itself or the presidency. Then she recalled the existence of a website, Compranet, on which all federal agencies were obliged to declare their purchases. Perhaps it might offer something of note about Los Pinos . . .

Bingo! Compranet listed all of the items bought on Martha's request. "It looked like a wedding registry, with everything super-expensive," Hernández would recall.

She discussed her find with the paper's top dogs: publisher Federico Arreola, editor in chief Raymundo Riva Palacio, and deputy editor Carlos Marín. Her immediate boss, Marín, dismissed it: Who would be interested in such

In its early years, *Milenio* was known for the first major exposé of the Fox administration and catchy headlines like "*Eat and Leave*, Fox Demands of Fidel [Castro]." Courtesy of *Milenio*.

trivia? But Arreola saw the news value. As Hernández argued, here was evidence that Los Pinos was failing to live up to Fox's pledges of austerity. Altogether, in just the first six months of the administration, Martha had spent some $850,000 of public money in spiffing up the mansion. The story ran as the lead on June 19, 2001, and included a screen shot from Compranet. Arreola cleverly encapsulated the profligacy with the headline, "Presidency Buys Towels at 4,025 Pesos [$400] Apiece."

Unsurprisingly, uproar followed, along with an equally unsurprising popular tag: "towel-gate." To much of the public, the revelation undermined Fox's image as a bringer of change, a task at which he was already struggling due to the obstacle of an opposition-led Congress. To much of the press, the story confirmed suspicions (or sexist-classist prejudices) that Martha was a grasping arriviste; such charges would hound her—with plenty to substantiate them—for the rest of the presidency.[3] For Fox, the scandal hit home, compelling him to fire his personal secretary, whom an official inquiry fingered as responsible for procurement violations involving excessive payments.[4] For *Milenio*, eighteen months after launch, the paper finally had a water-cooler scoop, giving it a boost in its aim to compete with *Reforma*.

As for Anabel Hernández, the story turned her into one of Mexico's best-known reporters and motivated her to specialize in political corruption. It also turned her into a headache, both for Los Pinos and for the man who paid her salary, Pancho González.

Anabel Hernández had always been on a mission.[5] Like Adela Navarro of Tijuana's *Zeta*, she had grown up in a home that read the press religiously, especially *Proceso*. Even as a teen she debated its stories with her father at the lunch table. On a high school exchange in San Francisco she experienced the earthquake of 1989, which tumbled bridges and kept the locals glued to their radios and televisions. She later reminisced, "I realized that being a journalist was a mission, a service to the community."[6] On returning to Mexico, when she told her father of her desired career, he was angry, considering most journalists corrupt. Anabel replied, "I will be a *different* journalist." She took a degree in communications and then joined the founding generation at *Reforma*.

Colleagues recall her as a head-turner: wide-eyed, wide smile, stylishly dressed, a commanding voice. Since she came from a well-to-do family, the city desk sometimes dispatched her to the richer parts of the capital. One of her stories gave voice to a citizens' group representing six neighborhoods, including ritzy Polanco, that opposed plans for an elevated train. Hernández's reporting helped nix the project. A city section lead highlighted apparent ballot rigging ahead of the 1994 election. Another report, foreshadowing a thematic turn she would take ten years later, exposed a police-protected narcotics network in the tough barrio of Tepito, Mexico City's black-market epicenter.[7]

While Hernández found her skills maturing within the competitive ethos of the *Reforma* newsroom, she took a break in 1996 to become a mother. Three years later she joined *Milenio* as it prepared for its launch on January 1, 2000. But the following December, disaster struck. Her father, a successful engineer, was kidnapped. Then the kidnappers killed him. Next, when Anabel and her family sought justice, the police replied that if they wanted an investigation, they would have to pay for it.

Anabel's father, the most important figure in her life, had always told her, "In this world, it's worthwhile being anything except corrupt." Having witnessed malfeasance firsthand, on electoral rolls, in Tepito, and now in the Mexico City police force, she honored her father's memory by devoting herself to exposing corruption wherever it might be found. And the time was right for her. Their investigative prowess honed during the 1990s, Mexico's more critical newspapers would dig into corruption as never before during the Fox years, fixing such work as a staple of civic-minded journalism.[8] Henceforth, presidents, governors, and their administrations would repeatedly be brought to account, the ensuing scandals causing prompt slides in approval ratings, as documented by the country's proliferating polling companies. Such fluctuations in popularity revealed a public much less tolerant of graft than during the golden age of the PRI, when it was typically met with a mix of fatalism and envy.[9]

"Towel-gate" was Hernández's first high-profile exclusive among many, but the rest would not come at *Milenio*. Despite the plaudits she garnered, her relationship with her bosses grew strained. They faced pressure from Los Pinos, first to remove her from the presidential beat, then to remove her altogether. They also fielded hate mail directed at the reporter. At the time, Martha was still popular, and her pending marriage to Fox—scheduled for July 2, the anniversary of his election—struck much of the public as a fairy tale.[10] Disenchanted at the switching of her beat and the spiking of some of her stories, Hernández hung on until the new year and then accepted an offer from *El Universal*.

———

Hernández's employer at *Milenio* was on a mission too. But his was driven less by journalistic ideals than by personal rivalries and political convenience, and in this second motive lay the fundamental reason for Hernández's exit.

Milenio was the brainchild of Francisco Antonio González, better known as Pancho, a son of the late magnate Dionisio González.[11] Despite their high profile in Monterrey, as owners of TV and radio stations across the North, newspapers across the country, and major real estate holdings, precious little is known about the González clan. Their companies are privately held; the family rarely speaks to the press; no investigative journalist, it seems, has ever profiled them. Late in life (he died in 1997) Dionisio told an in-house interviewer, "I am a man who does not like to show off." But what journalists who have met them agree on is that the González family hates the Juncos.

In 1933, a decade after Alejandro Junco's grandfather founded his first newspaper, the seed of what would become Grupo Reforma, Dionisio González bought his first radio station, the seed of Grupo Multimedios. For four decades, the Junco and González businesses prospered locally in parallel, the former in print media, chiefly with *El Norte*, the latter in radio, then television, and later billboards. According to Monterrey media chronicler José Luis Esquivel, "Dionisio had a business plan that was based on toeing the official line." But in some ways Dionisio and the Juncos were similar: Middle-class achievers, devoutly Catholic, and of course they competed for advertisers. The rivalry became more direct when the Luis Echeverría regime and the local governor encouraged Dionisio to undercut Junco's *El Norte* by creating *El Diario de Monterrey*.

By 1990, when Multimedios owned eighteen of Monterrey's thirty-seven radio stations, one of its top two TV stations, a modest movie theater chain, and sundry other businesses, Dionisio had handed management to Pancho. The son inherited Dionisio's expansionist drive and unshowy style. Jorge Zepeda Patterson, who visited him several times in the late 1990s, found him "rather like a gringo," if shorter in stature, with a fair and agreeable face and a straightforward, informal manner, happily perched in his simple office at *El Diario de Monterrey*. At one meeting, Zepeda realized González was not paying attention, distracted by a boxing match on the TV. "Wait a minute," said his host, and he made a phone call. "How much are they paying for the ad on the canvas? . . . What? Don't be an idiot! I can see the ad the whole time!"

Zepeda adds, "Pancho hated that while he had more money, Junco had the better paper. He told me he'd never rest until his was better." Further, if Junco could make a successful assault on Mexico City with *Reforma*, then so could he. Back in 1994 he had hired Arreola, one of Monterrey's leading columnists, to edit *El Diario*. Pancho told him it was his "dream" to launch a national paper. Arreola, who is similarly frank, told him he thought *El Diario* was terrible: poor design, inky text, awful photos. But he agreed to help Pancho realize his goal and advised him that the key to success was respectful criticism of power, as distinct from the sensationalistic tone of *El Norte* and *Reforma*.

Pancho González's dream was not just business but personal. He envied the influence of *Reforma* and perhaps the flattering attention that Junco reaped from *The New York Times* and *Wall Street Journal*; perhaps also he found Junco falling short in practicing the ethical journalism he liked to preach. Junco, meanwhile, resented González for encroaching; he himself had never set a toe in radio or TV. He resented him on personal grounds too: Some years before, *El Diario* had run a tell-all interview with Junco's father, who accused his son of having stolen *El Norte* from him.

As a former senior *Milenio* employee puts it, "Few things motivate Don Pancho more than his hatred for Alejandro Junco. And it's mutual."[12]

The second motive for creating *Milenio* was political. The González family had been growing their portfolio. They built up a northern movie theater chain called MM Cinemas, which owned dozens of multiplexes; they invested in theme parks, hotels, and real estate; they held local franchises for KFC and Pizza Hut; they would later launch a cable news channel and buy a 50 percent stake in the Monterrey Sultans baseball team.[13] The more they expanded, the more political friendships mattered, and not just in Monterrey. A Mexico City newspaper, once it had gained some street cred from several years of investigative coverage, could better curry favor with the federal establishment.

Pancho González set up a beachhead in 1997 with the magazine *Milenio Semanal*, whose design and prose cast a temporary shadow over *Proceso*. Before another year had elapsed, he bought Zepeda's Guadalajara daily *Público*, thereby beating Junco—who entered Mexico's second city with *Mural*—by three months. Grupo Multimedios would surpass Junco's four-city Grupo Reforma in the quantity of papers it published, but despite its promising recruitment of seasoned editors and reporters, it would always lag in prestige and influence. Perhaps this was largely because González hedged his bets from the start. First, the Mexico City paper that became the group's flagship tried to appeal simultaneously to most socioeconomic classes, from lower-middle to upper. Second, it had an estimated start-up budget of $8 million, less than a quarter of what Junco had ploughed into *Reforma*.[14]

The marginalizing of Anabel Hernández after "towel-gate" was a further indication of bets being hedged. An earlier one occurred in April 2000, just as Fox was drawing level with the longtime front-runner, Francisco Labastida of the PRI, in voter preferences. That month, *Milenio*'s in-house pollster, Rafael Giménez, produced data showing Fox taking the lead. Giménez would claim he was then fired.[15] Certainly, Pancho González was hoping for a Labastida victory. Once Fox was in power, he was happy to use the new era of unprecedented press freedoms to his advantage, printing revelations about the First Couple that sold papers. But *Milenio* was a balancing act: Access to Los Pinos had to be maintained.

Two Styles: Raymundo Riva Palacio and Carlos Marín

Mediating between Anabel Hernández and other prying reporters on the one hand and Pancho González on the other were three men who loomed large in Mexican media: Arreola, Marín, and Riva Palacio. Marín, with his stellar reporting career at *Proceso*, was perhaps the best known to the public.[16] Arreola, as González's trusted point man in print media, captained the paper as a business. On the editorial side, however, *Milenio* was Riva Palacio's ship.

Riva Palacio, by the time he joined the paper during its mid-1999 planning, had worked in journalism for a quarter century, across nine media.[17] He had accrued an unparalleled reputation as a creator and editor of investigative reports, a reputation that made him just the second Mexican invited to spend a year at Harvard University's Nieman Foundation for Journalism.[18] *Milenio* was his debut as an editor in chief.

Good journalism in Mexico is very often a matter of connections. Higher social status, being usually proportionate to the extra advantage of fairness of skin, opens doors more readily than in many other countries. And connections ran in Riva Palacio's blood. His patrilineal ancestors arrived from Spain in the eighteenth century as minor nobility, and their descendants allied themselves with liberal causes, which generally put them on the right side of history. Raymundo's ancestors included a number of state governors, and his father was governor of Morelos from 1964 to 1970. Three years after his father stepped down, Raymundo took his first job in journalism.

Connections mattered, but so did a keen eye, limpid prose, analytical acuity, and a gift for languages. After graduating from Mexico's top journalism school, the Carlos Septién, Riva Palacio swiftly passed through the mediocre *El Heraldo* to *El Sol*, which was also mediocre but named him its Washington correspondent. There he switched first to *Proceso* and then to *Unomásuno*. It was at his fifth job, with *Excélsior* for most of the 1980s, where he made his name, on assignment in Central America, Paris, Madrid, and Buenos Aires. And it was at *El Financiero* in the early 1990s, followed by *Reforma* in the mid-1990s, that he developed the two best investigative news teams of the decade. In parallel, he became an authority on the practice (and malpractice) of reporting. Like Marín, he penned a popular manual for students, calling his an "essay for a new journalism." A reporter who studied using both books recalls that Riva Palacio's is "more up-to-date and sophisticated, while Marín's is traditional and genre-based."[19]

Tall and corpulent, bearded and bookish-looking, like a wrestler turned academic, Riva Palacio cut a distinctive presence in the newsroom. He was friendly, generous with his time, less mercurial as an editor than Ramón Alberto Garza at *Reforma* and more attentive to ethical practice. "He would return your copy to you heavily marked up. Each revision was meticulous, checking if you were certain about what you'd written," recalls Rosie Arroyo, who worked under him at *El Financiero*.[20] His weakness, which helped explain his exit from several papers, was his defiant independent mindedness. He liked to do his own thing, whatever the orders from above, and when disagreements arose he would fight his corner to the irritation of his bosses. Now that he himself was editor in chief, having exerted a greater influence than anyone in its editorial design, *Milenio* might prove a happy home, a place he could stay, developing the daily into one of Mexico's very best over the course of many years. In fact, he would edit the paper for fewer than two.

Things started well for Riva Palacio, whose brief covered the whole *Milenio* chain: Mexico City, Monterrey, Guadalajara, Tampico, and Torreón.[21] With a design acquired and updated from Zepeda's *Público*, *Milenio* stood out with its red title, its Berliner format, and the large color photograph that often occupied a third of the front page. Altogether it had the look of a serious but entertaining paper, a direct contrast with the resolutely black-and-white *La Jornada*. Launching on day one of the new millennium gave the paper an extra sense of freshness, as did the early covers. One gave most of the page to a picture of Juan Ramón de la Fuente, rector of the National Autonomous University of Mexico (UNAM), with his head in his hands—instantly evoking the desperate situation at the university, which had been paralyzed by a student blockade for eight months. Others used long headlines to make a provocative statement. "The Valencia Family Cartel Takes Control of the Drug Business in Mexico," claimed one; "[Bishop] Samuel Ruiz Challenged the Vatican and Lost," declared another.[22]

Riva Palacio's team was fairly strong, many of them—to Pancho González's delight, no doubt—fellow disaffected veterans of *Reforma*. An early scoop, penned by Anabel Hernández and María Idalia Gómez in February 2000, printed the order to federal police to enter the UNAM and forcibly end the students' strike, which the paper published just hours before the maneuver happened. Of longer-lasting impact was a report on a State of México political clique—including future president Enrique Peña Nieto. The paper dubbed them *los golden boys*, and the phrase entered the popular lexicon. *Milenio* placed columns by well-known writers throughout the paper, rather than in dedicated pages, betting that in the twenty-first century opinion would draw readers as much as news. Other papers would copy the strategy.[23]

Milenio was well received by students, Riva Palacio and other staffers remember. It was more manageable than the bulky broadsheets *Reforma* and *El Universal*, with their multiple sections. It was more palatable than *La Jornada* to many of the UNAM students who had tired of a strike that had effectively set back their education a year, and of which the left-wing daily had been a supporter. *Milenio* was also priced a peso cheaper. *La Jornada* lost more than a quarter of its readership between 2000 and 2002, and defection to *Milenio* was a factor.[24] But it was perhaps not the main factor, for the paper was hardly left wing. Owing in part to the influence of the increasingly conservative Marín, when Subcommander Marcos and a cohort of Indigenous Zapatistas undertook a march from Chiapas to the capital in 2001, coverage in *Milenio* was negative.[25] At any rate, Riva Palacio claims that by its second year, daily circulation peaked at 70,000, placing it third in the capital's nontabloid market.[26]

Yet Riva Palacio did not get along well with Arreola—his superior, who resented his "lack of respect"—nor with Marín, his lieutenant. There were shouting matches in the newsroom.[27] And he soon felt the wrath of Marta (as Martha rewrote her name following her marriage to Fox; she deemed the new spelling "more biblical").[28] Popular rumor held that Riva Palacio took the fall for the "towel-gate" scoop. But he says the bone of contention was a new investigation, which he was directing, involving Marta's sons by her first marriage, Manuel and Jorge Alberto Bribiesca. The Bribiesca brothers seemed to be profiting from their links to Fox by peddling influence to businesses in Guanajuato state. Before anything appeared in print, says Riva Palacio, Marta summoned Pancho González to Los Pinos. Rather than firing his editor altogether, Pancho offered him a well-paid job representing his interests overseas. Of course, that did not interest Riva Palacio, so he took a settlement and departed in October 2001. A number of reporters quit in sympathy, and *Milenio* lost its investigative edge.[29]

In spring 2005, Arreola too would leave under political duress. Although something of a libertarian, he found himself siding with Andrés Manuel López Obrador, the left-wing mayor of Mexico City, in a mounting confrontation with Fox. The chief executive seemed bent on nixing the mayor's run for the presidency in 2006, betting on the legal ploy of a *desafuero*: having Congress remove his immunity from prosecution so he could be tried for abuse of office. Arreola saw this as an injustice, far out of proportion to the misdemeanor that López Obrador had committed. Arreola defended the mayor in the pages of *Milenio*. To Daniel Moreno, who arrived in 2003 as deputy editor, Arreola's partiality to López Obrador had been a problem for some time, acting as a brake on inquisitive coverage of the mayor's office. Things came to a head over an exclusive on March 28 claiming that Santiago Creel, Fox's secretary of government, had offered PRI bigwig Roberto Madrazo a series of political favors in exchange for a congressional bloc vote in support of the legal move of the National Action Party (PAN) against López Obrador.[30]

"Change your editorial line or things are going to go badly for you," Creel told Pancho González in response, so Arreola alleges. Arreola adds that Pancho resisted the powerful minister's threat. *Milenio*'s coverage of the *desafuero*, which dominated page 1 during April, continued broadly to sympathize with López Obrador. But on May 2, half the front page was given over to a letter of resignation by Arreola and a reply from González. Since he could tell that his employer was under great pressure from Los Pinos, Arreola had opted to quit and take a handsome payment. Then he joined López Obrador's nascent campaign for president.[31]

The departures of Riva Palacio and Arreola left Carlos Marín presiding over the *Milenio* chain. Thwarted in his desire to direct *Proceso*, Marín was finally lord of a periodical, and one with close to national reach. Soon *Milenio* shifted its headquarters downtown, next to the building of the late, unlamented *Novedades*.[32] Its relocation to the same vicinity as *El Universal* and *Excélsior* seemed to be a statement of intent.

But how would *Milenio* fare under the man whom Julio Scherer had passed over? The man whom Riva Palacio had brought in as his deputy, only to find out, after his departure, that he had been scheming against him? Could Marín revive a paper that, following a strong start, had sunk far back behind *La Jornada* in popularity?[33]

Marín, like Riva Palacio, was a graduate of the Carlos Septién journalism school, an author of a popular textbook, and a part-time teacher at the Iberoamerican University. There the similarities ended. Hailing from a middle-class home in Puebla, he lacked Riva Palacio's metropolitan-elite attitude and aspect; indeed, he was shorter and darker than most Mexican editors in chief. To some, it seemed he tried to compensate by dressing immaculately in suit and tie; Riva Palacio preferred a zip-up jacket. Seven years older than Riva Palacio, Marín had participated in the 1968 student movement and forged his career at left-wing media: *El Día*, Scherer's *Excélsior*, and *Proceso*. Marín's newsroom style was *buena onda*—talkative and humorous—whereas Riva Palacio alternated between avuncular, severe, and withdrawn. Marín lived modestly, for many years in a small apartment a stone's throw from *Proceso*, and he did not seem to colleagues to aspire to wealth. But his aspirations to prominence and power, as Scherer had once noted, were obvious.[34]

What followed, *Milenio* insiders and others mostly concur, was gradual journalistic decay and conservatism in all senses. Half of the problem owed to Pancho González: insufficient investment. Daniel Moreno, deputy editor for three years, found he had too few journalists to work with. He recalls, "It became a newspaper that merely registered the news, ceasing to win scoops, getting by on Marín's creativity and its columnists."[35] The other half of the problem was insufficient edginess. Whereas *Milenio* had been moderately critical of Fox, especially his *desafuero* machinations, under Marín the paper made a U-turn. On May 8, 2005, ten days after Fox dropped his persecution of López Obrador (having realized the affair was costing him politically), the paper led with "Fox: The PAN Will Win the Presidency in 2006." There was a photo of the president in full rally mode, along with the pull quote, "We don't want trickery or populism," in allusion to López Obrador.[36] In Arreola's view, the shift was largely Marín's doing—albeit with Pancho González's support—for he saw that the editor was cozying up to Fox, Marta, and Creel. Arreola adds, "He would tell his jokes, and politicians easily took to him."[37]

His unrelenting levity was not to everyone's taste. At one editorial meeting, Marín was upset that *Milenio* had been beaten to a business story. So he stood up, summoned the editor responsible, a woman, to his side of the table. Then he took off his belt and mimed giving her a beating. "He did things like this all the time," says another editor who was present. "Carlos disguises his sexism with humor."[38]

As well as Fox, Marín would support the two presidents who followed, while remaining hostile to their persistent rival: López Obrador. When officials protested a story in the paper, Marín would sometimes intervene to print the government's version; when they were rocked by scoops in other media, he would sometimes discredit the authors. He took a shine to members of the business elite, including Carlos Slim. It seemed to his peers that, in contrast to his former mentor Scherer, Marín subjugated his renowned reportorial instincts to his ambitions to hobnob with the powerful; he yearned to be famous. Above all, this elicited an old-school deference to the presidency, which of course suited Pancho González. By eight years or so into its nationwide project, with the newspaper business starting to shrink, the *Milenio* chain found it needed the crutch of federal advertising, just as the presidency was reverting to spending great sums on it.[39]

As *Milenio* succumbed to reportorial blandness, it became little more than a vehicle for big-name opinion columns—foremost among them, Marín's. In his op-eds, sometimes using salty language, the editor showed himself dogmatic, frequently outraged, keen to criticize other writers, and anxious to show off his learning. The latter tone was set in his very first effort, back at *Milenio Semanal* in 1999, which discussed global and national politics through the lens of philosopher György Lukács. On most weekdays as of 2006, his column, now short and spiky, would run on the front page.[40]

After the 2008 debut of Milenio Television, a digital news channel with Ciro Gómez Leyva as chief anchor, the *Milenio* chain seemed to lose importance. This was ironic because by then it counted an impressive fifteen dailies. But the chain was increasingly a money-loser.[41] Even Marín showed split loyalties: with a nightly interview show on the TV channel, he tried to reinvent himself as Mexico's Larry King. Marín's flattering biographer failed to produce evidence of him putting any stamp on the paper, beyond his own opinion columns and the odd memorable headline.[42]

Marín's peers suspected he compromised his independence in exchange for access. The *La Jornada* veteran Andrés Ruiz has said of a man he considers his friend, "To have insider sources helps you a lot, but at some point it may hinder you. The same sources that have given you information may later pressure you. I don't know if this has happened to Marín." Such willingness to compromise had been a charge against Marín during his latter days at *Proceso*. One former colleague claimed he wrote stories based on leaks from Ernesto Zedillo's attorney general, in exchange for protecting him from the same scrutiny that *Proceso* had applied to his predecessors.[43] Did Marín, at *Milenio*, do likewise with ministers? With presidents?

Fox and the Peak of Press Freedom

When did Mexican press freedom summit? Under President Carlos Salinas de Gortari, the media had experienced a gradual and general *apertura*—an opening up to watchdog journalism, a freeing from constraints, a freer flow of information—that came to a head in 1994. The floodgates having opened, Salinas's successor Zedillo presided over an unprecedentedly democratic media landscape. There were blots, like the heavy-handed Juan Francisco Ealy Ortiz arrest, the odd threat from a cabinet minister, and the frequent calls to editors from the president's private secretary. There were aggressions, such as the "express kidnapping" in consecutive weeks of two *Reforma* reporters, who were roughed up and interrogated by police over corruption stories they were working on. But such episodes were minor compared with what had gone on before. Official advertising continued to shrink, and with it the great incentive to self-censor. As for the most painful yardstick, the murder of journalists, eleven were killed on Zedillo's watch, roughly half the totals registered under either Salinas or Fox.[44]

By some measures, however, the Fox era was freer still. For one thing, private-sector advertising, depressed for most of the Zedillo era, finally exceeded its pre-recession level, hence media were even less dependent on state ad spend. Further, there was a freewheeling journalistic spirit and opening of space for dissident opinions during the Fox years; it built on the precedents of the 1990s and the invigorating end to a seven-decade quasi-dictatorship. Finally, greater freedom owed something to the president himself. The cowboy-booted vanquisher of the PRI made it clear that, among the things he was going to do differently, he would shun the strong-arm tactics of the past. The new modus operandi applied not only to intransigent peasant or worker leaders, whom his PRI predecessors had often bribed or jailed, but also to the press. Fox had drawn into his circle several veteran prodemocracy campaigners, including leftists such as Rubén Aguilar, a former publicist for Central American antifascist movements; the writer and academic Jorge Castañeda; and the political organizer Adolfo Aguilar Zinser. Their voices kept him to the new standard.[45]

One early change was an end to the fifty-year tradition of a Freedom of the Press Day banquet, in which the country's publishers and editors hobnobbed with the president; the final event took place in 2001. Moreover, no longer would the National Journalism Prizes, established by President Echeverría and first given in 1976, be awarded by a jury selected by the secretariat of government. A citizens' council would now choose the jury, and the awards would no longer be made on June 7, a date established under the PRI, but rather on May 3, the United Nations' World Press Freedom Day. In 1976, the winners had included Televisa's propagandist in chief, Jacobo Zabludovsky; in 2002, they included two journalists at *La Jornada*, the paper most critical of the Fox regime, and Anabel Hernández.[46]

Rubén Aguilar became the president's spokesman in 2004 and gained a reputation for openness, forgoing the threats that were the currency of his PRI-era forebears. He affirms, "The media understood that Fox wasn't going to be oppressive, so they felt free to be more critical. It was a virtuous circle." Roberto Rock of *El Universal* adds that the tonal shift was true of the Fox administration in general, for cabinet ministers and senior functionaries made fewer menacing calls to newsrooms. "Fox was easier to deal with than Salinas and Zedillo," he says, adding of Fox's successors, "Felipe Calderón was somewhat harder to deal with; Enrique Peña Nieto much harder." Lázaro Ríos of *Reforma* concurs on all counts: "Fox's phone calls were few and funny. Calderón showed disdain for the press. Peña behaved liked a governor; his people would complain even about little things."[47]

In another incentive to independent reporting, federal advertising declined yet further. Recalls Aguilar, "Fox basically decided: 'Here we don't buy media influence!'" Estimates of official ad spend now varied between 5 and 12 percent of the average Mexico City paper's revenue, compared with as much as 80 percent during the 1970s and 1980s. Deprived of their PRI-delivered lifeblood, two of the most decrepit dinosaurs still haunting the media landscape, *Novedades* and *El Heraldo*, finally keeled over.[48]

Another brontosaurus, the bloated, PRI-loving *Excélsior*, entered an existential crisis. Members of its cooperative fulminated at their once slick leader, Regino Díaz Redondo, for having run the paper as his fiefdom. There were accusations of corruption; some loans to *Excélsior* had reportedly been paid into his private account, allowing him to rake in some $2.5 million in interest. There was anger that the director had been unilaterally trying to sell the paper to Olegario Vázquez Raña, a hospital and hotel empresario and brother of *El Sol* owner Mario. Less openly admitted, but surely on everyone's mind, Díaz Redondo had obliged the paper during the presidential campaign to back the PRI and bash the PAN. One story claimed the Fox campaign took donations from the Legionnaires of Christ, a Catholic order tainted by a pederasty scandal, and the US Republican Party. A "psychological profile" had called Fox "a megalomaniac."[49] What hope was there now for continued state forgiveness of the paper's massive debts?

That October, the man who had done Echeverría's bidding and ousted Julio Scherer a quarter century before was himself, quite literally, thrown out on the street. There were insults—"Thief!"—and shoving. Chronicler Fabrizio Mejía Madrid caught the moment for the literary political magazine *Letras Libres*: "What impresses me are his eyes. They are dead. . . . The PRI having lost, the network of mutual understandings that moved Regino and made him talk became disconnected, and the eyes of the puppet are revealed to us as lifeless."[50]

Proceso revealed that the Salinas regime had forgiven *Excélsior* an accumulated debt of $9 million in 1992, only for it to have since racked up $30 million in debt to the Treasury alone. Meanwhile, Díaz Redondo's greed had reached beyond a predictable skimming off bank loans and advertising buys to even having the paper pick up his family's telephone bills. Circulation, once 95,000, had fallen to 35,000, about one-third of that of its former rival *El Universal*; half the *Excélsior* print run typically went unsold. When Díaz Redondo went with a company begging bowl to see Fox, the president-elect refused to meet him. Somehow the paper would stagger on until 2006, when it was bought out after all, for $55 million, by Olegario Vázquez Raña, and more than half of its bloated workforce of 800 was instantly laid off.[51]

During the Fox years, Mexico City's periodicals were mostly pluralistic and the larger ones (*Reforma*, *El Universal*, *Milenio*, and *Proceso*) more or less self-sustaining. Having launched websites and in some cases built regional chains, the capital's press could properly call itself "national" at last. *Reforma*, of course, was part of a Monterrey-based conglomerate that included dailies in Guadalajara and Saltillo. So was the upstart *Milenio*. *La Jornada* continued to decline in sales but grew outside the capital via further regional franchises, in Michoacán, Jalisco, Guerrero, Zacatecas, and soon Aguascalientes. *Proceso* too created regional editions: *Proceso Sur* and *Proceso Jalisco*.

Freestanding websites were another innovation. Print media had ventured into cyberspace as of 1995, when first *La Jornada*, then *El Norte* and *El Universal*, created basic digital editions. Most major papers had them by 1997. Now there appeared domains independent of any print or TV operation. Most were born during the era of the global dot-com bubble, whose giddy optimism prompted scores of Mexican start-ups between 1998 and 2000. But sound investment was hampered by a gold-rush mentality. Except for a few sites with deep-pocketed support, like Televisa's *Esmas* and Telmex's *T1msn*, this first wave soon crashed. The few independent sites that would endure started after the bubble burst, drew on more modest budgets, and usually targeted niche markets. These included the regional sites *E-Consulta* of Puebla (2002) and the Morelia-based *Quadratín* (2002), along with the business news site *Sentido Común* (2003).[52]

In each media arena—daily papers, supplements, magazines, books, and websites—Mexico's journalists were finding they were mostly free to write what they wanted. Even Televisa, still the main source of news for Mexico's majority, was breathing the oxygen of *apertura*. Having dropped PRI propagandist in chief Jacobo Zabludovsky as nightly news anchor in 1998, the broadcaster upgraded again in 2000 with a faster-paced newscast fronted by Joaquín López-Dóriga, a more probing journalist. Antiestablishment thinkers who had forged their careers in print began appearing on Televisa's news programs, even that hero of the liberal left Carlos Monsiváis. In June 2001 it launched a newsweekly, *Cambio*, in an eyebrow-raising partnership with Gabriel García Márquez, the celebrated left-wing Colombian novelist and pal of Fidel Castro.[53]

Press liberty advanced further with Mexico's first freedom-of-information act, in 2002. Laboriously named the Federal Transparency and Access to Governmental Public Information Act, the law owed little to Fox; he had promised such an act while campaigning but lacked both the votes and, critics claimed, the will to push a worthwhile bill through Congress. Rather, it was fostered by civil society activists.

Calling themselves the Oaxaca Group, after an academic conference in that city, they included some twenty professors and journalists; the latter involved an unlikely alliance of *El Universal* (led by Roberto Rock), *Reforma* (seldom a team player), and *La Jornada* (whose staffers derided *Reforma* and *El Universal* as bastions of neoliberalism), plus *El Informador* of Guadalajara. Fearing that Fox would settle for a weakly worded law in a bid for congressional consensus, the Oaxaca Group mobilized public support for muscular legislation that would compel federal agencies to release information on request—to the press, researchers, even the general public. It did so by writing up a "Oaxaca Declaration" that ran in more than 100 newspapers and then by drawing on the legal expertise of the academics to publish scores of articles and columns. International media also paid attention. The Oaxaca Group then drafted a bill and convinced opposition parties, as well as Fox and the PAN, to support it. The act, which included a strong supervisory body called the Federal Access to Information Institute (IFAI; later renamed the INAI), would be recognized across Latin America as a model disclosure law. *The Guardian*'s Jo Tuckman called it "the one big legislative success of Fox's administration."[54] The great irony was that the president who signed it into law would suffer more reputational damage than anyone as the press made use of it.

In practice, the law put an end to the PRI-era tradition of functionaries withholding data from journalists by whim or selectively feeding it to their favorites. It also democratized information more broadly. Within nine months of the law's activation in mid-2003, nearly 27,000 requests were registered, academics and lawyers being the most frequent petitioners. Journalists lodged just 7 percent of requests but scored notable results. At *El Universal*, Anabel Hernández continued her digging into abuse of office by Fox and Marta with a series of IFAI petitions, her findings including favors to an agricultural business of Fox's from a state development bank and Marta's tax-funded purchase of tens of thousands of dollars' worth of clothes in stores on Calle Masaryk, Mexico City's Rodeo Drive. Hernández collated and expanded on her findings in two popular books: *The Presidential Family* and *Party's End at Los Pinos*. The new magazine *Emeequis* used the IFAI to reveal how the presidential general staff, a military detachment housed at Los Pinos, spent the last three months of the Fox regime and the first month under Calderón placing dozens of fraudulent procurement orders that totaled at least $1 million.[55]

Fox's commitment to freedom of speech would wane toward the end. One sign was his surrender to the temptation to raise government ad spend, with the greater incentive to self-censorship that this implied. During his first two years, the sum spent was constant; it then jumped by 55 percent in 2003, presumably as the regime sought to trumpet PAN candidates in midterm elections. After receding somewhat, ad spend rose again in 2005 and 2006, finishing 73 percent higher than during Fox's first year.[56] Perhaps the barrage of criticism from an unrestrained press wore the president down.

"Fox found himself exposed in a way no president had even been before—and exposed in a particularly personal way," observed Jo Tuckman. The press assailed him for lacking gravitas when he wore his cowboy boots to a state dinner in Madrid; it ridiculed his claims of achievements by coining the term "Foxilandia" (an imaginary Mexico, akin to Disneyland, inside the president's head); it claimed he alternated between bouts of depression and Prozac-fueled gaiety; it derided him for verbal mishaps and repeatedly claimed he was not very bright.[57] On the other hand, Fox earned little credit and some derision for being the first president to regularly use gender-inclusive language: "Los y las mexicanos . . ."

Newscasts, on Televisa and TV Azteca alike, were benign. When Sallie Hughes analyzed three months of media coverage of Fox in 2003, she found only 1 percent of TV news items about the president to be negative, the vast majority balanced or neutral, and 25 percent positive. In *Reforma* and *El Universal*, by contrast, 32 percent of stories about Fox were negative. On the other hand, 29 percent were positive. The apparent contradiction owed to the fact that, while these papers more or less sympathized with the president's free-market agenda, they were swift to hold him to account over ethical breaches and policy failures: dubious donations to his Amigos de Fox campaign organization in 2000; an inability to get meaningful tax reform through Congress; inadequate job creation; ineffectual tackling of violent crime; and the perception that Marta was using her poverty relief charity Vamos México (Let's Go, Mexico) as a public relations platform for a presidential run.[58]

Proceso was irreverent and frequent in its skewering. Covers about the president included "The Economy: Deception upon Deception" (Fox with head bowed, his hand half covering his face); "The Fox Product" (Marta applying a comb to his moustache); "Politics in Pink" (Fox and Marta ironically framed within a heart, the story accusing them of frivolously catering to society magazines ahead of a European tour); "Two Years Later . . ." (Fox again with head bowed); "Goodbye to the Myth" (Fox looking glum, after the PAN's poor showing in midterm elections); "Three Years: The Agony" (Fox looking pained); and "The Candidate Who Was Not President" (Fox in silhouette during his campaign of 2000, flashing a victory sign).[59] Some criticism was substantial. *Proceso* obtained documents showing that Fox's presidential campaign had received millions of dollars in illegal corporate donations from Carlos Slim ($2 million), cement giant Cemex ($1.5 million), and other major companies. The magazine made the scandal its cover story for five successive issues, until a legal ploy by Fox's former campaign finance manager brought an investigation by the Federal Electoral Institute to a premature close.[60]

So swift was the press to criticize Fox, even during the months before his swearing in, that the pressure weighed on his cabinet. As early as August 2001, foreign minister Castañeda told the *Los Angeles Times* that Mexico's media wanted to bring down the president. More such allegations followed, along with Fox's counter that Mexicans who ignored the press and stuck to TV news would be happier.[61] Some observers felt that print media simply went too far, continuing the "drunken spree" of press freedom that Raúl Trejo and Marco Levario had decried in the Zedillo era. To Jorge Zepeda Patterson, politics had descended into a contest of public lynchings in which the press, happy to exploit sensational leaks to elevate sales, was entirely complicit. To Enrique Krauze, for whom Fox's "mediocre" performance paled next to the authoritarianism of predecessors from the PRI, the systematic animosity of *Proceso* smacked of prejudice.[62]

Readers seemed to agree, at least initially. In 2000, the World Values Survey found that Mexicans generally trusting in the press had declined to 39 percent, against 52 percent four years earlier. "Gotcha journalism" about Fox and Marta, who were very popular at the time of the election, likely accounts for this, along with a contempt for the naked support for the PRI by the likes of *Excélsior*, *Novedades*, *El Heraldo*, and many a regional paper. Five years later, however, the confidence level was back up to 49 percent, which suggests that a substantial portion of the public had come to believe that Fox and Marta merited much of the probing the media afforded them.[63]

Meanwhile, for most of Fox's term of office, critical periodicals faced few reprisals. Nor did the president launch verbal assaults on individual media.

As for Marta, the bad press was arguably harsher, and it took a visible toll. To some extent the barrage reflected unprecedented exercise of journalistic freedom, even to the point of malice; to some extent it was self-inflicted.

To begin with, Marta had never seemed to share Fox's ideas about press freedom. She persisted in giving reporters and columnists cause for critique: her lavish spending, which gave rise to "towel-gate"; her modeling of expensive fashions and her photo spreads in celebrity magazine ¡Hola!; her blasé complicity in the money-grabbing exploits of her sons; her routine use of Televisa newscasts to cast herself as Mexico's Evita Perón, hugging orphans, cancer patients, and lepers, sometimes shedding a tear as she did so.[64]

Then there was her clumsy management of Vamos México, which prompted a carefully assembled exposé in the *Financial Times* in January 2004. (It appeared shortly after she told *El Universal*, "I think Mexico is now ready to have a female president.") The London paper revealed that her foundation gave only 30 percent of its revenue to good works, augmenting the perception that it existed as a campaign vehicle and prompting an outcry in Congress and scrutiny in the local press; the scandal would prove a key factor in the eventual sinking of Marta's political dreams. She must have sensed that danger, for her initial reaction was to call a conference and dismiss the report as "lies, calumny, defamation [and] tendentious handling of information." Two days later, caving to political and media pressure, Vamos México released audited statements that showed the *Financial Times'* central "30 percent" claim to be correct.[65]

Proceso was nimble at needling the First Lady's queenly ego and ambitions, if sometimes using borderline-sexist tropes to do so. Several of the lasting public images of Marta owe to the magazine's covers: "Mrs. President" (smiling while holding a gaudy but expensive-looking bag); "Marta Accumulates Power" (smiling and waving while silhouetted against Fox's back); "Marta's Shopping Trip" (smiling while sporting a fancy turquoise jacket); "All the Power" (smiling while glancing upward and sporting a black top, perhaps a nod to Lady Macbeth); "The Threat Returns" (smiling amid a crowd, as though on campaign); and most damningly, "In Mourning, in Rome" (smiling in close-up, while bedecked in black, at an official event marking the death of Pope John Paul II). The cumulative message was clear: The First Lady was a walking exercise in gauche, and her designs on succeeding her husband were a peril to Mexico's fledgling democracy. Marta renounced her interest in running for president in July 2004.[66]

For Fox and Marta, a *Proceso* feature questioning the grounds for the annulment of her first marriage was the final straw. In May 2005, Marta sued both the writer, Olga Wornat, and the magazine, and at the same time *Proceso* lost most of its federal advertising. The quasi-boycott would persist until Fox left office. In fact, subsequent presidents have generally refused the magazine advertising to this day.[67]

Reforma and *El Universal* Go Head-to-Head

Grupo Reforma and *El Universal*, the twin market leaders in print, continued to enjoy under Fox the high levels of readership and influence they had established, or reestablished, as of the mid-1990s. They also dominated the capital's newspaper ad market, consuming well over half of the local pie between them.[68] Arguably, the intensity with which Juan Francisco Ealy Ortiz battled for readers with Alejandro Junco made for a qualitative peak in broadsheet journalism. It certainly gave the more experienced reporters new spaces in which to practice their art, in turn promoting an unprecedented trend of investigative journalism and book-length reportage. The two papers' dominance persisted despite consecutive earthquakes in each of their newsrooms.

On February 5, 2000, Grupo Reforma's hundreds of staffers were shocked to read in their very own papers that their high-energy boss, Ramón Alberto Garza, had quit.[69] He had fallen out with the man he called his "professional father," Alejandro Junco. The dispute, it emerged, centered on Junco's recent sale of financial news service Infosel (for close to $300 million), in which Garza, as a founder-executive, believed he held a 10 percent stake. But Junco informed him that he did not. Farewell letters from Garza to Junco and Junco to Garza, which omitted the cause of the rupture, appeared in the pages of *Reforma* and its sister papers, *El Norte*, Guadalajara's *Mural*, and *Palabra* of Saltillo; these were the four corners of an editorial fiefdom between which Garza had come to divide his time, visiting each during the course of every week. Twenty-seven years of collaboration had sharpened Junco and Garza's shared sense of being Mexico's apostles of a free press.

On the Monday, Garza said goodbye to his colleagues at *El Norte*, and on the Tuesday he did the same at *Reforma*. That afternoon there were tears in the atrium. Junco convened a meeting with the employees and made a lachrymose speech bidding Garza goodbye. "We are brothers," he said. Then Garza, equally tearful, reciprocated. A long queue formed of staff wishing to say goodbye to their captain. It took over an hour to pass. "It was like a funeral," Garza recalls. "Because we were like a family."

The shock of Garza's sudden exit was doubled for some by the identity of his replacement: Lázaro Ríos. The general manager was well liked, but he was not a journalist: He had forged his career in human resources. Time would show Junco's choice a wise one. Unlike the mercurial, sensationalism-prone, big-spending Garza, Ríos placed a steady hand on the ship's wheel and made more efficient use of the papers' assets. His managerial know-how—so evidently lacking among the journalists who rose to become editors in chief at most papers—would prove crucial to the company's health over the next decade or so, as newspapers in Mexico, like print media worldwide, found themselves buffeted by the internet and needing to cut costs. Further, the company now had senior editors who had absorbed much of what Garza might inspire and who could offer innovations of their own: Martha Treviño at *El Norte*; René Delgado and Roberto Zamarripa at *Reforma*.

"We all asked each other: What's going to happen?" remembers Ernesto Núñez, a *Reforma* founder-reporter. "But Junco made a good move by naming Lázaro Ríos as head of the [four] papers and René Delgado as editor in chief at *Reforma*." Set to endure for seventeen years, the Ríos–Delgado duo brought the paper propitious stability.[70]

Since Garza's exit shortly followed the official start of the presidential campaign season, there was a widespread fear in the newsroom that the paper would "deliver itself" to the PAN, the party Junco had long favored. But Delgado, who leaned leftward, worked to ensure that its reporting was fair. Grupo Reforma had a team of eighteen monitor TV and radio coverage, and it prepared a team of 100 to observe the Election Day process. The company also boasted what *The Washington Post* called "the most reliable public opinion polling operation in Mexico." Concerns about Junco's bias were answered by its final poll before the vote, which gave the PRI's Labastida a 3-point lead.[71]

After Fox won, *Reforma* employees were eager to display their independence by holding the victor to account. Núñez's own reporting, as one of those assigned to cover the PAN, offered a sharp example. On a weekend six weeks after the vote, Núñez was taking turns clocking the arrival of VIPs at Fox's ranch in Guanajuato, along with reporters from other media. Once they had interviewed the first secretary of the Chinese embassy, most of the press left, but Núñez and his photographer Paola García opted to stay on, just in case. At about three o'clock that afternoon, three pickup trucks arrived in the compound and boys and girls climbed out of the back of each. The reporters took pictures and interviewed the children: They were all field workers, coming to collect their pay. "Children and Youths Employed at the Fox Family Ranch," ran the damning headline, with Núñez's reports and García's photos filling a whole page. Stung by the story, which immediately got picked up by international media, Fox and Marta held a press conference the next day. Marta, essaying the crude defensiveness that would later turn the press against her, accused Núñez of having been sent by the PRI.

Junco, Núñez recalls, made hay from the revelation. For years afterward, whenever accused of being too pro-PAN, he would retort, "You're forgetting that we were the first to report that Fox's ranch employs child labor."[72]

Fears that *Reforma* might lose its mojo without Garza were dismissed once and for all by what was unquestionably the scoop of 2000. Watching the news on August 22, several Argentineans residing in Mexico caught an item featuring Ricardo Cavallo, director of the new national vehicle registry, Renave. It struck them that this man, clearly a compatriot, looked a lot like *Miguel Ángel* Cavallo, a military intelligence officer during Argentina's dictatorship two decades before. They had been political prisoners, and he had tortured them. Through an intermediary, they contacted Lázaro Ríos. The editor put his team to work. René Delgado had a facial-recognition expert examine photographs of the two Cavallos. One reporter contacted Baltasar Garzón, the celebrated Spanish judge who had issued an arrest warrant for former Chilean dictator Augusto Pinochet and was now pursuing former officers in Argentina, Cavallo included, over the killing of Spanish subjects. Another reporter went to interview the Renave director to ask him if he was indeed the same man ("It looks a lot like me, I can't deny it," Cavallo replied, amid terse answers). *Reforma*'s Buenos Aires stringer found an official identity number for Miguel Ángel Cavallo that matched the one that Ricardo Cavallo had used when applying for his Mexican residency permit. All this was done on a single day, and the story led on August 24. A graphic juxtaposed photographs of Cavallo from 1976 and the present, the latter modified to remove his moustache and glasses, together with numbers and notes from the expert that flagged matches in facial features. Companion pieces and a letter from Cavallo denying the accusations took up an inside page.[73]

After the paper hit the streets, the rest of the press swooped on the story, although not everyone gave *Reforma* credit. Cavallo himself boarded a flight home, declaring his intention to clear his name; he could do so without fear, due to Argentina's postdictatorship amnesty laws. However, Mexico's federal police force and the International Criminal Police Organization (Interpol) concocted a plan to detain Cavallo on the dubious charge of falsifying documents, so as to allow time for the Spanish judge Garzón to act. When the plane carrying Cavallo made a scheduled stop in Cancún, Interpol nabbed him. Garzón then issued an extradition request. Six months later, Spain's *El País* bestowed on the *Reforma* team its prestigious Ortega y Gasset Award. The prize was created in 1984 to honor journalistic achievement in the Spanish-speaking world. *Reforma* was the first Mexican paper to win it.[74]

As for coverage of the PAN, *Reforma* asked questions of the party in power as it had done when Mexico was governed by the PRI. Further stories by Ernesto Núñez, for example, showed that some of the local politicians who had ridden Fox's coattails to power were quite the rum bunch. By early 2002, Núñez had enough material on PAN politicians behaving badly to fill a full-page report. The State of México showed the party in a particularly poor light: the Ecatepec mayor who paid himself a $45,000 year-end bonus; the Atizapán mayor accused of killing a councilor of his who had uncovered corruption at city hall. Such scandals threatened the PAN's prospects in the 2003 midterms, and *Reforma* gave them due play.[75]

Observers including Riva Palacio did find that during the Fox years *Reforma* adopted a more PAN-sympathetic agenda overall.[76] But a favorable tone based on ideological compatibility and a continued holding to account are not incompatible goals for a self-confidently independent newspaper, as the relationships between Britain's *The Guardian* and its Labour Party or *The New York Times* and the Democrats amply attest.

———————

At *El Universal*, the newsroom shock came in February 2002, when the editor who had revolutionized the paper after decades of deferential mediocrity, Roberto Rock, was effectively demoted. And whom should Ealy import, in place of the man he treated as an adopted son, but the erstwhile adopted son of Junco: Ramón Alberto Garza.

After engineering the *El Universal* revamp of 1999, Rock had continued to shape Ealy's newspaper as the main rival to *Reforma* for the mantle of newspaper of record. In this, he was helped by his new right-hand man, Jorge Zepeda Patterson. A week before Fox's victory, the two men launched a glossy Sunday supplement, *Día Siete*, inspired by the *Semanal* insert at Spain's *El País* and *The New York Times Magazine*. After three or four years, some twenty papers were carrying it, the print run reaching 340,000, making *Día Siete* by far the most popular nontabloid periodical in Mexico. And it was profitable, its ad sales generating around $25 million per year.[77]

On the internet, *El Universal* caught up and overtook its rival. *El Norte* and *Reforma* had already launched real-time websites ElNorte.com and Reforma.com, in January and May 2000, respectively. *El Universal* went live in early 2001. Fortunately Ealy opted not to put up a paywall, something that Junco—at the insistence of his son, Alejandro Junco Elizondo—instituted from the start. Ably advised by Rosental Alves, a Brazilian consultant and academic who had helped launch the early-adapter website of the *Jornal do Brasil*, Rock's team paid unequaled attention to updating the paper's web pages during the day and permitting interactivity with readers. *El Universal* drew higher traffic online than any other paper.[78]

Finally, on February 18, 2002, Rock launched a revamped version of *El Universal Gráfico*, which since its debut in 1922 had served as the paper's evening edition. In the 1990s, it fell on hard times, so to cut costs it ceased to be a broadsheet. Now, partly inspired by the tabloid *Extra* published by *O Globo* of Brazil, it was a garish weekday morning tabloid. But for its banner headline and a few teasers, the front page was text-free and full color. Four of the first seven covers featured a dead body (three accidents, one murder). Once more this was a direct challenge to Grupo Reforma, which had struck commercial gold with the tabloid *Metro* in 1997. *Metro* drew on a similarly male-oriented, *nota roja* format—heavy on crime and grisly accidents, along with politicians misbehaving and soccer rivalries—that the Juncos had employed a decade earlier when launching a Monterrey tabloid of the same name. After a yet more sensationalist redesign in 2006, *Metro* would boast audited circulation across Mexico City, Monterrey, Guadalajara, and Saltillo of around 345,000.[79]

El Gráfico, as Ealy's tabloid was rebranded, also competed with *La Prensa*, long the capital's dominant scandal sheet. *La Prensa* had been bought in 1996 by Mario Vázquez Raña, publisher of the *Sol* chain, so it too had strong corporate backing. Like *Metro*, *El Gráfico* hit the bull's-eye at *La Prensa*'s expense: Within a year of relaunch, Rock claims, circulation zoomed from 12,000 (with sales of just 8,000) to 200,000.[80]

What followed was a race to the bottom, the three tabloids plumping for ever more sex and violence. As attacks between criminal gangs worsened in 2005 and 2006, dead bodies multiplied on page 1 of each. Seminaked women were often pasted next to them, teasing an inside "story." (By now, similar sex-and-violence principles governed tabloids across Latin America: *Extra* of Ecuador, *Ojo* of Peru, *Crónica* of Argentina, and so on.) And as the homicide rate soared during President Calderón's "war against drug traffickers," with readers apparently becoming inured, the cadavers on the covers of *Metro* and *El Gráfico* were sometimes accompanied by macabre wordplay: of a student killed outside his high school: "Lo dan de baja" (He's dismissed); of a man murdered at a soccer stadium: "Pena máxima" (Maximum penalty). The more literal-minded folk at *La Prensa* competed on shock value. This strategy reached a nadir in 2008, with a front page—visible to passers-by at the capital's thousands of newsstands—showing close-ups of three severed heads. These had been found inside an ice box that an unnamed gang had express mailed to a police station.[81]

The very day that the revamped *El Gráfico* debuted, Rock found himself sidelined. The entrance of Garza looked like a coup for Ealy in his head-to-head with Junco. *Reforma* was Mexico's most politically influential and most profitable paper, and Garza presumably knew all the secrets of its success. But the Garza era proved ephemeral. Within a year, the dutiful Rock would be back at his old job.[82]

Garza claims he was not at first an Ealy hire, for he arrived at *El Universal* as the envoy of potential buyers. As several sources attest, but for reasons unclear, Ealy had been seeking to sell a major stake in his paper or even sell out. Age was hardly a factor, for he was not yet sixty. But he may have tired of squaring his paper's finances, which were in poor shape. There was the expense of the 1999 revamp, the loss of ad market share to *Reforma*, and the long decline in the once hefty state subsidies on which the paper historically depended. Since Ealy had always been a lackey of the PRI, the new PAN regime might not help him with his debts. Then, in a seeming stroke of luck, a consortium of wealthy potential buyers appeared. One was Televisa, which Garza had swiftly joined as head of publishing after his *Reforma* exit; the others were Monterrey industrialists, Carlos Slim, a US newspaper, and Spain's Grupo Prisa, publisher of *El País*. Garza was tasked with working his magic to raise the paper's value to a sale price satisfactory to Ealy. First, he would further the improvements made by Rock to assail *Reforma*'s lead in sales and advertising; at the time, *El Universal* was selling about 70,000 copies a day to *Reforma*'s 120,000-plus. Second, he would plan a daily for Monterrey, a competitor to Junco's *El Norte*. Initially, Ealy liked what Garza was doing, for in June he made him vice president.

Garza's first act was to prioritize another makeover. Fewer than three years had passed since the last one, but the paper still looked traditional next to its younger rival. Garza's brief was, in effect, "Make *El Universal* look more like *Reforma*." One overt change of Garza's was switching the *El Universal* title from serious black to friendly blue, a counter to the salient green of Junco's paper. Similar modifications suffused the whole paper. Unveiled on July 1, 2002, the result, as press chronicler Cecilia González put it, "smelled of *Reforma* in design and content."[83]

Where the product differed was in tone. Per its editorial that day, *El Universal* was betting on journalism that "projects a healthy attitude, that proposes, that tells good news too, that encourages a culture of example-setting." That is, it would not muckrake at Los Pinos.[84] Was Ealy—knowing that Garza got along well with the First Couple—cozying up to Fox to facilitate the sale of his paper? Was he betting that the president, besieged by a broadly cynical press, would soon change course on government advertising and raise it? And if so, might it not behoove *El Universal* to treat the president more gently? Lo and behold, that same July 1, it ran a softball interview with Marta, teased on the front page with pictures of the First Lady in the Los Pinos kitchen, slicing a vegetable. The paper was deluged with criticism.[85]

On December 12, Garza at last met with Ealy and a Prisa executive and the sale was agreed. The following week, Ealy sent a lawyer to tell him the deal was off and his job was over. As well as being the target of complaints about the changes he had made, the high-energy editor was widely perceived as too much a stealer of the spotlight for Ealy's comfort. But what really brought his editorship to an end was politics.

The Prisa deal had begun to come undone when Slim withdrew from the consortium, which thus raised the profile of the Monterrey investors, who included the cement king Lorenzo Zambrano. Old-guard, left-of-center big-wigs within the PRI, which still weighed heavily in Congress, were set on preventing Zambrano and his northern cohort from holding editorial sway at the paper. It was bad enough having *Reforma* in the hands of a PAN-loving Monterrey industrialist. Then there was the *Milenio* chain, owned by a Monterrey sympathizer with the PRI's neoliberal wing; *El Financiero*, part-owned by Monterrey businessman Alfonso Romo; even the boards of Televisa and TV Azteca were heavy with northern magnates. To see the sole remaining major national paper in such hands was out of the question. So these men offered the cash to let Ealy solve his debts and a pledge for further subsidies. And they surely viewed Garza as too pro-PAN.

———

Despite the bonanza of the Fox era, clouds were gathering on the newspaper industry's horizon. Slowly, Mexicans were going online, and advertisers haltingly caught on. During the late 1990s, internet platforms had claimed just 1 percent of advertisers' budgets, and after the dot-com bust of 2000, there was a retreat from that tiny beachhead to legacy media. But in 2004, online advertising dramatically rebounded. It still represented a mere tenth of what companies spent on newspapers in Mexico (and a tenth of what they spent on magazines), but a long upward trend was set. The flight of readers and advertisers to the internet, which was about to hit the US press hard, was destined to become a Mexican worry too. Five years later, in recessionary 2009, Mexico's print media would seriously feel the pinch, and two years after that, online ad spend would outstrip spend on newspapers once and for all.[86]

La Jornada, with its student-heavy readership, felt the tide turn sooner. At *El Universal*, circulation apparently peaked in 2005. Junco's papers, including the *Metro* tabloids, hit a combined peak print run of 960,000 in 2006, with *Reforma* and *El Norte* both shipping around 150,000.[87] Thereafter—like its peers, if more gradually—*Reforma* and its sister papers would lose readers and advertisers.

Market contraction would mean cuts in page counts and layoffs, prompting a vicious cycle similar to the one already decimating newspapers and magazines in the United States, as ever more disaffected readers abandoned print for digital. It would not, however, mean a mass extinction in Mexico's papers. As early as 2003, business magazine *Expansión*, contemplating several recent closures, forecast that in five years' time Mexico City's cohort of dailies would shrink from around thirty to five or six. But its prediction rested on the common misconception that Mexican papers function as businesses, whereas the reality is that most are tools for special interests.[88]

In that regard, *El Universal* and *Reforma* were stand-out exceptions. The Fox era saw them consolidated as Mexico's two leading daily papers, and they emerged from the bonanza better equipped than most to face the pending market downturn. Yet even these two, in the long run, would face tough times and succumb to temptations—either to accept more federal advertising and thus veer toward *oficialismo*, or to assume the posture of chief organ of the opposition and thus adopt a more strident tone.

Chapter 8

The Press and the Powerful

AMLO, Calderón, Carlos Slim

From July 2, [the media] lose all sense of decency . . . they debase themselves, they stain themselves, and they give themselves up completely to lies and manipulation.

—Andrés Manuel López Obrador, on the 2006 presidential election

Reported expenditure [on federal advertising] almost tripled during the term of President Calderón.

—WAN-IFRA, *Comprando complacencia* [*Buying Complacency*]

You know when, how, and where to pressure and blackmail legislators, regulators, the media, judges, journalists, and the intelligentsia of the left.

—Denise Dresser, "Open Letter to Carlos Slim," *Proceso*, 2009

(Some of) the Media versus AMLO

Andrés Manuel López Obrador, the charismatic leftist politician popularly known as AMLO, reflected in a memoir on his dramatic defeat in the 2006 presidential election. Against Felipe Calderón of the incumbent National Action Party (PAN), the Party of the Democratic Revolution (PRD) candidate and former Mexico City mayor had lost—so the authorities claimed—by a margin of just 0.6 percent. This came after he had led in most polls for many months, after foul play by opposition actors including President Vicente Fox and captains of industry, and after the media had militated against him. He called his memoir *The Mafia Stole the Presidency from Us*, the mafia being a "political elite" made up of "influence traffickers, communicators, representatives of business, union leaders and traditional politicians."[1]

He had strong words for Mexico's press. As mayor, when he had held daily conferences, he had needed to keep his wits about him because editors sent "journalists linked to the political right" to provoke him and try to catch him out. In 2004, a covertly-filmed clip of his aide receiving wads of cash from a contractor favored by city hall was televised "an infinite number of times." During the *desafuero* case, which dragged on for a year as Fox sought to bar him from running for president, the media "rained down accusations" that he had no respect for the law. During the presidential campaign, business elites had paid off newspapers and broadcasters to run hate pieces comparing him to Hugo Chávez, the firebrand socialist leader of Venezuela; it was a period in which his team "knew that the media were completely given over to the right."[2]

In actual fact, for most of his time as mayor, López Obrador had enjoyed a calm and cordial relationship with the press. Nor, during the campaign season, had the media acted as massively against him as he claimed. But he could very well blame television, especially Televisa, for his defeat.

Once the 2006 contest started in earnest, most media were at least superficially fair. TV and radio stations more or less complied with their legal duty to give equal newscast time to the three leading candidates, including Roberto Madrazo of the Institutional Revolutionary Party (PRI), who never rose above third in the polls. In fact, they collectively gave greater coverage to López Obrador, presumably because he was the most controversial candidate. The newspapers granted more or less equal space too.[3]

Tone was another matter. Mexicans witnessed a barrage of political attacks the length and intensity of which were quite without precedent. The turning point was mid-March, when both the PAN, whose candidate Calderón lagged 10 points behind in the polls, and the PRD switched tactics. The PAN launched a devastatingly cutting TV attack ad, aired 500 times over the course of five weeks, which falsely accused its opponent of tripling Mexico City's public debt. It delivered the phrase, "López Obrador, a danger for Mexico." Meanwhile, López Obrador began criticizing Fox for illicitly involving himself in the contest by making speeches and running TV spots that trumpeted his achievements, to the obvious benefit of Calderón; Fox also warned of "populism," to the obvious detriment of López Obrador. The latter responded with public complaints that were legitimate in substance but abrasive in tone. At one point, he chided the president, "Cállate, chachalaca!" (Shut up, blabbermouth!).[4]

Such outbursts gave Calderón's backers the chance to brand their opponent an intolerant radical. The fearmongering attack ads continued, now likening López Obrador to the famously demagogic Chávez. And when the Venezuelan leader criticized this ploy, *Reforma* fueled the fire by leading with "Chávez defends López Obrador." Sensing the leftist might lose, several business moguls began to bank on Calderón, funding further attack ads. The combined effect was to generate what Sergio Aguayo termed a "moral panic" about the prospect of López Obrador entering Los Pinos. Within a month his lead in the polls had vanished.[5]

For the final four months of the race, studies commissioned by the Federal Electoral Institute (IFE) found a modest but important increase in negatively toned news items about López Obrador on TV and radio, especially on the national networks; these also increased their positive items about Calderón. Along with the Federal Electoral Tribunal, the IFE was also supposed to monitor and restrict attack ads, which, if found to be based on lies, are illegal in Mexico. But for nine weeks the two authorities declined to do anything about them, by which point the most damaging PAN ads had run their course. Political scientist Kathleen Bruhn attributed the foot-dragging to the fact that the IFE's governing council was stacked with appointees of the PAN and the PRI, to the exclusion of the PRD.[6]

Televisa became the channel of choice for anti-AMLO propaganda, including an ad from a leading business association warning that a change of economic model would put an end to the dreams of small-business owners. Televisa also used the underhand tactics of product placement. Three days before polling day, when campaigning was no longer permitted, the prime-time telenovela *La fea más bella* had two characters discuss the election; they concluded that a vote for Calderón would be a vote (quoting one of his slogans) for "the jobs president." On Televisa, PAN attack ads seemed to be synchronized with at least four softball interviews on its nightly newscast with President Fox, whose barely veiled comments in favor of Calderón and scaremongering about López Obrador were also found—after the vote—to have contravened electoral laws.[7]

The broadsheets were more balanced that spring, especially *El Universal*. Savvily playing both sides, Juan Francisco Ealy Ortiz's paper led one day with Fox forecasting an easy PAN victory and another day with new claims about the video scandals that had embarrassed López Obrador, but its top stories also included an electoral tribunal intervention against anti-AMLO attack ads and allegations of tax evasion by Calderón's brother-in-law. Six days before the vote, it splashed an interview with López Obrador by Roberto Rock, in which the leftist appeared conciliatory. Its polls variously put either man ahead or both of them tied. The overall balance was summed up in one banner: "Calderón and AMLO Collide."[8]

Reforma indulged in overt bias, pointing up López Obrador's insults toward Fox, depicting the attack ad controversy as a tussle between him and the private sector, revisiting the video scandals, and giving credence to a *Washington Post* editorial that said his victory would prompt greater migration. But Alejandro Junco's papers also did the leftist a couple of front-page favors, by making much of how the Fobaproa bank bailout scandal had yet to see any wrongdoers punished—a regular theme in López Obrador's attacks on Calderón—and by affording generous play to his closing rally. Further, their final opinion poll gave López Obrador a 2-point lead. Its columnists were as often supportive of him as critical. At the start of the campaign season, Junco told *Proceso* that he feared an "absolutist" presidency, should López Obrador win. He told meetings of editors and correspondents that his aim for his papers was to prevent an AMLO victory. Yet it seems Junco's ideological instincts were checked somewhat by his journalistic instincts—or by those of his editors.[9]

The most damning article appeared in the monthly *Letras Libres* (and in the US magazine *The New Republic*). Enrique Krauze wrote a cover-story profile that set the tone for most critical appraisals to come: "Tropical Messiah." Krauze was not the first to find that López Obrador drove some supporters to messianic devotion. But he may have been the first to allege that the leftist had a savior-like conception *of himself.* He concluded that López Obrador "represents an anti-modern left . . . : radical and populist, and with a disturbing element of political messianism."[10]

In the short run, more concerning for López Obrador were Mexico's business leaders, given their clout as campaign financiers. And yet, since the hard core of anti-AMLO activists belonged to this class, it was remarkable that Mexico's top business magazine, *Expansión*, gave equal play to interviews with the three main candidates, Calderón, López Obrador, and Madrazo.[11]

Altogether, given print media pluralism, the committed backing of *La Jornada*, and coverage by *Proceso* that (while raising awkward questions about the leftist) cast a much harsher light on his opponents, it could not be said that newspapers and magazines ganged up on López Obrador. The real assailant was television.

———

After the July 2, 2006, election, in what came to be a monthslong process of confirming the result, most media duplicated the official version of Calderón's narrow victory. *La Jornada* and *Proceso* were the main exceptions, backing López Obrador while he and his followers staged a massive sit-in protest in Mexico City's main plaza and along its main boulevard. Several press barons, having felt it good for business to offer impartial coverage before the election, now bet big on Calderón, trusting that another six years of the PAN would better serve their assets and expansion plans. One was Pancho González, whose *Milenio* ran many a postelectoral lead story favoring Calderón and many a page 1 column, by Carlos Marín, ridiculing López Obrador. González was planning his TV news network, and he presumably felt that given his lifelong support for the PRI, its prospects would be enhanced by a regime that was not of the Left.[12] Two others were Olegario Vázquez Raña and Olegario Vázquez Aldir, father-and-son owners of *Excélsior.*

By late 2005, Daniel Moreno had accumulated sixteen years of experience at six distinct media when he was invited to join *Excélsior,* once the sale to the Vázquez family went through, as editor in chief. "It was a chance to revive the most important newspaper of the twentieth century," he recalls.[13] Two things gave Moreno confidence. First, the offer came via Jorge Fernández Menéndez, his boss back at *Unomásuno*, and now an executive at the Vázquez media conglomerate, Grupo Imagen. Second, Vázquez Aldir offered him free rein, both editorially and managerially—he could hire whom he liked. The owner just had one small favor to ask: Could he refrain from touching Cardinal Norberto Rivera? Mexico's most powerful bishop was friends with his mother. This seemed normal to Moreno, as all magnates have pals they wish to protect.

Moreno's first few months went swimmingly. *Excélsior* was reborn on March 22, 2006, with an attractive redesign: new nameplate, black-and-gold trimmings, larger photos, and a four-story limit to the front page. Moreno hired respected veterans including Humberto Musacchio as a columnist and María Luisa Díaz de León and Pascal Beltrán del Río as deputy editors. He was able to maintain fair coverage of the election campaign. The day after the vote, *Excélsior* caught the national mood with an honest banner that simply said, "Who?"; underneath it was a shot of anxious-looking voters, along with rival claims of victory by Calderón and López Obrador. Moreno kept this up for two more days: "We Have to Wait" and "Everyone Demands Respect for the Count" ran the leads on July 4 and 5.[14]

But then came orders from above. On July 6, Moreno was forced to print, "It's Being Defined," next to a large portrait of a smiling Calderón. The editor was bothered, for the IFE had yet to issue a ruling; this was a politicized attempt to shape a situation still in flux. July 7 brought another front-page portrait of Calderón, next to an interview, and a headline—"Priority, Pact with the Left"—that depicted the conservative as magnanimous in victory.[15]

It all went downhill from there. "Instead of a *tough* newspaper, the owners now wanted a *mute* newspaper," says Moreno. "There was censorship daily. The paper delivered itself into the hands of the government." He found that the Vázquez-appointed publisher had placed spies in his newsroom. And the list of protected individuals, once confined to Cardinal Rivera, grew and grew as the owners' business relationships saw fit. The greatest of those, it became clear to Moreno, would be the one with the Calderón regime. Over the next six years, he could not help but notice that the main Vázquez-owned conglomerate, hotel and hospital operator Grupo Empresarial Ángeles, grew phenomenally. But he would ponder the exchange of favors that such rapid growth implied only from afar, because after nine months as editor in chief he quit.[16]

Raymundo Riva Palacio observes that for some media owners, government favors such as the granting of operating licenses, the transfer of real estate for development projects, and the awarding of contracts to procure goods or run public facilities—like prisons, for which the Vázquez family obtained long-term licenses—are much more important than official ad spend on their news-papers. He adds, "These parallel businesses shot up under Calderón."[17]

Calderón's "War on Drugs"

Ten days after his inauguration, Felipe Calderón fired the first salvo in a "war" (implying a righteous crusade that every patriot favored) against the so-called drug cartels. The president announced the dispatch of more than 5,000 troops, 1,500 police, and 60 aircraft to Michoacán. The state of his birth had become unruly: An upstart gang called La Familia—allied with the fear-some Zetas, ex-military commandos working for the Gulf Cartel—was en-gaged in a bloody turf battle with Los Valencia. For the first time, severed heads were being left in public places. That day, December 11, 2006, officials added that further military moves would soon occur in Sinaloa, Guerrero, Nuevo León, and Tamaulipas.[18] Calderón was surely satisfied at how the front pages saluted his boldness. "The Army Goes against *el Narco* in Michoacán" and "5 Thousand Troops to Michoacán against *el Narco*," informed *El Univer-sal* and *Milenio* ("*el narco*," as though the battling gangs were a single evil entity). "Federal Forces Take Michoacán," declared *Excélsior* (as though the subjugation of those gangs were a done deal). *Reforma* was equally conclusive: "Army Takes Michoacán." Adding a little sex to go with the violence, *Re-forma* posted alongside that headline a photo of three strippers taunting a seated policeman. It was a bit of fun, the caption claimed, organized by the mayor of a Mexico City suburb to celebrate Police Day. The mayor, it said, was from the PAN, the same conservative movement that had carried Calde-rón to Los Pinos.[19] Apparently, the PAN knew how to organize both a deploy-ment and a party.

Only *La Jornada*, among the capital's main dailies, declined to enthuse about Calderón's decree. It led instead with UNICEF criticism of his reduc-tion of the federal education budget, while merely flagging an inside story on the president's military maneuver. *Proceso* offered an ambiguous cover im-age that might have seemed a rare gesture of support: a squad of just-deplaned troops under the headline, "The Men of the President." But the accompany-ing features were less benign, one questioning Calderón's motives for cozy-ing up to the army, the other calling the Michoacán exercise a "theatrical operation" that would be "probably ineffective."[20]

Three weeks later, Calderón flew to Michoacán to inspect his troops, and it occurred to him to don a military cap and jacket. This was probably a bad idea. Bespectacled, balding, and short, Bismarck he was not. Far from it: Calderón was known as one of the PAN's careerist nerds, with an MA in economics from Mexico's technocratic Autonomous Technological Institute of Mexico (ITAM) and another in public administration from Harvard. While admired in political circles for high intelligence and a withering stare, he was fairly clueless in the art of PR. He wore the olive jacket unbuttoned, as though unsure of his own charade. Worse, the garment looked several sizes too big for him. Worse still, flanked by his physically imposing defense minister, Guillermo Galván, and the no less corpulent state governor, Lázaro Cárdenas Batel, the president looked almost boyish. History too condemned him: In a country long insistent on the separation of army and state, no sitting president had dared to dress in uniform, even those with the prior rank of general. All in all, it was hard for observers to escape the notion that this clumsy effort at martial gravitas was part of a strategy to regain legitimacy after the dubious election six months before.[21]

Mexico's political cartoonists, seeing the images that evening on television, must have issued a collective gasp of delight. Not since 1988, when US Democratic candidate Mike Dukakis sought to bolster his national security credentials by staging a photo op of himself grinning while driving a tank, had a North American politician lent himself so visibly to ridicule.[22]

Over the following week, images of a diminutive Calderón in army cap and jacket appeared in *Milenio*, *Proceso*, *La Jornada* (five times), and *El Universal*. Satirical magazine *El Chamuco*, relaunching after a seven-year hiatus, took it a step further. Its cover cartoon, by *La Jornada*'s El Fisgón, depicted a farcically miniature Calderón dressed in outsize purple military garb, clasping a blood-drenched sword and with his chest decorated with "medals" such as the Televisa logo, as he marched past an imposing portrait of nineteenth-century dictator Porfirio Díaz.[23]

The derision did not end there. The longer Calderón's "war" went on and the more murderous it got, with annual homicides eventually tripling, the wider the chasm yawned between the president's firmness of purpose and the reality of a country hobbled by improvised leadership and bathed in blood. The image of Calderón in his outsize fatigues became a metaphor for his presidency: the Little General Who Couldn't. It was recycled by cartoonists throughout the six-year term and sometimes pushed to absurdist heights. The cover of *El Chamuco* regularly let El Fisgón or *Proceso* cartoonist Hernández do their worst, rendering a stumpy Calderón in an assortment of ill-fitting uniforms, often accompanied by blood, skulls, or body parts.[24]

The two media moments—the announcement of the Michoacán maneuver and the visit to the troops—set a precedent for the dueling narratives of 2006 to 2012: a war of words that paralleled the gun battles in the provinces. Media that had been critical of López Obrador were not necessarily much enthused about Calderón. And many editors, now in their fourth presidential

After declaring a "war" on crime syndicates in late 2006, President Felipe Calderón met with a barrage of satirical cartoons, some of the most cutting by El Fisgón (Rafael Barajas) of *La Jornada*. Courtesy of Rafael Barajas.

era of media openness, were holding power to account as an automatic modus operandi. As the homicide rate spiraled, civic media relentlessly reminded the public that Calderón's regime had set off a human rights catastrophe.

Calderón and his team, having thrust themselves forward as tough on crime, came to see some in the media as wresting the story of his war from their grasp. They had to regain control of it. This they attempted to do, above all, with the most effective ploy of the PRI-era playbook: buying off owners and editors with ad spend. And the fates favored their strategy, for print media were becoming vulnerable, with the trickle of readers and advertisers to the internet turning into a rush.

The Return of Subsidies

Calderón's relationship with the press was somewhat the inverse of his predecessor's. Fox, together with his wife, Marta, had tried at first to charm the major papers. This worked to some extent, notably at *El Universal*. Even *La Jornada* was fairly kind to Marta. But as journalists grew critical of the couple, alleging an inability to get much done on his part and an excess of ambition on hers, the president and his wife withdrew somewhat, apparently hoping that modest increases in federal advertising would buy them kindness. Calderón, by contrast, was initially dismissive of journalists, rather like the similarly egg-headed Ernesto Zedillo, and he forbade most officials to give interviews without Los Pinos's consent. He had barely been in office two weeks when Raymundo Riva Palacio wrote in *El Universal*, "Political communication is strategic for every government that seeks consensus, and this is the great deficiency in design of the presidency of Calderón." What Calderón did do early on was try to buy favor. Federal ad spend increased by 23 percent in 2007.[25]

This initial boost likely had less to do with drug policy than with more mundane problems. Both *Reforma* and *La Jornada* leaned negative on the president during his first 100 days, and this had most to do with his budget cutting for education. *El Universal* did criticize Calderón for going after the narcos, but chiefly on account of the expense involved (fiscal conservatism guided its attitude to Calderón in general). By the end of 2007, moreover, the "drug war" was looking fairly successful. Kingpins had been arrested and others extradited; $207 million was seized in what was reportedly the biggest drug cash bust in history; marines snared twenty-four tons of cocaine in history's biggest coke bust; gang-related murders only climbed by a fraction and the overall homicide rate fell.[26]

But then, as expatriate British journalist Ioan Grillo put it in his bestseller *El Narco*, "Mexico exploded." During 2008, there arose a "full-scale criminal insurgency," with narco-related murders rocketing from 200 to 500 a month. Accounts differ as to why. The Calderón regime claimed its successes the year before put stress on criminal organizations that prompted both turf battles and reprisals against security forces. Academics and investigative journalists claimed that the Sinaloa Cartel of Joaquín "El Chapo" Guzmán and Ismael "El Mayo" Zambada went to war with weakened rivals in a bid for national supremacy, emboldened by a covert alliance with senior government officials.[27]

The violence of 2008 saw a shift in quality as well as quantity. Civilians were massacred for merely patronizing businesses owned by rival gangs. Executions of rival gunmen became performative: filmed and uploaded to You-Tube. The acting head of the federal police, Edgar Millán, was assassinated inside his home in Mexico City. Tijuana, Ciudad Juárez, and Culiacán became battlegrounds. Reporters and TV crews from the United States, Canada, Europe, and Japan descended on Mexico, breathless phrases at the ready. On the reliably sensationalist Fox News, an anchor introduced one report by claiming that the Juárez Cartel had "enough firepower to bring down *a whole country*" and calling the US-Mexico border "a line in the sand *between democracy and chaos*."[28]

On the home front, perhaps the most discomforting media response to Calderón's policy came from *Reforma*, with what it called the Ejecutómetro, or "Execution Meter." Noting that the bodies were piling up without any official effort to count them, senior editor René Delgado tasked a research assistant, Jésica Zermeño, with scouring every issue of the main national dailies since Calderón took office to produce a sum of drug-war-related deaths. Zermeño's research formed the basis for an extensive report, led by sociologist and crime expert Luis Astorga; it featured a double-page graphic of weekly homicides over the first six months of Calderón's initiative. Thereafter, with the interest and controversy this edition generated, the paper ran a weekly body count, eventually tagged the Execution Meter. With its provocative name and regular appearance, the graphic became a constant reminder that Calderón's war was spinning out of control. To the president's irritation, *Reforma* published the Execution Meter throughout his term; in November 2011, the bloodiest year to date, the table of figures went daily. The paper would persist with it for another ten years. Delgado was a little embarrassed about the name—which elicited criticism for normalizing the violence—but he was proud of what the meter achieved as a reference tool.[29]

Reforma reinforced the perception of a policy gone amuck. There were analytical essays with titles such as "The Spiral of Violence" and "War without a New Strategy." One lengthy feature explored abuses committed by the army, its assessment of civilian deaths as affordable "collateral damage," and the immunity from prosecution that it enjoyed. The horrific discovery in August 2010 that seventy-two Central and South American migrants had been shot to death by Zetas in San Fernando, Tamaulipas, prompted a shift in focus among civic media and freelancers toward the victims of violence. At *Reforma*, narrative reportage by Benito Jiménez and Daniela Rea exposed the tactical failings of Calderón's policy and the suffering of the populace. In one exemplary case, Jiménez offered a two-part portrait of Mier, Tamaulipas, a ghost town since locals had fled shoot-outs between the Gulf Cartel and its former allies the Zetas; it was still largely deserted despite the presence of the army. In another case, Rea described Cuernavaca, normally a paradisical getaway for Mexico City residents, transformed by the embedded Beltrán Leyva Cartel into a city of fear, with gang-related homicides more than tripling in a year to 251. Rea also helped spearhead the paper's exposure of clandestine "narcograves," used by criminals to bury multiple victims, of which 156 had been discovered by early 2011.[30]

One sign of Calderón's displeasure with *Reforma* came in the form of regular audits, or what might be termed fiscal harassment. These proved so lengthy and constant that Lázaro Ríos furnished the taxmen with their own office.[31]

La Jornada and *Proceso* opposed Calderón's policy more directly, highlighting its many failures and ridiculing the commander in chief, but that was to be expected from these left-wing publications, for whom Calderón was not only a conservative but an illegitimate president to begin with. In 2008 alone, *Proceso* dedicated twenty-one cover stories to state and crime syndicate violence.[32] Much less predictable was the critical posture of Alejandro Junco's newspapers, given this publisher's sympathy with the PAN. Asserts *Reforma* senior editor Delgado, "We had a very rocky relationship with the Calderón government, more so than with Fox."[33]

Calderón could do little about foreign takes on his policy, but he could try to steer domestic coverage. His main method was to buy his way into the media's good graces. In the bloody year of 2008, federal ad spending leaped 34 percent. It climbed in most subsequent years too. By 2012, Calderón had shelled out close to $3 billion, some two and a half times what Fox had spent. Most of it went to television, where bulletins never veered from the official narrative of Good Government versus Bad Narcos.[34]

Print media scooped up about 10 percent, or roughly $300 million, of the spend. Not all of that cash necessarily bought readily identifiable propaganda, for it probably paid for disguised-as-news *gacetillas* too. Letting his guard slip at a business leaders' event in 2010, Calderón decried some papers for reproducing *narcomantas* (publicly displayed bedsheets painted with threatening messages) on their front pages and added that such page 1 placement "costs any one of you, or the government . . . several million pesos."[35]

Reforma, surprisingly, was the third-ranked recipient of federal ad spend in 2011. But if Calderón thought that the $1 million spent on Junco's paper that year might elicit kinder treatment, he miscalculated. In March, Televisa persuaded 714 of the nation's media to join it in signing an Agreement for News Coverage of Violence. These newspapers, magazines, and broadcasters all pledged to avoid the kind of reporting that, among other things, made them involuntary spokespeople for organized crime, put victims or children at risk, endangered journalists, or interfered in the combatting of criminality. The first and last of these points were of course controversial. Should a paper *never* report a declaration made by a crime syndicate, as Calderón clearly wanted? And what constituted interference? Might not publishers and editors be tempted to err on the side of caution, especially those who depended on federal ad buys? On the other hand, there was a general hope that a more limited coverage would help reduce the murder rate. Whether this indeed occurred is debatable, but scholarly evidence shows that a rise in graphic attention by media to the violence between 2007 and 2010 had prompted crime syndicates to ramp up their public displays of brutality, no doubt in pursuit of greater publicity.[36]

Grupo Reforma refused to sign, despite the fact that several offices of *El Norte* had been targeted with gunfire and grenades and another one burned out by arsonists. The company claimed it had its own criteria for how to cover violence. That reaction surely reflected Junco's stubborn individualism, but there was also the suspicion—as voiced by Carmen Aristegui in a *Reforma* column—that Los Pinos was trying to monopolize the drug policy narrative so as to modify the perception of its failed strategy. As things turned out, front-page coverage of the violence declined dramatically across the Mexico City press over the two years following the pact, despite the fact that the homicide rate remained historically high. But the pact was not the only factor. Among the wide network of regional correspondents and photographers for *El Universal*, for example, personal security fears had grown with reprisal attacks on journalists by the crime syndicates. In addition, the paper's editors were baulking at pasting yet more blood on the page, feeling that the public was sick of it.[37]

Politically, the pact seemed to work. Calderón's approval rating, having declined from an early 2009 peak of 66 percent to 49 percent by May 2011, inched up again.[38]

A culture of self-censorship, having faded during the Salinas, Zedillo, and Fox years, made a comeback under Calderón. It was further evident in a tendency to exalt military offenses and to print—without fact-checking—the army's version of events. This "sin of omission" often coexisted with a "sin of commission," in that the press showed willing to adopt and even enhance the official discourse. Killings of actual or suspected criminal contingents during which soldiers suffered no casualties were reported as "clashes," a term that covered up the army's preference for massacring over taking prisoners, as an acclaimed study by freelancer Daniela Rea and *El País*'s Pablo Ferri illustrates. They observe that Calderón's government used discourse "as a symbolic wall between society and the dead." This logic applied to civilian deaths too: thus the frequency in press reports of the phrases "collateral damage," "up to no good," "in the wrong place at the wrong time." And hence, of course, the unthinking recycling of the US-inspired term with which Calderón baptized his whole policy: *la guerra contra el narcotráfico* (the war against drug trafficking), which in the press was frequently rendered *la guerra contra el narco*. As Oswaldo Zavala has argued, such language furthered a simplistic "narconarrative" that the state had been cultivating since the 1970s and which Calderón took to new heights of dissimulation. For one thing, the national homicide rate reached a historic low in 2007. It was Calderón's "pacification" (i.e., militarization) policy that reversed the trend.[39]

Despite a reputation for intolerance of criticism, Calderón generally did not strong-arm the press by urging owners or editors to fire reporters or switch them from a sensitive beat. According to Jorge Zepeda Patterson, by now editor in chief at *El Universal*, "Generally we had liberty. Calderón allowed criticism, except in rare cases."[40]

Junco, meanwhile, took the government's money. And rather more of it than he had done in the 1990s; back then, in libertarian fashion, he had preached the profitability of independent journalism. But the uncomfortable fact was that Grupo Reforma's revenues, like every other paper's, were shrinking. In the newsroom they could feel it.[41]

The cause of the squeeze was universal: the flight of readers and advertisers to the internet. While, in 2000, an estimated 38 percent of adult Mexicans read a paper and just 15 percent read news online, by 2011 newspaper readership had fallen to 27 percent and internet readership had doubled to 30 percent. The global recession of 2009 caused Mexico's advertisers to cut their collective budget for newspaper ads by about $75 million, a drop of 20 percent, spending almost all of the savings on digital platforms. The newspaper ad market never recovered. By 2012, digital media had overtaken newspapers as recipients of ad spend.[42] If Grupo Reforma, with its strong position in the capital and dominance in Monterrey, was having to tighten its belt, one could only imagine how more precarious media were faring—and thus how their publishers were enticed to sell sympathetic coverage to Calderón or state governors.[43]

Like *Reforma*, *Proceso* and *La Jornada* refused to sign the Agreement for News Coverage of Violence. *La Jornada* may have escaped the consequences; in 2011 it ranked fifth among print media recipients of federal largesse, ahead of the bigger *El Universal*. In the case of *Proceso*, there was nothing to lose, for the Calderón regime had emplaced on it a near-total ad boycott from the start. The magazine had angered the new incumbent by undertaking a legal battle seeking access to the 2006 ballots, in the hope of forcing the thorough recount that López Obrador was demanding. *Proceso*'s relentlessly negative coverage of the drug policy further soured Los Pinos. And so, for example, during 2008, federal agencies bought just 5 pages of ads in *Proceso*, compared with 166 pages in minor news magazine *Vértigo*, despite registered sales of 75,000 for the former and just 4,000 for the latter. This unjust apportioning of public money spurred *Proceso* editor Rafael Rodríguez Castañeda to lodge a formal complaint with the National Human Rights Commission. It took three years for the commission to find in *Proceso*'s favor—and propose a law to curb discretional awarding of advertising. Subsequent governments would pledge to remedy the problem and then fail to do so.[44]

When Calderón stepped down in late 2012, more than 120,000 Mexicans had met violent deaths, close to double the number under Fox. Another 26,000 had disappeared (a conservative estimate). The economy had edged up a mere

1.8 percent, the paltriest growth in four presidencies. The PAN was so unpopular after two terms in power that its candidate placed third in the 2012 election. And yet Calderón left office with a 53 percent approval rating.[45] In cynical PR terms, the nearly $3 billion he channeled to the media—coupled with the impact of the 2011 self-censorship pact—appeared to have been worthwhile.

Still, civic-oriented media ventured beyond the official narrative. So did a cascade of books by investigative reporters, for the publishing industry was giving unprecedented space to long-form journalism. They profiled the crime syndicates; probed the failures and contradictions of the "drug war," including the likely corruption of federal security chief Genaro García Luna (accused of siding with Guzmán and the Sinaloa Cartel); and gave voice to its victims. They also accused the Calderón regime of fomenting crony capitalism in such sectors as oil and mining.

The persistence in the public mind of such exposés would aid future president López Obrador in his vilification of his former electoral opponent. There were many opinion leaders ready to agree with him that Calderón had been not only inept but corrupt. He may have exited with a positive approval score, but by 2020 some 82 percent of Mexicans surveyed by *El Universal* wanted to see Calderón put on trial.[46]

Carlos Slim and the New Business Journalism

For twenty years, the identity of the world's richest person had been unveiled in the March issue of *Forbes*, with its annual "Billionaires" edition. For twenty years that person was always Japanese or American. But in June 2007 the esteemed US magazine, founded in 1917 and counting a staff of 1,000, was scooped by a journalist hunched over a screen in a small Mexico City apartment. Earth's greatest fortune was no longer that of Bill Gates, he announced on his website, but that of a Mexican: Carlos Slim.

The journalist was Eduardo García, and his website, *Sentido Común*.[47] Along with a staff of two, a reporter and a translator, García climbed an outdoor iron staircase to the roof of his house each morning, where the trio occupied a space designed as a maid's quarters. Along with friends, he had invested about $60,000 in the start-up, and since its 2003 launch it had gained 6,000 daily readers. Though the outfit was modest, García was well trained, with an MA in journalism from New York University and ten years' experience as local bureau chief for Bloomberg. He held a queasy fascination with Mexico's billionaire class: how they became so rich, what political cover they enjoyed, how they got away with monopolistic practices, how regulators were trying and usually failing to protect consumers and foster competition. He wanted to share his findings with a broader public than those who could afford Bloomberg's $1,000 monthly fee. He wanted to do so in Spanish.

The year before his scoop, struck by how telecoms magnate Slim had been shooting up the *Forbes* list (fourth in 2005, third in 2006), García told himself, "We can't be finding out from abroad how much this Mexican is worth!" So he started an occasional column called "Slim Watch" and studied the man's acquisitions and assets. He was aided by a recent Mexican law that obliged publicly traded companies to list anyone with at least a 5 percent shareholding in their annual reports. Revising his sums every few months on a spreadsheet, he found that *Forbes* was underestimating Slim's wealth. In April 2007, when *Forbes* had Slim $4 billion behind Gates, García put him at $0.5 billion higher than the Microsoft founder. He wrote a "Slim Watch" but it gained little notice. In late June, however, he saw that Slim's lead had yawned to $6 billion or so, largely due to the rocketing share price of his telephone conglomerate, América Móvil. Not only that, Slim's net worth of $59 billion was equivalent to almost 8 percent of Mexico's entire economy—and this in a country where half of the population of 110 million lived in poverty.

"The gap between Slim and Gates increases," announced "Slim Watch." But *Sentido Común* was a niche start-up, based in a glorified man cave. How was the story going to get traction? García had a couple of cards up his sleeve, which, being a modest sort of chap, he was reluctant to play, but this occasion called for it. The first was his wife, Elisabeth Malkin, who worked for *The New York Times*. Malkin tucked the finding into a story she was preparing on Slim's commitments to philanthropy. The second was Kieran Murray, a former colleague at the Mexico City *News*, García's employer before Bloomberg; Murray was now bureau chief at Reuters. Having fact-checked García's finding, Reuters ran a story on July 2 that began, "Mexican tycoon Carlos Slim is the world's richest man . . . according to a respected tracker of Mexican financial wealth."

"I remember [radio journalist] Carmen Aristegui reading out the Reuters story the next morning and hearing *Sentido Común's* name," García says. Within in a week, the BBC, Fox News, *BusinessWeek*, and *The Guardian* had paid attention. Within another month, *Sentido Común* was quoted about Slim in *Time*, the *Financial Times*, *La Vanguardia* of Barcelona, and local dailies *La Jornada* and *Reforma*. By year's end his readership had grown by a third. The following year, García rented an office and hired two more employees. *Sentido Común* was bona fide.

Perhaps more satisfying still was the story's impact in the public sector. As *Time* put it, "García's math has also grabbed the attention of federal regulators in Mexico, who finally have a substantive antitrust law at their disposal to pursue companies suspected of monopolistic market control—a chronic bane of the Mexican economy." Yet those regulators would move quite slowly against Slim's chief assets: the América Móvil subsidiaries Telmex, which owned 90 percent of landlines, and Telcel, which held close to 80 percent of the cellular market. After three years of changing places with Bill Gates and Warren Buffett, Slim cemented his number 1 ranking in 2010.

———

Business reporting was long the wasteland of Mexican journalism, where the principal venturers were publicists and mercenaries. Until *Reforma* introduced Mexico City to the well-informed business coverage that sister paper *El Norte* was already offering in Monterrey, few newspapers carried "Negocios" sections. Some had finance pages, in which the meagre space for business tended to take one of two forms: press releases written up as stories, probably for a *gacetilla*-style fee, and private-sector gossip columns, whose authors often sold column inches to corporate clients, just as many of their front-section counterparts did to political clients.[48]

Until *Reforma* emerged, more or less reliable daily business news could be found within *El Financiero* and *El Economista*, but as their names suggested, these papers were more interested in public finances and economic indicators than firms. To any reader but a specialist, their front-page stories, with rare exceptions, veered between the arcane and the numbers-heavy soporific. Captains of industry almost never appeared on page 1. What private-sector stories these papers did carry tended to be masked by the custom at Mexico City papers of keeping company names out of headlines. If a business wanted to appear in a headline, it should pay.[49]

Timothy Heyman, a British immigrant banker who had edited an investment newsletter for a thousand subscribers, felt that until the early 1990s, "business journalism in Mexico consisted of financiers who didn't know how to write and journalists who knew nothing of finance." Carlos Monsiváis more or less concurred. Reflecting on the poor job Mexico's papers did of explaining and pursuing the scandalous Fobaproa bank bailout of the mid- to late 1990s, the cultural critic put the problem down to "a journalism obsessively focused on the political and lacking reporters with training in economics."[50]

Eduardo García agonized over this problem; it was another motive for founding *Sentido Común*. Furthermore, articles often suffered from the same *declaracionitis* that pervaded political coverage: public declarations written up without questioning. Again, *Reforma* offered something different. It had the best-informed of the business columnists in Alberto Aguilar, who often reported what some tycoons might not want to be known, and it boasted the most fearless staff. When the mighty (and habitually arrogant) media conglomerate Televisa launched its direct-by-satellite TV service Sky, in partnership with Rupert Murdoch, the service fell short of the hundred-plus channels once promised; instead, due to technical delays, Sky was offering sixty and no pay-per-view. The headline in the *Reforma* business section poked fun: "Sky Launches Half-Heartedly." The reporter responsible promptly received an angry call from Televisa.[51]

As for magazines, the field was thin. Monthlies with names like *Mundo Ejecutivo* or *Líderes Mexicanos* were minor efforts whose business model allegedly rested on the selling of cover stories to vain executives and ambitious politicians.[52]

The exception was the oldest business magazine of them all, *Expansión*.[53] The brainchild of a San Francisco businessman called Harvey Poppel, *Expansión* launched in 1969. Mexico's economy had been enjoying fifteen years of continuous growth, and the initial idea was a fortnightly journal, wholly funded by advertising, that would explain economic and management trends to business owners and executives. Little by little, those men—for twenty years or so they were all men—became the magazine's main subjects. By the early 1990s, *Expansión* was easily Mexico's premier business publication, reputed as trustworthy and free of mercenary practices.

It was also pretty dull. Rarely did it publish anything that might challenge its readers, let alone the subject of a profile. Companies were portrayed in optimistic terms. CEOs were treated as visionaries. One item that generated broad controversy, in June 1990, was a ranking of Mexico's 100 most prominent businessmen.[54] Many of Mexico's most prominent businessmen, it turned out, did not like to be ranked. Some wrote privately to complain that the piece had turned them into kidnapping targets. Four years would pass before *Expansión* pulled that stunt again.

Things began to change for the better in 1994, when Poppel sold up. The buyer was the Chilton Company, part of the US media conglomerate Capital Cities/ABC and much less concerned than Poppel about causing offense with an incisive story. The climate was propitious for better business journalism, as foreign media interest in the North American Free Trade Agreement had greatly increased the number of reporters writing about Mexican firms. It also boosted reporters' autonomy, as García found when working at Bloomberg. After one of his reporters wrote a feature on how the global growth of Cemex had been funded by monopolistic profits at home, the cement giant pulled its ads from *Bloomberg Markets* magazine—but their employer did not care. The inquiring practices of Bloomberg, *The Wall Street Journal*, and others influenced their Mexican peers.[55]

Chilton soon named as editor in chief a twenty-eight-year-old, a reporter with a thirst for knowing what business leaders really thought and did behind the scenes. A transformation of *Expansión*, from PR vehicle to serious magazine, would distinguish his ten-year watch.

This young man was Javier Martínez Staines. Tall and fair enough to mix in Mexico's racially exclusive business arena without raising eyebrows, he had joined *Expansión* seven years earlier. In 1994 he had written critically of Agriculture Minister Carlos Hank González, a man with a long record of mixing politics and business; his article accused him of ensuring several trade agreements gave him exclusive rights to import sugar and grains.[56] Such efforts sharpened the young man's sense of what a business magazine could achieve. He also felt *Expansión* should do more to foster entrepreneurialism.

"Eighty percent of businessmen in Mexico were basically government contractors," Martínez Staines recalls. "The magazine was very close to advertisers. It was 100 percent about being a business, nothing about journalism."[57]

Martínez Staines figured that a more adventurous, proactive magazine needed an advisory board of senior figures to help engineer the changes. A board could also generate story tips. He invited a dozen or so leaders, including radio industry mogul Clemente Serna.

"When we did more neutral, objective work, we got pushback. This was a process that took a lot of convincing," says Martínez Staines.[58] While the magazine had not directly sold flattering stories, it had allowed companies to "buy goodwill" with the magazine via substantial ad placement. When *Expansión* began more of a warts-and-all coverage, some advertisers pulled out, among them breadmaking giant Grupo Bimbo. Martínez Staines remembers Bimbo saying, "The tone of *Expansión* has ceased to be encouraging and allied with the business world, instead becoming a medium of unnecessary questioning."

Soon there was a second change: Capital Cities/ABC merged with Disney, which had different priorities, and Mexico was in recession. The conglomerate put the magazine up for sale, and in 1998 Serna bought it. The radio magnate shared Martínez Staines's enthusiasm for a platform that did more than praise rich men in suits. A 1998 cover, for a series of features on Mexico's enormous informal economy, featured a smiling maid. "She is Eva," said the title. "She is 19. She earns 1,200 pesos [$130] a month."[59] Serna's ownership cemented the start of a golden age of reporting at *Expansión*.

Martínez Staines was able to triple his newsroom staff to eighteen and undertake more ambitious stories. A 2002 cover profiled the controversial Guadalajara entrepreneur Jorge Vergara, founder of a health products giant called Omnilife. Vergara was a curious example of a self-made man in a country whose business elite mostly passed their firms from generation to generation. But he was widely criticized for the dubious methods he had used to build his business, one modeled on the US health products behemoth for which Vergara

Top business magazine *Expansión* was for its first twenty-five years a cheerleader for Mexican business, but after a 1994 buyout it offered insightful coverage, such as this 2002 feature about Guadalajara-based mogul Jorge Vergara. Courtesy of *Expansión*.

had once worked: Herbalife (a firm itself attacked for false advertising and operating a pyramid scheme). Vergara was also deemed to have a massive ego, which led him to believe he could succeed at anything, even the notoriously high-stakes pursuit of film production. Martínez Staines signaled Vergara's high opinion of himself with his title for the cover, "I, Jorge," an allusion to the Robert Graves novel about imperial Rome, *I, Claudius*.[60] Vergara hated the article.

Having built the Grupo Expansión brand and expanded its stable of titles from four to fifteen, Serna chose to sell in 2005. As the group's leading publication, *Expansión* had seen its subscriber base grow to 45,000, strong for a Mexican periodical, and it shifted another 25,000 or so via stores and kiosks. The magazine's annual revenue was a decent $13 million, only a tiny fraction of which was government advertising. Now the buyer was Time Inc., whose strength and reach offered continued stability and partnering possibilities with its TV asset CNN. Martínez Staines, who was close to Serna, chose to leave that year. After two short-lived editorships, the magazine's tiller passed to Alberto Bello, a Spanish journalist, who would lead a successful embrace of digital platforms.

By the start of the Calderón era, Mexican business reporting was unprecedentedly rich and sophisticated. In bimonthly, daily, and online formats, *Expansión*, *Reforma*, and *Sentido Común* brought the public closer than ever to the inner workings and ups and downs of the private sector. So did a weekly newspaper, *El Semanario* (2003), founded by former *Reforma* business editor Samuel García. Short-lived but feisty—short-lived *because* it was feisty, some say—*El Semanario* ran critical features about leaders, including Slim as a financier (suspiciously influential in the corporate credit sector) and Ricardo Salinas Pliego as the CEO of several publicly traded companies ("arrogant," according to US regulators; resistant to transparency, according to Mexican observers).[61]

There remained the challenge, universal to newspapers and magazines, of balancing objective and inquisitive coverage with the need to retain advertisers. In Mexico that challenge had an unusual twist, because so much of the economy—and hence the ad pie—was controlled, directly or indirectly, by one man: Slim.

Carlos Slim and Media Capture

While Carlos Slim ruled the billionaires' roost, *Proceso* was strangely tepid in covering him. Strangely, because at the start of Slim's meteoric rise it had questioned his dealings the most. Much later, when *Forbes* placed Slim in the number three spot in its March 2007 billionaires issue, there was a flurry of media attention in Mexico, and *Proceso*, for the first time in twelve years, made him the focus of a hard-hitting cover: "The Wealth of Slim: Without Limits, without Shame, without Frontiers." These embarrassments, plus questioning coverage in US media ("You are engulfed by Slim in Mexico," political scientist George Grayson told the *Los Angeles Times*), pushed the billionaire to call a hasty press conference, where he told 100 assembled journalists that his galloping wealth owed merely to a rising stock market; Mexico's telecoms market was "competitive," he claimed.[62] Then *Proceso* mostly left him alone. Meanwhile, ads for what had become his profit center, cellular operator Telcel, regularly appeared in its pages.

Slim's winning of the 1990 auction of Telmex, the flagship privatization of the Salinas era, had put him in the public eye, and *Proceso* was an early monger of the rumor that his wealth owed to political alliances. A profile just after the Telmex result slyly noted, "Public slander explains Carlos Slim's wealth as a result of his being a front man for Miguel de la Madrid . . . and even Salinas de Gortari himself."[63]

The idea that the auction had been rigged would grow in the public mind as Slim used Telmex, including its seven-year protected monopoly over long-distance calls and its unique national cellular concession, as a money-spinner that took him to the top of Mexico's rich list within four years. *Proceso* encouraged that idea. Telmex was "a firm set up to win, with a [company] union that doesn't bother it," affirmed the title of a 1992 feature, which twice noted Slim's "closeness" to Salinas. In 1994, after Slim surpassed Emilio Azcárraga Milmo as Mexico's richest, the magazine assailed Telmex for "illegitimate" profits.[64]

Once Salinas left office, *Proceso* amped up the pressure. It platformed accusations that the Telmex auction had been tarnished by "favoritisms" toward Slim. It claimed that Slim and Azcárraga had been the moguls closest to Salinas, who helped make them the wealthiest; this story recorded the audacity of *El Financiero* reporter Alicia Salgado, who had recently put it to Slim point blank: Is it true that you were able to acquire Telmex because Salinas is your partner? ("That's foolishness," Slim replied.) *Proceso* then brought out a multipart cover story on the "turbidities of Salinas" in his privatization of Telmex and the banks. This issue elicited a lengthy letter of complaint from Slim. But *Proceso* went undaunted, with further features on Telmex's "fraudulent" auction and an attempt by PRD leader Cuauhtémoc Cárdenas to bring suit against Salinas and his functionaries for alleged crimes associated with it.[65] To cap it all, Rodríguez Castañeda published a book, *Operation Telmex*, an investigative account of the sale that fleshed out the magazine's claims.[66]

Abruptly, the focus and the accusations receded. In 1996, *Proceso* devoted to Slim less than half the space it had given him the year before. The subdued tone continued in 1997: His controversial telephone assets went unmentioned. This was the same year that Telmex—its protected monopoly at last expiring—began advertising in *Proceso*.[67] Slim would buy full-page ads in the journal for another twenty years. He would never again suffer the barrage of bad press that *Proceso* fired at him between 1992 and 1995.

Had Slim used ad spend to capture Mexico's most critical medium? The story may be more complex than that, due to an unlikely friendship between Slim and Julio Scherer that emerged around the time the editor retired. According to the evenhanded biography *Slim* by journalist Diego Osorno, the two men were reconciled by mutual friend Juan Antonio Pérez Simón, Telmex's vice chairman and, like Slim, an art collector. One irony of Slim's career is that, while often criticized as a poster boy for unregulated neoliberal excess, he was not by creed a Darwinistic libertarian but a social democrat. He cultivated friendships on the left; he dined several times with Fidel Castro; he would be the most visible business ally of López Obrador during the politician's mayorship, revitalizing with him Mexico City's colonial center.[68]

The friendship with Slim was put to the test in 1998, when one of Scherer's sons was kidnapped. Woken by the abductors' phone call and desperate to meet their demand for 300,000 pesos (some $33,000), the journalist dialed the richest person he knew. Slim moved at once, gathering the cash he held at home and mobilizing his friends. The ransom was paid within hours and the son returned in one piece. That year, *Proceso*'s only story about Slim was an interview with the head of the telephone workers' union, who recycled the magnate's line that long-distance phone competition was failing because rivals did not invest enough. Two years later, Slim bankrolled the first *Proceso* website.[69]

As of 2005, when Fox imposed on the magazine the federal ad boycott that subsequent presidents would more or less continue, and during the Calderón era, when circulation began to slide, *Proceso* found itself with a growing need for a Maecenas. Center-left moneybags Slim fit the bill.[70]

Slim's muscle as an advertiser, thanks to his holding companies América Móvil (Telmex, Telcel) and Grupo Carso (retail, construction, and much else), was felt in newsrooms across the capital. His declarations on the economy, his philanthropy, and his moves abroad gained copious column inches in the daily papers too. When Sallie Hughes interviewed editors during the Fox years, she found them all wary of offending Slim in print and unwilling to discuss him on the record. Said one, "There has been a shift from the government to the corporations in the capacity to influence the media." And it was not just Slim. Editors and reporters spoke about having to pussyfoot around broadcasters Televisa and TV Azteca, cement giant Cemex, the major banks, and other big corporate advertisers. Editors had to take special care not to offend with headlines. Reporters sometimes found their stories censored.[71]

Reforma coddled Slim, relates the magnate's biographer Osorno, because he was friends with its publisher Junco and had once helped the paper out of a hole by buying a year's advertising in advance. Slim was also on the board at *El Universal*.[72]

So who held Slim and his ilk to account? Who amped up pressure on the regulators, the courts, and Congress to put a leash on Mexico's monopolists and duopolists? The answer was a patchwork: a mix of foreign media, international organizations, and the minority of Mexican journalists who would not be cowed by the threat of ad boycotts, lawsuits, or loss of personal favors.

Eduardo García was one. Slim's standard defense of his 80 percent market share and 50 percent profit margins was that rival firms were not investing enough, and in 2008, as the criticisms of his business grew louder, Telmex launched a TV ad campaign featuring a voice that cried, "Invest already!" García made that phrase the title of a feature that deconstructed the ad and then exposed Slim's defense as a lie. Spain's Telefónica had already invested $9 billion but had repeatedly come up against Telmex obstructionism over connections to its network. Soon after his story appeared, Telmex dropped the ad. "It might have run its course," García says, "but my story *could* have been a factor."[73]

Jorge Zepeda Patterson was another. He edited a collection profiling eleven magnates, *The Masters of Mexico*, written by leading reporters. While admitting their entrepreneurship, this popular volume did not shy from showing the political favoritism that had helped them grow their billions. It flagged their near imperviousness to regulators and their proximity to presidents. Francesc Relea of *El País* penned the chapter on Slim, depicting him as a King Midas who promotes his own image as such and a monopolist who rejects the label.[74] A few years later, riffing on Relea's portrait, Zepeda posted to YouTube a widely seen video that showed through a series of common purchases how difficult it was to spend a day in Mexico without repeatedly putting money in Slim's pocket.

Slim's most fearless critic was Denise Dresser, a political scientist and *Reforma* columnist with lucid prose and a cutting turn of phrase. By now she was penning a second column, in *Proceso*, and often commenting on radio. Year on year she called for greater regulation of his telephone monopoly and greater willingness among her compatriots to criticize him publicly. In one column she alleged, "The loser in the construction of the Slim empire ... is the Mexican consumer." Slim eventually invited her for coffee, and he opened with a question: "Why don't you like me?" He tried to sway her with charts showing the comparative costs of his phone businesses. Seeing she was unconvinced, he asked, "Why are you so obsessed with competition?" To Dresser, this attitude typified Mexico's business elites, who viewed their sectors as rightful domains, like feudal lords.[75]

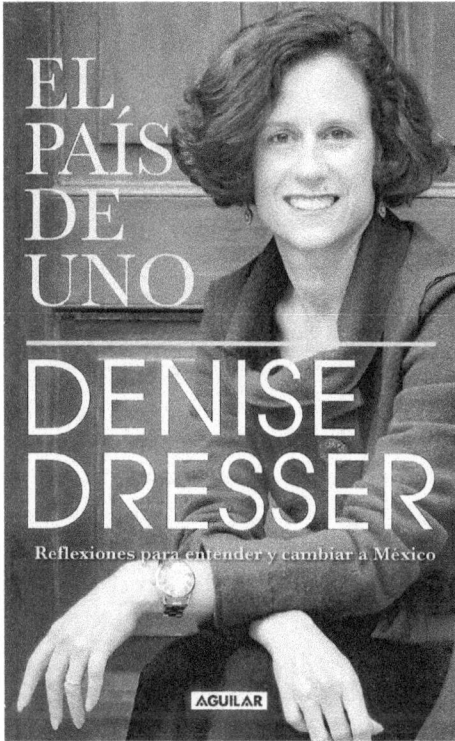

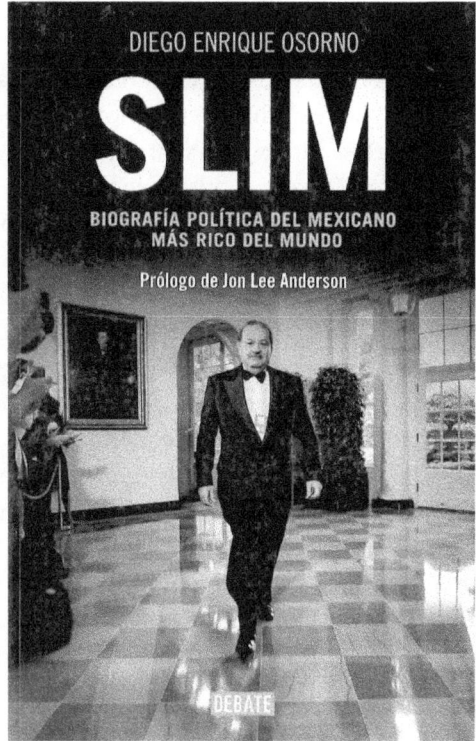

Until he was outed in 2007 as the world's richest individual, Carlos Slim received scant local critical attention. Pioneers of an evenhanded criticism included columnist Denise Dresser and freelancer Diego Osorno. Courtesy of Penguin Random House (México).

Dresser pursued her crusade and frequently consulted with regulators, who would admit the pressure they felt from Slim, Salinas Pliego, and other billionaires. Her 2009 "Open Letter to Carlos Slim" in *Proceso*, alleging the inconsistency and hypocrisy of his public declarations on competitivity and entrepreneurialism, earned a Nationalism Journalism Award. In a best-selling book, whose title approximately translates to *A Country of One's Own*, Dresser offered a diagnosis of Mexico's economic disparities, fueled by corruption and impunity, and had a lot to say on Slim. She noted the irony of his image as a promoter of economic development and the passivity with which many of her compatriots regarded him: "Perhaps he's a monopolist but he's our monopolist."[76]

Meanwhile, independent media put a spotlight on Eduardo Pérez Motta, the long-serving and oft-embattled head of the Federal Monopolies Commission (CFC). Frequently they interviewed him, casting a sympathetic light on his battle to rein in Mexico's worst-offending monopolies and sector-predominant corporations, especially those most obstructing competition.

His efforts helped reduce Slim's telephone hegemony by 13 percent and Cemex's share of cement sales by 4 percent, but he proved incapable of affecting Bimbo's 90 percent control of bread sales or Televisa's 70 percent broadcast share. When Pérez Motta stepped down after nine years, *Expansión* afforded him a hero's farewell with a seven-page profile. Media attention to Pérez Motta and other regulators fueled a public narrative that they were waging the war of the just in their efforts to undercut the privileges and protections long enjoyed by the billionaire class. Indeed, such regulators actively courted the press as a means to building public support for their work.[77]

Between 2009 and early 2013, the CFC, Supreme Court, and Congress all issued findings and resolutions on Slim's quasi-monopoly. América Móvil lost its PR battle, waged in part within Mexico's press, against a 2012 report by the Organization for Economic Cooperation and Development that claimed Telmex's monopoly pricing had slowed Mexico's economic development by nearly 2 percent per year. PAN, PRI, and PRD lawmakers together found the report's arguments persuasive enough to propose sweeping reforms to the telecoms sector in March 2013. These institutions' rulings had already caused América Móvil's stock price to gradually slide; now it plummeted. In May, Bill Gates retook the world's-richest title.[78]

Slim today is still a tremendously wealthy man. Profits lost in Mexico have been regained in South America. On the Bloomberg Billionaires Index (which since 2012 has updated the world's major fortunes at the close of Wall Street trading each day), he spent much of 2023 climbing from $80 billion to $100 billion, at which level he more or less remained during 2024, while oscillating between tenth and twentieth place. But he no longer exerts the sway over the Mexican stock market—where his firms once made up four-tenths of its entire worth—nor the grip over the telephone sector that he held during the Fox and Calderón eras. Making phone calls has become much cheaper for Mexicans. Most other long-standing monopolies and duopolies too, though still dominant, are neither as rapacious nor as outrageously profitable as before. Televisa, moreover, is much weakened. According to one study, "Between 1999 and 2018, the Mexican Competition Authority [i.e., the CFC] imposed more sanctions on monopolistic practices than the US antitrust authorities combined and was close to the revered record of the European Commission."[79] The evolution of reporting and commenting on business is part of that story.

Chapter 9

Reporting on Crime Syndicates and the Corrupt

> It's the great paradox of Mexican democracy: as the authoritarian regime disappears, the number of murders of journalists increases.
>
> —Jorge Carrasco, editor in chief, *Proceso*

> I maintain that investigative journalists are in the crossfire. On one side, the threat and lethality of drug trafficking and organized crime, and on the other, the repression and pressures of Mexico's [national and local] governments.
>
> —Adela Navarro, editor in chief, *Zeta*

Fragments from the Provinces

Ernesto Aroche lay face down on the floor while three men with guns ransacked the office of the news site he had founded. He was overwhelmed with anger and frustration. He thought, "What can I do? What can I do?"[1]

Lying near him, Mely Arellano, his partner in life and work, worried how Ernesto might react. They had been friends for a dozen years and colleagues at several of Puebla's newspapers. She knew he did not scare easily and feared he might do something rash.

After the burglars left, their arms full of loot, Aroche sprang up and chased them out onto the street. A colleague ran after him and restrained him. But the burglars were anyway too quick, a waiting car speeding them into the December dusk.

The three journalists took stock of the damage to their operation, the small and bold online newsmagazine *LadoB* (B side). The thieves had taken six laptops, several cell phones, backpacks, and a haul of company documents. They had been quick. They had yelled at the journalists to *"get down on the fucking floor!"* After that they had not spoken.

Having given their statements to the police and visited the district attorney's office, Aroche convened his editors and reporters at the home of a friend and they all debated what had happened. The professionalism of the thieves suggested off-duty cops. *LadoB* had only launched five months before, in July 2011. Whom had it offended?

The likeliest suspect, they came to agree, was the state's secretary for public security, Ardelio Vargas. A renowned hard-liner, Vargas was a Puebla native who had risen in national law enforcement, first in the army, then in the secret service, and finally in the federal police. In the last capacity, he gained infamy for involvement in the bloody repression of 2006 at Atenco in the State of México, where locals were protesting plans for a new Mexico City airport. Hundreds had been arrested, two killed, and many women allegedly abused or raped by police. Then, in early 2011, Vargas was called back to Puebla by the hard-line new governor, Rafael Moreno Valle Rosas.[2]

As chief of local law enforcement, Vargas lived up to his reputation for intolerance of social protest. His state police harassed and arrested marchers, made illegal searches of homes, and allegedly tortured detainees—in one case with electric shocks to the testicles. *LadoB*, founded on principles of public service, covered it all. "Vargas Accused of Being 'the Greatest Repressor That Puebla Has Had,'" ran one headline, quoting a complaint from thirty-five civic organizations.[3] A week before the burglary, the site ran a mocking cartoon of Vargas as a tubby version of Kalimán, a turbaned superhero of 1970s comics, known for his detective skills and great strength. A police-beat reporter told them that the picture bothered Vargas a lot. Nonetheless, Aroche and his team would never succeed in conclusively linking the burglary to Vargas, and the perpetrators would never be traced.

"The only thing we cannot do is give up, because then they win," Aroche told his colleagues on the night of the incident.

The immediate dilemma was that the theft had left them with a single desktop computer. *LadoB* published nothing for a month. But thanks to a fundraiser, the team acquired new laptops and returned to action in January. With a business model that did not rely on state largesse, their dedication to watchdog journalism remained. Announced the first headline, "A Year of Public Insecurity with Moreno Valle and Ardelio Vargas." Murder, kidnapping, theft, and rape had all risen in Puebla during 2011. Moreover, in Moreno Valle, *LadoB* had one of Mexico's most despotic governors to hold to account.[4]

———

Luis Carlos Santiago died from bullets to the head at two in the afternoon on Independence Day. He was interning as a photojournalist. He was twenty-one.[5]

That September 16, 2010, someone had been murdered at a shopping center, and Santiago accompanied a staff photographer, Carlos Manuel Sánchez, to take photos of the crime scene. Although the mall was very close to the offices of their employer, *El Diario de Juárez*, they arrived by car, and it was in the parking lot that they were shot at by several young men in another car. Santiago was at the wheel and he crashed the car as he died. Sánchez, hit several times, scrambled out and ran. One of the attackers gave chase, but after firing twice and missing he gave up.

Were Santiago and Sánchez shot at to stop them reporting the earlier murder? (Unlikely, as hit jobs in public places are usually designed to send a message.) Was the shooting of Santiago, as initial reports from local and federal authorities would have it, related to his "personal activities"? Or had the two young men been followed to the mall and targeted because they were employees of *El Diario*, the leading daily in the state of Chihuahua, which had a reputation for refusing to be silenced by threats?

The personnel of *El Diario* had endured the nightmare of a murdered colleague once too often. Back in 1991, their columnist Víctor Manuel Oropeza had been stabbed to death in his doctor's office, probably on the orders of a corrupt police commander, although the crime was never solved. In October 2008, another columnist, David García Monroy, numbered among a dozen killed when hooded gunmen burst into the bar where he was drinking and opened fire with machine guns; this crime too was never solved, but García Monroy's death looked like the random consequence of an unhinged narco mission.[6] Only a month later, one of the paper's top writers, crime reporter Armando "El Choco" Rodríguez, died one morning outside his home, at the wheel of his car. As his eight-year-old daughter sat watching, a hitman walked up and fired ten times through the driver's window.

Of the two gangsters eventually named in a federal bulletin as responsible for Rodríguez's murder, *El Diario* news editor Rocío Gallegos found that one had died in jail three months earlier and the other had complained to the National Human Rights Commission that he had "confessed" under torture. After another two years, federal prosecutors admitted that agents dispatched to Juárez were unable to find people willing to speak. Finally, in 2016, eight years after El Choco's murder, the alleged gunman (and possible torture victim) was sentenced to thirty years. The mastermind remained free—a situation unlikely to change. Just after the conviction, freelancer Témoris Grecko visited *El Diario* to research the murder for a book about the perils of Mexican journalism, *Killing the Story*. A reporter who had worked with Rodríguez told him, "Most of the people who participated in the investigation are dead." The first federal investigator appointed to the case, his successor, agents and experts from the state attorney's office—for one reason or another, they had all been killed.

In 2010, the year of Luis Carlos Santiago's death, Juárez recorded more than 3,000 murders, twice the total of two years earlier. This cemented its per capita ranking as the most homicidal city on earth.[7] The slaughter raised the siege mentality and daily anxiety of functionaries, law enforcement agents, and journalists alike. Two days after Santiago was murdered, several *narcomantas* were hung from footbridges across Juárez, directed at the press. To the editors of *El Diario*, this was the final straw. They wrote an anguished front-page editorial. Addressed to the "organizations" that were disputing the city's *plaza* (a narco term for exclusive territory), it amounted to a withering critique of federal and local governments: "You are, at present, the de facto authorities in this city because the legally instituted powers have not been able to keep our colleagues from dying." It went on, "We don't want any more dead. We don't want any more injured nor any more intimidation. It's impossible to do our jobs in these conditions. Tell us, therefore, what you expect from us as a media outlet."[8]

What struck observers most, spurring coverage around the country and abroad, was the editorial's desperate headline, more a cri de coeur than a literal question: "What do you want from us?"[9]

The complexity of *El Diario*'s plight explained the variety of responses. Toronto's *Globe and Mail*, supportive of President Felipe Calderón's policies, sniffed that "negotiating with criminal organizations is not an option." *The New York Times*, by contrast, empathized: "El Diario has shown great courage in the past." Sympathy among other Mexican papers based in high-violence regions led to similar editorials and opinion pieces. A year later, *El Diario* (along with Culiacán weekly *Río Doce*) was named a corecipient of the highest accolade in Latin American journalism, the Moors Cabot Prize from the Columbia University School of Journalism. As for Los Pinos, already upset at *El Diario*'s criticisms of Joint Operation Chihuahua, a scheme to combat the crime syndicates with hordes of soldiers and federal police, it restricted the paper's access to federal advertising in both 2011 and 2012.[10]

El Diario insisted in its editorial that asking what criminals wanted of it was "not a surrender." But how could the paper's editors and writers *not* now tread more carefully? Like all print media, the paper had also to deal with declining revenues. And like many in the provinces, it had to contend with often unsympathetic governors and mayors. Over subsequent years, observers (including Grecko) noted a decline in the paper's independence and journalistic standards. In 2013, news editor Gallegos was promoted to editor in chief, but in early 2018 she was demoted, as the paper's owners saw her critical journalism standing in the way of better advertising contracts from the state government. So she quit, asserting her belief that "journalism should neither be close to nor in the service of the authorities." She then founded the independent news site *La Verdad* (The Truth).[11]

––––––––––

Shortly before Jesús Blancornelas died of cancer, in 2006, he handed control of *Zeta* to Adela Navarro and one of his sons, René Blanco. Navarro handled editorial while Blanco supervised photography. On Navarro's watch, out of concern for reporters' safety, features about drug traffickers or their political protectors began to be bylined "Zeta Investigations"; papers elsewhere adopted a similar policy. Otherwise, *Zeta* remained fearless, whether

Jesús Blancornales (*far right*, interviewing Vicente Fox on the campaign trail in 2000) directed *Zeta* until 2006, when he turned editorial duties over to Adela Navarro (*second from the right*). Next to Navarro is senior editor Francisco Ortiz. Photograph by Ramón T. Blanco Villalón, courtesy of *Zeta*.

the subject was the Arellano Félix Organization, as a costly factional split led both sides to diversify into kidnappings; the Sinaloa Cartel, as it gained influence with Tijuana officials; or the paper's old foe, business leader Jorge Hank Rhon.[12]

Navarro received a blunt reminder of the peril in which she daily put herself in January 2010, with an unusually credible death threat. In the age of social media, death threats, often anonymous, are not uncommon for journalists of Navarro's profile, especially in states where organized crime is deep-rooted; most can be dismissed as insincere scaremongering or trolling. But the call that Navarro received that day came as a tip-off from an official at the US State Department. Via a phone tap, a joint DEA-FBI investigation had heard a lieutenant in the Arellano Félix Organization ordering the killing of three journalists: Navarro, her codirector Blanco, and their editor in chief. Given the authority of the tip-off, Navarro managed to get herself and her colleagues each assigned seven military bodyguards for several months. In years to come, they would hear of further death threats. Usually, it was their US contacts who supplied the tip-offs.[13]

Navarro's leadership of *Zeta* through the years of greatest violence—both in her city and for journalists in general—earned her many admirers. In 2007 the Committee to Protect Journalists honored her with its International Press Freedom Award. A slew of further honors followed: Spain's Ortega y Gassett Prize in 2008; Italy's Anna Politkovskaja Prize and Argentina's International Freedom of the Press Prize in 2009; the Honor Medal from the Missouri School of Journalism in 2010; the Courage in Journalism Award from the International Women's Media Foundation in 2011; inclusion among *Foreign Policy* magazine's Top 100 Global Thinkers in 2012 and a profile in the PBS documentary *Reportero* the same year. In the fall of 2021, Navarro was both a corecipient of the Moors Cabot Prize and the model for a key character in the final season of the Netflix series *Narcos: Mexico*.[14]

Perhaps a few of those prizes owed something to a bandwagon effect, given the appetite in the global North for photo ops with the heroes of the global South. But to Navarro, each one was valuable: "I've always said that awards constitute a network of protection for *Zeta*. Each one tells governments and criminals that we have allies."[15]

————

Pedro Argüello, Amancio Cantú, Miguel Domínguez Zamora, and Guillermo Martínez Alvarado all simply vanished. The four men were working for papers in Reynosa, Tamaulipas, across the Rio Grande from McAllen, Texas. On the night of March 1, 2010, they each received the same threatening phone call: "Meet us or we'll come for you."[16]

Perhaps fearing that the second option would put their families at risk, perhaps hoping for safety in numbers, these four and two other colleagues agreed to rendezvous at the designated place. There they were abducted by armed men. While two of them later escaped, the foursome were never heard from again.

Levantón is the term Mexicans use. Literally, the word means a "hoisting," as of a heavy object. Figuratively, it means abduction, usually by being forced at gunpoint into a vehicle, often by criminal elements, sometimes by state agents. Not all of the *levantados*—the taken—are killed. Among journalists, some are just given a warning; others are roughed up with it. Among more vulnerable victims, many are forced by the crime syndicates to work for them, as marijuana pickers, tunnel diggers, or sex slaves.

Since Argüello, Cantú, Domínguez, and Martínez Alvarado lived in one of the deadliest states in which to practice journalism, and since more than a decade has elapsed with no sign of them, the likelihood is that they were killed. Probably they were tortured first, for one of those who was kidnapped with them, but managed to escape, died in hospital nine days later from the beating he sustained. Yet the unknowability of the facts made the burden for their families especially hard to bear. "You can't imagine what it feels like," a relative of Domínguez told a reporter two years later. He added, "We can't say anything, because [the cartels] find out everything. They've bought off judges, police, taxi drivers . . ."

Muddying the picture further was the background of Argüello. When the Argentine author Gabriel Pasquini researched his disappearance, one of Argüello's employers told him, "I strongly doubt it's an attack on freedom of speech."[17] The reporter who had broken the story of the *levantón* said there had been no formal investigation, while Argüello had been one of a number of local reporters who had "involved themselves" in the climate of violence. The man's wife confirmed that he had worked part time in the Reynosa Police Department, a known criminal stronghold. Finally, Pasquini tracked down a former colleague of Argüello's who had fled the country. The source revealed that Argüello had a knack of arriving first at a crime scene; he would call reporters and encourage them to cover the stories "that he and the group that he worked for wanted"; and three months before his disappearance, Argüello had phoned his former colleague to convey a warning from some very upset members of the Zetas crime syndicate. Pasquini did not feel the need to draw conclusions. The evidence was clear: Argüello had been a *narcoperiodista*, a journalist in the pay of a crime syndicate. He had presumably worked as an *enlace*, or liaison, not only writing what they wanted but goading others to do likewise. So either Argüello had done something to displease his paymasters, or he had been hoisted by their rivals.[18]

The silence of the taken was met by the silence of the press. Six weeks earlier, Reynosa had witnessed the killing of a senior Zeta by a member of the Gulf Cartel, which until then had employed the Zetas as enforcers. The incident proved momentous, leading to a swift severing of ties between the two gangs, an orgy of urban violence (soon spreading to other states), and, after a series of threatening phone calls, the refusal of most local reporters to cover any of it. Their refusal hardened after the March 1 *levantón*.

"Before, if there was a shootout, the scene would be full of journalists," one Reynosa reporter told *The New York Times*. Fearing for his life, he had stopped covering narco violence. "Now . . . everyone stays away."

Said another reporter, who had recently quit the police beat, "I'm censoring myself. There's no other way to put it. But so is everybody else."[19]

Uniform self-censorship gave rise to another term: *zonas de silencio* (zones of silence). In such regions, news about narco violence was either nonexistent or limited to what the locally dominant crime syndicate told editors to publish. In Tamaulipas, the zone soon stretched throughout the state. Seven months after the Reynosa *levantón*, Mexico's military seized Tony Tormenta, the Gulf Cartel's Matamoros capo, following an eight-hour gun battle that brought the city to a standstill. No local paper reported the capture.[20]

Zones of silence also emerged in Michoacán, Guerrero, and Veracruz. Surveying Guadalajara in 2016, crime reporter Javier Valdez found that even major media in Mexico's second-largest city avoided narco themes. In some cities, the climate grew so oppressive that publishers announced that their papers would no longer cover organized crime. This was the call made in 2012 by Ninfa Deándar Martínez, publisher of *El Mañana* of Nuevo Laredo. For eight years *El Mañana* had been targeted: An editor in chief was stabbed to death in the street; a Deándar family member was abducted; gunmen stormed the paper's offices, spraying bullets and injuring several staff; three of its reporters numbered among the *levantados* of Reynosa, where *El Mañana* had a local edition. The final straw was another attack on its offices, which were raked by gunfire and hit by a grenade. Three years later, *El Mañana* dared to suspend its policy of silence and lead its Matamoros edition with a report on a three-day urban battle between factions of the Gulf Cartel. The day the paper hit the street, two gunmen entered its building, dragged the editor from his office, bundled him into a van, and beat him up while driving him around town. If he printed anything else on local violence, they said, they would return and kill him.[21]

———

Employees of the national media were rarely targeted. The infamous assassination of columnist Manuel Buendía in 1984 was a rarity. Part-time contributors could be vulnerable, but for all the growing strength of the crime syndicates and the delinquency of provincial power brokers, there persisted an unwritten agreement that full-time employees of the Mexico City press were not to be killed. Two days after the Reynosa *levantón* of March 2010, a reporter and cameraman for Milenio TV were hoisted in the same city, by members of the Gulf Cartel, after reporting on the violence. They were held overnight, beaten up badly, and let go with a warning.[22]

Yet in April 2012 the tacit accord that the national press is off-limits dramatically ruptured, with the murder of *Proceso*'s Veracruz correspondent, Regina Martínez.[23] Petite, Indigenous looking, and tough, a woman who struck her friends as married to her job, Martínez was found bludgeoned to death in the bathroom of her modest home in Xalapa, the state capital. Over twenty-five years she had gained a name for fearlessness and incorruptibility, going after politicians and functionaries whenever she sniffed malfeasance. But since 2004, the start of the gubernatorial term of Fidel Herrera, reporting on corruption in Veracruz had become unusually risky. Journalists were killed at a rate of one a year. And in 2010 the climate got more torrid still. Soon after the Zetas broke with the Gulf Cartel, stoking the firestorm of violence already assailing much of northern and central Mexico, the governor's chair came to be occupied by Javier Duarte. A rotund, guayabera-wearing bully, Duarte soon had journalists talking of a reign of terror, with his intolerance of dissent and heavy-handed co-option of the press. With the murder of Martínez, by which time Duarte had been in power for just seventeen months, the tally of journalists killed in his term rose to five; the following week, another three victims would be found, hacked into pieces, stuffed into plastic bags, and dumped in a sewage canal.[24]

Shortly before Martínez's death, *Proceso* had run a story by one of its top reporters, Jenaro Villamil, conveying allegations of corrupt practices by two politicians close to Duarte.[25] Although Martínez went uncredited, someone with a vengeful mindset might have supposed she had supplied Villamil with information. The fact that she had been beaten to death, rather than shot point-blank, suggested that her death was not a narco hit. It was either personal or political.

What followed was a catalog of miscarriages of justice. Within hours of the murder's discovery, investigators conjectured it was a crime of passion. This was a surprise to her friends, who had not seen her dating in years. Duarte offered to receive a delegation from *Proceso* the next day, and its retired founder editor, Julio Scherer, chose to head it. Having turned down Duarte's offer of luxury hotel accommodations and use of a helicopter, the eighty-six-year-old Scherer listened to the unctuous governor, a man less than half his age, compliment him on his "prestigious" magazine and make promises of "full transparency." Scherer was unimpressed with his prattling: "Mr. Governor, we don't believe you."

The day after that, federal prosecutor Laura Borbolla arrived in Xalapa. She found that the Veracruz forensics team had already bungled the collection of fingerprints. What evidence they had collected, they refused to share. *Proceso* entrusted its own investigation to Jorge Carrasco, a midcareer reporter known for being meticulous, and it made repeated requests to the Veracruz authorities to consider Martínez's work as a possible murder motive; they never did. A year after the killing, a court sentenced an alleged accomplice to the crime to a thirty-eight-year term. The state claimed that the perpetrator, a male sex worker and petty thief who it said was Martínez's lover, had gone missing. Soon after, Carrasco penned a blistering report, dissecting inconsistencies in the state's case. Its title echoed Scherer's skepticism: "We Don't Believe You. A Cover-Up of a Sentence."[26] The day the magazine appeared, Carrasco received texts on his phone, warning him that the Veracruz authorities were "coordinating with the Zetas" to find him. Information from Borbolla's office tended to confirm the threat's validity. With his wife and son, Carrasco fled the country for three weeks.

In 2015, with the case declared closed, US journalist Katherine Corcoran began her own investigation. A former Mexico City bureau chief for the Associated Press who had once tried to hire Martínez, Corcoran found that confessions had been forced with torture and witness statements had likely been coaxed with bribes. Four talented cub reporters to whom Martínez had been a mentor aided Corcoran in her quest; together and separately, they interviewed friends, witnesses, veteran journalists, and authorities. They were lied to and sometimes threatened. They found the official report salted with blame-the-victim fabrications. Among them: Shortly before her murder, Martínez had bought fabric for miniskirts and ginseng to enhance her libido. None of this was necessarily surprising, for as well as Mexico's tradition of poorly educated, ill-trained, and badly paid police, Corcoran had to contend with the mendacious tone set by Duarte. As Associated Press bureau chief, she had banned her reporters from quoting him on major breaking stories because his statements were often so patently false.

Years of investigating, replete with bogus leads, dead ends, intimidated witnesses, and creeping paranoia, did not provide Corcoran with firm answers. As to who ordered the hit, the evidence she was able to gather pointed to Duarte's first attorney general, Reynaldo Escobar, who, according to Villamil's *Proceso* story (just before Martínez was killed), had been fingered by a federal investigation as jointly responsible for allowing the Zetas to set up in Veracruz.[27] But Corcoran stopped short of a conclusion. For one thing, while it seemed clear to her that Martínez had been killed over some exposé she was working on, no one, not even her editors at *Proceso*, could say for sure what it was. Instead, Corcoran reproduced the saga of her troubled quest in a book, *In the Mouth of the Wolf*: a case study of Mexican impunity, at a time when only one in five murders resulted in a conviction (the rate has since worsened to fewer than one in ten).[28] The product of seven years of research by a veteran reporter, one with far greater resources—time and money—than the vast majority of her Mexican peers can muster, the book also serves as testimony to how the murder of Mexico's journalists almost always leads to one conclusion: unknowability.

"The realities of reporting in Mexico were far more complicated than anything I had encountered elsewhere," Corcoran writes in her preface. "A society without truth is a scary place to live."[29]

Narcopolítica: How Mexico Became So Dangerous

Mexican journalists have been killed on a more or less regular basis since the late nineteenth century. The numerical trend has not been consistent: The victim count inevitably rose during the revolution; declined as violence haltingly subsided in the 1920s and 1930s; became scarce during the "soft dictatorship" years of 1940 to 1968; and rose again thereafter, with a frightening acceleration after 2000.[30] Nor have the means of execution been consistent. Of the eleven killed during the long reign of Porfirio Díaz, three were the losing parties in duels, the consequence of offense taken over some article.[31]

In other ways, the Porfirian era set precedents. All of the murders took place outside the capital, as have more than 95 percent of cases since. Nine of the eleven victims worked for provincial media, as have the vast majority thereafter. In only two of the cases did the federal government intervene in the investigation, as again would prove the norm. None of the masterminds or perpetrators was incarcerated; and again, the pursuit of justice thereafter has continued to prove almost as ineffective.

Remarkably, in five or six of the Porfirian cases, the agitator was known to be the local governor. Impunity conformed to Díaz's custom of letting governors rule as petty dictators, as long as they remained loyal.[32] That sense of entitlement persisted after Díaz's ouster. During the revolution, Tabasco's Manuel Mestre Ghigliazza had a troublesome owner-editor bumped off, and years later he admitted it. In 1923, Filiberto Gómez, the brother of the governor of the State of México, shot a newspaper publisher in the lobby of the national Chamber of Deputies; six years later, he himself became governor. In 1924, Tabasco's iron-fisted Tomás Garrido Canabal was credited with the killing of an owner-editor whose body washed up in the Grijalva River. In 1930, the hardline Chiapas governor Raymundo Enríquez was similarly suspected of ordering a newspaper director's murder. And in 1939, the notoriously sociopathic governor of Puebla, Maximino Ávila Camacho, was credited with having his goons kidnap, strip naked, and shoot a publisher who dared to back a leading rival of his brother Manuel in the race for the presidency.[33]

Mexico's historians make much of 1940 as a watershed, and this is certainly true of power brokers' treatment of the press. Presidents still let governors rule as feudal lords, but they could no longer do entirely as they pleased. In 1947, when the Tamaulipas chief of police was found guilty of shooting publisher Vicente Villasana, the governor who had appointed him was removed by President Miguel Alemán. In 1956, conversely, the murder of two Baja California journalists was attributed to Governor Braulio Maldonado, for the assassins were men in his pay, and the politician got away with it, perhaps because of Institutional Revolutionary Party (PRI) concerns over the local rise of the National Action Party (PAN). Benjamin Smith blames that leniency for a five-year rise in media-worker murders: "Politicians now understood that it was possible to kill journalists, if one managed to cover up the crime."[34] Yet this episode was an instructive anomaly.

Between 1940 and 1969, only thirteen journalists were killed, and of those just nine were targeted for their work. Some of the relative calm surely had to do with governors setting the tone: When they were less aggressive toward the press, other authorities followed suit. The Maldonado episode somewhat supports this thesis, in reverse: Gubernatorial ruthlessness (and impunity) encouraged other powerful actors to do likewise. Both totals, of overall murders and of targeted victims, are comparable to the period 1920–39, but after 1940 far more newspapers were being published and journalists were far more numerous.[35] Thus, a much lower proportion were getting killed. The quantitative rise of the press owed to a fast-growing and increasingly literate population and the consolidation of federal and local subsidy schemes. Those schemes were likely another major reason why killing became less common: For autocratic politicians faced with critical journalists, it was much less hassle to buy them off than bump them off.

After 1970, in states where rule of law was weaker, the cozy arrangement began to fall apart. That decade, journalist murders tripled, and in the 1980s they doubled again. The key cause was drug trafficking, but—as Smith has again argued—this is not the straightforward cause that politicians have often led the public to believe. The creeping violence of the 1970s, first most evident in the poppy- and marijuana-growing state of Sinaloa, was triggered not by narcos double-crossing each other but by federal authorities competing over protection rackets. And so it was not necessarily the drug gangs who were responsible for the rise in journalist killings, of which Sinaloa was witness to ten in the 1970s and 1980s (before, it had only seen one since the revolution). Often, it was agents of the state. While in the majority of cases motive has never been clarified, nationwide data for those two decades yield sixteen cases of journalists likely or certainly murdered for their work; of these, the available evidence suggests that four were killed by narcos and five on the orders of politicians or police.[36]

Corrupt officials—or governors simply wishing to wash their hands of the matter—would cast the blame elsewhere. The fate of *Excélsior*'s Sinaloa stringer Roberto Martínez Montenegro is a case in point. He was killed in 1978 for having tried to blackmail two security federal chiefs by threatening to reveal their narco protection racket. Then one of those officials had a local police chief arrested and tortured into confessing the crime.[37]

For reasons unclear, the fast-growing murder rate of the 1970s (13 killed, compared with 4 in the 1960s) and the 1980s (28) leveled off in the 1990s (23), despite the continued growth of the news industry. Economics was perhaps part of it: The golden age of newspaper ad spend, between 1990 and 2000 or so, meant that reporters were better able to live on their salaries. Hence, "bad apples" were less inclined to seek payoffs or practice blackmail, a dangerous path if their targets were crime syndicates or corrupt politicians.

With the new century—and, ironically, the consolidation of electoral democracy—a whole series of factors converged to make reporting more dangerous. In the first decade, 65 journalists were murdered or disappeared. In the 2010s, the total reached 101.[38]

The resurgence of state governors as feudal lords was the first and perhaps the most important cause. Presidents from Emilio Portes Gil in 1929–30 to Carlos Salinas de Gortari in the 1990s had had little difficulty in ousting inept, ultracorrupt, or homicidal governors, due in part to a constitutional clause that allowed the Senate to dissolve any state government. Since Los Pinos controlled the Senate, the matter did not have to go to a vote; the president would snap his fingers and the governor would have no choice but to quit, usually requesting the face-saving device of "indefinite leave." But the senatorial mechanism ceased to function in 2000, for the victorious PAN failed to obtain a majority of senators. Unleashed politically, governors also found themselves empowered economically, thanks to a 1998 fiscal reform that greatly increased their budgets and their discretionary spending. These changes fueled a common gubernatorial culture of autocracy, arrogance, and acquisitiveness.[39]

Many governors thus set a tone for lax adherence to rule of law and contempt for independent journalism, which permeated their fiefs. They did so in part through their rhetoric, publicly shunning or deriding critical media. They also did so through their lavish spending on advertising, so as to co-opt the press—rather as Calderón was doing at the federal level—and to withdraw it when they did not like what they read. Moreno Valle of Puebla experimented with a so-called *tripack*: Ad buys from the state's three biggest spenders, the state university, Puebla's city hall, and the state government, were disbursed only to friendly media. Once Vicente Fox had set the precedent of using a governorship as a launchpad for a run at the presidency, a number of ambitious governors became more than usually image conscious. Often the amount of their outlays was covered up. When nongovernmental organizations Article 19 and Fundar asked every state government in 2011 to account for its ad spend over the previous five years, only two states gave a complete accounting, nineteen submitted partial figures, and eleven did not answer.[40]

Governors and their security chiefs also faced temptation to profit from protecting drug traffickers. Such rackets had ancient origins—dating from the revolution in the border states—but they spread southward as of the mid-1980s when the Colombian cartels switched their US-bound cocaine routes from the Caribbean to Mexico. Diversification of those routes within Mexico, or along its coast, meant that by 2000 many states were involved. Increased profits from the trade gave the crime syndicates the upper hand in their relations with state agents: The cash they wielded was simply too much for police, mayors, judges, and even some generals to resist. In turn, governors had a decision to make, a variation on the old offer of *plata o plomo* (silver or lead—i.e., a cash bribe or a bullet): They could accept payment for aiding the traffickers, risk a surge in local violence if they tried to stop them, or simply look the other way. A number chose the first option, as evidenced by how the government, sometimes under US duress, eventually went after them. By 2017, six former governors had been formally charged with narco links.[41]

None of this is to say that governors necessarily ordered journalists killed. But it is likely that, as governors let narco influence spread in their states, lower-level officials who were threatened with exposure of their complicity felt free to silence their critics. After all, the governor had their backs, through control of the state's police and judiciary and through steering of the narrative about the victim. One result of these networks of protection was something close to across-the-board impunity, which in turn gave corrupt officials and narcos alike the confidence to carry on killing. This is what happened most notoriously in Veracruz under Duarte (2010–16). As media historian Celia del Palacio demonstrates in her study of the Duarte-era press, aptly titled *To Shut Up or Die in Veracruz*, the governor excelled at crushing freedom of speech. In total, twenty media workers were killed and five disappeared. To date, the mastermind of the hit has been jailed in just one of those cases, making for an impunity rate of 96 percent.[42]

In 2015 a federal prosecutor's office conducted its own study of journalist killings and estimated that 40 percent owed to agents of the state. In Veracruz, the proportion was 80 percent.[43] But such figures may suggest a simplistic apportioning of blame. After all, another upshot of the protection networks was the difficulty in telling the agency of narcos from that of corrupt politicians. When murders occurred, to whom could local journalists point with any certainty as the guilty party? What about murders of which there was more than one mastermind, such as a crime capo and political protector making the call together?

Adela Navarro of *Zeta* once defined the trajectory of her paper thus: In the 1980s, its focus was on political corruption; in the 1990s, it was on drug trafficking; and from 2000 it was on the mixing of those two evils. She referred to the phenomenon as *narcopolítica*—that is, narcopolitics.[44]

For the regular journalist, especially the reporter or photographer on the crime beat, the risks of rising gubernatorial corruption and criminal influ-

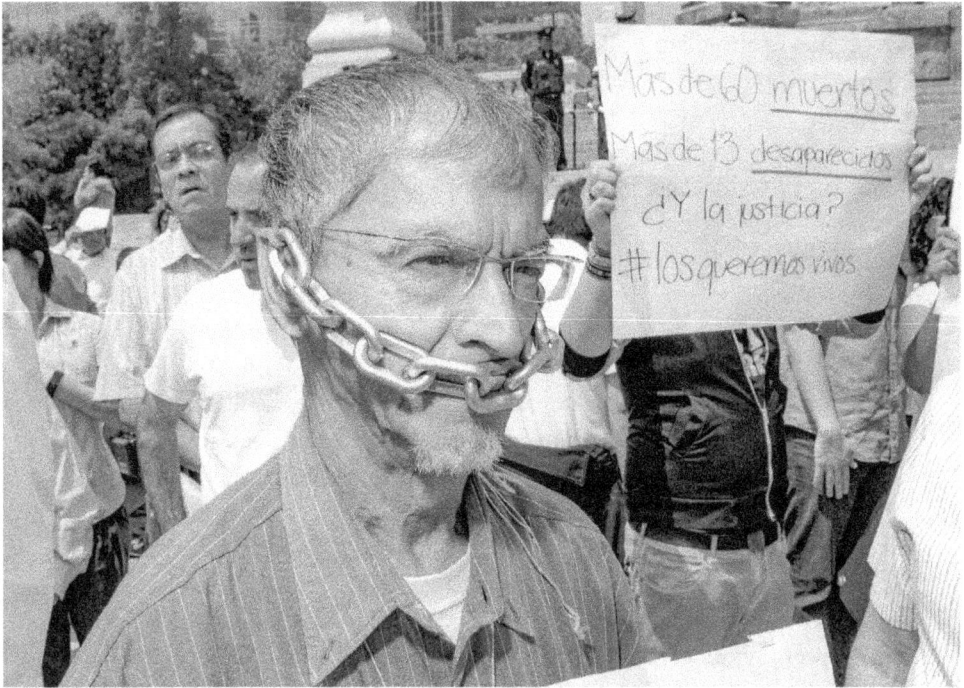

Journalists and sympathizers take to Mexico City's streets in August 2010 to protest the killings of provincial reporters, which soared in number under President Calderón. Courtesy of Keith Dannemiller.

ence were exacerbated in the Calderón years, when the elimination of journalists more than doubled to a rate exceeding one per month. Two of the factors making life more dangerous were directly attributable to the president himself.

First, Calderón's "war" against drug trafficking, declared in late 2006 and already spinning out of control by early 2008, made Mexico a much more violent place. In 2009, the annual homicide count reached around 20,000, double that of two years earlier. It was inevitable that journalists would be caught in the crossfire. That is, as crime reporters competed for stories, they incurred a greater risk of falling afoul of one gang or another, especially as those gangs themselves were now operating under greater stress. Turning up the pressure further was the state's "kingpin strategy"—targeting high-profile capos for arrest, in the hope of weaking their organizations and earning good press—which had the common side effect of fragmenting the syndicates into warring factions. Such disruptions made it yet harder for reporters to know what to report, with rival gangs calling newsrooms with conflicting instructions as to what to report and what not to.[45]

A second presidential initiative was a well-intentioned but in some respects harmful reform of the labor law. Calderón's purpose was to facilitate hiring and firing, after decades of clientelist cosseting of unions had made formal layoff processes prohibitively expensive, which encouraged companies to finagle employee resignations. Published in November 2012, on the final day of Calderón's term of office, the reform soon shook up the labor market.[46] Firms could now hire full-time workers as independent contractors rather than as employees with full benefits. With its income in decline, *El Universal* was an early adopter. In turn, reporters working for set fees, but lacking insurance and vacation pay, often felt the need to take greater risks, proving their worth as a hedge against getting laid off. Or they turned freelance, a relatively novel practice in Mexico, with its own innate pressures. Mass layoffs became more frequent. Among ill-paid and often disaffected reporters, "job precarity" became an issue of frequent complaint.[47] A poorer reporter, especially a poorer and overworked reporter, was more likely to make bad choices. *Nota roja* (police beat) photojournalists for some provincial papers were paid as little as three dollars for each dead body photographed, which both prompted physical burnout and took a psychological toll. Crime syndicates sometimes wanted their atrocities published and sometimes did not.[48] Could a tired photographer, in a rush between crime scenes, always make the right call?

Then there were circumstantial changes. The rapid rise of the spectacularly violent Zetas became the greatest threat. Mediocre traffickers but skilled extortionists, Zetas were already making themselves known outside their home base of Tamaulipas by 2004. Between 2010, when they completed their break with the Gulf Cartel, and 2012, when their most effective leader was gunned down by Mexican marines, the Zetas were in their bloody pomp, running the main protection rackets in a dozen northern and eastern states. Toward the press, the Zetas were swift to practice *plata o plomo*: take a bribe or take a bullet. *Narcoperiodistas* proliferated in the wake of their executions and abductions. Zones of silence resulted. Even as the syndicate weakened in Tamaulipas, its semiautonomous regional cells in Veracruz and other states continued to abduct or murder inconvenient journalists for years.[49]

(Despite its common association with the Zetas and the twenty-first-century coinage of the term, *narcoperiodismo* is not a recent phenomenon. In 1993, Attorney General Jorge Carpizo launched a series of investigations into editors, reporters, and columnists allegedly working on behalf of drug traffickers. One of the papers for which Carpizo gathered the most evidence of criminal association was *El Mañana* of Reynosa, including its publisher, Heriberto Deándar Martínez, whose successor and sister Ninfa would vow to stop covering narco violence in 2012.)[50]

As layoffs snowballed at legacy media, many journalists took jobs at the proliferating news websites. Most of these were standalone efforts, and while a few had big start-up budgets, the majority were tiny. A typical provincial news site (or *portal*, in Spanish) consisted of an editor-owner, usually an industry veteran, a midcareer deputy, and half a dozen or fewer young reporters, and the operation largely depended on the good graces of the governor, who might grant or withhold advertising on a whim. Not only were such reporters ill-paid, they lacked the backing of a publication with name and influence. Writers for dailies with small print runs were equally exposed. Amid a fast-mounting death toll, the killing of a part-timer with the likes of Reynosa site *Reporteros en la Red* or Tehuacán paper *Diario Puntual* (to cite actual examples) would soon be forgotten by all but friends and family. Surely that was part of their killers' calculus.

The explosion of news sites made covering the violence riskier still, for with reporting now occurring in real time, there was a premium on being first to an execution site or shoot-out scene. Sometimes this urgency had reporters showing up to take notes with hitmen lurking nearby or combatants still engaged. Such a misfortune led to the death-during-crossfire of Matamoros crime reporter Carlos Alberto Guajardo Romero, killed by soldiers in 2010.[51] After the start of Calderón's "war," a substantial number of the journalists slain were *nota roja* reporters and photographers, including half of those killed under Duarte in Veracruz.[52] *Nota roja* journalists were front-line observers of Mexico's plague of violence, vulnerable to crossfire, vengeful narcos, vengeful politicians, and exploitative employers.

———

Narcoperiodistas have been few compared with the thousands practicing journalism in Mexico. But their occasional appearance as victims of the violence that many of them cover fed a narrative—beloved of certain governors, security chiefs, attorneys general, and much of the public—that when reporters turned up dead, their own poor choices were at least partly to blame. As journalist killings grew to epidemic levels, phrases such as *andaba en malos pasos* (he took the wrong path—that is, by getting mixed up with some crime syndicate) became press conference clichés, standard means of deflecting bad publicity.[53]

Javier Duarte was especially quick to make such claims; it was an easy way to cover up the climate of impunity he had fostered in Veracruz. He once infamously used this language as a pretext for a further threat. At a lunch for local press in June 2015, by which point eighteen journalists had been killed or disappeared during his term, he warned the assembly that he knew that some of them were involved with organized crime. "Behave yourselves!

We all know who's taking the wrong path." He ominously added, "We're going to shake the tree and a lot of bad apples are going to fall."[54]

Yet the distressing truth remained that Duarte and his ilk were sometimes right. As Javier Valdez and other journalists and researchers have shown, some reporters indeed accepted narco cash. This made them vulnerable to a comeuppance. Widely credited examples include the TV Azteca Noreste reporter Gamaliel López (a reputed Zetas liaison, disappeared in 2007); Televisa's Orizaba correspondent Juan Santos Carrera (shot while drinking with Zetas in 2015); and southern Veracruz part-time writer Gumaro Pérez Aguilando (shot in 2017, probably by Jalisco hitmen because of his work for local Zetas). For some reporters, no doubt, the threat of *plata o plomo* had been too frightening to resist. Others, perhaps, had opted for *plata* by second nature. After all, many worked for media with mercenary traditions: criticizing local governments until they received a major ad buy, or accepting bribes from politicians. Katherine Cocoran certainly found this to be the case in Veracruz: "The narcos were tapping into a system of co-opting the media that was decades in the making."[55]

Owing to the popular memory of PRI-era *prensa vendida*—the sell-out press that dominated from the 1940s to the early 1990s—journalists in Mexico had never enjoyed a stellar reputation. The profession seemed untrustworthy. There was no Mexican cinematic parallel to *All the President's Men*, inspiring generations of students to become the local Bob Woodward or Carl Bernstein. Moreover, with noteworthy exceptions, regional media had never been able to wean themselves off state handouts. In the second decade of the new century, with advertisers fleeing to the internet, some that had managed to forge an independent path were seeking anew the governor's largesse, and readers noticed when critical coverage turned flattering.[56]

By 2018, when the World Values Survey (WVS) revisited Mexico, public confidence in the press had fallen again. Already trust had dropped from a neutral 49 percent in 2005 to a disapproving 29 percent in 2012, a decline that likely reflected the increasingly official tone in many media as they accepted ever-larger amounts of Calderón's advertising cash. Even by regional standards, faith in the press was low; a separate 2013 survey found that 33 percent of Mexicans trusted the press, compared with 47 percent of Latin Americans as a whole. Now, according to the WVS, trust stood at a paltry 26.8 percent. Advances in investigative journalism at digital media during the Enrique Peña Nieto presidency were likely outweighed by a retreat to political puffery at many regional papers and also at *El Universal*, *Milenio*, and even *La Jornada*.[57] And perhaps skepticism toward the media was so ingrained that even the hard-won scoops of watchdog journalists, exposing industrial-scale corruption among ruling elites, too often faced assumptions that such exposés were politically or economically motivated.

Whatever the case, it had become easy to dismiss reporters as habitual bribe-takers. The WVS of 2018 revealed that 50 percent of respondents believed "most" or "all" Mexican journalists and media were involved in corruption. So when authorities claimed that such-and-such a victim had been pally with the narcos or otherwise shady, their speculations found a receptive public. Del Palacio saw exactly this problem in Duarte-era Veracruz: a willingness to label journalists as "hitmen with pens," "extortionists," "pseudo-journalists," or "crooks." Or as one passerby put it, noting a march protesting the killing of a journalist, "They deserve it: they're a bunch of gossip-mongers." A 2017–18 nationwide survey of ninety-three journalists found them unhappy with public apathy over the risks they bore. Only civil-society organizations, whose activities they often reported, were regularly supportive. Members of the public frequently considered media to be just "another political institution." The respondents' general mood was succinctly phrased in the title of one of the articles based on this survey, which quoted a photographer reflecting on his local public: "They don't trust us; they don't care if we're attacked."[58]

Thus was the lot of the average twenty-first-century Mexican journalist, especially in the provinces, and more especially still among those who covered crime: precariously employed, poorly paid, threatened by crime syndicates, criticized and sometimes revictimized by politicians, and misunderstood by an uncaring nation or cynical public.

Lydia Cacho and the *Levantón*

Not all journalists who suffer the trauma of a *levantón*—forced into a car at gunpoint and taken God-knows-where—are the targets of crime syndicates. In December 2005, Lydia Cacho was hoisted by agents of the state. Bizarrely, given that she lived in Cancún on the Caribbean coast, it was police agents from Puebla who grabbed her. They then drove her 900 miles, a slow-burn torture trip of twenty hours' duration, while they repeatedly threatened Cacho with rape or murder, forced her to suck on the barrel of a gun, roughed her up in a gas station lavatory, pistol-whipped her in the ribs, and led her to believe that even if she made it alive to Puebla, she would probably be killed in the city's jail.[59]

Cacho was an experienced freelancer, with an activist approach to her work. As well as penning social justice pieces for local and national publications, she ran a high-security shelter for abused women and girls in Cancún, her home since the late 1980s. Her "crime" was to have written *The Demons of Eden*, an exposé of a sex-trafficking and child pornography ring based in this ostensible tropical paradise, and to have named names.[60] The ring was run by a Lebanese Mexican businessman, Jean Succar, who was already detained in Arizona, but she revealed that it included among its powerful protectors a Puebla-based compatriot of Succar's, Kemal Nacif. So Puebla governor Mario Marín sent state police to Cancún to detain Cacho for defaming Nacif, who was a major player in the Puebla textile industry. Swift work by her lawyers and *Día Siete* editor Jorge Zepeda Patterson, with whom she was then in a relationship, managed to get Cacho extricated from the Puebla prison on bail before further harm befell her.

Cacho's torment and her subsequent fight for justice would have made few waves outside Puebla were it not for a bombshell of a phone call between Nacif and Marín the day after the abduction, which someone had taped via a phone tap. In February 2006, one copy was mailed to *La Jornada* and another to radio journalist Carmen Aristegui. The paper led its front page with: "The plot against Lydia Cacho."[61] Penned by Blanche Petrich, the scoop centered on a lengthy transcription, which began with this damning exchange:

Marín: What's up, Kamel?
Nacif: My precious guv.
Marín: My hero, dammit.
Nacif: No, the hero of this movie is you, daddy.
Marín: Well, just yesterday I gave this bitch a damn good slapping.

Even the traditionally PRI-friendly Televisa, which interviewed Marín that night, would not let him off the hook. From that moment on, the governor would forever be known as "the Precious Guv." On the national stage, the diminutive, snake-eyed politician—who ludicrously claimed that the voice on the tape was not his—became an object of outrage and derision. In Puebla, his image was tarred less. The governor reportedly funneled extra sums to the press, and market leader *El Sol de Puebla* tended to back him, but a few papers, notably *La Jornada de Oriente*, remained suspicious and keen to pursue the truth. A protest march called for him to resign. Remarkably, the national scandal was insufficient to topple Marín, so determined were leaders of the PRI to keep all their chess pieces in place, in the hope of a return to Los Pinos that year.[62]

With the PRI protecting Marín and Marín protecting Nacif, Cacho remained exposed. Death threats against her multiplied. She would spend much of the next decade occupied with lawsuits, of which three were especially consuming. The first was a grueling defamation case brought against her by Nacif, whose high-paid lawyers laid siege to her, at one point engineering several summons requiring her to appear in court in Puebla, Cancún, and Mexico City on the very same day. The second was the case she brought against Marín and Nacif, for masterminding her abduction and psychological torture. The third was the government's case against Succar, who was extradited from Arizona in mid-2006. Here Cacho was called to testify, but her bigger contribution lay in counseling and coordinating witnesses among the dozens of victims and their mothers who had sought help from the shelter she had founded in Cancún.

For Cacho, it was an arduous trek. The years were punctuated by an attempt on her life; reversals before the Supreme Court; attacks by senior members of the PRI; the threat of personal bankruptcy; the removal of her uterus and ovaries, after prolonged stress contributed to tumors; periods of self-exile from Mexico, in response to death threats; and the breakdown of her relationship with Zepeda. But little by little, justice was more or less served. In 2007, she was acquitted of defaming Nacif (that year she won an Award for Freedom of Expression from the global writers' association PEN). In 2011, Succar was sentenced to 112 years in prison. In 2021, Marín was arrested in Acapulco on charges of ordering Cacho's illegal arrest and torture. The same year, Nacif was detained in Lebanon, where he had fled to escape the law.[63]

For Mexican journalism, the episode had major implications. First, it affirmed that women could match men as investigators. Cacho was in the vanguard of a generation of female writers, in their thirties and early forties, for whom exposing corruption or championing social justice was a mission and whose writing had a social impact. They included Anabel Hernández (corruption in Los Pinos), Ana Lilia Pérez (corruption in the PAN), Alejandra Xanic (corruption in business), Sanjuana Martínez (corruption in the Catholic Church), Beatriz Pereyra (corruption in sports), Laura Castellanos (armed movements), Sandra Rodríguez Nieto (the culture of violence in Ciudad Juárez), Daniela Rea and Marcela Turati (the victims and survivors of violence), Daniela Pastrana and Ángeles Mariscal (migrants), and Lilia Saúl (uses of the transparency law).[64] This was a far cry from the 1990s, when the *Proceso* newsroom was a bastion of masculinity and Mexico's most famous female investigative journalist, Alma Guillermoprieto, was one who chiefly wrote in English for *The New Yorker*. Further, by the 2010s, women formed the majority in many if not most of Mexico's newsrooms.

On a legal front, the Supreme Court ruled in 2013 that any potentially defamatory qualities in *The Demons of Eden* were secondary to the public interest. And on a commercial front, the scandal turned Cacho's book into a publishing sensation, affirming the viability of investigative books. When publishers Grijalbo first released it in spring 2005, they gave it a modest but typical print run of 4,000. Thanks to Cacho's victimization by Governor Marín, her story became front-page news, so another 30,000 were printed. Eventually sales would top 100,000—bestseller status twice over in a country in which the average adult read just two books per year.[65]

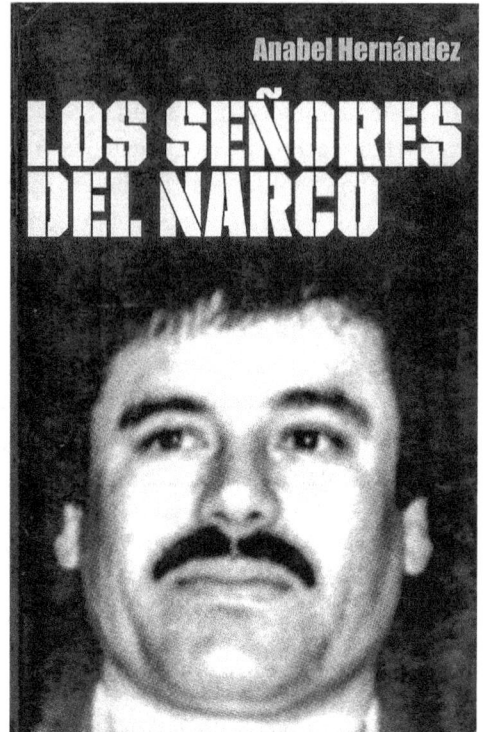

Bestsellers by two of Mexico's most valiant journalists: Lydia Cacho's 2005 exposé of the sex trafficking of minors in Cancún and Anabel Hernández's 2010 dive into the corruption of the state by the Sinaloa Cartel. Courtesy of Penguin Random House (México).

Anabel in Narcoland

Before 2000, the journalistic book was a minor genre in Mexico. It had been dominated by memoirs and collections of columns or interviews; such works were ephemeral.[66] The enduring exception was the *crónica*, a Latin American form of narrative journalism, often literary in style, sometimes embellished to the point of fiction. Some *cronistas*, as its purveyors are known, blended eyewitness immediacy with interviews, a style whose sovereign was Elena Poniatowska, with her chronicles of the 1968 student massacre and the 1985 earthquake. Some *cronistas* synthesized existing knowledge—of history, the arts, popular culture—and added witty observations and ironic commentary; here the masters were Salvador Novo, then Carlos Monsiváis. Yet the best-known *cronistas* were more analysts than investigators, and their books rarely pursued a single narrative or biographical subject. Nor did they venture much outside Mexico City.[67]

Narrative nonfiction got a boost from the 1994 Chiapas uprising. Within three years, at least fifteen local writers had authored books on the conflict. Many were impassioned quickies, but *The Rebellion of Las Cañadas* by Carlos Tello and *Rebellion from the Roots* by US expatriate John Ross would stand the test of time.[68] Another boost came with the entry to Los Pinos of Vicente Fox and Marta Sahagún. Their gaffes, self-indulgences, and inability to deliver on the promise of change inspired two muckraking books by Anabel Hernández and a best-selling biography of Marta by Olga Wornat.[69] Yet such subjects were low-hanging fruit: Their authors had reams of published stories on which to draw. A key investigative attribute of Cacho's *The Demons of Eden* was its broaching of a theme on which very little had been recorded. Another was its securing of interviews with sources difficult to reach or reluctant to speak, including victims of sexual assault. These daring and original qualities set a mark for writing about crime.

More or less coinciding with the Fox era was a multiplication of spaces for in-depth journalism, thanks to new magazines. These included *Milenio Semanal* (1997); Jorge Zepeda Patterson's *Día Siete* (2000) and Ignacio Rodríguez Reyna's *LaRevista* (2004), both backed by *El Universal*; and several standalone titles: the Colombian-owned *Gatopardo* (2000); Miguel Badillo's *Contralínea* (2002), and Rodríguez Reyna's follow-up project—after leaving *El Universal* due to Juan Francisco Ealy Ortiz's censorship—*Emeequis* (2006). Named for the Spanish letters MX, *Emeequis* won myriad awards.[70] Each of these titles became a seedbed for investigative books.

A final boost to long-form journalism came from the rise of drug-trafficking organizations, and with it a reportorial urge to document their crimes and uncover their protectors among politicians and the security forces. Blancornelas of *Zeta* helped kick-start the trend, with a trilogy that included the definitive history of the Arellano Félix family, *The Cartel*. Offering a more literary take and a wider-ranging vision of Mexico's violence was the author and arts writer Sergio González Rodríguez, who wrote on the femicide plague in Ciudad Juárez, decapitations performed by crime syndicate hitmen, and links between narco violence and US-driven neoliberalism. Even the veteran *cronista* Monsiváis got involved, headlining a collection of narratives.[71] The genre did not invite dilettantes. After González Rodríguez trialed excerpts of his Juárez investigation in *Reforma*, the fiftysomething writer was subjected to a *levantón*, told that his work was being monitored, and beaten to the point of a cerebral hemorrhage. He bravely went ahead and published the book, *Bones in the Desert*, and it cemented his reputation.[72]

By 2012, participants at the Guadalajara International Book Fair, the largest in the Spanish-speaking world, were talking of a "*narcolibro* boom." One report flagged eighteen recently released titles, including two to be presented at the fair: *El Narco*, by Ioan Grillo, soon a classic of the genre; and *The War of the Zetas*, by Diego Osorno, who had already scored a bestseller about the Sinaloa Cartel.[73] This *narcolibro* boom derived in part from commercialism: It catered to a public appetite for information—and conjecture—about the crime syndicates that much of the press, especially in the provinces, had been intimidated into withholding. *Nexos* online editor Esteban Illades sniped that such books, now "the main support of the publishing economy," in most cases offered "disposable" content.[74]

Nonetheless, like the nonfiction boom in general, these works were also the fruit of two decades of improved press freedom, which had encouraged veterans to throw off the shackles of self-censorship and nursed a younger cohort of inquisitive reporters. Many of the latter, admirers of global writers like Gabriel García Márquez and Ryszard Kapuściński, were keener than their forebears to develop their reportage into books, especially those who turned freelance.

And then there was *Los señores del narco* by Anabel Hernández. First released in 2010, and published in English as *Narcoland*, this 588-page tome was a brick through the palace window of the establishment.[75] It took as its premise that "semi-illiterate peasants" like "El Chapo" Guzmán "would not have got far without the collusion of businessmen, politicians, and policemen, and all those who exercise everyday power from behind a false halo of legality."[76] It named names.

The biggest name was Genaro García Luna, Calderón's minister of public security and point man in the "war on drugs." Hernández had begun to sense there was something awry about García Luna in the Fox years, when, as head of the federal police, he used to visit Los Pinos laden with gifts for Marta. For her third book, on corruption under Calderón, she zeroed in on two of the president's most trusted aides, García Luna and Secretary of Government Juan Camilo Mouriño, accusing both of self-enrichment.[77]

But in *Narcoland*, Hernández took her accusations to a more incendiary level. García Luna was the book's main villain, the chief protector or "godfather" of Mexico's most powerful crime syndicate, the Sinaloa Cartel. This explained both his undue wealth and the ability of El Chapo Guzmán—whose ghostly face adorned the cover—to expand his turf and avoid arrest. The war on drugs was therefore a lie, because the Calderón administration, like the Fox regime before it, was only going after the Sinaloans' rivals. The placement of García Luna at the center of the conspiracy was a daring piece of casting given that, when the book debuted, the fearsome security minister still had two years to run in his post. Perhaps it was doubly daring given that Hernández was a woman and a single mother, with all the vulnerabilities to harassment and other reprisals that her status entailed. The authors of previous high-profile books on the narcos had all been male.

Narcoland had a bigger impact than any of its predecessors because, as novelist Álvaro Enrigue wrote in a review, it "reads like a thriller." He lauded its use of "small, self-contained episodes" to develop the complex tale and its forgoing of maps, statistics, and sociological analysis in favor of a fast pace. The book afforded each character a dramatic arc and fleshed out even the cruelest criminals with roguish or ironic details. "El Mayo" Zambada counted among his money-laundering businesses the Happy Child Kindergarten. A hitman for the Zetas would sign the bodies of his victims with his less-than-macho nickname, "El Calabaza" (The Pumpkin). British war correspondent Ed Vulliamy praised the book for its "relentless narrative" and "depth of depiction" of Guzmán.[78] Beyond the conspiratorial revelations and deft storytelling, its commercial success was boosted by a lengthy dialectic in which state actors denounced the contents, made death threats against the author, and intimidated her family, and Hernández responded in public each time with denunciations of her own. Journalists at home and abroad—including an infirm Miguel Ángel Granados Chapa (who died of cancer a few months later)—came to her defense and praised her bravery. The Mexico City district attorney assigned her bodyguards. Hernández sought to protect herself chiefly by keeping herself in the public eye, and her media-intensive strategy had the secondary effect of sustained publicity for her book. Within six months sales reached 60,000. The total would eventually approach 200,000.[79]

Then came the lawsuit. In March 2012, Jorge Carpizo, an attorney general under President Salinas, sued Hernández and publisher Random House for defamation of character. Hernández was defiant, declaring that Carpizo's lawsuit was a general retaliation for her fingering of the powerful. "In a book of 600 pages, I mention Carpizo three times," she tellingly added, as though any laxness with minor players in her drama did not count. But Carpizo's suit was precise: Among other things, she had given credence to an anonymous claim that he had pocketed the $400,000 reward when Guzmán was first arrested in 1993. Carpizo, who had also served as rector of the National Autonomous University of Mexico and founder-president of the National Human Rights Commission, had a clean reputation and a brilliant mind. He may well have won in court, but he unexpectedly died a few weeks later from complications during a medical procedure. His family opted not to pursue the suit.[80]

Carpizo was not alone in questioning the book. No one doubted Hernández's valor, but many questioned her rigor. The claim about the $400,000 was prefaced with a cavalier "There are those who insinuate . . ." Despite the dropping of the lawsuit, that paragraph was cut from the second edition and the English translation. "Anabel's books are very carefully revised," says veteran Random House editor Ariel Rosales, "but she's very resistant to suggested changes." Balancing his review, Álvaro Enrigue noted the author's foggy approach to evidence, adding that "whole stretches of the book" relied on single, self-serving informants. He concluded, "*Narcoland* should be treated with caution."[81] Among academics, a consensus grew that the book could not be quoted as an authority.[82]

A case in point: In chapter 2, much is made of a confession by Guzmán upon his 1993 arrest, which "blew apart" the official version that Cardinal Juan Jesús Posadas Ocampo, killed that year at Guadalajara airport, died in the crossfire between Arellano Félix and Sinaloa hitmen.[83] Another: In the revised edition's chapter 1, testimony added from recently detained capo Benjamín Arellano Félix, claiming that the cardinal was actually shot by federal police because he was "supplying weapons to the guerillas," is quoted without comment, as though the claim were dependable.[84] A propensity to believe the worst of the powerful, take criminals' testimony at face value, and cater to a public appetite for conspiracy theory courses through the book.

Journalist turned academic Oswaldo Zavala felt *Narcoland* illustrated a broader flaw, for which he also criticized González Rodríguez, Osorno, and Mexican reporters in general: Such books perpetuate a "hegemonic discourse" created to justify state violence against the "cartels," a US-coined term suggesting a high degree of organization that does not actually exist. To Zavala, this war was insidious, and these journalists were complicit because their common narrative—also seen in novels, films, and TV series like *Narcos*—dampened urgent debates about inequality and corruption, criminalized the poor, and justified the militarization of the country.[85] At least as it applies to Hernández, Zavala's critique seems overstated; for one thing, her book is consistently *counter*hegemonic in its blasting of official corruption. But his criticism about media willingness to recycle the concept of the "cartel" and to stigmatize the have-nots echoed an evolving journalistic zeitgeist. Within a year of the release of Hernández's book, reporters like Marcela Turati and Javier Valdez began to publish studies of the victims of narco violence and humanizing portraits of subaltern combatants.[86]

Despite all the controversies, the most explosive accusation in *Narcoland*, of García Luna's self-enriching protection of the Sinaloa Cartel, would eventually be vindicated. On February 21, 2023, in the same New York courthouse where El Chapo Guzmán had been convicted four years earlier, a jury found García Luna guilty of taking millions of dollars in Sinaloa bribes during the Fox and Calderón eras. Prosecutors had included as evidence in their case García Luna's "multiyear campaign of harassment and threats" against Hernández.[87]

For Hernández, this final vindication arrived after a dozen or so years of trauma, including a death threat from García Luna himself, conveyed indirectly via government insiders, and the occasional deposit of headless animals on her doorstep. It came after a dozen armed men sealed off her street, broke into her home, and, failing to find the journalist, briefly abducted one of her bodyguards; this episode helped persuade her to leave Mexico with her children, first for a visiting gig at Berkeley's School of Journalism, then for residence in Italy. It came after eight years of visits to Mexico as she engaged in new projects, during which she always had to be accompanied by an armed escort.[88]

The afternoon the verdict was delivered, Hernández was seated in the courtroom. She had been commentating on the trial for Milenio TV and German broadcaster Deutsche Welle. She heard the five guilty counts read aloud. Then the judge, the jury, the prisoner, his family, the lawyers, and the press filed out. She stayed seated for another five minutes, quite alone, trying to make sense of her feelings. She wept. Then she got up, pen and notebook in hand, feeling empowered to carry on exposing corruption and impunity.[89]

Chapter 10

President Peña Nieto

Invented by Television, Crushed by the Internet

> Latin American media markets tend to be small and dominated by tycoons with other businesses, who prize cosy relationships with governments. They are being shaken up by digital media.
>
> —*The Economist*, 2018

> Sites like Animal Político, Sin Embargo, La Silla Rota, SDP Noticias, Aristegui Noticias and Reporte Índigo . . . have acquired prestige, and hence more and more readers, due both to the stories that they have decided to tell and the angles and perspectives that they have put forward in their reporting.
>
> —Manuel Alejandro Guerrero, *Democracy and Media in Mexico*, 2016

Aristegui Noticias and the Casa Blanca

The angelical face of Angélica Rivera peered smiling from the cover of *¡Hola!* The former actress struck an elegantly slinky pose in a shoulder-baring champagne top and lacy blue skirt. "First interview with the wife of the President of Mexico," promised one title. "The First Lady, Intimately," beckoned another.

Five and a half years later, her equally photogenic husband, Enrique Peña Nieto, would step down as the most reviled and ridiculed president in a century.

If a butterfly effect can have an engineer, this one was set in motion by a young reporter called Rafael Cabrera.[1] Lining up at the supermarket checkout one day in May 2013, he could not resist pulling *¡Hola!* off the rack and flicking through. He had a weakness for celebrity gossip; the feature might offer a few nuggets. For one thing, many photographs were taken not at Los Pinos but at a luxurious private residence. "There could be something here," Cabrera thought. He tossed the magazine into his cart.

A graduate of the *Reforma* night desk, Cabrera eventually found himself in the employ of Carmen Aristegui, the influential radio host. Aristegui, a grandchild of Basque Republican refugees from the Spanish Civil War, had carved a niche since the late 1980s as an unusually independent voice in broadcasting, and her unique setup would prove ideal for Cabrera and the story he wanted to tell. A petite, almost dainty woman, Aristegui possessed a remarkable tenacity: She would take hold of a controversy and grapple with it on air for days. She balanced this trait with one-on-one interviews, notable for her warmth and a wide smile, as viewers saw in her nighttime show on CNN en Español.

In April 2012 she launched the website *Aristegui Noticias*, which would play a crucial role in the story Cabrera wished to tell. It soon became one of Mexico's most consulted sites for real-time news.[2] This was thanks in large part to Daniel Lizárraga, her assignments editor. Another graduate of *Reforma*, Lizárraga had built a reputation for fact-checking rigor and astute use of the 2002 transparency law in the hunt for evidence of corruption. As their working relationship developed, Lizárraga convinced Aristegui to take her famously probing news show one step further by adding investigative journalism. Formalized in May 2014, Aristegui's investigative unit comprised a quartet. Lizárraga, in his forties, was in charge, and his young recruits included Irving Huerta and Sebastían Barragán, both studying for a master's in journalism at Mexico City's Center for Research and Teaching in Economics, and Cabrera. Lizárraga also supervised daily news for Aristegui. Another twenty reporters worked for MVS Radio, dividing their time between its various newscasts, including Aristegui's.

A year had gone by since Cabrera had picked up *¡Hola!*, and he had done enough poking around to know there was indeed "something here." The magazine reported that Rivera's private home was located in Las Lomas de Chapultepec, a zone of multimillion-dollar mansions. A search at the public property registry found that neither Peña nor Rivera was the owner, but a real estate company. Further digging revealed the company to be owned by Grupo Higa, a construction firm belonging to Juan Hinojosa, a magnate often favored by Peña when he was governor of the State of México; that regime had awarded Hinojosa contracts worth $3 billion. Had Hinojosa covertly returned such favors by building the First Couple a mansion? Might he be angling for more?

Lizárraga liked Cabrera's idea for a story on the subject. He dubbed Rivera's mansion the Casa Blanca, or White House, a literal descriptor that implied delusions of grandeur. Aristegui at once sensed the story's potential: "This is an atomic bomb," she told the foursome. Each of them delved into distinct aspects while continuing other investigations.

By October 2014, the Casa Blanca story was almost ready. Then news broke that a company of Hinojosa's was part of a Chinese-led consortium that had all but officially won a contract to build a 140-mile high-speed rail link between the capital and Querétaro, a signature project of Peña's, worth nearly $4 billion. With a little digging, Lizárraga's team found that competitors, including Germany's Siemens and Canada's Bombardier, had all dropped out, complaining they had been given insufficient time to assemble rival bids. Here was favoritism again. Meanwhile, Aristegui was involved in talks with MVS chief executive Joaquín Vargas about how to handle the Casa Blanca story. Vargas had already been getting heat from the president's office over what Lizárraga,

Cabrera, and company had been prying into. After two months of back-and-forth, Vargas and Aristegui reached a compromise: She would break the story on a Sunday, on her website. In what would become a bone of contention between the two, the journalist thus felt at liberty to take up the matter the next day on MVS Radio, discussing what had already been revealed.

But the sensitivity of the story required that Aristegui protect herself. Any single website was vulnerable to hacking. Any single outlet was vulnerable to reprisals. Furthermore, she wanted the story to create the biggest stir possible, lest Peña's communications team succeed in burying it. With media revenues in decline, editors could be leaned on by Los Pinos to ignore the story; on social media, Peña's staff were masters of the dark arts of fake news and Twitter bots.[3] So Aristegui met in turn with Carmen Lira of *La Jornada*, Rafael Rodríguez Castañeda of *Proceso*, and Roberto Zamarripa of *Reforma* to propose sharing the story for a synchronized release. She also reached out to Jo Tuckman of *The Guardian*, who arranged for her to meet with fellow correspondents from media including *The Wall Street Journal*, the *Los Angeles Times*, *The Washington Post*, the *Financial Times*, *Le Monde*, US TV network Univision, and the Associated Press.[4] This was a tactic her team had seen employed by *The Guardian* when publishing major exposés.

On Sunday, November 9, the media alliance began to break the story.[5] "The White House of Enrique Peña Nieto," ran the headline on *Aristegui Noticias*, while the subhead summed up the most damning material: "The President possesses a house in Las Lomas, Mexico City, valued at $7 million. It was built to his taste by Grupo Higa, one of the firms that won the bid for the Mexico City-Querétaro train, and that earlier constructed public works in the State of México, when he was governor."

Having been reached for comment on what Aristegui was about to reveal, Peña's team had killed the rail project three days before the article ran. It was an acutely embarrassing reversal, given that the president was about to visit China, whose government operated the construction company that was Grupo Higa's senior partner on the bid. And worse was to come. The following week, the First Lady uploaded a seven-minute video to her website, soon relayed on television and YouTube, addressing "all the accusations that have put my honor in doubt." In a subdued voice but with a look of disdain and a tone of self-righteous anger, she claimed that the house was hers, that Hinojosa had offered her a private mortgage, that she had already repaid 30 percent of it, and that she was in a position to buy a multimillion-dollar home "through all my hard work."[6]

For the better part of two years, Rivera had been showing off her jet-setting lifestyle and enviable wardrobe, not only to *¡Hola!* but also in posts to Facebook and Instagram. In the reading of *El Universal* veteran Roberto Rock, with the Casa Blanca scandal and images of the mansion echoing through the media,

La casa blanca de Enrique Peña Nieto (investigación especial)

El Presidente posee una casa en Las Lomas, DF, con valor de USD 7 millones. Fue construida a su gusto por Grupo Higa, una de las empresas que ganó la licitación del tren México-Querétaro, y que antes levantó obras en Edomex, cuando él fue gobernador.

Redacción AN
09 Nov, 2014 05:00

f   ☺   🐦   ✉

A 2014 scoop by *Aristegui Noticias* about a mansion dubbed "Casa Blanca," built for President Enrique Peña Nieto's wife by a contractor he had favored, marked the start of the collapse of his popularity. Courtesy of *Aristegui Noticias*.

"levels of repudiation, which had always been high, reached the stratosphere."[7] Whether or not she was telling the truth, the public reaction was plain. "Do you believe Angélica Rivera's explanation of how she acquired the Casa Blanca?" asked a poll in *Reforma*.[8] Only 13 percent said yes; 77 percent said no.

There was no apology from the president. In December he told reporters, "What conflict of interest? I don't see one at all!" Summing up the affair, along with a mounting collection of tone-deaf missteps, *The Economist* coined a phrase that would resonate for the rest of Peña's term: "A president who doesn't get that he doesn't get it."[9]

———

As Jenaro Villamil of *Proceso* revealed in many articles and two books, Peña had been groomed for the presidency since 2005—when he ran for governor of the State of México—by the media giant Televisa. He was telegenic and, in 2010, married Rivera, a Televisa star. Thanks in great part to Televisa's behind-the-scenes guidance and on-screen cheerleading, Peña built and maintained a formidable lead in the polls ahead of the 2012 election.[10]

Six weeks before the July vote, however, his perfect mask began to slip. On May 11, Peña suffered a scornful reception from many students at Mexico City's Iberoamerican University, or "Ibero," at one point reportedly taking refuge in a men's room. Not only Televisa but most print media omitted or played down the incident, a trend surely reflective of declining private-sector ad buys and a consequent thirst for campaign ad spend from the Institutional Revolutionary Party (PRI). Most sycophantic of all was Mario Vázquez Raña's *El Sol*, whose capital and regional editions all led with, "Success for Peña at the Ibero, Despite an Orchestrated Attempt at a Boycott."[11] Indeed, Televisa and *El Sol* went one step further than most in claiming that protesters at Peña's speech were not students. In response, 131 Ibero students created a YouTube video, displaying their Ibero IDs and reiterating their opposition. In turn this prompted the social media hashtag "#YoSoy132"—as in, "I'm the 132nd protestor"—and a movement was born. Nationwide, marches and rallies protested pro-Peña media bias, especially at Televisa. They demanded the full televising of a second candidates' debate (the first had been given only a marginal TV platform, probably because Televisa and TV Azteca guessed that their man Peña would do poorly). They called for a more thorough democratization of society.[12]

YoSoy132 members tended to shun print media too, preferring to share items from the independent news sites that had recently sprung up. And they were active on Twitter and Facebook, this being the first general election to be influenced by social media. Aguascalientes reporter Jennifer González, a journalism student at the time, recalls that among the minority in the press who paid close attention to the movement, most were editors and writers for online media. At local YoSoy132 marches and in social media messaging, she adds, it became common to "recommend and share content from SinEmbargo, Animal Político, ADN Político and Reporte Índigo," each of them standalone websites. Mexico, it seemed to some, had its own version of Occupy Wall Street or the Arab Spring. Andrés Manuel López Obrador, running for a second time with the Party of the Democratic Revolution (PRD), began to rise in the polls.[13]

Peña won the July 1 election by 7 points over López Obrador, a lead 16 points narrower than in the *Reforma* poll the previous November, but still decisive. He was helped by a common perception that López Obrador, despite his more conciliatory rhetoric, was not to be trusted; memories lingered of his tempestuous reactions to the 2006 defeat. Peña was helped by much if not most of the print media, as evidenced by their display of polls that exaggerated his lead to make his victory look inevitable; here the guilty parties included both the routinely submissive papers, such as *Excélsior* and the *El Sol* chain, and those that had lost their critical edge: the *Milenio* chain and *El Universal*.[14] Above all, Peña was helped by television. The weekend of the vote, *Proceso* editor Rafael Rodríguez Castañeda created what is arguably the magazine's most famous cover, one for which no title was needed: the presidential sash adorning the orange-eye logo of Televisa.[15]

Villamil followed up with a postelectoral autopsy: *Peña Nieto: The Great Staging*; the last word in Spanish, *montaje*, can also mean "farce." But for now, his was a minority view. Peña took office that December with some 55 percent of the public approving of him and, depending on the poll, just 22 to 35 percent disapproving.[16] Over the next six years—despite the pressures of yet another federal advertising boycott (prompted in part by *that* cover image)—*Proceso* would further hold Peña to account.

But the media that did most to expose his ineptness, together with the rife corruption of the PRI, were digital.

Two Visions of Digital: *Animal Político* and *SinEmbargo*

Daniel Moreno quit *Excélsior* in October 2006, despairing of the transactional intentions of its new owner, Olegario Vázquez Aldir, toward president-elect Felipe Calderón. Moreno never worked in newspapers again. For three years he directed news at W Radio, a station jointly owned by Televisa and Spain's Grupo Prisa, but the job was much less journalistic than administrative. So when two well-heeled Colombian TV executives called him from Miami with a plan for a digital project, Moreno was moderately interested.[17]

First, he needed a vacation. It was June 2010 and he had booked a hotel in Acapulco to coincide with the World Cup; he could alternately relax and watch the national soccer team make its usual progress to the first knock-out round and no further. Isaac Lee and Daniel Eilemberg were insistent, however. They flew down and met with him in the hotel lobby. Moreno, by now a slender man in his midforties, his boyish face and buzz cut at odds with his graying beard, met the investors in his T-shirt and flip-flops. As he later put it, "I didn't have Facebook and I didn't have Twitter. To me, digital media were absolutely exotic." But one point of the offer swung him: full editorial control.

A year earlier, Eilemberg had dreamed up a Twitter account called Pájaro Político (Political Bird), supplying real-time news bites about Mexico City, a novel idea at the time and a popular one. So the website would be *Animal Político*.[18] With a staff of just ten, *Animal Político* bowed on November 19, 2010. The idea was to offer a blend of daily news, mostly pulled from the wires and radio reports, and original reporting, some of it contributed by nongovernmental organizations (NGOs). The perspective would resemble *The Guardian*'s, center-left with a liberal take on social issues. It would do without opinion columns, preferring short informative takes from experts in a section called "Palenque." This was the easy part.

The challenges were multiple. First, standalone general news sites were thin on the ground, so hiring good people was hard and there were few places to look for inspiration. Moreno started with a design that he termed "a newspaper made on the internet," an unattractive idea that was ditched within a year. Second, even though the major dailies had been cultivating websites since the mid-1990s, most politicians paid little heed to news online—"The political class was very analog," Moreno recalls with a grim smile—which complicated landing interviews. Third, a similar bias held true for advertisers.[19] Fourth, there was the task of luring readers.

In early 2011, it was clear that *Animal Político*'s small audience was largely under thirty-five, little interested in the drug-war violence, and less in what politicians had to say about it. Experimentation followed, with a shift in emphasis to human rights, corruption, and the victims, rather than perpetrators, of the homicide epidemic. An innovative feature was a "lethality index," studying army encounters with crime syndicate gunmen. In one such case, the army killed twenty-five "aggressors" while incurring just two soldiers wounded. This suggested a custom of extrajudicial killings. At first there was no reaction, but several days later Televisa news presenter Denise Maerker took up the findings in a column in *El Universal*.[20] *Animal Político* was starting to register on the media map.

By the time YoSoy132 erupted a year later, the site had gained enough credibility among students to become a point of reference. Moreno claims its traffic doubled that summer thanks to its coverage of the movement, which was led by the young reporter Paris Martínez. While legacy media and social media users speculated about who might be "behind" the movement (López Obrador was the popular suspect), *Animal Político* focused on the students themselves.[21] When YoSoy132 held its first assembly at the National Autonomous University of Mexico, Moreno published their list of demands in full, which became one of his site's most read stories.

In late 2014, as Mexicans were reacting to news of Peña's Casa Blanca, the president was already under duress due to the September 26 disappearance, and likely murder, of forty-three trainee teachers from Ayotzinapa, Guerrero. Early reports suggested the abductors were either drug traffickers, municipal police, the army, or all three in cahoots. At any rate the government was slow to seek answers. No one media broke the story; the news trickled out until the scale of the crime was too glaring to hush up. But thanks again to Martínez, who went to Guerrero to talk to family members, *Animal Político*

Las empresas fantasma **ᴰᴱ VERACRUZ**

A 2016 exposé by *Animal Político* about misuse of public funds by Veracruz's Javier Duarte contributed to the governor's fall from grace, flight from Mexico, and eventual extradition and imprisonment. Courtesy of *Animal Político*.

was the first to humanize the victims by sketching each of them. A few weeks later, at a Mexico City demonstration convened by López Obrador's new party, Morena, writer Elena Poniatowska gave a speech titled "Give Them Back!," in which she cited Martínez and read out his profiles.[22]

What would distinguish *Animal Político* in the long run was its investigative journalism. The public and the political class got a taste of this in May 2016, when it published "Ghost Companies of Veracruz." This was the perilous Veracruz of Javier Duarte, the governor famed for fiddling while criminal gangs and local officials bumped off reporters. The story came to Moreno from a freelancer who had been alerted by local businessmen to how Duarte was awarding contracts to phony firms. Moreno dispatched his reporter Arturo Ángel to help investigate, while staffers in Mexico City made freedom-of-information requests to authorities. Duarte's initial response was to send a hack from a paper allied to his regime to meet with Ángel and ask him, "What can we do to sort this out?"—that is, Ángel should name his price.

"Ghost Companies of Veracruz" encapsulated the new digital journalism: It took seven journalists to produce, ran in three installments, and included interactive features and a video. The report found seventy-three contracts that had diverted the equivalent of $50 million in state funds to twenty-three fake companies. It prompted a follow-up by Mexicans Against Corruption and Impunity (MCCI), a new NGO, which in December unearthed another forty-five phony enterprises, recipients of $35 million. By then, Duarte was in hiding in Guatemala, having fled two months before his term was up; he had at last been abandoned by the PRI, which would no longer cover for him. Among the factors of his flight was an investigation by the Tax Administration Service, Mexico's IRS, prompted by *Animal Político*'s findings. Before long, Duarte was arrested and extradited, and in 2018 he was sentenced to nine years in jail for money laundering and criminal association.[23]

The following year *Animal Político* revealed an even bigger corruption case, which it dubbed "The Master Scam." Its report detailed systematic use of fake federal contracts for the funding of electoral campaigns by the PRI. The headline in Spanish, "La estafa maestra," was a play on words, suggesting the size of the operation and alluding to how the contracts were channeled via universities (*maestra* can mean both "expert" and "teacher"). Seventeen journalists joined the investigation. It was arguably the most complex of any undertaken by a Mexican news outlet, involving 517 freedom-of-information requests, 106 visits to companies or shareholders, and more than 100 interviews. The team included veterans Salvador Camarena and Daniel Lizárraga, now with the investigative unit at MCCI. The lead writers were three young guns, Miriam Castillo, Nayeli Roldán, and Manuel Ureste.[24]

In 2013 and 2014 alone, the report found, eleven federal dependencies contracted services worth some $600 million with eight public universities. None of those contracts had anything to do with education, so the universities in turn subcontracted 186 firms, of which 128 either lacked the legal foundation to receive public moneys or simply did not exist. Close to half of the total sum simply vanished. Fifty functionaries were implicated, including Pemex chief Emilio Lozoya Austin, the former social development minister (and one-time Mexico City mayor) Rosario Robles, and the rectors of the universities. Several media had already published snippets of the scam, using research from the federal audit office that inculpated the universities, but no prosecutions had been undertaken. *Animal Político*'s achievement was to pin most of the blame on the federal government, to map out the big picture in a visually digestible fashion, and to present corroborating evidence far beyond what either the government's supreme audit institution or other media had done.[25]

One measure of a story's impact is peer recognition. Like "The Ghost Companies of Duarte" the year before, "The Master Scam" earned *Animal Político* a National Journalism Award. A year later, it was honored in Spain with the prestigious Ortega y Gasset Award. These prizes together cemented the site's eminence in long-form political reportage.[26]

Susana Seijas, a media consultant who analyzed the impact of *Animal Político*'s reporting in 2017, was similarly impressed: "As a digital native, it was doing really exciting stuff and their data-driven content was something new—visually impactful and fresh." She found that Moreno was adept at boosting traffic via Twitter: "He took to the platform like a duck to water, with his online presence resembling one of a news influencer. His tweets would be trending topics."[27]

Another measure of impact is public interest, which for "The Master Scam" was initially strong but was muted two weeks later by a Mexico City earthquake that killed hundreds. Yet follow-up revelations and accusations over the course of two years would restore public attention, as would a well-received bestseller on the scandal by Roldán, Castillo, and Ureste.[28] The greatest measure, of course, is real-world impact, and here the record is disappointing. In 2019 Rosario Robles was jailed pending trial, but the judicial targeting of her and not anyone else seemed politicized (she was a long-standing rival of López Obrador), the specific charge against her was minor, and four years later she gained release on a technicality. Impunity in Mexico, even by Latin American standards, runs deep.[29]

September 2017 saw a huge spike in traffic at *Animal Político*, thanks to both "The Master Scam" and coverage of the earthquake, which badly hit the Condesa neighborhood near the website's offices; Moreno's team were quick to respond, with short video reports that went viral.[30] For Lee and Eilemberg, it was a good time to sell out. Moreno agreed: The staff had grown to twenty-five and the site needed a capital infusion to fulfill its promise. Besides, owing to its exposés of PRI skullduggery and such feats as fact-checking in real time Peña's State of the Nation addresses, the site was largely snubbed by the federal government. In fact, *Animal Político* had made a sticky start with the president by reporting that he had missed child-support payments for one of his extramarital sons, upon which the site received no federal advertising for a year. Under Peña as a whole, *Animal Político* would receive some $500,000 in official spend, about 15 percent of its total ad haul. But this was only one-twentieth of what was doled out to *SDP Noticias*, a once critical left-wing news site that had climbed into bed with Peña.[31]

Gerardo Márquez Camacho stepped up. A member of a wealthy Hidalgo boot-making family, Márquez owned the Pachuca daily *Criterio* and the Mexican franchise of *Newsweek*. The sale generated some controversy, given Márquez's close links to the PRI, from which he had allegedly benefited in real estate deals.[32] Moreno would assert that Márquez never interfered with editorial content. Eleven years after launch, buoyed by a combination of decent traffic and ad sales, paid content (always identified as such), consultancy fees and workshops, grants from NGOs such as the Ford Foundation, and a news verification contract with Facebook, *Animal Político* would at long last break even.

––––––––

Jorge Zepeda Patterson guessed that his time at *El Universal* was drawing to a close during 2010, when several things became obvious: After four years of Calderón's assault on the drug traffickers, the bloodshed was higher than ever, which meant the PRI could well return to power; the PRI's candidate would almost certainly be Enrique Peña Nieto; and Juan Francisco Ealy Ortiz wanted to be Peña's friend.[33]

Three years earlier, in a characteristically pompous ceremony followed by flashy play in the paper, Ealy had handed direction of *El Universal* to his son, the thirtysomething Juan Francisco Ealy Jr.[34] He said he was retiring and would travel the world with his wife. Ealy Jr. soon ousted editor in chief Roberto Rock, whom he personally disliked. To replace him, he hired Raymundo Riva Palacio, but the match proved awkward. Riva Palacio ran the paper as he saw fit, shaping its critical tone and handling relations with the Calderón regime with little thought of input from young Ealy Jr. So after less than a year Ealy Jr. fired Riva Palacio too. He asked Zepeda, who was directing the Sunday supplement *Día Siete*, to take the helm of the daily. Zepeda did so for two years, beginning in October 2008. According to the writer and broadcaster Ricardo Raphael, who entered as opinion editor, Zepeda convinced the publisher that Mexico City, home to the vast majority of the paper's readership, was a left-wing town and *El Universal* should thus be kinder to its PRD-affiliated mayor, Marcelo Ebrard. However, by summer 2010, Zepeda found himself having to deal each day with Ealy Sr., who, as Raphael puts it, "has always been a PRI sympathizer at heart." The magnate had evidently tired of traveling the world and yearned for the drama of hobnobbing and power brokering; he could help the PRI return to Los Pinos. After six months of this, Zepeda offered his resignation.

Zepeda was allowed to carry on editing *Día Siete*, along with his right-hand man Alejandro Páez. But with circulation of *El Universal* and its partners in the project tumbling, down by a third from its 2005 peak, the magazine's profit margins were much reduced. Its days were numbered. Ironically, it was one of those partners who offered Zepeda an alternative. Miguel Valladares, co-owner with his brother Pablo of *El Pulso*, the top paper in San Luis Potosí, invited him to lunch. Valladares asked him, "What's next?" He was keen on a new rival to *Proceso*, but better designed and more plural.

"Nothing on newsprint!" replied Zepeda. He related how *El Universal* had built up an online readership that vastly surpassed its print audience. The future was online. The Valladares brothers, who had inherited a fortune from their father's steelmaking business, agreed to finance a news site and take a two-thirds stake; Zepeda and Páez would commit their work in exchange for one-third. In June 2011, with a staff of thirty, they launched *SinEmbargo*, a pun on the Spanish for "however" and "without restriction."

Páez was perhaps as vital to the project's success as Zepeda, who in recent years had spent much of his time writing and editing books and consulting for regional papers. His current project was the second in a recurrent series of profiles of presidential contenders, *Los suspirantes 2012* (*suspirantes* is a made-up word suggesting "the yearning aspirants").[35] Páez, a generation younger, brought to *SinEmbargo* his personal passions—corruption, poverty, the concentration of wealth among elites—and his argumentative tone.

SinEmbargo proved a steady build rather than an instant success. At first, like *Animal Político*, it aimed to cover the news in full, including sports, culture, and showbiz. Its slant reflected Zepeda's leftist politics without being overbearing, which presumably came as a relief to the Valladares family, political centrists aligned with the PRI and friendly with Peña.[36] In an era of proliferating digital start-ups, *SinEmbargo* stood out with its professional reporting and tough line on the government, which made it a rival of *Animal Político*. One subeditor began his day checking the websites of *Reforma*, *El Universal*, *Milenio*, and, most carefully of all, *Animal Político*. As another subeditor admitted in 2013, "Our direct competition is Animal Político. . . . So far, they are our enemies. Why? Because they are the ones who are on our level, the highest level."[37]

Both sites made good use of freelancers. Multiple-award-winning feature writer Humberto Padgett was a frequent contributor to *SinEmbargo*. He kicked off with a moving, prize-winning chronicle about Zulema Hernández, an in-jail girlfriend of "El Chapo" Guzmán, who upon her release was raped, tortured, and killed by the Zetas. Another award-winning piece of his delved into the work and culture of opium poppy farmers in the remote mountainsides of Guerrero.[38] These features reflected the journalistic trend away from the drug lords and their clashes and toward the lived experience of the voiceless.

SinEmbargo distinguished itself from *Animal Político* by affording less coverage to socially liberal themes such as feminism and sexual diversity and by putting much more emphasis on political opinion. Zepeda assembled his "dream team" of columnists, most of them center-leftists: Zepeda's partner Lydia Cacho (who would continue after their amicable split), Ricardo Raphael, Jenaro Villamil of *Proceso*, and others. Zepeda and Páez also wrote columns.

The polemical style proved a good bet. By late 2016, *SinEmbargo* ranked sixth among Mexico's standalone news sites, with a monthly viewership of 3 million. Not counting platforms for culture or political satire, only three placed higher: *SDP Noticias*, *Aristegui Noticias*, and Carlos Slim's *UnoTV* (a bland site whose app was preinstalled on all Telcel cell phones).[39] But since advertisers in the private sector were slow to embrace digital, *SinEmbargo* still operated at a loss. So instead of hiring more reporters to compete with print, Zepeda and Páez eased the site from being a digital paper that exhaustively covered the news to something of a magazine format, offering a more interpretative take. This transformation consolidated *SinEmbargo*'s critical, left-wing credentials.

The Peña regime was not pleased. Already cut out of federal advertising—the site's take up to 2016 amounting to a measly $14,000—it received not a cent in 2017.[40] Further, the business continued to be subject to regular audits. Recalls Páez, "We gave the auditors a special desk, because we expected another team to arrive soon after one had departed."[41]

After nine years of red ink and cash injections from the Valladares brothers, *SinEmbargo* would break even in 2020. That put it a year ahead of *Animal Político*. By then López Obrador was president, and while Moreno's site was enduring a near-total federal advertising boycott, Zepeda's was not.

———

Digital platforms equaled if not surpassed print in influence during the Peña era, and *SinEmbargo*, *Animal Político*, and *Aristegui Noticias* offered a formidable holding to account. Their exposés and opinion columns made waves, not least because their work reverberated on social media and drove discussion in print, on radio, and on television. Some became the basis for popular books, such as *Peña's White House*, by Daniel Lizárraga and his *Aristegui Noticias* peers, and *The Master Scam*, by Nayeli Roldán and her *Animal Político* colleagues.[42]

Quantifying the sites' reach was not easy. Comscore, the top digital measurer in countries including Mexico and Spain, got flak for letting itself be gamed by sites either posting clickbait or using automated accounts on social media to inflate traffic.[43] But on Twitter, which had fake-account problems of its own but hosted a concentration of decision makers and university-educated users, *Aristegui Noticias* closed 2018 with an impressive 8.2 million followers. Also performing well were *Animal Político* with 1.9 million and *SinEmbargo* with 1.3 million. *SDP Noticias* had just 590,000, although its 5 million followers on Facebook showed its pull among the young and less discriminating.[44]

Except for *El Universal*, a perennial Comscore highflier, print media were generally slow to adapt to the new digital reality. And yet, quite in contrast to what was happening across the United States, Canada, the United Kingdom, and to a lesser extent other parts of Europe (where print media often received state subsidies), the flight of readers and advertisers to the internet did not produce a massive closure of newspapers.

The Paradoxical Persistence of Print

A visitor from New York or London in 2018 could walk along a few downtown Mexico City streets, stopping at the newsstands to note the titles, and tally twenty-seven distinct daily papers. The figure far exceeded the local sum on display back home—five in New York, eleven in London—even though Mexican purchasing power and newspaper readership were far lower. The same held true outside the metropolis. A visitor from Philadelphia to Puebla, both cities of 1.5 million, could spot thirteen dailies, as opposed to the three in the old burg where Benjamin Franklin once founded *The Pennsylvania Gazette*. Similarly sized San Diego and Phoenix produced one daily paper each.[45]

By the end of the Peña era, newspaper circulation in Mexico had been in decline for a dozen years, yet during that time the only papers to disappear in the capital were recently launched titles that failed either to read the signs of market decline or, more importantly, to pull down enough government advertising to be viable. Print persisted in Mexico because the vast majority of newspapers were never meant to be proper businesses in the first place. The economics of print were predicated on subsidies—chiefly from government sources, sometimes from the owners' pockets—and the leverage that papers ostensibly offered.

Most print media were created or acquired to wield political influence. Usually, such influence obtained favors that served an owner's core businesses: real estate, hotels, auto sales, telecoms, and all kinds of public contracting from drilling for oil to building transportation infrastructure. Less often, though more frequently in the provinces, papers served the ambitions of owners or family members who either held political office or aspired to.[46] Either way, they were what the business world calls "loss leaders": products sold below cost to benefit the sale of other goods and services. In the capital, only four periodicals significantly bucked this trend, for their owners were media players first and foremost, and these were the most influential: *Reforma*, *El Universal*, *La Jornada*, and *Proceso*.

Reforma and its Monterrey sibling *El Norte*, respectively edited by Lázaro Ríos and Martha Treviño, remained Mexico's newspapers of record. But due to financial duress—and after years of scrupulous trimming of overhead, in order to preserve jobs—both papers had found the need to scale down. By the early Peña years, they were diminished in both size and, given the rise of digital media, public influence. Gone were the literary, cultural, and political supplements that had made sitting with the paper an hours-long weekend pleasure, comparable to Manhattanites enjoying the Sunday *New York Times*. Even the main section was a good deal thinner, with less room for features and less attention to news outside the capital. (The latter trend could be seen in most of Mexico City's newspapers since the late Calderón years, which helps explain why such tragedies as the 2010 and 2011 massacres of 72 migrants and 193 citizens in San Fernando, Tamaulipas; the 2011 massacre of up to 300 townspeople in Allende, Chihuahua; and the general plight of Central American migrants received little timely attention.)[47] In 2016, Grupo Reforma laid off 130 employees, including most of its regional correspondents; of around 30, only 5 were kept on full time. In 2018, it lowered its payments to columnists, prompting star scribe Lorenzo Meyer to take his business to *El Universal*. During the Fox era, Alejandro Junco had employed 1,500 people between his news and design staff; now the total stood at 1,100 and would continue to shrink.[48]

Grupo Reforma still carried weight within the decision-making class, despite a rightward drift in its editorial line and a loss of pluralism among columnists, thanks to the quality of its papers' writing and their continued questioning of politicians of all stripes. But their broader reach via the internet was restricted by the decision to erect a paywall back in 2000; this was long before other market leaders did so, such as *The Times* of London (2010), *The New York Times* (2011), and *El País* (2020). The move was viewed by media observers as typical of Junco's arrogance and an economic and journalistic mistake, especially as it was a "hard" paywall that allowed no free visits. Of greater help in keeping afloat amid declining readership were the supplements "Club" and "Empresas": The first followed a custom begun at *El Norte* of charging the wealthy to have photographers sent to cover their gated-community birthday parties, bejeweled charity functions, and high-rent *quinceañeras*; the second charged corporate clients for advertorials.[49]

Reforma and *El Norte* had long gained a de facto subsidy from their popular *Metro* tabloid editions, with their cover images of bodies: murdered males and bikini'd females. *El Universal* likewise had help from its *Gráfico*, which like *Metro* once sold 200,000 to 300,000 a day in the capital. However, after smartphones became ubiquitous, Mexico's tabloids fast declined. In 2018, *Reforma* was the capital's top-selling "quality" paper, despite having slipped in circulation from its Fox-era peak of 150,000 to around 90,000; *Metro* was down to 120,000. In part, the broadsheet's resilience derived from an unusually strong subscriber base and its custom of having its street vendors buy their bundles, which explained why some of those green-clad personnel could still be seen hawking their wares in the early afternoon, after rivals had quit for the day.[50]

El Universal was in greater trouble. Its cash cow had always been its classified ads, yet despite transitioning the section online, the business was undercut by the rise of free alternatives, including via Facebook. By 2018, daily circulation was down to 40,000, from a peak of around 100,000. Although online traffic was strong, it was not very lucrative. To cut costs, the paper made notable use of low-paid reporters, hired as interns or casual labor, something that *Reforma* refused to do. Juan Francisco Ealy Ortiz, now in his seventies, was believed to have parlayed his decades of political influence into a collection of separate businesses and contracts, so he likely subsidized the paper from these. More obviously, Ealy looked for help to politicians, starting with the president. During the Peña years, *El Universal* took a whopping $86 million in federal advertising, more than any other paper and around five times the sum accorded to *Reforma*.[51] The difference showed on the page. While *Reforma* continued to run exposés, *El Universal* pulled its punches.

The investigative unit that Roberto Rock assembled in the 1990s was now headed by Salvador Frausto, and in January 2015 he supervised freelancer Laura Castellanos as she looked into the death of nine civilians in the violence-prone city of Apatzingán, Michoacán. The official version held that a federal police convoy suffered an ambush by the nine, resulting in the wounding of two police officers; despite having had the element of surprise, all the attackers died. Castellanos, a specialist in armed movements who knew Michoacán well, spent ten days tracking down witnesses, finding photographic and video footage, and even obtaining a taped statement from a local crime boss. As she and Frausto fact-checked and shaped the story, they endured burglaries, police surveillance, and a death threat. The story they assembled told of an extrajudicial execution of vigilante gang members, who had downed their arms for a peaceful protest, engineered by Peña's close friend and security point man, Alfredo Castillo. But once the exposé was ready, *El Universal* sat on it. After two months of editorial delay tactics, with the government moving to protect Castillo, Castellanos took the story to Carmen Aristegui. The radio host obliged by putting together an intermedia alliance like the one she had assembled for the Casa Blanca scoop: The piece ran simultaneously on *Aristegui Noticias*, on the website of human rights NGO Article 19, as a cover story in *Proceso*, and on Univision. The story went global.

Journalists at *oficialista* media tried to rubbish it, Carlos Marín at *Milenio* dismissing Castellano's brave work as "scavenger journalism." The juries of the National Journalism Award and the Latin American Investigative Journalism Award disagreed. As she accepted the former prize, Castellanos declared, "I think the moment the management of *El Universal* decided not to publish my investigation on the massacre for two months, for political reasons, they became de facto accomplices of the perpetrators."[52]

Perhaps smarting from being outmaneuvered by Castellanos, *El Universal* deputy editor David Aponte took greater care with another sensitive investigation. Later that year, the paper's freedom-of-information expert, Lilia Saúl, did a deep dive into the mounting tragedy of Mexico's disappeared citizens, victims of crime syndicates and state agents. In a joint investigation with Colombia's *El Tiempo*, she established that, since the start of Calderón's "war on drugs," some 25,000 Mexicans had vanished. Aponte ensured that the feature led the front page and jumped to an inside double spread. It would win an Ortega y Gasset Award. But Saúl felt its impact was muted by how the editor in chief, Francisco Santiago, had spun it. To her, the lead was that Peña had broken a promise to tackle the tragedy, which in fact was worsening. Yet the headline blamed his predecessor: "Crisis of the Disappeared Erupted with Calderón."[53]

Two years later Santiago was out, having gone too far in criticizing a citizen-led anticorruption initiative that discomfited the Peña regime; six columnists had quit in protest. Ealy replaced Santiago with Aponte. This represented his eighth change of editor in chief since the mid-1990s, during which time *Reforma* had had just two. And another storm struck when *The New York Times* ran a page 1 lead on the Peña government's media influence via massive advertising buys. The feature had much to say about *El Universal*. It detailed the censorship of Laura Castellanos. It described an extended defamation campaign, involving more than twenty front-page stories, against the leading National Action Party (PAN) precandidate for the 2018 presidential election, Ricardo Anaya. And it noted that after investigative director Salvador Frausto quit, fed up with all the pro-PRI bias, his replacement was a former press officer from the Ministry of Foreign Affairs.[54]

La Jornada, once a venerable institution of the Mexican left, had fallen on hard times. It lurched from one crisis to another, the result of a bloated employee count and unusually good salaries and benefits for staffers, which made redundancy packages very costly. Until 2015, the paper's coverage of hot-button issues such as Peña's free-market reform of the energy sector, the Casa Blanca, the forty-three disappeared students of Ayotzinapa, and massacres conducted by the army and police remained critical, although, per one academic study, not as critical as in *Proceso*. A degree of schizophrenia emerged, for by 2015 a smiling or commanding Peña appeared in a large page 1 photograph on average twice a month.[55]

During the second half of Peña's term, however, the crisis of credibility at *La Jornada* became acute. *The New York Times* reported it had accepted a $1 million-plus rescue package of extra federal advertising. When exactly that occurred is unclear, but as of May 2016 front-page photographs of Peña, already flattering in tone but fewer than once a month between January and April, leaped to thrice a month. The paper's core readership, die-hard leftist and nationalist, was treated to the man they regarded as Mr. Neoliberal shaking hands with Barack Obama (three times), saluting and later jogging with Justin Trudeau, and receiving an award for statesmanship from some US association. Further presidential poses had Peña addressing the United Nations, honoring writers and scientists, celebrating Day of the Dead, and saving the monarch butterfly.[56]

Given that the paper's columnists and cartoonists kept up their criticism, and given that its correspondents continued to report bravely on corruption in the states, the overall effect recalled the sell-out press of the 1970s: sycophancy toward the president and his cabinet on page 1, tempered by moments of inside-page feistiness. A veteran reporter lamented, "As of 2016, it was as though we were [state-owned press agency] Notimex, publishing the deeds of the government on a regular basis."[57]

Under Peña, *La Jornada* received $28 million in federal advertising, placing third behind *El Universal* and *Excélsior*. It apparently took in at least another $6 million from the PRD-run Mexico City government and ran thousands of *gacetillas* lauding the work of state governors, including 559 paid insertions (roughly two per week) bought by the notoriously corrupt Javier Duarte of Veracruz.[58]

Morale in the newsroom declined. It worsened as section heads and senior reporters got away with unethical practices, such as pocketing commissions on ad buys from Congress, and as senior editors earned luxurious salaries. De facto editor in chief Josetxo Zaldua was rumored to have accepted a beach house in Huatulco from Governor Alejandro Murat of Oaxaca. Rumors among the rank and file extended to nominal editor in chief Lira, who was believed to own at least three properties in Mexico City and a pied-à-terre in Paris. The latter may not be true, but amid a new austerity in the newsroom it became a common joke: "There are no batteries for my recorder, but Carmen sure has an apartment in Paris, right?"[59]

Since *La Jornada* had been founded on the basis of one vote per employee, Lira was supposedly first among equals, but in practice she was aloof and distant. Like a Marxist version of the late-in-life Queen Victoria, the septuagenarian Lira had become a figurehead, revered by senior courtiers and deferentially consulted each evening about the next day's front page but little involved in daily decisions and seldom seen in public. Beneath her persisted a patriarchal gerontocracy: editors in their sixties and seventies, four in five of them male. Some of them were given to sexist remarks and dismissive of reporters taking courses to improve their craft. They drove home in their luxury SUVs to the nicest neighborhoods, and every four years arranged the reelection of the sovereign who pampered them.[60]

Proceso too was weakened, although unlike *La Jornada* it remained consistently critical. Independent digital sites offering in-depth features eroded its historical dominion more than ever, and problems with distributors exacerbated the shrinkage. By 2018, weekly sales had slid to 60,000, down by a third since the Fox era. Regular ad buys from Carlos Slim helped compensate for yet another federal advertising boycott, but the magazine's uninspired website fared poorly. Many national and foreign correspondents were laid off and there was less money for freelance features. Altogether, the Peña presidency proved the least distinguished period in *Proceso*'s history. By the latter years, morale was low and editor in chief Rodríguez Castañeda suffered ill-health. In the verdict of then-reporter Jorge Carrasco, who would become editor in 2020, "The Master Scam and the 'Casa Blanca' were the two biggest themes of the administration—*and we weren't there*."[61]

As for the rest of the capital's papers, their editorial line was *oficialista* because publishers were reluctant to bite the hand that fed them most. Peña, who inherited a drug-war legacy of over 20,000 homicides per year and whose instincts were widely deemed somewhat authoritarian, had emulated Calderón's massive overspend on federal advertising. By the end of his term, his total outlay equally stood at around $3 billion.[62]

Milenio, born with such promise in 2000, typified the dependency. After Pancho González suffered a heart attack in 2016, he began to hand over to his similarly PRI-friendly son, Francisco Jr. The heir was said to be sharp and well liked, if lacking the vision of his father. He was also pals with Peña, once being photographed alongside a helicopter commandeered by the PRI's Senate leader for a golf date with the president. At times the paper ran good features. Milenio.com obtained strong traffic. But by now, with a front page that cheered for Peña, *Milenio* was much less distinguished for news than for its umpteen columnists. The contributors included Carlos Puig, Héctor Aguilar Camín, and top TV critic Álvaro Cueva; some were regulars on Milenio TV. In circulation, the daily lagged far behind *Reforma* and *El Norte*, the newspapers González had dreamed of equaling.[63]

A veteran Monterrey editor, who worked at both Grupo Reforma and *Milenio* corporate parent Grupo Multimedios, believes that for the González family, "*Milenio* is an expense. Its business model is based on arrangements with government departments. Their true business is real estate, shopping malls, hotels. The paper helps them with bureaucratic procedures and political leverage."[64]

Similar judgments could be made of most of the rest, where again there was little to distinguish them but their columnists. Oddly, given its low circulation, *Excélsior* enjoyed the second-highest federal advertising haul among newspapers. Meanwhile, its friends-of-Peña owners, Olegario Vázquez Raña and son Olegario Vázquez Aldir, obtained large federal contracts via their construction company Prodemex to build public works.[65]

Newer papers were often the most shameless in their politicking. In 2009 a wealthy Tamaulipas oil services contractor and PRI supporter, Ramiro Garza

Cantú, created the Mexico City tabloid *La Razón de México*. As editor in chief he hired Pablo Hiriart, who had steered *Crónica* during its first decade. *La Razón* boasted an attractive, uncluttered design with plenty of color, accessible graphics, and an admired cultural section. At first, it offered a plural selection of columnists and was unafraid to criticize President Calderón. But once the PRI regained the presidency, its owner's true colors showed through. It became overtly pro-Peña and critical columnists quit or were fired. A study of eleven media found *La Razón* to be the single most obsequious, backing the government narrative 83 percent of the time on legal reforms and 90 percent of the time during corruption and human rights scandals. In fact, to maximize its appeal to authorities and hence its take of official advertising, *La Razón* flattered both the right-wing PRI regime of Peña and the left-wing PRD regime that governed the capital.[66]

Print, Digital, and Persecution in the States

Print persisted outside Mexico City, too. Despite much talk of media in crisis, and much downsizing, few periodicals actually closed. In Puebla City, for example, the thirteen dailies circulating in 2018 were barely fewer than the fifteen available in 2006.[67] Many survived by courting greater ad spend from governors. As Leo Zuckermann put it in a *Proceso* column as early as 2003, governors were Mexico's "new viceroys," capable of using their expanded resources for influencing federal congressional elections to the benefit of their parties. A comprehensive 2015 report by the NGOs Article 19 and Fundar described "cartloads of cash" being annually dispensed, supposedly to promote the programs, achievements, and social campaigns of state governments, but effectively fostering the "personality cult" of some governors. Although a handful of states refused to reveal numbers, the report found that over the four years between 2010 and 2013, total state government ad spend approached $1.3 billion, about two-thirds the level of federal spending; print media scooped up around 30 percent of that, a more generous portion of the pie than at the federal level. Of course, this was a mixed blessing, for the discretionary manner with which all governors disbursed state cash led to greater submissiveness.[68]

What Zuckermann had not contemplated was that gubernatorial influence over elections might include their own—for president. Fox had become the first former state governor to gain the nation's highest office in half a century, and Peña repeated the feat twelve years later. Ambitious governors could now reasonably aspire to the presidency, or at least to high cabinet office. Courting local media with more cash than usual could help. So could courting the national press. Among governors of the Peña era with a record of massive self-promotion, outside as well as inside their states, were Manuel Velasco of

Chiapas and Rafael Moreno Valle Rosas of Puebla.[69] Both men, it soon became clear, harbored presidential ambitions.

"The tide of printed material that inundated the Federal District in late 2013 and early 2014 with the image of Manuel Velasco can only be compared with the level of opacity regarding expenditure [in Chiapas]," the Article 19 and Fundar report opined. The pretext for the blitz was Velasco's first State of the State address. It included ads in showbiz magazines, infomercials in movie theaters, and a cover-page feature in *Cambio* magazine, now owned by publisher Anuar Maccise. The *Cambio* story was almost certainly bought, using a model popularized by the magazines for executives *Líderes Mexicanos* and *Mundo Ejecutivo*: An ambitious politician (or his or her backers) would purchase coverage, and the magazine would have ads for the issue posted on billboards and painted on buses (presumably paid for by the client) across major cities. The ploy was, and remains, especially useful in the one or two years before an election, allowing politicians to skirt laws forbidding publicity until the formal campaign season begins.[70]

As for Moreno Valle, the report found that the Puebla governor made massive national-level outlays to promote at least two of his State of the State addresses, first via movie theater infomercials, then using radio and TV spots. Official data showed that Moreno Valle, who governed with the PAN, was not generous to print media, handing them just 12 percent of spend during his first three years. This was surely a consequence of his 2010 election campaign, during which most local papers overtly backed the incumbent PRI, the traditional source of their subsidies. But Armando Prida, the wily publisher of *Síntesis*, had dared to afford equal (some say favorable) coverage to Moreno Valle. During his first year of office, *Síntesis* reaped $800,000 in Puebla government advertising, while vocal opponent *El Heraldo de Puebla* got zero. The NGOs were unable to get at off-the-books outlays. But according to a former spokesman of his, Moreno Valle gave Mario Vázquez Raña more than $2 million to buy positive coverage in his national chain of *El Sol* papers as the politician prepared for a run at the presidency.[71]

When governors behaved badly, digital media often probed first, and not only *Animal Político* and *Aristegui Noticias* but equivalents in the states. The regional pioneers online included the daily news site *E-Consulta* and the newsmagazine *LadoB* in Puebla, and the sites *Raíchali Noticias* and *La Verdad* in Chihuahua, *Revista Espejo* in Sinaloa, *ZonaDocs* in Jalisco, *Plumas Libres* in Veracruz, *Página 3* in Oaxaca, and *Chiapas Paralelo*.

On a much lower-cost basis, often covering cities and regions beyond the metropolises, journalists who were usually part-timers set up blogs and Facebook pages to monitor municipal authorities, channel civil complaints, and report on local violence. A well-known early example was the border-focused

El Blog del Narco, which burned brightly between 2010 and 2013, offering frank coverage of crime syndicate battles and murders, replete with images of mutilated corpses but peppered with investigative panache. The editors asserted they were telling truths that other media did not dare to. The historian Paul Eiss called the blog "Mexico's premier venue for drug war content and the model for a certain kind of digitally enabled citizen journalism." Yet he also noted the censure it drew from other journalists for ethical disregard in what it posted, such as unsubstantiated rumors and uncredited stories pilfered from mainstream media. Arguably, *El Blog del Narco* offered a platform for crime syndicates to boast about their violence and send messages to rival gangs. Death threats to the anonymous pair who ran it, one of whom fled to Spain, caused it to all but flame out.[72]

Reporters who ran mini-sites on a labor-of-love basis very often had nowhere to run when threatened. A few relocated to Mexico City, with the help of a so-called government secretariat "Mechanism," set up by the Calderón regime in the wake of the Regina Martínez killing. But most were bound by family and the day jobs that kept them fed. Thus the Peña era saw a surge in killings of journalists active on the social network (a surge that continues to the present). Perhaps the worst case involved *Semanario Playa News*, set up on Facebook in the Caribbean resort of Playa del Carmen, a watchdog of both city and state governments. In summer 2018, within the space of a month, a reporter and the founding editor were murdered. Since they had all received death threats, in some cases from public officials, the site's small team had enrolled in the Mechanism—which by now registered some 300 journalists—and received remote support and a panic button. Yet the following May another of them was killed. By then, *Semanario Playa News* had disappeared. The initial double murder prompted freelance journalist Alejandra Ibarra to create Defensores de la Democracia, a site to warehouse the stories of murdered reporters before their blogs and Facebook pages expired and their work vanished.[73]

Compared with the Calderón era, the Peña years marked an overall dip in the murder of journalists, from a total of fifty-nine to forty-eight, and an abrupt decline in disappearances, from twenty to two.[74] The likeliest reason is that many papers simply refused to continue reporting on the crime syndicates, thus creating "zones of silence"; in particular, this explains the sharp drop in disappearances, a tactic favored by criminal gangs. Editors in general were taking greater care not to expose their reporters to risk. Reporters were becoming more proactive about self-protection, organizing themselves into collectives. Their goals varied, but in most cases collectives formed to share information and report risky stories in groups of two or more. They also lobbied authorities for greater protection and transparency, held press conferences when physical attacks and murders occurred, and organized workshops.

Periodistas de a Pie (Common Journalists), the first and best-known collective, was set up in 2007 by Marcela Turati and Daniela Pastrana, who had both turned freelance, along with five colleagues. All were women, which would set a tone for the leadership of collectives. Initially the plan was to hold workshops and diploma courses on how to write about poverty, a shared passion of the founders. But upon the 2008 murder of *El Diario de Juárez* reporter Armando "El Choco" Rodríguez, a friend to several of them, the collective began to organize freedom-of-speech protests, and after the 2012 killing of *Proceso*'s Regina Martínez the members went to Xalapa and Veracruz to give workshops on personal care—emotional as well as physical—amid the welter of criminal and state violence. Periodistas de a Pie was keen to promote collaborative journalism, and in 2015 it launched online the liberal-leaning magazine *Pie de Página*, with Pastrana as editor and a focus on human rights, education, migration, Indigenous peoples, and other social themes. Later, it began to share stories with regional sites like *LadoB* and to platform some of theirs. By 2018, at least twenty-one collectives had arisen, often as a local response to specific killings. Most appeared in the Peña era, in regions of concentrated attacks against the press: Veracruz, Sinaloa, Michoacán, Guerrero, Oaxaca, and all six of the border states.[75]

Meanwhile, other forms of aggression against the press—such as physical attacks, harassment, verbal threats, and phone tapping—dramatically grew under Peña, with Article 19 documenting 2,502 cases, compared with 1,092 under Calderón. Much of the increase derived from the growth of Facebook and Twitter as platforms conducive to threats and smear campaigns. Much of the aggression was attributable to public officials.[76] This in turn surely owed in part to signals from Los Pinos that PRI regimes in the states could act with impunity. The president openly tolerated the likes of Javier Duarte of Veracruz and Roberto Borge of Quintana Roo, sharing stages at events and posing for photos with these PRI governors, despite repeated media exposure of their graft.[77]

While murders were slightly fewer in number, more were high in profile. Under Calderón, the Regina Martínez killing had stood out for the attention it garnered, far more than for any other case, because the victim wrote for *Proceso*. Under Peña, there were several murders that prompted a similar level of outcry, two of the victims being writers for *La Jornada*: Miroslava Breach in Chihuahua and Javier Valdez in Sinaloa. Their demise in the spring of 2017 contributed to the bloodiest year on record for Mexico's press, with twelve documented murders. And the nature of their killing suggested the depth of Mexico's impunity problem, for both were gunned down in the street, in daylight.

Breach, aged fifty-four, was shot eight times at the wheel of her car on March 23, as she was about to drive her teenage son to school. For decades she had covered Indigenous rights and corruption in Chihuahua, with a recent focus on narcopolitics in the Sierra Tarahumara, the mountainous west from which she hailed. This range lies within the so-called Golden Triangle, which includes parts of Durango and Sinaloa, where opium poppy and marijuana are cultivated, forming a productive base for the Sinaloa Cartel. With valiant frankness, naming names, Breach described for *La Jornada* and *Norte de Ciudad Juárez* how traffickers, including the Sinaloa-affiliated Salazar crime family, had been placing allies as mayors with both the PRI and the PAN. A series on the topic, coauthored with *Proceso* contributor Patricia Mayorga, prompted months of threats, explicit ones from the gangsters and implicit ones from state officials. Governor Javier Corral of the PAN was a friend of the victim and at once promised an exemplary investigation into the killing. Meanwhile, Mayorga fled into exile, first to Mexico City, then to Peru.[78]

Despite Corral's pledge, not until December did the Chihuahua prosecutor's office present its case: the bemusing claim that a detained Salazar hitman known as El Larry, not family head Crispín Salazar, had ordered the hit; further, the triggerman had been murdered the week before. Fearing a cover-up, which might protect corrupt officials in the PAN as well as the Salazars, an ad hoc March 23rd Collective of thirty reporters converged on Chihuahua City and launched a parallel investigation; some even ventured into the Sierra Tarahumara, where state prosecutors had not dared tread. Given the risks, they strove for anonymity, but one who admitted to participating was John Gibler, a US specialist in Mexican social movements and regional violence. As Gibler had written elsewhere, "In Mexico, it's more dangerous to investigate a murder than to commit one."[79]

Published in September 2019 by Daniela Pastrana's online magazine, *Pie de Página*, the 28,000-word report revealed how prosecutors had ignored leads about Salazar agents and PAN officials. These included a former mayor of Breach's hometown, Hugo Schultz. More than seventy outlets in Mexico and abroad ran the story or parts of it. Evidently prompted by the publicity and likely by the collective's findings too, a federal prosecutor not only moved to put El Larry on trial but also indicted Schultz as an accomplice. This came as a surprise to the March 23rd Collective because Corral had recently named Schultz as his education czar for the Sierra Tarahumara. In 2021, with El Larry and Schultz behind bars, the federal prosecutor indicted the man the state prosecutor had sought to exculpate, Crispín Salazar. The crime boss remains at large.[80]

The murder of Javier Valdez caused more of a shock, because though he lived and worked in Culiacan, base of the Sinaloa Cartel, and although he had written about drug traffickers for twenty or more of his fifty years, he was not an investigative journalist but a chronicler. As fellow crime specialist Ioan

Grillo put it in an extended obituary for *Esquire*, "His favored subjects were the unseen faces of the cartel wars: the members of brass bands who played ballads to men in crocodile-skin boots and women with diamond-studded fingernails; children on dirt roads who dreamed of being hit men; crying mothers whose sons had been murdered." With his characteristic Panama hat and thick-rimmed glasses, Valdez was a Culiacán fixture, as was the column "Malayerba" ("Bad Herb," slang for marijuana) that he wrote for *Ríodoce*, a newsweekly he had cofounded.[81]

But in February 2017, Valdez made a possibly fateful decision to publish an interview with a lieutenant of Dámaso López, a right-hand man to "El Chapo" Guzmán, who had been warring for control of the Sinaloa operation with the sons of the capo following the latter's extradition to the United States. The sons, known as Los Chapitos, made it clear via an envoy that they did not want the piece to run, and after Valdez and codirector Ismael Bohórquez defied their wishes, Los Chapitos sent flunkies to follow the *Ríodoce* delivery vans and buy up all the copies from the newsstands. Then, for the edition of May 7, Valdez penned another risky piece, questioning the effectiveness of López's leadership. On May 15, as he walked at midday to the newsweekly's offices, he was shot twelve times. Grillo, who knew Valdez well, initially deduced that Los Chapitos authored the hit. Subsequent events—a declaration in the trial of one of the hitmen that fingered López as the mastermind, followed by an indictment against him—cast doubt. Two of the hitmen involved in the murder were eventually jailed (the third was found killed), in 2020 and 2021, but with Los Chapitos nowhere to be found and López in custody in the United States, that was as far as Mexican justice could proceed for now.[82]

Peña did make one concrete if belated advance. Back in 2010, under national and international pressures over the journalist mortality rate, Calderón had created the Special Prosecutor for Attention to Crimes against Freedom of Expression (FEADLE). Its remit allowed it to take part in—or even take over—an investigation, if the prosecutor deemed a killing was likely linked to the victim's work. This seemed to be good news, for NGOs and regional media felt that such cases were often compromised by local politics, with state prosecutors doing a governor's bidding. But FEADLE accrued a terrible record. In May 2017, the Committee to Protect Journalists secured a meeting with Peña, delivering a report on the "cycle of impunity" perpetuating murders. The same week, *SinEmbargo* published findings by Article 19 showing that of 798 inquiries into violence and threats against journalists opened by FEADLE during its first six and a half years, the agency had obtained convictions in just three cases.[83]

Two weeks after meeting with the Committee to Protect Journalists, Peña replaced his FEADLE chief with Ricardo Sánchez Pérez del Pozo, a young, ambitious lawyer with an MA in human rights from Northwestern University. Sánchez soon showed a greater willingness to "federalize" provincial cases and fight in the courts. Before his appointment, FEADLE had obtained just one murder conviction. During his first five years, Sánchez scored five, including against hitmen in the Breach and Valdez cases. In 2021, FEADLE announced that it had indicted 312 people for various forms of aggression, of whom two-thirds were public servants, the vast majority working at the state or municipal level, including a large number of police. These statistics gave the lie to the commonplace, peddled by governors and presidents, that violence against journalists was a simply a "narco" issue.[84]

And yet, nearly 90 percent of the 150 or so journalist killings between 2007 and 2024 failed to meet with any sort of justice (at a minimum, a hitman jailed). In 98 percent of cases, the masterminds remained at large.[85]

Peña Plunges, AMLO Ascends

Fifteen months after *Aristegui Noticias* dropped its Casa Blanca bomb, Adrián López, editor in chief of Sinaloa paper *Noroeste*, called it "an investigation that will go down in history as the journalistic catch that plunged Enrique Peña Nieto into the greatest presidential credibility crisis in this country's recent past."[86]

Subsequent scandals revealed a rotten regime at all levels. Disreputable governors came under the media microscope as never before. Cabinet ministers past and present were found to have erred and strayed. In retrospect, the Casa Blanca symbolized the whole house of cards of the late-era PRI, destined for a stunning collapse at the federal level, along with a chain reaction of defeats in gubernatorial elections. This time, unlike the millennial loss against the PAN, there would be no way back. Mexico was witnessing the rapid rise of the leftist party Morena, which had only been established in 2014, and the resurgence of its twice-defeated but charismatic leader, Andrés Manuel López Obrador—or AMLO, as almost everyone called him. The PRI's implosion would be all but complete following the midterms of 2021, with the party losing all eight of the governorships it fought to keep, leaving it with an all-time low of three. Morena by then held twenty, almost two-thirds of the total.[87]

Many revelations that destabilized Peña and the PRI resulted not from leaks—the kind that fueled the *Proceso* scoops of old—but from hard graft, carried out over months, by pairs if not teams of reporters, sometimes partially funded by NGOs, and published above all by the news sites. *Animal Político*'s MCCI-supported "Ghost Companies of Veracruz," on embezzlement by PRI governor Duarte of Veracruz, and "The Master Scam," on the PRI's diversion of public funds for electoral purposes, were just the highest-profile examples.[88]

Another gubernatorial scoop, a joint investigation between Mariel Ibarra of business magazine *Expansión* and Silber Meza of MCCI, was "Borge's Pirates," in July 2016. The Borge in question was Roberto, soon-to-depart PRI governor of Quintana Roo, and the "pirates" were a network of a dozen named officials, including three former governors, who seized buildings and land from smallholders on the Caribbean coast via dubious legal maneuvers. In August, Mexico's tax authority acknowledged that, in response to the exposé, it was investigating twenty-one officials. Borge's term ended the following month and by November, harried by this and other scandals, he had fled to Panama. Arrested in 2017 for money laundering, Borge was then exposed thrice more by Ibarra in *Expansión*: for two kinds of embezzlement (along with fifty partners, he stole $850 million from the state treasury and another $250 million from a rural development fund), then for financial abuse of office (he billed taxpayers $55 million for private flights for himself and his cronies). Borge was extradited to Mexico at the start of the election year of 2018. While his arrest owed to reasons distinct from the findings of "Borge's Pirates," Meza felt that the exposé forced the federal government to look at the governor's record in general.[89]

MCCI's involvement in the exposés of Duarte and Borge heralded the arrival of a major player in investigative journalism. The NGO was founded in 2015 by Claudio X. Gonzalez Jr., son of a business ideologue who ran Kimberly-Clark's Mexican operation. MCCI aimed to attack Mexico's ingrained culture of corruption, regardless of perpetrators' political affiliation; at the time, the country ranked 111th on Transparency International's Corruption Perceptions Index, worse than all other major Latin American nations bar Venezuela. The idea was to mobilize society through announcements, conduct and publish investigations, and bring lawsuits. The scandals that its joint investigations prompted, including "The Master Scam," collectively did as much as those engendered by any paper or news site to undermine the PRI, even though González Sr. had a history of coziness with the party. And MCCI was only the most visible of several NGOs whose investigations shone a light on the Peña regime's inadequacies, others including México Evalúa (i.e., Mexico Assesses), IMCO (the Mexican Institute for Competitiveness, whose analysis often appeared in *Reforma*), and Transparencia Mexicana (local arm of Transparency International).[90]

Intense media attention on corruption, together with public fatigue over narco violence, meant that coverage of the homicide epidemic was more subdued than under Calderón, but a decline in murders during Peña's first two years proved temporary and the numbers during his final two years were more horrific than ever, with annual homicides topping 30,000. Investigative journalists continued to focus on the victims, and again the best work emerged online. One standout report, by *La Silla Rota* and *E-Consulta*, spotlighted a narco "extermination camp" of at least twenty-two graves, discovered by relatives of disappeared people and hushed up by the Veracruz government. Another, by the new site *Quinto Elemento*, involved a massive collation of reports about the nearly 2,000 clandestine graves found across Mexico between 2006 and 2016. The discoveries, in twenty-four of Mexico's thirty-two states, included 2,884 bodies, with a new grave found every two days.[91]

Peña's approval rating, with a year to run before the 2018 election, hovered around 28 percent. Despite the huge sums he still lavished on the press, especially television and legacy media, his star did not recover. "Ayotzinapa" and "the 43"—bywords for both the trainee teacher disappearances of September 2014 and the government's inability to solve the case—haunted Peña for two-thirds of his presidency. The tragedy was kept in the public eye by the critical press, along with at least nine investigative books (including one by Anabel Hernández) and the media attention each one generated. In the states, the PRI plumbed new depths of disrepute. One report found that no fewer than fifteen former governors were under investigation, typically for embezzlement, self-dealing, or money laundering for organized crime. Of the fifteen, twelve belonged to the PRI.[92]

When López Obrador made corruption a central theme of his 2017–18 campaign, his ability to contrast himself with Peña met with a keen response.[93] On July 1, 2018, the PRI was pummeled, taking an all-time low of 16 percent of the vote. López Obrador cruised to victory with 53 percent, 30 points ahead of the PAN in second. His Morena party, with the help of smaller allies, also took both chambers of Congress.

López Obrador could thank the watchdog press for much of that swing. (But would he do so?) Civic-minded news sites had mushroomed, subjecting Peña and his peer group in the PRI to an extraordinary sum of sophisticated investigation. Both online and off, more editors and reporters than ever knew how to navigate freedom-of-information requests, court records, property registries, and statistical data mining. These were journalists for whom the formative epiphany was not the Tlatelolco massacre of 1968 or the *Excélsior* coup of 1976 but the Zapatista uprising of 1994, the dubious presidential election of 2006, or the YoSoy132 movement of 2012. For the most part, they were journalists for whom print was the past and digital the future.

Epilogue

The Fourth Estate and the "Fourth Transformation"

> Sometimes I consider it very paradoxical that López Obrador now is complaining about the critical and independent press when that critical and independent press contributed so much to forge the climate of rejection toward the previous regime.
>
> —Javier Garza Ramos, former editor, *El Siglo de Torreón*, 2019

> We said we were going to respect freedom of speech, and we did so. No journalist is persecuted or censored. One can even insult the president—and there's no repression. There are no longer pay-offs, because now the federal budget goes to the people. But there are freedoms: the right to dissent is guaranteed.
>
> —Andrés Manuel López Obrador, August 2021

> His [López Obrador's] failure to make Mexico safer for the press is notable as he was the first president who explicitly mentioned press freedom during his inaugural speech. He promised the killings would end. He promised an end to censorship. He promised an end to spying. He promised an end to impunity. Only in terms of *direct* censorship [has] his government delivered.
>
> —Jan-Albert Hootsen, Committee to Protect Journalists, September 2024

Mexico's Battered Watchdogs

In autumn 2024, as the term of Andrés Manuel López Obrador drew to a close, Mexico's press was battered but still resilient. Like media the world over, it had suffered from the market contraction caused by the COVID-19 pandemic and an accelerating generational shift from legacy media and websites to social media. It had also suffered a precipitous drop in federal subsidies and an unprecedented amount of public vitriol from the president himself.

López Obrador had come to power promising a "Fourth Transformation" of Mexico, equal in depth and radicalism to the shifts wrought by the War of Independence from Spain, the liberal Reform Era of the 1850s, and the revolution of 1910–20. Indeed, the government-elect styled itself the Fourth Transformation, or 4T for short. For the media, the 4T promised two broad changes. First, it would cut federal advertising by 50 percent from day one, in

December 2018; in actuality, for the presidential term as a whole, it would cut it by 80 percent.[1] Second, it would reform the law regulating what Mexicans call "social communication": how government departments advertise their activities and accomplishments. Among other things, federal ad spend would be apportioned on a transparent basis, according to each outlet's reach, circulation, or unique visits. This second change was never implemented.[2]

But a different kind of shift appeared on December 3, the first weekday of the presidency. López Obrador gave an early-morning press conference at the National Palace, similar to those he had given when mayor, the so-called *mañaneras* (a double entendre meaning one kind or another of early-morning activity). In marked contrast to his predecessors, he proceeded to speak from his podium almost every weekday for the next six years, a remarkable feat of nonstop agenda-setting that reduced the press to a secondary role. Via YouTube, on public television and radio, and in excerpts via a host of other media, López Obrador addressed the nation unfiltered.

The dynamic remained fairly constant. López Obrador would introduce a theme or two, hand over to a cabinet minister or other functionary for presentations accompanied by slides, and then resume, extemporizing, often for half an hour. He would underline points, he would wax historical, he would contrast the practice of his government with that of its neoliberal predecessors, he would pepper his discourse with memorable, often folksy phrases, and he would preach morality. He would identify critics, whom he labeled "our opponents," regardless of their ideology. He routinely responded to empirical criticism of his government with ad hominem criticism of its source. Such journalists and their media were "the snobbish press," "bribe-takers," even "criminals." Finally, the president would open the floor, choosing mostly from the front row, where his sympathizers gathered—a motley mix of old hands from leftist media, reporters from regional outlets, midcareer writers from marginal media looking to raise their profile, and influencers with newfangled platforms. Their softball questions often came giftwrapped with compliments for their dear leader. To the occasional hardball, his responses were often evasive and sometimes critical of the questioner. Altogether, the president himself spoke for one to two hours, and in doing so between seven and nine o'clock or so, his pronouncements, insults, and slogans dominated each day's news cycle.[3]

To the president's supporters within the press—easy to identify, as they tended to trumpet their pro-4T enthusiasm on social media—the *mañaneras* illustrated López Obrador's commitment to speaking directly to the people, unfiltered by self-interested media. The *mañaneras* were also a means of governing. When reporters from outside Mexico City asked López Obrador about problems in their states, the president's communications staff, led by Jesus Ramírez Cuevas, would take note and ensure follow-up. As for the president's

NACIONAL

Arremete contra REFORMA por faltante en Macuspana

Isabella González
Cd. de México (11 septiembre 2020) .-10:46 hrs

REFORMA es un pasquín inmundo.-AMLO

President Andrés Manuel López Obrador routinely applied a "shoot the messenger" tactic when media raised questions of his administration, with *Reforma* his favorite target. Courtesy of Grupo Reforma.

criticisms of specific media, they showed him exercising his right of reply, which was especially necessary given the bias and negativity of much of the press toward him. Yes, he singled out journalists, but his doing so was no harsher than their attacks on him. In the words of Ramírez Cuevas, the *mañaneras* also offered the viewing public "schools of citizenship . . . classes of history, and lessons in politics."[4]

To most professional observers, however, the president engaged in distasteful grandstanding at best, dangerous populism at worst. His frequent targets included many of those whose fearless investigations had done most to dismantle Institutional Revolutionary Party rule and help pave the way for his victory: *Reforma* (a favorite villain) and *Proceso*, *Animal Político* and *Aristegui Noticias*, the nongovernmental organizations Article 19 and Mexicans Against Corruption and Impunity (MCCI). He repeatedly named and shamed columnists and commentators, including some who in the past had been equally critical of the PRI and the National Action Party. He seldom admitted constructive criticism; those who questioned his inconsistencies or flagged apparent policy failures, even from a leftist perspective, were "conservatives." He preferred to shoot the messenger rather than address the points raised.[5]

Journalists decried in a *mañanera* were subject to torrents of abuse online, especially by YouTubers and an army of trolls on Twitter; some were harassed in public. Most troubling of all to most journalists and NGOs, López Obrador's discourse vilified a press still vulnerable to physical attack and murder. For at least fifteen years, since the killing of media workers began to rebound during the Vicente Fox era, the Committee to Protect Journalists, Article 19, and other concerned voices had been arguing and lobbying for more effective protections and prosecutions. López Obrador's attacks were widely considered a major step backward, even a de facto (if inadvertent) green light for continued impunity.[6]

Soon came an additional battering due to COVID-19. During 2020, a number of newspapers suspended their physical editions, including *El Economista* and *Crónica*. The magazine *Este País* abandoned print altogether. Outside the capital, six papers in Puebla City stopped printing (permanently in most cases), as did many dailies within the *El Sol* chain, such as *El Sol de Acapulco* and Guadalajara's once popular *El Occidental* (which restarted but then went weekly). Several news sites closed. Over the three years that followed, some print titles that were wounded by the pandemic and failed to recover at last called quits. The count of Mexico City dailies (excluding freesheets), which in 2018 had stood at twenty-seven, declined after six years to twenty.[7] The latter ebb was probably healthy, for none of those that vanished from newsstands had been practicing civic journalism; rather, their persistence fed the notion that the press only catered to vested interests.

Few media disappeared altogether, however. Rather, they bent over backward to remain afloat, if only online. Newspapers reduced their page counts. They made new rounds of mass layoffs, as did the regional newsrooms of Televisa, TV Azteca, and the biggest radio broadcaster, Grupo Radio Centro. At opposite ends of the spectrum of responses to hard times, *Animal Político* asked its reporters to take a 30 percent pay cut, while Grupo Imagen—the holding company of *Excélsior*, broadcaster Imagen TV, digital channel Excélsior TV, and several radio stations—laid off 400 employees.[8]

What had been true during times of shrinking sales under Felipe Calderón and Enrique Peña Nieto remained true under López Obrador: Many periodicals stayed in the game because they were loss leaders, affording politicians and industrialists leverage with federal and state governments.

Others were run by dedicated publishers for whom carrying on was a matter of pride and conviction, regardless of red ink, the more so because they considered López Obrador an inconsistent and semiauthoritarian president who needed to be watched. Still others were scrappy online outfits, their editors and reporters often working several jobs, even driving taxis. Altogether, although the media shrank during the López Obrador years, watchdog journalism did not consolidate in the hands of the few; rather, it remained fragmented. Those who had done most to hold Peña and the PRI to account investigated less, due to dwindling resources, while smaller players filled the gaps in piecemeal fashion.

Reforma, whose owner Alejandro Junco had long been suspicious of the leftist, did not play its watchdog role as carefully as in the past. The month before López Obrador took office, Junco handed the direction of Grupo Reforma to his son, Alejandro Junco Elizondo. Long-serving editor in chief Lázaro Ríos made way for Juan Pardinas, until then the head of the Mexican Institute for Competitiveness, a probusiness think tank. Under Pardinas, *Reforma* veered further to the right and toward hostility. The tone was set in early 2019, when a reporter found that the new secretary of government, Olga Sánchez Cordero, had failed to include a Houston apartment in her required declaration of assets—and the paper did not offer the minister right of reply. López Obrador's frequent vilification of *Reforma* likely hurt its reputation, if not its readership; its brand "trust score," as measured by the University of Oxford's Reuters Institute for the Study of Journalism, declined from 69 to 58 percent between 2018 and 2023. Only from October 2023, when Pardinas stepped down and veteran staffer Roberto Zamarripa took the helm, did the paper start to temper its stance, including by bringing aboard moderate pro-4T voices as columnists.[9]

A more persuasive holding to account emerged at *El Universal*, which arguably overtook *Reforma* as the newspaper of record of the López Obrador era. After a long history of self-interested *oficialismo*, punctured by periods of admirable journalism that usually ended with the abrupt removal of an editor, Juan Francisco Ealy Ortiz seemed finally to take seriously the guardian-of-democracy role he had spent so much of his life talking about. How much the decision was ideological, given Ealy's PRI-supporting convictions, and how much pragmatic, given the government's first-year cutting of his subsidy by 74 percent, is debatable. But by 2024, under editor in chief David Aponte, *El Universal* had spent six remarkably consistent years probing the 4T while largely avoiding the stridency that seeped into *Reforma*. In 2020 and 2021, the Reuters Institute ranked *El Universal* the most trusted source among Mexican newspapers, as well as the most read paper online. Also in 2021, Aponte revived the paper's investigative unit, which was now headed by Silber Meza, formerly of *Noroeste* and MCCI. One of the unit's successes was a ten-month, multipart investigation into fentanyl production and consumption in Mexico—problems publicly denied by López Obrador—which won a news coverage award from the Interamerican Press Association.[10]

Among digital media, the three that had risen to greatest influence in the Peña era—*Aristegui Noticias, Animal Político*, and *SinEmbargo*—were important but diminished. *Animal Político* remained the most reliable of the online watchdogs. Although it proved unable to match the resounding scoops of its recent past, the site provided unmatched coverage of the social impact of the 4T. Its data-driven monitoring of COVID-19 cases and deaths, packaged with arresting visuals, became a go-to reference tool. In Nayeli Roldán, it had a fearless reporter who gained fame as one of a small minority who dared question López Obrador incisively during *mañaneras* (which earned her reams of invective from pro-4T influencers). In 2023, Roldán won a special mention from the Moors Cabot jury. One of López Obrador's most repeated and most questioned claims, that he was shaping a health system that would be "as good as Denmark's," was thoroughly refuted by *Animal Político* in 2024. Led by Roldán, the ten-part investigation was called "We Were Not Denmark."[11]

Carmen Aristegui's exile from the airwaves, which persisted until October 2018, had not much dented her online popularity, for *Aristegui Noticias* remained within the top three news sites. The 2018 Reuters Institute study ranked her brand first in trustworthiness among native media. However, a public break with López Obrador, triggered by a story alleging corruption by his sons, cost her credibility among some on the left. By 2024, her site's Reuters "trust score" had steadily fallen from 76 to 57 percent and its ranking had dropped from second to seventh. These data reflected the force of López Obrador's bully pulpit, for the president denounced her (falsely) as having "never been in favor" of his movement, and by the end of his term she ranked as the sixth most criticized journalist or writer in his morning press conferences, with over 200 mentions.[12]

By contrast, *SinEmbargo* embraced the 4T almost as fully as *La Jornada* (like the paper, it retained a few critical columnists). It profited from the association, for its attacks on 4T opponents drew new readers. Importantly for its revenues, it used its YouTube channel to host *Los Periodistas* (The journalists), a polemical two-hour daily talk show launched in 2021 and featuring the site's editor, Alejandro Páez, and Álvaro Delgado, whom Páez had lured away from *Proceso*. By its third year, some episodes were drawing half a million viewers and several reached twice that. *SinEmbargo*'s investigative work was largely directed not at questioning the 4T but at exposing malfeasance by its predecessors or its opponents. When Páez was asked in 2023 to name the site's recent investigative achievements, five of the six features he chose fit this description.[13]

In the context of plummeting subsidies, a pandemic, and, for most of the López Obrador era, a weak economy, it was no surprise that new launches were few beyond the domains of pro-4T propagandists and influencers. These people tended anyway to prefer YouTube, where they could best monetize their stridency. But there was one high-impact arrival: *Latinus*. With a mix of barbed criticism and investigative journalism, most of it directed at the president and Morena, Latinus was chiefly a platform for the charismatic former Televisa anchor Carlos Loret de Mola. It bowed in early 2020 with the covert backing of an investor group led by the sons of Tabasco politician Roberto Madrazo, an old and bitter rival of the president. Attacks on Loret in the *mañaneras* helped raise the site's visibility. By the end of his term, the president had criticized Loret more than 700 times (on average, every other morning). While *Latinus* garnered a decent but not leading place in the Comscore rankings, its video clips racked up tens of millions of monthly views on YouTube and TikTok.[14]

By contrast, a few media lived on federal life support, in exchange for almost unalloyed devotion to the 4T, most of all *La Jornada*. The left-wing daily's proximity to power was evident not only in its fawning tone and its criticism of those whom López Obrador dubbed "opponents" but also in the access several of its old hands enjoyed to the National Palace, sometimes meeting with the president. López Obrador awarded the paper $60 million in subsidy support, more than twice what it received under Peña and 9 percent of the government's entire ad budget; no other print medium got more than 3 percent.[15] The once mighty Televisa, for decades a broadcast behemoth, had come to rely to some extent on handouts too, given profit margins and borrowing capacity eroded by audience flight; its New York stock price fell from forty dollars in 2015 to less than two dollars by August 2024.[16]

La Jornada and *Latinus*, by trading in pro- and anti-4T polemic, epitomized much of Mexico's new journalistic reality. Albeit less invariably, so did *SinEmbargo*, *SDP Noticias*, and *Contralínea* on the one hand, and *Reforma*, *El Universal*, *Animal Político*, and *Aristegui Noticias* on the other. That is, print and digital media tended to retreat from balance and plurality. They both reflected and accentuated the polarization of the public sphere, especially among the university educated, where most of the readership lay. They also attacked each other, though this was chiefly a tactic of pro-4T media and influencers against perceived opponents, rather than the other way around. Some of the impetus was likely commercial, much was ideological. López Obrador himself played a key role. In an apparently dialectical fashion, criticisms leveled at his government drew presidential attacks against those that made them, which fueled more impassioned criticism. And the president's invective against the press in general—albeit accompanied by the phrase "with a few honorable exceptions"—fomented a greater public distrust of the media as a whole.

In June 2021, the government's stigmatization of the press and individual journalists reached a new low with the launch of the *mañanera* segment "Who's Who among the Lies." Each Wednesday, a spokeswoman purported to answer the president's critics by finding fault in their claims and accusing them of bad faith. While some rebuttals were fair or at least a valid matter of opinion, many were disingenuous or mendacious, as even some supporters of the regime admitted. A study of "Who's Who" by fact-checking website *Verificado* found that during the segment's first year, almost half of its claims were false or misleading. Evidently, "Who's Who" took a page from the Donald Trump playbook: Label whatever coverage one dislikes as "fake news." It also masked the president's own Trump-like proclivity for falsehoods and unsubstantiated affirmations.[17] Nonetheless, the fact that the other half of the segment's claims were deemed by *Verificado* to be legitimate shows that critical media often took to unsubstantiated AMLO bashing.

We await the results of the first World Values Survey poll in six years, which is underway in Mexico at this writing. But the 2024 *Digital News Report* from the Reuters Institute found that trust in the news had declined by 15 points to 35 percent on López Obrador's watch.[18]

Some of Mexico's journalists were left questioning their role. As moderate 4T sympathizers conceded, while López Obrador had succeeded in bringing millions of Mexicans out of poverty—more than any president in memory—and lifted the economies of the poorer southern states, he also deserved criticism. He had made major missteps (his handling of COVID-19, leaving Mexico with one of the world's worst excess-death rates), taken a U-turn on militarization (placing yet more troops on the streets, rather than returning the army to the barracks), implemented questionable policies (doubling down on fossil fuels by building an oil refinery; doing the United States' bidding by obstructing flows of Central American migrants), and failed to keep reiterated promises (to bring justice to the forty-three disappeared of Ayotzinapa; to give Mexico a Danish-style health system; to put an end to corruption). He had launched a sustained assault on the checks and balances of executive power: the independence of the judiciary, the autonomy of regulators, the dignity of the press. And yet, despite ample reporting on such issues in civic-minded media, as well as by his more strident critics on radio and online, López Obrador's average favorability ratings never dipped below 60 percent and finished at 74 percent.[19]

As Nayeli Roldán of *Animal Político* put it, "Journalism does not seek to topple anyone from power. . . . [However,] in this presidential period it did not play as effective a role in demanding accountability as in those previous. . . .

This may owe to the need for those of us in the media to reconsider the way in which we reach our audiences or because we haven't known how to adapt ourselves to technological changes."[20] One might add, it may also owe to how Mexico had never witnessed as effective a political communicator, for better or worse, as López Obrador.

The Challenges Ahead

Fundamental structural, regulatory, and cultural problems continue to hobble Mexico's press. What might the government of President Claudia Sheinbaum—and the media itself—do to tackle them?

The biggest structural challenge is economic. Very few news outlets are self-sustaining, due to a combination of low readership, public reluctance to pay subscriptions, the persistence of Google and Facebook as hegemons of the private-sector ad market, an excess of press that means the little private advertising left over is split between myriad periodicals and websites, and a culture of state dependence that disincentivizes entrepreneurialism. This is even truer of media based in metropolitan areas outside Mexico City and Monterrey, whose dependence on state advertising is more pronounced. In the United States, a traditional answer to market shrinkage has been mergers between newspapers and acquisitions by chains such as Gannett or McClatchy, but most Mexican publishers are so politically or personally invested in their media, a merger or sale would be anathema.

In much of Europe, the answer has been government subsidies. Given the reliance of most of Mexico's press on official advertising, along with a general discontent in recent decades over its discretionary disbursement, federal and state governments would best commit to bolstering a civic press by setting up autonomous bodies to transparently allocate funds. Such institutions, run by a pluralistic group of counselors, should evaluate applicants on a combined quantitative and qualitative basis, taking into account not only size of readership—thus refusing to prop up vanity publications and minor political tools—but also reputation and the need to preserve ideological diversity. UNESCO has advisory experience in this field. Mexico might also study the long-standing history of autonomous media subsidy bodies in such midsize economies as Norway, Sweden, Denmark, Austria, and the Netherlands, along with newer funds in France, Italy, and Spain.[21]

The fair, autonomous, and transparent allocation of subsidies would strengthen the standards and the investigative capacity of Mexican journalism. It would also go some way to building public trust in the media as the "Fourth Estate," a necessarily powerful component of a healthy democracy. Greater trust would in turn curb the general apathy over violence against the press. The ingrained nature of such violence would also be tempered if the president and state governors were to resist ad hominem attacks against specific reporters, commentators, and media. Crime syndicates and corrupt politicians would no longer be given to understand that journalists are fair game.

More concretely, the Special Prosecutor for attention to crimes against Freedom of Expression needs the resources and the political support to regain the level of accomplishment seen in 2017 and 2018 in bringing the killers of journalists to justice. While the capable lawyer Ricardo Sánchez Pérez del Pozo was kept in charge of the office under López Obrador, and while he retained the respect of freedom-of-speech activists, his budget was cut; Peña gave him an average $1.1 million per year, but López Obrador gave him an average $700,000. The pace of convictions slowed.[22] Even in the high-profile murder cases of Armando "El Choco" Rodríguez, Regina Martínez, Miroslava Breach, and Javier Valdez, in which federal agents got involved, no mastermind has been convicted. Meanwhile, media workers continue to be killed at a horrific pace. According to Article 19, forty-seven were murdered during the López Obrador presidency, the same number as under Peña.[23]

To be viable, the press needs legal protections on more mundane levels too. One concern is the trend, pronounced in recent decades, of deadbeat employers. Established players and sweet-talking promoters alike have set up papers or news sites that fail within a few years, upon which they lay off their staff without due severance.[24] A clampdown would reduce the frequency of new launches—no bad thing given the saturated media landscape—and temper the deep concern among journalists about job precarity.

Another issue is plagiarism. The boom in news sites since the 2010s has been accompanied by a routine copying of stories from other media, without attribution and often without a byline other than "Staff" or "Newsroom." The practice is rife at the personal sites of columnists and influencers. At such sites, original content is mostly limited to the columns and video clips of the media personality whose name and face typically adorn the masthead. A related trend, observable at the same sites, is the use of uncredited photographs, which jeopardizes the livelihood of photojournalists. Some sites repackage information in bylined articles that evidence no original reporting, enabling them to generate large amounts of content per writer each day. This technique helps explain the meteoric rise of *InfoBAE*, an Argentina-based operation that entered Mexico in 2017 with a staff of twenty. By 2024, it topped the local Comscore chart with 17 million monthly visits, knocking *El Universal*'s site into second place.[25]

On the legal front, concerns persist about libel laws. As the press has become more independent and inquisitive, these laws have been used by the powerful to try to silence or punish those who write about corruption.

The most celebrated recent case involved *Reforma* columnist Sergio Aguayo, who in 2016 wrote of former Coahuila governor Humberto Moreira that "he emits a corrupt stench." Despite having recently been arrested in Spain on charges of money laundering for the Zetas and embezzlement, Moreira sued. Three years later, a civil court ordered Aguayo to pay Moreira damages of $500,000, a decision that elicited a statement of concern from Mexico's UN Human Rights Office. A few months after that, a judge ordered the embargo of Aguayo's assets and obliged him to pay a $20,000 guarantee, at which Article 19 and Amnesty International demanded that the judges and lawyers involved in the prosecution be investigated for conflict of interest. From there, the case went to the Supreme Court, which in March 2022 found in Aguayo's favor. Still, very few journalists have either the resources or the support network with which Aguayo was able to fight his case, which cost him about $25,000, most of that donated by friends and sympathizers, along with a legal team working pro bono.[26]

As for the agency of the press itself, the greatest challenge is to win back public trust. Many attempts to hold López Obrador or his government to account were strident, unbalanced, lacking in right of reply, inadequate in their recourse to professional expertise (legal, medical, economic, environmental), or incomplete in context (especially the social conditions that the president inherited in 2018). Biased attacks were like softballs to López Obrador; at his *mañanera*, he could whack them out of the park, claiming with some reason that such criticisms were made in bad faith, which allowed him to get away with ignoring the problem raised. Worse, when he or his followers labeled a journalist or a paper *chayotero* (bribe-taking), it did not matter that they offered no factual evidence, for the label tapped into inaccurate but deep-rooted stereotypes of the press as entirely *vendida* (in it for the money). Altogether, substandard journalism, presidential hostility, the social media echo chamber, and popular prejudice made for a heady cocktail of distrust.

As the Reuters Institute recommends, the building of trust in news broadly requires four kinds of initiative: editorial strategies that better align topics covered with what the public say they want to read; transparency about ethical standards, along with a reduction of bias and apparent conflicts of interest; management policies that ensure journalistic independence and staff diversity; and engagement with the public, including response to audience feedback. And there's a warning: Trust "is even more challenging to restore where it has dissipated."[27]

Both to regain trust and to improve effectiveness, Mexican media could do more to better train their journalists. The age-old phenomenon of *declaracionismo*—single-source stories based on public declarations— broadly persists today and is generally worse in the provincial press. Part of the problem is that most of Mexico's numerous communications schools provide inadequate preparation. Further, amid the economic asphyxiation of the López Obrador era, opportunities for journalists to improve their craft diminished. During the pandemic, Grupo Reforma suspended its traditional summer workshops for new recruits; they have yet to resume. A government-imposed president at the Center for Research and Teaching in Economics halted its prestigious journalism program, which offered an MA and annual diploma courses. Where professionalizing programs do exist, editors are often reluctant to give reporters time off to take them.[28]

To further improve quality, Mexico's press could also commit greater resources to investigative journalism. This genre boomed between the mid-1990s and 2018, but under López Obrador it suffered from depleted funding and ever-fewer spaces. The economic decline of the sector as a whole was a major factor, but so was the almost automatic discrediting of exposés by the president and his social media allies. Publications still willing to regularly devote resources to the genre are few. Among print media, there are *El Universal* and to a lesser extent *Reforma*, *Milenio* (still primarily a forum for columnists), and *Proceso* (driven by crisis to switch from a weekly to a monthly format). In the states, only *Zeta* of Tijuana and *Noroeste* of Sinaloa stand out. Digital practitioners include *Animal Político*, *Pie de Página*, *Quinto Elemento*, and a new project founded by Ignacio Rodríguez Reyna called *Fábrica de Periodismo* (The Journalism Factory), plus a few regional sites such as *ZonaDocs* of Guadalajara, Guanajuato-based *POP Lab*, and *La Verdad* of Ciudad Juárez. Most of these media are able to put out only a few investigations per year.[29]

Since financial duress has led most media to cut back on investigative reports, it has increasingly fallen to columnists to assume the watchdog role. But with the proliferation of opinion mongers in legacy media, most of them criticizing López Obrador (often quite viscerally), the phenomenon arguably became counterproductive.[30] Instead of continuing to pay high retainers to so many columnists, publishers might better channel some of that outlay to complementary and potentially profitable forms of journalism online, as *SinEmbargo* did with *Los Periodistas*. Sinaloa's *Noroeste* began to do so in February 2024 with its YouTube and Facebook channel Noticiero Noroeste; after six months its videos were accumulating 11 million monthly views, thanks in great part to a thematic emphasis on everyday people, including the victims of Sinaloa's notorious narco violence.[31]

Much of the best investigative work of the past two decades has been financed in whole or in part by Mexican and foreign NGOs. Their continued support is vital, but it needs to be regularly evaluated. The boards of Mexico's

NGOs are largely dominated by business elites, most of whom have overtly or covertly opposed the 4T—notoriously so in the case of MCCI founder Claudio X. González Jr., whose open partisanship called into question the rigor and validity of this NGO's investigations of corruption within the president's circle.[32]

Almost absent from Mexico's media landscape have been the interventions by rich philanthropists that helped reinvigorate or rescue major titles in the United States: Jeff Bezos of Amazon buying *The Washington Post*, investment manager John W. Henry buying *The Boston Globe*, digital entrepreneur Marc Benioff buying *Time* magazine. In each case, the purchase owed more to altruism than hope of profit and the buyer pledged editorial independence (although Bezos, eleven years after his purchase, changed his mind during the 2024 campaign season).[33] In Mexico such gestures are exceedingly rare, the best known involving Alejandro Legorreta, an heir to a banking family, who in 2020 bought *Gatopardo*. Legorreta took the movie stars off its cover and gave the magazine a greater focus on social issues like migration and the environment, thus preserving a rare venue for long-form reporting and photojournalism. Multiple prizes for its writers and freelancers followed.[34]

Will other business leaders step in and help preserve the mission and autonomy of the Fourth Estate? Will Sheinbaum, who took office on October 1, 2024, prove less averse to an independent press than López Obrador and allocate subsidies more fairly? Will media themselves succeed in diversifying their revenue streams and cracking the riddle of monetizing their digital presence? Perhaps all three kinds of action are necessary for Mexico to avoid becoming a bifurcated nation of media consumers: The well-informed wealthy and the ill-informed rest. Like many countries, Mexico risks regressing toward a society akin to eighteenth-century Europe, in which an elite pays for reliable information, written and edited by specialists, and the large majority contents itself with a freely available mix of unfiltered reports, polemic, and rumor.[35]

Notes

Abbreviations

AGN   Archivo General de la Nación
DFS   Dirección Federal de Seguridad

Preface

1. "International Editor of the Year Award," WorldPress.org, Dec. 11, 2006; cf. González de Bustamante and Relly, *Surviving Mexico*, 1–3. "Drug cartels" is a misnomer because Mexico's criminal organizations do not collude to fix prices, are less centralized than popular portrayals contend, and (increasingly) have multiple revenue streams. On "syndicates," see Reuter and Paoli, "How Similar?"

2. Gillingham et al., introduction, 6–8.

3. Hallin and Papathanassopoulos, "Political Clientelism."

4. Guerrero and Márquez-Ramírez, *Media Systems*; Moreno, "Big Missing Link," 154, 172.

5. Article 19, *Negación*, 109–14; Cortés, *El choque inevitable*, chap. 4. In 2021 alone, Article 19 documented seventy-one denigrating phrases used by López Obrador or cabinet members during the president's morning press conferences.

6. "Esta es la lista de chayoteros de Peña Nieto," Polemon.mx, May 23, 2019; "Con AMLO incrementan 85% los ataques contra la prensa: Artículo 19," AnimalPolitico.com, Apr. 5, 2022; "Attacks on Press in Mexico Hit Record Level during López Obrador's Presidency," TheGuardian.com, Apr. 5.

7. Committee to Protect Journalists, *No Excuse*; Impunidad Cero, *Impunidad en homicidio*, 18; author's database.

8. Gillingham and Smith, *Dictablanda*; Gillingham et al., *Journalism, Satire*, chaps. 3–10; Smith, *Mexican Press*.

9. I develop this argument in "Milestones: 1968, 1976" in chapter 1.

10. Freije, *Citizens of Scandal*.

11. For an analysis of this specific era, see Paxman, "Salinas Years, 1988–1994."

12. See, e.g., Leñero, *Los periodistas*; Burkholder, *La red*, chap. 5; Musacchio, *Historia crítica*, 234–38, 241–42; and Smith, *Mexican Press*, 276.

13. Chiefly using a series of case studies rather than a continuous narrative, Smith's *Mexican Press* covers 1940 to 1976 and Freije's *Citizens of Scandal* covers 1963 to 1987.

14. Lawson, *Building the Fourth Estate*; Hughes, *Newsrooms in Conflict*; González, *Escenas del periodismo Mexicano*.

15. Waisbord, *Watchdog Journalism*; Alves, "From Lapdog to Watchdog."

16. Owing to considerable variations in the value of Mexican currency over the decades, all peso amounts are converted into dollars at the then-prevailing rate, unless specifically indicated.

17. Cortés, *El choque inevitable*, 310–47.

18. Freedom House, *Freedom and the Media*, 1; Herscovitz, "Leading Newspapers," 112–15; Márquez-Ramírez, "Mapping Anti-Press Violence."

19. Schiffrin, introduction, 1.

20. Comisión Interamericana de Derechos Humanos, *Informe anual*; "American Journalism Sounds Much More Democratic Than Republican" "When the New York Times Lost Its Way," Economist.com, Dec. 14, 2023.

21. World Values Survey, Wave 1 (1981–84) to Wave 7 (2017–22), www.worldvaluessurvey .org; cf. Moreno, "Big Missing Link," 172 (citing surveys in 2013 and 2014).

22. Herman and Chomsky, *Manufacturing Consent*; Starkman, *Watchdog That Didn't Bark*; Davies, *Hack Attack*.

23. Reyna et al., "Beyond Exogenous Models."

24. The sum of journalist murders during the presidency of López Obrador was forty-seven, the same number as under Peña; "Periodistas asesinadxs en México," Articulo19 .org/periodistasasesinados.

25. Salazar Rebolledo, *Más allá*; Echeverría and González, *Media and Politics*, chaps. 5–8.

26. Paxman, *Los Gobernadores*.

27. Piccato, *History of Infamy*, 64; Gerardo Albarrán de Alba, "Ética y doble moral de los medios," *Zócalo*, Jan. 2020, pp. 6–10.

Introduction

1. My recollections, based in part on a diary I kept at the time, have been enriched by conversations and emails with the following former colleagues, for which I am most grateful: Andrew Cawthorne, Andrew Downie, Eduardo García, Kelly Garrett, Laurence Iliff, David Luhnow, Elisabeth Malkin, Shayne McGuire, Sam Quinones, Jim Silver, Starr Spencer, Mark Stevenson, and Michael Zamba. A lengthier version of this chapter can be read at the author's website, www.andrewpaxman.com.

2. Cole, "Unique English-Language Daily," 555.

3. Marshall, *Watergate's Legacy*.

4. Brad Hamilton, "Cornerman: A Tribute to Pete Hamill," TheHatchInstitute.org, Feb. 15, 2019.

5. "El edificio de Milenio y Multimedios cumple 110 años," Milenio.com, Dec. 18, 2019.

6. Musacchio, *Historia crítica*, 182, 189–90; Fernández and Paxman, *El Tigre*, 74–75.

7. Fernández Christlieb, *Los medios*, 69–70; Alexander, *Sons of the Mexican Revolution*, 48–49, 183–88.

8. Rodríguez Castañeda, *Prensa vendida*, 80–81; Hinds and Tatum, *Not Just for Children*, 128n4, 187, 190.

9. Cole, "Unique English-Language Daily," 554.

10. Rodríguez Castañeda, *Prensa vendida*, 80–81; Fernández and Paxman, *El Tigre*, 428–33; Musacchio, *Historia crítica*, 205, 211; "Periódicos chilangos que ya no existen," Chilango .com, June 7, 2016; Víctor Hugo O'Farrill Toscano (grandson of Rómulo O'Farrill Jr.), email to author, July 18, 2020.

11. Stoub, "Self-Censorship," 30; cf. Riva Palacio, "Culture of Collusion," 31–32.

12. *The News*, May 3, 1992, p. 2.

13. *The News*, Dec. 22, 1992, p. B7; Apr. 6, 1993, pp. 35, 38.

14. A recent survey had found that the vast majority of *News* readers were over fifty, most of them retired; Stoub, "Self-Censorship," 31.

15. The phrase was coined by magazine publisher José Pagés Llergo (1910–89), director of *Siempre!*

16. *The News*, Oct. 31, 1992, p. 5.

17. Secretary of government (*secretario de Gobernación*) is a post with no US equivalent but akin to the UK home secretary; under the PRI, it was the most powerful cabinet post, responsible for the legal initiatives of the executive, relations with social and religious organizations, security and policing, and media regulation.

18. *The News*, Nov. 4, 1992, p. 2.

19. Zach Margulis, untitled draft, [Nov. 4, 1992], author's collection.

20. Stoub, "Self-Censorship," 32; letter, McGuire to Bambarén, Jan. 6, 1993, author's collection.

21. *The News*, Nov. 12, 1992, p. 2; Nov. 13, 1992, p. 2.

22. *Newsweek*, Nov. 23, 1992, p. 3.

23. *El Norte*, Nov. 17, 1992, p. 1.

24. *New York Times*, Nov. 28, 1992, p. 19; Stoub, "Self-Censorship," 33.

25. *New York Times*, Dec. 4, 1992, p. 6; *Síntesis* [Puebla], Dec. 4, 1992, p. 7; *Proceso*, Dec. 6, 1992, pp. 11–12; *El Financiero*, Dec. 9, 1992, p. 48.

26. *Christian Science Monitor*, Mar. 22, 1993, p. 6.

27. Stoub, "Self-Censorship," 33; McGuire to Bambarén, Jan. 6, 1993.

28. The best histories of *Excélsior* are Burkholder, *La red*; and González, *Escenas del periodismo mexicano*, chap. 2.

29. Ortiz Garza, "Fighting for the Soul."

30. "Así se construyó el Palacio de 'El Periódico de la Vida Nacional,'" Excelsior.com .mx, Jan. 22, 2020.

31. *Proceso*, Oct. 28, 2000, pp. 32–33; "Cinco monstruos de la arquitectura en Ciudad de México," ElPais.com, Aug. 30, 2017.

32. Aguayo Quezada and Acosta, *Urnas y pantallas*, 14; Lawson, *Building the Fourth Estate*, 71–76; Hughes, *Newsrooms in Conflict*, 15, 110–11; Garza Ramos, "Democratization and the Regional Press," 266.

33. Rodríguez Castañeda, *Prensa vendida*.

34. *Mexico Insight*, Sept. 12, 1993, pp. 13–15; a shorter version ran in the *Houston Chronicle*, Oct. 3, 1993, p. A24.

35. "Fighting to Tell the Truth," *Chicago Tribune*, June 18, 1997.

36. Rivard, *Trail of Feathers*.

Chapter 1

1. The sketch of Ealy draws on El Universal, *El Universal*, 12, 173–75; Rodríguez Munguía, *La otra guerra secreta*, 86–94; Smith, *Mexican Press*, 71–72; Fernández Christlieb, *Los medios*, 60–61; *Proceso*, Sept. 15, 1996, pp. 8–9; and report, July 25, 1985, Archivo General de la Nación (hereafter AGN), Dirección Federal de Seguridad (hereafter DFS), Versión Pública: Juan Francisco Ealy Ortiz.

2. Others who studied economics at the UNAM in the 1960s include future president Carlos Salinas.

3. Camp, *Mexican Political Biographies 1884–1934*, 119.

4. Smith, *Mexican Press*, 71; González, *Escenas del periodismo mexicano*, 27; *Proceso*, Sept. 15, 1996, pp. 8–9.

5. El Universal, *Juan Francisco Ealy Ortiz*, 39; reports, Jan. 29 and Feb. 3, 1973, AGN, DFS, Versión Pública: Ealy Ortiz.

6. Smith, *Mexican Press*, chap. 2.

7. Rodríguez Munguía, *La otra guerra secreta*, 69, 95–98; Cano Andaluz, "Los libros y la prensa"; *El Universal*, Oct. 3, 1968, p. 1.

8. Rodríguez Castañeda, *Prensa vendida*, 15. This book details each banquet and squirm-inducing speech from 1951 to 1992; as of 1952, June 7 was officially known as Press Freedom Day; Rodríguez Castañeda, *Prensa vendida*, 24.

9. Rodríguez Castañeda, *Prensa vendida*, 123, 130; Secanella, *El periodismo*, 157–59.

10. Rodríguez Castañeda, *Prensa vendida*, 140–43.

11. Freije, "Censorship in the Headlines," 239–40; Krauze, *Mexico*, 742–43.

12. Rodríguez Castañeda, *Prensa vendida*, 140–43.

13. On *Excélsior*'s critical edge under Scherer: Scherer García and Monsiváis, *Tiempo de saber*, 39–48, 53–54, 67–71; Musacchio, *Historia crítica*, 224–30; Burkholder, *La red*, 147–55; Castillo, *La biografía secreta*, 62, 66–68.

14. On *El Universal* in the Echeverría era: Luis Javier Solana and Luis Gutiérrez Rodríguez, in Ana María Serna, *"Se solicitan reporteros,"* 101, 123, 130, 267–68, 277–78; Guízar García, "Los titulares," 42, 173–75; Freije, *Citizens of Scandal*, 79–84; Bohmann, *Medios de comunicación*, 151; González, *Escenas del periodismo mexicano*, 29–32; Rodríguez Munguía, *La otra guerra secreta*, 94–95; *Proceso*, Sept. 15, 1996, pp. 8–9; report, Sept. 10, 1971, AGN, DFS, Versión Pública: Ealy Ortiz.

15. Secanella, *El periodismo*, 32; Scherer García and Monsiváis, *Tiempo de saber*, 233.

16. Scherer García, *Estos años*, 43–46; Bohmann, *Medios de comunicación*, 195; González, *Escenas del periodismo mexicano*, 71–72; Hughes, *Newsrooms in Conflict*, 142.

17. Scherer García, *El poder*, 11, 65–66; Secanella, *El periodismo*, 157, 163–67; González, *Escenas del periodismo mexicano*, 30.

18. *El Universal*, Sept. 2, 1982, p. 1.

19. Scherer García, *La terca memoria*, 124; González, *Escenas del periodismo mexicano*, 30–32; *Proceso*, Sept. 15, 1996, p. 11; former *El Universal* editors, interviews by the author, Mexico City, Sept. 2018 and Aug. 2024; Wilbert Torre, interview by the author, Mexico City, Oct. 16, 2019.

20. González, *Escenas del periodismo mexicano*, 30; Scherer García, *Estos años*, 48–49; Scherer García, *La terca memoria*, 124.

21. John Preston, *Fall*.

22. *El Universal*, Jan. 13, 1987, pp. 1, 10; Jan. 14, 1987, pp. 1, 14; Rodríguez Castañeda, *Prensa vendida*, 283–85; González, *Escenas del periodismo mexicano*, 32–33.

23. One of the most famous journalists to be fired by Ealy was columnist Manuel Buendía, over a column about Mexico City mayor Carlos Hank, in 1978; Granados Chapa, in Ana María Serna, *"Se solicitan reporteros,"* 179. On further firings by Ealy, see my discussions in chapters 6 (of Benjamín Wong), 7 (of Ramón Alberto Garza), and 10 (of Jorge Zepeda Patterson).

24. Fernández Christlieb, *Los medios*, 69; Musacchio, *Historia crítica*, 7–8.

25. Fernández Christlieb, *Los medios*, 59–60; Musacchio, *Historia crítica*, 152; Garner, *British Lions*, 254n72, 294n39.

26. Garciadiego, "¿Cuándo, cómo?"; Garner, *British Lions*, 209–11.

27. Musacchio, *Historia crítica*, 152–53.

28. Bohmann, *Medios de comunicación*, 66–67; Musacchio, *Historia crítica*, 39–47, 132–37, 150–51; Piccato, "Notes for a History," 41–43.

29. Musacchio, *Historia crítica*, 157–59.

30. Scherer García and Monsiváis, *Tiempo de saber*, 182.

31. Musacchio, *Historia crítica*, 153; Smith, *Mexican Press*, 28.

32. Reavis, "Stop the Presses"; Riding, *Distant Neighbors*, 124–26; Singer, *Mordaza de papel*, 25–26; Rodríguez Castañeda, *Prensa vendida*, 229–31, 291–92, 312; Torres A., *El periodismo mexicano*, 92–102; Lawson, *Building the Fourth Estate*, 34–37; Musacchio, *Historia crítica*, 183–84, 190–92, 211, 227, 229; Smith, *Mexican Press*, 20–25, 70–78; *Proceso*, May 23, 1983, pp. 20–23; Jan. 25, 1988, pp. 6–15.

33. Jean-François Revel, "Democratie mexicaine," *Esprit*, May 1952, quoted in Krauze, *Mexico*, 578–79.

34. Hallin and Papathanassopoulos, "Political Clientelism," 175, 179, 182–83, 188–89; cf. Guerrero and Márquez-Ramírez, *Media Systems*.

35. Musacchio, *Historia crítica*, 167, 174–75.

36. Smith, *Mexican Press*, chap. 6, esp. 207–14; Reavis, "Stop the Presses," 194–95; interviews with Rodolfo Ruiz, Puebla, Oct. 30, 2019; Manuel Appendini, Aguascalientes, July 1, 2020; anonymous *La Jornada reporter*, Mexico City, Oct. 30, 2020.

37. Musacchio, *Historia crítica*, 33–110.

38. Rodríguez Munguía, *La otra guerra secreta*, 98, 172; report on Benjamín Wong Castañeda, [1985], and report, July 25, 1985, AGN, DFS, Versión Pública: Ealy Ortiz; former *El Universal* editor, interview, Mexico City, Sept. 27, 2018.

39. Ortiz Marín, *Los medios*, 70–71; Bohmann, *Medios de comunicación*, 149.

40. Erwin Macario, interview, Villahermosa, Oct. 12, 2022; Víctor Sámano, interview, Villahermosa, Oct. 13, 2022.

41. Camp, *Mexican Political Biographies 1835–1993*, 241, 412, 483–84; "Flores Tapia, Oscar," 241; "Loret de Mola Mediz, Carlos," 412; "Morales Blumenkron, Guillermo," 483–84.

42. Niblo, *Mexico in the 1940s*, 214, 346–47; Fernández and Paxman, *El Tigre*, 74–77; Bess, *Routes of Compromise*, 124, 136–37.

43. *El Heraldo de México*, Nov. 9, 1965, p. 1; Rodríguez Castañeda, *Prensa vendida*, 93; Paxman, *Jenkins of Mexico*, 311–12, 343, 360–61.

44. González Casanova, *Democracy in Mexico*, 216; Freije, *Citizens of Scandal*, 32; Smith, *Mexican Press*, 28, 126.

45. Smith, *Mexican Press*, 31, 47; Piccato, "Notes for a History," 48–49; Benjamin Smith, email to the author, Jan. 6, 2018.

46. By around 1980, *Alarma!* reportedly sold more than 1 million copies a week; Secanella, *El periodismo*, 22.

47. Musacchio, *Historia crítica*, 203, 208, 239; Bohmann, *Medios de comunicación*, 124; Trejo Delarbre, "Periódicos."

48. Martínez Mendoza, "El periodismo en Chiapas."

49. Hallin and Mancini, *Comparing Media Systems*, 28–30; Brüggemann et al., "Hallin and Mancini Revisited."

50. Sparrow, *Uncertain Guardians*, 115–16; Tiffen, *Rupert Murdoch*, 136–37.

51. Aguayo Quezada, *La charola*, 76–80.

52. Quoted in Secanella, *El periodismo*, 14.

53. World Values Survey, Wave 1 (1981–1984), www.worldvaluessurvey.org; Musacchio, *Historia crítica*, 197–98; "Nuestra escuela," www.septien.mx/acerca-de-la-escuela.

54. Alejandro C. Manjarrez, interview, Puebla, Nov. 12, 2018.

55. Scherer García and Monsiváis, *Tiempo de saber*, 147.

56. Fromson, "Mexico's Struggle," 118.

57. Smith, *Mexican Press*, 43; Mijangos y González, *Historia mínima*, 153.

58. The sketch of Musacchio and his experiences draws, except where indicated, on the interview with him in Ana María Serna, *"Se solicitan reporteros,"* 203–27.

59. Allier Montaño, *68: El movimiento que triunfó en el futuro*.

60. Musacchio, *Historia critica*, 216; Volpi, *La imaginación*.

61. Rodríguez Castañeda, *Prensa vendida*, 120, 123, 126–27.

62. Interview with Musacchio in Ana María Serna, *"Se solicitan reporteros,"* 203–27.

63. Zolov, *Refried Elvis*, chap. 6.

64. Secanella, *El periodismo*, 32–35; Hughes, *Newsrooms in Conflict*, 5, 33; Musacchio, *Historia crítica*, 236–38; González, *Escenas del periodismo mexicano*, 72; Smith, *Mexican Press*, 276.

65. The story of *Unomásuno* draws on Flores Quintero, *Unomásuno*; Scherer García and Monsiváis, *Tiempo de saber*, 240–41; González, *Escenas del periodismo mexicano*, 84–93; Musacchio and Gutiérrez, in Ana María Serna, *"Se solicitan reporteros,"* 218–24, 284–86; Freije, *Citizens of Scandal*, 91–92; and Héctor Aguilar Camín, interview (via videocall), May 2, 2024.

66. Riva Palacio, *La prensa*, 67–68; Julia Preston and Dillon, *Opening Mexico*, 91–92; Freije, *Citizens of Scandal*, 91, 96–97; René Delgado, interview, Mexico City, Feb. 1, 2023; Héctor Aguilar Camín, interview (via videocall), May 2, 2024.

67. This opinion of *Unomásuno* is shared by Secanella, *El periodismo*, 35; Riva Palacio, *La prensa*, 68; various sources quoted in González, *Escenas del periodismo mexicano*, 88–90; and Freije, "Censorship in the Headlines," 255.

68. Freije, *Citizens of Scandal*, 2–3, chap. 3, chap. 4.

69. Musacchio, *Diccionario enciclopédico de México*. See also Musacchio, *Milenios de México*.

70. The sketch of Granados Chapa draws on Musacchio, *Granados Chapa*; and the interview with him in Ana María Serna, *"Se solicitan reporteros,"* 143–69.

71. Secanella, *El periodismo*, 45, 48, 59–77, 120.

72. *Unomásuno*, Aug. 24, 1981, p. 4; Aug. 27, 1981, p. 1.

73. On Becerra's alcoholism and the broader drinking culture within *Unomásuno* and the press in general, see Flores Quintero, *Unomásuno*, 161–66; cf. Smith, *Mexican Press*, 53, 160.

74. Musacchio, *Granados Chapa*, 116–30; Secanella, *El periodismo*, 157–59, 168–72; Rodríguez Castañeda, *Prensa vendida*, 236–37, 317; González, *Escenas del periodismo mexicano*, 93–99; Gutiérrez, in Ana María Serna, *"Se solicitan reporteros,"* 281–88.

75. Quoted in Ana María Serna, *"Se solicitan reporteros,"* 222.

76. Flores Quintero, *Unomásuno*, 305, 308–10; Freije, *Citizens of Scandal*, 124, 147, 154.

77. Trejo Delarbre, *Mediocracia sin mediaciones*, 206–7; González, *Escenas del periodismo mexicano*, 99, 101–2; Gutiérrez, in Ana María Serna, *"Se solicitan reporteros,"* 288–91; *Unomásuno*, Aug. 14, 1986, pp. 1, 7.

78. *Proceso*, Oct. 2, 1989, pp. 6–11; Gutiérrez, in Ana María Serna, *"Se solicitan reporteros,"* 289–92.

79. Alegría Martínez, *Manuel Becerra Acosta*, 99, 137; Trejo Delarbre, "Periódicos," III; González, *Escenas del periodismo mexicano*, 100–107; Flores Quintero, *Unomásuno*, 303–4; José Carreño Carlón, interview, Mexico City, Oct. 18, 2019; Carlos Salinas de Gortari, interview, London, June 29, 2021.

80. Riding, *Distant Neighbors*, 83.

81. Fromson, "Mexico's Struggle," 118.

Chapter 2

1. The sketch of Navarro draws on "In Treacherous Tijuana, Editor Adela Navarro Bello's Risks Are Life-or-Death," WashingtonPost.com Oct. 26, 2011; "A Mexican Journalist in the Crosshairs," SanDiegoUnionTribune.com Dec. 2, 2011; and Adela Navarro, interview, Mexico City, June 20, 2019, and via telephone, Sept. 12, 2023.

2. Adela Navarro, interview, Mexico City, June 20, 2019, and via telephone, Sept. 12, 2023.

3. Moncada Ochoa, *Oficio de muerte*, 89–95, 99–100, 104–8, 142–44, 158–68; Smith, *Mexican Press*, 171, 181–84.

4. Adela Navarro, "El presente del periodismo: 8," Horizontal.mx, Mar. 15, 2016.

5. *Zeta*, April 11, 1980, p. 1.

6. William Murray, "To the Left of Zero," *New Yorker*, July 31, 1989, pp. 57–66; Bautista Castillo, "*Zeta*," chap. 2; *Los Angeles Times*, Mar. 24, 2006.

7. On Héctor Félix Miranda, his killing, and the inquiry: Murray, "To the Left," pp. 57–58; Bautista Castillo, "*Zeta*," chap. 3; Moncada Ochoa, *Oficio de muerte*, 176–81; *Zeta*, Apr. 29, 1988.

8. *Proceso*, Apr. 25, 1988, p. 18.

9. On gubernatorial machismo, see Andrew Paxman, introduction to Paxman, *Los gobernadores*, 9–10. On federal technocrats: Riding, *Distant Neighbors*, 79–81.

10. Blancornelas, quoted in Murray, "To the Left," p. 66.

11. *Zeta*, May 6, 1988, p. 1.

12. Rodríguez Castañeda, *Prensa vendida*, 298.

13. In 2015, Félix Miranda's killers were released from jail, upon which they returned to work for Hank Rhon; *Zeta*, May 1, 2015, pp. 23–25; Adela Navarro, "Covering the Cartels," Reuters Institute seminar, Oxford, March 3, 2021.

14. *La Opinión*, Jan. 16, 1957, p. 6. On the co-option of Puebla's press, see Paxman, "Changing Opinions."

15. Monsiváis, *A ustedes les consta*, 71–72.

16. Trejo Delarbre, "Democracia por escrito," 188, 198.

17. Erwin Macario and Audelino Macario, interviews, Villahermosa, Oct. 12 and 16, 2022.

18. José Carreño Carlón, interview, Mexico City, Oct. 18, 2019; various journalists, interviews, Puebla, Oct. 2019, Aguascalientes, Feb. 2020, Tabasco, Oct. 2022.

19. "Relación de periódicos de las diferentes entidades federativas de la república," June 11, 1960, AGN, Dirección General de Investigaciones Políticas y Sociales, 1279, cited in Gillingham et al., introduction, 16.

20. Gillingham, "Regional Press Boom"; Garza Ramos, "Democratization and the Regional Press," 263-74; Smith, *Mexican Press*, chaps. 5, 6; Freije, *Citizens of Scandal*, chap. 1.

21. Smith, *Mexican Press*, chaps. 7, 8; Paxman, "Changing Opinions," 165-75; Gillingham, "Regional Press Boom."

22. Musacchio, *Historia crítica*, 163; Smith, *Mexican Press*, 118-20; Freije, *Citizens of Scandal*, 25-32; Garza Ramos, "Democratization and the Regional Press," 268.

23. Gillingham, "Regional Press Boom," 165, 170-72.

24. Camp, *Entrepreneurs and Politics*, 25-27, 166-67; Garza Ramos, "Democratization and the Regional Press," 268-70. An early precedent for press influence is that of Hermosillo's *El Imparcial*, which helped elect a PAN mayor in 1967; Garza Ramos, "Democratization and the Regional Press," 270.

25. Freije, *Citizens of Scandal*, chap. 6; Fernández and Paxman, *El Tigre*, 381-83; Rodríguez Castañeda, *Prensa vendida*, 280-81.

26. Merchant Ley, "Una negociación sutil," 55-61; Bautista Castillo, "Zeta," 50.

27. Bautista Castillo, "Zeta," 65, 68, 126, 128; Hernández Ramírez, "La formación universitaria," 116-18, 132-35.

28. Meyer, "El presidencialismo," 77; Espinoza Valle, "Alternancia y liberalización política," 28-30; Merchant Ley, "Una negociación sutil," 56.

29. Osorno and Aldrete, *La muñeca tetona*. Further details of the encounter are from "La muñeca tetona, documental de Diego Enrique Osorno," Chilango.com, July 27, 2017; and "Monsiváis y el Ateneo de Angangueo," Museo del Estanquillo, Aug. 1, 2020, youtube.com.

30. Krauze, *Mexico*, 763, 772-73; Castañeda, *Perpetuating Power*, 64-70.

31. Julia Preston and Dillon, *Opening Mexico*, 419; *La Jornada*, July 19, 1988, p. 7.

32. Osorno and Aldrete, *La muñeca tetona*.

33. Osorno and Aldrete, *La muñeca tetona*.

34. Reding, "Mexico at a Crossroads," 615; Dick Reavis, "How Do You Say 'Perestroika' in Spanish?," *Texas Monthly*, Oct. 1989, p. 135; Salinas, *México*, 95; Julia Preston and Dillon, *Opening Mexico*, 420; William Orme, interview (via videocall), Feb. 27, 2021.

35. Lawson, *Building the Fourth Estate*, 39; Julia Preston and Dillon, *Opening Mexico*, 419-22; Carlos Salinas, interview, London, June 29, 2021.

36. Salinas, *México*, 269-71; Roberto Blancarte, "Adios a Milenio," Milenio.com, Apr. 19, 2022.

37. Julia Preston and Dillon, *Opening Mexico*, 420-21.

38. Abello, quoted in Osorno and Aldrete, *La muñeca tetona*.

39. Krauze, *La presidencia imperial*, 459; Reding, "Mexico at a Crossroads."

40. Lawson, *Building the Fourth Estate*, chap. 6; Otto Granados, interview, Mexico City, May 9, 2019; José Carreño Carlón, interview, Mexico City, Oct. 18, 2019.

41. I further develop the "Salinas watershed" argument in Paxman, "Salinas Years."

42. Hughes, *Newsrooms in Conflict*, chap. 6; Lawson, *Building the Fourth Estate*, 82-88.

43. Freije, *Citizens of Scandal*. See also Lawson, *Building the Fourth Estate*, 21–22, 70, 125–37.

44. I sketch these economic variables below and discuss them in greater detail in Paxman, "Salinas Years."

45. Carlos Salinas, interview, London, June 29, 2021.

46. Scherer García, *Estos años*, 51; Camp, *Politics in Mexico*, 56; William Orme, interview (via videocall), Feb. 27, 2021; Carlos Salinas, interview, London, June 29, 2021.

47. Rodríguez Castañeda, *Prensa vendida*, 307–9, 313–14; Lawson, *Building the Fourth Estate*, 76–77; cf. Trejo Delarbre, "Periódicos."

48. Hughes, *Newsrooms in Conflict*, 132.

49. Article 19, *In the Shadow of Buendía*; Dallas Morning News, *Credibility*; Americas Watch, *Human Rights in Mexico*, chap. 8; Canadian Committee to Protect Journalists, *Press and the Perfect Dictatorship*; Committee to Protect Journalists, *Free Trade?*

50. Orme, introduction, 9; Lawson, *Building the Fourth Estate*, 77; *Proceso*, Feb. 10, 1992, pp. 18–19; Dudley Althaus, email exchange, Sept. 2021; Mike Tangeman, email exchange, Oct. 2021, Mar. 2022.

51. Lawson, *Building the Fourth Estate*, 76.

52. Haber et al., *Mexico since 1980*, 75 (table 3.6).

53. Paxman, "Salinas Years"; *Forbes*, July 5, 1993, p. 76. The figures may be conservative, for a marketing magazine put newspaper ad revenue for 1994 at $171 million; *Adcebra*, Sept. 1994, pp. 1, 30.

54. Castañeda, "Limits to Apertura," 140; Samuel García, interview, Mexico City, May 6, 2017.

55. Krauze, *La presidencia imperial*.

56. Rodríguez Castañeda, *Prensa vendida*, 341.

57. Examples include Guerrero under Governor Francisco Ruiz Massieu banning *Proceso* 697 in March 1990 and Puebla under Governor Manuel Bartlett banning *Proceso* 840 in December 1992; Rodríguez Castañeda, *Prensa vendida*, 325–26; author's diary, Dec. 1992.

58. Rodríguez Castañeda, *Prensa vendida*, 301, 331–32, 345–46; Esquivel Hernández, *Cien años*, 62–63; Raymundo Riva Palacio, "Recambio de portavoz," *Este País*, May 1992, pp. 56–57; José Luis Esquivel Hernández, interview, Monterrey, Oct. 2, 2019; Sara Lovera, interview (via videocall), Jan. 28, 2021; Lázaro Ríos, communication with the author, Dec. 20, 2023.

59. Conger, "From Intimidation to Assassination," 103; Castillo, *La biografía secreta*, 364; Michael Zamba, interview (via videocall), May 25, 2020.

60. Paxman, "Changing Opinions," 96–98.

61. Moncada Ochoa, *Oficio de muerte*; Conger, "From Intimidation to Assassination," 99–101.

62. Rodríguez Castañeda, *Prensa vendida*, 335; Conger, "From Intimidation to Assassination," 101; Moynihan, "Mexican News," 113; Committee to Protect Journalists, "Mexican Journalists Murdered," 146; Moncada Ochoa, *Oficio de muerte*, 193–97.

63. On the commonalities of murder inquiries: Moncada Ochoa, *Oficio de muerte*; Committee to Protect Journalists, *No Excuse*.

64. Until 2018, when President López Obrador opted against living in the presidential mansion, Mexicans referred to the presidency as Los Pinos, much in the way that Americans speak of "the White House" and Britons speak of "Number 10" or "Downing Street."

65. Otto Granados, interview, Mexico City, May 9, 2019.

66. Ignacio Rodríguez Reyna, interview, Mexico City, Oct. 19, 2021; Roberto Zamarripa, interview, Mexico City, Dec. 2, 2022.

67. Rodríguez Castañeda, *Prensa vendida*, 335, 342, 344; Lawson, *Building the Fourth Estate*, 226n44; *New York Times Magazine*, Oct. 6, 1991, pp. 40–48; *New York Times*, Feb. 9, 1996, p. A4.

68. For cases of PIPSA cutting newsprint or calling in debts, see Smith, *Mexican Press*, 66–67, 74, 109, 130, 140, 147; Rodríguez Castañeda, *Prensa vendida*, 276, 319; and Lawson, *Building the Fourth Estate*, 33–34.

69. Rodríguez Castañeda, *Prensa vendida*, 322, 330; Lawson, *Building the Fourth Estate*, 33–34, 77, 236n48; Luis Javier Solana, quoted in Ana María Serna, *"Se solicitan reporteros,"* 105.

70. Zacarías, "El papel del papel," 80–81; World Values Survey, Waves 1 (1981–84) and 2 (1990–94), www.worldvaluessurvey.org.

71. Lawson, *Building the Fourth Estate*, 77.

Chapter 3

1. Padilla and Reguillo, *Quién nos hubiera dicho*, 10, 27, 502; Julia Preston and Dillon, *Opening Mexico*, 430–31; *El Informador*, Apr. 22, 1992, p. 1; *Siglo 21*, Apr. 22, pp. 1, 5; Alejandra Xanic, interview (via telephone), June 5, 2024.

2. Xanic won a 2013 Pulitzer Prize as coauthor of a *New York Times* exposé of widespread bribery by Walmart during its expansion in Mexico.

3. The stories of Zepeda and the *Siglo 21* launch draw on Fregoso Peralta and Sánchez Ruiz, *Prensa y poder en Guadalajara*, 127–33; Larrosa-Fuentes, "Los periódicos," 192–98; Lawson, *Building the Fourth Estate*, 73–75; Julia Preston and Dillon, *Opening Mexico*, 427–32; Ángel Melgoza and Luis Sánchez Barbosa, "El fin de siglo en Guadalajara," Territorio. mx, June 15, 2015; Alejandra Xanic, interview (via telephone), Mexico City, Nov. 29, 2018, and June 5, 2024; Jorge Zepeda Patterson, interview, Mexico City, May 22, 2019; Salvador Camarena, interview, Mexico City, May 24, 2019; Rubén Martín Martín, interview, Guadalajara, June 6, 2019; Diego Petersen Farah, interview, Guadalajara, June 7, 2019; Luis Miguel González, interview, Mexico City, Feb. 1, 2023.

4. Ruiz Castañeda, *La prensa*, 243.

5. Larrosa-Fuentes, "Los periódicos," 193, 231–33; Smith, *Dope*, 309–10.

6. Larrosa-Fuentes, "Los periódicos," 200–202, 229; Salvador Camarena, interview, Mexico City, May 24, 2019; Oliver Meza, conversation with author, Aguascalientes, May 2019.

7. Paxman, "Guadalajara Film Festival," 68–70. *La Mamá del Abulón* is an *albur* (sexual pun), sounding like a fusion of slang terms for fellatio and large vagina.

8. *Siglo 21*, Nov. 8, 1991, p. 1.

9. Hernández Ramírez, "Siglo 21," 180–83.

10. Lomelí Meillón, "Gobernantes y gobernados," 219–54; Reguillo, "Comunicación irruptiva," 510–11.

11. Alonso, "Sociedad y gobierno," 176–90; *Proceso*, Feb. 17, 1992, pp. 26–29, 808 (cover story), April 27, 1992, pp. 6–11.

12. Larrosa-Fuentes, "Los periódicos," 196–99; *El Occidental*, Apr. 23, 1992; *El Informador*, Apr. 23, 1992.

13. The 1985 earthquake, its social impact, and coverage by *La Jornada* are subjects of chapter 6.

14. Larrosa-Fuentes, "Los periódicos," 191, 195–99.

15. On *Siglo 21* between 1992 and 1995: Lawson, *Building the Fourth Estate*, 75; Larrosa-Fuentes, "Los periódicos," 199–204; Hernández Ramírez, "*Siglo 21*," 168, 178–80; Jorge Zepeda Patterson, interview, Mexico City, May 22, 2019; Salvador Camarena, interview, Mexico City, May 24, 2019; Rubén Martín Martín, interview, Guadalajara, June 6, 2019; Diego Petersen Farah, interview, Guadalajara, June 7, 2019, and email to the author, Aug. 16, 2024; Luis Miguel González, interview, Mexico City, Feb. 1, 2023.

16. Jorge Zepeda Patterson, interview, Mexico City, May 22, 2019.

17. Luis Miguel González, interview, Mexico City, Feb. 1, 2023.

18. Juan Angulo, interview, Mexico City, May 4, 2019.

19. Lawson, *Building the Fourth Estate*, 141; *El Informador*, May 25, 1993, pp. 1, 3, May 27, p. II-1, May 28, p. II-1, May 29, p. II-1; *El Occidental*, May 25, 1993, pp. 1, 2; *Siglo 21*, May 25, 1993, pp. 1, 3, May 26, p. 1, May 28, p. 1. For conspiracy theories about the cardinal's killing see, e.g., *El Chapo*, season 1, episode 4, aired May 7, 2017, on Netflix.

20. *Siglo 21*, May 25, 1993, p. 3; Jorge Zamora, interview (via telephone), Sept. 28, 2024.

21. The 200 staffers included a newsroom of 100, along with teams in administration, sales, marketing, circulation and delivery, and the printing press; Luis Petersen, email to the author, Aug. 15, 2024.

22. *Siglo 21*, Feb. 2, 1995, p. 1.

23. *Siglo 21*, Feb. 12, 1995, p. 1.

24. *Siglo 21*, July 22, 1996, p. 1.

25. Rubén Martín, interview, Guadalajara, June 6, 2019.

26. Merchant Ley, "Una negociación sutil," 62; Diego Petersen Farah, email to the author, Aug. 16, 2024.

27. On the Zepeda–Dau schism and launch of *Público*: Julia Preston and Dillon, *Opening Mexico*, 435–36; Melgoza and Sánchez Barbosa, "El fin de siglo"; Larrosa-Fuentes, "Los periódicos," 209–11, 214–18; *Proceso*, Aug. 10, 1997, p. 39; Rubén Martín Martín, interview, Guadalajara, June 6, 2019; Diego Petersen Farah, interview, Guadalajara, June 7, 2019; Jorge Zepeda Patterson, interview, Mexico City, June 19, 2019.

28. Larrosa-Fuentes, "Los periódicos," 206–9.

29. Hernández Ramírez, "*Siglo 21*," 184–86.

30. Jorge Zepeda Patterson, interview, Mexico City, June 19, 2019.

31. *Público*, Sept. 8, 1997, p. 1.

32. Larrosa-Fuentes, "Los periódicos," 215, 218–19.

33. Larrosa-Fuentes, "Los periódicos," 215–17.

34. Federico Arreola, interview, Mexico City, Oct. 21, 2021; Rubén Martín Martín, interview, Guadalajara, June 6, 2019.

35. Lawson, *Building the Fourth Estate*, 85–86; Hughes, *Newsrooms in Conflict*, 41; Larrosa-Fuentes, "Los periódicos"; Hernández Ramírez, "*Siglo 21*."

36. Hernández Ramírez, "Franquicias periodísticas"; Federico Arreola, interview, Mexico City, Oct. 21, 2021.

37. Larrosa-Fuentes, "Los periódicos," 199–200; Hernández Ramírez, "*Siglo 21*," 163–64; *La Jornada*, Sept. 20, 2021, p. 9A; Salvador Camarena, interview, Mexico City, May 24, 2019.

38. Jorge Zepeda Patterson, ed., *Los suspirantes* (Mexico City: Planeta, 2005); *Los amos de México* (Planeta, 2007); *Los intocables* (Planeta, 2008); *Los suspirantes 2012* (Planeta, 2011); *Los suspirantes 2018* (Planeta, 2017).

Chapter 4

1. On the launch of *Reforma*: Esquivel Hernández, *Reforma*, 139, 153–58; Fromson, "Mexico's Struggle," 132–33; Lawson, *Building the Fourth Estate*, 77–78; González, *Escenas del periodismo mexicano*, 188–95; *New York Times*, June 29, 1993, p. D22; *Reforma*, Nov. 20, 1993; "Primer aniversario" (supplement), *Reforma*, Nov. 20, 1994; Daniel Moreno, interview, Mexico City, May 24, 2019; José Landeros, interview, Monterrey, Oct. 2, 2019; Ramón Alberto Garza, interview, Mexico City, Oct. 15, 2019; Daniela Pastrana, interview (via videocall), Mar. 25, 2021.

2. Fromson, "Mexico's Struggle," 132.

3. *New York Times*, June 29, 1993, p. D22.

4. Carlos Marichal, conversation with the author, Mexico City, Nov. 11, 2019; former *Reforma* editor, conversation with the author, Dec. 2023.

5. *Reforma*, Nov. 20, 1993, p. 1; cf. *El Día*, June 26, 1962 (López Mateos), *El Sol de México*, Oct. 25, 1965 (Díaz Ordaz), *El Heraldo de México*, Nov. 9, 1965 (Díaz Ordaz), *La Jornada*, Sept. 19, 1984 (Arsenio Farell, labor secretary).

6. Lawson, *Building the Fourth Estate*, 78; González, *Escenas del periodismo mexicano*, 195; Esquivel Hernández, *Reforma*, 156–57.

7. *New York Times*, Dec. 20, 1993, p. D6.

8. Esquivel Hernández, *Reforma*, 139; "Primer aniversario" (supplement), *Reforma*, Nov. 20, 1994, pp. 4–5.

9. On Junco, his family, and *El Norte*: Oppenheimer, *Bordering on Chaos*, 280–81; Fromson, "Mexico's Struggle," 131–33; Esquivel Hernández, *Reforma*, 25–42, 58–59, 65–72, 77–86, 100–113, 135–47; José Luis Esquivel Hernández, José Landeros, Rubén Hipólito, and Ramón Alberto Garza, interviews, Monterrey, Oct. 2–4, 2019.

10. Smith, *Mexican Press*, 7, 118–19, 163.

11. Nolan, "Relative Independence"; Cobb, "Provincial Journalism"; José Luis Esquivel Hernández, email to the author, Apr. 18, 2021.

12. Lawson, *Building the Fourth Estate*, 44, 72, 229n84; *El Norte*, Sept. 2, 1982, pp. 1, B1.

13. On Ramón Alberto Garza: González, *Escenas del periodismo mexicano*, 185–87, 207; Esquivel Hernández, *Reforma*, 97–101, 221; Ramón Alberto Garza, interview, Monterrey, Dec. 8, 2023.

14. Lawson, *Building the Fourth Estate*, 72; *New York Times*, July 16, 1988, p. 6; Samuel García, interview, Mexico City, May 6, 2017.

15. On *El Porvenir* under Jesús Cantú: Esquivel Hernández, *Cien años de El Porvenir*, 57–63; Rodríguez Castañeda, *Prensa vendida*, 260–61, 297–80, 345–46; Arreola, "Jesús (pero no Ramírez), el verdadero resentido de la vocería de AMLO," SDPNoticias.com, May 30, 2019; Juan Alberto Cedillo, interview, Monterrey, Oct. 2, 2019; Jesús Cantú Escalante, interview (via videocall), Mar. 28, 2023.

16. Aguilar and Terrazas, *La prensa*, 91.

17. See "A Watershed Emerges" in chapter 2.

18. Fregoso Peralta, *Prensa regional y elecciones*, 114–16; Lawson, *Building the Fourth Estate*, 72–73, 212; *New York Times*, July 16, 1988, p. 6.

19. Toussaint, *Recuento de periódicos fronterizos*, 97.

20. Rodríguez Castañeda, *Prensa vendida*, 261, 293, 319; Lawson, *Building the Fourth Estate*, 76–77.

21. Jarvenpaa and Leidner, "Information Company in Mexico," 349, 353, 356; Fromson, "Mexico's Struggle," 132; Samuel García, interview, Mexico City, Aug. 2, 2018.

22. González, *Escenas del periodismo mexicano*, 188–89; *New York Times*, June 29, 1993, p. D22; Ramón Alberto Garza, interviews, Monterrey, Oct. 4, and Mexico City, Oct. 15, 2019.

23. Ana María Serna, "José Carreño Carlón," unpublished article, 2005; María Elena Hernández Ramírez, interview, Guadalajara, Oct. 20, 2018; Sara Lovera, interview (via videocall), Jan. 28, 2021; Carlos Salinas de Gortari, interview, London, June 29, 2021.

24. Rodríguez Castañeda, *Prensa vendida*, 366–69; Lawson, *Building the Fourth Estate*, 36, 76; González, *Escenas del periodismo mexicano*, 193; *The News*, Jan. 14, 1993, p. 1, Feb. 20, 1993, p. 3.

25. Espino Sánchez, "Periodistas precarios"; Lawson, *Building the Fourth Estate*, 36; Otto Granados, interview, Mexico City, May 9, 2019.

26. Castañeda, "Limits to Apertura," 137; *Proceso*, Nov. 29, 1992 (cover story); Miguel Basáñez and José Agustín Ortiz Pinchetti, "El Grupo de los Nueve, 1985–2000," EstePais .com, Oct. 2020.

27. *El Economista*, Feb. 26, 1993, pp. 1, 51; *Proceso*, Mar. 7, 1993 (cover story).

28. Oppenheimer, *Bordering on Chaos*, 137; Riva Palacio, *La prensa*, 161–63; González, *Escenas del periodismo mexicano*, 73.

29. Hughes, *Newsrooms in Conflict*, 118, 132, 142.

30. Lawson, *Building the Fourth Estate*, 77–78; Riva Palacio, *La prensa*, 78–79; González, *Escenas del periodismo mexicano*, 72–73, 192–95; Hughes, *Newsrooms in Conflict*, 15–16, 83.

31. Daniela Pastrana, interview (via videocall), Mar. 25, 2021; Ernesto Núñez, interview, Mexico City, Dec. 15, 2021; Ramón Alberto Garza, interview, Monterrey, Dec. 8, 2023.

32. *Reforma*, Jan. 6, 1994, p. 5E; Jan. 11, 1994, p. B7.

33. On the history of *periodismo de denuncia*, often serving special interests, see Freije, *Citizens of Scandal*, 10–14.

34. Daniel Moreno, interview, Mexico City, May 24, 2019; González, *Escenas del periodismo mexicano*, 191.

35. On the early years of *El Financiero*: Riva Palacio, *La prensa*, 72–78, 171–72; González, *Escenas del periodismo mexicano*, 119–40; Musacchio, *Granados Chapa*, 173–76; *La Jornada*, July 27, 2003, p. 17; and interviews with Daniel Moreno, Mexico City, May 24, 2019; José Martínez, Mexico City, Nov. 12, 2019; Rosa Elba Arroyo, Mexico City, Dec. 10, 2019; José Reveles, Mexico City, Feb. 27, 2020; Claudia Fernández (via telephone), May 2, 2021; Ignacio Rodríguez Reyna, Mexico City, Oct. 19, 2021; Raymundo Riva Palacio, Mexico City, Feb. 27, 2020, Oct. 21, 2021, Aug. 28, 2024; and Alejandro Ramos Esquivel (via email), Aug. 30, 2024.

36. *El Financiero*, July 7, 1988, p. 1.

37. In the Zedillo era (1994–2000), *El Financiero* drew little more than 10 percent of its revenue from official advertising; Lawson, *Building the Fourth Estate*, 90, 213.

38. Loaeza, *Las niñas bien*; Loaeza, *Las reinas de Polanco*; *La Jornada*, Sept. 3, 2010, p. 7.

39. Lawson, *Building the Fourth Estate*, 140–41; *El Financiero*, Nov. 11, 1991, p. 61; Nov. 15, 1991, p. 33; Nov. 22, 1991, p. 34; Nov. 28, 1991, p. 43; "Recomendación 126/1991," Comisión Nacional de Derechos Humanos, Dec. 6, 1991, www.cndh.org.mx.

40. Riva Palacio, "Culture of Collusion," 32.

41. Lawson, *Building the Fourth Estate*, 71, 84; González, *Escenas del periodismo mexicano*, 135–37; René Delgado, interview, Mexico City, Feb. 1, 2023.

42. Raymundo Riva Palacio, "Back to the Present," *Neiman Reports*, Summer 1994, pp. 76–77; Riva Palacio, "Culture of Collusion," 27–28.

43. Sergio Sarmiento, "Chiapas y los medios," *Este País*, April 1994, pp. 38–40; Sarmiento, "Trial by Fire," 35–37. Cf. Trejo Delarbre and Becerra, *Chiapas*.

44. Hughes, *Newsrooms in Conflict*, 122–24.

45. César Romero Jacobo, interview (via videocall), Dec. 10, 2021.

46. Tim Padgett, "Confessions of a Gringo Correspondent: 'Salinas Fooled Me Too,'" lecture, Wabash College, Crawfordsville, IN, Feb. 15, 1996.

47. Coverage of the 1968 Tlatelolco massacre and the 1985 earthquake are discussed in chapters 1 and 5 (in the context of the story of *La Jornada*), respectively.

48. On *La Jornada* and its coverage of Chiapas, see chapter 6.

49. Sherman, "Mexican Media"; Oppenheimer, *Bordering on Chaos*, 110, 128–34, 150–55, 158–60; Fernández and Paxman, *El Tigre*, 497–500.

50. Oppenheimer, *Bordering on Chaos*, 154, 159–60.

51. Trejo Delarbre, *Mediocracia sin mediaciones*, 302–10.

52. Daniel Moreno and Salvador Camarena, interviews, Mexico City, May 24, 2019; Roberto Zamarripa, interview, Mexico City, Dec. 2, 2022; Ciro Gómez Leyva, interview, Mexico City, Sept. 21, 2021.

53. Ernesto Núñez, interview, Mexico City, Dec. 15, 2021.

54. Julia Preston and Dillon, *Opening Mexico*, 433; Fromson, "Mexico's Struggle," 133–35; Sarmiento, "Trial by Fire," 35; *New York Times*, Dec. 20, 1993, p. D6; Ramón Alberto Garza, interview, Mexico City, Oct. 15, 2019.

55. Lawson, *Building the Fourth Estate*, 90, 213; Hughes, *Newsrooms in Conflict*, 110; Ramón Alberto Garza, interview, Mexico City, Oct. 15, 2019.

56. On the Voceadores conflict: Aguilar and Terrazas, *La prensa*, 11–14, 41–42, 105–19, 155–72; Fromson, "Mexico's Struggle," 133–34; Jarvenpaa and Leidner, "Information Company," 352–53; "Primer aniversario" (supplement), *Reforma*, Nov. 20, 1994, p. 3; "Reforma 10 años" (supplement), *Reforma*, June 5, 2004, p. 24; Daniel Moreno, interview, Mexico City, June 21, 2019; Ernesto Núñez, interview, Mexico City, Dec. 15, 2021; Lázaro Ríos, correspondence with the author, Dec. 20, 2023.

57. Daniel Moreno, interview, Mexico City, June 21, 2019.

58. Levario Turcott, *Primera plana*, 28–32; *New York Times*, Nov. 20, 1994, p. 3.

59. Ernesto Núñez, interview, Mexico City, Dec. 15, 2021.

60. Oppenheimer, *Bordering on Chaos*, 276–78; Lawson, *Building the Fourth Estate*, 144; *Reforma*, Dec. 9, 1994, p. 1; *New York Times*, Jan. 24, 1995, p. 9; Raymundo Riva Palacio, interview, Mexico City, Oct. 21, 2021.

61. Fromson, "Mexico's Struggle," 134; Jarvenpaa and Leidner, "Information Company," 350; Lawson, *Building the Fourth Estate*, 78; *Advertising Age*, Dec. 5, 1994, p. 35; Ramón Alberto Garza, interview, Mexico City, Oct. 15, 2019.

62. Sarmiento, "Trial by Fire"; Riva Palacio, "Culture of Collusion," 26–28; Hughes, *Newsrooms in Conflict*, 81–82, 121–22, 195–96; Lara Klahr and López Portillo Vargas, *Violencia y medios 2*, 29–30, 33, 45.

63. Antonio Ocaranza, interview, Mexico City, May 20, 2019.

64. Rodríguez Castañeda, *Prensa vendida*, 343–44, 349, 364; González, *Escenas del periodismo mexicano*, 33–36; Hughes, *Newsrooms in Conflict*, 135–38.

65. Vanden Heuvel and Dennis, *Changing Patterns*, 21–24, 28; Oppenheimer, *Bordering on Chaos*, 139; Wilbert Torre, interview, Mexico City, Sept. 26, 2018.

66. Krauze, *La presidencia imperial*, 457.

Chapter 5

1. The story of Scherer and the succession at *Proceso* draws on Oster, *Mexicans*, chap. 13; Scherer García, *Estos años*; Jacinto Rodríguez Munguía, "*Proceso*, la ruptura," *Milenio Semanal*, Mar. 29, 1999, pp. 30–35; Castillo, *La biografía secreta*, 305–14, 332–35, 415–42; María Scherer Ibarra, interview, Mexico City, Feb. 14, 2020; Carlos Puig, interview, Mexico City, Sept. 22, 2021; and Rafael Rodríguez Castañeda, interview (via videocall), Dec. 20, 2021.

2. See, respectively, *Proceso*, May 13, 1991; Apr. 23 and 30, 1990; Mar. 8, 1993.

3. Castillo, *La biografía secreta*, 282–86.

4. Daniel Moreno, interview, Mexico City, May 24, 2019; Antonio Ocaranza, interview, Mexico City, May 10, 2019.

5. Lawson, *Building the Fourth Estate*, 69.

6. Rodríguez Munguía, "*Proceso*, la ruptura"; Margarita Carreón, interview (via telephone), Jan. 4, 2022.

7. Rodríguez Castañeda, *Prensa vendida*.

8. Leñero and Marín, *Manual de periodismo*.

9. The sketch of Scherer draws on Oster, *Mexicans*, chap. 13; Scherer García, *La terca memoria*, 95–97, 141–48, 155–72; Vicente Leñero, "Treinta y cinco años alrededor de Julio," *Proceso*, Jan. 11, 2015, pp. 28–35.

10. Julio Scherer: Versión Pública, AGN, DFS, Caja 47 (entries: May 5, Aug. 15, Aug. 22, 1959); cf. Smith, *Mexican Press*, 67, 129, 151, 201–11, 222.

11. Cf. Oster, *Mexicans*, 185–86.

12. Secanella, *El periodismo*, 31–32; Burkholder, *La red*, 134–38.

13. Scherer García, *Los presidentes*, 36; Brewster, "Student Movement"; *Excélsior*, Oct. 3, 1968, pp. 1, 6–7, 13–14.

14. Scherer García, *La terca memoria*, 39–80; Scherer García, *Los presidentes*.

15. Riva Palacio, *La prensa*, 171; Freije, *Citizens of Scandal*, 92–94, 101; Castillo, *La biografía secreta*, 102, 109, 153–57; *Bajo Palabra*, Aug. 2000, pp. 14–15.

16. Riva Palacio, *La prensa*, 170.

17. *Proceso*, Nov. 6, 1976.

18. Freije, *Citizens of Scandal*, chap. 3; Castillo, *La biografía secreta*, 122–24, 183.

19. Rodríguez Castañeda, *Prensa vendida*, 218.

20. Rodríguez Castañeda, *Prensa vendida*, 218, 220; Lawson, *Building the Fourth Estate*, 69; Castillo, *La biografía secreta*, 160–66; Arellano Mora, "¿La publicidad oficial?," 150–56.

21. Freije, *Citizens of Scandal*, 79–81, 84–86, 103, 118, 125–31; Castillo, *La biografía secreta*, 169–74, 181–86; Grecko, *Killing the Story*, 103–6; *Proceso*, Sept. 13, 1982, pp. 20–25, July 25, 1983, pp. 6–12; anonymous *Proceso* veteran, interview, Oct. 2020.

22. Oster, *Mexicans*, 189; Arellano Mora, "¿La publicidad oficial?," 150–58; Freije, *Citizens of Scandal*, 180–81.

23. Castillo, *La biografía secreta*, 278–80; *Proceso*, Nov. 4, 1991, Nov. 21, 1994; "Leñero comenta las mejores portadas de Proceso," *Viceversa*, Sept. 1998; anonymous *Proceso* veteran, interview, May 2019.

24. Torres, *El periodismo mexicano*, 138–39; Reavis, "Stop the Presses," 198; *Expansión*, Aug. 19, 1992, p. 240; *Proceso 30 años* (special issue), Oct. 2006, pp. 229, 240; anonymous *Proceso* veteran, interview, Oct. 2020; Armando Guzmán, interview, Villahermosa, Oct. 12, 2022.

25. Anonymous *Proceso* veteran, interview, May 2019; Carlos Puig, interview, Mexico City, Sept. 22, 2021.

26. Oster, *Mexicans*, 189–90; Lawson, *Building the Fourth Estate*, 35; Burkholder, *La red*, 141, 163; Castillo, *La biografía secreta*, 29, 203; *Proceso* (Scherer cover story), Jan. 11, 2015, pp. 38, 47, 65.

27. Campbell, in Ana María Serna, *"Se solicitan reporteros,"* 200.

28. Alejandro Junco, "Newspaper Publishing in Mexico Is a Perilous Business," *Presstime*, April 1989, p. 42, and *Wall Street Journal*, Dec. 4, 1992, p. A7; Payán, *Memorial del viento*.

29. Leñero, "Treinta y cinco"; *Proceso*, Jan. 11, 2015, pp. 41, 69–70, 75, 80–81, 84; Campbell, in Ana María Serna, *"Se solicitan reporteros,"* 201–2.

30. Krauze (quoting Paz), "Proceso a *Proceso*," p. 219.

31. Humberto Musacchio, in Ana María Serna, *"Se solicitan reporteros,"* 222; *Proceso*, Jan. 11, 2015.

32. Castillo, *La biografía secreta*, 131–32; cf. Levario Turcott, *Primera plana*, 109, 150–51, 173–75.

33. Trejo, quoted in Castillo, *La biografía secreta*, 156–57.

34. Trejo Delarbre, "Democracia por escrito," 194; José Reveles, interview, Mexico City, Feb. 27, 2020; Eduardo García, email to the author, Oct. 26, 2020.

35. *Proceso*, Jan. 9, Jan. 16, Jan. 23, Jan. 30, Feb. 6, 1995.

36. *Proceso*, Nov. 6, 1976, p. 5, Jan. 11, 2015, p. 60; Daniel Moreno, interview, Mexico City, May 24, 2019; María Scherer Ibarra, interview, Mexico City, Dec. 16, 2021; Anne Marie Mergier, conversation with the author, Paris, May 21, 2022. On Mergier: García, *Ellas, tecleando su historia*, 218–31.

37. Viétnika Batres, interview (via videocall), Oct. 23, 2020; Carlos Marín, interview, Mexico City, July 10, 2024.

38. Arellano Mora, "¿La publicidad oficial?" 103–9, 152–56; Benavides, *"Gacetilla,"* 95; *Proceso 30 años*, Oct. 2006, p. 228.

39. Oster, *Mexicans*, 188–89; *Proceso 30 años*, Oct. 2006, p. 228.

40. Lawson, *Building the Fourth Estate*, 67; Campbell, in Ana María Serna, *"Se solicitan reporteros,"* 201; *Los Angeles Times*, Apr. 18, 1999, p. 26; Álvaro Delgado, interview, Mexico City, Sept. 23, 2021.

41. *Bajo Palabra*, July 1, pp. 6–9, July 16, pp. 15–16, Aug. 1, pp. 14–17, Sept. 1, 2000, pp. 42–44; cf. Castillo, *La biografía secreta*, 443–44.

42. *Reforma*, Oct. 3, 1995, p. 1.

43. Esquivel Hernández, *Reforma*, 168; *Reforma*, Sept. 28, 1995, p. 1.

44. Oppenheimer, *Bordering on Chaos*, 43, 266–67; González, *Escenas del periodismo mexicano*, 202–3.

45. González, *Escenas del periodismo mexicano*, 203; *Proceso*, Oct. 9, 1995, pp. 6–7, 18–19.

46. González, *Escenas del periodismo mexicano*, 203.

47. Levario Turcott, *Primera plana*; cf. Rubio, "Coping with Political Change," 27–28; Riva Palacio, *La prensa*, 244n39.

48. Levario Turcott, *Primera plana*, 46–50, 60–62, 221–24, 227–33.

49. Riva Palacio, *La prensa*, 244n39.

50. González, *Escenas del periodismo mexicano*, 205; *Los Angeles Times*, Dec. 7, 1997, p. 1; Daniel Moreno, interview, Mexico City, June 21, 2019; Raymundo Riva Palacio, interview, Mexico City, Oct. 21, 2021; anonymous former *Reforma* editor, interview, Dec. 12, 2023.

51. Former *El Financiero* reporter, interview, Mexico City, May 2019; Daniel Moreno, interview, Mexico City, June 21, 2019; Ignacio Rodriguez Reyna, interview, Mexico City, Oct. 19, 2021; Ernesto Núñez, interview, Mexico City, Dec. 15, 2021.

52. Ciro Gómez Leyva, interview, Mexico City, Sept. 21, 2021.

53. Daniela Pastrana, interview (via videocall), Mar. 25, 2021; Arturo Cano, interview, Mexico City, Dec. 16, 2021.

54. Alejandro Páez, interview, Mexico City, Oct. 19, 2021.

55. Julia Preston and Dillon, *Opening Mexico*, 393–401, 557; *Reforma*, Mar. 25, p. 6, Mar. 26, p. 6, Mar. 27, p. 4, June 3, pp. 1, 4, Aug. 19, 1998, pp. 1, 7; René Delgado, interview, Mexico City, Feb. 1, 2023.

56. Hughes, *Newsrooms in Conflict*, 57–58.

57. Arce Barceló, "Análisis del periódico mexicano," 358; Hughes, *Newsrooms in Conflict*, 118; *New York Times*, Jan. 3, 1999, p. 3; *Washington Post*, June 22, 2000, p. 20; Lawson, *Building the Fourth Estate*, 224–25; Esquivel Hernández, *Reforma*, 8.

58. Levario Turcott, *Primera plana*, 156–63, 257–95; Hughes, *Newsrooms in Conflict*, 83, 143; Riva Palacio, *La prensa*, 244n39; Roberto Rock, interview, Mexico City, Oct. 19, 2021.

59. *El Universal*, May 3, 1995, p. 1; Carlos Salinas de Gortari, interview, London, June 29, 2021.

60. Rodríguez Castañeda, *Prensa vendida*, 361–62; Álvaro Delgado, interview, Mexico City, Sept. 23, 2021; Roberto Rock, interview, Mexico City, Oct. 19, 2021.

61. The sketch of Rock and his editorship draws on Riva Palacio, *La prensa*, 166–67; Hughes, *Newsrooms in Conflict*, 24, 126–27, 139–46; Ana María Serna, *"Se solicitan reporteros,"* 321–44; interviews with Jorge Zepeda Patterson, Mexico City, Nov. 14, 2019; Raymundo Riva Palacio, Mexico City, Sept. 21, 2021; Roberto Rock, Mexico City, Sept. 22 and Oct. 19, 2021; Claudia Fernández (via telephone), May 2, 2021; and Marco Lara Klahr (via videocall), Feb. 10, 2022.

62. The account of the tax fraud case against Ealy draws on Orme, introduction, 1–2; Levario Turcott, *Primera plana*, 38–46; Hughes, *Newsrooms in Conflict*, 143–45; González, *Escenas del periodismo mexicano*, 37–38; *El Universal*, Sept. 13, 1996, p. 1; *New York Times*, Sept. 14, 1996, p. 5, Aug. 27, 1997, p. 5; and Roberto Rock, interview, Mexico City, Sept. 22, 2021.

63. Lawson, *Building the Fourth Estate*, 90; Hughes, *Newsrooms in Conflict*, 137; anonymous former politician, interview, June 2021; anonymous former *El Universal* editors, interviews, Sept. and Oct. 2021.

64. Castillo, *La biografía secreta*, 189f, 292; "Mexican Press Still on the Take," *Nieman Reports*, Fall 1997, p. 76; anonymous *Reforma* editor, interview, Dec. 2022.

65. Scherer García and Monsiváis, *Tiempo de saber*, 284, 288; Moncada, *Oficio de muerte*, 198, 201–6, 212; Antonio Ocaranza, interview, Mexico City, May 10, 2019.

66. *El Universal*, Aug. 8–Sept. 12, 1996.

67. *Proceso*, Mar. 20, 1995, Aug. 27, 1995, Mar. 31, 1996; Arellano Mora, "¿La publicidad oficial?," 154.

68. World Values Survey, Wave 3 (1995–98), www.worldvaluessurvey.org.

69. Riva Palacio, *La prensa*, 165; *El Universal*, Jan. 12, 1999, p. 1; Claudia Fernández, interview (via telephone), May 2, 2021; Roberto Rock, interview, Mexico City, Oct. 19, 2021.

70. *El Universal*, Sept. 30, 1999, p. 1.

71. Levario Turcott, *Primera plana*, 47, 69–70, 86–88, 123, 161–63, 202, 263–64, 267, 273–74, 283, 286, 294–95, 319–20, 339–40, 387. On Salinas as favorite villain, see "The Man Mexico Loves to Hate; Salinas," BaltimoreSun.com, Apr. 7, 1999.

72. Riva Palacio, *La prensa*, 82–84, 165–67, 171; González, *Escenas del periodismo mexicano*, 38–39; Hughes, *Newsrooms in Conflict*, 61–66, 125–27, 141–42; *New York Times*, Jan. 3, 1999, p. 3; Jorge Zepeda Patterson, interview, Mexico City, Nov. 14, 2019; Claudia Fernández, interview (via telephone), May 2, 2021; Roberto Rock, interview, Mexico City, Oct. 19, 2021.

73. The account of the schism of 1999 at *Proceso* draws on Scherer García, *Vivir*, 89–98; Rodríguez Munguía, "*Proceso*, la ruptura"; Raymundo Riva Palacio, "Regresa Julio Scherer," *Milenio Semanal*, Apr. 5, 1999, p. 6; *Los Angeles Times*, Apr. 18, 1999, p. 26; interviews with María Scherer Ibarra, Mexico City, Feb. 14, 2020; anonymous *Proceso* veteran, Oct. 29, 2020; Carlos Puig, Mexico City, Sept. 22, 2021; Margarita Carreón (via telephone), Jan. 4, 2022; Carlos Marín, Mexico City, July 10, 2024.

74. *Milenio Semanal*, Sept. 1, 1997, p. 2 (directory), Feb. 2, 1998 (cover); *La Jornada*, June 27, 1999, p. 46; Federico Arreola, "Milenio, aquel periodista estalinista y la cena en casa de Riva Palacio con AMLO" and "Sí, tiene derecho López-Gatell a pachanguear en la playa," SDPNoticias.com, Jan. 1, 2020, Jan. 4, 2021; Federico Arreola and Raymundo Riva Palacio, interviews, Mexico City, Oct. 21, 2021.

75. *Milenio Semanal*, June 29, 1998, pp. 16–17.

76. *Proceso*, Jan. 7, 1980, July 20, 1997, July 27, 1997, Mar. 1, 1998 (all are cover stories). On Marín: Scherer García, *Vivir*, 91; Núñez Jaime, *Carlos Marín*, 16–21, 40–42, 178–79; *El Universal*, Aug. 18, 2021, p. 9.

77. *Proceso*, "Edición Especial: Testimonios de Tlatelolco," Oct. 1998.

78. Scherer García, *Vivir*, 89–98; Raymundo Riva Palacio, interview, Mexico City, Sept. 21, 2021.

79. Rodríguez Munguía, "*Proceso*, la ruptura," 31.

80. Rodríguez Munguía, "*Proceso*, la ruptura," 31.

81. Rodríguez Munguía, "*Proceso*, la ruptura," 35.

82. Rodríguez Munguía, "*Proceso*, la ruptura"; Julia Preston and Dillon, *Opening Mexico*, chaps. 9, 11, 12; Krauze, "Proceso a *Proceso*," 214–15, 218.

83. Núñez Jaime, *Carlos Marín*, 163, 179; *Milenio Semanal*, Mar. 29, 1999, pp. 36–37 (cf. Apr. 5, 1999, pp. 24–26); Ricardo Sevilla, "Carlos Marín: El enemigo de sí mismo," Polemon.mx, Jan. 22, 2020.

84. *Reforma*, Mar. 29, 1999, p. B1; *Los Angeles Times*, Apr. 18, 1999, p. 26.

85. Castillo, *La biografía secreta*, 36–37, 408, 413–15; "Las glorias pasadas de 'Proceso': Entrevista con Moisés Castillo," Etcetera.com.mx, March 2019; Carlos Puig, interview, Mexico City, Sept. 22, 2021; Álvaro Delgado, interview, Mexico City, Sept. 23, 2021; Raymundo Riva Palacio, interview, Mexico City, Oct. 21, 2021.

86. The story of *Proceso*'s renewal in 1999–2000 draws on Castillo, *La biografía secreta*, 339–56, 455–56; Scherer Ibarra, "Revista *Proceso*," 90–96; and interviews with Rafael Rodríguez Castañeda (via videocall), Jan. 1, 2022; anonymous *Proceso* veteran, Nov. 2019; María Scherer Ibarra, Mexico City, Feb. 14, 2020, and Dec. 16, 2021; Margarita Carreón (via telephone), Jan. 4, 2022; and Jorge Carrasco, Mexico City, Mar. 23, 2023.

87. Ortiz Pinchetti, and Ortiz Pardo, *El fenómeno Fox*, 63.

88. Ortiz Pinchetti and Ortiz Pardo, *El fenómeno Fox*, 59–66, 193–99; Julia Preston and Dillon, *Opening Mexico*, 490–91; Kuschik, "Las encuestas"; *Proceso*, Apr. 9, 2000.

89. *Proceso*, June 27, 1999; Julia Preston and Dillon, *Opening Mexico*, 380–82.

90. Margarita Carreón, interview (via telephone), Jan. 4, 2022.

Chapter 6

1. Sánchez Ruiz, "El público de la prensa," 168–71; Lawson, *Building the Fourth Estate*, 61, chap. 7; Levario Turcott, "¿Crisis en *La Jornada*?"; Margarita Carreón, interview (via telephone), Jan. 4, 2022.

2. Granados Chapa, *Buendía*; Smith, *Dope*, chap. 19; Alcalá, *Red privada*; Héctor Aguilar Camín, "Manuel Buendía y los idus de mayo," *Nexos*, July 1984, pp. 5–9.

3. On Denegri, see Luis Gutiérrez, in Ana María Serna, "Se solicitan reporteros," 260–62, 271; and Enrique Serna, *El vendedor de silencio*.

4. Moncada Ochoa, *Oficio de muerte*, 133–34; Aguilar Camín, "Manuel Buendía"; Rodríguez Castañeda, *Prensa vendida*, 246; De la Rosa, "Manuel Buendía."

5. Musacchio, *Granados Chapa*, 133–36; González, *Escenas del periodismo mexicano*, 147–50; Arce Barceló, "Análisis del periódico mexicano," 350; *La Jornada*, Dec. 4, 2020, p. 17; Humberto Musacchio, interview, Mexico City, June 18, 2019.

6. Rodríguez Castañeda, *Prensa vendida*, 240–41; Musacchio, *Granados Chapa*, 135–37; Granados Chapa, in Ana María Serna, "Se solicitan reporteros," 169–70; Humberto Musacchio, interview, Mexico City, June 18, 2019.

7. Riding, *Distant Neighbors*, 302; Scherer García and Monsiváis, *Tiempo de saber*, 233; José Carreño Carlón, interview, Mexico City, Oct. 18, 2019; Héctor Aguilar Camín, interview (via videocall), May 2, 2024.

8. Riva Palacio, *La prensa*, 73; Musacchio, *Granados Chapa*, 135; García, *Ellas, tecleando su historia*, 187–90.

9. Héctor Aguilar Camín, "Pasaje de ida" (unpublished manuscript, [2024]); Arturo Cano, interview, Mexico City, July 10, 2024.

10. González, *Escenas del periodismo mexicano*, 143–50; Hughes, *Newsrooms in Conflict*, 114–15, 251n12; *La Jornada*, Nov. 23, 2019, p. 4; Juan Angulo, interview, Mexico City, Apr. 5, 2019; Viétnika Batres, interview (via videocall), Oct. 23, 2020.

11. The sketch of Payán draws on González, *Escenas del periodismo mexicano*, 95, 155–56, 168–70; Musacchio, *Granados Chapa*, 159–69; Granados Chapa and Gutiérrez, in Ana María Serna, *"Se solicitan reporteros,"* 169–74, 280–81; report on the founding of *La Jornada*, Aug. 15, 1984, Manuel Becerra Acosta: Versión Pública, AGN, DFS, Caja 3; "Carlos Payán Velver: Doctor honoris causa," Universidad de Guadalajara, 2013, www.udg.mx/sites/default/files/brochure_payan_cs.pdf; *La Jornada*, July 15, 2018, p. 7; Humberto Musacchio, interview, Mexico City, June 18, 2019; and Sara Lovera, interview (via videocall), Jan. 28, 2021.

12. Sara Lovera, interview (via videocall), Jan. 28, 2021.

13. Rodríguez Castañeda, *Prensa vendida*, 292, 366; Oppenheimer, *Bordering on Chaos*, 135, 138; González, *Escenas del periodismo mexicano*, 155–56; Granados Chapa, in Ana María Serna, *"Se solicitan reporteros,"* 170–71.

14. González, *Escenas del periodismo mexicano*, 150; Arce Barceló, "Análisis del periódico mexicano," 399; *La Jornada*, Nov. 21, 1984, pp. 1, 3, 19–21, 32; Nov. 22, pp. 1, 4–5, 32; Nov. 27, p. 32.

15. Morales Flores, "25 años de fotografiar"; *La Jornada*, May 25, 1985, pp. 1, 6, 9.

16. Fernández and Paxman, *El Tigre*, 319–20; Julia Preston and Dillon, *Opening Mexico*, 100–101; William Orme, interview (via videocall), Feb. 27, 2021.

17. Freije, *Citizens of Scandal*, 139, 161–63; cf. Secanella, *El periodismo*, 109–17.

18. Walker, *Waking from the Dream*, 197; *La Jornada*, Sept. 19, 1984, p. 1.

19. Lawson, *Building the Fourth Estate*, 125, 132–37; Julia Preston and Dillon, *Opening Mexico*, 110.

20. *La Jornada*, Sept. 20, 1985, pp. 18–19 (photo spread), Sept. 23, 1985, p. 1; Morales Flores, "25 años de fotografiar."

21. Freije, *Citizens of Scandal*, 146–51, 243n30.

22. Poniatowska, *Nada, nadie* ("The state . . . ," 182); Julia Preston and Dillon, *Opening Mexico*, 109–11; Freije, *Citizens of Scandal*, 159–65.

23. Rodríguez Castañeda, *Prensa vendida*, 266–67; Lawson, *Building the Fourth Estate*, 42; González, *Escenas del periodismo mexicano*, 43–44; anonymous former *El Universal* editor, interview, Mexico City, Oct. 2019; Raúl Trejo Delarbre, interview (via videocall), Nov. 15, 2023.

24. Freije, *Citizens of Scandal*, 2, 138–39, 165–66.

25. González, *Escenas del periodismo mexicano*, 150–51; Freije, *Citizens of Scandal*, chap. 5; *La Jornada*, Sept. 17, pp. 1, 4–9, Sept. 19, 1995, "Perfil" (supplement).

26. Arce Barceló, "Análisis del periódico mexicano," 375–76.

27. Trejo Delarbre, *Mediocracia sin mediaciones*, 204–6 (all percentages are rounded); Rodríguez Castañeda, *Prensa vendida*, 291–92; Lawson, *Building the Fourth Estate*, 57.

28. Julia Preston and Dillon, *Opening Mexico*, 157–58, 533n157–58; "Encuesta" (supplement), *La Jornada*, July 5, 1988; Miguel Basáñez, interview, Mexico City, Nov. 7, 2023.

29. *La Jornada*, July 7, 1988, p. 1.

30. Trejo Delarbre, *Mediocracia sin mediaciones*, 207, 219–20.

31. Oppenheimer, *Bordering on Chaos*, 138; Hughes, *Newsrooms in Conflict*, 204–5; *La Jornada*, Sept. 2, 1985, p. 1; cf. *La Jornada*, Sept. 2, 1986; Sept. 2, 1987; Nov. 2, 1989; Nov. 2, 1990; Nov. 2, 1991; Nov. 2, 1992; Nov. 2, 1993; Sept. 2, 1995.

32. Lawson, *Building the Fourth Estate*, 57. On anti-Americanism in Mexican cartoons (including El Fisgón), see Morris, *Gringolandia*, chap. 4.

33. González, *Escenas del periodismo mexicano*, 165–68; Arce Barceló, "Análisis del periódico mexicano," 377.

34. Musacchio, in Ana María Serna, *"Se solicitan reporteros,"* 224–25; Musacchio, *Granados Chapa*, 151–52; Juan Angulo, interview, Mexico City, April 5, 2019; Humberto Musacchio, interview, Mexico City, June 18, 2019.

35. Morales Flores, "25 años."

36. Julia Preston and Dillon, *Opening Mexico*, 419–22; *La Jornada*, Sept. 6, p. 6, Sept. 8, 1988, p. 2.

37. Julia Preston and Dillon, *Opening Mexico*, 209–10; Lawson, *Building the Fourth Estate*, 32; *Christian Science Monitor*, Mar. 22, 1993, p. 6.

38. Lawson, *Building the Fourth Estate*, 57, 70–71; Humberto Musacchio, interview, Mexico City, June 18, 2019.

39. Musacchio, *Granados Chapa*, 159–69; González, *Escenas del periodismo mexicano*, 166; Rodríguez Castañeda, *Prensa vendida*, 365–66; *La Jornada*, Nov. 12, 1992, p. 11.

40. Granados Chapa, in Ana María Serna, *"Se solicitan reporteros,"* 173–74; Humberto Musacchio, interview, Mexico City, June 18, 2019.

41. Riva Palacio, "Culture of Collusion," 32; Riva Palacio, *La prensa*, 77; Lawson, *Building the Fourth Estate*, 79; Musacchio, *Granados Chapa*, 173–74.

42. Lawson, *Building the Fourth Estate*, 57, 70–71; Salinas de Gortari, *México*, 817; *La Jornada*, Jan. 2, 1994, pp. 1, 2; Humberto Musacchio, interview, Mexico City, June 18, 2019; anonymous informant, interview, June 2021.

43. Genoveva Flores Quintero, *La seducción*, 87–88, 153, 252; *La Jornada*, Jan. 19, 1994; "Perfil" (supplement), *La Jornada*, Jan. 21, p. 13, Feb. 23, 1994, pp. 1, 6, 16.

44. Sarmiento, "Trial by Fire," 35–36; Levario Turcott, "¿Crisis en *La Jornada*?"; Hughes, *Newsrooms in Conflict*, 117–18 (cf. 57–58); Arce Barceló, "Análisis del periódico mexicano," 379–82; *La Jornada*, Jan. 13, 1994, p. 1.

45. Sarmiento, "Trial by Fire," 37; García, *Ellas, tecleando su historia*, 165–79; report on the founding of *La Jornada*, Aug. 15, 1984, Manuel Becerra Acosta: Versión Pública, AGN, DFS, Caja 3.

46. Oppenheimer, *Bordering on Chaos*, 65; *La Jornada*, Feb. 5, pp. 1, 6–7, Feb. 6, pp. 1, 6–7, Feb. 7, pp. 1, 8–9, Feb. 8, 1994, pp. 1, 8–9.

47. Flores Quintero, *La seducción*, 85–88, 140.

48. Ross, *War against Oblivion*, 3; Flores Quintero, *La seducción*, 264; "Chiapas: Reprimidos y premiados," CGTChiapas.org, Aug. 18, 2010.

49. Galaz Ramírez, *Los primeros veinte*, 178–83 (1994), 284 (1995–98).

50. Oppenheimer, *Bordering on Chaos*, 135, 138; Lawson, *Building the Fourth Estate*, 57; *La Jornada*, June 27, July 11, 22, 23, 30, Aug. 2, 4, 9, 10, 11, 15, 16 (page 1 *gacetillas* about Zedillo); *La Jornada*, June 15, pp. 16, 22, June 24, p. 44, July 2, p. 37, July 17, p. 19, July 30, p. 20, Aug. 5, p. 41, Aug. 13, p. 24, Aug. 14, p. 24, Sept. 1, p. 14, Sept. 8, p. 38, Sept. 19, p. 22, 1994 (Tabasco coverage).

51. Hughes, *Newsrooms in Conflict*, 5–7, 13.

52. Crovi et al., *Periodismo digital en México*, 75; Arce Barceló, "Análisis del periódico mexicano," 409, 439.

53. *El Chamuco*, Feb. 14, 1996; Hernández, "El Chamuco," Mi Blog Tamaño Carta, Feb. 25, 2009, http://monerohernandez.blogspot.com; *La Jornada*, Mar. 3, 2012, p. 6.

54. Minnesota Advocates for Human Rights, *Massacre in Mexico*; Lawson, *Building the Fourth Estate*, 138, 150, 154–55.

55. Levario Turcott, "¿Crisis en *La Jornada*?," p. 5.

56. González, *Escenas del periodismo mexicano*, 162–63.

57. Lawson, *Building the Fourth Estate*, 157–70; González, *Escenas del periodismo mexicano*, 161–62; *La Jornada*, July 7, 1997, p. 1.

58. Quinones, *True Tales*, 182; Lawson, *Building the Fourth Estate*, 213, 238n70; Wilbert Torre, interview, Mexico City, Oct. 16, 2019; Sam Quinones, interview (via telephone), July 31, 2020.

59. The sketch of Lira and her leadership draws on Monsiváis, *A ustedes les consta*, 295–308, 361; González, *Escenas del periodismo mexicano*, 166–70; Granados Chapa, Luis Gutiérrez Rodríguez, and Raúl Trejo Delarbre in Ana María Serna, "*Se solicitan reporteros*," 174–75, 280–81, 301–2; report on the founding of *La Jornada*, Aug. 15, 1984, Manuel Becerra Acosta: Versión Pública, AGN, DFS, Caja 3; Humberto Musacchio, interview, Mexico City, June 18, 2019; and Sergio Aguayo, interview, Mexico City, Dec. 16, 2021.

60. The sketch of Aguayo draws on Oppenheimer, *Bordering on Chaos*, 170–71; Julia Preston and Dillon, *Opening Mexico*, 86–87, 208–10, 236–38; González, *Escenas del periodismo mexicano*, 166–67; and Sergio Aguayo, interviews, Mexico City, Dec. 16, 2021, and via videocall, Feb. 10, 2022.

61. *La Jornada*, July 21, 1987, pp. 10, 32, Sept. 13, 1989, pp. 1, 8, Aug. 25, 1991, p. 17, Apr. 27, 1994, pp. 1, 10; cf. Julia Preston and Dillon, *Opening Mexico*, 209–14.

62. Sergio Aguayo, interview, Mexico City, Dec. 16, 2021.

63. *La Jornada*, Sept. 18, 1996, p. 8.

64. See, e.g., Article 19 and Fundar, *El costo* and *Contar "lo bueno."*

65. Aguayo Quezada, *1968*; Aguayo Quezada, *La charola*.

66. Grayson, *Mexican Messiah*, 146–47, 156.

67. Alberto Nájar, interview, Mexico City, Sept. 20, 2021; Arturo Cano, interview, Mexico City, Dec. 16, 2021.

68. "Luis Hernández Navarro," in Llopis, *Plumas rebeldes*; Hernández Navarro, "Acteal"; *La Jornada*, Masiosare, Dec. 14, 1997.

69. Arturo Cano, interview, Mexico City, Dec. 16, 2021.

70. Riva Palacio, *La prensa*, 172; González, *Escenas del periodismo mexicano*, 169–70; Hughes, *Newsrooms in Conflict*, 61–63, 68, 204–5; Levario Turcott, "¿Crisis en *La Jornada*?," p. 5; Alberto Nájar, interview, Mexico City, Sept. 20, 2021.

71. Levario Turcott, "¿Crisis en *La Jornada*?"; Granados Chapa, in Ana María *Serna*, "*Se solicitan reporteros*," 172–74; anonymous *La Jornada* veteran, interview, Sept. 2021.

72. Sara Lovera, interview (via videocall), Jan. 28, 2021; Alberto Nájar, interview, Mexico City, Sept. 20, 2021.

73. González, *Escenas del periodismo mexicano*, 170; García, *Ellas, tecleando su historia*, 141–42, 145, 183; and interviews with Daniela Pastrana (via videocall), Mar. 25, 2021; Alberto Nájar, Mexico City, Sept. 20, 2021; and Héctor Aguilar Camín (via videocall), May 2, 2024.

74. *La Jornada*, June 16, 1997, p. 1 and "Perfil" (supplement); Ricardo Cayuela Gally, "ETA y La Jornada," *Letras Libres*, Jan. 2012, pp. 40–44.

75. García, *Ellas, tecleando su historia*, 144–45, 183, 212–13, 243–44; Levario Turcott, "¿Crisis en *La Jornada*?"

76. González, *Escenas del periodismo mexicano*, 167–68; Jean Meyer, conversation with the author, Mexico City, Feb. 7, 2019; anonymous Monsiváis confidant, interview, Dec. 2, 2020.

77. Anonymous *La Jornada* veteran, interview, Oct. 2020.

78. Pew Research Center, *What the World Thinks*, 55; Riva Palacio, *La prensa*, 173; *La Jornada*, Sept. 13, 2001, p. 5.

79. García, *Ellas, tecleando su historia*, 243–44; *La Jornada*, Aug. 11, 2016, p. 10. As of this writing (May 2025) Lira, at age 82, remains *La Jornada*'s editor in chief.

80. Julia Preston and Dillon, *Opening Mexico*, 274–79, 296–97, 496–500.

81. Trejo Delarbre, *Mediocracia sin mediaciones*, 387–404, 422–27, 446–63; Julia Preston and Dillon, *Opening Mexico*, 489–96; Fernández and Paxman, *El Tigre*, 596–600; "Adiós al PRI" (PAN campaign ad), 2000, www.youtube.com/watch?v=rbw00Rn69a8.

82. Julia Preston and Dillon, *Opening Mexico*, 477–79, 500; Trejo Delarbre, *Mediocracia sin mediaciones*, 445.

83. Estrada, *La ley de Herodes*; José Martínez, *Las enseñanzas del profesor*; Fernández and Paxman, *El Tigre*.

84. "Mexican Press Still on the Take," *Nieman Reports*, Fall 1997, p. 76.

85. On the presidential debate: Trejo Delarbre, *Mediocracia sin mediaciones*, 403, 426. On the rise of civic-minded talk radio as of 1985: Lawson, *Building the Fourth Estate*, 99–103.

86. Lara Klahr, *Diarismo*, 190; *Reforma*, Mar. 20, 1998, p. 6; Raúl Trejo Delarbre, email to the author, July 30, 2024.

87. *Crónica*, Dec. 8, 1997, p. 1, Jan. 27, 1999, p. 1; Daniel Moreno, interview, Mexico City, Mar. 23, 2023.

88. On the story of *Milenio*, see "'Towel-Gate' and the *Milenio* Dream" in chapter 7.

89. Fernández and Paxman, *El Tigre*, 551, 598–600; Trejo Delarbre, *Mediocracia sin mediaciones*, 448–51; Levario Turcott, *Primera plana*, 165–71; Hughes, *Newsrooms in Conflict*, 179–81.

90. Ward and Durden, "Government and Democracy," 32, 34; Lara Klahr, *Diarismo*, 191–94.

91. Arce Barceló, "Análisis del periódico mexicano," 344; anonymous *La Jornada* veteran, interview, Oct. 2020; Alberto Nájar, interview, Mexico City, Sept. 20, 2021.

Chapter 7

1. Julia Preston and Dillon, *Opening Mexico*, 15–16; *Los Angeles Times*, July 5, 2001, p. 11.

2. The story of Martha Sahagún and "towel-gate" draws on Riva Palacio, *La prensa*, 177–78; García, *Ellas, tecleando su historia*, 113–16; *Milenio*, June 19, 2001, p. 1; Raymundo Riva Palacio, interview, Mexico City, Oct. 21, 2021; and María Scherer Ibarra, interview, Mexico City, Dec. 16, 2021.

3. Wornat, *La jefa*; Hernández and Quintero, *La familia presidencial*; Tuckman, *Mexico*, 63–64, 196–97.

4. Morris, *Political Corruption in Mexico*, 258.

5. The sketch of Anabel Hernández draws on García, *Ellas, tecleando su historia*, 107–19; *Dirty Money*, season 1, episode 4, "Cartel Bank," dir. Kristi Jacobson, aired January 26, 2018, on Netflix; and former colleagues of Hernández, interviews, 2019–21.

6. *Dirty Money*, season 1, episode 4, "Cartel Bank," directed by Kristi Jacobson, aired January 26, 2018, on Netflix.

7. *Reforma*, Feb. 26, 1994, p. B1; Mar. 10, 1994, p. B8; Mar. 26, 1994, p. B5; June 9, 1995, p. B1; June 11, 1995, p. B1.

8. Morris, *Political Corruption in Mexico*, 58–60, 247–68 (appendix B).

9. Riding, *Distant Neighbors*, chap. 6; Morris, *Corruption and Politics*, chap. 6.

10. *Los Angeles Times*, July 5, 2001, p. 11; *Guardian*, Nov. 10, 2001, p. 15.

11. The sketch of the González family and Multimedios draws on Toussaint, *Recuento de periódicos fronterizos*, 92–96; Hernández Ramírez, "Franquicias periodísticas," 81–83; "Grupo Multimedios," Media Ownership Monitor Mexico, https://mexico.mom-rsf.org; "'La vida me llamó a la radio,'" Milenio.com, Sept. 14, 2020; and interviews with Jorge Zepeda Patterson, Mexico City, June 19, 2019; José Luis Esquivel Hernández, Monterrey, Oct. 2, 2019, and via email, Sept. 9, 2021; Carlos Puig, Mexico City, Sept. 22, 2021; and Federico Arreola, Mexico City, Oct. 21, 2021.

12. Former *Milenio* employee, interview, Sept. 2021.

13. Hernández Ramírez, "Franquicias periodísticas," 82; *Milenio*, Oct. 2, 2006, p. 25, Feb. 20, 2017, "La Afición," p. 10, Oct. 23, 2018, p. 33.

14. The estimate is that of the paper's first general director (or publisher), Federico Arreola; Arreola, interview, Mexico City, Aug. 26, 2022.

15. Julia Preston and Dillon, *Opening Mexico*, 495, cf. 487.

16. Núñez Jaime, *Carlos Marín*, 67–94, 151.

17. The sketch of Riva Palacio draws on Lawson, *Building the Fourth Estate*, 35–38, 87; Téllez Cuevas, "Los Riva Palacio"; *Etcétera*, July 2014, pp. 34–42; and interviews with Raymundo Riva Palacio, Mexico City, Feb. 27, 2020, Sept. 21, 2021, Oct. 21, 2021; Rosa Elba Arroyo, Mexico City, Dec. 10, 2019; Federico Arreola, Mexico City, Aug. 26, 2022; and anonymous former colleagues of Riva Palacio, 2019–21.

18. "Knight Latin American Nieman Fellows," Nieman.harvard.edu.

19. Riva Palacio, *Más allá de los límites*; Riva Palacio, *Manual para un nuevo periodismo*; Mirna Servín, conversation with the author, Mexico City, Jan. 22, 2024.

20. Rosa Elba Arroyo, interview, Mexico City, Dec. 10, 2019.

21. Hernández Ramírez, "Franquicias periodísticas," 92–93.

22. *Milenio*, Jan. 2, 3, 4, 12, 2000, p. 1.

23. *Milenio*, Feb. 6, 2000, pp. 1, 4, 5; *Los Angeles Times*, July 9, 2012, p. 1; Carlos Marín, interview, Mexico City, July 10, 2024.

24. Núñez Jaime, *Carlos Marín*, 156; Levario Turcott, "¿Crisis en *La Jornada*?"; Alberto Nájar, interview, Mexico City, Sept. 20, 2021; Raymundo Riva Palacio, interview, Mexico City, Oct. 21, 2021.

25. Núñez Jaime, *Carlos Marín*, 113, 148–49; Raymundo Riva Palacio, interview, Mexico City, Oct. 21, 2021.

26. Raymundo Riva Palacio, interview, Mexico City, Oct. 21, 2021.

27. Núñez Jaime, *Carlos Marín*, 140, 149–50, 155; Federico Arreola and Raymundo Riva Palacio, interviews, Mexico City, Oct. 21, 2021; Carlos Marín, interview, Mexico City, July 7, 2024.

28. Hernández and Quintero, *La familia presidencial*, 90–92.

29. Andrés Ruiz, quoted in Núñez Jaime, *Carlos Marín*, 149 (cf. 35); Raymundo Riva Palacio, interview, Mexico City, Aug. 28, 2024.

30. *Milenio*, Mar. 28, 2005, p. 1; Federico Arreola, interview, Mexico City, Oct. 21, 2021; Daniel Moreno, interview, Mexico City, Mar. 24, 2023.

31. *Proceso*, Apr. 3, 2005, pp. 22–23; *Milenio*, May 2, 2005, p. 1; Federico Arreola, interview, Mexico City, Oct. 21, 2021.

32. Núñez Jaime, *Carlos Marín*, 42, 94, 163; Castillo, *La biografía secreta*, 33–35, 454.

33. Zepeda Patterson put *La Jornada* circulation at 50,000 and the capital edition of *Milenio* at around 20,000; Zepeda Patterson, "La prensa en México o la soberbia de la víctima," *Cuadernos de periodistas* [Madrid], Jan. 2005, p. 149.

34. Núñez Jaime, *Carlos Marín*, 19–20, 33, 125, 129; Scherer García, *Vivir*, 91; Ricardo Sevilla, "Carlos Marín: El enemigo de sí mismo," Polemon.mx, Jan. 22, 2020; interviews with Carlos Puig, Mexico City, Sept. 22, 2021; Raymundo Riva Palacio, Mexico City, Oct. 21, 2021; Carlos Marín, Mexico City, July 10, 2024.

35. Daniel Moreno, interview, Mexico City, Mar. 24, 2023.

36. *Milenio*, May 8, 2005, p. 1.

37. Francisco Arreola, interview, Mexico City, Aug. 26, 2022.

38. Anonymous interview, Mexico City, Mar. 2023.

39. Grecko, *Killing the Story*, 108–10, 151–52; Sevilla, "Carlos Marín"; Raymundo Riva Palacio, interview, Mexico City, Oct. 21, 2021; Federico Arreola, interview, Mexico City, Aug. 28, 2022.

40. Núñez Jaime, *Carlos Marín*, 28–32, 39, 104–9; Sevilla, "Carlos Marín."

41. Milenio TV may have lost money too, but it likely served more effectively to curry favor with the PRI. Gómez Leyva later became chief anchor at Imagen TV.

42. Núñez Jaime, *Carlos Marín*, 28, 39, 102–24, 155–57.

43. Núñez Jaime, *Carlos Marín*, 150; Federico Arreola, interview, Mexico City, Aug. 26, 2022.

44. Moncada Ochoa, *Oficio de muerte*, 198–213, 306–7; *Reforma*, Sept. 6, 1997, p. 1; Lázaro Ríos, email to the author, Dec. 20, 2023.

45. Hughes, *Newsrooms in Conflict*, 116; Julia Preston and Dillon, *Opening Mexico*, 506, 508–9, 514–15; Moreno, "Big Missing Link," 162–63.

46. Rodríguez Castañeda, *Prensa vendida*, 165, 234, 288; Julián Vázquez and Carmen de la Rosa, "A 8 Columnas," Premio Nacional de Periodismo, 2002, 41–48, www.periodismo.org.mx/assets/historia.pdf.

47. Ivonne Melgar, "Rubén Aguilar, vocero de Anaya," Excélsior.com.mx, Mar. 15, 2018; interviews with Rubén Aguilar, Mexico City, May 9, 2019; Roberto Rock, Mexico City, Oct. 19, 2021; Lázaro Ríos (via videocall), Dec. 12, 2023.

48. Riva Palacio, *La prensa*, 181; Hughes, *Newsrooms in Conflict*, 137; Rubén Aguilar, interview, Mexico City, May 9, 2019.

49. *Excélsior*, June 7, 2000, pp. 1, 10.

50. González, *Escenas del periodismo mexicano*, 71–76; Hughes, *Newsrooms in Conflict*, 135–38; *Letras Libres*, Dec. 2000, pp. 109–10.

51. *Proceso*, Oct. 22 (cover story), Oct. 29, 2000, pp. 28–37; *El Semanario*, Feb. 27, 2006, p. 6.

52. Curry et al., "Mexican Internet"; Harlow, *Digital-Native News*, chap. 2; "Mexico's Net Upstarts," *Industry Standard*, Apr. 24, 2000; Eduardo García, interview, Mexico City, Apr. 6, 2019; Carlos Puig, interview, Mexico City, Sept. 22, 2021.

53. Paxman, "Mexican Democracy's Awkward Partner," 396–97; Castillo, *La biografía secreta*, 372–77; Daniel Moreno, interview, Mexico City, Oct. 17, 2019.

54. Escobedo, *Comunicación y transparencia*, 5–6, 91–94; Hughes, *Newsrooms in Conflict*, 198–99; Tuckman, *Mexico*, 57; Michener, "FOI Laws," 150–51; "Ley Federal de Transparencia y Acceso a la Información Pública Gubernamental," *Diario Oficial*, June 11, 2002.

55. Hughes, *Newsrooms in Conflict*, 199–200; Hernández and Quintero, *La familia presidencial* (see, e.g., 38–44, 100–102); Hernández, *Fin de fiesta*; García, *Ellas, teclando su historia*, 117–19; *El Universal*, Sept. 29, 2003, pp. 1, G5; *Emeequis*, May 28, 2007, pp. 32–39.

56. WAN-IFRA, *Comprando complacencia*, 21.

57. Hughes, *Newsrooms in Conflict*, 191–92; Tuckman, *Mexico*, 63.

58. Hughes, *Newsrooms in Conflict*, 192–96.

59. *Proceso*, May 13, 2001; June 17, 2001; Oct. 21, 2001; June 30, 2002; July 13, 2003; Nov. 30, 2003; July 3, 2005.

60. *Proceso*, May 26, 2002, pp. 8–13; cf. *Proceso*, June 2, 9, 16, 23, 2002.

61. Levario Turcott, *Primera plana*, 240–43; Riva Palacio, *La prensa*, 178–79; Hughes, *Newsrooms in Conflict*, 191.

62. Zepeda Patterson, "La prensa en México,"150–51; Krauze, "Proceso a *Proceso*," 215.

63. World Values Survey, Waves 4 (1999–2004) and 5 (2005–9), www.worldvaluessurvey.org.

64. Riva Palacio, *La prensa*, 178; Tuckman, *Mexico*, 63–64; *Los Angeles Times*, July 5, 2001, p. 11; *Guardian*, Nov. 10, 2001, p. 15.

65. Morris, *Political Corruption in Mexico*, 59, 266–67; *El Universal*, Jan. 12, 2004, pp. 1, 10; *Financial Times*, Jan. 31, 2004, FT Weekend, pp. 1, 16–21, Feb. 5, 2004 (US edition), p. 1; *Reforma*, Feb. 3, 2004, pp. 1, 4; *Proceso*, Feb. 8, 2004, pp. 6–9.

66. *Proceso*, July 29, 2001; Aug. 11, 2002; Oct. 19, 2003; Feb. 8, 2004; Oct. 10, 2004; Apr. 17, 2005.

67. Anonymous *Proceso* veteran, interview, Nov. 2019; María Scherer Ibarra, interview, Mexico City, Feb. 14, 2020.

68. *Expansión*, Jan. 22, 2003, p. 25.

69. The story of the episode of Garza's exit and Ríos's appointment draws on González, *Escenas del periodismo mexicano*, 207–8; Esquivel Hernández, *Reforma*, 177–79, 221–22; and interviews with Daniel Moreno, Mexico City, June 21, 2019; Ramón Alberto Garza, Monterrey, Oct. 4, 2019, and Dec. 8, 2023; Wilbert Torre, Mexico City, Oct. 16, 2019; and Lázaro Ríos (via videocall), Dec. 12, 2023.

70. Interviews with Daniel Moreno, June 21, 2019; Ernesto Núñez, Dec. 15, 2021; and René Delgado, Mexico City, Nov. 7, 2023.

71. Rockwell, "Mexico," 116–18; *Washington Post*, June 22, 2000, p. 20; Ernesto Núñez, interview, Mexico City, Dec. 15, 2021.

72. *Reforma*, Aug. 13, 2000, p. 10; "Mexico President Uses Child Workers," AbcNews.go .com, Aug. 13, 2000; "Un diario mexicano desvela que Fox emplea en su finca a menores de 14 años," EFE (ElPais.com), Aug. 13, 2000; Ernesto Núñez, interview, Mexico City, Dec. 15, 2021.

73. González, *Escenas del periodismo mexicano*, 211–12; Trevino-Rangel, *Policing the Mexican Past*, 253–36; *Reforma*, Aug. 24, 2000, pp. 1, 10; René Delgado, interview, Mexico City, Nov. 7, 2023.

74. González, *Escenas del periodismo mexicano*, 211, 213; Trevino-Rangel, *Policing the Mexican Past*, 254–55; *Reforma*, Aug. 25, 2000, p. 1; *Milenio*, Aug. 25, 2000, p. 17 (*Reforma* credited); *El Universal*, Aug. 25, 2000, p. 18 (*Reforma* not credited); *La Jornada*, Aug. 25, 2000, pp. 1, 8 (*Reforma* not credited); "Premios Ortega y Gasset de Periodismo," ElPais .com.

75. *Reforma*, Feb. 9, 2002, p. 6; "Faltan a evento panistas incómodos," Reforma.com, Feb. 10, 2002; *Reforma*, Mar. 14, 2002, p. 2 (cf. Mar. 6, 2002, p. 1); Ernesto Núñez, interview, Mexico City, Dec. 15, 2021.

76. Riva Palacio, *La prensa*, 84–85.

77. Interviews with Jorge Zepeda Patterson, Mexico City, Nov. 14, 2019; Alejandro Páez, Mexico City, Oct. 19, 2021; and anonymous former colleague of Zepeda, June 5, 2024.

78. Crovi et al., *Periodismo digital en México*, 122, 128–33; Esquivel Hernández, *Reforma*, 7, 189, 225; Jorge Zepeda Patterson, interview, Mexico City, Nov. 14, 2019; anonymous *Reforma* editor, interview, Dec. 2022.

79. Mondragón Aguilar, "Prensa popularizada," 56, 64–66; Esquivel Hernández, *Reforma*, 7, 133, 174; *El Gráfico*, Feb. 21, 22, 25, 26, 2002, p. 1; Lázaro Ríos, interview (via video-call), Nov. 16, 2023. *Metro* launched in Monterrey in 1988.

80. Roberto Rock, interview, Mexico City, Sept. 22, 2021.

81. Hughes, *Newsrooms in Conflict*, 204; Mondragón Aguilar, "Prensa popularizada," 26, 66–78, 173–75; *La Prensa*, Oct. 22, 2008, p. 1; Roberto Rock, interview, Mexico City, Sept. 22, 2021.

82. The story of Garza at *El Universal* draws on Riva Palacio, *La prensa*, 167, 173–74; González, *Escenas del periodismo mexicano*, 46–51; Osorno, *Slim*, 202; Esquivel Hernández, "Prensa de papel"; and interviews with Samuel García, Mexico City, Dec. 12, 2014, Sept. 27, 2018; Daniel Moreno, Mexico City, Oct. 17, 2019, Mar. 24, 2023; and Ramón Alberto Garza, Monterrey, Dec. 8, 2023.

83. González, *Escenas del periodismo mexicano*, 46.

84. *El Universal*, July 1, 2002, p. 1.

85. González, *Escenas del periodismo mexicano*, 47; *El Universal*, July 1, 2002, pp. 1, 8.

86. "Inversión en medios" (annual report), *Adcebra*, Sept. 1999–2001; "Inversión en medios" (annual report), *Merca2.0*, Apr. 2003–15.

87. Esquivel Hernández, *Reforma*, 7; Hernández Medina, "El desarrollo," 190–91; Jorge Zepeda Patterson, interview, Mexico City, Nov. 14, 2019.

88. *Expansión*, Jan. 22, 2003, pp. 24–32.

Chapter 8

1. López Obrador, *La mafia nos robó*, 12.

2. López Obrador, *La mafia nos robó*, 105, 156, 161–64, 203, 245.

3. Trejo Delarbre, "La actuación."

4. Aguayo, *Vuelta en U*, 167–73; Grayson, *Mexican Messiah*, 247–51.

5. Villamil and Scherer Ibarra, *La guerra sucia*, 26–32, 102–9; Bruhn, "López Obrador," 174–79; Aguayo, *Vuelta en U*, 172; *Reforma*, Mar. 22, 2006, p. 1.

6. Villamil and Scherer Ibarra, *La guerra sucia*, 34–36; Bruhn, "López Obrador," 173–75, 180–84; Aguayo, *Vuelta en U*, 168–69, 174–75, 329nn12, 13.

7. Villamil and Scherer Ibarra, *La guerra sucia*, 33, 103; López Obrador, *La mafia nos robó*, 207–8; Aguayo, *Vuelta en U*, 176–77, 180, 185–86, 213; *Reforma*, May 27, 2006, p. 1.

8. *El Universal*, May 15, 19, 24, June 6, 7, 9, 12, 23, 26, 2006 (all p. 1).

9. Esquivel Hernández, *Reforma*, 202; Bruhn, "López Obrador," 180; *Proceso*, Nov. 20, 2005, pp. 18–20; *Reforma*, Apr. 17, May 15, 19, 27, June 5, 13, 24, 29, 2006 (all p. 1); Manuel Appendini, conversation with the author, Aguascalientes, June 28, 2023.

10. Enrique Krauze, "El mesías tropical," *Letras Libres*, June 2006, pp. 12–24; Enrique Krauze, "Tropical Messiah," *New Republic*, June 19, 2006, pp. 22–27.

11. *Expansión*, June 14, 2006, pp. 56–76.

12. For postelectoral bias in *Milenio*, see the front-page leads of Aug. 4, 19, and 20; Sept. 14 and 16; and (more obviously) Marín's front-page columns of July 4, 7, 12, and 18; Aug. 8, 10, 24, and 25; and Sept. 1, 2006.

13. Daniel Moreno, interview, Mexico City, Mar. 24, 2023.

14. *Excélsior*, Mar. 22, 2006, pp. 1, 11 (directory), July 3, p. 1, July 4, p. 1, July 5, 2006, p. 1.

15. *Excélsior*, July 6, p. 1, July 7, 2006, p. 1.

16. Daniel Moreno, interview, Mexico City, Mar. 24, 2023. After Moreno's exit, his place was taken by Pascal Beltrán del Río, who remains *Excélsior*'s editor today.

17. *La Jornada*, Feb. 7, 2022, p. 17; Raymundo Riva Palacio, interview, Mexico City, Sept. 21, 2021.

18. Grillo, *El Narco*, 106, 112–13; Tuckman, *Mexico*, 44–46; *Reforma*, Dec. 12, 2006, p. 1; *La Jornada*, Dec. 12, 2006, p. 14.

19. *El Universal*, *Milenio*, *Excélsior*, and *Reforma*, Dec. 12, 2006, p. 1.

20. *La Jornada*, Dec. 12, 2006, pp. 1, 14; *Proceso*, Dec. 17, 2006, pp. 10–16, 18, 11.

21. Grillo, *El Narco*, 111–13; Tuckman, *Mexico*, 67–68; *Reforma*, Jan. 4, 2007, pp. 1, 4; *Proceso*, Jan. 7, 2007, pp. 8–9; Luis Medina, communication with the author, July 7, 2023.

22. Seifert, *Politics of Authenticity*, 118–20, 125.

23. *Milenio*, Jan. 4, 2007, p. 3; *Proceso*, Jan. 7, 2007, p. 11; *La Jornada*, Jan. 8, pp. 7, 11, Jan. 9, p. 5, Jan. 10, 2007, pp. 5, 6; *El Universal*, Jan. 9, 2007, p. 15; *El Chamuco*, Feb. 14, 2007.

24. Loeza Landa, "Una representación," 117–82.

25. Tuckman, *Mexico*, 68, 72; WAN-IFRA, *Comprando complacencia*, 21; *El Universal*, Dec. 15, 2006, p. 30.

26. Heredia Gayosso, "De Felipe Calderón," 84–90; Grillo, *El Narco*, 112–16, 149–51.

27. Grillo, *El Narco*, 116–18.

28. Grillo, *El Narco*, 116–26; *Fox Report Weekend*, Fox News, Mar. 7, 2009 (emphasis in original).

29. *Reforma*, Enfoque, June 17, 2007, pp. 4–13, June 23, 2007, p. 1; Jésica Zermeño, interview (via telephone), Mar. 6, 2023; René Delgado, interview, Mexico City, Feb. 1, 2023.

30. Meade, "Plaza Is for the *Populacho*," 299–304, 310; *Reforma*, May 23, 2010, Enfoque, Aug. 26, 2010, p. 1, Sept. 24, 2010, Revista R, Dec. 8, 2010, p. 10, Dec. 9, p. 9, Dec. 19, Enfoque, Apr. 10, 2011, p. 18, Apr. 19, p. 1; Jésica Zermeño, interview (via telephone), Mar. 6, 2023.

31. Lázaro Ríos, "Las amenazas cumplidas contra Reforma," LetrasLibres.com, May 19, 2020.

32. The title of the last of these cover stories sums up the general tone: "The Lost War." *Proceso*, Dec. 28, 2008.

33. René Delgado, interview, Mexico City, Feb. 1, 2023.

34. Villamil, *El sexenio de Televisa*, 214–16; Grillo, *El Narco*, 129; WAN-IFRA, *Comprando complacencia*, 21, 26.

35. *La Jornada*, Feb. 26, 2010, p. 3; WAN-IFRA, *Comprando complacencia*, 24.

36. Lozano Rendón, "El Acuerdo"; Ríos and Rivera, "Media Effects."

37. Merchant Ley, "Una negociación sutil," 72–73; *Reforma*, Mar. 25, 2011, p. 15; Ríos, "Las amenazas"; Lilia Saúl, interview (via videocall), Oct. 17, 2023.

38. Campos, *El juicio ciudadano*, 24. By November 2011, Calderón's approval rating stood at 54 percent.

39. Rea and Ferri, *La tropa*, 69–73, 236–41, 256–58; Zavala, *La guerra*, 21–24, 38–46, 250, 320–21, 327.

40. Campos, *El juicio ciudadano*, 37–38; Jorge Zepeda Patterson, interview (via videocall), Dec. 6, 2022.

41. Jésica Zermeño, interview (via telephone), Mar. 6, 2023; René Delgado, interview, Mexico City, Nov. 7, 2023.

42. *Merca2.0*, Apr. 2008, 2009, 2013; WAN-IFRA, *Comprando complacencia*, 34.

43. On spending by governors: Article 19 and Fundar, *Libertad de expresión*.

44. WAN-IFRA, *Comprando complacencia*, 17–18, 26; "En la primera mitad del sexenio persisten las malas prácticas en publicidad oficial," Article 19 MX-CA, Aug. 16, 2022, https://articulo19.org; María Scherer Ibarra, interview, Mexico City, Feb. 14, 2020; Jorge Carrasco, interview, Mexico City, Mar. 23, 2023.

45. Campos, *El juicio ciudadano*, 24; "Nuestra tragedia humanitaria comenzó en el gobierno de Calderón," AristeguiNoticias.com, Sept. 3, 2020.

46. López Obrador, *La mafia que se adueñó*, 11, 24, 34, 60, 84–84, 93–94; *El Universal*, Aug. 27, 2020, pp. 1, 6.

47. The story of García and *Sentido Común* draws on *New York Times*, June 28, 2007, p. C1, June 15, 2009, p. B1; Reuters, "Mexican Carlos Slim Zips Past Gates in Rich Ranks: Report," CNBC.com, July 3, 2007; "Carlos Slim's Embarrassment of Riches," Time.com, July 11, 2007; "SC en los medios," SentidoComun.com.mx [Apr. 2009]; Eduardo García, interviews, Mexico City, Apr. 6, 2019, Feb. 28, 2020.

48. Secanella, *El periodismo*, 119–21.

49. Eduardo García, interview, Mexico City, Mar. 7, 2019.

50. Scherer García and Monsiváis, *Tiempo de saber*, 290–93; Timothy Heyman, conversation with the author, Mexico City, Dec. 15, 2021.

51. Riva Palacio, *La prensa*, 163; *Reforma*, Dec. 10, 1996, p. 36; María Fernanda Matus, conversation with the author, Mexico City, April 1997; Eduardo García, interview, Mexico City, Mar. 7, 2019.

52. *Expansión* veteran, interview, May 2021.

53. The *Expansión* story draws on "50 años" (cover story), *Expansión*, Apr. 1, 2019; León, "Las mujeres empresarias"; and interviews with Eduardo García, Mexico City, Mar. 7, 2019; Alberto Bello, via videocall, May 5 and 6, 2021; and Javier Martínez Staines, Mexico City, Jan. 31, and via email, Feb. 8, 2023.

54. *Expansión*, June 6, 1990, pp. 31–41.

55. *Bloomberg Markets*, Aug. 2001; Eduardo García, interviews, Mar. 7 and Apr. 6, 2019.

56. *Expansión*, Nov. 9, 1994, pp. 139–41.

57. Javier Martínez Staines, interview, Mexico City, Jan. 31, 2023.

58. Javier Martínez Staines, interview, Mexico City, Jan. 31, 2023.

59. *Expansión*, Nov. 18, 1998 (cover); cf. reports on pp. 22–36, 38–42, 45–55.

60. *Expansión*, Nov. 13, 2002, cover and pp. 54–68.

61. *El Semanario*, Jan. 24, 2005, pp. 16–19, May 9, 2005, pp. 15–19.

62. *Proceso*, Mar. 4, 2007 (cover); *La Jornada*, Mar. 11, 2007, p. 25; *Los Angeles Times*, Mar. 13, 2007, p. C4.

63. *Proceso*, Dec. 15, 1990, pp. 20–22.

64. *Proceso*, May 18, 1992, pp. 20–21, July 23, p. 34, July 30, pp. 34–37, Nov. 26, 1994, p. 71.

65. *Proceso*, Feb. 20, 1995, pp. 40–42, June 26, pp. 36–38, Sept. 18 (cover), Oct. 1, pp. 36–37, Dec. 3, pp. 20–21, Dec. 10, p. 31.

66. Rodríguez Castañeda, *Operación Telmex*.

67. Castillo, *La biografía secreta*, 325.

68. Osorno, *Slim*, 201, 211, 244–46.

69. Osorno, *Slim*, 200–201; *Proceso*, Apr. 11, 1998, pp. 28–31.

70. Osorno, *Slim*, 204–5; *Proceso*, Oct. 5, 2003, pp. 6–10.

71. Hughes, *Newsrooms in Conflict*, 84, 89–90, 98–99.

72. Osorno, *Slim*, 202, 204, 211–12.

73. "Telmex: ¡Inviééértale! (léase con acento norteño)," *Sentido Común,* Apr. 18, 2008, www.AxisNegocios.com; Eduardo García, interview, Mexico City, Apr. 6, 2019.

74. Relea, "Carlos Slim."

75. Relea, "Carlos Slim," 35–37, 43–46; *Reforma*, Mar. 28, 2005, p. 15; *Proceso*, Mar. 4, 2007, pp. 11–13.

76. Dresser, *El país de uno*, 165–78, 190–204; *Reforma*, June 1, 2009, p. 19, Feb. 6, 2012, p. 11; *Proceso*, Feb. 14, 2009, pp. 50–51; Denise Dresser, email to the author, July 3, 2024.

77. Arslan, "Mexico's Battle with Monopolies," 15–16; *El Semanario*, Apr. 27, 2006, p. 14; *Reforma*, June 29, 2006, Negocios, p. 1, Apr. 7, 2010, Negocios, p. 4, Mar. 13, 2013, Negocios, p. 1; *Expansión*, Sept. 13, 2013, pp. 112–18.

78. *Wall Street Journal*, May 4, 2011, p. B1; *Expansión*, Apr. 12, 2013, p. 150; "Bill Gates Retakes World's Richest Title from Carlos Slim," Bloomberg.com, May 17, 2013.

79. Arslan, "Mexico's Battle with Monopolies," 2; "Bloomberg Billionaires Index," Bloomberg.com/billionaires; "Mexico's Slim Joins $100 Billion Club Thanks to Super Peso," Bloomberg.com, Dec. 14, 2023; Fernández and Paxman, *El Tigre*, 16–19. As of this writing (May 2025), Slim had an eighteenth-ranked fortune of $92 billion.

Chapter 9

1. The story of the assault on *LadoB* draws on interviews with Ernesto Aroche and Mely Arellano, Puebla, Mar. 20 and Oct. 29, 2019.

2. *Proceso*, May 14, 2006, pp. 6–12; "Ardelio Vargas, el funcionario que renunció por señalamientos de AMLO por vínculos con García Luna," ElFinanciero.com.mx, July 4, 2023. Moreno Valle Rosas was the son of *El Financiero* coinvestor Javier Moreno Valle.

3. "Acusan a Ardelio Vargas de ser 'el máximo represor que ha tenido Puebla,'" LadoBe.com.mx, Oct. 10, 2011; cf. "Ardelio Vargas: el regreso a los viejos tiempos," LadoBe.com.mx, Oct. 17, 2011.

4. Salazar Rebolledo, *Más allá*, 15; "Un año de inseguridad pública con Moreno Valle y Ardelio Vargas," LadoBe.com.mx, Jan. 10, 2012. On Moreno Valle, who died in 2018, see Aroche, "Rafael Moreno Valle Rosas."

5. The story of the murders of Luis Carlos Santiago and Armando Rodríguez draw on Moncada, *Oficio de muerte*, 214–18, 272–73; Bosch and Vélez Salas, *Tú y yo*, 279–80, 307–8; Grecko, *Killing the Story*, 113–20; and "¿Quiénes somos?," Diario.mx/nosotros.

6. Moncada, *Oficio de muerte*, 263–64; Bosch and Vélez Salas, *Tú y yo*, 115–16.

7. Grillo, *El Narco*, 127; "Mexico's Ciudad Juárez Is No Longer the Most Violent City in the World," Time.com, Oct. 15, 2012.

8. *El Diario de Juárez*, Sept. 19, 2010, p. 1.

9. Corcoran, *In the Mouth*, xiv. Cf., e.g., *La Jornada*, Sept. 20, 2010, p. 5; *New York Times*, Sept. 24, 2010, p. A20.

10. "Mexican Journalists, Seeking Mercy from the Merciless," TheGlobeAndMail.com, Sept. 21, 2010; *New York Times*, Sept. 24, 2010, p. A20; WAN-IFRA, *Comprando complacencia*, 17; "Past María Moors Cabot Prizes Winners," Journalism.Columbia.edu, Jan. 26, 2021; Abraham Rubio, email to the author, Feb. 11, 2019.

11. Grecko, *No se mata*, 302–3; Jan-Albert Hootsen (Committee to Protect Journalists), interview, Mexico City, Feb. 21, 2019; Abraham Rubio, interview, Mexico City, Apr. 4, 2019.

12. Jones, "Unintended Consequences"; Grecko, *Killing the Story*, 136; Navarro, "El presente del periodismo"; Adela Navarro, interview (via telephone), Sept. 12, 2023.

13. Grecko, *Killing the Story*, 136; "40 años de ZETA," ZetaTijuana.com, Apr. 11, 2020; Adela Navarro, interview (via telephone), Sept. 12, 2023.

14. "Adela Navarro Bello," n.d., TheGlobalJournal.net; "'Our Commitment Is to Our Murdered Colleagues, to Freedom of Expression, to Journalism and to the Society We Serve': Adela Navarro, 2021 Cabot Prize," LatAmJournalismReview.org, Oct. 13, 2021.

15. Adela Navarro, interview (via telephone), Sept. 12, 2023.

16. The story of the Reynosa disappearances draws on Bosch and Vélez Salas, *Tú y yo*, 51–53, 87–88; González de Bustamante and Relly, *Surviving Mexico*, 45–47, 63; *New York Times*, Mar. 14, 2010, p. 1; Raymundo Pérez Arellano, "El periodista que volvió de la muerte," CosechaRoja.org, Feb. 23, 2012. On the *levantón* practice, see Valdez Cárdenas, *Taken*.

17. Bosch and Vélez Salas, eds., *Tú y yo*, 51–53, 87–88.

18. On the *narcoperiodista* phenomenon in Tamaulipas, see Valdez Cárdenas, *Narcoperiodismo*, 21–48.

19. *New York Times*, Mar. 14, 2010, p. 1.

20. Comisión Interamericana de Derechos Humanos, *Zonas silenciadas*, 32; Grecko, *Killing the Story*, 124.

21. Valdez, *Narcoperiodismo*, 51–83; González de Bustamante and Relly, *Surviving Mexico*, 45–47, 53–56, 83–84; Grecko, *Killing the Story*, 124–25. On zones of silence, see also Comisión Interamericana de Derechos Humanos, *Zonas silenciadas*, 26–39.

22. Moncada, *Oficio de muerte*, 200, 238–39, 257, 280, 282; Smith, *Dope*, 285 (cf. 281); Raymundo Pérez Arellano, "México: El periodista que volvió de la muerte," CosechaRoja.org, Feb. 23, 2012.

23. The story of the Regina Martínez murder and cover-up draws except where noted on Corcoran, *In the Mouth*.

24. For portraits of Duarte and his regime, see del Palacio, *Callar o morir*; and Pastrana, "Javier Duarte."

25. *Proceso*, Apr. 8, 2012, p. 18–19.

26. *Proceso*, Apr. 14, 2013, pp. 22–25.

27. Under Fidel Herrera (2004–10), Escobar was general secretary of government, the number two post in the state; *La Jornada*, Oct. 8, 2011, p. 12.

28. *Este País*, Dec. 2016, pp. 13–22.

29. Corcoran, *In the Mouth*.

30. Numbers and numerical trends in this section are drawn from the author's database, compiled with reference to Moncada, *Oficio de muerte*; Bosch and Vélez Salas, *Tú y yo*; Smith, *Mexican Press*; the databases of nongovernmental organizations Article 19 MX-CA (Articulo19.org/periodistasasesinados) and the Committee to Protect Journalists (Cpj.org /data/killed); and many case-specific sources.

31. Escudero, *El duelo en México*, 81–84, 109–14.

32. Garner, *Porfirio Díaz*, 107–10; Moncada, *Oficio de muerte*, 30.

33. Moncada, *Oficio de muerte*, 40–46, 54–56, 76–79, 84; Paxman, "Maximino Ávila Camacho," 113.

34. Moncada, *Oficio de muerte*, 70–76; Smith, *Mexican Press*, 184.

35. Smith, *Mexican Press*, chap. 1.

36. Smith, *Dope*, chap. 16; author's database (see note 30, above).

37. Smith, *Dope*, 285 (cf. 281). On the attention the case garnered, see Moncada, *Oficio de muerte*, 115–20.

38. As in previous instances, these per-decade totals do not include cases in which journalists appear to have been killed for reasons unrelated to their work.

39. Moncada, *¡Cayeron!*; Andrew Paxman, introduction to Paxman, *Los Gobernadores*, 10–18; Salazar Rebolledo, *Más allá*, 87–89, 131–37.

40. Aroche, "Rafael Moreno Valle Rosas," 153–56; Article 19 and Fundar, *Diagnóstico sobre*.

41. Smith, *Dope*, 43–58, 333–35, 338–41; "15 exgobernadores bajo la lupa," Politico.MX, July 17, 2017.

42. Del Palacio, *Callar o morir*, 11–12, 295–306.

43. "Informe estadístico de la Fiscalía Especial para la Atención de Delitos cometidos contra de la Libertad de Expresión" (Mexico City: FEADLE, 2015), cited in Corcoran, *In the Mouth*, 103, 304n103.

44. Navarro, "El presente del periodismo."

45. Grillo, *El Narco*, 127–30, 220; "Homicidios a nivel nacional: Serie anual de 1990 a 2020," www.Inegi.org.mx, 2021.

46. Velasco Arregui, "Precarización del empleo."

47. Espino Sánchez, "Periodistas precarios"; Valdez Cárdenas, *Narcoperiodismo*, 63, 79–80.

48. Valdez Cárdenas, *Narcoperiodismo*, 91–97; Corcoran, *In the Mouth*, 40.

49. Valdez Cárdenas, *Narcoperiodismo*, 21–48; Del Palacio, *Callar o morir*, 107–11; Corcoran, *In the Mouth*, 21–22.

50. Carpizo, *Un año*, 383–420.

51. "Mexican Reporter Killed in Matamoros Crossfire," Cpj.org, Nov. 8, 2010.

52. Del Palacio, *Callar o morir*, 119.

53. Article 19, *Democracia simulada*, 18; González-Macías and Salazar Rebolledo, "Confianza en la prensa mexicana," 13–15.

54. Duarte, quoted in Grecko, *Killing the Story*, 43; Corcoran, *In the Mouth*, 199.

55. Valdez Cárdenas, *Narcoperiodismo*, 27, 40–48; Corcoran, *In the Mouth*, 21. The examples are from Moncada, *Oficio de muerte*, 248–49; Bosch and Vélez Salas, *Tú y yo*, 147–48; Del Palacio, *Callar o morir*, 114–17, 301, 305; "Mexico: Latest Murder Highlights Blurred Lines in Journalism," Associated Press, Jan. 1, 2018, https://apnews.com; and Juan Alberto Cedillo, interview, Monterrey, Oct. 2, 2019.

56. Once critical regional media that became submissive to local governments include *El Diario* of Ciudad Juárez, *Milenio Jalisco* (formerly *Público*) of Guadalajara, and *Síntesis* of Puebla.

57. World Values Survey, Waves 5 (2005–9), 6 (2010–14), and 7 (2017–22), www.worldvaluessurvey.org; Alejandro Moreno, "Confianza en las instituciones," *Este País*, Dec. 2013, pp. 8–9. On advances in digital-media journalism and retreats within print media, see chapter 10.

58. Del Palacio, *Callar o morir*, 175–77; González-Macías and Reyna García, "'They Don't Trust Us'"; González-Macías and Salazar Rebolledo, "Confianza en la prensa mexicana."

59. Except where noted, Lydia Cacho's story draws on her memoir *Infamy*.

60. Cacho, *Los demonios del Edén*.

61. *La Jornada*, Feb. 14, 2006, pp. 1, 3.

62. Tuckman, *Mexico*, 85–87; Solares Orgas, "Tratamiento periodístico"; *El Sol de Puebla*, Feb. 16, 2006, p. 1.

63. "Detienen al exgobernador de Puebla, Mario Marín," AnimalPolitico.com, Feb. 3, 2021; "7 datos sobre el caso Lydia Cacho y Kamel Nacif," ElFinanciero.com.mx, May 13, 2021.

64. On Hernández, Pérez, Pereyra, Turati, and Saúl, see García, *Ellas, teclando su historia*; on Rea, Rodríguez Nieto, and (again) Turati, see Polit Dueñas, *Unwanted Witnesses*; on Xanic, see chap. 3.

65. Ariel Rosales (Penguin Random House), interview, Mexico City, Feb. 2, 2023.

66. Ariel Rosales, interviews, Mexico City, Feb. 13, 2020, Feb. 2, 2023; Consuelo Sáizar, conversation with the author, Oxford, May 17, 2021.

67. Secanella, *El periodismo*, 53–57, 79–84. For an analysis of the *crónica* genre, see Corona and Jörgensen, *Contemporary Mexican Chronicle*; and Stephen, *Stories That Make History*.

68. Flores Quintero, *La seducción*, 8, 23; Tello Díaz, *La rebelión*; Ross, *Rebellion from the Roots*; *New York Review of Books*, Mar. 2, 1995, pp. 34–43.

69. Hernández and Quintero, *La familia presidencial*; Hernández, *Fin de fiesta*; Wornat, *La jefa*.

70. González, *Escenas del periodismo mexicano*, 40–41; Toche, "Revista Emeequis."

71. Jesús Blancornelas, *Horas extra: Los nuevos tiempos del narcotráfico* (Mexico City: Plaza y Janés, 2003); Jesús Blancornelas, *En estado de alerta: Periodistas y gobierno frente al narcotráfico* (Mexico City: Plaza y Janés, 2005); Sergio González Rodríguez, *Huesos en el desierto* (Mexico City: Anagrama, 2002); Sergio González Rodríguez, *El hombre sin cabeza* (Mexico City: Anagrama, 2013); Sergio González Rodríguez, *Campo de guerra* (Mexico City: Anagrama, 2014); Carlos Monsiváis et al., *Viento rojo* (Mexico City: Plaza y Janés, 2004).

72. Lida, introduction to *Field of Battle*, 11.

73. Grillo, *El Narco*; Osorno, *El Cártel de Sinaloa*; Osorno, *La guerra de los Zetas*; "Llega a la FIL el boom de los narcolibros," ReporteIndigo.com, Oct. 15, 2012; "Narcolibros en la FIL de Guadalajara," LaTercera.com [Santiago], Nov. 21, 2012.

74. *Nexos*, Jan. 2017, pp. 83–87.

75. Hernández, *Los señores del narco* (2010 and 2014); Hernández, *Narcoland*.

76. Hernández, *Narcoland*, 6.

77. Hernández, *Fin de fiesta*; Hernández, *Los cómplices del presidente*; "García Luna declaró casas y Mustangs . . . luego escondió su patrimonio," Politica.Expansion.mx, Jan. 24, 2022.

78. "When a Corpse Is a Message," *London Review of Books*, 36:9 (May 8, 2014), pp. 21–23; Ed Vulliamy, "'Mexico's War on Drugs Is One Big Lie,'" *Observer* (London), Sept. 1, 2013.

79. García, *Ellas, teclando su historia*, 109; "Quieren matarme: Anabel Hernández," CIMAC.org.mx, Jan. 10, 2011; "Narco, fenómeno editorial," ElUniversal.com.mx, Apr. 17, 2011; *Proceso*, May 9, 2011, pp. 65–66; Vulliamy, "'Mexico's War'"; Ariel Rosales, interview, Mexico City, Feb. 2, 2023.

80. "Bestselling Author Sued for Libel after Suggesting Corruption," IndexOnCensorship .org, Mar. 7, 2012; *El Universal*, Mar. 31, 2012, pp. 1, 10; Gómez Gallardo, "Sobre el ejercicio"; *Reforma*, Apr. 4, 2012, p. 13.

81. Hernández, *Los señores del narco* (2010), 46 (cf. Hernández, *Narcoland*, 26; Hernández, *Los señores del narco* [2014], 47); Ariel Rosales, interview, Mexico City, May 22, 2023; Álvaro Enrigue, "When a Corpse Is a Message," *London Review of Books*, pp. 21–23; Esteban Illades, "El periodismo en los tiempos del narco," *Nexos*, Jan. 2017, p. 84.

82. I base this claim on exchanges with seven colleagues, the caveats of Enrigue, and the analysis of Oswaldo Zavala, who in *Los cárteles no existen* (70) observes, "Her lack of rigor in the sources of information she uses makes her research simply unverifiable."

83. Hernández, *Los señores del narco* (2010), 50–72; Hernández, *Narcoland*, 29–37; cf. Grillo, *El Narco*, 80.

84. Hernández, *Los señores del narco* (2014), 44; Hernández, *Narcoland*, 24.

85. Zavala, *Los cárteles no existen*, 46–75; Zavala, *La guerra en las palabras*, 405–16.

86. Turati, *Fuego cruzado*; Valdez Cárdenas, *Los morros del narco*. See also Tercero, *Cuando llegaron los bárbaros*; Turati and Rea, *Entre las cenizas*; and Valdez Cárdenas, *Taken*.

87. *New York Times*, Feb. 22, 2023, p. 10.

88. Vulliamy, "'Mexico's War'"; "Comando irrumpe en el domicilio de la periodista Anabel Hernández," Proceso.com.mx, Dec. 30, 2013.

89. Anabel Hernández, "Veredicto contra García Luna, epílogo de mi búsqueda," DW.com, Feb. 22, 2023.

Chapter 10

1. The story of Rafael Cabrera, Carmen Aristegui, and the "Casa Blanca" scandal draws on Torre, *El despido*, chap. 2; Rock, *La historia detrás*, 110–13; Grecko, *Killing the Story*, chap. 8; ¡Hola!, May 1, 2013; Irving Huerta, interview, London, July 11, 2019; and Rafael Cabrera, interview (via videocall), Oct. 5, 2023.

2. "Carmen Aristegui inaugura su portal de noticias," Proceso.com.mx, Apr. 16, 2012; "10 titulares sobre los medios digitales de México en julio," ElEconomista.com.mx, Sept. 8, 2015.

3. "Pro-Government Twitter Bots Try to Hush Mexican Activists," Wired.com, Aug. 23, 2015; "How to Hack an Election," Bloomberg.com, Mar. 31, 2016.

4. Jo Tuckman, email to the author, July 28, 2019.

5. See, e.g., "La casa blanca de Enrique Peña Nieto," AristeguiNoticias.com, Nov. 9, 2014; *Proceso*, Nov. 9, 2014 (cover); *La Jornada*, Nov. 9, 2014, p. 13; and *Washington Post*, Nov. 10, 2014, p. 10.

6. In 2021 Rivera's video was reposted by the news site *La Política Online* at www .youtube.com/watch?v=TQzEg64gl3k.

7. Rock, *La historia*, 112.

8. Grecko, *Killing the Story*, 157.

9. *Economist*, Jan. 24, 2015, p. 45; cf. Torre, *El despido*, 179; Grecko, *No se mata*, 124; Rock, *La historia*, 21, 223.

10. *Proceso*, Oct. 23, 2005, pp. 6–9; Villamil, *Si yo fuera presidente*; Villamil, *Peña Nieto*.

11. *El Sol de México*, May 12, 2012, p. 1; cf. "Tuiteros acusan a Vázquez Raña de minimizar hechos en Ibero," Terra.com.mx, May 12, 2012.

12. Díaz-Domínguez and Moreno, "Effects of #YoSoy132"; *Wall Street Journal*, May 24, 2012, p. 13.

13. González Posadas, "Construcción social," 205; Díaz-Domínguez and Moreno, "Effects of #YoSoy132"; "Student Movement Dubbed the 'Mexican Spring'," TheNation.com, May 29, 2012.

14. Villamil, *Peña Nieto*, chap. 3; Hurtado Razo, "¿Encuestas o Propaganda?"

15. *Proceso*, July 2, 2012; Jorge Carrasco, interview, Mexico City, Mar. 23, 2023.

16. Villamil, *Peña Nieto*; "Poll of Polls: Aprobación presidencial EPN," Parametria .com.mx, Dec. 10, 2015.

17. The story of *Animal Político* draws on "Animal Político y los retos de informar en en siglo XXI," Forbes.com.mx, June 16, 2017; Daniel Moreno, interviews, Mexico City, June 21 and Oct. 17, 2019, Feb. 1, 2023; Mael Vallejo, interview, Mexico City, Oct. 16, 2019; and Susan Seijas, email to the author, Sept. 23, 2024.

18. *Animal Político* continues to tweet as @Pajaropolitico.

19. "Inversión en medios 2010," *Merca2.0*, Apr. 2011, pp. 34–38.

20. *El Universal*, June 1, 2011, p. 8.

21. González Posadas, "Construcción social," 205; "La peculiar 'guerra sucia' online contra #YoSoy132," Proceso.com.mx, June 18, 2012; "#YoSoy132: jóvenes regidos por viejos," Razon.com.mx, June 26, 2012.

22. Hernández Santos, "Cuerpos sin nombre"; Paris Martínez, "Iguala: 43 desaparecidos, 43 historias" and "Iguala: Los desaparecidos no son un número, tienen rostro y sueños," AnimalPolitico.com, Oct. 7 and 8, 2014; "Intervención de Elena Poniatowska en Zócalo: 26 de octubre de 2014," YouTube.com, 2014.

23. "Reportaje: Empresas fantasma de Veracruz," www.periodismo.org.mx/assets/2016 -Reportaje.pdf; Arturo Ángel and Víctor Hugo Arteaga, "El caso de las empresas fantasma de Veracruz," AnimalPolitico.com, May 24, 2016; Raúl Olmos, "Surgen otras 45 empresas 'fantasma' de Javier Duarte," MCCI (ContraLaCorrupcion.mx), Dec. 7, 2016; "El exgobernador mexicano Javier Duarte es condenado a nueve años de prisión tras declararse culpable," ElPais.com, Sept. 27, 2018.

24. "La estafa maestra," AnimalPolitico.com, Sept. 5, 2017 (since updated).

25. "La estafa maestra"; "'La estafa maestra' ya estaba en los medios," Etcétera.com .mx, Sept. 5, 2017.

26. "Ganadores 2016" and "Ganadores 2017," Premio Nacional de Periodismo (Periodismo.org.mx); "Animal Político, Univisión, David Armengou, Marcela Miret y Soledad Gallego-Díaz, Ortega y Gasset 2018," ElPais.com, Apr. 4, 2018.

27. Susan Seijas, email to the author, Sept. 23, 2024.

28. Grecko, *Killing the Story*, 199; Roldán et al., *La estafa maestra*.

29. Roldán and Ureste, *La estafa maestra*; *Reforma*, Dec. 7, 2023, p. 13. As another example of Mexican impunity, former presidents have been jailed for graft in Brazil, Argentina, Peru, Venezuela, Ecuador, Paraguay, and most of Central America but have never even been put on trial in Mexico.

30. "Animal Político entra a la terna de los más leídos en digital," ElEconomista.com. mx, Mar. 5, 2018.

31. "Difunde Presidencia lista de empresas y periodistas que tuvieron contratos con gobierno de EPN," AnimalPolitico.com, May 25, 2019; Daniel Moreno, interview (via telephone), Sept. 9, 2024; Alberto Tavira, email to the author, Sept. 16, 2024. Cf. "SDP Noticias, haciendo de la polémica un buen negocio," ElEconomista.com.mx, Nov. 29, 2016.

32. "Nuevo dueño de Animal Político, ligado al PRI de Osorio Chong," Polemon.mx, Sept. 11, 2019; Marco Lara Klahr, interview (via videocall), Feb. 10, 2022.

33. The stories of Zepeda's exit from *El Universal* and of *SinEmbargo* draw on González Posadas, "Construcción social," chaps. 5–8; "Sin Embargo S. de R.L. de C.V.," Media Ownership Monitor Mexico (Mexico.mom-gmr.org), 2018; and interviews with Jorge Zepeda Patterson, Mexico City, June 19, 2019, Nov. 14, 2019, Dec. 6, 2022; Alejandro Páez, Mexico City, Oct. 19, 2021, May 24, 2023; and Ricardo Raphael (via telephone), Nov. 14, 2023.

34. *El Universal*, Oct. 24, 2007, pp. 1, 14–15.

35. Zepeda Patterson, *Los suspirantes 2012*.

36. González Posadas, "Construcción social," 101–2; *El Universal*, Apr. 17, 2017, Revista Clase (supplement).

37. Quoted in González Posadas, "Construcción social," 182; cf. 121.

38. Humberto Padgett, "Zulema y 'El Chapo': Amor, SMS y tragedia," SinEmbargo. mx, July 23, 2013; Humberto Padgett, "Guerrero: Caminando por los campos de la goma," SinEmbargo.mx, Feb. 16, 2015.

39. "Por falla, Aristegui Noticias presenta subregistro de visitas," AristeguiNoticias. com, Mar. 7, 2017. On *UnoTV*: "UnoTV, una marca construida con mensajes de texto," ElEconomista.com.mx, Sept. 8, 2015.

40. "SinEmbargo ha recibido en 5 años, del Gobierno federal, 280 mil pesos en contratos de publicidad oficial," SinEmbargo.mx, Dec. 28, 2017.

41. Alejandro Páez, interviews, Mexico City, Oct. 19, 2021, May 24, 2023.

42. Lizárraga et al., *La Casa Blanca*; Roldán et al., *La estafa maestra*.

43. Víctor Hernández, "OJO, @jandradej; Si en Comunicación Social de CDMX creen que ComScore sirve, están equivocados y arriesgan fraude," BlogDeIzquierda.com, Apr. 1, 2016; "Si odias el 'clickbait' tienes que leer esto," ElEspanol.com, Nov. 8, 2019.

44. Follower counts as recorded by the author on Dec. 31, 2018.

45. Andrew Paxman, "Why Does Mexico Have So Many Newspapers?," paper presented at the History Seminar, Latin American Centre, University of Oxford, Feb. 18, 2021, www

.academia.edu/45155004. The totals do not include freesheets: four in Mexico City; three in New York, London, and Puebla; and one in Philadelphia.

46. Examples include Oaxaca's *Diario Despertar*, founded in 2006 as a propaganda organ by embattled governor Ulises Ruiz, and the Zacatecas franchise of *La Jornada*, launched by investors including Jorge Álvarez Maynez, two years before his election to the Zacatecas congress.

47. Marcela Turati, interview (via videocall), Apr. 17, 2020; Benjamin Smith, email to the author, Apr. 10, 2024.

48. Francisco Pazos, "El ciudadano Junco," *Eje Central*, July 20, 2017; Carlos Marí, interview, Villahermosa, Oct. 12, 2022; René Delgado, interview, Mexico City, Nov. 7, 2023; Lázaro Ríos, email to the author, Nov. 30, 2023.

49. Interviews with Ariel Rosales, Mexico City, Aug. 2, 2018; anonymous former TV Azteca executive, Mexico City, May 2019; and Alejandro Páez, Mexico City, May 24, 2023.

50. Interviews with Ariel Rosales, Mexico City, Aug. 2, 2018; Raymundo Riva Palacio, Mexico City, Sept. 21, 2021; Carlos Marí, Villahermosa, Oct. 12, 2022; and Lázaro Ríos (via videocall), Dec. 12, 2023.

51. *Reforma*, Oct. 15, 2017, p. 11; "Fin de ciclo para la prensa mexicana," ElPais.com, May 3, 2019; Jorge Zepeda Patterson, interview, Mexico City, Nov. 14, 2019; Lázaro Ríos, interview, Mexico City, Sept. 24, 2024; former *El Universal* reporter, conversation with the author, May 20, 2020.

52. Grecko, *Killing the Story*, chap. 8; Laura Castellanos, "Fueron Los Federales," AristeguiNoticias.com, Apr. 19, 2015; Castellanos, *Proceso*, Apr. 19, 2015, pp. 12–19; *New York Times*, Dec. 25, 2017, pp. 1, 10.

53. *El Universal*, Sept. 22, 2015, pp. 1, E6–7; Lilia Saúl, interview (via videocall), Oct. 17, 2023.

54. "El Universal corrió a su director editorial por atacar al Sistema Anticorrupción," LaPoliticaOnline.com, July 12, 2017; "Cambio de timón en El Universal," EjeCentral.com.mx, July 12, 2017; *New York Times*, Dec. 25, 2017, pp. 1, 10.

55. Guerrero, *¿Cómo se informa?*, chaps. 2, 3.

56. *New York Times*, Dec. 25, 2017, pp. 1, 10; *La Jornada*, Jan. 30, Feb. 9, Apr. 30, May 18, 23, June 7, 28, 29, 30, July 19, 23, 30, Sept. 1, 2, 5, 8, 20, Oct. 12, Nov. 2, 16, 21, 28, Dec. 2, 6, 13, 16, 2016.

57. Anonymous *La Jornada* veteran, interview, Oct. 2020.

58. Angélica Recillas, "Cómo la 4T rescató a La Jornada con recursos públicos," Etcetera.com.mx, July 16, 2024.

59. Anonymous *La Jornada* veterans, interviews, July 10, 18, 2024.

60. Anonymous *La Jornada* veteran, interview, Oct. 2020.

61. Interviews with anonymous *Proceso* veteran, May 2019, Oct. 2020; Álvaro Delgado, Mexico City, Sept. 23, 2021; María Scherer Ibarra, Mexico City, Dec. 16, 2021; Jorge Carrasco, Mexico City, Nov. 9, 2023.

62. Rodríguez García, *El regreso autoritario*; "Fin de ciclo para la prensa mexicana," ElPais.com, May 3, 2019.

63. "González Family," Media Ownership Monitor Mexico (Mexico.mom-gmr.org), 2018; José Luis Esquivel Hernández, email to the author, Feb. 17, 2021; Alberto Bello, interview (via videocall), May 6, 2021; anonymous *Milenio* columnist, interview, Sept. 2021.

64. Anonymous informant, interview, Monterrey, Oct. 2019.

65. *New York Times*, Dec. 25, 2017, pp. 1, 10; "Vázquez Raña Family," Media Ownership Monitor Mexico (Mexico.mom-gmr.org), 2018; "Fin de ciclo para la prensa mexicana," ElPais.com, May 3, 2019.

66. Guerrero, *¿Cómo se informa?*, 97; "Ramiro Garza Cantú," Media Ownership Monitor Mexico (Mexico.mom-gmr.org), 2018; *La Razón* columnist, conversation with the author, Mexico City, Nov. 2018.

67. Author's observations, on living in Puebla in 2006 and returning in 2018 and 2019.

68. Article 19 and Fundar, *Libertad de expresión*, 7, 27, 37; Garza Ramos, "Democratization and the Regional Press," 274–76; *Proceso*, July 13, 2003, pp. 20–21.

69. *Proceso*, Mar. 6, 1995, pp. 44–46; Article 19 and Fundar, *Libertad de expresión*, 7, 48–53.

70. Article 19 and Fundar, *Libertad de expresión*, 77; "El Gobernador de Chiapas se autopromueve en el DF y en estados del centro del país," SinEmbargo.mx, Dec. 17, 2013; "Otra vez Manuel Velasco . . . Chiapas insiste en ocultar los contratos de publicidad oficial," AnimalPolitico.com, Feb. 4, 2014; *Expansión* veteran, interview, May 2021.

71. WAN-IFRA, *Comprando complacencia*, 41; Article 19 and Fundar, *Libertad de expresión*, 38, 49; interviews with Fernando Crisanto, Raúl Torres Salmerón, and Armando Prida, Puebla, Oct. 30, 2019.

72. Eiss, "Front Lines"; Paul Eiss, conversation with the author, Guadalajara, Oct. 20, 2018.

73. "Playa News anuncia cierre tras asesinato de Rubén Pat," EjeCentral.com.mx, July 25, 2018; "Asesinado un periodista en Playa del Carmen, el sexto en México en 2019," ElPais.com, May 16, 2019; "Sin trabajo, desplazados y pendientes de un botón de pánico," AnimalPolitico.com, Sept. 19, 2019; "Journalists Keep Getting Killed in Mexico after Posting on Facebook," Vice.com, Nov. 11, 2021; Alejandra Ibarra, conversation with the author, Mexico City, Sept. 9, 2019.

74. These counts, drawn from the author's database, exclude journalists confirmed as killed for reasons other than their work.

75. Ramos Rojas, *En defensa*, esp. 137–48; González de Bustamante and Relly, *Surviving Mexico*, 90–92; "Quienes somos," PeriodistasDeAPie.org.mx; Marcela Turati, interview (via videocall), Apr. 17, 2020; Daniela Pastrana, interview, Mexico City, Jan. 31, 2023.

76. Article 19, *Ante el silencio*, 16, 23, 141–43, 146–50.

77. Corruption charges were brought against Duarte and Borge only after they had stepped down; "15 exgobernadores bajo la lupa," Politico.mx, July 18, 2017.

78. *Norte de Ciudad Juárez*, Apr. 2, 2017, p. 1; Melissa del Bosque, "The Bunker," *New Yorker*, Apr. 17, 2023, pp. 30–41; Jan-Albert Hootsen, interview, Mexico City, Feb. 21, 2019; Abraham Rubio, interview, Mexico City, Apr. 4, 2019.

79. John Gibler, *To Die in Mexico* (San Francisco: City Lights, 2011), cited in Grecko, *Killing the Story*, 15; del Bosque, "Bunker."

80. "Proyecto Miroslava," PiedePagina.mx, Sept. 4, 2019; del Bosque, "Bunker."

81. Ioan Grillo, "The Man Who Wrote His Own Death Sentence," *Esquire*, Oct. 2018, pp. 62–67.

82. Grillo, "Man Who Wrote"; *La Jornada*, June 18, 2021, p. 14; Ioan Grillo, conversation with the author, Nov. 29, 2023.

83. Rogelio Hernández López, "La Feadle se torció," EjeCentral.com.mx, Mar. 2, 2015; Article 19, *Libertades en resistencia*; Committee to Protect Journalists, *No Excuse*; "EPN deja un burócrata en FEADLE y la prensa lo paga," SinEmbargo.mx, May 6, 2017; "Mexican Special Prosecutor for Crimes against Freedom of Expression Has a Long History, but Produces Few Results," LatAmJournalismReview.org, July 29, 2022; Jan-Albert Hootsen, interviews, Mexico City, Feb. 21, 2019, and via email, Nov. 15, 2023.

84. "Mexican Special Prosecutor"; del Bosque, "Bunker"; Jan-Albert Hootsen, interviews, Mexico City, Feb. 21, 2019, and via email, Nov. 15, 2023.

85. As in previous instances, these figures exclude journalists confirmed as killed for reasons other than their work.

86. Adrián López, "El presente del periodismo: 3," Horizontal.mx, Feb. 16, 2016.

87. Uribe Mendoza, *México Elecciones 2021*, 14–15.

88. On these stories, see the earlier section "Two Visions of Digital: *Animal Político* and *SinEmbargo*."

89. Silber Meza, "Los Piratas de Borge," MCCI (ContraLaCorrupcion.mx), July 6, 2016; *Expansión*, Aug. 1, 2016, pp. 88–96; "El SAT investiga a 21 funcionarios de Quintana Roo involucrados en despojo de bienes," AnimalPolitico.com, Aug. 22, 2016; Mariel Ibarra, "Los Piratas de Borge y el robo del tesoro de 16,000 millones de pesos," "El programa fachada de Borge para desviar recursos," and "Los vuelos millonarios de Borge y sus empresas favoritas," Expansion.com.mx, Aug. 15, 16 and 18, 2017; "Roberto Borge es vinculado a proceso por delincuencia organizada," Expansion.mx, Mar. 16, 2023; Silber Meza, interview, Mexico City, Feb. 29, 2020. In 2024, Borge remained in jail, facing charges including organized crime.

90. Rock, *La historia*, 107–10, 121–23; "Corruption Perceptions Index: Mexico," Transparency International, www.transparency.org/en/cpi/2015/index/mex; *Expansión*, Dec. 15, 2016, pp. 92–104.

91. Miguel Ángel León Carmona, "El campo de exterminio que gobierno de Veracruz ocultó," LaSillaRota.com, Apr. 26, 2017; Alejandra Guillén et al., "El país de las 2 mil fosas," *Quinto Elemento* (Quintoelab.org), Nov. 12, 2018; "'El país de las 2000 fosas' gana el Premio Breach/Valdez de Periodismo y Derechos Humanos 2019," UN Office on Drugs and Crime (Unodc.org), May 3, 2019.

92. Hernández, *La verdadera noche*; Rock, *La historia*, 97–103; "15 exgobernadores bajo la lupa," Político.mx, July 18, 2017; "Peña Nieto vs AMLO: aprobaciones históricas," Parametria.com.mx, Nov. 30, 2018; Article 19, *Ante el silencio*, 175–87.

93. Regidor and Iber, "New Hope for Mexico?"; *Economist*, June 23, 2018, pp. 20–22.

Epilogue

1. "La publicidad del gobierno de López Obrador," Economicon.mx, Sept. 17, 2024.

2. Schwartz, "Intermediary"; *Reforma*, July 20, 2018, p. 4; Jesús Cantú, interview, Monterrey, Dec. 7, 2023.

3. Estrada, *El imperio*, chaps. 3–5; Morín, *Prensa inmunda*, 229–35; Cortés, *El choque*, chap. 1; Maza, *Estado de Silencio*; "Mexico's López Obrador Holds Daily Briefings Rivalling Trump's," TheGuardian.com, May 4, 2020.

4. "Jesús Ramírez," interview by Sabina Berman, ADN Opinión, Feb. 12, 2019, YouTube .com. I base the defense of the *mañaneras* on personal observations and conversations with

progovernment journalists at two such press conferences, Mexico City, Nov. 7, 2023, and Aug. 27, 2024.

5. Cortés, *El choque*, chap. 4; León Krauze, "AMLO vs. 'Fake News,'" Slate.com, Mar. 14, 2019.

6. Article 19, *Disonancia*, 53–58, 117–27; Morín, *Prensa inmunda*, 235–40; "López Obrador's Anti-Press Rhetoric Leaves Mexico's Journalists Feeling Exposed," CPJ.org, May 6, 2019; "Hampa del periodismo," AnimalPolitico.com, May 23, 2019; Maza, *Estado de silencio*.

7. "Coronavirus desata crisis en diarios impresos en México," LaOpinion.com (Los Angeles), Apr. 8, 2020; Center for Research and Teaching in Economics journalism students, conversations with the author, Spring 2020; Samuel García, emails to the author, Feb. 16, 2021; Ernesto Aroche, email to the author, Feb. 18, 2021; Juan Larrosa-Fuentes, interview (via telephone), Jan. 9, 2024.

8. Rodelo, "Putting Context"; "COVID 19, amenaza el periodismo," SEMMexico.com, June 29, 2020; *El Pulso de los Medios*, Nov. 2021, p. 3, Dec. 2021, pp. 2–3; Center for Research and Teaching in Economics journalism students, conversations with the author, spring 2020.

9. Grecko, *No se mata*, 326–27; Reuters Institute for the Study of Journalism, *Digital News Report 2018*, 123, *Digital News Report 2023*, 121; *Reforma*, Feb. 6, 2019, p. 1, Oct. 7, 2023, pp. 1, 2.

10. Reuters Institute for the Study of Journalism, *Digital News Report 2020*, 93, *Digital News Report 2021*, 125; *Proceso*, Apr. 12, 2020; *El Universal*, Aug. 22, 2022, pp. 1, 6 (etc.); *El Pulso de los Medios*, Sept. 2023, p. 3.

11. "'Hago periodismo porque es mi forma de vida,' dice Nayeli Roldán," LatAmJournalismReview.org, Sept. 26, 2023; "Reyna Haydee Ramírez: la periodista que cuestiona a AMLO," Grupo Fórmula, Feb. 9, 2024, YouTube.com; "No fuimos Dinamarca" (series), AnimalPolitico.com, Feb. 26–Mar. 13, 2024.

12. Reuters Institute for the Study of Journalism, *Digital News Report 2018*, 123, *Digital News Report 2024*, 127; "El regreso de Carmen Aristegui," ElEconomista.com.mx, Jan. 20, 2017; *El Universal*, Nov. 30, 2021, p. 4; "Los periodistas más atacados por el Presidente," Spin, Sept. 2024 (courtesy of Luis Estrada); Alejandro Páez, interview, Mexico City, May 24, 2023.

13. "Los Periodistas," Youtube.com/hashtag/losperiodistas; Alejandro Páez, email to the author, Nov. 25, 2023.

14. *Washington Post*, Feb. 17, 2022, p.20; "Una red de políticos prominentes y empresas (con acceso a dinero público) está detrás de *Latinus*," SinEmbargo.mx, Mar. 29, 2021; *El Pulso de los Medios*, June 2023, pp. 1, 3, Sept. 2023, p. 2.

15. "Los amigos (muy amigos) de López Obrador," ElPais.com, Oct. 25, 2020; Andrew Paxman, "*La* larga *Jornada* hacia el oficialismo," *Nexos*, Sept. 2024, pp. 36–48.

16. Fernández and Paxman, *El Tigre*, 17–20; "La publicidad oficial en 2022," Funder.org.mx, Aug. 8, 2023; "Grupo Televisa S.A.B.," Finance.yahoo.com/quote/TV.

17. Comisión Interamericana de Derechos Humanos, *Informe anual*, 270, 280–84; Estrada, *El imperio*, chap. 6; Reyna, "'A Mercenary, a Thug'"; "A un año de su creación, 47% del 'Quién es Quién' es falso o engañoso," Verificado.com.mx, June 29, 2022.

18. Reuters Institute for the Study of Journalism, *Digital News Report 2024*, 127.

19. "Aprobación presidencial," Oraculus.mx, Sept. 27, 2024.

20. Nayeli Roldán, "¿Para qué sirve el periodismo y por qué no incidió en este sexenio?," LetrasLibres.com, Sept. 26, 2024.

21. Trappel, "Subsidies."

22. "Periodismo en México: Informar para vivir, morir por informar," SinEmbargo. mx, July 18, 2020; "Mexican Special Prosecutor for Crimes against Freedom of Expression Has a Long History, but Produces Few Results," LatAmJournalismReview.org, July 29, 2022; Jan-Albert Hootsen, email to the author, Nov. 15, 2023.

23. "Periodistas asesinados en México," Articulo19.org.

24. See, e.g., Esquivel Hernández, "Prensa de papel"; "Denuncian extrabajadores de *La Jornada Michoacán* incumplimientos de su directivo," Proceso.com.mx, Feb. 17, 2016; "El caso de Max Trejo y Mexico.com," DistintasLatitudes.net, Aug. 22, 2019.

25. "Daniel Hadad, en la asamblea de la SIP," InfoBAE.com, Oct. 20, 2018; José Soto Galindo, interview (via telephone), Sept. 24, 2024.

26. *Reforma*, Jan. 20, 2016, p. 9, Oct. 18, 2019, p. 10, Jan. 28, 29, 2020, p. 1, Mar. 22, 2022, p. 1; Sergio Aguayo, interview (via telephone), Sept. 9, 2024.

27. Banerjee et al., *Strategies for Building Trust*, 4, 67.

28. I taught in the Center for Research and Teaching in Economics journalism program between 2015 and 2020.

29. Carlos Bravo Regidor, "El fin de una era periodística," *Reforma*, Aug. 25, 2022, p. 10; emails to the author from Frida Rodelo, Dec. 21, 2023, Carlos Bravo Regidor, Dec. 28, 2023, and José Soto Galindo and Ignacio Rodríguez Reyna, Sept. 26, 2024; Daniel Moreno, interview (via telephone), Sept. 9, 2024; Daniela Pastrana, interview (via telephone), Sept. 17, 2024.

30. René Sánchez Huitrón, "El auge de la opinión," ArenaPublica.com, June 24, 2024.

31. Adrián López, interview (via email), Sept. 11, 2024.

32. Alejandra Salas-Porras, "De la guerra de ideas a la guerra jurídica," paper presented at Colegio de México, Aug. 30, 2023; "Claudio X. presidía MCCI y recibía fondos de EU cuando formó bloque político opositor," SinEmbargo.mx, July 6, 2022; "Mexicanos Contra la Corrupción pagó 619 mil pesos por nota de 'casa gris' de hijo de AMLO," Contralinea .com.mx, July 8, 2023.

33. "Washington Post opinion editor departs as Bezos pushes to promote 'personal liberties and free markets,'" TheGuardian.com, Feb. 26, 2025.

34. Alejandro Legorreta, "Una nueva era para Gatopardo," Gatopardo.com, Dec. 29, 2020; "Los galardonados de 2023," Gatopardo.com, Dec. 2023.

35. On the risk of a "two tier" media environment in the United States, United Kingdom, and elsewhere, see Reuters Institute, *Digital News Report 2018*, pp. 9–31; House of Lords, *The Future of News*.

Bibliography

Archives in Mexico City

Archivo General de la Nación
   Dirección Federal de Seguridad
   Dirección General de Investigaciones Políticas y Sociales
   Fototeca
Biblioteca Miguel Lerdo de Tejada
Fototeca Nacional
Hemeroteca Nacional

Interviews by the Author

Sergio Aguayo
Rubén Aguilar
Héctor Aguilar Camín
Juan Angulo
Leticia Ánimas
Manuel Appendini
Mely Arellano
Ernesto Aroche
Federico Arreola
Rosa Elba Arroyo
Miguel Basáñez
Viétnika Batres
Alberto Bello
Rafael Cabrera
Salvador Camarena
Arturo Cano
Jesús Cantú
Jorge Carrasco
José Carreño Carlón
Margarita Carreón
Juan Alberto Cedillo
Fernando Crisanto
Raúl Trejo Delarbre
Álvaro Delgado
René Delgado
Claudia Fernández

Eduardo García
Samuel García
Ramón Alberto Garza
Ciro Gómez Leyva
Luis Miguel González
Otto Granados
Maribel Gutiérrez
Armando Guzmán
José Luis Esquivel Hernández
María Elena Hernández Ramírez
Timothy Heyman
Rubén Hipólito
Jan-Albert Hootsen
Irving Huerta
José Landeros
Marco Lara Klahr
Juan Larrosa-Fuentes
Sara Lovera
Audelino Macario
Erwin Macario
Alejandro C. Manjarrez
Carlos Marín
Rubén Martín Martín
José Martínez
Javier Martínez Staines
Anne Marie Mergier

Silber Meza
Daniel Moreno
Humberto Musacchio
Alberto Nájar
Adela Navarro
Ernesto Núñez
Antonio Ocaranza
William Orme
Diego Enrique Osorno
Alejandro Páez
Daniela Pastrana
Diego Petersen Farah
Luis Petersen Farah
Armando Prida
Carlos Puig
Sam Quinones
Alejandro Ramos Esquivel
Ricardo Raphael
José Reveles
Lázaro Ríos
Raymundo Riva Palacio

Roberto Rock
Rafael Rodríguez Castañeda
Ignacio Rodríguez Reyna
César Romero Jacobo
Ariel Rosales
Abraham Rubio
Rodolfo Ruiz
Carlos Salinas de Gortari
Víctor Sámano
Lilia Saúl
María Scherer Ibarra
José Soto Galindo
Wilbert Torre
Raúl Torres Salmerón
Marcela Turati
Mael Vallejo
Alejandra Xanic
Roberto Zamarripa
Michael Zamba
Jorge Zepeda Patterson
Jésica Zermeño

Dissertations, Theses, and Unpublished Manuscripts

Arce Barceló, María Esther. "Análisis del periódico mexicano *La Jornada*." PhD diss., Universidad de Murcia, 2011.

Arellano Mora, Angelita Gisel, "¿La publicidad oficial puede posibilitar la crítica periodística? El caso de la revista *Proceso* de 1976 a 2018 en México." MA thesis, Universidad Iberoamericana, 2019.

Bautista Castillo, Virginia, "*Zeta*: Su historia, sus hombres." BA thesis, Universidad Nacional Autónoma de México, 1993.

Cobb, Phillip. "Provincial Journalism and National Development in Mexico." PhD diss., University of Texas, Austin, 1971.

Curry, James, Oscar Contreras, and Martin Kenney. "The Mexican Internet after the Boom: Challenges and Opportunities." BRIE Working Paper 159, Berkeley Roundtable on the International Economy, University of California, Berkeley, June 2004.

De la Rosa, Yared. "Manuel Buendía, el columnista que marcó el periodismo." Unpublished paper, masters of journalism, Centro de Investigación y Docencia Económicas, 2019.

González Posadas, Jennifer Carolina. "Construcción social de la noticia: Negociación de los criterios de noticiabilidad en el cibermedio mexicano." MA thesis, Universidad Autónoma de Aguascalientes, 2014.

Guízar García, Elizabeth. "Los titulares en la prensa mexicana del siglo XX." MA thesis, Universidad Nacional Autónoma de México, 2007.

Heredia Gayosso, Enrique Israel. "De Felipe Calderón a presidente de México: Análisis de contenido en prensa mexicana durante los primeros 100 días de gobierno." BA thesis, UNAM, 2014.

Hernández Medina, Sergio. "El desarrollo de la prensa en México." PhD diss., Universidad Complutense, 2019.

León, Carla. "Las mujeres empresarias en las páginas de la revista *Expansión*." Unpublished paper, master of journalism, Centro de Investigación y Docencia Económicas, 2019.

Loeza Landa, Jorge Eduardo. "Una representación de la narcoviolencia." MA thesis, Universidad Veracruzana, 2015.

Merchant Ley, Diana Denisse. "Una negociación sutil: Relaciones de cortesía entre actores del campo periodístico de Baja California." PhD thesis, CIESAS (Centro de Investigaciones y Estudios Superiores en Antropología Social) Occidente, Guadalajara, 2017.

Mondragón Aguilar, Susana Jeanine. "Prensa popularizada: *El Gráfico* y *Metro* y su construcción periodística del sujeto popular." PhD diss., Universidad Nacional Autónoma de México, 2017.

Nolan, Sidney. "Relative Independence of Two Mexican Dailies." MA thesis, University of Texas, Austin, 1965.

Scherer Ibarra, María. "Revista *Proceso*, en busca de un rediseño organizacional." MA thesis, Universidad Iberoamericana, 2010.

Solares Orgas, María Elvira. "Tratamiento periodístico de la información del caso Marín—Cacho, Puebla." BA thesis, Universidad Iberoamericana, Puebla, 2007.

Toche, Nelly. "Revista Emeequis, un modelo centrado en el producto y que descuidó el modelo de negocio." Unpublished paper, masters of journalism, Centro de Investigación y Docencia Económicas, 2020.

Published Works

Aguayo Quezada, Sergio. *La charola: Una historia de los servicios de inteligencia en México*. Mexico City: Grijalbo, 2001.

———. *1968: Los archivos de la violencia*. Mexico City: Grijalbo, 1998.

———. *Vuelta en U: Guía para entender y reactivar la democracia estancada*. Mexico City: Taurus, 2010.

Aguayo Quezada, Sergio, and Miguel Acosta. *Urnas y pantallas*. Mexico City: Océano, 1997.

Aguilar, Gabriela, and Ana Cecilia Terrazas. *La prensa, en la calle: Los voceadores y la distribución de periódicos y revistas en México*. Mexico City: Grijalbo, 1996.

Alcalá, Manuel, dir. *Red privada*. Netflix, 2021.

Alexander, Ryan M. *Sons of the Mexican Revolution: Miguel Alemán and His Generation*. Albuquerque: University of New Mexico Press, 2016.

Allier, Eugenia. *68: El movimiento que triunfó en el futuro*. Mexico City: Bonilla Artigas, 2021.

Alonso, Jorge. "Sociedad y gobierno en la coyuntura de las explosiones." In *Quién nos hubiera dicho: Guadalajara 22 de abril*, edited by Cristina Padilla and Rossana Reguillo. Guadalajara: ITESO, 1993.

Alves, Rosental Calmon. "From Lapdog to Watchdog: The Role of the Press in Latin America's Democratization." In *Making Journalists: Diverse Models, Global Issues*, edited by Hugo de Burgh. London: Routledge, 2005.

Americas Watch. *Human Rights in Mexico*. New York: Americas Watch, 1990.

Aroche, Ernesto. "Rafael Moreno Valle Rosas." In *Los Gobernadores*, edited by Andrew Paxman. Mexico City: Grijalbo, 2018.

Arslan, Melike. "Mexico's Battle with Monopolies: Reputation-Based Autonomy and Self-Undermining Effects in Antitrust Enforcement." *Socio-Economic Review* (2024): mwae036.

Article 19. *Ante el silencio, ni borrón ni cuenta nueva: Informe anual 2018*. Mexico City: Article 19, 2019.

———. *Democracia simulada, nada que aplaudir*. Mexico City: Article 19, 2018.

———. *Disonancia: Voces en disputa*. Mexico City: Article 19, 2020.

———. *In the Shadow of Buendía*. London: Article 19, 1989.

Article 19 and Fundar. *El costo de la legitimidad*. Mexico City: Article 19 and Fundar, 2013.

———. *Libertades en resistencia*. Mexico City: Article 19, 2017.

———. *Negación*. Mexico City: Article 19, 2022.

Article 19 and Fundar. *Diagnóstico sobre el gasto en comunicación social y publicidad en las entidades federativas*. Mexico City: Article 19 and Fundar, 2011.

———. *Libertad de expresión en venta*. Mexico City: Article 19 and Fundar, 2015.

Banerjee, Sayan, Camila Mont'Alverne, Amy Ross Arguedas, Benjamin Toff, Richard Fletcher, and Rasmus Kleis Nielsen. *Strategies for Building Trust in News: What the Public Say They Want across Four Countries*. Oxford: Reuters Institute for the Study of Journalism, 2023.

Benavides, José Luis. "*Gacetilla*: A Keyword for a Revisionist Approach to the Political Economy of Mexico's Print News Media." *Media, Culture and Society* 22, no. 1 (2000): 85–104.

Bess, Michael K. *Routes of Compromise: Building Roads and Shaping the Nation in Mexico, 1917–1952*. Lincoln: University of Nebraska Press, 2017.

Bohmann, Karin. *Medios de comunicación y sistemas informativos en México*. 1986; Mexico City: Conaculta, 1989.

Bosch, Lolita, and Alejandro Vélez Salas, eds. *Tú y yo coincidimos en la noche terrible*. Barcelona: Nuestra Aparente Rendición, 2012.

Bravo Regidor, Carlos, and Patrick Iber. "A New Hope for Mexico?" *Dissent* 65, no. 2 (2018): 94–105.

Brewster, Claire. "The Student Movement of 1968 and the Mexican Press: The Cases of *Excélsior* and *Siempre!*" *Bulletin of Latin American Research* 21, no. 2 (2002): 171–90.

Brüggemann, Michael, Sven Engesser, Florin Büchel, Edda Humprecht, and Laia Castro. "Hallin and Mancini Revisited: Four Empirical Types of Western Media Systems." *Journal of Communication* 64 (2014): 1037–65.

Bruhn, Kathleen. "López Obrador, Calderón, and the 2006 Presidential Campaign." In *Consolidating Mexico's Democracy: The 2006 Presidential Campaign in Comparative Perspective*, edited by Jorge I. Domínguez, Chappell Lawson, and Alejandro Moreno. Baltimore: Johns Hopkins University Press, 2009.

Burkholder, Arno. *La red de los espejos: Una historia del diario Excélsior, 1916–1976*. Mexico City: Fondo de Cultura Económica, 2016.

Cacho, Lydia. *Infamy: How One Woman Brought an International Sex Trafficking Ring to Justice*. Berkeley: Soft Skull, 2016.

———. *Los demonios del Edén: El poder que protege a la pornografía infantil.* Mexico City: Grijalbo, 2005.

Camp, Roderic A. *Entrepreneurs and Politics in Twentieth-Century Mexico.* New York: Oxford University Press, 1989.

———. *Mexican Political Biographies, 1835–1993.* Austin: University of Texas Press, 1995.

———. *Mexican Political Biographies, 1884–1934.* Austin: University of Texas Press, 1991.

———. *Politics in Mexico.* 2nd ed. New York: Oxford University Press, 1996.

Campos, Roy. *El juicio ciudadano: Evaluación de la presidencia de Felipe Calderón en México, 2006–2012.* Mexico City: Mitofsky, 2012.

Canadian Committee to Protect Journalists. *The Press and the Perfect Dictatorship.* Toronto: Canadian Committee to Protect Journalists, 1992.

Cano Andaluz, Aurora, ed. *Las publicaciones periódicas y la historia de México: Ciclo de conferencias.* Mexico City: Universidad Nacional Autónoma de México, 1995.

———. "Los libros y la prensa." In *Diálogos sobre el 68,* edited by Silvia González Marín. Mexico City: Universidad Nacional Autónoma de México, Instituto de Investigaciones Bibliográficas, 2003.

Carpizo, Jorge. *Un año en la procuración de justicia, 1993.* Mexico City: Porrúa/PGR, 1994.

Carreño Carlón, José. *Los medios de comunicación.* Mexico City: Nostra, 2007.

Castañeda, Jorge G. "Limits to Apertura: Prospects for Press Freedom in the New Free-Market Mexico." In *A Culture of Collusion: An Inside Look at the Mexican Press,* edited by William A. Orme Jr. Coral Gables, FL: North-South Center Press, 1997.

———. *Perpetuating Power: How Mexican Presidents Were Chosen.* New York: New Press, 2000.

Castillo, Moisés. *La biografía secreta de un semanario polémico.* Mexico City: El Salario del Miedo / Universidad Autónoma de Nuevo León, 2018.

Cole, Richard. "Unique English-Language Daily Succeeds in Mexico City." *Journalism Quarterly* 47, no. 3 (1970): 553–56.

Comisión Interamericana de Derechos Humanos. *Informe anual de la relatoría especial para la libertad de expresión.* Washington, DC: Organización de los Estados, 2022.

———. *Zonas silenciadas: Regiones de alta peligrosidad para ejercer la libertad de expresión.* Washington, DC: Organización de los Estados, 2017.

Committee to Protect Journalists. *Free Trade without a Free Press?* New York: Committee to Protect Journalists, 1994.

———. "Mexican Journalistes [*sic*] Murdered in the Line of Duty between 1984 and 1995." In *A Culture of Collusion: An Inside Look at the Mexican Press,* edited by William A. Orme Jr. Coral Gables, FL: North-South Center Press, 1997.

———. *No Excuse: Mexico Must Break Cycle of Impunity in Journalists' Murders.* New York: Committee to Protect Journalists, 2017.

Conger, Lucy. "From Intimidation to Assassination: Silencing the Press." In *A Culture of Collusion: An Inside Look at the Mexican Press,* edited by William A. Orme Jr. Coral Gables, FL: North-South Center Press, 1997.

Corcoran, Katherine. *In the Mouth of the Wolf: A Murder, a Cover-Up, and the True Cost of Silencing the Press.* New York: Bloomsbury, 2022.

Corona, Ignacio, and Beth E. Jörgensen, eds. *The Contemporary Mexican Chronicle: Theoretical Perspectives on the Liminal Genre.* Albany, NY: State University of New York Press, 2002.

Cortés, Raúl. *El choque inevitable: Prensa, discurso y poder en el sexenio de López Obrador.* Mexico City: Grijalbo, 2022.

Crovi, Delia, Florence Toussaint, and Aurora Tovar. *Periodismo digital en México.* Mexico City: Universidad Nacional Autónoma de México, 2006.

Dallas Morning News. *Credibility: A Look at the Mexican Press Today.* Dallas: Dallas Morning News, 1989.

Davies, Nick. *Hack Attack: How the Truth Caught Up with Rupert Murdoch.* London: Chatto and Windus, 2014.

Del Palacio Montiel, Celia. *Callar o morir en Veracruz: Violencia y medios de comunicación en el sexenio de Javier Duarte (2010–2016).* Mexico City: Juan Pablos, 2018.

Díaz-Domínguez, Alejandro, and Alejandro Moreno. "Effects of #YoSoy132 and Social Media in Mexico's 2012 Presidential Campaigns." In *Mexico's Evolving Democracy: A Comparative Study of the 2012 Elections*, edited by Jorge I. Domínguez, Kenneth F. Greene, Chappell H. Lawson, and Alejandro Moreno. Baltimore: Johns Hopkins University Press, 2014.

Domínguez, Jorge I., Kenneth F. Greene, Chappell H. Lawson, and Alejandro Moreno, eds. *Mexico's Evolving Democracy: A Comparative Study of the 2012 Elections.* Baltimore: Johns Hopkins University Press, 2014.

Dresser, Denise. *El país de uno.* Mexico City: Aguilar, 2011.

Echeverría, Martín, and Rubén Arnoldo González, eds. *Media and Politics in Post-Authoritarian Mexico.* Cham, Switzerland: Palgrave Macmillan, 2024.

Eiss, Paul. "Front Lines and Back Channels: The Fractal Publics of *El Blog del Narco*." In *Journalism, Satire, and Censorship in Mexico*, edited by Paul Gillingham, Michael Lettieri, and Benjamin T. Smith. Albuquerque: University of New Mexico Press, 2018.

El Universal. *El Universal, espejo de nuestro tiempo.* Mexico City: El Universal / MVS Editorial, 2006.

———. *Juan Francisco Ealy Ortiz: 50 años de vida periodística.* Mexico City: El Universal, 2019.

Escobedo, Juan Francisco, ed. *Comunicación y transparencia de los poderes del Estado.* Mexico City: Universidad Iberoamericana, 2003.

Escudero, Ángel. *El duelo en México.* 1936; Mexico City: Porrúa, 1998.

Espino Sánchez, Germán. "Periodistas precarios en el interior de la república mexicana: Atrapados entre las fuerzas del mercado y las presiones de los gobiernos estatales." *Revista Mexicana de Ciencias Políticas y Sociales* 61, no. 228 (2016): 91–120.

Espinoza Valle, Víctor Alejandro. "Alternancia y liberalización política." *Frontera Norte* 8, no. 16 (1996): 21–35.

Esquivel Hernández, José Luis. *Cien años de El Porvenir.* Monterrey: Cerda, 2019.

———. "Prensa de papel." *Revista Mexicana de Comunicación* 80 (Mar. 2003): 40–46.

———. *Reforma: Un grupo con Ángel.* Monterrey: Cerda, 2008.

Estrada, Luis. *El imperio de los otros datos: Tres años de falsedades y engaños desde palacio.* Mexico City: Grijalbo, 2022.

Estrada, Luis, dir. *La ley de Herodes.* Bandidos Films, 1999.

Fernández, Claudia, and Andrew Paxman. *El Tigre: Emilio Azcárraga y su imperio Televisa*. 4th ed. Mexico City: Grijalbo, 2021.

Fernández Christlieb, Fátima. *Los medios de difusión masiva en México*. Mexico City: Juan Pablos, 1982.

Flores Quintero, Genoveva. *La seducción de Marcos a la prensa: Versiones sobre el levantamiento zapatista*. Mexico City: M. A. Porrúa, 2004.

———. *Unomásuno: Victorias perdidas del periodismo mexicano, 1977–1989*. Mexico City: Universidad Iberoamericana / Fractal, 2014.

Freedom House. *Freedom and the Media 2019*. Washington, DC: Freedom House, 2019.

Fregoso Peralta, Gilberto. *Prensa regional y elecciones*. Guadalajara: Universidad de Guadalajara, 1993.

Fregoso Peralta, Gilberto, and Enrique E. Sánchez Ruiz. *Prensa y poder en Guadalajara*. Guadalajara: Universidad de Guadalajara, 1993.

Freije, Vanessa. "Censorship in the Headlines: National News and the Contradictions of Mexico City's Press Opening in the 1970s." In *Journalism, Satire, and Censorship in Mexico*, edited by Paul Gillingham, Michael Lettieri, and Benjamin T. Smith. Albuquerque: University of New Mexico Press, 2018.

———. *Citizens of Scandal: Journalism, Secrecy, and the Politics of Reckoning in Mexico*. Durham, NC: Duke University Press, 2020.

Fromson, Murray. "Mexico's Struggle for a Free Press." In *Communication in Latin America: Journalism, Mass Media, and Society*, edited by Richard R. Cole. Wilmington, DE: Scholarly Resources, 1996.

Fundar. *Contar "lo bueno" cuesta mucho: El gasto en publicidad oficial del gobierno federal 2013 a 2016*. Mexico City: Fundar, 2017.

Galaz Ramírez, Lourdes, ed. *Los primeros veinte, 1984–2004*. Mexico City: DEMOS, 2004.

García, Elvira. *Ellas, tecleando su historia: Conversaciones con mujeres periodistas*. México City: Grijalbo, 2012.

Garciadiego, Javier. "¿Cuándo, cómo, por qué y quiénes hicieron la Constitución de 1917?" *Historia Mexicana* 66, no. 3 (2016): 1183–270.

Garner, Paul. *British Lions and Mexican Eagles: Business, Politics, and Empire in the Career of Weetman Pearson in Mexico, 1889–1919*. Stanford, CA: Stanford University Press, 2011.

———. *Porfirio Díaz*. London: Longman, 2001.

Garza Ramos, Javier. "Democratization and the Regional Press." In *Journalism, Satire, and Censorship in Mexico*, edited by Paul Gillingham, Michael Lettieri, and Benjamin T. Smith. Albuquerque: University of New Mexico Press, 2018.

Gillingham, Paul. "The Regional Press Boom, ca. 1945–1965." In *Journalism, Satire, and Censorship in Mexico*, edited by Paul Gillingham, Michael Lettieri, and Benjamin T. Smith. Albuquerque: University of New Mexico Press, 2018.

Gillingham, Paul, Michael Lettieri, and Benjamin T. Smith, eds. *Journalism, Satire, and Censorship in Mexico*. Albuquerque: University of New Mexico Press, 2018.

Gillingham, Paul, and Benjamin T. Smith, eds. *Dictablanda: Politics, Work, and Culture in Mexico, 1938–1968*. Durham, NC: Duke University Press, 2014.

Gómez Gallardo, Perla. "Sobre el ejercicio responsable de la libertad de expresión." *Revista Mexicana de Comunicación* 25, no. 130 (Apr. 2012): 42–43.

González, Cecilia. *Escenas del periodismo mexicano: Historias de tinta y papel*. Mexico City: Fundación Manuel Buendía, 2006.

González Casanova, Pablo. *Democracy in Mexico*. New York: Oxford University Press, 1970.

González de Bustamante, Celeste, and Jeannine Relly. *Surviving Mexico: Resistance and Resilience among Journalists in the Twenty-First Century*. Austin: University of Texas Press, 2021.

González Macías, Rubén Arnoldo, and Víctor Hugo Reyna García. "'They Don't Trust Us; They Don't Care If We're Attacked': Trust and Risk Perception in Mexican Journalism." *Communication and Society* 32, no. 1 (2019): 147–60.

González Macías, Rubén Arnoldo, and Grisel Salazar Rebolledo. "Confianza en la prensa mexicana: Hacia un mejor entendimiento sobre el nexo entre periodistasy audiencias." *Improntas de la Historia y la Comunicación* 11 (2023): e051.

Granados Chapa, Miguel Ángel. *Buendía: El primer asesinato de la narcopolítica en México*. Mexico City: Grijalbo, 2012.

Grayson, George W. *Mexican Messiah: Andrés Manuel López Obrador*. University Park: Pennsylvania State University Press, 2007.

Grecko, Témoris. *Killing the Story: Journalists Risking Their Lives to Uncover the Truth in Mexico*. New York: New Press, 2020.

———. *No se mata la verdad: El peligro de ser periodista en México*. Mexico City: HarperCollinsMéxico, 2020.

Grillo, Ioan. *El Narco: The Bloody Rise of Mexican Drug Cartels*. London: Bloomsbury, 2013.

Guerrero, Manuel Alejandro. *¿Cómo se informa hoy en México? Cinco tendencias noticiosas ante la narrativa oficial*. Mexico City: Universidad Iberoamericana, 2018.

———. *Democracia y medios en México*. Mexico City: Instituto Nacional Electoral, 2016.

Guerrero, Manuel Alejandro, and Mireya Márquez-Ramírez, eds. *Media Systems and Communication Policies in Latin America*. London: Palgrave Macmillan, 2014.

Haber, Stephen, Herbert S. Klein, Noel Maurer, and Kevin J. Middlebrook. *Mexico since 1980*. Cambridge: Cambridge University Press, 2008.

Hallin, Daniel, and Paolo Mancini. *Comparing Media Systems: Three Models of Media and Politics*. New York: Cambridge University Press, 2004.

Hallin, Daniel C., and Stylianos Papathanassopoulos. "Political Clientelism and the Media: Southern Europe and Latin America in Comparative Perspective." *Media, Culture and Society* 24 (2002): 175–95.

Harlow, Summer. *Digital-Native News and the Remaking of Latin American Mainstream and Alternative Journalism*. Abingdon, UK: Routledge, 2022.

Herman, Edward S., and Noam Chomsky. *Manufacturing Consent: The Political Economy of the Mass Media*. New York: Pantheon, 1988.

Hernández, Anabel. *Fin de fiesta en Los Pinos*. Mexico City: Grijalbo, 2006.

———. *La verdadera noche de Iguala*. Mexico City: Grijalbo, 2016.

———. *Los cómplices del presidente*. Mexico City: Grijalbo, 2008.

———. *Los señores del narco*. 2010; rev. ed., Mexico City: Grijalbo, 2014.

———. *Narcoland*. London: Verso, 2013.

Hernández, Anabel, and Arelí Quintero. *La familia presidencial*. Mexico City: Grijalbo, 2005.

Hernández Navarro, Luis. "Acteal: Impunidad y memoria." *El Cotidiano* 172 (2012): 99–115.

Hernández Ramírez, María Elena. "Franquicias periodísticas y sinergias productivas en la prensa mexicana." In *Estudios sobre periodismo: Marcos de interpretación para el contexto mexicano*, edited by María Elena Hernández Ramírez. Guadalajara: Universidad de Guadalajara, 2010.

———. "La formación universitaria de periodistas en México." *Comunicación y Sociedad* 1 (2004): 109–38.

———. "*Siglo 21*: Periodistas diferentes." In *Medios de Comunicación y Derecho a la Información en Jalisco, 2021*, edited by Juan S. Larrosa-Fuentes. Tlaquepaque, Jalisco: ITESO, 2023.

Hernández Santos, Marcelo. "Cuerpos sin nombre, nombres sin cuerpo: Los 43 desaparecidos de la normal rural de Ayotzinapa, Guerrero (2014)." In *De Tlatelolco a Ayotzinapa: 50 años de insurgencía estudiantil*, edited by José Eduardo Jacobo Bernal. Zacatecas: Universidad Autónoma de Zacatecas, 2019.

Herscovitz, Heloiza. "Leading Newspapers in Brazil as Political Actors (1994–Present)." *Estudios Interdisciplinarios de América Latina* 30, no. 2 (2019): 93–122.

Hinds, Harold, and Charles Tatum. *Not Just for Children: The Mexican Comic Book in the Late 1960s and 1970s*. Westport, CT: Greenwood, 1992.

House of Lords. *The Future of News*. London, 2024.

Hughes, Sallie. *Newsrooms in Conflict: Journalism and the Democratization of Mexico*. Pittsburgh: University of Pittsburgh Press, 2006.

Hurtado Razo, Luis Ángel. "¿Encuestas o Propaganda? La estrategia política, elecciones 2012." *Razón y Palabra* 87 (July 2014).

Impunidad Cero. *Impunidad en homicidio doloso y feminicidio 2022*. Mexico City: Impunidad Cero, 2022.

Jacobson, Kristi, dir. Dirty Money. Season 1, episode 4, "Cartel Bank." Aired on Netflix on January 26, 2018.

Jarvenpaa, Sirkka L., and Dorothy E. Leidner. "An Information Company in Mexico: Extending the Resource-Based View of the Firm to a Developing Country Context." *Information Systems Research* 9, no. 4 (1998): 342–61.

Jones, Nathan. "The Unintended Consequences of Kingpin Strategies: Kidnap Rates and the Arellano-Félix Organization." *Trends in Organized Crime* 16, no. 2 (2013): 156–76.

Krauze, Enrique. *La presidencia imperial*. Mexico City: Tusquets 1997.

———. *Mexico: Biography of Power*. New York: HarperCollins, 1997.

———. "Proceso a Proceso." *Proceso 30 años*. Oct. 2006.

Kuschik, Murilo. "Las encuestas y la elección del año 2000." *Revista Mexicana de Ciencias Políticas y Sociales* 44, no. 180 (2015): 120–37.

Lara Klahr, Marco. *Diarismo: Cultura e industria del periodismo impreso en México y el mundo*. Mexico City: Editorial E, 2005.

Lara Klahr, Marco, and Ernesto López Portillo Vargas, eds. *Violencia y medios 2: Reporteros de policía*. Mexico City: Insyde / Centro de Investigación y Docencia Económicas, 2006.

Larrosa-Fuentes, Juan. "Los periódicos de Guadalajara entre 1991 y 2011: El ocaso de la prensa industrial." In *Estudios sobre periodismo en México: Despegue e institucionalización*, edited by María Elena Hernández Ramírez. Guadalajara: Universidad de Guadalajara, 2018.

Lawson, Chappell. *Building the Fourth Estate: Democratization and the Rise of a Free Press in Mexico*. Berkeley: University of California Press, 2002.

Leñero, Vicente. *Los periodistas*. Mexico City: Joaquín Mortiz, 1978.

Leñero, Vicente, and Carlos Marín. *Manual de periodismo*. Mexico City: Grijalbo, 1986.

Levario Turcott, Marco. "¿Crisis en *La Jornada*?" *Etcétera*, Apr. 2003, pp. 5–11.

———. *Primera plana: La borrachera democrática de los diarios*. Mexico City: Cal y Arena, 2002.

Lida, David. Introduction to *Field of Battle*, by Sergio González Rodríguez. Los Angeles: Semiotext(e), 2019.

Lizárraga, Daniel, Rafael Cabrera, Irving Huerta, and Sebastián Barragán. *La Casa Blanca de Peña Nieto: La historia que cimbró un gobierno*. Mexico City: Grijalbo, 2015.

Llopis, Enric. *Plumas rebeldes: Periodistas contra la corriente*. Valencia: n.p., 2019.

Loaeza, Guadalupe. *Las niñas bien*. Mexico City: Océano, 1987.

———. *Las reinas de Polanco*. Mexico City: Cal y Arena, 1988.

Lomelí Meillón, Luz. "Gobernantes y gobernados: Una reflexión política." In *Quién nos hubiera dicho: Guadalajara 22 de abril*, edited by Cristina Padilla and Rossana Reguillo. Guadalajara: ITESO, 1993.

López Obrador, Andrés Manuel. *La mafia nos robó la presidencia*. Mexico City: Grijalbo, 2007.

———. *La mafia que se adueñó de México*. Mexico City: Grijalbo, 2010.

Lozano Rendón, José Carlos. "El Acuerdo para la Cobertura Informativa de la Violencia en México: Un intento fallido de autorregulación." *Comunicación y Sociedad* 26 (2016): 13–42.

Márquez-Ramírez, Mireya. "Mapping Anti-Press Violence in Latin America: Challenges for Journalists' Safety." In *The Routledge Companion to News and Journalism*, 2nd ed., edited by Stuart Allan. Abingdon, UK: Routledge, 2023.

Marshall, Jon. *Watergate's Legacy and the Press: The Investigative Impulse*. Evanston, IL: Northwestern University Press, 2011.

Martínez, Alegría. *Manuel Becerra Acosta: Poder y periodismo*. Mexico City: Plaza y Janés, 2001.

Martínez, José. *Las enseñanzas del profesor*. Mexico City: Océano, 1999.

Martínez Mendoza, Sarelly. "El periodismo en Chiapas durante el gobierno de Absalón Castellanos Domínguez." *Revista Pueblos y Fronteras* 2, no. 3 (2007): 251–93.

Maza, Santiago, dir. *Estado de silencio*. La Corriente del Golfo, 2024.

Meade, Everard. "The Plaza Is for the *Populacho*, the Desert Is for Deep-Sea Fish: Lessons from *la Nota Roja*." In *Journalism, Satire, and Censorship in Mexico*, edited by Paul Gillingham, Michael Lettieri, and Benjamin T. Smith. Albuquerque: University of New Mexico Press, 2018.

Meyer, Lorenzo. "El presidencialismo: Del populismo al neoliberalismo." *Revista Mexicana de Sociología* 55, no. 2 (1993): 57–81.

Michener, Greg. "FOI Laws around the World." *Journal of Democracy* 22, no. 2 (2011): 145–59.

Mijangos y González, Pablo. *Historia mínima de la Suprema Corte de Justicia de México*. Mexico City: Colegio de México, 2019.

Minnesota Advocates for Human Rights. *Massacre in Mexico: Killings and Cover-Up in the State of Guerrero*. Minneapolis: Minnesota Advocates for Human Rights, Dec. 1995.

Moncada Ochoa, Carlos. *¡Cayeron!* Mexico City: n.p., 1979.

———. *Oficio de muerte: Periodistas asesinados en el país de la impunidad*. Mexico City: Grijalbo/Proceso, 2013.

Monsiváis, Carlos, ed. *A ustedes les consta*. Mexico City: Era, 1980.

Morales Flores, Mónica. "25 años de fotografiar: Pedro Valtierra, fotógrafo de prensa." *Letras históricas* 16 (2017).

Moreno, Daniel. "The Big Missing Link for Promoting the Rule of Law." In *The Missing Reform: Strengthening the Rule of Law in Mexico*, edited by Viridiana Ríos and Duncan Wood. Washington, DC: Woodrow Wilson Center, 2018.

Morín, Edgar. *Prensa inmunda: Breviario de engaños, crimen y propaganda*. Mexico City: Grijalbo, 2022.

Morris, Stephen D. *Corruption and Politics in Contemporary Mexico*. Tuscaloosa: University of Alabama Press, 1991.

———. *Gringolandia*. Lanham, MD: SR Books, 2005.

———. *Political Corruption in Mexico: The Impact of Democratization*. Boulder, CO: Lynne Rienner, 2009.

Moynihan, Mary C. "Mexican News and American Diplomacy: U.S. State Department Monitoring of Press Freedom Violations in Mexico." In *A Culture of Collusion: An Inside Look at the Mexican Press*, edited by William A. Orme Jr. Coral Gables, FL: North-South Center Press, 1997.

Musacchio, Humberto, ed. *Diccionario enciclopédico de México*. 4 vols. Mexico City: Andrés León, 1989.

———. *Granados Chapa: Un periodista en contexto*. Mexico City: Planeta / Temas de hoy, 2010.

———. *Historia crítica del periodismo mexicano*. Mexico City: Luna Media, 2016.

———, ed. *Milenios de México*. 3 vols. Mexico City: Hoja Casa Editorial, 1999.

Niblo, Stephen. *Mexico in the 1940s: Modernity, Politics, and Corruption*. Wilmington, DE: SR Books, 1999.

Núñez Jaime, Víctor. *Carlos Marín: Un periodista ante el espejo*. Mexico City: Planeta/ Temas de hoy, 2011.

Oppenheimer, Andrés. *Bordering on Chaos: Guerrillas, Stockbrokers, Politicians, and Mexico's Road to Prosperity*. Boston: Little, Brown, 1996.

Orme, William A., Jr., ed. *A Culture of Collusion: An Inside Look at the Mexican Press*. Coral Gables, FL: North-South Center Press, 1997.

Ortiz Garza, José Luis. "Fighting for the Soul of the Mexican Press: Axis and Allied Activities during the Second World War." In *¡Américas unidas! Nelson A. Rockefeller's Office of Inter-American Affairs (1940–46)*, edited by Gisela Cramer and Ursula Prutsch. Madrid: Iberoamericana/Vervuert, 2012.

Ortiz Marín, Ángel Manuel, ed. *Los medios de comunicación en Baja California*. Mexicali: Universidad Autónoma de Baja California, 2006.

Ortiz Pinchetti, Francisco, and Francisco Ortiz Pardo. *El fenómeno Fox: La historia que Proceso censuró*. Mexico City: Planeta, 2001.

Osorno, Diego Enrique. *El Cártel de Sinaloa: Una historia del uso político del narco*. Mexico City: Grijalbo, 2009.

———. *La guerra de los Zetas: Viaje por la frontera de la necropolítica*. Mexico City: Grijalbo, 2012.

———. *Slim: Biografía política del mexicano más rico del mundo*. Mexico City: Debate, 2015.

Osorno, Diego Enrique, and Alejandro Aldrete, dirs. *La muñeca tetona*. Detective, 2017.

Oster, Patrick. *The Mexicans: A Personal Portrait of a People*. New York: William Morrow, 1989.

Padilla, Cristina, and Rossana Reguillo, eds. *Quién nos hubiera dicho: Guadalajara 22 de abril*. Guadalajara: ITESO, 1993.

Pastrana, Daniela. "Javier Duarte." In *Los Gobernadores*, edited by Andrew Paxman. Mexico City: Grijalbo, 2018.

Paxman, Andrew. "Changing Opinions in *La Opinión*: Maximino Ávila Camacho and the Puebla Press, 1936–1941." In *Journalism, Satire, and Censorship in Mexico*, edited by Paul Gillingham, Michael Lettieri, and Benjamin T. Smith. Albuquerque: University of New Mexico Press, 2018.

———. "Guadalajara Film Festival." In *The Variety Guide to Film Festivals*, edited by Steven Gaydos. New York: Perigee, 1998.

———. *Jenkins of Mexico: How a Southern Farm Boy Became a Mexican Magnate*. New York: Oxford University Press, 2017.

———, ed. *Los Gobernadores*. Mexico City: Grijalbo, 2018.

———. "Maximino Ávila Camacho." In *Los Gobernadores*, edited by Andrew Paxman. Mexico City: Grijalbo, 2018.

———. "Mexican Democracy's Awkward Partner: Televisa as a De Facto Power." In *Mexico in Focus: Political, Environmental and Social Issues*, edited by José Galindo. Hauppauge, NY: Nova Science, 2015.

———. "The Salinas Years, 1988–1994: Watershed in the Opening of Mexico's Print Media." In *Media and Politics in Post-Authoritarian Mexico*, edited by Martín Echeverría and Rubén Arnoldo González. Cham, Switzerland: Palgrave Macmillan, 2024.

Payán, Carlos. *Memorial del Viento*. Mexico City: Secretaría de Cultura de la Ciudad de México, 2018.

Pew Research Center. *What the World Thinks in 2002*. Washington, DC: Pew Research Center, 2002.

Piccato, Pablo. *A History of Infamy: Crime, Truth, and Justice in Mexico*. Berkeley: University of California Press, 2017.

———. "Notes for a History of the Press in Mexico." In *Journalism, Satire, and Censorship in Mexico*, edited by Paul Gillingham, Michael Lettieri, and Benjamin T. Smith. Albuquerque: University of New Mexico Press, 2018.

Polit Dueñas, Gabriela. *Unwanted Witnesses: Journalists and Conflict in Contemporary Latin America*. Pittsburgh: University of Pittsburgh Press, 2019.

Poniatowska, Elena. *Nada, nadie: Las voces del temblor*. Mexico City: Era, 1988.

Preston, John. *Fall: The Mystery of Robert Maxwell*. London: Viking, 2021.

Preston, Julia, and Sam Dillon. *Opening Mexico: The Making of a Democracy*. New York: Farrar, Straus and Giroux, 2004.

Quinones, Sam. *True Tales from Another Mexico: The Lynch Mob, the Popsicle Kings, Chalino, and the Bronx*. Albuquerque: University of New Mexico Press, 2001.

Ramos Rojas, Diego Noel. *En defensa de la libertad de expresión: Estudio sobre acciones y trayectorias de los Colectivos de Periodistas en México*. Guadalajara: Universidad de Guadalajara/CIESAS, 2022.

Rea, Daniela, and Pablo Ferri. *La tropa: Por qué mata un soldado*. Mexico City Aguilar, 2019.

Reavis, Dick. "Stop the Presses." *Texas Monthly*, Nov. 1978, pp. 192–98.

Reding, Andrew. "Mexico at a Crossroads: The 1988 Election and Beyond." *World Policy Journal* 5, no. 4 (1988): 615–49.

Relea, Francesc. "Carlos Slim." In *Los amos de México*, edited by Jorge Zepeda Patterson. Mexico City: Planeta, 2007.

Reuter, Peter, and Letizia Paoli. "How Similar Are Modern Criminal Syndicates to Traditional Mafias?" *Crime and Justice* 49, no. 1 (2020).

Reuters Institute for the Study of Journalism. *Digital News Report*. Oxford: Oxford University, 2018–. Published annually.

Reyna, Víctor Hugo. "'A Mercenary, a Thug . . . Not Even a Journalist': The Stigmatization of News Workers in Mexico." *Journalism Practice* (2024).

Reyna, Víctor Hugo, Martín Echeverría, and Rubén Arnoldo González. "Beyond Exogenous Models: Mexican Journalism's Modernization in Its Own Terms." *Journalism Studies* 21, no. 13 (2020): 1815–35.

Riding, Alan. *Distant Neighbors: A Portrait of the Mexicans*. New York: Vintage, 1985.

Ríos, Viridiana, and Johanna Rivera. "Media Effects on Public Displays of Brutality: The Case of Mexico's Drug War." *Politics, Groups, and Identities* 7, no. 1 (2019): 194–206.

Riva Palacio, Raymundo. "A Culture of Collusion: The Ties That Bind the Press and the PRI." In *A Culture of Collusion: An Inside Look at the Mexican Press*, edited by William A. Orme Jr. Coral Gables, FL: North-South Center Press, 1997.

———. *La prensa de los jardines: Fortalezas y debilidades de los medios en México*. Mexico City: Plaza & Janés, 2004.

———. *Manual para un nuevo periodismo: Desafíos del oficio en la era digital*. Mexico City: Grijalbo, 2013.

———. *Más allá de los límites: Ensayos para un nuevo periodismo*. Mexico City: Fundación Manuel Buendía, 1988.

Rivard, Robert. *Trail of Feathers: Searching for Philip True*. New York: Public Affairs, 2005.

Rock, Roberto. *La historia detrás del desastre: Crónica de una herencia envenenada*. Mexico City: Grijalbo, 2019.

Rockwell, Rick. "Mexico: The Fox Factor." In *Latin Politics, Global Media*, edited by Elizabeth Fox and Silvio Waisbord. Austin: University of Texas Press, 2002.

Rodelo, Frida-V. "Putting Context at the Forefront: A Critical Case Study of Journalists' Layoffs in Mexico." *Communication and Society* 36, no. 2 (2023): 17–31.

Rodríguez Castañeda, Rafael. *Operación Telmex: Contacto en el poder*. Mexico City: Grijalbo, 1995.

———. *Prensa vendida: Los periodistas y los presidentes*. Mexico City: Grijalbo, 1993.

Rodríguez García, Arturo. *El regreso autoritario del PRI: Inventario de una nación en crisis*. Mexico City: Grijalbo, 2015.

Rodríguez Munguía, Jacinto. *La otra guerra secreta: Los archivos prohibidos de la prensa y el poder*. Mexico City: Debate, 2007.

———. "*Proceso*, la ruptura." *Milenio Semanal*, Mar. 29, 1999, pp. 30–37.

Roldán, Nayeli, Miriam Castillo Moya, and Manuel Ureste Cava. *La estafa maestra*. Mexico City: Temas de hoy, 2018.

Roldán, Nayeli, and Manuel Ureste. *La estafa maestra: La historia del desfalco*. Rev. ed. Mexico City: Planeta, 2022.

Ross, John. *Rebellion from the Roots: Indian Uprising in Chiapas*. Monroe, ME: Common Courage, 1995.

———. *The War against Oblivion: The Zapatista Chronicles, 1994–2000*. Monroe, ME: Common Courage, 2000.

Rossana Reguillo, "Comunicación irruptiva: El 22 de abril a través de los medios de comunicación." In *Quién nos hubiera dicho: Guadalajara 22 de abril*, edited by Cristina Padilla and Rossana Reguillo. Guadalajara: ITESO, 1993.

Rubio, Luis. "Coping with Political Change." In *Mexico under Zedillo*, edited by Susan Kaufman Purcell and Luis Rubio. Boulder, CO: Lynne Rienner, 1998.

Ruiz Castañeda, María del Carmen, ed. *La prensa, pasado y presente de México*. Mexico City: Universidad Nacional Autónoma de México, 1990.

Salazar Rebolledo, Grisel. *Más allá de la violencia: Alianzas y resistencias de la prensa local mexicana*. Mexico City: Centro de Investigación y Docencia Económicas, 2022.

Salinas de Gortari, Carlos. *México: Un paso difícil a la modernidad*. Barcelona: Plaza y Janés, 2000.

Sánchez Ruiz, Enrique E. "El público de la prensa: La insoportable levedad de casi no ser." *Anuario de Investigación de la Comunicación CONEICC* 1 (1994): 165–85.

Sarmiento, Sergio. "Trial by Fire: The Chiapas Revolt, the Colosio Assassination and the Mexican Press in 1994." In *A Culture of Collusion: An Inside Look at the Mexican Press*, edited by William A. Orme Jr. Coral Gables, FL: North-South Center Press, 1997.

Scherer García, Julio. *El poder*. Mexico City: Grijalbo, 1990.

———. *Estos años*. Mexico City: Océano, 1995.

———. *La terca memoria*. Mexico City: Grijalbo, 2007.

———. *Los presidentes*. 3rd ed. Mexico City: Grijalbo, 2015.

———. *Vivir*. Mexico City: Grijalbo, 2012.

Scherer García, Julio, and Carlos Monsiváis. *Tiempo de saber: Prensa y poder en México*. Mexico City: Aguilar, 2003.

Schiffrin, Anya. Introduction to *In the Service of Power: Media Capture and the Threat to Democracy*, edited by Anya Schiffrin. Washington, DC: Center for International Media Assistance, 2017.

Schwartz, Leo. "The Intermediary." *Columbian Journalism Review*, Jan. 8, 2020.

Secanella, Petra María. *El periodismo político en México*. Mexico City: Prisma, 1983.

Seifert, Erica. *The Politics of Authenticity in Presidential Campaigns, 1976–2008*. Jefferson, NC: McFarland, 2014.

Serna, Ana María. *"Se solicitan reporteros": Historia oral del periodismo mexicano en la segunda mitad del siglo XX*. Mexico City: Instituto Mora, 2015.

Serna, Enrique. *El vendedor de silencio*. Alfaguara, 2019.

Sherman, Scott. "The Mexican Media and the 1994 Elections." In *Changing Patterns: Latin America's Vital Media*, by Jon Vanden Heuvel and Everette E. Dennis. New York: Freedom Forum Media Studies Center, 1995.

Singer, Leticia. *Mordaza de papel*. Mexico City: El Caballito, 1993.

Smith, Benjamin T. *The Dope: The Real History of the Mexican Drug Trade*. London: Ebury, 2021.

———. *The Mexican Press and Civil Society, 1940–1976: Stories from the Newsroom, Stories from the Street*. Chapel Hill: University of North Carolina Press, 2018.

Sparrow, Bartholomew. *Uncertain Guardians: The News Media as a Political Institution*. Baltimore: Johns Hopkins University Press, 1999.

Starkman, Dean. *The Watchdog That Didn't Bark*. New York: Columbia University Press, 2014.

Stephen, Lynn. *Stories That Make History: Mexico through Elena Poniatowska's Crónicas*. Durham, NC: Duke University Press, 2021.

Stoub, Jeffrey. "Self-Censorship and the Mexican Press." *Mexico Policy News* 9 (Fall 1993): 30–34.

Téllez Cuevas, Rodolfo. "Los Riva Palacio, su presencia de dos siglos en la política Mexicana." *Espacios Públicos* 14, no. 32 (2011): 103–27.

Tello Díaz, Carlos. *La rebelión de Las Cañadas*. Mexico City: Cal y Arena, 1995.

Tercero, Magali. *Cuando llegaron los bárbaros*. Mexico City: Temas de hoy, 2011.

Tiffen, Rodney. *Rupert Murdoch: A Reassessment*. Sydney: University of New South Wales Press, 2014.

Torre, Wilbert. *El despido: La verdad detrás de salida de Carmen Aristegui del noticiero más escuchado en México*. Mexico City: Temas de hoy, 2015.

Torres A., Francisco Javier. *El periodismo mexicano: Ardua lucha por su integridad*. Mexico City: Ediciones Coyoacán, 1997.

Toussaint Alcaraz, Florence. *Recuento de periódicos fronterizos*. Mexico City: Fundación Manuel Buendía, 1990.

Trappel, Josef. "Subsidies: Fuel for the Media." In *Comparative Media Policy, Regulation and Governance in Europe: Unpacking the Policy Cycle*, edited by Leen d'Haenens, Helena Sousa, and Josef Trappel. Bristol: Intellect, 2018.

Trejo Delarbre, Raúl. "Democracia por escrito: La prensa mexicana entre 1970 y 1994." In *Las publicaciones periódicas y la historia de México*, edited by Aurora Cano Andaluz. Mexico City: Universidad Nacional Autónoma de México, 1995.

———. "La actuación de los medios." In *2 de julio: Reflexiones y alternativas*, edited by Jacqueline Peschard. Mexico City: Universidad Nacional Autónoma de México, 2007.

———. *Mediocracia sin mediaciones: Prensa, televisión y elecciones*. Mexico City: Cal y Arena, 2001.

———. "Periódicos: ¿Quién tira la primera cifra?" *Nexos*, June 7, 1990, Cuadernos de Nexos, I–III.

Trejo Delarbre, Raúl, and Ricardo Becerra. *Chiapas: La comunicación enmascarada, los medios y el pasamontañas*. Mexico City: Diana, 1994.

Trevino-Rangel, Javier. *Policing the Mexican Past: Transitional Justice in a Post-authoritarian Regime*. Cham, Switzerland: Palgrave Macmillan, 2022.

Tuckman, Jo. *Mexico: Democracy Interrupted*. New Haven, CT: Yale University Press, 2012.

Turati, Marcela. *Fuego cruzado: Las víctimas atrapadas en la guerra del narco*. Mexico City: Grijalbo, 2011.

Turati, Marcela, and Daniela Rea, eds. *Entre las cenizas: Historias de vida en tiempos de muerte*. Mexico City: Sur+, 2012.

Uribe Mendoza, Cristhian. *México Elecciones 2021*. Mexico City: Reformas Políticas, 2021.

Valdez Cárdenas, Javier. *Los morros del narco*. Mexico City: Aguilar, 2011.

———. *Narcoperiodismo: La prensa en medio del crimen y la denuncia*. Mexico City: Aguilar, 2016.

———. *The Taken: True Stories of the Sinaloa Drug War*. Translated by Everard Meade. 2012. Lincoln: University of Nebraska Press, 2017.

Vanden Heuvel, Jon, and Everette E. Dennis. *Changing Patterns: Latin America's Vital Media*. New York: Freedom Forum Media Studies Center, Columbia University, 1995.

Velasco Arregui, Edur. "Precarización del empleo y régimen neoliberal." *Alegatos* 92 (2016): 175–200.

Villamil, Jenaro. *El sexenio de Televisa*. Mexico City: Grijalbo, 2010.

———. *Peña Nieto: El gran montaje*. Mexico City: Grijalbo, 2012.

———. *Si yo fuera presidente*. Mexico City: Grijalbo, 2009.

Villamil, Jenaro, and Julio Scherer Ibarra. *La guerra sucia de 2006: Los medios y los jueces*. Mexico City: Grijalbo, 2007.

Volpi, Jorge. *La imaginación y el poder*. Mexico City: Era, 1998.

Waisbord, Silvio. *Watchdog Journalism in South America: News, Accountability and Democracy*. New York: Columbia University Press, 2000.

Walker, Louise E. *Waking from the Dream: Mexico's Middle Classes after 1968*. Stanford, CA: Stanford University Press, 2015.

WAN-IFRA. *Comprando complacencia: Política y censura indirecta en México*. Mexico City, 2014.

Ward, Peter M., and Elizabeth Durden. "Government and Democracy in Mexico's Federal District, 1997–2001: Cárdenas, the PRD and the Curate's Egg." *Bulletin of Latin American Research* 21, no. 1 (2002): 1–39.

Wornat, Olga. *La jefa: Vida pública y privada de Marta Sahagún de Fox*. Mexico City: Grijalbo, 2003.

Zacarías, Armando. "El papel del papel de PIPSA en los medios mexicanos." *Comunicación y Sociedad* 25–26 (1995–96): 73–88.

Zavala, Oswaldo. *La guerra en las palabras*. Mexico City: Debate, 2022.

———. *Los cárteles no existen*. Barcelona: Malpaso, 2018.

Zepeda Patterson, Jorge, ed. *Los suspirantes 2012*. Mexico City: Planeta, 2011.

Zolov, Eric. *Refried Elvis: The Rise of the Mexican Counterculture*. Berkeley: University of California Press, 1999.

Index

drug cartels. *See* crime syndicates

Drug Enforcement Administration, US (DEA), 12–13, 14, 113, 219

Duarte, Javier (Gov), 223–24, 228, 231–32, 233, 249–50, 259, 264, 267, 268, 314n24, 320n77

Durazo, Arturo "El Negro," 43–44, 119

Ealy Ortiz, Juan Francisco, xvi, 24–32, 33, 35, 40–42, 92, 112, 121, 126, 130–32, 146, 182, 185–88, 252, 257–58; firing of editors by, 32, 147, 187–88, 252, 258, 286n23; and pluralism, 128–30, 132–33, 192, 237, 274–75

earthquake of 1985, xi, xvii, 6, 62, 80, 106, 144–49, 236

Echeverría, Luis, 25–26, 27–29, 34, 35, 40, 43, 56, 93–94, 113, 118, 131, 134, 168, 175; and "coup" against *Excélsior*, xi, 16–17, 29, 42, 47, 115, 117, 121, 139, 176, 269

Economist (magazine), 242, 245

El Economista, 19, 76, 87, 99, 102, 153, 154, 205, 273

E-Consulta (Puebla), 177, 262, 269

Eilemberg, Daniel, 247, 251

embute (form of government bribe), 9, 34, 39, 50, 69, 84, 95, 98, 145, 154. See also *chayote*

Emeequis (magazine), 179, 237

Enrigue, Álvaro, 239, 240

Enríquez, Raymundo (Gov), 225

Este País (magazine), 99, 273

ETA (Euskadi Ta Askatasuna), 158–59

Etcétera (magazine), 126, 158

Europe, 3, 43, 123, 161, 278; Mexican journalists in, 46–47, 58, 241

European press, xiv, 34–35, 43, 62, 74–75, 95, 123, 126, 150–51, 198, 241, 254–55, 278. See also British press; French press; Spanish press

Excélsior, 1, 4, 15–21, 25, 26, 33, 37, 116, 285n28; and Echeverría's "coup," xi, 16–17, 29, 42, 47, 110, 115, 117, 121, 139, 176, 269; "diaspora" of employees; xi, 42, 45, 115, 122, 123; under Regino Díaz Redondo, 17–21, 39, 42, 43, 64, 66, 68, 70, 99, 108, 112, 133, 139, 142, 145, 148, 154, 176–77, 180; under Julio Scherer, 5, 16, 27, 28, 29, 43,

116–18, 120–21, 123; under Vázquez family ownership, 193–95, 195, 247, 259, 260, 273, 310n16

"excess of press," xvi, 37; in Mexico City, 37, 89, 150, 188, 255, 273; in state capitals, 37, 255, 261, 278

Expansión (magazine), 188, 193, 206–9, 214, 268

Fábrica de Periodismo, 281

Facebook, 244, 246, 247, 252, 254, 256, 262, 263, 264, 278, 281

Falcón (cartoonist), 77, 81

Federal Access to Information Institute (IFAI), 178–79

Federal Electoral Institute (IFE), 160, 180, 191–92, 194

Federal Judicial Police (PJF), 67, 68, 103

Federal Security Directorate (DFS), 29, 38, 66–67, 98–99, 116, 134, 140

Federal Transparency and Access to Governmental Public Information Act, 178–79

Félix Gallardo, Miguel Ángel, 13, 140

Félix Miranda, Héctor, 49–54, 57

Fernández, Claudia, 103, 132, 133, 161

Fernández Menéndez, Jorge, 101–2, 194

Figueroa, Raúl (Gov), 153

Financial Times, 181, 204, 244

El Financiero, 19, 66, 69, 70, 102–4, 105, 112, 123, 127, 130, 132, 142, 144, 148, 151, 170, 188, 205, 210

El Fisgón (cartoonist), 149, 159–60, 196–97, 303n32

Fobaproa (bank bail-out fund), 127, 136, 192, 205

Forbes (magazine), 65, 203, 204, 209

Ford Foundation, 129, 157, 251–52

"Fourth Transformation" (4T), 270, 271, 274–76, 277, 282

Fox, Vicente, 69, 172, 190, 227, 261; election of, 137–38, 160–63, 169, 176; in media, 133, 160, 164–66, 169, 173, 178–80, 183, 185, 187, 190, 192, 237; and media opening, xii, xviii, 163, 167, 175–81, 182, 200; and media restrictions, 164, 181, 211

Building Service-Oriented Government

Lessons, Challenges and Prospects

NCPA Research Series

ISSN: 2315-4896

In the new millennium, governments worldwide are experiencing a series of challenges posed by social, economic and technological changes such as globalization, financial crises, global warming, population ageing and Internet and social media. Addressing these "wicked problems" requires a fundamental transformation in public administration from traditional government-centric model to collaborative governance. This transformation provides public administration scholars with unprecedented opportunities in playing a significant role in influencing public policy making, implantation and bring about social changes through their scholarship. This book series is part of the efforts of Nanyang Centre for Public Administration (NCPA) in taking advantage of the expertise of its scholars and collaborators to examine thorny policy and management problems governments are dealing with. Paying special attention to Asia, particularly China and Singapore, the series focuses on cutting-edge public policy and management issues in urban planning and development, public service delivery, public crisis management, public budgeting, public sector performance management, E-government and social media and collaborative governance. Not only does the series aim to contribute to the scholarship in the increasing important discipline in Asia, but also emphasize its social relevance and impacts in and on the quality of public policy making and implementation and most important, people's quality of life.

Published

Building Service-Oriented Government: Lessons, Challenges and Prospects
edited by Wu Wei (Nanyang Technology University, Singapore)

Building Service-Oriented Government

Lessons, Challenges and Prospects

NCPA Research Series

1

Editor

Wu Wei
Nanyang Technological University, Singapore

World Scientific

NANYANG CENTRE FOR
PUBLIC ADMINISTRATION

Published by

World Scientific Publishing Co. Pte. Ltd.

5 Toh Tuck Link, Singapore 596224

USA office: 27 Warren Street, Suite 401-402, Hackensack, NJ 07601

UK office: 57 Shelton Street, Covent Garden, London WC2H 9HE

British Library Cataloguing-in-Publication Data
A catalogue record for this book is available from the British Library.

BUILDING SERVICE-ORIENTED GOVERNMENT
Lessons, Challenges and Prospects

ISBN 978-981-4434-53-9 (pbk)

In-house Editor: Alisha Nguyen

Typeset by Stallion Press
Email: enquiries@stallionpress.com

Preface

The 2012 Lien International Conference on Public Administration was held in Nanyang Technological University (NTU), Singapore, March 10–11, 2012. Sponsored by Singapore's Lien Foundation, the conference was organized by NTU's Nanyang Centre for Public Administration (NCPA) in collaboration with the School of International and Public Affairs of Shanghai Jiao Tong University, and the Section on Chinese Public Administration of American Society for Public Administration (ASPA). With the theme of "Forging Service-Oriented Government: Challenges and Prospects," the conference aims to provide a platform for participants to exchange ideas, views, knowledge, experiences and practices on forging a service-oriented government from a comparative perspective.

During the two-day conference, over 30 leading politics and public administration experts from the United States, Mainland China, Taiwan, Hong Kong and Singapore presented their studies and participated in panel discussions. Professor Tom Liou, the first Chinese-American President of ASPA, who was invited as the Conference distinguished speaker, delivered a keynote speech "Public Ethical Values and Service-Oriented Government."

To create more-rounded discussions and bring in new perspectives, senior scholars and government officials from China and Singapore were invited as roundtable discussions panelists. They gave very insightful views on some of the critical public administration issues faced in their own countries, and shared many important lessons drawn from their experiences. For the closing session, we were honored to have Mr. Li Zaiyong, Mayor of Guiyang City, China, to share his experience on achieving good governance in China.

While conference participants highlighted the difficulties in establishing a service-oriented government, they all agreed that an efficient service-oriented government is essential for sustainable growth and economic development, as well as the well-being of the people. The government and civil society have to actively cooperate with each other in order to forge an efficient service-oriented government.

All in all, the 2012 Lien International Conference on Public Administration was very successful. After a peer review process, ten papers presented in the conference are included in this book. We are pleased to see a variety of relevant topics and are grateful to the professionalism, expertise and insightful views contributed by the authors in the book. We hope these papers will contribute to the scholarship and practice in building service-oriented government and good governance in China and beyond.

This conference was just one of our ways to facilitate dialogue and knowledge sharing. There are still many areas that we can learn from one another. We hope this event will stimulate even greater collaboration and cooperation among the researchers, practitioners and government leaders across the borders.

Lastly, we would like to acknowledge Singapore's Lien Foundation for their kind support and sponsorship for this conference.

Contents

Chapter 1

Evaluating Public Service Performance in Urban China: Findings From the 2011 Lien Chinese Cities Service-Oriented Government Project

Wu Wei*, Yu Wenxuan†, Lin Tingjin‡, Wang Jun§
and Tam Waikeung¶

China has made remarkable economic and social progress within three decades of the market-oriented reform. However, the country is still facing numerous challenges. During this period of profound transformation, building a service-oriented government and a harmonious society has become central to China's ongoing administrative reform and has been gradually embraced by government of all levels (Gao and Wang, 2009). A service-oriented government represents a governance mode that places service in the center of government functions, which requires a fundamental transformation of government functions for Chinese public administration. The service-oriented government requires a sufficient understanding of the needs of citizens and businesses that is critical to meet the goals of creating a

---
*Associate Professor, Director of Nanyang Centre for Public Administration, Nanyang Technological University
†Assistant Professor, School of Humanities and Social Sciences, Nanyang Technological University
‡Research Fellow, Nanyang Centre for Public Administration, Nanyang Technological University
§Research Associate, Nanyang Centre for Public Administration, Nanyang Technological University
¶Former Research Fellow, Nanyang Centre for Public Administration, Nanyang Technological University

favorable socio-economic environment and providing quality public services. Building a service-oriented government is one of the important themes of China's 12th Five-Year Plan. Therefore, it has become imperative for public administration practitioners, public administration scholars and the public to understand the concept of service-oriented government from a comprehensive survey of how the development of service-oriented government proceeds in China and learn the lessons from both successes and failures.

In 2010, with the generous support from the Lien Foundation in Singapore, the Nanyang Centre for Public Administration (NCPA) at Nanyang Technological University (NTU) and the School of Public Affairs (SPA) at Xiamen University jointly developed the Lien Public Service Excellence Index for Chinese Cities and used it to assess and rank the quality of public service delivery in 32 major Chinese cities. On September 19, 2010, NCPA and SPA introduced the index and reported the ranking in a press conference in Guangzhou. The index and the ranking attracted widespread interest and discussion within China and beyond (Wu *et al.*, 2011). In 2011, based on the latest international and national research and practices and China's 12th Five-Year Plan, NCPA systematically updated the index to the "Lien Chinese Cities Service-Oriented Government Index." The new index reflects the efforts Chinese government makes in building service-oriented government that cannot be sufficiently evaluated by the prior index. According to the "Lien Chinese Cities Service-Oriented Government Index" (the Index hereafter), NCPA and the School of International and Public Affairs at Shanghai Jiao Tong University in China conducted a telephone survey of urban citizens and businesses in 32 major Chinese cities including municipalities directly under the central government, provincial capitals, sub-provincial cites[1] and some important cities during April–June 2011. Based on the data collected, we examined the trajectory of building service-oriented government in China and identified successful practices. The findings of this project do not only illustrate Chinese local governments' efforts in building service-oriented government but also test the internal and external validity of the Index.

---

[1] For the translation of "副省级市", three different translations coexist, namely, "vice-provincial city," "deputy-provincial city" and "sub-provincial city." To avoid confusion, we adopt the translation, sub-provincial city in this report.

This chapter presents the Lien Chinese Cities Service-Oriented Government Index and analyzes data collected from the 2011 Lien Survey of Service-Oriented Government in Chinese Cities. The chapter has five sections. The first section reviews the existing literature, defines the concept of service-oriented government, and highlights the theoretical backgrounds of the Lien Chinese Cities Service-Oriented Government Index. The second section introduces the Lien Chinese Cities Service-Oriented Government Index. The third section discusses the methodologies adopted by the 2011 Lien Survey of Service-Oriented Government in Chinese Cities, followed by the section presenting the main findings. The final section concludes.

1.1. Public Service, Service-Oriented Government and Evaluation

The Lien Chinese Cities Service-Oriented Government Index was developed as a scientific, practical and localized evaluation scheme for continuously assessing the performance of Chinese cities in building service-oriented government. Developing the Index requires comprehensive examination and comparison of relevant international and national studies and evaluation frameworks on public service delivery and service-oriented government in order to establish its practical relevance and distinguish it from existing similar schemes.

In 2010, we systematically examined the scope, nature and design of the following international or national evaluation schemes on public service quality: Global Competitiveness Index by World Economic Forum (Schwab, 2011), World Competitiveness Index by International Institute for Management Development in Lausanne (World Competitiveness Centre, IMD, 2010), Global Cities Index by *Foreign Policy* (Foreign Policy, 2008), Quality of Life Index by the Intelligence Unit of *Economist* (Economist Intelligence Unit, 2005), World Bank's Doing Business project (The World Bank Group, 2010), Accenture's Leadership in Customer Service project (Accenture, 2009), Mercer's 2010 Global Quality of Living survey (Mercer, 2010), the annual *Blue Book of City Competitiveness* by Chinese Academy of Social Sciences since 2003 (Chinese Academy of Social Sciences, 2010), the annual *Strategic Report of China's Sustainable Development* by Chinese Academy of Sciences (Chinese Academy of Sciences, 2010), the 2010 Chinese City Public Service Index developed by Antai College of Economics and Management in Shanghai Jiao Tong University (Antai

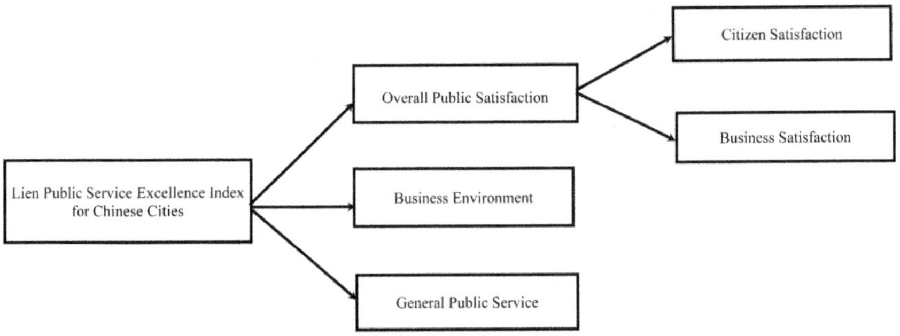

Figure 1.1.   2010 Lien Public Service Excellence Index for Chinese Cities.

College of Economics and Management, SJTU, 2010), and the 2009 Index for Public Assessment of Public Service developed by Horizon Research Consultancy Group in China (Horizon Research Consultancy Group, 2009).

Drawing upon existing literature and relevant evaluation schemes and fully considering the Chinese characteristics of public service provision, we developed the Lien Public Service Excellence Index for Chinese Cities in 2010. This index has three dimensions: overall public satisfaction, business environment, and general public service (see Figure 1.1). The three dimensions consist of several sub-dimensions. For instance, overall public satisfaction includes citizen satisfaction and business satisfaction. The index has total 106 measurements.

In 2011, after reviewing latest official reports, documents and speeches delivered by Chinese leaders, and reflect on the new development in theory and practice in Chinese public administration. We realized that public service provision is only one of many dimensions of a service-oriented government. The building of service-oriented government in China not only involves the provision of quality public service, but also entails other dimensions such as rule-of-law and democratic governance. A service-oriented government is a government that is effective and transparent, allows democratic participation, provides a favourable environment for sustainable development, produces quality public goods and services, and enjoys a high level of public trust and support. A viable index for service-oriented government should include the aforementioned elements, reflecting Chinese government's efforts in carrying out administrative reforms, enhancing administrative capacity, empowering citizens' political participation, and improving the accessibility of government information.

1.2. 2011 Lien Chinese Cities Service-Oriented Government Index

Based on the extant research and a understanding of the nature and scope of a service-oriented government, we developed the 2011 Lien Chinese Cities Service-Oriented Government Index. The Index is an upgrade of the 2010 Lien Public Service Excellence Index for Chinese Cities. In addition to the three dimensions in the previous index — overall public satisfaction, business environment, and general public service, the new index include four additional dimensions: government efficacy, citizen participation in policy making and implementation, government transparency, and government trust (see Figure 1.2).

The 2011 Lien Chinese Cities Service-Oriented Government Index comprises three dimensions: citizen perspective, business perspective, and

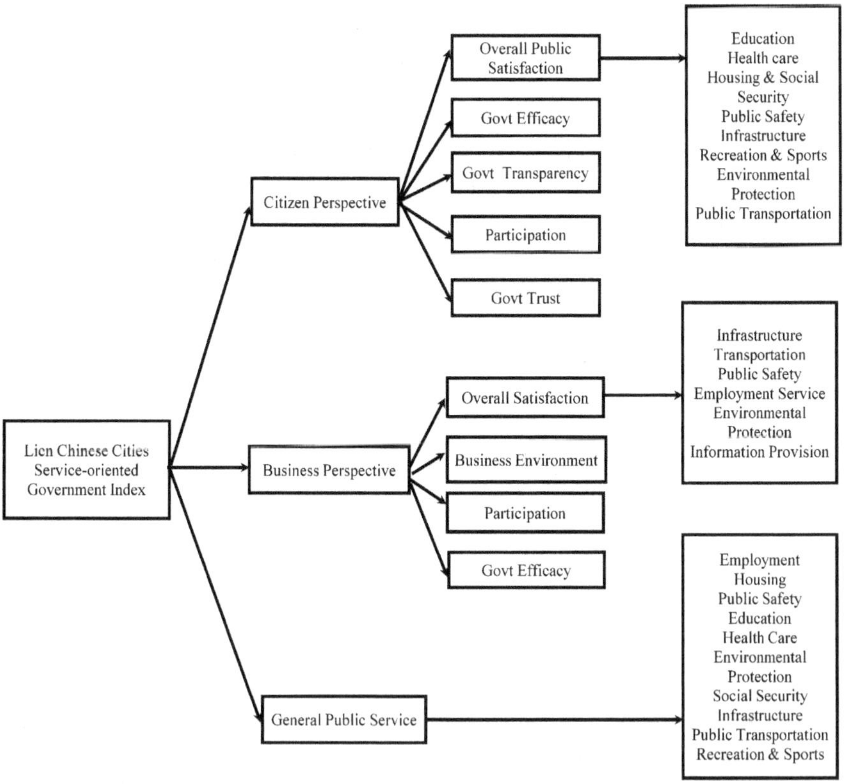

Figure 1.2. 2011 Lien Service-Oriented Government Index.

general public service. The citizen perspective includes five sub-dimensions:

1) overall public satisfaction: how citizens are satisfied with eight types of public services: education, health care, housing and social security, public safety, infrastructure, recreation and sports facilities, environmental protection, and public transportation;

2) government efficacy: how citizens perceive government's efficiency, effectiveness and competency in providing public service;

3) government transparency: how citizens perceive the accessibility of information in policy making, policy outcomes, and implementation;

4) citizen participation in policy making and implementation: how citizens perceive to what extent government allows them to participate in the process of policy making and implementation.

5) government trust: how citizens perceive the trustworthiness of government, i.e. whether government sincerely pursues public interest and does right things even in the absence of constant scrutiny.

The business perspective includes four sub-dimensions:

1) overall satisfaction: business assessment of infrastructure, transportation, public safety, employment service, environmental protection, and information provision that are crucial to their development;

2) business environment: business assessment of ten important public services, including annual industrial-commercial registration service, taxation, and protection of intellectual property rights, and so forth;

3) participation in policy making and implementation: business assessment of the degree to which government allows them to participate and influence policy making and implementation; and

4) government efficacy: business assessment of government efficiency and capacity in providing public service.

General public service covers ten types of public services, including employment, housing, public safety, education, health care, environmental protection, social security, infrastructure, public transportation, and recreation and entertainment facilities. Data on inputs and outputs of these public services come from official statistical yearbooks and relevant government reports and archives.

Following the principles of comprehensiveness, feasibility, localization, non-redundancy, cost-sensitivity and data accessibility, we adopted a variety of qualitative and quantitative research methods including Delphi method and focus group for constructing and selecting measurements. As a result, we included 75 measurements in the Index.

As highlighted in Figure 1.2, the 75 measurements are grouped within 10 different sub-dimensions. Because these 75 measurements have different units of measurement, on the one hand, we need to standardize different units of measurement using z-score, on the other hand, given that standardization tends to lose some information of the original data, however, we also need to avoid using z-scores as possible as we can. Accordingly, when the measurements within one dimension (or sub-dimension) had the same unit of measurement, we used raw scores of each measurement for further calculation. Only when the measurements within one dimension (or sub-dimension) have different units did we convert all raw scores of each measurement into dimensionless z-score for further analysis.

When a sub-dimension consists of three or more measurements, each measurement was weighted by a component score obtained by the Principal Component Analysis (PCA); otherwise, measurements were assigned equal weights. In aggregating the scores of the two general categories — Citizen Perspective and Business Perspective, we used PCA to weight the dimensions within the two perspectives.

Finally, in calculating the total scores of building service-oriented government (i.e., assigning weights to the three general dimensions of the Index), we adopted Delphi method and consulted public administration experts and government officials in Singapore and China. They agreed that there were no sound theoretical and practical guidelines regarding assigning weights to the three dimensions. Accordingly, we assigned equal weight to each dimension.

1.3. 2011 Lien Survey of Service-Oriented Government in Chinese Cities

During April–June 2011, using the Lien Chinese Cities Service-Oriented Government Index as the framework for survey design, NCPA and the School of International and Public Affairs at Shanghai Jiao Tong University conducted telephone survey of urban citizens and businesses in 32 major Chinese cities (for details, please refer to Table 1.1)

1.3.1. *Telephone survey of urban citizens*

The telephone survey was conducted in a two-month period (April–June) in 2011. In 9 of the 32 cities in China (Beijing, Shanghai, Shenyang, Chongqing, Guangzhou, Chengdu, Xi'an, Shenzhen, and Wuhan), we sampled about 1,000 residents in each city. In each of the other cities, we chose about 700 residents. A total of 25,222 valid telephone interviews

Table 1.1.   Sample Size of Each City.

Municipalities directly under the central government

Beijing (1003)   Shanghai (1000)   Tianjin (701)   Chongqing (1000)

Provincial capital cities and sub-provincial level cities

Changchun(701)	Changsha (705)	Chengdu (1005)	Dalian (700)
Fuzhou (702)	Guangzhou (1000)	Guiyang (706)	Harbin (702)
Haikou (704)	Hangzhou (704)	Hefei (701)	Jinan (700)
Kunming (700)	Lanzhou (710)	Nanchang (704)	Nanjing (700)
Nanning (701)	Ningbo (700)	Qingdao (703)	Shenyang (1042)
Shenzhen (1004)	Shijiazhuang (714)	Taiyuan (702)	Wuhan (1000)
Xi'an (1000)	Xiamen (702)	Zhengzhou (702)	

Other important city

Suzhou (704)

Table 1.2.   Demographics of Survey Respondents (Citizens).

Variable	(N)	Percentage %
Gender		
Male	13824	54.8
Female	11398	45.2
Education		
Junior secondary school or below	4518	18.0
Senior secondary school, vocational school	6504	26.0
College, University graduates or above	13966	55.9
Age		
18–29	11444	45.9
30–39	6002	24.1
40–49	3716	14.9
50–59	1885	7.6
60 or above	1892	7.6
Individual monthly income (RMB)		
1999 or below	6132	25.9
2000–3999	8796	37.2
4000–5999	3006	12.8
6000–7999	781	3.3
8000–9999	388	1.7
10000 or above	1043	4.3
No fixed income	3449	14.6

were conducted. Table 1.3 reports the socio-economic characteristics of the respondents. Compared China's Sixth National Population Census' data on resident population with the demographic data of our survey respondents, our respondents were representative in their respective urban population.

Table 1.3.   Socio-economic Characteristics of Survey Respondents (Businesses).

Variable	(N)	Percentage %
Ownership		
State-owned	159	5.2
Collectively-owned	59	1.9
Joint ventures	49	1.6
Sole foreign-owned	42	1.4
Private	1913	63.1
Individually-owned	808	26.7
Number of employees		
1–200	2568	89.6
201–400	76	2.7
401–600	41	1.4
601–800	13	0.5
801–1000	55	1.9
1001 or above	112	3.9
Nature of Business		
Agriculture and mining	96	3.5
Manufacturing and construction	657	24.1
Transportation, retail and hotel	640	23.5
Finance and property	270	9.9
Communication, computer and software	374	13.7
Scientific research and geology	66	2.4
Education	54	2.0
Health care and social welfare	88	3.2
Management of citizen facilities and citizen services	482	17.7
Length of business operation in the city		
Less than 2 years	776	26.3
2–5 years	988	33.4
6–10 years	576	19.5
More than 10 years	615	20.8

1.3.2. *Telephone survey of businesses*

In the same period we also conducted a telephone survey of businesses in the 32 cities. With around 100 business representatives being interviewed in each city, we finally have a total of 3,203 valid telephone interviews. The sampling frame was the 2011 edition of the "Phone Number Directory of the Legal Representatives of Business Enterprises" (the Directory) of each selected city. In each city, we randomly chose 1,000 telephone numbers from the Directory and made phone calls. If we failed to complete 100 successful telephone interviews out of the 1,000 telephone numbers, we drew another 1,000 telephone numbers from the Directory and make another round of calls. The process would continue if we could not complete 100 successful

interviews in a city. Table 1.3 shows the characteristics of our business respondents.

1.4. Findings of the 2011 Lien Survey of Service-Oriented Government in Chinese Cities

1.4.1. *The citizen perspective*

The overall public satisfaction dimension is composed of 19 measurements that evaluate eight types of public services. Respondents rated each type of public services on a 10-point scale, with the highest score (most satisfied) being 10 and the lowest (most dissatisfied) 1. 5 and 6 represent a medium level of satisfaction. The overall citizen assessment of public service quality are 6 or higher in all the 32 selected cities, which means that citizens are relatively satisfied with public services of their respective cities. Citizens in 10 cities (Xiamen, Hangzhou, Qingdao, Ningbo, Suzhou, Dalian, Jinan, Nanjing, Beijing and Chongqing) have relatively higher satisfaction with public service, as these cities scored 7.78–8.53 (see Table 1.4). It should also be noted that no city scored 9 or higher, implying room for further improvement.

To measure citizens' perception on the other four sub-dimensions, citizen participation in policy making and implementation, government transparency, government efficacy, and government trust, we asked the respondents to what extent they agree with a number of statements. These statements were assessed by a five-point Likert scale, ranging from completely disagree (1), disagree, neutral/so-so, agree, to completely agree (5). For the convenience of comparison, we coded the above five options as 2, 4, 6, 8, 10 in our final analysis. In the spectrum, 6 is in the middle and refers to a neutral assessment of public service. The data in Table 1.4 show that citizens' attitudes toward these dimensions, to a large degree, are neutral. The majority of cities scored 6 or 7 on each of the dimensions and none of the cities obtained scores higher than 7.5. Moreover, citizens have a relatively low rating on government efficacy. Only nine cities scored above 6 and the highest score was only 6.44. The scores of the remaining 23 cities range from 5.2 to 6.0. In sum, all city governments (including the top ten) need to further improve their performance in citizen participation, government transparency, government efficacy, and government trust.

In the citizen perspective, Xiamen performs much better than other cities, ranked the first on all the five dimensions. Jinan and Qingdao, two cities in Shandong province, were ranked among the top ten on all the five

Table 1.4. Rankings of the Sub-dimensions of Service-Oriented Government in Citizen Perspective.

Ranking	Public Service Satisfaction	Government Citizen Participation	Information Transparency	Government Efficacy	Government Trust
1	Xiamen 8.53	Xiamen 7.18	Xiamen 7.28	Xiamen 6.44	Xiamen 7.34
2	Hangzhou 8.25	Chongqing 7.06	Guiyang 7.02	Guiyang 6.30	Guiyang 7.16
3	Qingdao 8.20	Qingdao 7.00	Qingdao 7.00	Qingdao 6.10	Qingdao 7.12
4	Ningbo 8.12	Guiyang 6.88	Jinan 6.92	Hangzhou 6.08	Shijiazhuang 7.08
5	Suzhou 8.10	Changsha 6.82	Changsha 6.90	Dalian 6.08	Hefei 7.02
6	Dalian 8.02	Kunming 6.80	Suzhou 6.90	Suzhou 6.08	Haerbin 7.00
7	Jinan 7.87	Changchun 6.78	Haerbin 6.88	Hefei 6.08	Changsha 6.98
8	Nanjing 7.85	Shijiazhuang 6.76	Nanning 6.86	Ningbo 6.06	Changchun 6.98
9	Beijing 7.84	Jinan 6.76	Shijiazhuang 6.86	Jinan 6.04	Jinan 6.96
10	Chongqing 7.78	Suzhou 6.76	Changchun 6.82	Changsha 6.02	Nanning 6.96
11	Chengdu 7.75	Nanning 6.74	Chongqing 6.80	Changchun 6.00	Zhengzhou 6.94
12	Shijiazhuang 7.74	Hangzhou 6.74	Ningbo 6.78	Nanning 5.98	Chongqing 6.92
13	Changchun 7.65	Shanghai 6.74	Hangzhou 6.72	Zhengzhou 5.98	Suzhou 6.88
14	Shenyang 7.63	Ningbo 6.72	Dalian 6.70	Chongqing 5.96	Ningbo 6.86
15	Shanghai 7.63	Haikou 6.70	Hefei 6.68	Kunming 5.96	Nanchang 6.82
16	Changsha 7.60	Wuhan 6.66	Kunming 6.66	Chengdu 5.94	Taiyuan 6.80
17	Nanning 7.58	Hefei 6.60	Nanchang 6.60	Shijiazhuang 5.92	Chengdu 6.78
18	Hefei 7.56	Haerbin 6.58	Zhengzhou 6.58	Haikou 5.90	Lanzhou 6.78
19	Tianjin 7.56	Dalian 6.56	Nanjing 6.58	Nanchang 5.84	Kunming 6.76
20	Fuzhou 7.45	Zhengzhou 6.54	Haikou 6.58	Shenyang 5.82	Shenyang 6.74

(Continued)

Table 1.4. (*Continued*)

Ranking	Public Service Satisfaction		Government Citizen Participation		Information Transparency		Government Efficacy		Government Trust	
21	Zhengzhou	7.43	Nanchang	6.54	Tianjin	6.56	Chongqing	5.78	Tianjin	6.74
22	Xi'an	7.43	Nanjing	6.54	Fuzhou	6.52	Nanjing	5.76	Hangzhou	6.68
23	Kunming	7.37	Chengdu	6.52	Taiyuan	6.50	Nanchang	5.72	Beijing	6.66
24	Haikou	7.34	Fuzhou	6.50	Chengdu	6.48	Tianjin	5.68	Haikou	6.64
25	Haerbin	7.32	Taiyuan	6.46	Shenyang	6.46	Beijing	5.64	Nanjing	6.62
26	Guangzhou	7.24	Shenzhen	6.46	Wuhan	6.42	Shenzhen	5.60	Dalian	6.60
27	Shenzhen	7.23	Shenyang	6.44	Lanzhou	6.28	Taiyuan	5.54	Fuzhou	6.60
28	Wuhan	7.15	Xi'an	6.44	Beijing	6.24	Lanzhou	5.54	Shanghai	6.58
29	Nanchang	7.06	Beijing	6.36	Shanghai	6.22	Shanghai	5.54	Xi'an	6.42
30	Taiyuan	7.03	Tianjin	6.34	Shenzhen	6.18	Guangzhou	5.48	Guangzhou	6.28
31	Guiyang	6.92	Guangzhou	6.28	Xi'an	6.16	Wuhan	5.26	Wuhan	6.24
32	Lanzhou	6.50	Lanzhou	6.24	Guangzhou	6.10	Xi'an	5.24	Shenzhen	6.12

dimensions. Suzhou was ranked among the top ten on the dimensions of overall public satisfaction, citizen participation, and government efficacy. Dalian, a city, located in northeastern China also performed well regarding overall public satisfaction and government efficacy. Moreover, a number of inland cities, especially those in the southwest did a good job. For example, Shijiazhuang was ranked relatively high in terms of government transparency, citizen participation, and government trust. Changsha was among the top ten in citizen participation, government transparency, government efficacy, and government trust. Guiyang was one of the top five cities on three sub-dimensions, including citizen participation, government transparency and government trust. Chongqing also performed quite well in overall public satisfaction and citizen participation.

Geographically, the top ten cities in the five dimensions of the citizen perspective are mainly located in eastern (Xiamen, Qingdao, Suzhou, Jinan, and Ningbo) and southwestern China (Chongqing and Guiyang). Another three cities are located in central (Changsha), northern (Shijiazhuang), and northeastern China (Changchun). Citizens living in the first-tiered cities (Beijing, Shanghai, Tianjin, Guangzhou, and Shenzhen) had a quite negative assessment of their governments in building service-oriented government and none of these cities was part of the top ten. Similar assessments were found in the Pearl River Delta area and the south.

As mentioned before, the total score of the Citizen Perspective was obtained by the PCA for weighing and aggregating the five sub-dimensions. However, because these sub-dimensions were measured with different scales, scores of each sub-dimension and the total score of the perspective were actually standardized scores. To help the audience understand the total score and the scores of each sub-dimension in a more intuitive way, we de-standardize these scores to scores with a 10-point scale. As a result, the final scores, with their distributions around the true mean, reflect the actual ranking of these cities.[2] As can be seen in Figure 1.3, in the citizen perspective, Xiamen, Qingdao, Suzhou, Jinan, Changsha, Chongqing, Ningbo, Shijiazhuang, Guiyang, and Changchun performed

---

[2]According to the Central Limit Theorem, a standard score usually ranges from -3 to $+3$, which in our case indicates the distance (measured by standard deviation) of a city's total scores from the mean scores of the 32 cities. Considering that all the five sub-dimensions are measured by a 10-point scale, we calculated the means and standard deviations of the raw scores, based on which we "de-standardized" the total standard scores, that is, obtained the final total scores through the formula (standardized total scores * standard deviation + the mean).

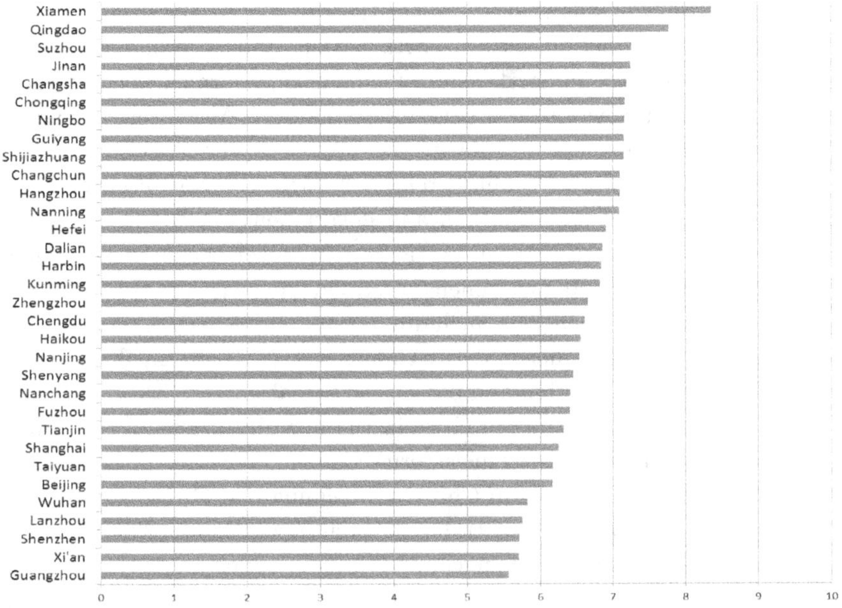

Figure 1.3.   Ranking of Service-Oriented Government in Citizen Perspective.

better in building service-oriented government. But it seems difficult to find the common geographical or economic characteristics these ten cities share. Some cities are located in the coastal regions, whereas others are in the central and western regions. Suzhou, Ningbo and Xiamen are economically developed, whereas Guiyang, Changchun and Shijiazhuang are not. In addition, citizens in the so-called first-tiered cities like Beijing, Shanghai, Guangzhou, and Shenzhen got a relatively poor evaluation in building service-oriented government.

Our data show that among the five sub-dimensions of the citizen perspective, only "overall public satisfaction" and "GDP per capita of each city," "overall public satisfaction" and "FDI as percentage of GDP" are positively correlated with each other, but the correlations are quite weak. It should be highlighted that neither the total score of the citizen perspective of a service-oriented government nor the four sub-dimensions (citizen participation, government transparency, government efficacy, and government trust) have any strong correlation with GDP per capita. The findings suggest that although economic prosperity provides financial support for public service provision, more developed economies do not necessarily lead to more citizen satisfaction with public services.

Table 1.5. Correlation Analysis of Dimensions of Service-Oriented Government in Citizen Perspective and City Economic Factors (Pearson Correlation Coefficient).

	Overall Public Satisfaction	Citizen Participation	Govern- ment Transparency	Govern- ment Efficacy	Govern- ment Trust	Citizen Perspective of Service- Oriented Government
GDP per capita	0.401*	−0.110	−0.162	0.051	−0.327	−0.055
FDI as percentage of GDP	0.381*	0.009	−0.016	0.146	−0.189	0.063
FDI per capita	0.331	−0.073	−0.154	0.072	−0.373*	−0.063
Fiscal Expenditure per capita	0.108	−0.120	−0.356*	−0.142	−0.441*	−0.238

*$p < 0.05$ (Two-tailed Test)

FDI per capita had a negative correlation with government trust. Similarly, per capita government fiscal expenditure has a negative correlation with government transparency and government trust (see Table 1.5). Considering the multidimensional nature of service-oriented government, although promoting economic development is likely to increase citizen satisfaction with urban public services, economic development alone is far from sufficient to bring a service-oriented government into effect. In fact, overemphasizing FDI and economic development and overlooking the development in non-economic areas and governance capacity would have significant negative impacts on building service-oriented government. Therefore, from both theoretical and practical view points, our focus should not be restrained in the single dimension of public service provision and citizens' satisfaction with the provision. This also explains why we decided to revise and upgrade the "2010 Lien Public Service Excellence Index for Chinese Cities" to the "Lien Chinese Cities Service-Oriented Government Index" in 2011.

To sum up, while we should not completely deny the important role of economic development in building service-oriented government (especially improving citizen satisfaction with public services), we clearly recognize that there are more important elements (such as government transparency, citizen participation in policy making and implementation, government efficacy, and government trust) besides economic development, contributing to the building of service-oriented government. Our data show that these elements do not have strong correlations with economic growth, fiscal capacity, and FDI.

1.4.2. *The business perspective*

Among the four sub-dimensions, "overall business satisfaction" is composed of 21 indicators that measure government's performance in six types of public services, and "business environment" is composed of 10 indicators. Respondents were asked to rate their satisfaction with each statement on a 10-point scale, ranging from "most dissatisfied" (1) to "most satisfied" (10). Overall, all 32 cities obtained scores more than 7, indicating that they are generally satisfied with their governments' performance on the two dimensions.

Regarding business overall satisfaction, Xiamen, Hangzhou, Qingdao, Ningbo, Chongqing, Shanghai, Suzhou, Hefei, Dalian, and Beijing are the top ten, having scores ranging from 8.66 to 9.66. In particular, the scores of Xiamen, Hangzhou, Qingdao, and Ningbo are impressive, scoring over 9 out of 10.

Regarding business environment, Xiamen, Qingdao, Hangzhou, Ningbo, Dalian, Hefei, Nanjing, Chengdu, Beijing, and Chongqing obtained scores ranging from 8.14 to 9.19, among which Xiamen, Qingdao, and Hangzhou in particular scored over 9.

Compared to the scores from the citizen perspective, the scores from the business perspective seem higher. This difference may be attributed to local governments' strong commitment to promoting economic growth. Compared to public services provided for citizens, public services that target businesses are more tangible, easier to be quantified (i.e., easier to be measured by higher administrative level), and pro-economic development. By contrast, public service provided for citizens tend to be consumable and distributive (e.g., health care, education, and social security), and thus is irrelevant or even conflicting to the holy grail of economic growth pursued by local governments. The difference between citizen assessment and business assessment of public service provision also illustrates our previous finding that the correlation between economic development and citizen satisfaction with public services is weak.

Regarding the other two sub-dimensions, participation in policy making and implementation and government efficacy, we asked respondents to indicate whether they agree with a number of statements on a five-point Likert scale, ranging from "completely disagree" (1) to completely agree (5). To facilitate further comparison, we coded responses as 2, 4, 6, 8, 10 points in our final analysis. Accordingly, "6" refers to a neutral/so-so assessment of public services.

Table 1.6. 4 Rankings of the Sub-dimensions of Service-Oriented Government in Business Perspective.

Ranking	Public Service Satisfaction		Business Environment		Business Participation		Government Efficacy for Business	
1	Xiamen	9.66	Xiamen	9.19	Shijiazhuang	7.60	Xiamen	7.40
2	Hangzhou	9.54	Qingdao	9.08	Hangzhou	7.48	Qingdao	6.88
3	Qingdao	9.50	Hangzhou	9.06	Xiamen	7.40	Hangzhou	6.84
4	Ningbo	9.13	Ningbo	8.76	Hefei	7.40	Ningbo	6.64
5	Chongqing	8.94	Dalian	8.31	Nanjing	7.38	Shanghai	6.60
6	Shanghai	8.84	Hefei	8.26	Kunming	7.20	Jinan	6.56
7	Suzhou	8.79	Nanjing	8.24	Changsha	7.18	Hefei	6.44
8	Hefei	8.72	Chengdu	8.19	Qingdao	7.18	Chengdu	6.40
9	Dalian	8.72	Beijing	8.14	Guangzhou	7.16	Haikou	6.34
10	Beijing	8.66	Chongqing	8.14	Changchun	7.10	Nanning	6.32
11	Chengdu	8.63	Shanghai	8.08	Dalian	7.04	Shijiazhuang	6.30
12	Nanjing	8.57	Jinan	8.08	Chongqing	7.04	Changchun	6.30
13	Shenzhen	8.51	Shenzhen	8.07	Guiyang	6.98	Nanjing	6.18
14	Changchun	8.51	Suzhou	8.06	Suzhou	6.94	Wuhan	6.18
15	Jinan	8.43	Changsha	8.04	Taiyuan	6.92	Zhengzhou	6.12
16	Shenyang	8.42	Shijiazhuang	8.02	Ningbo	6.86	Guiyang	6.10
17	Changsha	8.40	Zhengzhou	7.90	Jinan	6.84	Suzhou	6.08
18	Zhengzhou	8.39	Guiyang	7.86	Shenzhen	6.78	Xi'an	6.08
19	Guangzhou	8.37	Guangzhou	7.85	Tianjin	6.76	Kunming	6.06
20	Shijiazhuang	8.29	Haikou	7.81	Shanghai	6.66	Dalian	6.06
21	Haikou	8.28	Changchun	7.81	Nanchang	6.62	Chongqing	6.00
22	Fuzhou	8.26	Fuzhou	7.75	Nanning	6.60	Lanzhou	6.00
23	Guiyang	8.25	Tianjin	7.74	Haikou	6.60	Shenzhen	6.00
24	Tianjin	8.20	Shenyang	7.67	Chengdu	6.60	Changsha	5.96
25	Nanning	8.04	Nanchang	7.60	Haerbin	6.58	Guangzhou	5.96
26	Taiyuan	7.95	Taiyuan	7.59	Beijing	6.56	Shenyang	5.94
27	Nanchang	7.95	Nanning	7.59	Shenyang	6.54	Nanchang	5.94
28	Xi'an	7.93	Wuhan	7.51	Wuhan	6.48	Beijing	5.92
29	Haerbin	7.76	Lanzhou	7.41	Lanzhou	6.14	Fuzhou	5.90
30	Kunming	7.76	Xi'an	7.40	Fuzhou	6.12	Taiyuan	5.66
31	Lanzhou	7.34	Haerbin	7.31	Zhengzhou	6.00	Haerbin	5.62
32	Wuhan	7.34	Kunming	7.22	Xi'an	5.80	Tianjin	5.46

Table 1.6 shows that the scores of the two dimensions, participation in policy making and implementation and government efficacy, are lower than those of public service for business and business environment. Most cities scored between 6 and 8 in the two dimensions. It shows that our business respondents generally tended to have a relatively neutral attitude on the two dimensions. As shown in Table 1.6, no city scored more than 8. Especially, our business respondents assigned the lowest scores to government efficacy (nine cities scored lower than 6), indicating their general negative assessment on government efficacy.

It is noticeable that no matter in which perspective, either the citizen perspective or the business perspective, "overall satisfaction with public services" obtained the higher scores than "government efficacy." It shows that both citizens and businesses have high expectation toward their governments in efficacy and capacity. Additionally, our analysis shows that businesses generally have more favourable attitudes towards their city government than citizens (including overall satisfaction with public service, participation, and government efficacy), which to some extent reflects the impact of local governments' sole pursuit for higher GDP.

In the top ten cities along the business perspective, Xiamen is ranked the first on "overall satisfaction," "business environment," and "government efficacy," and the third on "participation in policy making and implementation." Hangzhou is ranked the fourth in all the four sub-dimensions; Qingdao is among the top three cities on all the sub-dimensions, except for business participation; Ningbo is among the top ten in the sub-dimensions other than participation; Shanghai performs well in terms of government efficacy.

In the business perspective, inland cities and cities in southwest region, including Hefei, Shijiazhuang, Chengdu, and Chongqing, are impressive as well. For individual city's performance on the four sub-dimensions of business perspective, please refer to Table 1.6.

As what we did on the scores of the citizen perspective, we applied the de-standardization method to the standard scores of the business perspective and used the final total scores obtained from the process to rank city governments.[3] As illustrated in Figure 1.4, in the business perspective, Xiamen, Hangzhou, Qingdao, Ningbo, Hefei, Nanjing, Shanghai, Shijiazhuang, Dalian, and Chongqing are the top ten cities in terms of building service-oriented government. Geographically, seven of the top ten cities ranked along this general dimension are located in eastern China. The remaining three cities are located in northern (Shijiazhuang), northeastern (Dalian), and southwestern China (Chongqing).

This finding demonstrates that, in the business perspective, the eastern region has stronger commitment to building service-oriented government.

---

[3]We first calculated the mean and the standard deviation of the four sub-dimensions using the raw scores, and used the obtained mean and standard deviation to de-standardize the standardized total scores (using factor analysis), which can be expressed mathematically as the formula: final total scores = standard total scores * standard deviation + the mean.

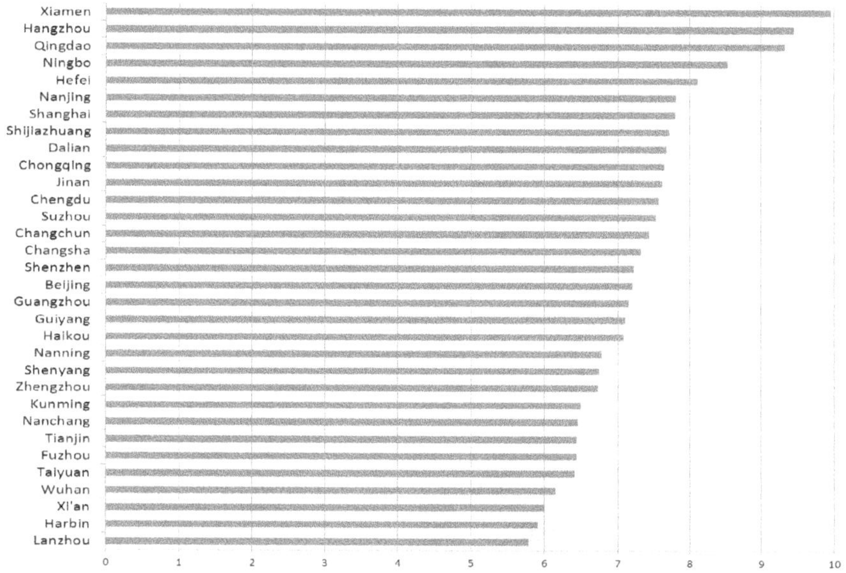

Figure 1.4. Ranking of Service-Oriented Government in Business Perspective.

It should be noticed that although cities in eastern China tend to have a higher level of economic development than their counterparts in central and western China, cities in eastern region that were ranked as the top ten are not all economically advanced. Examples include Hefei, Shijiazhuang, and Chongqing. Even though a service-oriented government from the business perspective may be more related to economic development (compared to the citizen perspective of service-oriented government), our data analysis shows that the correlation is weak. We found that GDP per capita, fiscal expenditure per capita, and FDI per capita might not adequately explain the variation of the total scores of the business perspective. Correlation analysis reveals that only the three pairs of the factors including business environment and GDP per capita, business overall satisfaction with public service and GDP per capita, business environment and FDI per capita, are positively correlated and the correlation coefficients are quite small (see Table 1.7). This again suggests that GDP-oriented development is not the only determinant of building a service-oriented government. Apart from economic factors, the building of service-oriented government also depends on governance capacity and a strong orientation towards providing quality service.

Table 1.7. Correlation Analysis of the Business Perspective and City Economic Factors (Pearson Correlation Coefficient).

	Overall Satisfaction with Public Service	Business Environment	Business Participation	Government Efficacy	Citizen Perspective of Service-Oriented Government
GDP per capita	0.431*	0.399*	0.225	0.100	0.346
FDI as percentage of GDP	0.309	0.235	0.035	0.055	0.198
FDI per capita	0.373*	0.321	0.123	0.061	0.268
Fiscal Expenditure per capita	0.278	0.244	0.051	0.064	0.197

$^*p < 0.05$ (Two-tailed Test)

1.4.3. *General public service*

The general public service dimension includes 20 measurements grouped in eight types of public services. The data came from government statistical yearbooks, government reports, and other government archives. This dimension primarily reflects government inputs and outputs in the eight types of public services. Since the units of measurement of these 20 items are different, we had to standardize all raw data for further aggregation. After converting the raw data to z-scores, we used the component scores of PCA to assign weights to the eight types of public services. The initial total scores of the general public service dimension, therefore, are standardized scores for each city. Again, to make sure the scores can be understood in a more intuitive way, we de-standardize the scores subsequently. However, different from the other two general dimensions, citizen perspective and business perspective (their sub-dimensions have the same 10-point scale in spite of different measurements), this dimension, general public service, consists of twenty items that have not only different units but also different range of scales. This means that two parameters, the mean and the standard deviation, are not available for de-standardization. But given the logical relationship between this dimension (totally based on objective data) and two sub-dimensions, citizen satisfaction and business satisfaction, (based on subjective assessment), we adopted the mean and the standard deviation of all cities on these latter two sub-dimensions as the parameters for the de-standardization treatment. It has to be pointed out that the treatment did not change the ranking of the 32 cities or the relative differences on total scores between cities. It only allows the cities to be distributed around the

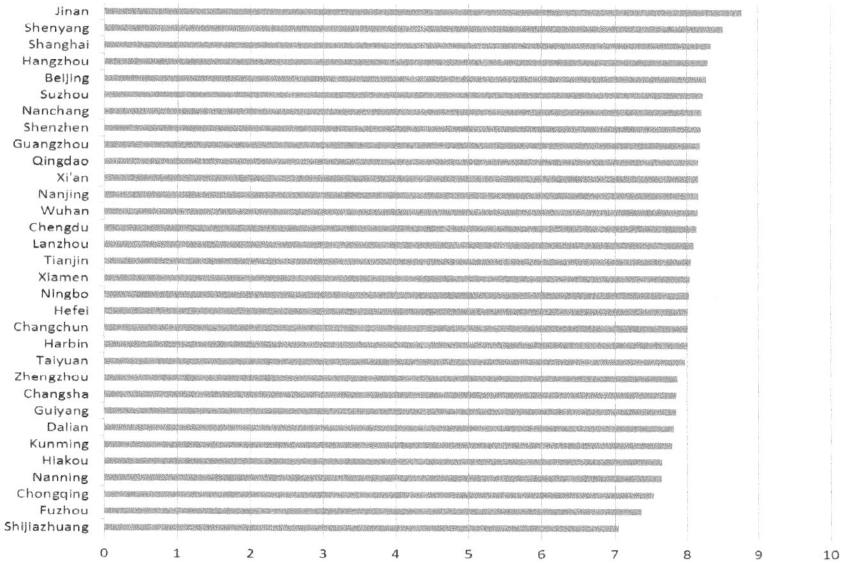

Figure 1.5. Ranking of General Public Service.

true mean (on "citizen satisfaction" and "business satisfaction") in order based on their actual differences.

Figure 1.5 displays the ranking of the 32 cities along the "general public service" dimension. The top ten cities are: Jinan, Shenyang, Shanghai, Hangzhou, Beijing, Suzhou, Nanchang, Shenzhen, Guangzhou, and Qingdao. This ranking is somewhat different from those from the citizen perspective and business perspective, as some cities in the Pearl River Delta and some first-tiered cities are ranked among the top ten. This is the case because the scores of the "general public service" are based on objective hard data.

Further correlation analysis reveals a strong and positive correlation between a city's performance in "general public service" and its GDP per capita (see Table 1.8), i.e., economically developed cities tend to have a higher level of inputs and outputs of public service. However, we must also notice that "general public service" does not have a correlation with the total scores of the citizen perspective and business perspective, which suggests that while financial supports can increase the quantity of public service provision, the increase may still fail to meet the expectations of citizen and businesses. The finding shows that in addition to providing more public services, governments have a lot more to do. Particularly,

Table 1.8. Correlation Analysis of the General Public Service Dimension and City Economic Factors.

	General Public Service
Citizen Public Service Satisfaction	0.100
Citizen Perspective of Service-Oriented Government	−0.174
Business Public Service Satisfaction	0.131
Business Perspective of Service-Oriented Government	0.100
GDP per capita	0.464**
FDI as percentage of D+GDP	0.168
FDI per capita	0.321
Fiscal Expenditure per capita	0.312

**$p < 0.01$ (Two-tailed Test)

city governments need to develop a comprehensive understanding of the demands of citizens and businesses with regard to different aspects of service-oriented government.

1.4.4. *Overall ranking of service-oriented government*

The overall ranking of 32 cities is obtained by summing up the scores of the three dimensions of the service-oriented government index, the citizen perspective, the business perspective and the general public service. Without existing theoretical or practical guidelines on how to weigh the three dimensions, we decided to assign the same weight to each dimension. More specifically, we first obtained the averages of the standardized total scores of the three dimensions. Then, we calculated the mean and the standard deviation using the total scores obtained from the de-standardization method. Finally, we de-standardized the aggregated scores of the three dimensions of each city to scores with a 10-point scale. It has to be emphasized again that the mathematic transformation did not change the ordering of the raw data or the relative differences between data.

The top ten cities of the 2011 Lien Chinese Cities Service-Oriented Government are Xiamen, Qingdao, Hangzhou, Jinan, Ningbo, Suzhou, Hefei, Changchun, Shanghai, Nanjing and Chengdu (Nanjing and Chengdu tie in the ranking) (see Figure 1.6).

Chengdu (a city located in the Southwest) and Changchun (a city located in the northeast) have been ranked among the top ten. Changchun is the only city in northeastern China that enters the list. Different from other top 10 cities, Chengdu's performance is quite impressive. Its performance in each sub-dimension is equally well, while some other cities in the top ten

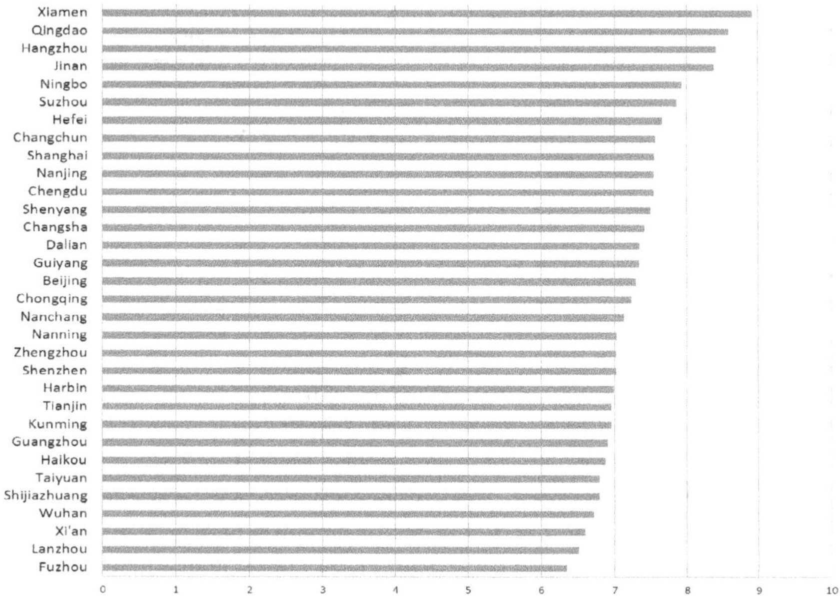

Figure 1.6.   Overall Ranking of 32 Cities in Service-Oriented Government.

perform extremely well in some areas but not that well in other areas. It shows that the social and economic development of Chengdu is all rounded.

Except for Changchun and Chengdu, all the top ten cities are located in eastern China, marking the strength of the eastern region in building service-oriented government. Although the Yangtze River-centric eastern region is a crucial economic powerhouse in China, other regions including the Pearl River Delta (the south), Beijing and Tianjin (the north), Chengdu and Chongqing (the southwest) nonetheless are also vibrant economic centres. Why do cities in the eastern region perform relatively well in building service-oriented government, compared with the other regions? This finding re-emphasizes that economic development can only partially explain the progress in building service-oriented government. Indeed, our analysis shows that except for GDP per capita, other economic indicators do not have significant correlations with the Index (see Table 1.9). Moreover, the correlation between GDP per capita and the total score of the index is not strong.

Moreover, almost all the top ten cities are nationally or internationally well-known tourist destinations having long and unique history, and

Table 1.9.   Correlation Analysis of the Lien Chinese Cities Service-Oriented Government Index and City Economic Factors (Pearson Correlation Coefficient).

	GDP per capita	FDI Ratio to GDP	FDI per capita	Fiscal per capita
Lien Chinese Cities Service-Oriented Government Index	0.367*	0.209	0.256	0.132

*$p < 0.05$ (Two-tailed Test)

picturque ecological environment. Qingdao, Hangzhou, Chengdu, Shanghai and Ningbo were elected as the "2011 Best City for Leisure in China" by China Tourism Research Institute. In addition, Shanghai won the accolade of "The Most Fashion City," Xiamen "The Most Romantic City," and Hefei "The Most Innovative City in Leisure and Entertainment." The development of these hot tourist destinations requires high level of openness, excellent sense of service, and strong capabilities in providing quality public services and social management. These capacities have a spill-over effect out of the tourist industry, helping a local government nurture the service-oriented management culture and holistic social and economic development. It is no surprise that Xiamen, Ningbo and Suzhou are ranked as the top three cities in holistic development, according to the "2011 Report on China City Holistic Development" released recently by the Academy of Chinese City Development.

1.5. Conclusion

We developed the "Lien Chinese Cities Service-Oriented Government Index" and conducted the 2011 Lien Survey on Service-Oriented Government in 32 major Chinese cities based on the Index. Our findings would be of use for Chinese city governments to better understand the concept of service-oriented government and further improve their practices. In addition, our findings are also informative for multi-national corporations and Chinese enterprises to make investment decisions.

Findings of the 2011 Lien Survey show that economic development plays an important role in increasing public service inputs and outputs as well as improving citizen satisfaction with public service. Public service provision, however, is only one of many dimensions of service-oriented government. Not only does a service-oriented government in China require

a sustainable economic development, but also strong government efficacy, government transparency, citizen participation, and social management capacity. Moreover, local governments must pay more attention to the demands of citizens and businesses. Actually, China's 12th Five-Year Plan requires Chinese government ". . . broadly mobilize and organize people to participate in social management according to law, nurture civic awareness, fulfil civic duty, realize self-management and self-development, enlarge public participation, and enhance both quality and quantity of public service."

The findings of the 2011 Lien Survey also have significant practical implications for the urbanization and city development in China. An ideal service-oriented city envisioned by citizens and businesses does not simply pursue economic development without any concerns with its culture and tradition. Instead, such an ideal city should have beautiful landscape, unique historical-cultural characteristics, quality public service, comfortable and vibrant living environment, and sufficient employment and development opportunities. And such an ideal can only be turned into reality with a service-oriented government able to provide quality public services and a facilitating environment for citizens and businesses to pursue sustainable development with a high level of efficacy, transparency, democratic participation, and public trust and support.

In the future, we will continually fine tune the Index to further improve its validity and reliability. We will also continually improve the Lien Survey by including more localities at different administrative levels in order to have a more holistic view in the development of service-oriented government in China. We believe that our research will serve as an important reference for Chinese cities to further enhance their governance capacity, transform their governance mode, and further improve the building of service-oriented government in China.

References

Accenture (2009). Leadership in customer service report: Creating shared responsibility for better outcomes. Dublin: Accenture.

Antai College of Economics and Management, Shanghai Jiao Tong University (2010). 2010 Chinese City Public Service Index. Shanghai: Shanghai Jiao Tong University.

Chinese Academy of Sciences (2010). *Strategic Report of China's Sustainable Development*. Beijing: Science Press.

Chinese Academy of Social Sciences (2010). *Blue Book of City Competitiveness*. Beijing: Social Sciences Academic Press.

Economist Intelligence Unit (2005). The Economist Intelligence Unit's Quality of Life Index. London: Economist.

Foreign Policy (2008). The 2008 Global Cities Index. Foreign Policy, 68–77.

Gao, XP and LP Wang (2009). *Introduction of Service-Oriented Government.* Beijing: People's Publishing House.

Horizon Research Consultancy Group (2009). 2009 Index for Public Assessment of Public Service. Beijing: Horizon Research Consultancy Group.

Mercer (2010). Quality of Living Worldwide City Rankings 2010. NewYork: Mercer.

Schwab, Klaus (2011). The Global Competitiveness Report 2010–2011. Geneva: World Economic Forum.

The World Bank Group (2010). Doing Business 2010. Washington: World Bank.

World Competitiveness Centre, IMD (2010). World Competitiveness Yearbook (WCY). Lausanne: International Institute for Management Development.

Wu, W, WX Yu, TJ Lin and J Wang (2011). Improve public service quality, nurture service-oriented government: Lien's survey 2010. *Urban Insight,* 1(1), 10.

Chapter 2

Public Ethical Values and Service-Oriented Government

Kuotsai Tom Liou*

The author of this chapter has a great honor to attend the 2012 Lien International Conference on Public Administration hosted by the Nanyang Centre for Public Administration at Nanyang Technological University. The theme of this conference, "Forging Service-Oriented Government — Challenges and Prospects," is important because of suggestions in developing a service-oriented government to address challenging issues in China, especially for its 12th Five-Year Plan (2011–2015) (Xinhuanet, 2010). Similar ideas about the importance of public services have also been emphasized by American public administration scholars (e.g., Denhard and Denhard, 2003) in recent years.

This chapter will focus on the relationship between public ethical values and service-oriented government. As we all know, the environment of public administration has changed because of the explosion of new information and communication technologies, the change of social norms, and the development of democratization movement. The public today demands higher standards of ethics, transparency and accountability in the public sector. The chapter consists of two parts: (1) ethical values in public service, and (2) challenging issues in service-oriented government.

---

*Professor, School of Public Administration, University of Central Florida, President, American Society for Public Administration.

2.1. Ethical Values in Public Service

Public ethical values have been emphasized in the literature of public administration for many years (e.g., Rohr, 1978; Waldo, 1994). While there is no general agreement on the definition of ethics, social scientists have emphasized three basic ethical principles in their research: (1) respect for persons, (2) beneficences (i.e., doing good and making all efforts to improve an individual's well being), and (3) justice (i.e., equal distribution) (US Department of Health, Education and Welfare, 1978).

Public administration scholars have identified sources and purposes of public ethical values. For example, Van Wart (1998) identified five ethical sources in terms of (1) individual values, such as honesty and respect, (2) professional values, such as code of ethics of professional associations (e.g., ASPA), (3) organizational values, including organizational health, design, leadership style, (4) legal values, such as constitution, laws, and specific responsibilities of public agencies, employees, and citizens, and (5) public interest values, such as a representational democracy, a separation of political power through federalism, protection of individualism. Focusing on public service professionalism, Caiden (2000) indicated such values as: providing public benefits, enforcing the rule of law, ensuring public responsibility and accountability, improving professional performance, and promoting democracy.

Besides public ethical sources, types and purposes, researchers provide additional information about motivations for unethical practice and problems of ethical dilemma. For example, Steinberg and Austern (1990) discussed motivations for individual unethical practice, which include personal greed, ideology, financial problems, ignorance of laws, friendship (i.e., helping a friend), good intention (i.e., cutting some red tape), and going along with others (i.e., bureaucrats loyalty). Closely related to unethical motivations, researchers (e.g., Ayee, 1998; Menyah, 2010) also emphasized ethical dilemma in the public service as they are related to administrative discretion, corruption and nepotism, administrative secrecy, information leaks, public accountability, and policy dilemmas.

To promote or ensure ethical behavior, public administration researchers and institutions (e.g., Ayee, 1998; OECD, 1998) have emphasized various managerial strategies or administrative changes and reforms. These strategies or reforms are: ethical codes and trainings, civil service reforms (e.g., improved remuneration), procedure requirements and changes (e.g., disclosure of income/assets/gifts, auditing and investigation,

improved procurement procedures), structural and institutional arrangements (e.g., independent watchdog agencies, audit institutions, and anti-corruption agencies), policy and program rationalization, civic society organizations and the media support.

The review of major ethical issues in public service indicates not only different types of ethical values and unethical practices, but also strategies to promote ethical behavior. It should be noticed that ethics is not just based on individual value judgments, but also related to organizational management and effectiveness and policy dilemmas and conflicts.

2.2. Challenging Issues in Service-Oriented Government

To explain the relationship between pubic ethical values and service-oriented government, this chapter explains ethical challenges in government's policy option, service delivery, and service attitude to promote such values as equity, accountability, and transparency.

2.2.1. *Equity issues in policy option*

Focusing on economic development and growth, China's past reform policies have resulted in some ethical concerns and value arguments. For example, one of the strategies is the uneven regional development approach to promote the development of China's coastal regions and cities. Under this strategy, governments in these regions have authority to develop preferential policies to attract business development (e.g., Liou, 2009). While these policies are efficient in attracting business investments, negative consequences of the uneven development policies are increasing regional disparities and income gaps in the society. For example, when comparing per capita GDP between the coastal and interior provinces, Liou (2009) reported that, in 2006, Shanghai had the highest per capita GDP of 56,733 RMB and Guizhou had the lowest per capita GDP of 5,750 RMB. The income disparity between the richest area and the poorest area is about 10 times. Similar income gap problems also occurred between China's urban and rural areas. In 2009, the urban per capita net income stood at 17,175 yuan ($2,525), while the rural per capita net income was 5,153 yuan. The income gap between the urban and rural areas showed a ratio of 3.33 : 1 (e.g., Fu, 2010). The inequality issues have been related to social problems in the areas of food safety, environmental pollution, and labor dispute (Liou and Wu, 2010).

The equity issue of income gap has also been emphasized in the US as one of the policy concerns in the presidential election. According to a study by the US Congressional Budget Office (2011, p. 1), the income gap in America has been growing for 30 years. Between 1979 and 2007, the study showed that the top 1% of Americans with the highest incomes have seen their incomes grow by an average of 275%; that the 60% of Americans in the middle of the income scale saw their incomes increase by just 40%; and that the poorest fifth of Americans saw their income rise by 18%. The issue of social inequity has been further emphasized by policymakers because Americans are also angry over the recent financial crisis and related recession and unemployment problems.

From the perspective of ethical concerns, equity and social issues are related to policy dilemmas between economic and social development. Public policies designed to promote economic growth may be unfair to the general public because of special incentive policies to business communities. Successful economic development may result in social problems of income gap and environment pollution. The challenge here is the balance between economic and social development, business and pubic interests, market efficiency and social equity concerns.

2.2.2. *Accountability concerns in service delivery*

Closely related to policy option problems, the second challenging issue for the service-oriented government is accountability concerns in the service delivery system. Accountability includes different types, such as hierarchical, legal, professional and political accountability, because public employees have to be accountable to various authorities, interest groups, and to the rule of law in general (Romzek and Dubnick, 1987). The new governance theory emphasizes that civil servants, public organizations, and politicians are held accountable for their decisions and performance (World Bank, 1994).

Unlike objective measurements in economic activities, the development of social programs in China will be challenging, because these programs are sophisticated in their subject issues (e.g., education, health, social welfare) and require long-term efforts to see their changes and effects. It is important to enhance managerial capacity of government agencies to promote administrative efficiency, accountability and transparency in the design, implementation, supervision and evaluation of these programs. One important ethical issue here is the continuing pervasiveness of official

corruption cases. Many corruption cases were reported in government agencies that provide direct services to the public. In the area of food safety, for example, a former head of China's State Food and Drug Administration was executed on July 10, 2007 for taking bribes from various firms in exchange for state licenses related to product safety (National Public Radio, NPR, 2007).

The accountability concerns will also be emphasized, even if we consider an alternative, market-based approach in the service delivery system. For example, it is popular to use various privatization options (e.g., contracting out/outsourcing, franchising, public-private partnerships, volunteer services) to provide some public service programs. While there may be different arguments about motivation and effectiveness of privatization policy, especially its role in the Chinese society, accountability concerns are important in the process of implementing privatization options to avoid corruption and mismanagement cases. Implementation issues include the decision to privatize public services, the selection of private service providers, the supervision of private operations, and the evaluation of performance quality.

One example about accountability concerns in the United Sates is about the relationship between financial deregulation and the recent financial crisis. The developments of regulatory legislations and institutions since the Great Depression and financial deregulation policies since the late 1970s have resulted in a fragmented and complex arrangement of the US regulatory system (US GAO, 2009). Government regulators failed to adequately oversee the sale of new investment products, such as different derivative instruments (e.g., credit default swaps, bond insurance) and new types of mortgages (e.g., sub-prime, Alt-A, no doc, etc), to protect the consumers and to avoid problems of the financial system. This regulatory gap problem has been considered as one of contributory factors to financial crisis. The issue of accountability has been a major concern of new regulations, because the Dodd–Frank Wall Street Reform and Consumer Protection Act of 2010 introduced new policy measures to regulate those unregulated investment products and to protect the consumer with new agencies and requirements (US Senate Committee on Banking, Housing, and Urban Affairs, 2010).

One factor contributing to accountability is the application of communication and information technology in providing these services. For example, electronic government (EG) is the application of information technologies to the work of government to make public services and management more

effective and accountable to citizens and businesses (Howard, 2001; Karen and Lee, 2001). The benefits of using information technologies in China's administrative system include improving communication between departments at all levels, helping pubic and business communities understand policy changes, and enhancing administrative capacity (e.g., transparency and accountability) among all local governments (especially those in the Western and interior region) (Liou, 2008). But, the development of information technology may not change traditional problems of bureaucratic culture and may bring new social problems, such as on-line rumors and related anti-official conflict or unrest.

2.2.3. *Transparency emphasis in service attitude*

The final concern for the service-oriented government is public employees' attitude in providing public service and in interacting with the general public. It is important to emphasize that service-oriented government focuses on the people. Denhard and Denahrd (2003) indicated that the new public service is about serving, not steering; we need to value people, not just productively; and we value citizenship and public service above entrepreneurship. It is important that public employees recognize the citizen as the focus of their work, and that they need to care about citizen's needs and respect citizen's rights during the process of their service.

One example about the importance of service attitude is the declines of American's trust in government and public institutions. According to the survey of Pew Research Center (2010), only 22% of Americans surveyed say they can trust government in Washington "almost always or most of the time," which is among the lowest measures in the half-century. Regarding the public's feelings about the federal government, the survey reveals that 56% say they are frustrated with the federal government, 21% say they are angry and only 19% say they are basically content.

One managerial strategy to respect the citizen's needs and rights is the idea of citizen participation. Promoting participatory and transparent governance, public administration researchers (e.g., Hickey and Mohan, 2004; Kim *et al.*, 2005) argue that the institutionalization of participation by all people is a cornerstone of good governance. Citizen participation gives governments the opportunity to know important information about the needs and priorities of citizens, communities, and businesses. Through the participation, governments will be in a better position to make good decisions and will receive more public support when implementing the decisions.

In addition, transparency and open attitudes are especially important in the government's response to conflicts and crisis. For example, in 2011, China's railway accident in Wenzhou has resulted in the official review of technology and safety issues as well as the revision of the overall development plan. But, major critiques were about the lack of transparency in the government's immediate response and the lack of awareness of new media (e.g., microblogs) influence among government officials (Xinhuanet, 2011). During his trip to Wenzhou, Premier Wen Jiabao emphasized that the government's investigation into the train crash will be open, transparent and under public supervision (Wong, 2011).

2.3. Conclusion

To support the development of service-oriented government, we need to promote not only professional management concepts and techniques to enhance operational efficiency, but also important public ethical values to address challenges of economic and social development. Professional management concepts and techniques, such as performance measurement and e-government, are useful tools and strategies to support efficient operations in public agencies. Public ethical values, such as anti-corruption, social justice, transparency and participation, are important factors for us to rebuild public's trust and confidence in the public sector.

This chapter provides a review of conceptual issues about public ethical values and theoretical arguments about challenging issues for the service-oriented arguments. This chapter also mentioned several cases in the US and China to emphasize the relationship between public ethical values and service-oriented government. While conceptual and theoretical arguments are useful to understand the importance of this relationship, future research on this topic may need to collect data to conduct case studies or empirical analyses to test and verify the arguments and to make contributions to the related theories and policy and managerial implications.

Dear friends, it is an exciting time to study public administration. It is wonderful this year that we study these issues at Nanyang Technological University in Singapore. I learned that the Nanyang Centre for Public Administration has provided professional education and training to Chinese public employees for many years. Congratulations on your outstanding achievements. For more than 70 years, ASPA has also provided professional education, training, and research opportunities to support the development of democratic government in the US and abroad. It is interesting to notice

that the theme of ASPA's 2012 conference focuses on civic engagement and the theme of the 2013 conference promotes governance and sustainability to address public ethical issues that are related to economic and social development. We welcome your participation in the 2013 ASPA conference in New Orleans.

Finally, thank you for the invitation and the opportunity to share with you my ideas on the service-oriented government. I look forward to learning new ideas from your papers and panels. Best wishes to the success of the conference.

References

Ayee, J (1998). *Ethics in the Public Service*. Second Pan-African Conference of the Ministers of Civil Service. Rabat, Morocco, December 13–15.

Caiden, G (2000). The essence of public service professionalism. In *Promoting Ethics in the Public Service*, Department of Economic and Social Affairs, Division for Public Economics and Public Administration, United Nations Public Administration Network. NY: United Nations, pp. 21–31.

Denhardt, JV and RB Denhardt (2003). *The New Public Service: Serving, not Steering*. Armonk, NY: ME Sharpe.

Fu, J (2010). Urban-rural income gap widest since reform. *China Daily*. March 2. Available at http://www.chinadaily.com.cn/china/2010-03/02/content_9521611.htm.

Hickey, S and G Mohan (eds.) (2004). *Participation, From Tyranny to Transformation? Exploring New Approaches to Participation in Development*. London: ZED Books.

Howard, M (2001). E-government across the globe: How will "e" change government? *Government Finance Review*, 17(4), 6–9.

Karen, L and J Lee (2001). Developing fully functional e-government: A four-stage model. *Government Information Quarterly*, 18(2), 122–137.

Kim, P-S, J Halligan, N Cho, CH Oh and AM Eikenberry (2005). Toward participatory and transparent governance: Report on the sixth global forum on reinventing government. *Public Administration Review*, 65(6), 646–654.

Liou, KT and J Wu (2010). Government-business relations in China's economic development. *International Journal of Organizational Theory and Behavior*, 13(3), 354–377.

Liou, KT (2009). Local economic development in China and the United States: Strategies and issues. *Public Administration Review*, 69(S1), S29–S37.

Liou, KT (2008). E-government development and China's administrative reform. *International Journal of Public Administration*, 31(1), 76–95.

Menyah, D (2010). Ethics, ethical dilemmas and the public service. *Ethical Dilemmas in the Public Service*, Commonwealth Association for Public Administration & Management, pp. 5–9. Ottawa, ON Canada: CAPAM.

National Public Radio (NPR) (2007). *China Executes Ex-Food and Drug Chief.* July 10. Available at http://www.npr.org/templates/story/story.php? storyId=11846089#11656278.

Organization for Economic Cooperation and Development (OECD) (1998). *Principles for Managing Ethics in the Public Service.* PUMA Policy Brief. No. 4. Public Management Service. May. Paris: OECD.

Pew Research Center (2010). Distrust, Discontent, Anger and Partisan Rancor, The People and Their Government. April 18. Available at http://pewre search.org/pubs/1569/trust-in-government-distrust-discontent-anger-partisan-rancor.

Rohr, J (1978). *Ethics for Bureaucrats.* New York: Marcel Dekker.

Romzek, BS and MJ Dubnick (1987). Accountability in the public sector: Lessons from the challenger tragedy. *Public Administration Review,* 47, 227–239.

Steinberg, SS and DT Austern (1990). *Government, Ethics, and Management: A Guide to Solving Ethical Dilemmas in the Public Sector.* NY: Praeger.

US Congressional Budget Office (CBO). (2011). *Trends in the Distribution of Household Income Between 1979 and 2007.* Washington, DC: USCBO.

US Department of Health, Education, and Welfare (USDHEW), (1978). *The Belmont Report: Ethical Principles and Guidelines for the Protection of Human Subjects of Research.* Publication No. (OS) 78-0012. Washington, DC: USDHEW.

US Government Accountability Office (GAO). (2009). *Financial Regulation: A Framework for Crafting and Assessing Proposals to Modernize the Outdated US Financial Regulatory System.* January 2009. Available at http://www.gao.gov/new.items/d09216.pdf.

US Senate Committee on Banking, Housing, and Urban Affairs. (2010). *Brief Summary of the Dodd-Frank Wall Street Reform and Consumer Protection Act.* Available at http://bankingsenate.gov/public/_files/070110_Dodd_Frank_Wall_Street_Reform_comprehensive_summary_Final.pdf.

Van Wart, M (1998). *Changing Public Sector Values.* New York: Garland Publishing, Inc.

Waldo, D (1994). Public administration and ethics. In FS Lane (ed.), *Current Issues in Public Administration,* pp. 176–180. New York: St. Martins Press.

Wong, F (2011). *China's Wen Visits Train Crash Site, Vows Thorough Probe.* Available at http://uk.reuters.com/article/2011/07/28/us-china-train-idUKTRE76R07120110728.

World Bank (1994). *Governance: The World Bank's Experience.* Washington, DC: Author.

Xinhuanet (2011). China orders transparent handling of major accidents after fatal train crash. Available at http://news.xinhuanet.com/english2010/china/2011-08/03/c_131027624.htm.

Xinhuanet (2010). China at key stage of reform, development. Available at http://news.xinhuanet.com/english2010/china/2010-10/18/c_13561781.htm.

Chapter 3

The Role of Emotional Labor in Public Service

Meredith A Newman[*,†]

This chapter addresses an emerging issue in the field of public administration that has been missing from public management scholarship and training — the concept of emotional labor. The main body of public administration literature is on how best to deliver public services in the most effective, efficient, economical, and ethical manner — at a time when public expectation about the quality of service delivery is growing. What is often overlooked is recognition of the emotive skills in the performance of much of this work, especially in the human services and in crisis response and disaster management — and how its performance can lead to burnout. If we are to achieve "public service-oriented government," whether we are in Singapore, China or the US, recognition of the centrality of emotion work in the citizen-state exchange is essential.

The chapter discusses three points: 1) What emotional labor is and is not; 2) its relationship to burnout; and 3) implications for practice. It draws from Newman's ongoing research into emotional labor with her colleagues Mary Guy (University of Colorado, Denver) and Sharon Mastracci (University of Illinois, Chicago) and their two recent books on the subject (Guy, Newman and Mastracci, 2008; Mastracci, Guy and Newman, 2012).

---

[*]This chapter draws from the collaborative work of Meredith A Newman, Mary Guy and Sharon Mastracci. The research assistance of Professor Jue Wang, Nanyang Technological University, is gratefully acknowledged.

[†]Professor and Chair, Florida International University, newmanm@fiu.edu

3.1. What Emotional Labor Is and Is Not

Cool heads, warm hearts. Isn't that what we want when public workers meet citizens? To achieve that combination requires not only cognitive labor but also emotional labor. To clarify what emotional labor is, I will first tell you what it isn't. It isn't emotional intelligence; it isn't motivation; nor is it leadership. What differentiates emotional labor from these other topics is that it is an attribute of a job, while public service motivation, leadership, and emotional intelligence are personal attributes of the worker. In other words, the job requires emotional labor.

3.1.1. *It is not emotional intelligence*

Emotional labor is confused most often with emotional intelligence due to the similarity of the words, but the two differ considerably. Emotional intelligence is a broader term than emotional labor in that it denotes the individual's *capacity* to recognize emotions in oneself and others, much as cognitive intelligence measures the capacity to perform analytic and verbal tasks. It is emotional intelligence that makes it possible to recognize emotions in oneself and others and to use this knowledge for improved self-management and relationships with others. Some of the key skills characterizing emotional intelligence are active listening, acknowledging others, and mindful speaking. Emotional intelligence provides the substrate by which a worker has the ability to perform emotional labor. Again, the former is located in the person while the latter is located in the job. The latter is a noun: "She exerts emotional labor"; and the former is an adjective: "She possesses emotional intelligence."

3.1.2. *It is not public service motivation*

The fundamental difference between the constructs of public service motivation and emotional labor is where each is "located." While the former is not anchored in a particular job and may not involve formal employment at all, the latter is specific to a job. Public service motivation is what drives a person to serve. It is not a required element of a public service job. One's inspiration to serve the public lies within oneself; it is neither an attribute of a job, nor a condition to obtain one.

3.1.3. *It is not leadership*

Leadership is similarly conflated with emotional labor, but it is intertwined between the individual and the context of the job. The emotive component

of leadership is an essential one, because it is "a series of social exchanges in which the leader can drive the other person's emotions into a better or worse state" (Goleman, 2006, p. 276). Leadership has been described as "relationship management that involves effective communication, teamwork, and conflict management skills, as well as the ability to help people work toward common objectives" (Berman and West, 2008, p. 743). Leadership is a personal attribute exercised in a complementary context that suits the individual's style. Emotional labor, on other hand, is an element of the job. While emotional labor comes from the nature of the work, leadership, public service motivation, and emotional intelligence are qualities of the worker.

3.2. Emotional Labor: What It Is

Having carved out the negative space surrounding emotional labor, I will now fill in its center.

The term "emotional labor" refers to the management of one's own feelings as well as those of the other in order to get the job done. It has multiple facets, ranging from authentic expression of the worker's emotional state, to requiring workers to don masks and display an emotion that they do not actually feel. The purpose is to affect how the citizen feels. Successful performance depends on it. Law enforcement needs citizens to be deferential and to trust their authority. Social services need citizens to feel that there is a constructive way to deal with their problems. Emergency responders need citizens to trust their expertise and be confident of their actions. In these terms, the jobs of a social worker and correctional officer can be viewed as opposite poles. One employs a smile and requires its incumbents to be "nicer than natural." The other employs toughness and requires "tougher than natural" behavior. Acting in a neutral manner also demands emotion work as workers suppress their true feelings in order not to under- or over-react and to present an air of fairness and lack of bias.

Emotional labor includes analysis and decision making in terms of the expression of emotion, whether actually felt or not, as well as its opposite: the suppression of emotions that are felt but not expressed. More specifically, emotional labor comes into play during communication between worker and citizen and it requires the rapid-fire execution of:

- Emotive sensing, which means detecting the affective state of the other
- Analyzing one's own affective state
- Judging how alternative responses will affect the citizen, and then selecting the response that is likely to elicit the desired response

- Behaving, such that the worker suppresses or expresses an emotion — in order to elicit the desired response.

Service exchanges between worker and citizen require the worker to sense the right tone and medium for expressing a point and/or feeling and then to determine whether, when, and how to act on that analysis. To ignore this combination of analysis, affect, judgment, and communication is to ignore the social lubrication that enables rapport, elicits desired responses, and ensures that interpersonal transactions are constructive.

In Newman, Guy and Mastracci's previous research on emotional labor, they discovered several important dimensions of emotional labor. First, at varying levels of intensity, it plays a role in nearly all government jobs. Civil servants probably recognize that the work entails emotion work, even though they may not be familiar with the term emotional labor itself. Frontline workers deal with the day-to-day needs of an increasingly demanding public; management handles the inter- and intra-agency demands of subordinates and superiors on everything from budget and human resources to agency turf battles. Second, they found that the performance of emotional labor need not lead to burnout. Public servants are as energized by intense emotional labor demands as they are exhausted. The difference lies in how management and workers address the emotive labor demands of these jobs. This led them to a third conclusion: Emotional labor is part of an occupation, not simply something that a person brings to the job (or not) — compared with emotional intelligence, which is located in the person. The characteristics of the job — its purpose and role in the organization, its demands and requirements — determine whether or not job holders will find themselves exerting emotional labor. This led to a fourth conclusion: Agencies can screen, train, retrain, and evaluate employees on the quality of emotional labor that they exercise on the job. But it is the rarest office that even recognizes the emotive demands of its workers, much less evaluates and compensates for them.

3.3. The Relationship Between Emotional Labor and Burnout

Why should senior public servants and academics care about emotional labor and burnout? From multiple perspectives — employee wellness, quality of work life, performance, citizen trust, service outcomes — management has an important role to play ensuring that the emotive aspects of work are appreciated and acknowledged, that there are systems in place to reward

its good performance, and that there are systems in place to address its downside. Our research makes it obvious that agencies should be screening, training, evaluating, and rewarding employees on the quality not just of their cognitive (technical) skills but also of their emotive (affective) skills and on their ability to mitigate overloads when the stress is too much.

Newman, Guy and Mastracci have been researching emotional labor for almost a decade, introducing it into the lexicon of public administration theory and practice. In 2008, they published *Emotional Labor: Putting the Service in Public Service.* Their next book, *Working on the Razor's Edge: Emotional Labor in Crisis Response* (2012), probes the actual performance of emotional labor more deeply. They focus on *how* it is done, and they go to extremes to find answers. They query public servants working in dangerous, emotionally intense crises every day: work that is on the razor's edge.

Burnout is a critical occupational hazard for those in the helping professions (such as social work, teaching, health care, criminal justice, crisis response and emergency services). Burnout is an indication of the employees growing inability to adequately manage their emotions when interacting with clients. Burnout is an issue of primary concern in "high-touch" occupations, those that involve lots of face-to-face contact — in other words, those with heavy emotional labor demands. Today, more and more jobs can be characterized as high-touch and as requiring emotional labor. References to "soft skills," "interpersonal skills," or simply "people work" contain an admission that the job requires some kind of emotional labor.

This is illustrated by reference to an interviewee, an immigration officer at an inspection station in Shenzhen, China. This job entails heavy emotional labor demands. The officer needs to greet and serve hundreds of passengers each day. In addition to the technical aspects of the job (for example, ensuring the validity of travel documents), his job requires that he treat every passenger in a professional and friendly manner — irrespective of whether he feels like doing so or not. As he puts it: "our work used to be managing people ... now it is serving people" (personal interview with Jue Wang, February 2012). Immigration officers need to stay calm when they encounter unexpected situations or rude and unruly passengers — all for the purposes of doing their job.

Burnout is increasingly costly in human and economic terms. In order to burnout, a person needs to have been on fire at one time. One of the greatest costs of burnout is the reduction of the effective service of the very best people in a given profession, and the resultant loss of productivity.

Emotion work is not negative *per se*. Rather, empirical studies show that emotion work has both negative and positive outcomes. Accordingly, burnout and engagement may be viewed as opposite ends of a continuum in the relationship people establish with their jobs.

Another interviewee, a director of a regional division in the Committee of Youth League in Shanghai, provides an illustration of the *duality* of emotion work. His responsibilities include frequent interactions with young people — dealing with troubled teenagers, motivating others to participate in events, and developing trust with his clientele. He states that he values his work and he can see how it is appreciated by others. "The working environment is rather positive and friendly. It is a happy scenario. However, the work is not as simple as it seems." The job requires him to be patient and positive in his interactions with his charges. He needs to listen to them, hear their needs, and understand their concerns. He states that he feels "the stress of being professionally friendly to everyone. The stress does not only come from the relationship with clients but also from the relationship with colleagues" (personal interview with Jue Wang, February 2012).

Emotional exhaustion (individual stress), cynicism (negative reaction to others and the job), and ineffectiveness (negative self-evaluation) are the principal dimensions of burnout. At the other end of the continuum stands the positive state of engagement with work, with its three dimensions of energy, involvement, and efficacy. These dimensions may be viewed as mirror images of the other. The focus here is on burnout.

3.3.1. *First dimension: Emotional exhaustion*

Emotional exhaustion is the main symptom of burnout and its most obvious manifestation. It refers to feeling overextended and depleted of one's emotional and physical resources. Workers feel drained and unable to unwind and recover. They experience a general malaise that accompanies a paradoxical combination of weariness and sleep problems.

Within the human services, the emotional demands of the work can exhaust a service provider's capacity to be involved with, and responsive to, the needs of recipients. Moreover, workers who perform emotional labor under conditions of low job autonomy and high job involvement are more at risk of emotional exhaustion than others. This means that burnout is a serious risk in impossible jobs, such as in family services agencies in the United States where caseworkers have huge caseloads, little discretion, and service budgets that cannot possibly cover all needs.

3.3.2. *Second dimension: Cynicism*

People use cognitive distancing to protect themselves from repeated emotional demands that are overwhelming. They become cynical and, in colloquial terms, become *crispy* in that they are negative, callous, or excessively detached from their jobs. They are "absent on the job," going through the motions in a detached, uncaring, even robotic manner. They depersonalize the citizens they work with, treating them as objects and they become mechanical in their discussions with coworkers. Such "hardening" and "deadening" is expressed as becoming numb to the repeated adrenalin "highs" that accompany so much of high-stakes people work.

3.3.3. *Third dimension: Ineffectiveness*

Ineffectiveness is the third dimension of burnout and is the tendency to evaluate one's work negatively. The belief that one is no longer able to achieve one's goals is accompanied by feelings of inefficiency, poor professional self-esteem, and a growing sense of inadequacy. For many public service workers who spend each day working with citizens who are in dire need, they may feel that no matter how hard they try and what actions they take, they will not have a lasting impact. This causes a discouraging sense of fatalism. And seeing so much need and deprivation on a daily basis can make it difficult to maintain a professional "edge" and psychic balance.

In order to hear first-hand how public service workers engage in emotional management, we turn to Newman, Guy and Mastracci's fieldwork in Illinois, US.

For any one of us who has ever felt apathetic towards their government, spending time at the Chicago Office of Public Guardian (OPG) or a similar human service agency provides a powerful antidote. This can be better illustrated than explained by the vignettes that follow.

For people in human service professions, helping others gives a sense of meaning to life; not being able to help is most stressful. The vicarious involvement in clients' lives can produce over-identification, unrealistic expectations, and finally a painful letdown. Over-involvement can also upset the delicate balance of "detached concern" and cause a loss of objectivity. An attorney at the OPG provides an illustration (Guy, Newman and Mastracci, 2008, pp. 32–33):

> One of my sex abuse clients ... she's been raped by her father for seven, eight years — was a straight-A student and nobody

knew what was going on at home. She finally cried out in junior high school and an aunt had taken her in with her siblings, and she got a full scholarship [to the university] and I had her in the office — she's been my client for eight years and she called me in May because she's come back after her sophomore year pregnant and, you know, I hung up the phone and just sobbed and thought, you know, here's — of all the things that are going on in her life and I thought we were on track and that things are better and I realized how emotionally attached I am to [her]. And I've only got 13 clients left and many of them are in my life a long time and I don't know how younger attorneys do this job.

The absence of concrete evidence of success causes feelings of insignificance, disillusionment, and helplessness, which are the hallmarks of burnout. For many of Newman, Guy and Mastracci's respondents, irrespective of their particular job, there was a feeling that no matter how hard they tried, they could not have a lasting impact on the lives of their clients. This sense of fatalism is expressed by an attorney as he describes the state of a co-worker (Guy, Newman and Mastracci, 2008, p. 32):

We can't control what happens to our clients ... He's being tortured by this job — he feels out of control — that whatever he does, he can't help these kids ... The outlooks for our clients are mostly bleak ... Ninety-nine percent of what we do has been done before.

Law enforcement provides a fertile ground for examining the management of emotions on the job. Burnout among correctional staff is legion. The dangerous working conditions and the lack of support from the public or the system combine to produce enormous emotional labor demands upon these workers. Emotion management is the modus operandi for correctional workers. Not being able to "set it down" takes its toll (Guy, Newman and Mastracci, 2008, p. 30):

Our jobs are far more difficult emotionally because you have to overcome your own feelings and their feelings and try to make something happen at the same time ... One thing I do really stress for myself is not flying off the handle, but remaining calm and that takes a great deal sometimes out of me. Sometimes I go home at night and I'm just exhausted because I've had to be professional when I sometimes would like very much not to be ... All that

tension just goes right into you. And it's like you carry it around with you. Because I'm not allowed to shout, scream, yell, carry on like a fool, it just kinda goes around with you.

When physical distancing is impossible, correctional staff use emotional withdrawal — time outs — as a respite from the stressors of their work. Negative "absence behavior" and "time abuse," such as taking longer breaks, calling in sick, spending more time on paperwork, leaving work early, and tardiness, are all examples of withdrawal by means of spending less time with clients. An employee of the Illinois Department of Corrections provides an example (Guy, Newman and Mastracci, 2008, pp. 34–35):

This staff member has called in sick all week. She is always giving me excuses on why she can't be on her unit at the time she's supposed to be there ... there's an issue that I have with staff and that issue is the use of time ... I mean they're calling in at the last minute — just won't come to work ... [Discussing another worker:] He's never here. He's always calling in. He's always trying to find a way to get off from work ... The counselors that give me the biggest problems are those that don't come to work.

3.4. Implications for Practice

Emotional labor is "real work." The voices heard here lead us to the primary practical implication, namely that emotional labor must be recognized, acknowledged, and compensated. Selection mechanisms that capture the goodness of fit between job demands and worker characteristics, the development of more accurate and complete job descriptions, and meaningful performance evaluation procedures for human service workers are necessary first steps. A second implication is to respond to the evidence that emotional labor has both positive and negative outcomes. A focus on both engagement and burnout can lead to workplace interventions that aim to increase worker energy, involvement, and efficiency, and alleviate emotional exhaustion, cynicism, and ineffectiveness. Job autonomy represents a key point of intervention. Autonomy and control over one's work and hence over the expression of "display rules" becomes a crucial factor in determining which outcome is likely to prevail.

Four strategies that are effective for avoiding or minimizing the effects of burnout are: critical incident debriefings, self-care plans, job redesign, and time outs.

3.4.1. *Critical incident debriefings*

A strategy used frequently by law enforcement, firefighters, and emergency rescue squads in the US is what is called critical incident debriefings or critical stress debriefings. These meetings serve a valuable function in dealing with vicarious trauma, compassion fatigue, and post-traumatic stress by helping workers deal with intense emotions they suppressed while the work was ongoing or afterward. The debriefings may be required or voluntary. They provide an opportunity to talk with peers and/or trained professionals about lingering images, memories and emotions in a manner that suits the workplace culture. They may be one-on-one with a counselor or they may be group meetings that involve all workers who were involved in the incident. To be successful, they require support and encouragement from supervisors and directors. It is often preferable for management to require debriefings rather than letting them be "on demand." This way, workers must attend and they do not lose face by appearing "weak" by requesting a session.

3.4.2. *Self-care plans*

Used predominantly among female dominated workforces such as victim assistance workers and domestic violence workers, the purpose of a self-care plan is to serve as a preemptive means for keeping employees healthy. It may be required by the employer or it may be optional. Where most effective, the plan requires employees to specify personal goals for themselves on an annual basis. The goals may or may not be work-related and always relate to personal growth. The ultimate purpose of the plan is to remind workers that their lives and personal growth are separate from the emotional crises they deal with on the job.

When workers have their annual performance appraisal, they are evaluated on their progress toward achieving goals in their self-care plan, just as they are evaluated on the various dimensions of their specific job. A plan includes personal stretch goals in the area of physical, emotional, financial, intellectual, and/or spiritual health. Within the first thirty days of employment, workers are required to create their plan and state it in measurable, outcome oriented terms.

3.4.3. *Redesign of jobs*

The purpose of job redesign is to relieve emotional pressure on workers. One way of doing this is to rotate responsibilities so that the individual

alternates between work that is intensely involved with citizens and administrative work that removes the worker from the emotive demands of daily face to face contact. For example, at a prison in Illinois, correctional officers and counselors routinely divide their time between interacting with offenders in the housing units, and performing administrative tasks in offices in a different building. Administrators can also reduce demands on workers by varying the work load. They can structure "time-outs" that enable workers to temporarily escape from usual job demands, giving them a change of pace during which they "recharge their batteries."

3.4.4. *"Time-outs"*

Time-outs are opportunities for staff to voluntarily choose to do less stressful work while others take over their responsibilities with service recipients. What makes this form of withdrawal a positive one is that good care can be maintained even while the professional is getting a temporary emotional breather. As noted above, when physical distancing is impossible, workers use emotional withdrawal as a coping mechanism. The dysfunctional side of time outs includes "absence behavior" and "time abuse." But if there is a proactive schedule that provides for time outs, the break can fit within the patterns of the organization.

Other strategies employers can use to mitigate the risks of emotional labor are recruitment processes that emphasize the importance of the job applicant being self-aware, and attention to social support. The importance of training and supervision cannot be overemphasized. Workshops that focus on "risk and crisis management," "communication and expression skills" and "emotion management" directly speak to the performance of emotive skills. There is also preemptive training that can forestall or prevent the downside to emotion work. Alerting workers that it is normal to experience intense, lingering images of horrific scenes helps them to understand that their reaction is predictable, rather than being a sign of weakness.

Interpersonal skills and emotional labor are at the heart of service delivery. Emotion work produces benefits, including a heightened sense of personal and professional accomplishment, a more productive interpersonal exchange, and a facility to achieve workplace goals. The downside to the "masks of impression management" is a tendency towards worker stress and burnout.

3.5. Conclusion

What have we learned from Newman, Guy and Mastracci's research in the US and Wang's interviews in China, and what does it mean? First, Newman, Guy and Mastracci have long argued the importance of recognizing emotional labor. Emerging research in this area underscores its crucial importance. It is a "comes with" for all jobs where public servant meets citizen. Not only are cognitive skills essential, emotive skills are as well. If we are to hire, train, develop, and evaluate workers on the basis of their performance, we must include consideration of the whole job, not just its technical aspects. Workers must be able to suppress, control, or elicit their own and others' emotions as the job demands. In other words, their capacity to engage in, and their efficacy in, exerting emotional labor is essential to job performance.

Second, Newman, Guy and Mastracci challenged mainstream management theory, proverbs, and principles, because we are still left with a fairly barren landscape when it comes to explaining emotional labor in public service. We are still stuck with an image of work forged during the industrial age by management scientists blind to the *human processes* by which work gets done.

In emotion work, the highs are high and the lows can be very low. Employers and supervisors need to acknowledge the highs and anticipate the lows. They can do this by providing mechanisms that celebrate the upside while not ignoring the downside and leaving individuals to rebound on their own. In the absence of strategies for coping with haunting recollections long after the job is done, workers too often turn "crispy" engaging in dysfunctional behaviors, losing interest in their work, and seeking work elsewhere. Losing trained, competent workers is expensive and, with forethought, avoidable.

For those working in academia, they may consider including coverage of emotional labor and emotive skills in their curricula. Emotion work fits comfortably into courses that focus on interpersonal relations, as well as overview courses that describe the nature of public service work. These include introductory courses such as "The Profession of Public Service," "Introduction to Public Administration," "Leadership in Public Service," and similar subjects. Courses that focus on organizational dynamics include "Organization Development," "Administrative Theory," "Human Resource Management, "Managing People, "Public Management," and so forth. For

a discussion on how to teach emotional labor, in terms of both content and style, see Mastracci, Newman and Guy (2010).

Whether public servants come in contact with citizens over a reception desk, at the tax assessor's office, at a zoning hearing, or in a crisis — in Singapore, Beijing, Chicago or Miami — emotional labor will be required. While the upside to emotion work is more prevalent, there is a downside. All public servants would do well to have at their disposal self-care plans and critical incident stress management in some form.

The implications for emotional labor in public service are thus: Through selective recruitment of applicants who are technically skilled and emotionally self-aware, the workforce is better equipped to deliver public services and realize the promise of a public service-oriented government. Training and development that targets worker knowledge about emotional labor and the feelings that are normal in such work will advance the performance of emotion work and proactively reduce its downside. Emotional labor is a skill. It can be learned and developed. Management can provide training that can improve workers' job performance and mitigate the negative effects of emotional labor on their lives outside of work. This is possible — whether or not you work on the razor's edge or manage or teach those who do.

References

Berman, EM and JP West (2008). Managing emotional intelligence in US cities: A study of social skills among public managers. *Public Administration Review*, 68(4), 742–758.

Goleman, D (2006). *Emotional Intelligence: Why It Can Matter More Than IQ*. 10th Anniversary Ed. New York: Bantam Books.

Guy, ME, MA Newman and SH Mastracci (2008). *Emotional Labor: Putting the Service in Public Service*. Armonk, New York: ME Sharpe.

Mastracci, SH, ME Guy and MA Newman (2012). *Emotional Labor and Crisis Response: Working on the Razor's Edge*. Armonk, New York: ME Sharpe.

Mastracci, SH, MA Newman and ME Guy (2010). Emotional labor: Why and how to teach it. *Journal of Public Affairs Education*, 16(2), 123–141.

Chapter 4

Irrationality, Bricolage, Quality and Performance Measurement: Unpacking the Conundrum in a Comparative East–West Context

Paul Higgins*

4.1. Introduction

Recent explorations into the causes of the post-2008 global financial crisis have unearthed the irrationality of the underpinning "system" of finance and the opportunistic bricolage that characterizes extant practice amongst city traders and other market intermediaries (Engelen *et al.*, 2010; Hildyard, 2008). While analogous reference has been made to the more adversarial forms of regulation typical under new public management (NPM), critical academic commentaries of the business of financialization fall short of advocating more regulation as a means to overcome the problems of global finance (Engelen *et al.*, 2011). This is because regulation in the financial sector is not considered to be an external constraint on the adverse behavior of practitioners but rather a major input to their continued malfeasance (*Ibid.*). The list of opportunistic improvisation techniques that financial actors have used to creatively respond to regulatory confinement is both impressive and on-going. To date their notoriety has included the creation of such innovative products and processes as collaterized debt obligations, short selling, mortgage default bets and private finance initiatives (Hildyard, 2008).

However, if financial agents have used a range of derivatives and securitization vehicles to profit from evading or "playing" regulations then

* Assistant Professor, Department of Public and Social Administration, City University of Hong Kong, p.higgins@cityu.edu.hk

what scope has there been for the long-chain of performance management[1] to reap analogous benefits in the even more heavily regulated public sector? A wealth of empirical research has, for instance, highlighted the often contradictory results of public sector regulation, developed initially as a means of compensating for the mistrust inherent in the market relations between principals and agents (Hood, James and Scott, 2000), but then only to transpose into a far less rationalist experience of gaming, tunnel vision, system irresponsibility and other perverse incentives (Cutler and Waine, 1997; Propper and Wilson, 2003; Bird *et al.*, 2005; Bevan and Hood, 2006).

An important dimension to Lévi-Strauss' original nomination of the bricoleur, in this regard, concerns its animation through comparison with an opposite figure he labelled the *ingénieur* (roughly translated into English as "engineer") (Duymedjian and Ruling, 2010). Whereas the spirit of the engineer is implicated in the realization, maintenance and Panglossian refinement of those instrumental forms of public accountability fashioned on technocratic lines to measure and seek continuous performance improvement (or standards or targets), the spirit of the bricoleur is caught up in those creative responses that then require further regulatory curtailment and so on. Such engagement potentially secures the presence of an elongated rationalist: bricoleur nexus performing an action-response fixture of "cat and mouse" (i.e., a contrived relationship involving constant pursuit, near captures, and repeated escape). This raises the question of why does the bricoleur emerge in this regulatory context given that, in contrast to the finance sector, affected practitioners are unlikely to be able to ring-fence personal profits from negatively externalised liabilities (Hildyard, 2008)?

Utilizing critical comparative examples taken from the UK, Hong Kong and China, the theoretical reach of this chapter grapples with the rationality: bricolage nexus particularly acknowledging the fundamentally different levels of bricolage behavior, varied motivations, competing values and forms of institutionalism that shape this realm. The three cases are, furthermore, chosen to gain a small but detailed spectrum of insights which accommodate both the "most different" comparative public policy design logic (Faure, 1994) and the literal replication model of case study design methodology (Yin, 1994). Taken together, the chapter predicts that *similar*

---

[1]Here the practice of instrumental performance measurement is considered to be a long-chain of activity that implicates the breadth of government from central authority through senior and middle layers of bureaucracy including front-line and back-of-office staff.

findings will emerge across the three *different* settings but for predictable reasons.[2]

That is to say, instantly recognizable, authentic and convincing examples of the bricoleur in action will emerge across the three case study contexts but in ways that require further elaboration and context to be fully appreciated. The theoretical premise that lies behind this chapter's claim of rationality-bricolage manifestation derives from the argument that the fundamental underpinning or foundational knowledge of instrumental performance measurement is not tantamount to some genuine scientific "system" of largely free-standing and confined technical knowledge with detached feedback mechanisms — such as unmanned space travel or the functionality of a television set — but an embedded system of contingent outcomes, grounded in social-cultural-political issues. The confirmatory potential of this claim, furthermore, stems from the fact that the ensuing evidence base is composed entirely of "actually existing" practice unobtrusively obtained from peer-reviewed published empirical research findings collected in the domain of interest and from amongst the three cultures considered.

According to this methodological design choice, the UK is considered to be a relative groundbreaker of the NPM doctrine even adapting the essence, if not the ideological baggage, of its "Citizen's Charter" initiative to the distinct milieu (and second case study context) of Hong Kong, via the performance pledge scheme in the early 1990's (Lo, 1993). In fact, what makes these two related case studies particularly intriguing is that Hong Kong has not subsequently produced the intense Panglossian performance measurement refinement of the UK. Instead, Hong Kong's institutional framework of performance pledges has remained fairly dormant in terms of refinement, redefinition and re-targeting. Mainland China, meanwhile, provides a further critical case study scenario; a relative newcomer to centrally sanctioned instrumental performance measurement (Chan and Gao, 2008; Burns and Zhou, 2010; Yang and Modell, 2011), and with a different set of agendas and rationales to pursue; some top-down and collective others bottom-up and localized. In all cases, however, while

---

[2]Although the author has traded depth for breadth in the "small number" of case studies chosen the theoretically generalizable themes arising should be instantly recognizable both in the cases of focus and amongst those countries deploying similar forms of instrumental performance measurement. Thus, if this study was extended to, say, the US, Japan and Finland similar themes of higher-order bricolage, data and activity manipulation would materialize.

broadly consistent examples of bricolaged improvisation, opportunism and creativity are found to persist cross-examination of the emergent data reveals that particular nuances arise which can be further explained by reference to the broader political and historical context in which public management reform is conjectured.

The argument is constructed as follows. In the first part, the chapter begins by undertaking the somewhat ambitious task of relating Levi-Strauss' (1966) primitive and technological contextualisation of bricolage to the realm of NPM and therein to the more specific domain of instrumental performance measurement. This process duly informs this chapter's initial conceptualization of the *ingénieur* (engineer) and the *bricoleur*, of which respective manifestations are associated, first, with the micro-foundational (Stoker, 2009) promotion of rationalist public accountability systems, and second, with the opportunistic "pick and mixing" of subordinates' repertoire as they respond to the modernist infrastructure of their super-ordinates. Against this backdrop, the chapter critically engages with empirically-derived information drawn from the three critical cases to secure a degree of consistency in bricoleur identification and to facilitate the theoretically generalizable gain of literal replication (Yin, 1994). The data that emerges from this examination is then further organized around the three emergent themes of "higher order bricolage," "data and practice manipulation" and "the rationality: bricolage nexus" to reveal further insights about the behaviors, motivations, values and institutions that shape this realm of activity.

4.2. The Engineer and Bricoleur in Instrumental Performance Management

In *The Savage Mind* (1966), Claude Lévi-Strauss defines the concept of "bricolage" as a method of expression through the selection and synthesis of components culled from surrounding culture (Laventure, 2012). The bricoleur uses all the concrete materials and experiences encountered in everyday life and through others around them, to make sense of the world he/she is living in and to find solutions for the problems he/she is confronted (Frissen and Slot, 2009). The bricoleur thus creatively and intuitively combines and recombines his/her repertoire or stock of resource elements — the bits and pieces collected *independently* of any particular project or utilization — to respond to unravelling circumstances (*Ibid.*, emphasis added).

Lévi-Strauss original nomination of the bricoleur is contra-positioned with the *ingénieur* (engineer) whose value positioning is grounded in a specific belief in the superiority of rationality and scientific reasoning. Compared to the bricoleur, the engineer is conceptualized as deploying a more systematic, structured and rational way of thinking that is fundamentally open in the sense that it is characterized by a constant move toward transgressing prevailing boundaries to enlighten humanity (Duymedjian and Ruling, 2010). One need only consider the language of rationality, certainty and system coherence that pervades the conventional justification of performance regulation in all three economies studied here — and others beyond — to gain recognition of this mode of thinking.

In Hong Kong, for instance, the Efficiency Unit un-problematically describes the process of performance measurement as "setting strategic objectives based on customer needs, identifying key result areas, formulating measurement criteria, gathering performance data and trying to bridge performance gaps" (Cited in Cheung, 2005). In the UK, the Audit Commission for England and Wales (Audit Commission.gov.uk) displays an equally assured discourse in its mission statement explaining that its function is to "independently" drive economy, efficiency and effectiveness in local public services to deliver better outcomes for everyone ... (while) ... providing authoritative, unbiased, evidence-based analysis and advice. Finally, in China, the policy document promulgated by the Central Party Organization Department, which heralded the implementation of performance measurement across local areas (Chan and Gao, 2008), explicitly proposed that a "scientific assessment system and assessment standards be formulated" (Translation Wang, 2008, p. 11) with "specific methods of information collection, calculation, assessment, spot checks, and supervision ... studied and formulated in accordance with the relevant stipulations of the Statistics Law to ensure the truthfulness, accuracy, and time-effectiveness of the figures" (*Ibid.*, p. 13). In fact, in 2006, the Central Committee of the Communist Party of China issued a new set of guidelines to instill an even more "scientific" and "objective" approach to performance evaluation including a refined performance scorecard with stronger emphasis on professional performance (Yang and Modell, 2011).

What aligns all three examples of assumed "system rationality," then, is the confidence of certainty, coherence and comprehensible feedback loops. In contrast, the boundaries of the bricoleur's repertoire are considered to be constrained by the limits imposed by a particular state of civilization which rarely exceeds the class of actions and significances he/she is accustomed

Table 4.1.   Comparing the Bricoleur and Ingénieur.

	Bricoleu	Ingénieu
Metaphysics	Everything matters Complex, interconnected system Closed universe	A-priori hierarchical order Reduction/decomposition Openness, transcending boundaries

Epistemology	Intimate knowledge, familiarity
	Knowledge about relationships
	  implying a low functional
	  fixedness
	Versatility implying resilience
		Distant knowledge, representation
		Knowledge about structural bias
		  characteristics entities
		
		Specialization

Practice	Collection through unplanned
	  encounters
	Unclear outcomes
	Dialogue with elements in
	  stock, diversion of resources
	Assemblage, substitution "it's
	  working"
	Creation and use cannot be
	  dissociated
	Outcomes look unlike anything
	  else
		Search for adequate,
		  project-oriented means
		Project and design
		Respect of prior specifications
		
		Seamless integrated system
		
		Evaluation through expected level
		  of performance/quality
		Separation of creation and use
		
		Outcomes respond to field norms

Source: Duymedjian and Ruling (2010).

to, and "by inclination or necessity always remains within [the constraints]" (Lévi-Strauss in Duymedjian and Ruling, 2010, p. 140). In no sense, however, should this demarcation be seen to imply that the practice of bricolage is somehow inferior to the "rationalism" of the engineer. Rather, Lévi-Strauss (1966) depicts bricolage and rationalism as parallel forms of acquiring knowledge (see Table 4.1) to the extent that compared with the holistic, all-embracing and complex metaphysics of the bricoleur, the engineer is reductionist in his/her appeal and exhibits structural bias with an (erroneous) tendency to exclude objects deemed external to their cause and deemed to have no value.

Such a description is particularly apt when, as contemplated in this chapter, it is leveled at the notion of the engineer as rationalist champion of contemporary NPM. This is because by adopting a micro-foundational approach to public accountability the rationalist fails to demonstrate sensitivity to the possibilities of community-orientated and holistic notions of quality relying abstractly instead on specialization, focus and system manageability. As Sanderson (1996, p. 91) aptly observed in the context

of the UK's Citizen's Charter initiative, officially stated performance achievement may not necessarily concur with reported experience:

> on the one hand, a picture portrayed by the Government's Citizen's Charter of public services "reaching standards of performance that would have been unthinkable only a few years ago"; on the other hand, a totally different picture portrayed with newspaper features of public services starved of resources and suffering severe problems due to backlogs of maintenance and repairs and inadequate resources to provide services to decent services.

Whereas the "engineer" can thus reasonably be construed as being formally responsible for introducing the rationalist, system-encompassing forms of regulation characteristic of both the financial and public sectors, the bricoleur's conterminous manifestation involves responding to these pressures in a "softer," more opportunistic manner. In some of these cases, the bricoleur's motivations appear to be genuinely concerned with seeking ways to cover gaps in service derived from the narrow, "tunnel envisioned," performance management perspective regulated; that is to say, to overlook the pressures to obtain high performance scores in a bid to protect *real* (holistic) service quality.[3] In other cases, the bricoleur's motivations seem to stem from a different set of values; such as the need to attain centrally imposed targets, to demonstrate continuous improvement and/or to achieve some other benchmark or standard. Under these institutionalized motivational circumstances (extrinsic rather than intrinsic), the irrational system of public sector performance measurement is in danger of succumbing to the problem of Goodhart's law (1975) which states that "performance indicators lose their usefulness when used as objects of policy."

Both types of motivation intrinsically motivated to protect holistic quality or externally institutionalized to achieve some target or standard, thus help to explain why a bricoleur may materialize in this realm of instrumental public accountability rather than allowing the process to proceed smoothly akin to some scientific rational process. Another scenario would be the case where "blind" compliance is merely administered

---

[3]In fact, it was precisely this "traditional" (Pfeffer and Coote, 1991) line of argument that was vehemently pursued by opponents of the Citizen's Charter initiative in the UK and which was duly criticized for measure fixation and holistic quality loss (Bellamy and Greenaway, 1995). Interestingly, these criticisms do not appear to materialize in Hong Kong or China for reasons explained in more detail below.

by subordinates to produce as an objective account of performance as permitted within the confines of the system (e.g., not incentivized in anyway by its structured manifestation). Except for these circumstances, considered in more detail below, the more widely reported (i.e., Western derived) form of improvisational practice produces the bricoleur as an agent in the long-chain of performance management creatively responding to the pressures of principal regulation in a bid to demonstrate institutional achievement or motivated safeguards. One is not suggesting that either approach — to safeguard holistic quality or to attain targets — is capable of achieving the aims set out for it but rather to highlight the different types of behavior that usually materializes.

This indeterminate bricolaged activity, furthermore, has the potential to produce an on-going regulator: regulated nexus where the curtailments of the former become an input to further regulated bricolage of the latter, as per the financialization analogy mentioned above. However, it is also the contention of this paper that such bricolaged activity operates at a variety of levels along the performance management chain depending precisely on what the objectives of its highest order determination are and how well these can subsequently be controlled by principals. In other words, the principal's rationale for establishing the performance management framework needs first to be ascertained and one factor that appears to be universally apparent in all three cases is the co-existence of market values.

4.3. Higher Order Bricolage

Although regulation and performance measurement of public services is by no means a new phenomenon (Cutler, 2007), NPM manifestations of it derived initially following efforts on the part of central authorities to liberalize and commercialize the public sector (Pollitt, 1986; Pfeffer and Coote, 1991; Bellamy and Greenaway, 1995). In the UK, a NPM pioneer, the introduction of instrumental performance management arose not with the aim of *improving* public services *per se* but rather in response to the problem of how to legitimize the antecedent of a cutback management strategy in the face of a skeptical electorate. As Pollitt (1986) maintained during the emergence of the NPM phenomenon, the pursuit of quality and performance improvement in public services provides a more positive sounding political agenda than one merely focusing on cutting costs; it has an "aroma of action, dynamism, and purposeful effort" about it.

However, if the origins of contemporary forms of instrumental performance management derive from the conjecture of NPM then despite its rationalistic overtones, it too was probably born of the bricolage mode. In other words, public sector performance measurement represents the materialization of the highest-ordered bricolaged assemblage derived from a fusion of quantitative management knowledge and engineering sciences (i.e., quality control in manufacturing) and its application to a professionally established or traditional domain of largely Weberian bureaucracy. According to this interpretation, the rise of instrumental performance measurement represents part of the imposition of one set of values (managerial modernization) over another (traditional public administration); a battle manifested materially in what has been described in the UK as the corporate takeover of the public sector (Johnson and Callender, 1999; Whitfield, 2001).

But if this is so, then what of the legitimizing rationale for instrumental performance measurement in "free-market" Hong Kong, an economy that did not go through a "politics of privatization" grounded in the issues of, say, ownership, the scope of government and holistic quality, as per the UK (Ascher, 1987)? In Hong Kong, the nature of the higher-order performance measurement bricolage seems to have adopted a different form having been *opportunistically* modeled on the UK's "Citizen's Charter" initiative (Lo, 1993) following adaptation (Rose, 2005) by the, then, Governor Chris Patten in 1992. In this case, the higher-order bricolage re-assemblage entailed the deployment of the existing repertoire of the Citizen's Charter initiative, and its supporting foundational knowledge, amongst an extended realm of oversight (i.e., Hong Kong) to make a separate political gain (e.g., to promote the air of 'outward-looking, customer-orientated' government) in an economy lacking popular democracy and subjected to fading colonial rule. As per the UK Citizen's Charter initiative Hong Kong's performance pledge scheme also represents a "packaged" reform (i.e., a defined set of performance pledges having been distributed across 75 departments/bureaux, especially customer-facing ones). Similarly, "packaged" features are also apparent in the UK post-citizen charter regimes of best value performance indicators, comprehensive performance assessment and comprehensive area assessment.

The situation in China is more difficult to decipher since, compared to fairly dormant Hong Kong which has not experienced the on-going Panglossian refinement of the UK, it is still very much embroiled in an unraveling situation. Yang and Modell (2011) describe the circumstances

of China akin to an incomplete shift between moral (post-1949) and merit (post-1978) conceptions of performance, which has fostered considerable ambiguity enabling various actors to exercise power in more or less explicit ways. Hence, it is possible to identify both top-down and bottom-up approaches to performance management that are able to co-exist within the "spirit" of central preferences. Thus, at the local government level, the spawning of instrumental performance measurement of a nature akin to the form if not substance of NPM doctrine can be seen very much as a spontaneous, opportunistic and individualistic endeavor born of the unplanned prospect that promotion is performance-based (Burns and Zhou, 2010). According to this form of institutionalism, the bricoleur (i.e., promotion candidate) adopts Western notions of performance management (such as, performance pledges or user satisfaction surveys) to boost his/her promotion credentials (*Ibid.*). In this sense, the toolkit or repertoire of performance measurement is merely one of a number of fads and fashions that might be adopted by local officials to "look good" as cutting edge or "outward looking" candidates.

Sensitive of such localism overstepping the centrist line, however, the Chinese state authorities (Central Party Organization Department) are also eager to dictate that "local benefits obtained by disregarding overall benefits, by violating the state's macro-regulation and control policies, and by disregarding laws and regulations are not regarded as work achievements" (Translation Wang, 2008, p. 11). Accordingly, performance measurement in China is also used to ensure that local officials comply with higher-level policy priorities, which are then allocated and distributed downwards through the administrative hierarchy (Chan and Gao, 2008). China's performance measurement system thus incorporates central directives on the one hand but illuminates local features on the other. Ultimately, however, if a city official fails to meet certain targets, especially those with veto or priority power, he/she would not be evaluated for annual bonuses or promotion and could even face a salary cut or dismissal (*Ibid.*).

In addition to the commonality of rationalist scientific discourse that pervades the three cases two further points emerge from this initial analysis of higher-order bricolage. First, all three forms of instrumental performance measurement co-exist with the rise or consolidation of market mechanisms in public services. Thus, in the UK, the Citizen's Charter initiative helped to legitimize the shift to market, whereas best value performance indicators were part of a package of reforms, known as best value, that instigated more flexible and extended forms of contracting and private sector involvement

compared to compulsory competitive tendering. In Hong Kong, meanwhile, the performance pledge scheme could be simply transferred and applied from the UK without obstruction since it both reinforced the positive non-intervention stance of the then incumbent colonial government and despite stressing the role of the user in its prescriptions was, somewhat ironically, a largely imposed agenda. Accordingly, the "citizenship" debate of the UK which centered on the question of where to place the apostrophe to denote either individualism (i.e., the citizen's charter) or collectivism (i.e., citizens' charter) was simply not part of the Hong Kong discourse. China's performance management system, finally, has again "in step with the prescriptions of the market economy," developed relatively quickly since the mid-1990s (Burns and Zhou, 2010, p. 26). Thus, akin to core NPM experiences expressed around the world, the use of the market and instrumental performance measurement seem to move in tandem with both features deriving from the same stock or repertoire of higher-ordered bricolage.

The second observation is that all three sets of performance measures take the form of a supposedly coherent package of indicators (i.e., citizen's charters indicators, performance pledges and China's target based responsibility system), which is of course entirely consistent with the logic of a "system." However, unlike the certainty of a free-standing and confined system of rationality with a specific aim to, say, "fly" or to "transmit analogue or digital signals" it is far less clear where the parameters of instrumental performance measures really begin and end. This is because in an explicitly social-cultural-political climate one is confronted with such normative issues as the scope and purpose of government. Here, even the creation of a single indicator such as "GDP" or "happiness" becomes problematic owing to difficulties of calculation and interpretation. For instance, an increase in GDP may not concur with improved and sustainable well-being (which is surely the ultimate aim of assessment) given the potential deleterious source of its rawer and realistic attainment, while comparative happiness performance could be a function of expectation of conditioning. Likewise, the incorporation of multiple indicators in a bid to provide a more rounded or complete view, as per this chapter's examples of "packaged" datasets, can still not overcome the problem of exclusivity.

4.4. Data and Activity Manipulation

Moving further down the performance management chain attention can turn to the regulated agent and the possibility that instrumental

forms of public accountability spawn system irrational data and practice manipulation. This occurs owing either to the *extrinsic* motivational pressure that agents feel to achieve institutionalized targets or the *intrinsic* motivational pressure that is exerted to protect holistic quality in the light of a declining moral (Chinese)/traditional (UK) accountability framework. In "ideal" terms one can contrast these two positions according to their appeal to either a professionalized set of values — e.g., notions of need, fairness and judgement — or to some managerialist appeal to value for money, openness and customer service.

According to the "traditional" quality or professional view the problem with the practice of instrumental performance measurement is not, as is *conventionally* regarded in the global finance literature, born of the *lack* of regulation owing to the excessive faith placed in market operators but rather from the very obsessive modernist concern with control, monitoring and surveillance. In other words, regulation in the traditional public sector is performed at the *expense* of *métis* — the practical knowledge derived from everyday experience — not to its advantageous curtailment. Notice here that the terms *métis* and *bricolage* denote different meanings despite their shared distinctiveness from conceptions of rationality. Accordingly, in the face of instrumental performance measurement, such intrinsically-motivated responses of the professional kind seem harder to detect from the available literature especially in the UK where such "traditional" objections to NPM were at least apparent early on.

Fifteen years ago, for instance, case study research by McIntosh and Broderick (1996) in the UK produced interesting evidence of the "holistic quality" aspirations of personnel working in the relatively "simple" context of refuse collection (whose managerialist quality prescriptions are usually reduced to a mere consideration of whether "waste has been collected or not collected" and "from which precise location" via abstracted notions of asset specificity, bounded rationality and information asymmetry). In particular, McIntosh and Broderick (1996) found that citizens' of the refuse collection service in the UK may actually value those aspects of service performance not encapsulated by standardized definitions of quality (i.e., instrumental performance measures) including such "hidden" or un-specifiable tasks as "checking upon the well-being of elderly people in their homes" or refuse collectors doubling up as an early morning security squad. Seen in this light, the refuse collection service becomes part of the community just as "Postman Pat" the popularized cartoon character might have been to residents of Greendale.

With the passing of time, however, such rich contextual studies of holistic quality and community are harder to find as the academic emphasis has tended to switch to an assessment of instrumental outputs framed in managerialist terms. One only need explore the wealth of studies devoted to exploring whether the performance of public services has improved or deteriorated since NPM, without proper recognition as to the limits of such operationalization (see Cutler and Waine, 1997 for an authoritative overview). For China, however, such targets seem to be designed for a different purpose, namely to strengthen and improve "the Evaluation of Practical Work Accomplishment of the Leadership Corps of Party Committees and Government at the County (Municipal) Level" or to achieve "the Target-Based Responsibility System" via the attainment of certain tasks — whether it be population birth control, dealing with corruption or state tax collection — rather than necessarily the precise means or standards by which certain functions of government are performed as per some of Hong Kong's performance pledges; many of which relate to the speed of service delivery (Legislative Council Panel on Public Service, 2009).

This, then, leaves the prospect of extrinsically-motivated target achievement spawning what is termed here the possibilities of data and practice manipulation. Whereas "data manipulation" involves the process of presenting one's *already collected* figures in their best possible light "practice manipulation" relates to those first-order organizational activities that *generate* the initial data. All three case studies produce clear evidence of both data and practice manipulation.

In the Chinese objective responsibility system, for instance, because local governments are permitted to assign weights and scores to the measures local authorities are able to negotiate over these aspects to some extent (Gao, 2007, p. 58, cited in Burns and Zhou, 2008). This allows officials not only engage in a process of data "mushrooming" — "a tactic of agency information overload designed to obfuscate real performance to the principal" (Van Dooren *et al.*, 2010, p. 160) but also to unjustifiably dis-aggregate or aggregate figures to hide problematic aspects of performance through attention or lack of attention to detail, respectively (*Ibid.*).

Likewise, in England, the creation and reportage of a composite quality of life index could also be used to mask an underlying problem such as a comparatively high crime rate or an unsustainable lifestyle (Higgins and Campanera, 2011). Alternatively, attention to an overall increase in crime rates in a city can be diverted by pointing to an improvement in a district (*Ibid.*).

Taylor (2006), meanwhile, cites the example of how the Television and Entertainment Licensing Authority in Hong Kong used the dates of "interim replies" (standard responses to complainants informing them that their complaints are under investigation) as the dates of "substantive replies" (which provide information on the results of the investigations) to produce misleading, but better sounding, performance information. Again, both sets of data had already been produced in this example with the resulting data manipulation concerning the form of how such data was then presented.

Concerning the issue of practice manipulation, Van Thiel and Leeuw (2002, p. 272) cite the case where the British National Health Service (NHS) agreed that patients should be on a waiting list for an operation no longer than 2 years. At first, this measure appeared successful, as the average waiting time decreased (*Ibid.*). However, on further examination it was found that because the waiting time only began to be counted after the first hospital consultation, consultation was postponed to decrease the waiting time (*Ibid.*). Consequently, the average waiting time did not decrease at all but was merely shifted in time, while an improvement was able to be reported where there was none (*Ibid.*). Hood (2006) even more remarkably observes how fake hospital rooms on NHS corridors were created by the physical assemblage of curtains in order to help fulfill a national target. Turning to Asia, Cheung (2005, p. 364) details how regular attainment of the Hong Kong's postal service "three telephone rings response pledge," though impressive, has to be qualified thus producing further evidence of practice manipulation:

> Our test call was indeed picked up within three rings by the interactive voice message system, and prompted to choose the language option. Next, followed a recorded message introducing one of the latest services offered by HK post, then a series of instructions on which tone buttons to press for different types of service inquiry, which altogether lasted about 30 seconds, before the final instruction was given on pressing the button for direction communication with customer service. Yet that was not the end of the encounter with the system — two recorded messages were then heard, one soliciting the caller's willingness to participate in the entire conversation being recorded for quality assurance purpose. In the end approximately 3 minutes elapsed before the caller was able to speak to a real person from HK post.

Thirdly, reporting on the China situation as a whole, Gao (2010, p. 71) suggests that stories describing the way in which "figures are made by officials, and officials are in turn produced by figures" are hardly new for Chinese people. Burns and Zhou (2008) also observe that since local leaders whose counties, districts, or provinces do well on the economic indicators, tend to have a greater chance of promotion some officials have been perversely incentivized to use whatever means, including violating labor and environmental protection laws or illegally accumulating huge public debt, to achieve their goal. Such deleterious practice thus has affinity with those financial practitioners who hide (and externalize) their "risks" (read financial losses, actual or potential) by passing them on to less savvy retail clients such as pension holders and the State, while ring-fencing their own profits from liabilities (Hildyard, 2008). The only difference in the case of instrumental performance measurement is that the form of "risk" hiding (read reduced quality but, possibly, *enhanced* performance) involves manipulating or masking the real picture while the form of negative externalization involves the environmental and social degradation arising.

To conclude, then, the deleterious by-products of public sector performance measurement described here do not usually amount to some physical or tradable commodity, as per the personalized gains of the financial sector, but rather to *foregone* (and usually important *ex-ante*) service activity as well as the creation of adverse by-products. However the extent to which such deleterious outcomes actually materialize seems to reflect, on the one hand, the strength of officials' appeal to potentially declining professional values and, on the other hand, the severity of the carrot and sticks pertaining to achieve or not to achieve the targets set.

4.5. Rationality: Bricolage Nexus

Compared to the constant revisions and adjustments to performance measurement found in the UK, the Hong Kong situation is reported as being far less active. For instance, over a period of three years the Legislative Council Panel on Public Service (2009) estimates that 3% of indicators had been deleted, 8% of indicators represented new additions and 20% of indicators had faced minor refinements. In contrast, across a similar time period in English local government an entire regime of comprehensive performance assessment had been replaced with a new regime of comprehensive area assessment (Audit Commission *et al.*, 2009). As Taylor (2006, p. 300) suggests perhaps the Hong Kong "statutory

bodies" preoccupation with the need to meet their performance targets and
to avoid attracting unfavorable publicity has led many to establish easy and
unchallenging targets. Thus, about 70–80% of Hong Kong's performance
pledges have remained the same for several years and there has been nothing
like the academic/political debates heard in the UK about the substantive
limitations of performance indicators. As such, the rationalist: bricolage
nexus performed in Hong Kong, and to some extent China, seems to be one
of fairly abrupt asymmetrical consent. This would suggest that there is a
fine line between notions of top-down compliance and the fostering of an
underlying accord between principal and agent to ensure that targets are
met. Cheung (2005) even asks whether Hong Kong's performance pledge
scheme was designed simply to serve bureaucratic/managerial imperatives
such as compliance with top-down directives so that units look good as
"responsive" agencies.

Meanwhile, in Zhouzhi (X'ian, China), Gao (2010, p. 61) observes
that because accomplishment of non-mission-based targets was hard to
compare and difficult to monitor, local officials tended to worry less about
these relatively "soft" targets, even though most officials were well aware
of the *importance* of these tasks (emphasis added). Witness here, then,
none of the traditional professional reservations voiced by some of their
UK counterparts (Pfeffer and Coote, 1991; Bellamy and Greenaway, 1995;
McIntosh and Broderick, 1996), despite China's long-standing tradition of
professional civil service training and imperial civil examination (Tsang,
2007) and its post-1949 moral performance scheme (Yang and Modell,
2011).

The rationality: bricolage nexus in the UK, meanwhile, corresponds
more closely with the situation depicted in the financial sector where
regulation is not considered to be an external constraint on the adverse
behavior of finance but rather a major input to its continued malfeasance.
Here, Greener (2009) cites the example of British healthcare where an on-
going "cat and mouse" game of constant pursuit, near capture and repeated
"escape" is manifested. Thus, at Stage one (initial regulation):

> Doctors might be told that they must see a patient within
> 30 minutes of their arrival for an appointment ... (Stage two,
> opportunistic escape). Looking at the target, doctors do not have to
> treat the patient, but merely to "see" them. As such an easy way
> of meeting the target would be for doctors, in-between treating
> patients, to periodically (every 30 minutes) to emerge from their

treatment rooms, greet all the patients waiting, and then to return to their room again. They will have "seen" the patients, and so met the target ... (Stage three, re-pursuit). Where policymakers become aware of the "seeing" patients ruse, and change the target to say that all patients should have their treatment begun within 30 minutes of arriving for an appointment (Stage four, revised opportunistic escape). A devious public manager might again look at the exact wording of the target, and put in a place a system whereby, because the new target does not specify a doctor will treat the patient, a triage nurse instead will be tasked with meeting every new patient as they arrive, interviewing them, and where possible dealing with the patient problems without the doctor. The hospital might argue that diagnosing the patient is a crucial part of treatment, and interviewing the patient is an important part of diagnosis. Although no doctor has been near a patient, the process of treatment therefore has begun as soon the triage nurse sits down with the patient, and the target has been met.

Although it is not entirely clear why the rationality: bricolage nexus materializes in this context the behavior described certainly does not concord with conventional views of public service professionalism. This raises the question whether professional medical doctors should really be getting themselves tangled up in the irrationalities of practice that such a situation produces. In other words, should not managerially regulated medical professionals be doing more useful things with their time? Note also in the above example how the regulator falls short of specifying that a doctor must treat the patient in the most overtly of humanistic terms and with the care and precision of a Harley Street Practitioner. Similarly, in the education sector the British government does not revert to a non-negotiable position that selection is a merely geographical proximity/local school based decision because, although this might be the most holistically welcome possibility (whereby national standards permeate through all schools), it is also inconsistent with the underlying policy objective to instill "choice" and "selection" in schools (i.e., to mimic the market).

Consequently, it is a lack of *principle* (and quality) that governs the NPM regime of instrumental performance measurement not its assumed fostering and/or abundance. Thus, despite the rhetoric of continuous performance improvement that has pervaded the UK's public sector during the New Labor era the parameters of the bricoleur's action always seems

to stay within the "limits" of its higher order objective. In this sense at least, public sector performance measurement becomes part of Lévi-Strauss' "myth making," not some genuine authentic article of rationalist oversight but part of the politics of simulation.[4]

Along similar lines, Wong and Wan (2009, p. 445) observe that while Hong Kong's Environmental Protection Department "does list performance pledges on the target times for responding to complaints and enquiries, processing applications for permits/licenses/approvals, providing waste management services, and providing environmental information, it does not stipulate, for example, its targets for reductions in the amount of pollutants discharged in a given year." By failing to address such pressing substantive issues (i.e., pollution control), it begs the question whether Hong Kong's performance pledges are even measuring the right performance and those aspects of performance most important to citizens (Cheung, 2005)?

Again, using the financial analogy, the failure to report on some of society's most grave concerns (i.e., climate change, pollution, poverty, unsustainability) could be construed as tantamount to "hiding" the prevailing "risk" of contemporary modernization. Such a higher-ordered example thus reflects not so much a case of data and practice manipulation but an episode of agenda setting. Seen in this light, the long-chain of performance regulation is designed to produce both compliance *and* legitimacy although these two objectives may not always move in tandem. Elsewhere the rationality: bricolage nexus merely disrupts the real task of getting on with the job (as per the aforementioned hospital example) a situation which seems to demand the re-instigation of trust and public professional practice to remedy the situation.

4.6. Conclusion

As China continues to grapple with its moral and merit performance dilemma the UK, one of the leading proponents of instrumental performance management, is reigning in some of its technical accountability arrangements. The most striking manifestation of the latter concerns the announcement that the Audit Commission for England and Wales faces

---

[4]Here one is reminded of Weber's distinction between substantive and instrumental rationality; albeit whereas Weber feared that substantive rationality might become enclosed by instrumental rationality (trapped in an "iron cage"), in the Strauss mode the deployment of instrumental performance management displays rationality as myth.

imminent abolition (Parry and Sear, 2010). This begs the question why given all that has been said above about the growth of the market, NPM and instrumental performance measurement. Three particular insights come to mind.

First, the cost of maintaining the Audit Commission's performance management regime has proven to be overbearing, especially in the context of major public sector austerity. Interestingly, this explanation precisely contradicts the managerialist logic of NPM that the gains of regulation (i.e., stimulants to performance improvement in the absence of market pressures) should outweigh its costs. Although it is reasonable to expect decreasing returns from instrumental performance measures such an abrupt abolition does raise the question of what happens next? One major danger in the UK in this regard is that in the light of a declining traditional professional accountability framework the quality of public services will simply continue to deteriorate, possibly at an accelerated rate. The explanation for this is that while the strict, top-down and antagonistic nature of national headlining performance standards might have generated their fair share of criticism they at least maintained a degree of commitment to the notion of citizenship entitlements, proposed as a way of tackling postcode lotteries (Bogdanor, 2010). Although the UK coalition government would claim that the big society of communities, social enterprises and the private sector will be able to perform the functions of the retracting public sector (Cabinet Office, 2010), this claim is simply born of the desperation that the quality of public services really are deteriorating. Despite the collectivist spirit of "we are all in *this* together" that pervades the populist rhetoric of the UK's big society position the word "this" (austerity demise) is hugely downbeat and negative in connotation.

Second, performance management simply does not work and is not worth pursuing anymore. Again this would be a major admission which undoes much of the aforementioned "scientific" assumptions of, say, New Labor's best value scheme or comprehensive performance assessment. Here one need only observe the type of language that the Conservative Party (2009, p. 19) used when announcing the abolition of the Audit Commission to appreciate how consistent it is with the discussion of the bricoleur threaded throughout this chapter:

> Despite persistent general reductions in user satisfaction, the Government's most recent inspection scores show three quarters of councils to be "improving strongly or well" suggests that the main

effects of the inspection regimes has been to teach local authority officers how to play the inspection regime, rather than reflect local performance. This is a classic example of councils' energy and resources being diverted away from delivering local services into delivering a tick in a government box.

Third, relatedly, and perhaps most profoundly, performance measurement has served its higher-order legitimizing purpose in the UK and can thus be disbanded. More specifically, now that the party politics of privatization in the UK has been superseded by the tri-partisanship of place-based community empowerment (i.e., localism), there is no longer a need for political elites to legitimize the neo-liberal project. In other words, liberated from the party politics of privatization the associated legitimizing infrastructure of attainment can be dismantled (Pollit, 1986).[5] This is not yet the case in health and education, whose politics of privatization are still very much contested and performance, audit and inspection regimes still persist. Whatever the exact reason, it all seems to provide only part of the answer since such an explanation does not seem to work in Hong Kong, and to some extent China, where the prevalence of instrumental performance measurement continues to co-exist with the consolidation or rise of the market as a governing principle. However, as noted above, the higher-order legitimizing bricolage in these conterminous Asian contexts seems to be designed to perform some other function, standard or objective as further mediated by stronger notions of top-down compliance and/or the fostering of an underlying accord between principal and agent.

There is, however, another more fundamental sense in which public sector performance measurement does not seem to be working and that is that it is emblematic of a society in which only rationalistic principles rather than political tradition are valued. However, as Gao (2009) observes in China, the way that performance measurement is conducted — governing by goals and numbers — does not address the substantial governance issues and fundamental social and political tensions that exist in Chinese society. Accordingly, the failure of Planning, Programming, and Budgeting System (PPBS), zero-based budgeting (ZBB), management by objectives (MBO) and other such initiatives to become institutionalized can be attributed to

---

[5] Nothing has yet materialised to fill the ensuing accountability gap; presumably because the emerging principles of localism are inconsistent with the notion of national standards and accountability now being proposed under the guise of the "big society."

the inability of those processes to integrate themselves into the decision-making processes that really matter to managers and stakeholders (Van Dooren *et al.*, 2010, p. 177).

Here, Massey (2011, p. 71) alludes to Raymond Plant's view that traditionally the spirit of the public sector was to trust producer groups "as professionals bound by an ethical code or ethos, and that they are gentlemen who are seeking to do the public good". Under these conditions the real issue is not a technical one about commercialized modernization but a democratic issue about public control of our economic and social futures. Given the increasingly "hollowed out" direction of UK that the UK has taken since Thatcher such a transformation will demand more than a leap of faith, one tantamount to a new phase of substantive bricolage intervention willing to look backwards as well as forwards to cover the ensuing vacuum. In fact, according to the arguments presented in this paper such a shift may demand the next bout of higher order substantive bricolage re-invention:

> In many organizations, documenting an arrangement's functioning (through users' manuals) and structure (for maintenance reasons) is seen as the principal way to ensure the sustainability of its exploitation beyond the point when the initial bricoleurs disengage. From a knowledge perspective, formalization is based upon reification and postulates that knowledge can exist as a delimited entity that can be stated formally. Thus the arrangement created through bricolage collapses into standardized industrial production means, losing the particularity that characterized its realization process. We hypothesize that the utilization and the maintenance of a bricolage outcome arrangement will always, at some point, demand interventions based on the bricolage mode, and that whenever bricolage is involved, an approach towards organizational knowledge as emerging from a network of social relations, experiences, and personalized memory will remain essential (Duymedjian and Ruling, 2010, p. 147).

References

Ascher, K (1987). *The Politics of Privatisation: Contracting out Public Services.* Macmillan: London.

Audit Commission, Care Quality Commission, HM Inspectorate of Constabulary, HM Inspectorate of Prisons, HM Inspectorate of Probation and OFSTED

(2009). *Comprehensive Area Assessment Framework Document*. London: Audit Commission.

Bellamy, R and J Greenaway (1995). The new right conception of citizenship and the citizen's charter. *Government and Opposition*, 30(4), 469–491.

Bevan, RG and C Hood (2006). What's measured is what matters: Targets and gaming in healthcare in the English public health care system. *Public Administration*, 84(3), 517–538.

Bird, S, D Cox, V Farewell, H Goldstein, T Holt and P Smith (2005). Performance indicators: Good, bad, and ugly. *Journal of the Royal Statistical Society A*, 168(1), 1–27.

Bogdanor, V (2010). *On Forms of Accountability*. London: Public Services Trust.

Burns, JP and Z Zhou (2010). Performance management in the government of the People's Republic of China: Accountability and control in the implementation of public policy. *OECD Journal on Budgeting*, 2, 1–28.

Cabinet Office (2010). *Full Policy Programme Statement*. Available at http://www.cabinetoffice.gov.uk/media/407789/building-big-society.pdf

Chan, H and J Gao (2008). Performance management in China. *Chinese Law and Government*, 41(2–3), 1–126.

Cheung, ABL (2005). What's in a pamphlet? Short falls and paradoxical flaws in Hong Kong's performance pledges. *Public Management Review*, 7(3), 341–366.

Conservative Party (2009). *Control Shift: Returning Power to Local Communities*. London: Conservative Party.

Cutler, T (2007). A necessary complexity: History and public management re-form. Available at http://www.historyandpolicy.org/papers/policy-paper-67.html.

Cutler, T and B Waine (1997). *Managing the Welfare State*. Berg: Oxford.

Duymedjian, R and CC Ruling (2010). Towards a foundation of bricolage in organization and management theory. *Organization Studies*, 31, 133–151.

Engelen, E, I Erturk, J Froud, A Leaver and K Williams (2010). Reconceptualizing financial innovation: Frame, conjuncture and bricolage. *Economy and Society*, 39(1), 33–63.

Engelen, E, I Erturk, J Froud, S Johal, A Leaver, M Moran, and K Williams (2011). *Misrule of Experts: The Financial Crisis as Elite Debacle*. Open University: Milton Keynes.

Faure, AM (1994). Some methodological problems in comparative politics. *Journal of Theoretical Politics*, 6(3), 307–322.

Frissen, V and M Slot (2009). The return of the bricoleur: Redefining media business: The good, the bad and the challenging. In *Conference Proceedings*, B Sapio, L Haddon, E Mante-Meijer, L Forunati, T Turk and E Loos (eds.), Koper: ABS Center.

Gao, J (2009). Governing by goals and numbers: A case study in the use of performance measurement to build state capacity in China. *Public Administration and Development*, 29, 21–31.

Gao, J (2010). Hitting the target but missing the point: The rise of non-mission-based targets in performance measurement of Chinese local governments. *Administration and Society*, 42(1), 56–76.

Goodhart, CAE (1975). Monetary relationships: A view from threadneedle street. Papers in Monetary Economics, Reserve Bank of Australia.

Greener, I (2009). *Public Management: A Critical Text*. Palgrave: Basingstoke.

Higgins, P and JM Campanera (2011). (Sustainable) quality of life in English city locations. *Cities*, 28(4), 290–299.

Hildyard, N (2008). *A (Crumbling) Wall of Money: Financial Bricolage, Derivatives and Power*. The Cornerhouse: Sturminster Newton.

Hood, C (2006). Gaming in targetworld: The targets approach to managing British public services. *Public Administration Review*, 66(4), 515–520.

Hood, C, O James and C Scott (2000). Regulation of government: Has it increased, is it increasing, should it be diminished? *Public Administration*, 78(2), 283–304.

Johnson, J and G Callender (1999). Globalizing economic and managerial reforms in public sectors; Towards a universal theory of governance, strategic sovereignty, vulnerability, de-skilling, relearning? In A Kouzmin and A Hayne (Eds.), *Essays in Economic Globalization, Transnational Policies and Vulnerability*, pp. 41–73. Amsterdam: IOS Press.

Laventure, D (2012). Bricolage. *International Collaborative Dictionary of Communications*. Available at http://mediaresearchhub.ssrc.org/icdc-content-folder/bricolage/

Lévi-Strauss (1966). *The Savage Mind*. Chicago: University of Chicago Press.

Legislative Council Panel on Public Service (2009). Review of performance pledges. LC Paper No. CB(1)1959/08-09(01)

Lo, JMK (1993). Reflections on responsive public administration in Hong Kong: The citizen's charter, performance pledges and beyond. *Asian Journal of Public Administration*, 15(2), 201–224.

Massey, A (2011). Nonsense on stilts: United Kingdom perspectives on the global financial crisis and governance. *Public Organization Review*, 11, 61–75.

McIntosh, I and J Broderick (1996). Neither one thing nor the other: Compulsory competitive tendering and southborough cleaning services. *Work Employment and Society*, 10(9), 359–78.

Parry, K and C Sear (2010). *Audit Commission Abolition*. London: House of Commons Library.

Pfeffer, N and A Coote (1991). *Is Quality Good for You?* London: IPPR.

Pollitt, C (1986). Beyond the managerial model: The case for broadening performance assessment on government and the public services. *Financial Accounting and Management*, 2(3), 155–169.

Propper, C and D Wilson (2003). The use and usefulness of performance measures in the public sector. *Oxford Review of Ecomic Policy*, 19(2), 250–267.

Rose, R (2005). *Learning From Comparative Public Policy: A Guide to Lesson Drawing*. London: Routledge.

Sanderson, I (1996). Evaluation, learning and the effectiveness of public services. *International Journal of Public Sector Management*, 9(56), 90–108.

Stoker, G (2009). The microfoundations of governance: Why psychology rather than economics could be the key to better intergovernmental relations. Conference Paper, University of the West Indies, Mona, January 8–9.

Taylor, J (2006). Statutory bodies and performance reporting: Hong Kong and Singapore experience. *Public Organization Review*, 6, 334–357.

Tsang, S (2007). *Governing Hong Kong*. Hong Kong: Hong Kong University Press.

Van Dooren, W, G Bouckaert and J Halligan (2010). *Performance Management in the Public Sector*. London: Routledge.

Van Thiel, S and F Leeuw (2002). The performance paradox in the public sector. *Public Performance and Management Review*, 25(3), 267–281.

Wang, T (2008). Notice on strengthening and improving the evaluation of practical work accomplishment of the leadership corps of party committees and government at the county (municipal) level. *Chinese Law and Government*, 41(2–3), 10–22.

Whitfield, D (2001). *Public Services or Corporate Welfare*. London: Pluto Press.

Wong, TK-Y and P-S Wang (2009). Lingering environmental pessimism and the role of government in Hong Kong. *Public Administration and Development*, 29, 411–451.

Yang, C-L and S Modell (2011). Power and performance: Institutional embeddedness and performance management in a Chinese local government organization. Available at http://www.hec.edu/var/fre/storage/original/application/2639eaa6ddafdb56f7cd49611ebecd88.pdf.

Yin, RK (1994). *Case Study Research: Design and Methods*. London: Sage Publication.

Chapter 5

Social Accountability for Public Service in Higher Education: A Text Analysis of Chinese Research Universities' Undergraduate Teaching-Learning Quality Annual Reports

Tian Linghui and Xiong Qingnian*

5.1. Introduction

The requirement of submitting *Quality of Undergraduate Teaching-Learning Annual Report for Project 985 Universities* was announced on 11 July 2011 by Chinese Ministry of Education. With the aim of instilling the spirit of long-term development and education reform policy, to establish the annual reporting system according to *National Guidelines for Medium and Long-Term Education Reform and Development (2010–2020)*, to enhance the status of education center and to improve the quality of teaching. Those universities identified under Project 985 will take the lead of releasing annual reports to the public. At the same time, the guidelines also stated the requirements on writing, submission timeline and format: (a) All universities should compile the report based on their individual situation. There is no constraint on the submission format and length. (b) All reports should be submitted to the Department of Higher Education during the summer holiday. The Ministry of Education will publish the report on its website, while the relevant universities shall publicize their submissions simultaneously (Department of Higher Education, 2011). By the end of September 2011, all 39 universities had submitted the reports and published the content on their websites.

---
*Assistant Professor, Institute of Higher Education, Fudan University; Professor, Director, Institute of Higher Education, Fudan University

Public university shoulders national responsibility for innovating knowledge, developing human resources and enhancing social equity. However, prior to the announcement of report submission, the accountability to the quality had been in existence only in the form of internal accountability and government's administrative accountability. The 2010 Annual Report for undergraduate teaching and learning quality released marked the beginning of social accountability for public higher education sector in China.

The aim of initiating Project 985 was to strengthen Chinese higher education system by founding world-class universities. Between 1999 and 2008, the central government had injected 23.9 billion RMB into the project. The funding package invested by the local government had also been increased by 7 folds. The figures as of 2008 indicated that the total number of Project 985 universities, which represented only 2% of total number of universities for the whole nation, had more than 64% of National Talent Development Base, and harnessed 51% of total number of Distinguished Teacher at national level. More than half of the doctoral degree was awarded by these universities. The Project 985 universities also undertook 40% of Project 973 and nearly 50% of research funding granted by National Natural Science Foundation of China. More than 50% of the recipients of Outstanding Young Scientist Award were from Project 985 universities. The number of Yangtze River Scholar Chair professors and visiting professors engaged also occupied more than 80% nationwide. More than 85% and 60% of academicians of Chinese Academy of Sciences and Chinese Academy of Engineering were from these 39 public research universities (Project 985 Report Team, 2010, pp. 79–80). The Project 985 universities, being heavily invested by the central and local government, should naturally bear higher public responsibility.

This chapter aims to view from the perspective of social accountability and provide analysis from all the 39 reports submitted by the Project 985 universities, to gain a better insight to the missions and behaviors of Chinese top universities when examined under systematic social accountability.

5.2. Analysis

The reports from all the 39 universities had been submitted before the guideline for scope, content and format were announced. In this regard, it becomes more apparent for the reports to reflect clearly how these first class universities understand their missions on teaching and learning, and to what extent they are accountable when facing the first social accountability.

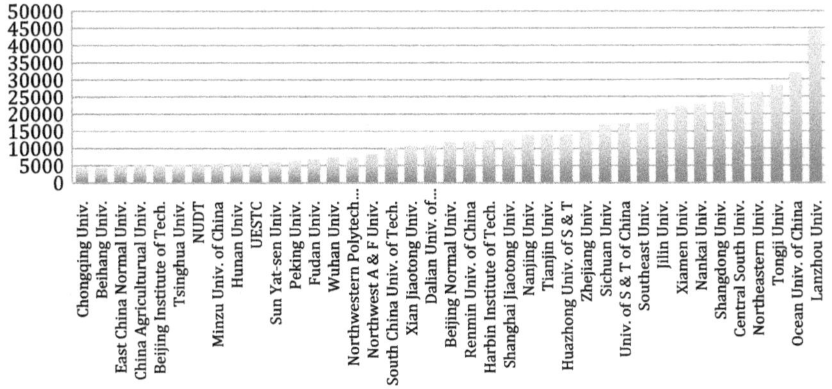

Figure 5.1. The Length of 2011 Annual Reports on Undergraduate Teaching-Learning Quality.

The word "accountability" implies the minimum requirement, whether it is viewed from the perspective of administrative level, consumer level, social level, or from a third party such as the independent and professional agency. It requires somebody or something to have the "ability" and "possibility" to be "accounted for" or "counted up." With this understanding, the information of accountability should at least akin to account book and maintain a principle of "minimum exposure" (World Bank, 2009, p. 7). With these considerations, our analysis will be carried out according to the presentation format, content and degree of exposure.

The length of reports from the 39 Project 985 universities varies from 4,384 to 44,481 words. In Figure 1, where the longest report is ten times longer than the shortest one. Although it may be unfair to judge the quality of a report by its thickness, however, it is apparent that a too short passage may not convey adequate information and elaboration.

Statistically, the reports for quality of undergraduate teaching and learning cover the goal of undergraduate education, the budget, student population, the size of teaching workforce, and teaching facilities, etc. Other factors include the quality assurance system for teaching, teaching reform initiatives, Innovative Student Cultivation Program, internationalization of undergraduate education, moral education, social engagement, campus culture, the implementation and achievement of Undergraduate Teaching Quality and Teaching Reform Project (UTQTRP),[1] awards and

---

[1]Undergraduate Teaching Quality and Teaching Reform Project (UTQTRP) was launched by the Ministry of Education and Ministry of Finance. The project aims

commendation, employment of graduates, etc. The future direction of reform and initiatives are also being considered.

From the 39 reports, it can be seen that the top five programs received the highest attention are, namely, UTQTRP, Innovative Students Program, goal of undergraduate education, Innovative Student Cultivation Program, Student's Participation in national and international competition. All the 39 universities have presented the achievement of UTQTRP, such as the number of National Excellent Course, special study program, and distinguished teaching staff, etc. The results of student's participation in competition event were presented in the form of number and level of awards received. Most of the universities have also formed a special column to register such achievements. Whether the awards were given to the teachers or students, they were only the minority in the campus. The Innovative Student Cultivation Program was also another item being discussed. The quality shown in the program could only reflect the small group of elite students who were heavily subsidized by the government. It did not cover the main cohort of students who formed the majority and also did not take care of the welfare of students and general public. 30 reports clearly elaborated their goals of undergraduate education, which implies that these first class universities have a common understanding that identifying goal of undergraduate education has a positive impact on the remaining population toward recognition and action. However, when we conducted analysis into the individual goals, we discovered that 18 of them adopted a system with high flexibility and solid foundation. Such a highly homogeneous goal is the result of reflection commonly found among the universities that have realized the disadvantage of elite-targeted training model. On the other hand, it has also reflected the area for improvement in multi-disciplinary training and innovative exploration in the area of university education system.

---

to improve the undergraduate teaching, through mobilization of resources from the government, schools and various sectors in the society. The basic task is to encourage all to work toward improving the quality of undergraduate teaching by looking at it positively. UTQTRP emphasizes that the quality of teaching and learning is central to a university's mission. The approach is to categorize and highlight the field of specialization. In UTQTRP, 3000 types of National Excellent Course will be identified. Over 500 National Experimental Teaching Center is under construction. Initiating Undergraduates Innovative Experimental Program to support 15,000 innovative experiments conducted by outstanding students. 100 winners for distinguished teaching staff will be identified annually. The program also encourages and funds students to participate in national and international competitions, and to provide assistance to the universities at the Western region.

Table 5.1. Keywords Used in the Report for Quality of Undergraduate Teaching-Learning and the Frequency of Distribution.

	Theme	Frequency	Percentage
Concept	Goal of Undergraduate Education	30	76.92%
Input Factors	Budget	17	43.59%
	Student Population	19	48.72%
	Size of Teaching Workforce	19	48.72%
	Teaching Facilities	20	51.28%
	Scholarship	2	5.13%
Process Factors	Admission & Enrollment	12	30.77%
	Quality Assurance System	22	56.41%
	Training Policy for teachers	17	43.59%
	Teaching Reform Initiatives	23	58.97%
	Quality Survey	22	56.41%
	Involvement in Scientific Research	25	64.10%
	Moral and Physical Education	10	25.64%
	Campus Culture	3	7.69%
	Internationalization of Undergraduate Education	21	53.85%
	Innovative Student Cultivation Program	31	79.49%
Output Factors	Employment	24	61.54%
	Achievement of UTQTRP	39	100%
	Awards	30	76.92%
Quality Improvement	Problem and Improvement Measures	11	28.21%

Other areas of concern exceeded 50% are the employment rate, initiatives in teaching reform, quality assurance system for teaching, student population, quality survey, internalization of undergraduate education, facilities such as classrooms, library, internet access, etc.

Those items with lowest degree of visibility are the scholarships program, campus culture, moral and physical education, existing problem and the improvement measures, and admission and enrollment. The frequencies were found to be 5.1%, 7.69%, 25.64%, 28.21% and 30.88% respectively. The scholarships program is being used as a mechanism to assist those outstanding students from poor families, it is meant to ensure that the students could study in peace. However, this item was given the lowest priority. Only 2 universities have reported such an indicator. Few words were mentioned on the moral and physical education for students that reflects the high focus of universities on knowledge and scientific research but neglecting the moral and physical aspects of education. That could have attributed to compartmentalized function in the organizational structure of

the universities. The universities have also proposed various improvement measures and initiatives; 11 universities highlighted their problems and future implementation measures, 5 universities indicated with different degrees of details, 3 of them discussed about the problems faced and the last 3 analyzed the problems and proposed future reform measures. The status of admission and enrollment was expressed in terms of the minimum score above the municipal or city average from which the students will be admitted. On this aspect, only one university provided the distribution pattern of source of student. Compared with a similar report from the University of California in the same year, the figures in that report cover the ratio of application, admission and matriculation since 1995, the GPA value from 2000 till mid-term of this year, SAT score, and the distribution pattern of student since year 2000 (categorized as international, local and other states). The statistics also cover the proportion of first undergraduate in individual family as compared with those from public research universities such as Harvard University and Stanford University (University of California, 2011). University of California uses comparable statistics, which explains the importance of multi-dimensional transparency for a first class university on the admission performance and social accountability.

Those below 50% mark cover the funding, student population, size of teaching workforce and training policy for teaching staff. The source of funding, amount and budgeting status, student and teacher population are the basic information and should be covered for minimum visibility. However, more than half of the universities did not mention or even provide any explanation. As the funding is part of the security and quality assurance system, only 43.59% of the universities provided scattered information in these aspects. There are 10 universities reported selectively the investment in the facilities for teaching and learning, the implementation of UTQTRP, teaching operating and increasing research opportunity. Two universities reported the growth of fund investment without citing any evidence. Two universities reported the total investment and partial renovation for facilities. Only 7.69% of the universities reported the funding and distribution of specific projects. Less than half of the reports covered the student population and size of teaching workforce; only total population of students was mentioned, but there was no analysis about the composition of student population, for example, proportion of students from cities compared with those from villages, their socio economic status, student-teacher ratio, etc. Only 2 reports mentioned about the allocation of facilities. The size and quality of teaching force is one of the important security measures for human resources in education system. 19 reports mentioned

about the number of professional teachers and the distribution hierarchy. One special observation is that the number of universities reporting the number of academicians, Yangtze River Scholars, Distinguished Teachers and Distinguished Youth Scholar Award winners has far exceeded the number of universities reporting the total number of teaching staff. When more focus was being placed on assessment than cultivation of teaching workforce, it explains why only 43.59% of universities emphasized the area of human resources development.

According to the Ministry of Education, all universities must publish Undergraduate Teaching-Learning Quality 2011 Annual Reports via internet simultaneously. However, until February 2011, 5 of them have not published their reports yet. As shown in Figure 2, 12 of the universities published their reports on their websites, 18 of them published on the Office of Teaching and Learning Affairs column, the other 4 published on the column for Party Administration Office, School Public Affairs column, Public Service and History column respectively. Among 34 universities that made the publicity, 16 of them installed a hit counter (Figure 3). 3 of them

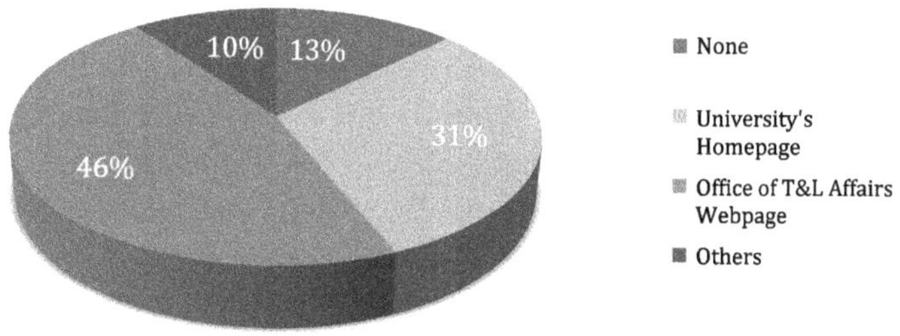

Figure 5.2.   Publication of 2010 Annual Report.

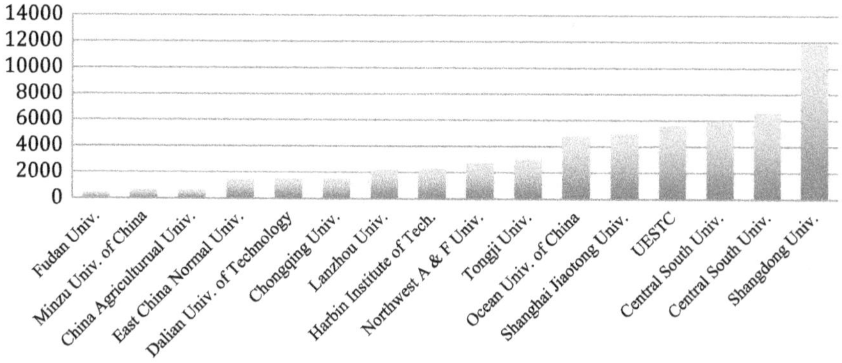

Figure 5.3.   The Web Traffic Analysis of 16 Project 985 Universities' Annual Reports.

received less than 1,000 hits, 4 of them received more than 5,000 hits and the Shandong University's webpage received more than 10,000 hits.

5.3. Conclusion

The public research universities in China have been designated by the government to provide premium higher education. The definition, production and evaluation of educational quality have over a long time been involved in the stakeholders only from the universities and the government. The publicity of report under Project 985 pilot universities is one of the government's innovative efforts to establish a social accountability system, to elevate the effectiveness of administrative accountability, and to improve the quality and responsiveness of public service in providing a higher education. According to the World Bank (2004, p. 1), "Social Accountability" is being defined as a channel to enhance accountability through the public's supervision. Public's participation can be made directly or indirectly. Social accountability has been reckoned as the government's new approach to good governance. This approach is based on significant conceptual, empirical, and policy-related work on why top-down development approaches alone are insufficient and why combined government and citizen effort is more effective (World Bank, 2009, p. 124). However, an effective social accountability system requires both good accountability behavior and accountability tools and they should be improved gradually as well. By analyzing the first-year Report on Undergraduate Teaching-Learning Quality, it is able to help to improve the feasibility, effectiveness and sustainability of social accountability for public service in higher education.

5.3.1. *University, government and the public: Who is the quality for? Who to report to?*

(1) *Government-oriented quality*

From the 39 reports submitted, it was found that the following programs had been ranked in the first three positions and being heavily subsidized by the government: The achievement of UTQTRP, such as National Excellent Course, Distinguished Teacher Award, and National Experimental Teaching Center, Innovative Student Cultivation Program, and students' participation in local and international competition events. However, there are lesser emphases on the scholarship, admission and enrollment, and the employment of graduates, which are of the public concern. Furthermore, the

above information was a result of government's reform effort. There was no longitudinal data to help us track the trend in the recent years. It appears that all the publicized information was made to response to the government's performance accountability instead of citizens' social accountability.

(2) *Who was being ignored?*

In the reports, students as the clients were found marginalized. Firstly, there is a lack of concern over comprehensive development for the general cohort of students. In the topic of comprehensive student development, almost 80% of Project 985 universities reported the Innovative Student Cultivation Program, but there are less than 50% of them mentioned about the total number of students, and no mention about any concern over those students who need more attention. All the universities reported the National Excellent Course programme, but the percentage of course run was only 28.2%. When compared with the absolute number for teaching facilities, academicians and Distinguished Teacher Award winners, National Excellent Course, it could be seen that the service provided on per-student usage is generally low. 94.87% of the universities chose to report absolute figures selectively. On the effect to promote comprehensive development for students, the statistics have shown that 64.1% of the universities announced the performance of student's participation in national and international competition events. One of the universities requires all undergraduate students to engage into research activities. Students are the service clients for qualified higher education. First class university should aim to provide comprehensive education to students, but not substitute it with achievements in research development.

Secondly, the public nature of education service was being neglected. To be fair to all students, the Project 985 universities, which have been designated and subsidized by public funding, should undertake higher responsibility of providing excellent education services, in addition to implementing Innovative Student Cultivation Program. However, none of the universities have indicated clearly in their analyses the student resource and distribution between countries and cities, and the allocation of scholarships and bursaries.

5.3.2. *Transparency*

The transparency and openness of information is a prerequisite for accountability. In the first issue of Project 985 report, some problems were

detected, such as the basic data is of lower standard and lack of comparable longitudinal data. A lower standard of reported basic data refers to low transparency of implementation status of budget funding and execution, student population, size of teaching workforce, admission status and career status of graduates. There is a wide disparity in content among the reports provided, which makes it difficult for the public to raise questions on the quality and cost-effectiveness, and even more difficult to make comparison. Comparable longitudinal data refers to that basic information generated for the public and government, for the purpose of comparing the stability and development status of training quality from the university concerned. 6 of them were found having shown such data at different levels and indicators. 3 of them reported the changes of scores for admission, career status of graduates and fund expenditure. Other 3 universities reported comparison with the previous 3 or 5 years data.

5.3.3. *Depth of involvement and inclusiveness of participation*

Annual Report on Undergraduate Teaching-Learning Quality was arranged to be announced in sufficient publicity to enable the public's scrutiny and to widen the scope to general public. Such an arrangement should promote stakeholders' dialogue for higher educational quality. The Inclusiveness of Participation was found mainly from internal than external personnel. Nearly 87% of the universities have chosen to publicize the reports simultaneously on the internet, and 35%, 53% and 12% of them published their reports on the university homepages, Teaching and Learning Affairs Office's webpage and Party Administrative Office respectively. The discrepancy in the approach on publishing the information had, to a certain extent, reflected the degree of control. Other than those published on the homepage, those published on other columns reflect the intention to control the involvement toward the internal staff level. For those 5 universities that chose not to publish at the prescribed deadline, their openness toward public participation remains questionable.

Due to the fact that most of the reports generated were centered around the government's requirements but not on students, low transparency of information, coupled with the use of professional terminology and abstract concept, has limited public participation. Use of special terms such as six systems and ten key projects for undergraduate education, success rate of first-stage course selection, which could at the most be understood by

internal staff who are directly involved in the projects. As a comparison, in the University of California's report, each comparison table is supplement with simple key words and explanation, such as SAT, professional scores and credit scores, etc.

5.4. Discussion

Under the direction of Ministry of Education, publication of *Undergraduate Teaching-Learning Quality Annual Report* has become an initiation of social accountability system for public higher education services. With the establishment of such a system, it implies that it is significant to provide a fair and high-quality undergraduate education. From a macro-perspective, the function of social accountability provides an approach for citizens to voice out, so as to supervise the quality improvement process of public services. A good social system lays a good foundation for effective social accountability. We are still at the primary stage of constructing a social accountability system for public services in higher education. More efforts are still needed, especially from the government, for it to be refined and become a mature system.

The government serves as the promoter and designer for social accountability system. It does not only need to improve the accountability system, but also need to look into cultivating the citizens' awareness and participation capability. A closed-loop social accountability consists of identifying the entry point, mobilizing support, obtaining information, analyzing information, disseminating information, negotiating change (World Bank, 2009, p. 124). It could be observed from the announcement issued by Ministry of Education: there was a lack of explanation and understanding for a new system, there was no proper communication and publicity, no elaboration of the intent and the rationale of publishing the quality report. The reports were generated under a two-month notice without full understanding of the intent. So it is inevitable to reveal all those disparity among the reports submitted by the universities. The publication of public services information is not an end goal by itself, but it is to enhance the quality of public services through involvement of stakeholders. In order to have a full-fledged social accountability system, as a minimum requirement, the government must provide guidelines, which spell out the requirements to cover the intent of innovation, define the role and responsibility of public service supplier and accountable body, and any approach used to promote interaction between the main bodies. The institution of higher education

must deviate away from the traditional concept of using professionalism as the fortress, and to clearly understand the role as a public service provider and its relevant responsibility, to be more open and transparent in providing internal quality information, and to be more responsive in answering public queries. All reform and innovation must be viewed to contribute to promote fairness and quality enhancement. Public participation has never been less active in China. It should therefore be used as a good cultural basis to begin instilling necessary training and practice. With adequate public training and practice in place, we will have a good system of social accountability with effective public participation. The impact of such an effective system will certainly contribute to quality improvement to a perfect social accountability system.

References

Department of Higher Education (2011). *Notice on The Project 985 University Releasing Undergraduate Teaching-Learning Quality 2010 Annual Report.* Beijing: Ministry of Education.

Project 985 Report Team (2010). *Project 985 Ten-Year Report.* Beijing: Higher Education Press, 79–80.

The Academic Planning, Programs and Coordination Department of the Academic Affairs Division (2011). *University of California Annual Accountability Report 2011.* LA: UC.

World Bank (2004). *Social Accountability: An Introduction to the Concept and Emerging Practice.* Washington, DC.

World Bank (2009). *Social Accountability in the Public Sector: A Conceptual Discussion and Learning Module.* Beijing: China Renmin University Press.

Chapter 6

Integrated Development of Metropolitan Governance and Public Service: A Case Study of the Pearl River Delta Region[†]

Lin Ye[*]

6.1. Introduction: Urbanization in China — A Call for Change

Urbanization in China took a significant turn in 2011 when the country's urban population exceeded its rural population for the first time in the history. With its unprecedented urbanization rate of the last three decades, China is marching through the stage of fast urbanization and entering a stable urbanization process. If this trend of urbanization continues, China will have an urbanization rate of over 70% in 2050 and enter the so-called "post-urbanization era." Urbanization brought profound economic, social, and cultural impacts to the country and its population. Many have argued that China's urbanization is a joint force of marketization, privatization, and industrialization (Heikkila, 2007; Zhang, 2008). Urbanization in China is characterized by the fast land development from rural to urban uses (Lin, 2007). The country's industrialization and its populations' integration into urban areas are lagging behind. This poses serious question on how urbanization is benefiting the populations and whether such benefits are distributed equitably.

[†]This research is supported by Sun Yat-sen University's 985 Project, "Hundred Talent Program" research start-up grant, the 2010 Humanities and Social Science Young Scholar Tongshan Program Fund, and China Center for Public Administration Research's Excellent Research Fund and Key Project Fund.
[*]Associate Professor, China Center for Public Administration Research, Institute of Urban Governance and Urban Development, School of Government, Sun Yat-sen University, ylljc@hotmail.com.

According to the recent China Urbanization Report published by the China Development Foundation, urbanization has brought multiple social conflicts and problems to the country. One of the issues is that wealth accumulation of Chinese cities far exceeds the improvement of public service delivery and residents' quality of life. According to the national statistics, the average Chinese citizen spends over 60% of their income on basic needs, such as food, clothing, and housing, leaving not much for improving their quality of life (China Development Foundation, 2011). This dilemma, together with income gaps, social stratification, and housing price spikes, leads to wide-spread social unrest in Chinese cities. These conditions put China's city management in the hot seat and require aggressive reform. One of the strategies is to adjust local government's functions from promoting economic development to serving pubic need. According to Pierre (1998) city governments ought to have two basic functions of producing and providing public services, and maintaining political institutions and democratic systems at the local level. As a provider and (or) producer of public services, a significant issue is whether the services delivered meet the needs of local residents. One of the impacts urbanization brought to Chinese cities has been the dominant place-making and entrepreneurial mentality of urban development and management. Lin (2007) argues that since the mid-1990s, China's urban spaces have been reproduced through a city-based and land-centered process of urbanization in which large cities managed to reassert their leading positions in an increasingly competitive, globalizing and urbanizing economy. Local government has become the key stakeholder in urban development and a leader of the pro-growth coalition since decentralization in 1990. Both financial autonomy and land-use authority have devolved to local government. Exhibiting achievements to the central government and promoting economic development to serve interest groups and the constituency have become the primary driving forces for China's urban development (Zhang, 2002). Under this growth-driven paradigm, the goal of urbanization in China is to pursue economic growth and maximize returns on capital investment. Cities are considered capital for profit making for interest groups, largely the government, businesses, and developers. The delivery of public services was not always at the top of the urban development agenda. Therefore urbanization brought a wide range of problems to Chinese cities. Problems persist in many policy areas including household registration, social welfare, public infrastructure, and environmental protection. Such conditions call for a fundamental change to China's urban development and management focus. Public service delivery needs to become the priority of Chinese cities in order to fulfill the true

benefits of urbanization equitably and improve the quality of life for urban residents. Cities' functions are to be changed from primarily promoting economic growth to delivering desirable public services. This will call for a new mode of urban management to facilitate the future urbanization of the country.

6.2. Metropolitan Development and Public Service Delivery

One important feature of urbanization in the global economy is the development of metropolitan regions. The openness and competitiveness brought by globalization asserted the importance of urban agglomeration in many different areas of the world. The role of cities and metropolitan regions has become more important and contributes significantly to economic growth in both developed and developing countries. Metropolitan regions are the sites of dense masses of interrelated economic activities that tend to have high levels of productivity because of their jointly-generated agglomeration economies and innovative potential (Scott and Storper, 2003). In many advanced countries, major metropolitan areas are key sites of the national economy. For example, over 40% of US employment is concentrated in 15% of the country's land area (Porter, 2001). Mega city-regions are extremely important in their national economies. In 1990, Barcelona held 7% of its nation's Gross Domestic Product (GDP), Seoul held 23%, Sydney held 19%, and New York held 2.5% (Savich, 1996). In developing countries, such as Brazil, China, India, and South Korea, the effects of agglomeration on productivity are also strongly apparent, and economic growth typically proceeds at an especially rapid rate in the large metropolitan regions. These metropolitan regions are the most important foci of national growth and the places where export-oriented industrialization is most likely to occur (Scott and Storper, 2003).

In China, the national government developed aggressive policies to promote regional economic development after its adoption of reform and open-door policies. The coastal (eastern) areas enjoyed favorable national policies to explore new forms of economic and social development. Historically, these areas were more open to the outside world because of their easy access to water transportation. By adopting more aggressive and flexible economic policies and opening up to foreign investment and global capital, these areas were the first regions to develop modern industrial and informational economies in China. The three most developed regions, the Jing-Jin-Ji, the Yangtze River Delta, and the Pearl River Delta metropolitan region, are all located in the coastal (eastern) region (Ye, 2009).

As China is entering a new stage of urbanization it maintains a strong impetus for urban cluster and metropolitan region development. The integrated development between cities is an important task at this stage of urbanization. China's 12th Five-Year Plan specified the "Two Horizontal and Three Vertical Axis" (*Liang Heng San Zong*) for urban cluster development. The two horizontal (east-west) axes are planned along the Luqiao corridor and Yangtze River. The three vertical (north-south) axes are mapped by the coastal highway, the highway between Beijing and Guangzhou, and the highway between Baotou and Kunming. Urban cluster development has become one of the most important trends of China's urbanization. China has developed several giant urban clusters, including the Beijing-Tianjin, the Yangtze River Delta, and the Pearl River Delta urban clusters. Besides these three leading urban clusters, China is also developing more than 10 other mega urban regions to organize economic and social development.

An urban cluster can consist of one or more metropolitan areas. A metropolitan area is an agglomeration of population, infrastructure, and economic activities. Diverse populations living in a metropolitan area demand a wide range of public services. Lack of desirable public services has been identified as one of the major challenges urbanization has brought to Chinese cities. As the urban economy further develops, populations tend to move more frequently within metropolitan regions. For example, the Jing-Jin-Jin metropolitan region in China had over 80% of its residents who did not have local resident registrations and were considered "floating" population (Ye *et al.*, 2008). More diverse populations will demand different types and levels of public services. For example, low-income families are in need of more affordable public services while medium- and high-income households demand more amenable living environment. As people move more freely within a metropolitan area, "voting with their feet" may happen when people choose to live and work in neighboring small cities to avoid undesirable conditions such as high housing price, congested traffic, and worsening air quality in the big city. Thus it has become more difficult but important to develop a metropolitan-wide public service network.

6.3. A Case Study of Public Transportation Development in the Pearl River Delta

The Pearl River Delta region is the one of the largest and most developed regions in China. Located in the southeast of China, the PRD

region includes nine major cities in the Guangdong Province: Guangzhou, Shenzhen, Foshan, Jiangmen, Huizhou, Zhaoqin, Zhuhai, Dongguan, and Zhongshan. In 2009, this region had a total population of 48 million and a GDP of almost 30 trillion RMB. The Pearl River Delta region underwent a spatial transformation from a uni-centric region to a multi-layer urban agglomeration system during the last two decades. In 1990, the Pearl River Delta region only had one city with over one million people and the other with over half a million. Most cities in the region were medium-size or small-size cities at that time (Lin, 2001). Twenty years later, in 2010, there were eight cities with populations over one million and five with over half a million people. The number of medium or small cities remained relatively stable. The population concentration process indicates a spatial transformation under which the peripheral cities in the Pearl River Delta region grew faster in the early stage of regional development while the major cities have gradually taken over demographic and economic dominance in the last decade (Ye, 2011).

There are three major metropolitan areas in the Pearl River Delta: the Guangzhou–Foshan metropolitan area; the Shenzhen–Hong Kong metropolitan area; and the Zhuhai–Macao metropolitan area. This section will focus on the Guangzhou–Foshan metropolitan area to analyze its public service arrangement, using public transportation as an example.

Table 6.1 lists the socio-economic statistics of these two cities. Guangzhou has been the political, economic, and cultural center in the Pearl River Delta region although Shenzhen, the second largest city in this region is quickly developing itself from a small fishing village to the fourth largest city in China and competing with Guangzhou in all areas (Lin, 2007; Ye, 2011). Facing the competition from Shenzhen and Hong Kong, Guangzhou gradually lost its leading position in the Pearl River Delta region in the 1980s (Lin, 2007). Since the late 1990s, the Guangzhou government has

Table 6.1.   Statistics of Guangzhou and Foshan 2010.

City	Total Population	Land Area (Sq. km)	Population Growth 2000–2009 (%)	Gross Domestic Product (billion yuan)	GDP Per Capita (yuan)	GDP Growth 2000–2009 (%)
Guangzhou	10.3 million	7287	3.9	913.8	88718	266.5
Foshan	6.0 million	3848	12.3	482.1	80391	359.1

Source: Guangdong Statistics Yearbook 2010.

taken major steps to rectify its problems in an attempt to regain the city's status as a regional center with a high level of prosperity, efficiency, and civilization. To realize this objective, the government initiated a three-phase urban development strategy in the first decade of the 21st century (Xu and Yeh, 2005). As the host of the 16th Asian Games in 2010, Guangzhou's urban development received international recognition, with the city winning the 2002 Dubai International Award for Best Practices in Improving the Living Environment. Foshan has been historically tied to Guangzhou as a neighboring second-tier community for many years. As Guangzhou is quickly becoming a modern city with over 60% of its economic production from tertiary industries, secondary industries made up almost two-thirds of Foshan's GDP. Guangzhou's GDP almost doubled that of Foshan. Politically Guangzhou is the provincial capital. Foshan is only a prefecture city.

Both cities realized the importance of adopting a region-wide governance and development strategy. Guangzhou and Foshan are the central area for the Lingnan (Southern China) culture, which goes back thousands of years. The two cities were one municipality in ancient China and have a strong historical and cultural bond. In the contemporary era, Guangzhou is positioning itself as an international metropolis while Foshan has promoted a garden city and green development strategy. These two cities offer distinct but complimentary cultural styles for residents.

In 2009, the mayors from both cities organized a joint meeting every six months to discuss metropolitan region issues. This Joint Mayoral Meeting has become the main institution to design and implement metropolitan development in this area. This meeting requires attendance from most city-level agencies that are involved in city-wide service delivery and policy planning, including the mayor's office, development and reform, human resources, transportation, construction, finance, education, health, environmental protection, planning, food and drug, and tourism departments. The Joint Mayor Meeting is held every six months with representatives from each department attending and reporting progress in metropolitan-wide issues. The operational office of this meeting is set up under the powerful Development and Reform Bureau in each city and places full time staff to be in charge of the coordination of metropolitan development projects.

In May 2011, the Joint Mayoral Meeting announced the Guangzhou-Foshan Metropolitan Area Development Plan 2010–2020. This ten-year plan established a three-phase target for metropolitan development. The

first two years are set for a comprehensive development planning stage. Institutional arrangements and government policies are going to be implemented in the following five years. A highly integrated metropolitan region is the overall goal for 2020. This plan outlines eight policy areas that these two cities will work on together: infrastructure building, economic restructuring, technology advancement, environmental protection, social services, government affairs, regional cooperation, and policy innovation.

Following this strategic plan, an annual plan is set up by the Joint Mayoral Meeting to select targeted projects. In 2010, nineteen major projects were completed to promote integrated development in this metropolitan area, including announcing a three-year working plan, building several inter-city highways and extending the inter-city subway, organizing a shopping festival for residents from two cities, cooperative training of government employees from two cities, and the adjustment of the water zone protection plan along the two cities' border (Guangzhou Municipal Development and Reform Commission, 2010).

One of the major policy areas that has been under significant development is the public transportation network. In the latest annual plan of metropolitan development signed by two cities, over 50 programs were established with 6 inter-city transportation projects. Developing this inter-city transportation network will enable the Guangzhou–Foshan metropolis to construct a comprehensive transportation network consisted of regular railroads, high-speed rails, and city rail transit. The goal is to cover over 70% of the total transportation needs by rail transit and establish a one-hour commuting radius between two cities.

Such ambitious planning has started to achieve outcomes. In November 2010, the first subway connecting the two cities opened. This subway construction started in 2007, with a total investment of almost 15 billion yuan. Two cities share the costs with Guangzhou paid for 51% and Foshan provided 49% of the funding. The provincial government subsidized the remaining of the funding. It is the first inter-city subway in China and has a total route length of 32 km. The opening attracted wide public attentions. Within the first month of operation, over 3.3 million passengers rode the subway. A survey indicated that, over 16% of the passengers commuted between these two cities. The subway made a single day trip for work a reality for residents in two cities (Guangzhou Daily, 2010). It is suggested that this subway would be further improved if it can be better connected with bus and bike routes, provide easier access for elderly and disabled, and have more frequent runs (Foshan Daily, 2011). It can be seen that

such metropolitan-wide public service is highly demanded by residents in both cities. The opening of the inter-city subway provides residents an opportunity to travel freely between two cities to enjoy leisure time and diverse cultural activities. The combination of the transportation network and cultural integration helps develop an integrated metropolitan area.

Inter-city highway is another area that has been under aggressive development in Guangzhou and Foshan. In the 2010 annual development plan of the two cities, six major highways are designed to be constructed to provide an easy connection between two cities. The Reform and Development Commission, Construction Bureau, and Transportation Bureau are the three primary agencies that are responsible for the implementation of the annual plan. A detailed design plan, construction schedule, and completion time was set up for each project. Each project was assigned to a specific agency as the responsible party for the project implementation. The Joint Mayoral Meeting serves as the communication and coordination point for necessary cooperation among agencies.

In addition to transportation infrastructure development, the two city governments also established innovative policies for residents to travel more freely between the cities. For example, an integrated computer system was put into operation in 2010 to enable drivers to pay for tolls in two cities. By the end of 2012, most highway and road toll stations in both cities will be integrated into this system. Divers between these two cities will no longer need to use two different toll systems.

6.4. Discussion and Conclusion

From the above discussion, integrated metropolitan development and service delivery has become a top-priority issue in the Guangzhou–Foshan metropolitan area. Multiple agencies are involved to establish a cross-city governance network to promote such development. Public transportation has been one of the policy focuses. However, it is not an accident why public transportation was selected to be the front-running area. In late 2008, Guangdong Province and the NDRC made another regional plan for the PRD region, the Outline of the Plan for the Reform and Development of the Pearl River Delta 2008–2020. This plan is widely considered the master plan for the region in the next 20 years and directs the region's development path. Following the announcement of this strategic plan, five Regional Integration Plans were implemented, covering the policy areas of environmental protection, infrastructure building, urban–rural planning,

economic restructuring, and public service delivery. Under the public service delivery plan, ten categories of services were identified: education, health, cultural, transportation, low-income welfare, housing subsidy, employment assistance, medical insurance, environmental, and professional services. Public transportation is the area that received the most attention and fastest development. There are several reasons for this.

First of all, one of the driving forces for regional integrated development is the gap of service levels among cities. As the regional center, Guangzhou has significantly higher levels of education, health, and other welfare coverage than other cities in the region. Guangzhou is home to most of the prestigious universities, desirable hospitals, and cultural centers of southern China. The "integration" of such services will require that the city of Guangzhou share its precious resources with other cities. To charge for residents from other cities for such services is not easy, which means that many "free rider" problems will emerge. The city of Guangzhou is going to pay for a high proportion the expenses.

However, public transportation presents a different case. The cost of the construction is evenly shared by two city governments. More importantly, transportation systems provide relatively equal access for residents and businesses from both cities. It has been argued that the integration process between Guangzhou and Foshan had a significant impact on the real estate market in Foshan. Many developers in Foshan were not able to compete with "big brands" from Guangzhou and had to give up their development projects in the center of Foshan. Developers from Guangzhou aggressively took control of the high-end real estate market. Convenient inter-city transportation systems also allow more residents from Guangzhou to purchase housing in Foshan while working in Guangzhou. Such trends more than tripled the housing price in Foshan in recent years and put heavier burden on Foshan's residents.

Secondly public transportation constructions are counted as infrastructure investment and drive up economic figures of local production. Such investment is also widely accepted as an incentive for economic growth, which has always been the primary task of local governments in China. Therefore, public transportation development tends to achieve consensus among cities and was more easily to be chosen as the front-runner of metropolitan service policies.

Nevertheless, the case from the Pearl River Delta represents the trend of integrated metropolitan development and public services in China. There are some points worth learning from the case. Citizen participation

is an important factor of metropolitan development in Guangzhou and Foshan. Governance at the metropolitan level addresses the problem of incorporating the participation of a growing number of increasingly diverse interests in the decision-making process. Understanding the informal as well as the formal dimensions of participation is crucial (Sellers and Hoffmann–Martinot, 2008). During the process of developing the metropolitan governance structure in Guangzhou and Foshan, citizen participation has been an important factor. For example, university professors, community leaders, and regular citizens were invited to comment on the transportation, communication, education, and medical services policies in the development of the Guangzhou and Foshan metropolitan region (Foshan City Government, 2010). After the inter-city subway was open, both cities administered passenger questionnaires to collect feedback and comments for improvement (Foshan Daily, 2011; Guangzhou Daily, 2010). An open citizen participation scheme helped identify the most important policy areas and facilitate an effective governance structure.

Another worthwhile tool is the effective coordination and cooperation among multiple agencies cross cities. The establishment of Joint Mayoral Meeting serves as the central plan design and policy implementation hub, which provides a strong government leadership and institutional power for metropolitan development. In a country like China, where government authority is very strong in carrying out new policies, such an arrangement is necessary.

References

Foshan City Government (2010). Public discussion of Guanghzou–Foshan integration. Available at http://www.foshan.gov.cn/foshangov/xxgk/ztjs/guangfo tongcheng/wangyoureyi/201010/t20101025_1917250.html, accessed February 10, 2012.

Foshan Daily (2011). The inter-city subway ridership survey. Available at http://www.citygf.com/gftc/02/201106/t20110602_1678274.html.

Guangzhou Daily (2010). Residents' lifestyle changed with the inter-city subway. Available at http://www.citygf.com/FSNews/FS_002008/201012/t20101203_965770.html.

Guangzhou Municipal Development and Reform Commission (2010). *Guangzhou-Foshan Integration 2010 Main Tasks*. Available at http://www.gzplan.gov.cn/bmln/ghc/gzdt/201006/t20100630_11097.htm.

Heikkila, E (2007). Three questions regarding urbanization in China. *Journal of Planning Education and Research*, 27, 65–81.

Lin, GCS (2001). Metropolitan development in a transitional socialist economy: Spatial restructuring in the Pearl River Delta, China. *Urban Studies*, 38(3), 383–406.

Lin, GCS (2007). Reproducing space of Chinese urbanization: New city-based and land-centered urban transformation. *Urban Studies*, 44(9), 1827–1855.

Porter, ME (2001). Regions and the new economics of competition. In AJ Scott (Ed.), *Global City-Regions: Trends, Theory, Policy*, pp. 139–157. Oxford, UK: Oxford University Press.

Savitch, HV (1996). Cities in a global era: A new paradigm for the next millennium. In M Cohen, B Ruble, J Tulchin and M Garland (Eds.), *Preparing for the Urban Fortune: Global Pressures and Local Forces*, pp. 39–65. Washington, DC: Woodrow Wilson Center Press.

Scott, A and M Storper (2003). Regions, globalization, development. *Regional Studies*, 37(6–7), 579–593.

Sellers, J and V Hoffmann-Martinot (2008). *Metropolitan Governance*. United Cities and Local Governments.

Xu, J and AGO Yeh (2005). City repositioning and competitiveness building in regional development: New development strategies in Guangzhou, China. *International Journal of Urban and Regional Research*, 29(2), 283–308.

Ye, L (2011). *Metropolitan Region and Governance in the Pearl River Delta*. Proceedings of the 7th International Conference on Public Administration, 399–404.

Ye, L (2009). Regional Government and Governance in China and the United States. *Public Administration Review*, December, S116–S121.

Ye, YM, YJ Li and K Ni (2008). Metropolitan population migration and regional integrated development in the Jing-Jin-Ji region. *China Population Science*, 2, 57–64.

Zhang, L (2008). Conceptualizing China's urbanization under reforms. *Habitat International*, 32(4), 452–470.

Zhang, T (2002). Urban development and a socialist pro-growth coalition in Shanghai. *Urban Affairs Review*, 37, 475–499.

Chapter 7

The Role of NGOs in Maintaining Social Stability in China — Based on the Perspective of Public Security Service Delivery

Han Lin*

7.1. Introduction

7.1.1. *Current social stability situation in China*

Chinese society is experiencing a critical period in its reform process — known as the double transitional period — simultaneous social and economic transition. The emotions of the masses are sensitive and small incidents are able to trigger large-scale social conflicts and contradictions. Accordingly, a number of mass incidents have broken out in recent years, which means that the Chinese government's pressure of maintaining social stability has grown drastically. The authoritative *Social Blue Book 2006* shows that the social stability indicator of China has been growing negatively since 1979. According to the book's definition, the social stability indicator is composed of inflation rate, urban unemployment rate, social security coverage, the percentage of poor population, the wealth difference, and income gap between urban and rural area. Between 1979 and 2004, the social stability index reduced by an average of 1.1% per year, and from 1991 to 2004 it decreased by 2.9% per year.

In addition, there has been a lot of empirical evidence indicating that the instability of Chinese society has increased. The most striking example of this is that the number of mass incidents[1] has been raising in recent

---

*Department of Social and Public Administration, City University of Hong Kong.
[1] "Mass incidents" are officially defined as any kind of planned or impromptu gathering that forms because of "internal contradictions," including mass public speeches, physical conflicts, airing of grievances or other forms of group behavior that may disrupt social

years. Between 1993 and 2003 the number of mass incidents increased from 10,000 to 60,000, and the number of participants from 700,000 to over 3,000,000.[2] In 2004, the number of mass incidents rose to 74,000 with a total of 3.7 million citizens taking part and then to 87,000 incidents in 2005.[3] In addition to the mass incidents, lone individuals are increasingly taking part in protest activity. The share of mass incidents includes: peasants appealing for rights (35%); workforce dispute (30%); residential conflicts in cities (15%); social conflicts[4](10%); social disturbance[5] (5%) and organized crime and others (5%).[6]

From the standpoint of Chinese government such unstable and disharmonious factors prevent the national economic development progressing in a harmonious way. Consequently, central and local governments regard "reducing social stability risk" or "maintaining social stability" as an administrative priority. For example, central government has set up an official and permanent institution to carry out the task of maintaining social order and stability. The leading group of maintaining social stability was set up in the 1990s and the office of maintaining social stability is responsible for the group's daily operations. At present, the head of the group is Zhou Yongkang, one of nine numbers of the Politburo Standing Committee monitoring the country's law enforcement, which reports directly to Vice President Xi Jinping tipped to succeed Hu as president on issues concerning the maintenance of social order. Furthermore, social instability has come to be regarded as a nationwide problem, and governments at different levels have also set up their own groups in recent years normally headed by the local party secretaries overseeing law enforcement.

Besides establishing special task forces, China has also allocated special funds for maintaining social stability. At 2010's annual session of the National People's Congress (NPC) in March, the State Council revealed its budget for maintaining social stability for the first time, which amounted

---

stability. In practice, there is no agreement on the definition of a "mass incident." Police generally use a wider definition which enables them to document how effective their enforcement is; government officials tend to use a narrow definition to minimize the apparent scale of the problem.

[2] Ta Kung Pao, 12 July 2005.

[3] Wang (2006).

[4] Social conflict is the struggle for agency or power in society.

[5] Social disturbance refers to a broad of range of non-violent and violent political activity ranging from peaceful demonstrations and strikes to organized warfare or acts of terrorism.

[6] 于建嵘，威权政治面临的挑战---中国的骚乱事件与管治危机。美国加州大学伯克利分校演讲

to 514 billion yuan (US$72 billion) in 2010, up 8.9% compared to 2009. This figure is almost equal to the central government's 518.6 billion yuan budget for defense.[7] On 5 March 2011, the Financial Ministry published the budget for maintaining public security 624.4 billion, which is 21.5% higher than 2010. This exceeded the 601.1 billion yuan budget for defense in 2011.

7.1.2. *The relationship between social stability and public security*

According to the authoritative social blue book, social issues affecting social stability situation include economic stability, leadership stability, political stability, public security stability and so on eight categories. Therefore, social stability is closely related with the local public security situation, and enhance of public security service will be beneficial for maintaining social stability.

On the other hand, the decreasing performance of the social stability indicator and social order indicator indicate the deficiency of public service in some fields concerned by people. In conjunction with progressive economic development, people's incomes have been improved substantially and thus their demands on education, medical treatment, social security which are supposed to be provided by government have also increased. However, the deficiency of relevant public policies and the lag of social reform results in an imbalance between public policies and public demand, which will aggravate the discontent that people have of government. According to a research report conducted by Horizon Company at the end of 2005, Chinese people's sense of social order and public security has been decreasing in the last three years, and rural people's condition is worsening.[8] According to the research, the score of people's sense of public security. which is an important subjective indicator measuring social stability situation, was 3.53 in 2005, while it is 3.61 in 2004 and 3.66 in 2003. The growing discontented emotions are prone to triggering social conflicts and contradictions, which are regarded by Chinese governments as potential risks threating social stability and preventing the construction of harmonious society. Among all kinds of public services, the quality of public security service aiming to secure social protection against risks and

---

[7]Available at http://www.atimes.com/atimes/China/LD28Ad01.html.
[8]Available at http://politics.people.com.cn/GB/1026/4120532.html.

vulnerabilities is the most directly related with social order and social stability situation. According to an academic paper "Social control versus social stability,"[9] social stability can be defined as "the actual observance of governmentally formalized, regulated and enforced laws, rules, and norms for social relations."

Therefore, improving the "quality" of public security service is an effective way of maintaining social stability. The logic of this position is that the less socially stable the situation, the more public security service is required, whereas better quality public security leads to enhanced socially stability.

7.2. Literature Review

7.2.1. *Theory of public security*

Public security is the function of government that ensures the protection of citizens, organizations and institutions against threats to their well-being and to the prosperity of their communities.[10] Government, public organizations and businesses closely collaborate to guarantee public security and maintain a stable environment for economic prosperity.

Although public security significantly contributes to the attractiveness of an area, the productivity of its people, and hence the overall success of an economy, the sector frequently suffers from low budgets, limited resources and inadequate information systems. Large events, pandemics, serious accidents, environmental disasters and terrorism attacks pose additional threats to public security and order. For contemporary China, which holds that "maintaining social stability" is a national policy priority, the content of "public security" is of major and increasing importance.

As mentioned above, with the rapid social transition of Chinese society, economic and political transition simultaneously, some new issues affecting public security have emerged. According to the firstnational research report "Social stability risk assessment indicator system," the sources of social stability risk in contemporary China include:

a. *Nine types of social disputes*: land acquisition dispute; demolition dispute; tenement dispute; restructuring dispute; medical dispute; labor

---

[9] Available at http://www.acrwebsite.org/volumes/display.asp?id=7420.
[10] Available at http://en.wikipedia.org/wiki/Public_security.

dispute; pollution dispute; lending dispute; dispute between local and provincial residences.

b. *Five types of security problems*: food security; medicine security; medical security; production security; internet security.

c. *Two integrity problems*: governments losing public trust and the society losing integrity.

Accordingly, the frequent occurrence of mass incidents, skip-level petitions (*YueJi Shang Fang*) and the conflicts between local governments and unsatisfied residents, all provide new challenges for public security and threaten social stability also. Thus, the quality of public security service provided by governments at different levels of delivering public security service is closely related with its capacity to maintain social stability. "Maintaining stability" is equal to "maintaining security" to a certain extent.

7.2.2. *Delivery of public security service*

Public security is generally regarded as "pure" public goods and therefore supposed to be provided by government monopolistically. As Sabina Alkire argues: "Governments have the responsibility and authority to provide human security to their citizens" (2002). It is one of the basic societal pacts that bind state and society together.

In China, public security service is provided by a public security bureau (Gong An Ju) which refers to the government offices while the smaller offices are called police posts (Pai Chu Suo). They are responsible for policing (law enforcement), public security, and social order, and other duties including residence registration as well as immigration and travel affairs of foreigners.[11] The specific role of public security bureaus includes, amongst others, fire services, disrupting public protests, crime control and public safety.

Among multiple social actors, governments are perhaps the most appropriate and capable actors to ensure the security of their populations, while they are often neither able, nor appropriate, institutions for the task (Sarah, 2002). In urban areas, the community is the grass roots of China's administrative system, though the quality of its public security service is often unable to satisfy local resident's growing needs. Inrural areas, especially the more remote ones, the situation is even worse. Some services are not available or are available at considerably higher cost and

---

[11] Available at http://en.wikipedia.org/wiki/Public_security_bureau.

lower quality than in urban locations. In China, the frequency of crime in rural area is much higher than in urban areas.

The gap between supply and demand has been enlarging and a single government actor is not considered to be able to provide qualified public security services. The previous regulatory public service mechanism is not suitable for the contemporary situation. Thus, innovative and cooperative public service delivery mechanisms involving multiple social actors have become a potentially effective and essential method of improving the quality of public security service. Some parts of the government are cooperating with other social actors such as enterprises, NGOs, individuals and other social organizations. In this chapter, a pro-typical case will be used to show the role of NGO in the public security service delivery mechanism. NGOs can act as a vehicle to bring different types of social actors together to share the responsibility of improving the quality of public security service thus maintaining social stability.

7.2.3. *Cooperative public security service delivery mechanism*

Public service delivery is critical to ensure the well-being of people and to stimulate economic development. A modern public service delivery system entails: appropriate analytical tools to determine the right mix of services — essential public goods or competitiveness public goods — and matching them to the right regions, in a manner that considers efficiency/equity tradeoffs and is coherent with the overall regional strategy. What's more, modern service delivery mechanism calls for an adaptable governance frame-work that embraces the shifting role of stakeholders at all levels; improves the capacity of local authorities, facilitates participation and introduces mechanisms to ensure proper horizontal and vertical coordination as well as knowledge and resource pooling (OECD, 2004).

Co-design and co-delivery are mainly about the questions of which services are to be provided and how they are to be provided. In the public service delivery system, government plays a central role among different providers including some private firms and the voluntary sectors. In rural regions, it is more challenging for the government to provide extra services as result of the pervasive problems such as low density, distance and lack of critical mass (OECD, 2010).

The models of cooperation include public-public cooperation; public-private cooperation; public-non-profit cooperation. In certain service sectors, most notably health and human services, non-profit service

organizations are a major (sometimes sole) agent of service delivery at the community level (Sharon and Ophelia, 2004). In Western countries, these relationships are characterized by free-for-service or annual contracts. Now some countries are beginning to see joint development of service programs in which the public and non-profit participants share the responsibility for program design, performance and evaluation. In China, with the progress of market-oriented economy and the construction of public service-styled government, governments have gradually opened up the public service to market and let different types of social actors participate in the delivery of public services. Especially for public security service, which is endowed more timely content as result of its close connection with "maintaining social stability."

Organizations usually belong to one of three sectors of society: the government sector; for-profit/private sector, and the NGO/third sector. For a society to achieve its full potential and for citizens to fulfill their goals, all three sectors must cooperate with one another. Each sector has strengths and weaknesses in providing what citizens need:

a. The government sector drafts and enforces laws and regulations.
b. The business sector most effectively delivers goods and services.
c. The third sector which consists of non-governmental organizations provides services that the business and government are unwilling to or unable to deliver, and they provide venues for citizens to come together and be heard on issues that they feel are important.

7.2.4. *The role of NGOs*

Definition of NGOs

A non-governmental organization (NGO) is any non-profit, voluntary citizens' group which is organized on a local, national or international level. Task-oriented and driven by people with a common interest, NGOs perform a variety of services and humanitarian functions, for example, bringing citizen's concerns to governments, advocating and monitoring policies, and encouraging public participation through provision of information. Some are organized around specific social issues, such as human rights, environment or healthy issues. They provide analysis and expertise, serve as early warning mechanisms and help monitor and implement international agreements. Their relationship with offices and agencies of the United Nations system differs according to their goals, their venue and the mandate

of a particular institution.[12] NGO can also be called as "third sector" or "not-for-profit" organizations. In recent years, NGOs have become a critical actor within public policy landscapes at local, national and global levels (Lewis, 2001). Around the world, there is an increasing trend of the delivery of social services through the participation of voluntary organizations, which are neither government agencies guided by the state nor organizations committed to the profits (Salamon and Anheier, 1999).

Special role of NGOs

Different social actors are thought to cooperate and share responsibilities to ensure an active, inclusive and diversified public participation process: the government is proactive in expanding opportunities for public participation and all individuals have the right to be part of the decisions influencing their quality of life; special efforts are made to include women, indigenous people, youth and other marginalized groups, such as disadvantaged racial and ethnic minorities; transparency ensures all motives and objectives are apparent and information vital to a decision is presented and is reliable; openness to informal and formal routes of communication broadens the scope of public participation.

In most NGO/business and NGO/government partnerships, the NGOs retain their independence. Beyond providing services, one of the most important functions of NGOs is to facilitate citizens' participation in their societies. NGOs enable all voices to be heard when individuals form a group with others who have similar values and interests. NGOs often aim to promote understanding between citizens and the state. NGOs contribute to a civil society by providing a means for expressing and actively addressing the various and complicated needs of a society. They are seen as serving several essential functions:[13]

a. NGOs promote pluralism, diversity and tolerance in society while protecting and strengthening cultural, ethnic, religious, linguistic and other identities;
b. NGOs advance science and thought; develop culture and art; protect the environment; support all activities that make a vibrant civil society. NGOs motivate citizens in all aspects of society to act, rather than depend on state power and beneficence;

---

[12] Available at http://www.ngo.org/ngoinfo/define.html.
[13] Available at http://www.peacecorps.gov/multimedia/pdf/library/M0070_mod1.pdf.

c. NGOs create an alternative to centralized state agencies and provide services with greater independence and flexibility;

d. NGOs establish the mechanisms by which governments and the market can be held accountable by the public.

Why are NGOs important? One often quoted answer is that: NGOs increase "social capital"[14] by providing people with opportunities to build trust in each other and the capacity to work together towards common goals. NGOs are essential partners for governments, the private sector, and social organizations in meeting people's needs. NGOs are an expression of people's beliefs that through their own initiative, they can better fulfill their potential by working together, and in doing so, to shorten the opportunity gap between the advantaged and disadvantaged groups in society.

Development of NGOs in China

NGOs with Chinese characteristics:

According to the above definition of NGOs, non-governmental organizations are not only formal, private and non-profit-distributing, they are also self-governing and voluntary (Salamon and Anheier 1992, p. 134). Based on this definition, Chinese NGOs, as a whole, are not yet consistent with this type of organizations as described. Kang Xiaoguang concluded in his study of Chinese social organizations that very few Chinese organizations meet the Western conceptions of NGOs (Kang, 1999). Unlike independent organizations or third sectors in many countries with a long history of civil society, China's NGOs do not command the degree of organizational autonomy in the democratic countries. Against Chinese political and institutional context, Chinese NGOs do not consider themselves as the vanguards of society battling state intrusion or as an independent sector with distinct sectors. Rather, the great majority of Chinese NGOs see their roles as complementing and assisting the state. It is necessary to maintain a good NGO-government relationship in order to survive, and as survivors, many of them know how to play political games under China's CCP-state. Actually, in many countries, the government and non-profit sector maintain a cooperative rather than a conflicting relationship. In 1981, Salamon coined the term "third party government" to depict the fundamental pattern of

---

[14]Putnam (2000) defines social capital as those "features of social organization, such as trust, norms, and networks that can improve the efficiency of society by facilitating coordinate actions."

relationships between government and the private sector in the delivery of public services in the US. "In this model, private, non-profit organizations serve as partners with government in the provision of public services rather than as substitutes or gap fillers."(Young, 2001, p. 365).

The official classification of NGOs in China is based on the regulation approved by the state council. They can be divided into three categories: social organizations, private non-enterprise entities and foundations. According to official statistics, there were 431,000 NGOs registered in China at the end of 2009, including 239,000 social organizations, 190,000 private non-enterprise entities and 1,843 foundations.[15] At present, Chinese NGOs are involved in many fields related to social development. According to the report by Wang Ming of Tsinghua University, we can see that NGOs are active mainly in: social service (45%), survey and research (43%), industrial associations' and societies' work (40%), legal counseling and service (25%), policy consulting (22%) and poverty reduction (21%).[16]

Profound changes in social and economic structures of Chinese society have created public and private spheres that allow NGOs to emerge and grow. An increasing number of organizations become self-sufficient and self-governing and their normal operation independent of government control. The case in this chapter indicates that NGOs are becoming increasingly powerful instruments through which Chinese people participate in public affairs, develop personal interests, and express their petitions. Although Chinese NGOs do not have a substantial effect on government policy-making and political matters, they do present an obvious political trend that people are gaining control of their lives in an unseen fashion. According to Qiusha Ma's study, she concluded that NGO development has been a crucial step in the emergence of a new state-society relationship, and that non-governmental institutions are indeed facilitating the formation of civil society in China (Ma, 2006). On the other hand, NGO growth in China is highly unbalanced, with the non-governmental organization playing an active role in economic and social development while possessing almost no voice in political and religious issues. According to the blue book, the services areas provided by social organizations are become broader in 2009 to encapsulate technology, education, culture, health,

---

[15] Annual Report on Chinese Civil Organizations (2010–2011). Beijing: Social Science Academic Press (China).
[16] Huang, H. NGO Development trends in China. Available at http://docs.china-europa-forum.net/doc_616.pdf.

environmental protection and legal services. Among all of these categories, social organizations of agricultural and rural development account for 18.98%, and the percentage of social service organizations is 12.91%.

7.3. Case Study of Ping An (Safety) Association, Xintai City, Shandong Province

As mentioned previously the social stability situation of China is delicate and one potential means of addressing the problem is to incorporate NGO's into the delivery of public security services. This section explores the context, objectives, functions, characteristics and impacts of the Association and the advantages of the Association in delivering public security service and in maintaining social stability.

7.3.1. *Establishment of Ping An association*

Xin Tai city, Shandong province is one county city owning relatively larger area and population, and list on China's Economic Hundred Counties and Shandong Province's Economic Thirty Counties. Xintai city's area is 1946 square kilometers, population is 137.8 ten thousand, 20 administrative towns and streets, 917 administrative villages and one provincial high-tech development zone.

The first Ping An Association was established in Wennan town, Xin Tai city, in February 2006 and funded by 55 entrepreneurs in local area. Wen Nan town is located in the junction area of three counties, and the geographical environment is complicated, therefore, theft crimes happened frequently especially at night. The police force was insufficiently prepared to protect people's property and life safety. Therefore, some entrepreneurs proposed to fund a professional association aiming at sharing the responsibility of protecting public security and social order which were supposed to be undertaken by police officers. This suggestion was supported by other entrepreneurs, and social organizations. Then dozens of peasant entrepreneurs, enterprises and town people funded to establish Ping An Association and funded 485,000 yuan immediately.

The primary objectives of Ping An Association" are to make up the shortage of public security service provided by local government especially in the rural areas. Its primary task is to guard people's life and properties against crimes. After five years' practice, its functions have changed a lot, moving from simply maintaining public security into defusing social

conflicts, handling emergency incidents, and conducting legal education which are beneficial for maintaining social stability. In the light of these possibilities, this section explains how the Association is able to mediate social events affecting social stability to become an important linkage between the government and lay people. In June 2008, the Safety Association of Xin Tai city was constructed, and until now, more than 20 towns of Xin Tai have built the Safety Association, 602 communities (countries) have built sub-associations, and industry-associations were established in electric and health sectors. In all, there are 1,152 sub-associations and 11,830 individual memberships forming a four-level network system covering city, town, county and industry.

7.3.2. *Characteristics of Ping An association*

Ping An Association is a non-profit social organization, under the guidance of party committee and government. It was voluntarily established by the social organizations and individuals of a certain area, and members who take part in the maintenance of public security. Safety Association is a kind of autonomous organization that has the normative regulations, clear rights and obligations, and implements self-government legally. Safety Associations at different levels organize activities based on the relevant regulations and insist on democratic principles, namely "self-management, self-education, self-supervision, and self-development."

The most obvious innovation of Safety Association is to mobilize multiple social actors taking part in the social management system, and collaborating with the government sectors to keep social stability. Safety Association creates an innovative social stability risk management framework — "people's security is safeguarded by people, social stability is maintained by the society." Depending on the Safety Association, Xin Tai established the innovative social stability risk governance system characterized on the principle of "social collaboration, public participation."

Through motivating the social resources, Safety Association becomes an effective non-government mechanism of maintaining social stability, and forms the new social stability risk governance system combining political and legal sectors in the local government with autonomous non-government organizations. Based on Safety Association," Xin Tai city government built the innovative social risk handling system, which means connecting government regulation with social mediation, and complementing governments' administrative functions with social autonomous resources. In 2009,

compared to 2005, the number of petitions and petitioners passing through local authorities reduced by 59.3% and 55.9% respectively in Xin Tai city. The number of criminal cases reduced by 11.76%, major malignant cases decreased by 36%, and the number of unsolved petition events reduced by 44.3%. The social stability risk was also well controlled thus effectively promoting the economic and social harmonious development. In the past three years, Xin Tai's economy increased by 14.8% every year to the extent that in 2009, the GDP was 50.1 billion, and local financial input is 23.3 billion, thus ranking the county-level city 23rd among the top 100 developed counties.

7.3.3. *Innovative public security service delivery mechanism — Multi-dimensional prevention and control system of public security*

The population of Xintai city is 1.37 million, while the number of policemen is 600, therefore the power and funds of public police cannot meet people's increasing needs on public security service. Xintai city relies on Ping An Association to expand the channel of funds, and built police patrols with multiple formats. The system of public security in the city is composed of four parts:

- Super Patrol — Ping An Association set aside 1 million special funds on supporting villages and communities to form the professional and combining patrols with multiple formats. The number of patrol officers in the village areas has reached 6,100, and achieving the combination between professionals with masses, policemen with people and build prevention and control system with strength of masses. The forms of patrols include professional patrols officers, patrols of armed police, and patrols of volunteers from Ping An Association.
- Project of Ping An Lamp — Electric power company of Xintai city who is one of the unit members of Ping An Association paid 9.27 million membership fee to install 30 thousands Ping An lights for 917 administrative villages.
- Projects of "Tian Mu" — Xintai Unicom Company who is one unit member of Ping An Association invested 57 million and financial bureaucracies at city and town levels joint with Ping An Association financed 10.5 million yuan to install 1,200 monitoring cameras across villages and realize the real-time monitoring at security situation through the networking.

- Ping An Mutual Aid Network — Xintai Unicom Company invested 270 thousands yuan to install mutual aid telephones in 870 administrative villages across Xintai city.

7.3.4. *The role of NGOs — Taking Ping An Association as an example*

The advantages of NGOs in delivering public security service

a. Advantage of trust

The members of NGOs mainly come from lay people who have more connections with local people and know more about their requirements, which potentially means that their thoughts, minds and methods of handling emergencies are "softer" than the civil servants and more easily accepted by the people. They also find it easier to build mutual-trust relationship with the masses and possess the advantage of trust when handling problems and crises. The trust advantage also includes the financial aspect which means that NGO's financial operation is under the co-supervision of governments, enterprises and society, therefore its financial situation is relatively open and transparent. For example, in Ping An Association, its individuals members are mainly composed of veteran cadres, veteran party members and old labor models from different industries — "three olds," and they are familiar with the grass roots situation and own high prestige among masses so that they easily gain close contact with masses.

b. Advantage of resources

The most obvious characteristic of NGOs is non-profit and capable of mobilizing different kinds of social resources. When confronted with emergencies and crisis, public interests of NGOs make them possible to mobilize broad social capitalbeyond the capacity of governments while indulging in handling emergencies and making up the shortage of official emergency resources. The voluntary characteristic of NGOs also attracts a large number of volunteers to offset the government's human resources deficiency and to undertake the function of diverting masses and logistical support.

For Ping An Association, the principle of membership fee is "from people, giving back to people," and the funding sources include paying membership fee, social donation, and government grants. There are almost 10 million yuan membership fee every year. In the project of "Ping An lights," Ping An Association specially set aside 800,000 yuan to subsidy

the electric fee of towns and communities without charging people any money. "Ping An lights" not only compressed the possible space of crimes, but also provided great convenience to people's life and production, and enhanced the quality of public security service. It has become a popular project gaining broad mass support.

c. Advantage of efficiency

When emergencies and crisis happen, governments always make reaction lag behind as result of its rigid bureaucracy, while NGOs are able to act flexibly and rapidly based on different areas and different fields. NGOs could take advantage of various soft methods like demonstration, persuasion and innovation to improve the efficiency of social resources. For example, in December 2008, there were more than 300 Hui minority people who blocked Ci Lai railway as result of a train accident. Leaders of Municipal Party Committee arranged public police power to be prepared firstly, and then Zhang Lu who is the Chairman of sub-association of Yu Cun town and XuZongguang who is the Associate Chairman with other members belonging to Hui minority consulted with relevant people. After 24 hour negotiation, the two parties finally arrived at consensus and signed agreement. The discontented people left railway before the train passes by and a mass incident was resolved successfully.

d. Advantage of equity

The government represents public interests and is the actor of public power, therefore its standpoint is supposed to be based on the whole country, society and people. When handling emergencies, the government should balance the advantages and disadvantages and coordinate the whole social relations in order to maintain social stability and keep economic growth to the maximum extent. As a result of integrity and politics requirements, the government sometimes ignored the interests and appeals from certain disadvantaged group and diverse needs from different social groups cannot be satisfied timely and appropriately. Unlike the government, NGOs' behavior follows the principle of "demand–satisfaction". Especially some NGOs specially serve certain disadvantaged group and provide more physical and mental assistances to people lacking channels of expressing their appeals, and make up the shortage of official power and promote social equity. For example, Yu Cun town owns the biggest Hui minority population, the contradictions between Han people and Hui people frequently happened that brought about negative effects on local public security and

economic development. Ping An Association of Yu Cun town attracted 57 individuals members and among them, 17 are Hui people. Since its establishment in May 2007, Ping An Association has mediated in more than 90 contradictions and most of them were resolved successfully.

The role of NGOs in maintaining social stability

a. NGOs could act as the bridge and link between government
   and mass people

In the construction of harmonious society, Chinese governments are transforming their functions into the mode of public service-oriented government and this involves handing over some social management functions to NGOs. NGOs become the bridge linking enterprises, individuals, and governments. On the one hand, NGOs can express the requirements of their respective groups to the upper level, which is the orientation of from bottom to top; on the other hand, they could convey public policies from upper level to lower group and coordinate different groups' interests and interaction.

b. NGOs could promote the democratization and scientific of public
   policies

NGOs always represent certain group's interests, and they will take part in the policy formulation process in order to realize their respective groups' needs. For NGOs, the channels of taking part in public policies formulation process include: First, NGOs could report problems and put forward requirements to related departments representing their groups, and promote authoritative departments to make policies; second, NGOs could express their viewpoints about the formulation and implementation of some public policies; third, when their respective groups' benefits were damaged by certain policies, NGOs will negotiate with relevant actors and defend their interests.

c. NGOs could alleviate social contradictions and enhance
   social harmony

The baseline of harmonious society is social stability and equity, and NGOs' autonomy, non-governmental nature, voluntary, and public benefits decide them play a critical role in maintaining social stability, alleviating social contradictions and promoting social harmony. On the one hand, Ping An Association will take part in the mediation of serious social disputes according to the arrangement of party committee and governments. On the other hand, Ping An Association will voluntarily mediate some disputes and

conflicts around us. Members of Ping An Association mostly come from the masses who own broad personal connections and information sources. They can easily communicate with normal people and make use of moral, religious and regulative methods to handle conflicts except law and policy methods.

d. NGOs could handle emergencies immediately and reduce
   social conflicts

With the emergency of new conflicts of interest and types of social contradictions, the occurrence of emergencies increases rapidly. The direct intervention of government and public police would probably bring about the negative effect on the crisis and aggravate the situation. The role of Ping An Association in handling emergencies include: first, the function of breakwater which means to build the first line of defense avoiding the head-on collision between the masses and judicial officers from the government; second, the function of "pressure reducing valve" which means to reduce people's discontent emotions and prohibit the rapid spread of emergencies; third, the function of "bridge" to listen people's suggestions and reflect their appeals; finally, the function of adhesives of creating opportunities of making interactions between governments and masses.

7.3.5. *The disadvantages of Ping An association*

On the one hand, just as stated above, Ping An Association has made a large number of contributions for the local social stability and economic development. On the other hand, by its nature, Ping An Association is a voluntary organizations established by the masses, therefore it owned some incapability on some issues.

Firstly, Ping An Association is an NGO with Chinese characteristics and under the guidance of party committee and local government. Therefore, it is short of the law enforcement and political authority compared with government. When handling some events threatening social stability, the method of flexible mediation is invalid sometimes.

Second, the membership of the association is complicated and difficult to unify. Members of the association are composed of individuals, unit members, and community members. The identities of members are multiple and broad, and the composition of membership changes frequently; therefore it is difficult to realize unified management.

Finally, the financial sources of association which mainly depend on membership fee are unstable. Ping An Association is a kind of voluntary organization which does not have coercive power, and members submit fee

or not depending on their own willingness. Therefore, the financial situation
of Ping An Association is unstable to a certain extent.

7.4. Conclusion

Human security concerns are increasingly becoming a priority across the
globe, especially in China, which is endowed with particularly political
implication relating with maintaining social stability.

Among the range of actors that stands to make a positive contribution
to enhance security for people, governments are often the most able and the
most appropriate. However, in many countries and contexts, governments
are unable to address certain security issues or are themselves the root
cause of these issues. If it attempts to control social stability directly
through government delivered public security, it may increase hostility
toward the state. Thus, Chinese authorities see the use of collaborators such
as NGOs and individuals as a way to ensure social stability both because
they are non-direct government oriented and because their mechanism of
inclusion is seen as promoting a harmonious society. In some situations,
NGOs can be of crucial relevance, supplementing or replacing the efforts of
governments.

This chapter has mainly demonstrated the impact of one such government — NGOs' collaboration in the form of Ping An (Safety) Association.
The chapter explores the contexts, objectives, functions, advantages and
role undertaken by the association in delivering public security service and
maintaining social stability in China. At the same time, this chapter also
states the disadvantages and inabilities faced by the association in its practices. Overall, NGOs have obvious advantages compared with other social
actors in handling social stability risk in China, such as the advantages of
trust, efficiency and equity. The objectives of Ping An Association aiming to
maintain social stability have been achieved successfully and the innovative
collaboration created by Ping An Association provides an implication for
China's local government to shift to social governance.

In China, there actually exist many political obstacles to full and
effective NGOs' participation in public security and social stability initiatives, and the costs and difficulties of building strong NGOs' networks are
obvious. Addressing these problems will be one task for governments and
other interested actors to undertake and require the considerable dialogue
between NGOs, governments and aid agencies. Despite the pressure which
NGOs already face, the connections and resources that NGOs stand to

gain from their involvement in public security and maintaining social stability initiatives will all encourage NGOs to make a full and meaningful commitment to social development.

References

Alkire, S (2002). Conceptual framework for human security. Discussion Paper for the Commission on Human Security, February 16.

An NGO Training Guide for Peace Corps Volunteers. Module 1: The Role of NGOs in a Civil Society. Available at http://www.peacecorps.gov/multi media/pdf/library/M0070_mod1.pdf.

Cunningham, I and P James (2011). *Voluntary Organizations and Public Service Delivery*. London: Routledge.

Dawes, SS and O Eglene (2004). New models of collaboration for delivering government services: A dynamic model drawn from multi-national research. Center for Technology in Government, University at Albany/SUNY.

IRGC (2006). Risk governance: Towards an integrative approach. White Paper NO. 1 by Ortwin Renn with Annexes by Peter Graham.

Krahmann, E (2009). The commodification of security in the risk society. School of Sociology, Politics, and International Studies, University of Bristol. Working Paper No. 06–08.

Ma, Q (2006). *Non-Governmental Organizations in Contemporary China: Paving the Way to Civil Society?* London and New York: Routledge.

Michael, S (2002). The role of NGOs in human security. The Hauser Center for Non-Profit Organizations and the Kennedy School of Government, Harvard University.

OECD (2007). Enhancing the Delivery of Justice and Security. Availalble at http://www.oecd.org/dataoecd/27/13/38434642.pdf.

OECD (2010). Strategies to Improve Rural Service Delivery. OECD Rural Policy Reviews. Available at http://www.oecd-ilibrary.org/docserver/download/fulltext/0410051e.pdf?expires=1329379242&id=id&accname=ocid195699&checksum=05805B6EB25B601AB64F4BF5E8EC6F68.

OECD (2010). Governance and Public Service Delivery in Rural Areas. OECD Rural Policy Reviews. Available at http://www.oecd-ilibrary.org/docserver/download/fulltext/0410051ec003.pdf?expires=1329378731&id=id&accname=ocid195699&checksum=A5271616041E24FCFD43F992C2EA03C9.

OECD (2010). Designing Services for Rural Communities: The Role of Innovation and Co-design and Co-delivery in Improving Outcomes.

OECD. Innovative Service Delivery: Meeting the Challenges of Rural Regions. Available at http://www.oecd.org/dataoecd/14/42/41063088.pdf.

Ott, JS and LA Dicke (2012). *The Nature of the Non-Profit Sector*. Boulder, CO: Westview Press.

Salamon, LM and HK Anheier (1992). In search of the non-profit sector I: The question of definitions. *Voluntas*, (2), 125–151.

Scheye, E (2009). State-Provided Service, Contracting Out, and Non-State Networks: Justice and Security as Public and Private Goods and Services. OECD.

Wang, I (2006). Incidents of social unrest hit 87,000 in 2005. *South China Morning Post*, January 20.

Xiaoguang, K (1999). *Power Shifting: The Change of China's Power Structure During a Time of Transition*. Zhejiang: Zhejiang People's Publishing House.

Young, DR (2001). Third party government. In JS Ott (Ed.), *The Nature of the Non-profit Sector*. Boulder, CO: Westview.

Chapter 8

Political Trust, Public Service Performance and Government Transparency in China

Wenxuan Yu*

8.1. Introduction

Political trust, trust in government, has been declining worldwide in recent decades (Cheema, 2005; Levi and Stoker, 2000; Nye, 1997). Even China, a country with deeply rooted culture of trust in political authority, is also experiencing declining political trust. How to enhance political trust so as to facilitate collective action in this turbulent time is one of the big questions of public administration (Kirlin, 1996). Policy-makers and some scholars believe that improving public service quality and promoting government transparency are two effective strategies to restore political trust (Hood *et al.*, 2006). However, studies have emerged to challenge the positive causal relationship between public service performance, administrative transparency and political trust (Curtin and Meijer, 2006; Grimmelikhui-jsen, 2009; Kampen, Van de Walle and Bouckaert, 2006; Van de Walle and Bouckaert, 2003, Yang and Holzer, 2006). Kampen, Van de Walle and Bouckaert (2006) found that the relationship between public service performance and political trust was moderated by the predisposition toward government. Van de Walle and Bouckaert (2003) pointed out that better public service performance did not necessarily lead to higher political trust. Recently some scholars have begun to question the long-held belief that

---

*Assistant Professor, School of Humanities and Social Sciences, Nanyang Technological University

administrative transparency will enhance political trust (Curtin and Meijer, 2006; Grimmelikhuijsen, 2009, Worthy, 2010).

The impacts of public service performance and government transparency on political trust, in fact, are empirical questions and need to be empirically explored with a variety of different data and methods. Due to the complexity of the relationships, current empirical studies, more or less, suffer from problems such as problematic research design, inferior data and unsophisticated research methods. More empirical studies with improved data and research methods, therefore, are needed. In addition, according to postmodernism (Miller and Fox, 1995), the influence of public service performance, government transparency on political trust may be culturally dependent. So exploring the relationship between public service performance, transparency and political trust in different culture will not only enrich our understanding of the relationship, but also has significant practical implications for policy makers and practitioners in ascertaining how to improve political trust in specific cultural context. In this chapter, I try to conduct a preliminary multilevel investigation in the influence of public service performance, and administrative transparency on political trust, using data collected from a large-scale public service quality evaluation project conducted in China in 2011.

This chapter has six sections. In the first section, literature on the relationships between political trust and public service performance and administrative transparency is reviewed. In the second section, a theoretical model is presented and discussed. In the third section, research methods are introduced. In the fourth section, findings from a series of hierarchal linear models (HLM) are presented. In the fifth section, I discuss the findings. In the sixth section, I conclude with research limitations and future research direction.

8.2. Literature Review

8.2.1. *Trust, political trust and its determinants*

Trust is a multifaceted construct. It is essential to all human interaction in a society (Tonkiss, Passe, Fenton and Hems, 2000). In general, trust mainly refers to political trust and social trust. Political trust is the trust that political scientists and public administration scholars pay particular attention to. Political trust could be defined as "judgment of the citizenry that the system and the political incumbents are responsive, and will do what is right even in the absence of constant scrutiny" (Miller and Listhaug, 1990, p. 358). This definition implies that political trust can be developed at

three levels. The first level is at system level, where political trust is directed toward the overall political system and regime; in the second level, political trust involves certain political organizations; in the third level, political trust reflects people's confidence in individual government officials. A comprehensive literature review in political trust shows that political trust has three main dimensions: trust in competence, benevolence and honesty (Grimmelikhuijsen, 2009, Kim, 2005). Political trust in competence refers to the public's perception on the capability of the overall political system, government organizations or individual government officials in designing, implementing public policy and delivering public service efficiently and effectively (Berman, 1997; Carnevale, 1995); political trust in benevolence concerns to what extent the public perceive the government and its officials show their genuine interest in improving their welfare (Berman, 1997; Hart, 1984); political trust in honesty means whether the public believe the overall political system, government organizations and individual government officials will behave according to public interest even without their monitoring (Barns and Prior, 1996; Berman, 1997; Carnevale, 1995).

Any failure in the three dimensions will dramatically deteriorate political trust. Studies have shown that government's incapability in dealing financial crises, economic development and providing quality public services including education, environmental protection, public health care and public safety etc., significantly contribute to the declining political trust in both developed countries and developing countries (Nye and Zelikow, 1997). Berman (1997) found that poor quality of public service in local government undermined the political trust. La Porte and Metlay (1996) also observed that the declining competence of agency members caused political distrust. In addition to government's incompetence in providing public services and improving their quality of life, consecutive political scandals, rampant political and administrative corruption that damage the public's trust in benevolence and honesty, are considered as one of the most important political factors contributing to the continually deteriorating political trust worldwide (Mishler and Rose, 2001).

Moreover, trust scholars have also found that individual social and demographic variables such as age, sex, education attainment and income, are important determinants of political trust (Christensen and Per Lagreid, 2005; Kim, 2005; Thomas, 1998). Different people at different age, with different sex and income go through different process of socialization, leading to different confidence and perception in government's competency, benevolence and honesty.

8.2.2. *Political trust and public service performance*

Improving public service quality has been proposed as an effective strategy to improve political trust (Berman, 1997; The Panel on Civic Trust and Citizen Responsibility, 1999; Van deWalle *et al.*, 2003; Yang, 2005). It is believed that by working hard in providing quality public service, public officials show the citizens their competency and benevolence in improving their quality of life so as to win political trust. Vigoda-Gadot and Yuval (2003) empirically found that better managerial quality improve public service performance and then improve political trust.

The central tenet of administrative reforms in the past three decades, New Public Management Movement (NPM) in the Commonwealth Countries such as the UK, Australia and New Zealand and Reinventing Government Movement in the US, is to improve government performance and provide quality public service in an efficient way in order to improve public trust and support. In China, under the administration of President Jintao Hu, "service-oriented government"became the urgent goal Chinese public administration aims to accomplish. Chinese Communist Party (CCP), the ruling party in China since 1949, is endeavoring to promote economic development, provide quality public services and improve people's quality of life in order to restore the drastically declining political trust and its legitimacy. The logic reasoning underneath the administrative reforms is that better quality of public service delivery leads to higher citizen satisfaction and higher citizen satisfaction with public service provision subsequently improves political trust toward government (Van deWalle *et al.*, 2003).

The positive causal relationship between public service performance and political trust, however, is dubious. The performance-trust link, in fact, may be compromised by a variety of mediating factors. For example, citizens who have higher expectation toward government may not be satisfied by the quality of public service their government is providing, although the quality is objectively good or better than other neighboring governments. Even though citizens are satisfied with public service performance, the satisfaction is not the only component of their overall satisfaction toward government. Moreover, political trust may be highly influenced by factors other than public service satisfaction. In a culture that is characterized with a deeply-rooted distrust in government, it is likely that no matter how satisfied citizens are with public service delivery, they still distrust the government. The distrust is considered as necessary for a healthy democracy (Kim, 2005; Yang and Holzer 2006; Van de Walle *et al.*, 2003).

In addition, citizens' demographic and social profile may also interact with public service quality to influence their political trust (Christensen and Per Lagreid, 2005).

8.2.3. *Government transparency and political trust*

Government Transparency refers to the availability of information in the process and outcome of government policy making and implementation. The extent to which a government is transparent can be measured by "... the depth of access it allows and the depth of about process it is willing to reveal, and the level of attention to citizen response it provides" (Curtin and Meijer 2006, p. 111). Not only is government transparency considered as the *sine qua non* of democracy (Vleugels, 2008), it is also believed that government transparency has crucial instrumental values such as increasing accountability, improving the quality of government decision-making, improving public communication, increasing public participation and curbing corruption (Piotrowski *et al.* 2009; Worthy, 2010). All these benefits government transparency can achieve arguably contribute to restoring political trust. Therefore, it is no surprise to see that since 2006, the international right to know movement has been accelerating and sweeping the world (Yu, 2011). So far between 80 and 90 countries around the world now have some form of Open Government Information (OGI) legislation. An intriguing standout in this trend is the case of China, a country long regarded as closed, authoritarian and having long history of secretive public administration. China passed its nationwide OGI law, the Regulations of the People's Republic of China on Open Government Information (the "Regulations") in 2007 (Horsley, 2007).

Some empirical studies, however, have begun to challenge the transparency-trust link that has been taken for granted in political discourse (Curtin *et al.*, 2006; Grimmelikhuijsen, 2009; Worthy, 2010). According to data collected from official documents, interviews, survey of requesters and media analysis, Worthy (2010) found that government transparency did not increased political trust in government in Canada, the US and New Zealand. There is a paradox between government transparency and trust. The more transparent government is, the more government incompetence, inconsistency and policy failure will be unearthed, which further deteriorate the already declining political trust. In addition, even for the beneficiaries of government transparency policy, information requesters, only 3% of them surveyed reported that OGI policy increased their trust

in government, while 40% felt that it had decreased their trust. In China, Yu (2011) also found that although public officials embraced the idea of open government information, the worries about the detrimental effects of revealing government wrong doings and misconduct on political trust by implementing OGI policy was reasonable and ubiquitous.

In China, the enactment of the Regulations has sparked research on OGI in China. OGI scholars have begun to explore the reasons why the Chinese government initiated the Regulations and how it has implemented the Regulations (Ding, 2009; Horsley, 2007; Hubbard, 2008; Piotrowski *et al.*, 2009). Several national studies have been carried out to systematically evaluate the government transparency or, more specifically financial transparency and environmental transparency (CPPSS, 2010; CPPS,2009, 2010; IPE and NRDC, 2009). Based on the evaluations, Lorentzen, Landry and Yasuda (2010) constructed a regression model including three categories of explanatory variables, the ability (e.g, fiscal revenue, GDP growth rate) willingness (e.g, FDI to GDP ratio, Single-firm dominance) and leadership characteristics (e.g, tenure of CCP secretary as mayor, mayor appointment date of cities) to explain the variation in environmental transparency in Chinese cities. Drawing upon the study of Lorentze *et al.* (2010), Ma and Wu (2011) developed the most comprehensive model to explain the variation of fiscal transparency between Chinese provincial governments. In their model, 18 independent variables are grouped into four perspectives, external demand perspective, fiscal performance perspective, resources and capacity perspective and strategic leadership perspective. Nonetheless, there are still lack of empirical studies using quantitative methods to explore whether or not enhancing government transparency will achieve acclaimed goals, especially pubic trust, in China.

8.3. Theoretical Model

In this study, based on literature review on the performance-trust link, transparency-trust link and literature on government transparency in China, particularly the study of Lorentze *et al.* (2010) and Ma *et al.* (2011) and available data, I developed a multilevel model to examine the relationship between political trust in Chinese cities and its determinants at individual level and city level.

Figure 8.1 indicates that political trust is the dependent variable of the hierarchical linear model (HLM). Political trust in this model has three dimensions, trust in competence, trust in benevolence and trust in

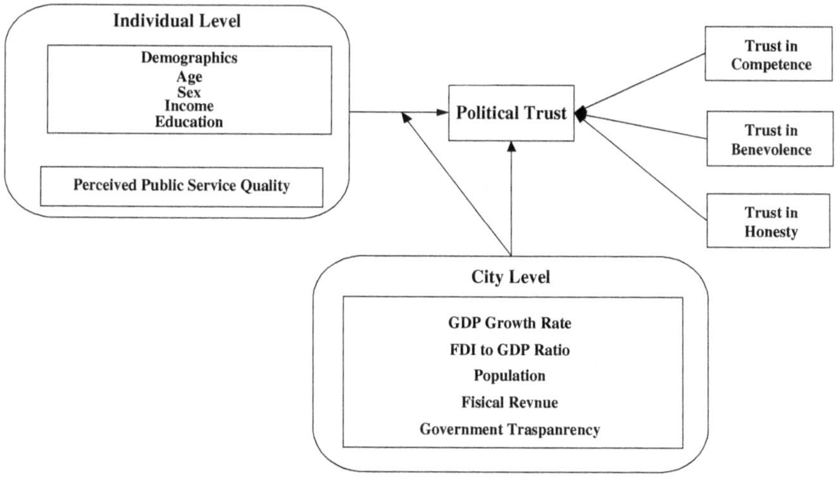

Figure 8.1.   A Multilevel Model of Political Trust.

honesty. At individual level, perceived public service quality (i.e., subjective measure of public service performance) is the independent variable, while individual demographic factors such as age, sex, income, tenure (the number of years living within the city) education are control variables. At city level, government transparency is the independent variable, GDP per capita, FDI to GDP ratio; population and fiscal revenue are covariates. The arrows in the model indicate the direction of influence between variables. In the model, individual level variables influence political trust, while city level variables not only influence political trust directly and but moderate the relationship between individual level variables and political trust.

In the section below, details in variable description and operationalization are explained.

8.4. Methods

8.4.1. *Data and measurement*

Data utilized by this study mainly come from a national public service performance evaluation project conducted in 2011 by Nanyang Technological University (NTU) and Shanghai Jiaotong University. Sponsored by a well-known charity foundation in Singapore, The Lien Foundation, researchers from NTU developed an evaluation framework to assess the public service performance in China's 32 major cities. The scheme includes

both subjective and objective indicators to measure residents' subjective performance assessment in nine service areas and the output and input of public service delivery in each city respectively. A questionnaire containing 27 items was developed so as to measure residents' subjective assessment on the quality of public services. Residents were asked to evaluate the performance of the 27 public services within the nine service areas using a 10 points scale, 1 referring to very bad and 10 referring to very good. Based on the questionnaire, researchers at Shanghai Jiaotong University conducted phone surveys in respective cities from May to July 2011. Finally, a total of 25,222 valid questionnaires were returned.

In this study, dependent variable, political trust and individual level variables such as perceived public service quality, age, sex, income, education and tenure are obtained the Lien project, while group level independent variables, GDP per capita, FDI to GDP ratio, population are collected by 2010 Chinese city statistical yearbooks and fiscal revenue is collected from respective government websites. The group level independent variable, administrative transparency, is measured by data obtained from "2011 Ranking of Government Transparency in China" published by the Chinese Academy of Social Sciences (CASS). Because of the incompatibility of the datasets, a data set containing 27 cities with the total of 20817 observations was finally compiled and employed (See Table 8.2). For the details of the dependent and independent variables such as variable name, measurement, data source, please see Table 8.3, Table 8.4 and Table 8.5.

8.4.2. *Data analysis*

In this study, Hierarchical Linear Models (HLM) were constructed to test the theoretical model because of two characteristics of the available data. First, residents are nested in their respective cities. It is very likely that the variance of residents' political trust within their own cities is different across cities, because of the common influence of political, social and economic factors at city level. If the data are analyzed at the individual level, thereby ignoring the nesting of individuals within cities, the estimated standard errors will be too small, and the risk of type I errors inflated (Raudenbush and Bryk, 2001). Second, the data on government transparency of Chinese cities are measured at city level. Running regular OLS by assigning a constant score to each individual within a city, therefore, will significantly reduce the standard deviation of government transparency and also lead to the risk of type I errors.

Table 8.1.   Public Service Areas and Public Services.

Public Service Areas	Public Services
Education	Education facility
	Education quality
	Education equity
Employment	Employment information provision
	Employment training
	Job creation
Health Care	Hospital facility
	Health care resources
	Contagious disease prevention and treatment
Housing and Social Welfare	Medical insurance
	Medicare
	Public housing
Public Safety	Public safety in your residential district
	Public safety in your city
Infrastructure	Road and highway
	Postal and telecommunication facility
	Public restroom
	Parking facility
Cultural, Sports and Recreational Services	Cultural, sports and recreational facility
	Cultural, sports and recreational activities Management
Environmental Protection	Air quality
	Road cleanliness
	Water quality of rivers and lakes
	Garbage collection and waste Management
Public Transportation	City public transportation
	City public bus routes
	City traffic congestion

Three HLM models were constructed and tested in this study, using statistics software package HLM 7.0. 1) The one-way ANOVA model (see Figure 8.2); 2) The random-coefficients regression model (see Figure 8.3), 3) The intercepts and slopes-as-outcomes model (see Figure 8.4). The one-way ANOVA model aims to test whether the "nested effect" exists between cities, i.e., citizens living in the same city tend to have similar political trust. The "null model" served as the basis for the subsequent analysis. The random-coefficients model is to explore the effects of level 1 variables on

Table 8.2.   Sample Cities and the Distribution of Valid Responses.

Sample Cities	Valid Responses
Changchun	701
Fuzhou	702
Haikou	704
Kunming	700
Zhengzhou	702
Changsha	705
Xiamen	702
Hangzhou	704
Lanzhou	710
Ningbo	700
Shijiazhuang	714
Guiyang	706
Hefei	701
Nanchang	704
Qingdao	703
Suzhou	704
Dalian	700
Harbin	702
Jinan	700
Nanjing	700
Taiyuan	702
Shenyang	1042
Chengdu	1005
Shenzhen	1004
Guangzhou	1000
Wuhan	1000
Xi'an	1000
Total	20817

political trust and explore what the coefficients of level 1 variables varying across different cities are. The intercepts and slopes-as-outcomes model is the full model examining how level 1 and level 2 variables and their interactions influence the dependent variable, political trust at individual level in this study. In the HLM models, level 1 variables were centered on the grand means, while level 2 variables are not centered.

Before running the three HLM models, Pearson correlation coefficients among independent variables at individual and city levels were checked. It turned out that no serious correlations existed, therefore avoiding the multi-culinearity problem (see Table 8.5 and Table 8.6).

Table 8.3.   Descriptions of Individual and City level Variables.

Variables	Variable Name	Description	Data Source
Political Trust	TRUST	A composite measure. It is the average of the three residents' responses about their agreement on three statements about public officials' competency, benevolence and honesty, based on 5 Likert scale.	2011 Lien Project
Individual Level			
Age	AGE	An ordinal variable. Residents were asked to place themselves in 6 categories ranging from 15 years old to 65 years old and above.	2011 Lien Project
Sex	SEX	A dummy variable (male = 1, female = 0)	2011 Lien Project
Income (Household Monthly Income)	INCOME	An ordinal variable. It has 7 categories ranging from no regular income(= 0) to more than 10 thousand	2011 Lien Project
Education	EDU	An ordinal variable. It has 6 categories ranging from the lowest (Primary school and lower = 1 to Above University = 6)	2011 Lien Project
Perceived Public Service Quality	PSQ	A composite measure of the subjective assessments on the quality of 27 public services. It is the average of residents' assessments on the 27 services, according to 1 10 points scale.	2011 Lien Project
Tenure	TENURE	An interval variable. Residents were asked how many years they had lived in current cities.	2011 Lien Project

(Continued)

Table 8.3. (*Continued*)

Variables	Variable Name	Description	Data Source
City Level			
GDP Growth Rate	**GDPGR**	A measure of the GDP growth rate in the city	2011 Chinese City Statistics Yearbook
FDI to GDP Ratio	**FDI.GDP**	It is the ratio of foreign direct investment to GDP in each city in 2010	2011 Chinese City Statistics Yearbook
Population	**POP**	The log of number of residents in the city	2011 Chinese City Statistics Yearbook
Fiscal Revenue	**FISREV**	The log of fiscal revenue of the city. Fiscal revenue in Chinese cities includes budget revenue, off-budget revenue and other source of revenue.	Respective government websites
Administrative Transparency	**TRANSP**	A standardized variable measuring administrative transparency in the city. The original transparency score assigned by CASS is in 100-points scale.	2011 Ranking of Government Transparency in China http://news.xinhuanet. com/politics/2011-02/24/ c_12111450.htm

Table 8.4.   Descriptive Statistics, City Level Variables.

	N	Minimum	Maximum	Mean	Std. Deviation
GDPGR	27	2.60	17.80	12.0696	2.95984
FISREV	27	4.79	6.93	5.9224	.52167
POP	27	5.06	7.04	6.3269	.49092
TRANSP	27	−3.19921	1.31778	.0000000	1.00000000
FDL_GDP	27	.00	.09	.0385	.02529
Valid N	27				

Table 8.5.   Descriptive Statistics, *Individual Level Variables*.

	N	Minimum	Maximum	Mean	Std. Deviation
TRUST	20101	1.00	5.00	2.9472	.69572
PSQ	16183	1.00	10.00	6.6699	1.25268
TENURE	15441	.50	90.00	15.6205	15.31647
AGE	16769	18	91	36.67	14.454
SEX	20817	.00	1.00	.4553	.49801
EDU	20659	1	6	3.69	1.249
INCOME	19687	1	15	5.41	4.516
Valid N	10230				

Level-1 Model

$$TRUST_{ij} = \beta_{0j} + r_{ij}$$

Level-2 Model

$$\beta_{0j} = \gamma_{00} + u_{0j}$$

Mixed Model

$$TRUST_{ij} = \gamma_{00} + u_{0j} + r_{ij}$$

Figure 8.2.   One-way ANOVA Model.

8.5. Findings

8.5.1. *One-way ANOVA model*

The one-way ANOVA model (the null model) is presented in Figure 8.2. β_{0j} is the mean political trust of residents in city j. γ_{00} is the grand mean of residents' political trust. Table 8.8 shows that P-value of u_0 is less than 0.001, which means the mean political trust of residents in city j, $B0j$, is significantly different across cities. Therefore, residents' political trust is

Level-1 Model

$$TRUST_{ij} = \beta_{0j} + \beta_{1j}{}^*(PSQ_{ij}) + \beta_{2j}{}^*(AGE_{ij}) + \beta_{3j}{}^*(SEX_{ij})$$
$$+ \beta_{4j}{}^*(EDU_{ij}) + \beta_{5j}{}^*(INCOME_{ij}) + \beta_{6j}{}^*(TENURE_{ij}) + r_{ij}$$

Level-2 Model

$$\beta_{0j} = \gamma_{00} + u_{0j}$$
$$\beta_{1j} = \gamma_{10} + u_{1j}$$
$$\beta_{2j} = \gamma_{20} + u_{2j}$$
$$\beta_{3j} = \gamma_{30} + u_{3j}$$
$$\beta_{4j} = \gamma_{40} + u_{4j}$$
$$\beta_{5j} = \gamma_{50} + u_{5j}$$
$$\beta_{6j} = \gamma_{60} + u_{6j}$$

Mixed Model

$$TRUST_{ij} = \gamma_{00} + \gamma_{10}{}^*PSQ_{ij} + \gamma_{20}{}^*AGE_{ij} + \gamma_{30}{}^*SEX_{ij} + \gamma_{40}{}^*EDU_{ij}$$
$$+ \gamma_{50}{}^*INCOME_{ij} + \gamma_{60}{}^*TENURE_{ij} + u_{0j} + u_{1j}{}^*PSQ_{ij}$$
$$+ u_{2j}{}^*AGE_{ij} + u_{3j}{}^*SEX_{ij} + u_{4j}{}^*EDU_{ij} + u_{5j}{}^*INCOME_{ij}$$
$$+ u_{6j}{}^*TENURE_{ij} + r_{ij}$$

Figure 8.3.   Random Coefficient Model.

nested within cities and HLM analysis is required. The inter-city correlation coefficient, $0.02/(0.02+0.47) = 0.04$, shows that 4% of variance in residents' political trust is between cities, while 96% of the variance exists at the resident level. Given the large sample size within city (700–1000) and the small sample size of cities (27), the explained variance between cities is rather significant, which requires HLM analysis.

8.5.2. Random-coefficients model

According to the results shown in Table 8.10, PSQ, perceived public service quality, Age, AGE and education attainment, EDU, are statistically significant at 0.01 level. The positive signs of PSQ and Age, mean that the better residents perceive their cities' public service performance, the more

Level-1 Model

$$TRUST_{ij} = \beta_{0j} + \beta_{1j}{}^{*}(PSQ_{ij}) + \beta_{2j}{}^{*}(AGE_{ij}) + \beta_{3j}{}^{*}(SEX_{ij})$$
$$+ \beta_{4j}{}^{*}(EDU_{ij}) + \beta_{5j}{}^{*}(INCOME_{ij}) + \beta_{6j}{}^{*}(TENURE_{ij}) + r_{ij}$$

Level-2 Model

$$\beta_{0j} = \gamma_{00} + \gamma_{01}{}^{*}(TRANSP_j) + \gamma_{02}{}^{*}(GDPGR_j) + \gamma_{03}{}^{*}(FDI\_GDP_j)$$
$$+ \gamma_{04}{}^{*}(FISRV_j) + \gamma_{05}{}^{*}(POP_j) + u_{0j}$$

$$\beta_{1j} = \gamma_{10} + \gamma_{11}{}^{*}(TRANSP_j) + \gamma_{12}{}^{*}(GDPGR_j) + \gamma_{13}{}^{*}(FDI\_GDP_j)$$
$$+ \gamma_{14}{}^{*}(FISRV_j) + \gamma_{15}{}^{*}(POP_j) + u_{1j}$$

$$\beta_{2j} = \gamma_{20} + \gamma_{21}{}^{*}(GDPGR_j) + \gamma_{22}{}^{*}(FDI\_GDP_j) + \gamma_{23}{}^{*}(FISRV_j)$$
$$+ \gamma_{24}{}^{*}(POP_j) + u_{2j}$$

$$\beta_{3j} = \gamma_{30}$$

$$\beta_{4j} = \gamma_{40} + \gamma_{41}{}^{*}(GDPGR_j) + \gamma_{42}{}^{*}(FDI\_GDP_j) + \gamma_{43}{}^{*}(FISRV_j)$$
$$+ \gamma_{44}{}^{*}(POP_j) + u_{4j}$$

$$\beta_{5j} = \gamma_{50}$$

$$\beta_{6j} = \gamma_{60} + \gamma_{61}{}^{*}(GDPGR_j) + \gamma_{62}{}^{*}(FDI\_GDP_j) + \gamma_{63}{}^{*}(FISRV_j)$$
$$+ \gamma_{64}{}^{*}(POP_j) + u_{6j}$$

Mixed Model

$$TRUST_{ij} = \gamma_{00} + \gamma_{01}{}^{*}TRANSP_j + \gamma_{02}{}^{*}GDPGR_j + \gamma_{03}{}^{*}FDI\_GDP_j$$
$$+ \gamma_{04}{}^{*}FISRV_j + \gamma_{05}{}^{*}POP_j + \gamma_{10}{}^{*}PSQ_{ij}$$
$$+ \gamma_{11}{}^{*}TRANSP_j{}^{*}PSQ_{ij} + \gamma_{12}{}^{*}GDPGR_j{}^{*}PSQ_{ij}$$
$$+ \gamma_{13}{}^{*}FDI\_GDP_j{}^{*}PSQ_{ij} + \gamma_{14}{}^{*}FISRV_j{}^{*}PSQ_{ij}$$
$$+ \gamma_{15}{}^{*}POP_j{}^{*}PSQ_{ij} + \gamma_{20}{}^{*}AGE_{ij} + \gamma_{21}{}^{*}GDPGR_j{}^{*}AGE_{ij}$$
$$+ \gamma_{22}{}^{*}FDI\_GDP_j{}^{*}AGE_{ij} + \gamma_{23}{}^{*}FISRV_j{}^{*}AGE_{ij}$$
$$+ \gamma_{24}{}^{*}POP_j{}^{*}AGE_{ij} + \gamma_{30}{}^{*}SEX_{ij} + \gamma_{40}{}^{*}EDU_{ij}$$
$$+ \gamma_{41}{}^{*}GDPGR_j{}^{*}EDU_{ij} + \gamma_{42}{}^{*}FDI\_GDP_j{}^{*}EDU_{ij}$$
$$+ \gamma_{43}{}^{*}FISRV_j{}^{*}EDU_{ij} + \gamma_{44}{}^{*}POP_j{}^{*}EDU_{ij} + \gamma_{50}{}^{*}INCOME_{ij}$$
$$+ \gamma_{60}{}^{*}TENURE_{ij} + \gamma_{61}{}^{*}GDPGR_j{}^{*}TENURE_{ij}$$
$$+ \gamma_{62}{}^{*}FDI\_GDP_j{}^{*}TENURE_{ij} + \gamma_{63}{}^{*}FISRV_j{}^{*}TENURE_{ij}$$
$$+ \gamma_{64}{}^{*}POP_j{}^{*}TENURE_{ij} + u_{0j} + u_{1j}{}^{*}PSQ_{ij} + u_{2j}{}^{*}AGE_{ij}$$
$$+ u_{4j}{}^{*}EDU_{ij} + u_{6j}{}^{*}TENURE_{ij} + r_{ij}$$

Figure 8.4.　Intercepts-and Slopes-as-Outcomes Model (Full Model).

Table 8.6. Pearson Correlations Between Independent Variables at Individual Level.

		TRUST	PSQ	AGE	SEX	EDU	INCOME	TENURE
TRUST	Pearson Correlation	1	0.432**	0.117**	0.021**	-0.151**	-0.041**	0.055**
	Sig. (2-tailed)		0.000	0.000	0.002	0.000	0.000	0.000
	N	20101	16099	16099	20101	19969	19076	14945
PSQ	Pearson Correlation	0.432**	1	0.080**	0.038**	-0.094**	-0.025**	0.008
	Sig. (2-tailed)	0.000		0.000	0.000	0.000	0.002	0.355
	N	16099	16604	16604	13883	16183	15460	12162
AGE	Pearson Correlation	0.117**	0.080**	1	-0.004	-0.258**	-0.171**	0.664**
	Sig. (2-tailed)	0.000	0.000		0.564	0.000	0.000	0.000
	N	16099	16604	20817	16769	16117	16395	12586
SEX	Pearson Correlation	0.021**	0.038**	-0.004	1	-0.015*	-0.038**	0.008
	Sig. (2-tailed)	0.002	0.000	0.564		0.034	0.000	0.316
	N	20101	13883	16769	20101	16710	16395	15441
EDU	Pearson Correlation	-0.151**	-0.094**	-0.258**	-0.015*	1	0.106**	-0.128**
	Sig. (2-tailed)	0.000	0.000	0.000	0.034		0.000	0.000
	N	19969	16183	16117	16710	20659	19562	14658
INCOME	Pearson Correlation	-0.041**	-0.025**	-0.171**	-0.038**	0.106**	1	-0.113**
	Sig. (2-tailed)	0.000	0.002	0.000	0.000	0.000		0.000
	N	19076	15460	16395	16395	19562	19687	14658
TENURE	Pearson Correlation	0.055**	0.008	0.664**	0.008	-0.128**	-0.113**	1
	Sig. (2-tailed)	0.000	0.355	0.000	0.316	0.000	0.000	
	N	14945	12162	12586	15441	14658	14658	15441

**. Correlation is significant at the 0.01 level (2-tailed).

*. Correlation is significant at the 0.05 level (2-tailed).

Table 8.7. Pearson Correlations Between Independent Variables at City Level.

		GDPGR	FDL_GDP	FISREV	POP	TRANSP
GDPGR	Pearson Correlation	1	0.098	−0.218	0.402*	0.062
	Sig. (2-tailed)		0.628	0.275	0.038	0.760
	N	27	27	27	27	27
FDL_GDP	Pearson Correlation	0.098	1	0.061	−0.234	0.184
	Sig. (2-tailed)	0.628		0.762	0.240	0.357
	N	27	27	27	27	27
FISREV	Pearson Correlation	−0.218	0.061	1	0.190	0.287
	Sig. (2-tailed)	0.275	0.762		0.343	0.146
	N	27	27	27	27	27
POP	Pearson Correlation	0.402*	−0.234	0.190	1	0.161
	Sig. (2-tailed)	0.038	0.240	0.343		0.421
	N	27	27	27	27	27
TRANSP	Pearson Correlation	0.062	0.184	0.287	0.161	1
	Sig. (2-tailed)	0.760	0.357	0.146	0.421	
	N	27	27	27	27	27

*Correlation is significant at the 0.05 level (2-tailed).

Table 8.8. One-way ANOVA Model.

Fixed Effect	Coefficient	Standard Error	t-ratio	Approx. d.f.	p-value
Final estimation of fixed effects:					
For INTRCPT1, β_0					
INTRCPT2, γ_{00}	2.950608	0.024225	121.799	26	< 0.001

Random Effect	Standard Deviation	Variance Component	d.f.	χ^2	p-value
Final estimation of variance components					
INTRCPT1, u_0	0.12331	0.01521	26	647.15648	< 0.001
level-1, r	0.68522	0.46953			

Statistics for current covariance components model
Deviance = 41938.684579
Number of estimated parameters = 2

they will trust their government, while the older the residents are, the more they would trust their government. The negative sign of residents' education attainment, EDU, suggests that the higher education level residents possess, the less likely they would trust government. Compared with the null model, in this model, by introducing level 1 variables the proportion reduction in variance at level 1, $(0.47 - 0.39)/0.47 = 0.17$, indicates that level 1 variables

Table 8.9. Random-Coefficients Model.

Fixed Effect	Coefficient	Standard error	t-ratio	Approx. $d.f.$	p-value
Final estimation of fixed effects (with robust standard errors)					
For INTRCPT1, β_0					
INTRCPT2, γ_{00}	2.969019	0.009356	317.331	25	< 0.001
For PSQ slope, β_1					
INTRCPT2, γ_{10}	0.243159	0.006494	37.444	25	< 0.001
For Q12_2AGE slope, β_2					
INTRCPT2, γ_{20}	0.003866	0.000582	6.639	25	< 0.001
For SEX slope, β_3					
INTRCPT2, γ_{30}	-0.012265	0.013723	-0.894	25	0.380
For EDU slope, β_4					
INTRCPT2, γ_{40}	-0.064612	0.007151	-9.035	25	< 0.001
For INCOME β_5					
INTRCPT2, γ_{50}	0.000653	0.001083	0.603	25	0.552
For TENURE, β_6					
INTRCPT2, γ_{60}	-0.001290	0.000644	-2.002	25	0.056

Random Effect	Standard Deviation	Variance Component	$d.f.$	χ^2	p-value
Final estimation of variance components					
INTRCPT1, u_0	0.03434	0.00118	25	41.23965	0.022
PSQ slope, u_1	0.02158	0.00047	25	36.90068	0.059
AGE slope, u_2	0.00154	0.00000	25	21.01561	> 0.500
SEX slope, u_3	0.03578	0.00128	25	32.58709	0.142
EDU slope, u_4	0.02496	0.00062	25	45.56774	0.007
INCOME, u_5	0.00245	0.00001	25	16.89177	> 0.500
TENURE u_6	0.00198	0.00000	25	34.78079	0.092
level-1, r	0.62190	0.38676			

Statistics for current covariance components model
Deviance $= 19438.882485$.
Number of estimated parameters $= 29$.

account for 17% of variance in political trust within cities. This model also shows that the variance components of the intercept, EDU are statistically significant at 0.05 level, which means that the coefficients of intercept and EDU significantly vary across cities and should be random coefficients and explained by level 2 variables. Although the variance components of PSQ and Tenure are not significant at 0.05 level, its p-value is pretty close to 0.05 and PSQ and Tenure are theoretically supposed to be influenced by city level political, social and economic characteristics and vary across cities.

Table 8.10.   Intercepts-and Slopes-as-Outcomes Model.

Fixed Effect	Coefficient	Standard error	t-ratio Approx.	$d.f.$	p-value
Final estimation of fixed effects (with robust standard errors)					
For INTRCPT1, β_0					
INTRCPT2, γ_{00}	3.180480	0.109731	28.984	20	<0.001
TRASP_OB, γ_{01}	0.000149	0.000478	0.313	20	0.758
GDPGR, γ_{02}	0.007397	0.001529	4.839	20	<0.001
FDL_GDP$_{03}$	−1.227967	0.292399	−4.200	20	<0.001
FISRV$_{04}$	0.027159	0.020094	1.352	20	0.192
POP, γ_{05}	−0.066434	0.019415	−3.422	20	0.003
For PSQ slope, β_1					
INTRCPT2, γ_{10}	0.187644	0.080239	2.339	20	0.030
TRANSP$_{11}$	0.000209	0.000474	0.441	20	0.664
GDPGR, γ_{12}	0.001686	0.003158	0.534	20	0.599
FDL_GDP$_{13}$	−0.037768	0.248150	−0.152	20	0.881
FISRV$_{14}$	−0.012318	0.016369	−0.753	20	0.460
POP, γ_{15}	0.015546	0.016977	0.916	20	0.371
For AGE slope, β_2					
INTRCPT2, γ_{20}	0.003809	0.000557	6.843	20710	<0.001
For SEX slope, β_3					
INTRCPT2, γ_{30}	−0.012321	0.013492	−0.913	20710	0.361
For EDU slope, β_4					
INTRCPT2, γ_{40}	−0.343834	0.091903	−3.741	21	0.001
GDPGR, γ_{41}	0.005427	0.002663	2.038	21	0.054
FDL_GDP$_{42}$	−0.032228	0.275003	−0.117	21	0.908
FISRV$_{43}$	0.034936	0.015072	2.318	21	0.031
POP, γ_{44}	0.001468	0.015955	0.092	21	0.928
For INCOME, β_5					
INTRCPT2, γ_{50}	0.000654	0.001112	0.588	20710	0.556
For TENUREβ_6					
INTRCPT2, γ_{60}	−0.004831	0.005926	−0.815	21	0.424
GDPGR, γ_{61}	0.000162	0.000155	1.044	21	0.308
FDL_GDP$_{62}$	−0.020822	0.009973	−2.088	21	0.049
FISRV$_{63}$	−0.002723	0.000965	−2.821	21	0.010
POP, γ_{64}	0.002928	0.000829	3.531	21	0.002

Random Effect	Standard Deviation	Variance Component	$d.f.$	χ^2	p-value
Final estimation of variance components					
INTRCPT1, u_0	0.02674	0.00071	20	33.59187	0.029
PSQ slope, u_1	0.02115	0.00045	20	32.18461	0.041
EDU slope, u_4	0.01468	0.00022	21	26.91996	0.173
TENURE, u_6	0.00042	0.00000	21	15.34289	>0.500
level-1, r	0.62223	0.38717			

Statistics for current covariance components model
Deviance = 19543.662602
Number of estimated parameters = 11

Therefore in the full model below, Table 8.11, I allow them to be random coefficients.

Testing the level 1 and level 2 models at the same time, Table 8.11 indicates that fiscal revenue, age, perceived public service performance have statistically significant positive impact on political trust. The more fiscal revenue a city has, the more its residents trust its government and public officials; The older a resident is, the more trustful she is; the better a resident perceive her city's public service performance, the higher her political trust.

Table 8.11 also shows that the interaction between population (POP) and sex (SEX), the interaction between fiscal revenue (FISCAL), and sex (SEX), are statistically significant with positive signs. Because men are more trusting than women, according to the HLM analyses, it means that men tend to trust their city government and officials more than women in cities with larger population and more fiscal revenue.

Although given other variables constant, this model shows that administrative transparency has a positive relationship with political trust, which is different from the means-as-outcome model, the interaction effects of government transparency between sex, education, age, income and perceived public service performance on political trust are negative. The positive sign of government transparency and its negative signs of the interaction terms indicate that men, people with higher education attainment, older and higher public service satisfaction and richer will have lower political trust in a city with more government transparency. The finding shows that the impact of government transparency on political trust is moderated by other determinants of political trust, such as age, sex, education, income and perceived public service performance. The relationship between administrative transparency and political trust is different for different people with different age, sex, education, income and different views in public service quality.

8.6. Discussion

This study finds that at city level, in China, city residents in a city with faster GDP growth rate and more fiscal revenue tend to have higher political trust and at individual level, better quality of public service delivery will make them trust government more. In the data analyses not shown in the article, a city's revenue is highly correlated with public expenditure, which to some extent equals to more government spending in public service delivery. These finding actually suggests that on average faster economic

Table 8.11. Intercepts-and Slopes-as-Outcomes Model.

Fixed Effect	Coefficient	Standard error	t-ratio Approx.	$d.f.$	p-value
Final estimation of fixed effects (with robust standard errors)					
For INTRCPT1, β_0					
INTRCPT2, γ_{00}	3.180480	0.109731	28.984	20	< 0.001
TRASP_OB, γ_{01}	0.000149	0.000478	0.313	20	0.758
GDPGROWR, γ_{02}	0.007397	0.001529	4.839	20	< 0.001
FDI_RATI, γ_{03}	−1.227967	0.292399	−4.200	20	< 0.001
LGFR, γ_{04}	0.027159	0.020094	1.352	20	0.192
LGPOP, γ_{05}	−0.066434	0.019415	−3.422	20	0.003
For PSQ slope, β_1					
INTRCPT2, γ_{10}	0.187644	0.080239	2.339	20	0.030
TRASP_OB, γ_{11}	0.000209	0.000474	0.441	20	0.664
GDPGROWR, γ_{12}	0.001686	0.003158	0.534	20	0.599
FDI_RATI, γ_{13}	−0.037768	0.248150	−0.152	20	0.881
LGFR, γ_{14}	−0.012318	0.016369	−0.753	20	0.460
LGPOP, γ_{15}	0.015546	0.016977	0.916	20	0.371
For Q12_2AGE slope, β_2					
INTRCPT2, γ_{20}	0.003809	0.000557	6.843	20710	< 0.001
For SEX slope, β_3					
INTRCPT2, γ_{30}	−0.012321	0.013492	−0.913	20710	0.361
For Q13EDU slope, β_4					
INTRCPT2, γ_{40}	−0.343834	0.091903	−3.741	21	0.001
GDPGROWR, γ_{41}	0.005427	0.002663	2.038	21	0.054
FDI_RATI, γ_{42}	−0.032228	0.275003	−0.117	21	0.908
LGFR, γ_{43}	0.034936	0.015072	2.318	21	0.031
LGPOP, γ_{44}	0.001468	0.015955	0.092	21	0.928
For Q16AVG_M slope, β_5					
INTRCPT2, γ_{50}	0.000654	0.001112	0.588	20710	0.556
For LIVINGP slope, β_6					
INTRCPT2, γ_{60}	−0.004831	0.005926	−0.815	21	0.424
GDPGROWR, γ_{61}	0.000162	0.000155	1.044	21	0.308
FDI_RATI, γ_{62}	−0.020822	0.009973	−2.088	21	0.049
LGFR, γ_{63}	−0.002723	0.000965	−2.821	21	0.010
LGPOP, γ_{64}	0.002928	0.000829	3.531	21	0.002

growth and more and better quality public service delivery lead to more political trust in Chinese cities. It supports the arguments of political economic development literature that in developing countries, higher levels of political trust are associated with wealthier regions and people trust

their government more when their government can promote economic growth faster and provide more and better public services (Leigh, 2006, Nye, 1997). This finding, to some extent, provides evidence to the classic positive link between public service performance and political trust, i.e. the better public service performance perceived by the residents, the more they trust their government. It seems like the efforts of Van de Walle (2003) in demystifying the dubious relationship are in vain in China. The finding also show that in Chinese cities, residents' political trust is heavily relied on government competency, which implies that as long as government is competent in promoting economic development and improve public service delivery, political trust could be continually improved without considering the other two dimensions of political trust, benevolence and honesty.

On the one hand, the positive and direct relationships between public service quality, economic development and political trust reflect that China is still a developing county. Even in its major cities, similar with other developing countries, government competency in pursing economic development and provide public service probably is still the single most important driver for political trust; On the other hand, it could be the result of CCP's political propaganda and education. Since 1980s, CCP had been putting its political legitimacy primarily on economic development and improvement in quality of life (Yang, 2006). After 2008 financial crisis, the quick economic recovery from the crisis strengthens the image of CCP as one the most competent ruling parties in developing economy and improving quality of life in the world, and the only political group that can provide China with a better tomorrow.

One of the most noteworthy findings of this study is the significant negative relationship between government transparency and political trust. It challenges the long-held belief in public discourse that government transparency leads to higher level of political trust and supports Worthy's finding that government transparency could not enhance political trust (2010). Given all the evidence, I postulate that probably the relationship between government transparency and trust is not linear but U-shaped. Grimmelikhuijsen (2009) provided some evidence to support the postulation. His findings from an experiment showed that more transparency lead to higher level political trust, only given the high level of transparency exists. The U-shaped curvilinear relationship suggests that in a country with low government transparency and deeply ingrained culture of secrecy, in the short run, more transparency will lead to lower political trust. It is the case of China, UK and Australia (Snell, 2006; Worthy, 2010; Yu, 2011).

The study also finds that the relationship between political trust and government transparency is also moderated by other variables such as social demographic variables and subjective public service quality. The study finds that in China, men are more trusting than women, though not statistically significant. And the discrepancy between men and women in political trust becomes larger in larger and richer cities. The findings on the gender difference are at odds with existing trust literature in Western countries where women living in smaller communities tend to be more trusting. It suggests political trust is a culture sensitive construct. In this study, however, the finding that people with higher education attainment, older and higher public service satisfaction and richer will have lower political trust in a city with more government transparency suggests that China and the US share a lot of commonalities in this regard. I postulate that according to the idea of post-positivism, there exists an underlying complicated model about political trust, probably the curvilinear relationship between political trust and government transparency belonging to model.

8.7. Conclusion

This study provides a preliminary multilevel model to test the relationship between political trust, public service performance and government transparency using data collected from China. The findings of the study enrich our understanding of the spurious relationships between two important conceptual links of public administration, the trust and transparency link and the performance-trust link, and how the relationship work in China, a place with distinctively different culture from the West.

This study also has significant practical implications for policy makers and implementers in China. The findings that promoting economic development and providing quality public services are the main drivers for political trust and more government transparency will lead to lower level of political trust may provide justification for Chinese government and CCP's continuing efforts in placing their political legitimacy in promoting economic development and the unsatisfactory implementation of OGI regime. I argue that because the findings are based on historical data, it cannot provide prediction for what will happen in the future. China is entering a historical junction given the changed international political, social, economic environment, increasing income discrepancy, regional disparity and rampant corruption. Chinese government and CCP really need to change their mindset, political ideology and the ways of

governance. While keeping developing economy and provide quality public service, they also need to pay more attention to address those increasing thorny problems caused by super-fast economic development in the past three decades and further improve government transparency to improve the quality of public policy decision making and curb rampant corruption, even though at the cost of lower political trust in short run (Yao, 2010).

This study also has several limitations. First, because of the limitation of the data available, some important city level and individual level variables are left out. It would cause some statistical problems because of missing variables. Second, although at individual level, the sample size of each city satisfies the large sample criterion for HLM analysis, at city level only 26 cities are included. Third, the 26 cities are key Chinese cities. Whether or not the findings of this study could be generalized to all Chinese cities are problematic. Fourth, the authors develop the operationalization and measurement of political trust and public service quality by themselves. Their internal validity and external validity are questionable. More studies need to be conducted to verify their effectiveness.

In the future, I will collect more data, include more important variables in the model and verify some interesting findings that still wait for explanation, such as why in China men are more trusting than women, the difference between men and women in political trust is bigger in richer cities with more population and more importantly the postulated curvilinear relationship between political trust and public transparency.

References

Barnes, M and D Prior (1996). From private choice to public trust: A new social basis for welfare. *Public Money and Management*, 16(4), 51–57.

Berman, EM (1997). Dealing with cynical citizens. *Public Administration Review*, 57(2), 105–112.

Carnevale, D (1995). *Trustworthy Government: Leadership and Management Strategies for Building Trust and High Performance*. San Francisco: Jossey-Bass.

Carnevale, DG and B Wechsler (1992). Trust in the public sector: Individual and organizational determinants. *Administration and Society*, 23(4), 471–494.

Cheema, G (2005). *Building Democratic Institutions: Governance Reform in Developing Countries*. Conn: Kumarian Press.

CPPS (2009). *2009 Annual Report on China's Fiscal Transparency — An Assessment of Open Information on Provincial Government Finance*. Shanghai: Shanghai University of Finance and Economics Press.

CPPS (2010). *2010 Annual Report on China's Fiscal Transparency — An Assessment of Open Information on Provincial Government Finance*

and *Departmental Administrative Revenue and Expenditure*. Shanghai: Shanghai University of Finance and Economics Press.

CPPSS (2010). *Summary of the 2009 Annual Report on China's Administrative Transparency*. Beijing: Center for Public Participation Studies and Supports, Law School, Peking University.

Christensen, T and P Lagreid (2005). Trust in government: The relative importance of service satisfaction, political factors, and demography. *Performance and Management Review*, 28(4), 487–511.

Curtin, D and AJ Meijer (2006). Does transparency strengthen legitimacy. *Information Polity*, 2006 (11), 109–122.

Grimmelikhuijsen, S (2009). Do transparent government agencies strengthen trust? *Information Polity*, 14(3)

Hart, DK (1984). The virtuous citizen, the honorable bureaucrat, and "public" administration. *Public Administration Review*, 44(11).

Hood, C and D Heald (2006). *Transparency: The Key to Better Governance?* Oxford, UK: Oxford University Press.

Horsley, J (2007). *China Adopts First Nationwide Open Government Information Regulations*. Available at http://www.freedominfo.org/features/20070509. htm.

IPE and NRDC (2009). *Breaking the Ice on Environmental Open Information: The 2008 Pollution Information Transparency Index (PITI) First Annual Assessment of Environmental Transparency in 113 Chinese Cities*. Beijing: Institute of Public and Environmental Affairs (IPE) and Natural Resources Defense Council (NRDC).

Kampen, JK, S Van de Walle and G Bouckaert (2006). Satisfaction with public service delivery and trust in government: The impact of the predisposition of citizens toward government on evalutations of its performance. *Public Performance and Management Review*, 29(4), 387–404.

Kim, S (2005). The role of trust in the modern administrative state. *Administration and Society*, 37(5), 611–635.

Kirlin, JJ (1996). The big questions of public administration in a democracy. *Public Administration Review*, 56(5), 416–423.

La Porte, TR and DS Metlay (1996). Hazards and institutional trustworthiness: Facing a deficit of trust. *Public Administration Review*, 56(4), 341–347.

Leigh, A (2006). Trust, inequality and ethnic heterogeneity. *Economic Record*, 82, 268–280.

Levi, M and L Stoker (2000). Political trust and trustworthiness. *Annual Review of Political Science*, 3(1), 475–507.

Lorentzen, PL, PF Landry and JK Yasuda (2010). Transparent authoritarianism?: An analysis of political and economic barriers to greater government transparency in China. Paper Presented at the APSA 2010 Annual Meeting.

Ma, L and J Wu (2011). What drives fiscal transparency? Evidence from provincial governments in China. In the 1st Global Conference on Transparency Research. New Jersey: Newark.

Miller, AH (1974). Political issues and trust in government: 1964–1970. *The American Political Science Review*, 68(3), 951–972.

Mishler, W and R Rose (2001). What are the origins of political trust? *Comparative Political Studies*, 34, 30–62.

Nye, J (1997). Introduction: The decline of confidence in government. In *Why People Don't Trust Government?* J Nye, S Joseph, PD Zelikowand DCKing (Eds.), pp. 1–19. Cambridge, MA: Harvard University Press.

Piotrowski, S, Y Zhang, W Yu and W Lin (2009). Key issues for implementation of Chinese open government information regulations. *Public Administration Review*, 69, S129–S135.

Raudenbush, SW and AS Bryk (2002). *Hierarchical Linear Models: Applications and Data Analysis Methods: Applications and Data Analysis Methods.* New York: Sage Publications.

Snell, R (2006). Freedom of information practices. *Agenda*, 13(4), 291–307.

The Panel on Civic Trust and Citizen Responsibility. (1999). *A Government to Trust and Respect. Rebuilding Citizen-Government Relations for the 21st Century.* Washington, DC: National Academy of Public Administration.

Thomas, CW (1998). Maintaining and restoring public trust in government agencies and their employees. *Administration and Society*, 30(2), 166–193.

Tonkiss, F, A Passey, N Fenton and LC Hems (2000). *Trust and Civil Society.* London: Macmillan.

Van de Walle, S and G Bouckaert (2003). Public service performance and trust in government: The problem of causality. *International Journal of Public Administration*, 26(8–9), 891–913.

Vigoda-Gadot, E and F Yuval (2003). Managerial quality, administrative performance and trust in governance revisited: A follow-up study of causality. *International Journal of Public Sector Management*, 16(7), 502–522.

Vleugels, R (2008). Overview of All 86 FOIA Countries. Available at http://www. freedominfo.org/features/FOIA_overview_vleugels.pdf.

Worthy, B (2010). More open but not more trusted? The effect of the freedom of information act 2000 on the United Kingdom central government. *Governance*, 23(4), 561–582.

Yang, D (2006). Economic transformation and its political discontents in China: Authoritarianism, unequal growth, and the dilemmas of political development. *Annual Review of Political Science*, 9, 143–164.

Yang, K and M Holzer (2006). The performance-trust link: Implications for performance measurement. *Public Administration Review*, 66(1), 114–126.

Yao, Y (2010). The End of the Beijing consensus. *Foreign Affairs.* Available at http://www.foreignaffairs.com/articles/65947/the-end-of-the-beijing-consensus.

Yu, W (2011). Open government information: Challenges faced by human resource management in China. *International Journal of Public Administration*, 34(13), 879–888.

Chapter 9

Explaining Citizens' Satisfaction With Public Service Quality in Chinese Cities 2010: Citizen-Level Predictors vs. City-Level Predictors*

Tingjin Lin[†]

9.1. Introduction

Providing quality public service is the *raison d'être* of government. International empirical evidences indicate that economic development and high quality of life have strong and significant positive correlation with the capacity of government in providing quality public service. Provision of quality public service not only satisfies citizen demand and enhances their quality of life, but also critically affects human capital development and international capital flow. This in turn determines whether a city or region can achieve sustainable economic and social development.

Provision of quality public service is particularly important under authoritarian regimes, given that the legitimacy of authoritarian regimes is primarily based on their capacity to promote economic development and enhance citizens' livelihood. China is a case in point (Yang, 2006). The implementation of the market-oriented economic reforms since the 1980s led to the weakening of the state-owned enterprises and the collapse of the rural commune system — two pillars of public service providers during the Mao era. Starting from the 1990s, the Chinese government has sought to re-build its public service delivery system in order to provide quality public service more effectively (Saich, 2008).

---

*The chapter was presented on the 69th MPSA Annual Conference, March 2011, Chicago.
[†]Research Fellow, Nanyang Centre for Public Administration, Nanyang Technological University.

While much research has been conducted on various aspects of China's public service provision, empirical studies of how citizens in urban China evaluate the quality of public service provision is still an academic vacancy. As the first step to examine how citizens across urban China evaluate public service quality and their determinants, the Nanyang Centre for Public Administration (NCPA) at the Nanyang Technological University in Singapore, with the financial support from the Lien Foundation in Singapore, developed the "Lien Public Service Excellence Index for Chinese Cities" and used it to conduct surveys of citizens' evaluation of public service quality in 32 major Chinese cities in 2010.[1]

Paying attention to the respective strengths of different methods of designing indexes, NCPA adopted literature review, Delphi method, and surveys to construct the assessment scheme. The index covers three major dimensions of the quality of public service delivery such as Overall Public Service Satisfaction (Citizens and Business), Business Environment, and General Public Service Provision. The index consists of 34 indicators and 106 measurements aiming to assess the performance of public service delivery in Chinese cities.

The sub-index focusing on citizens' overall satisfaction assesses ten types of public service, including: education; employment; health care; housing and social security; public safety; basic infrastructure; culture, sport and

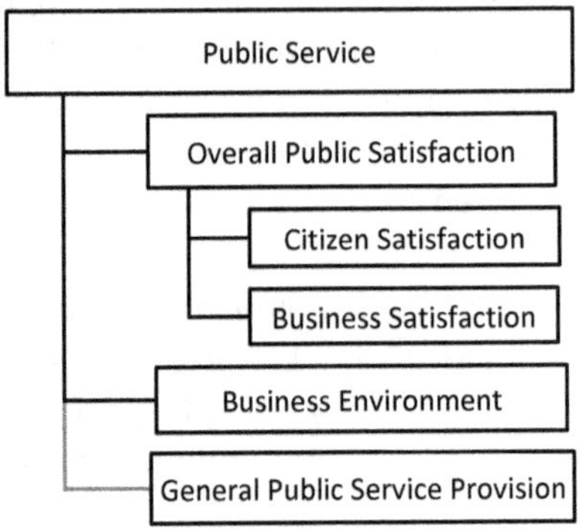

Figure 9.1.   Public Service Excellence Index for Chinese Cities.

---

[1] These 32 cities included: Beijing, Changchun, Changsha, Chengdu, Chongqing, Dalian, Fuzhou, Guangzhou, Guiyang, Haikou, Harbin, Hangzhou, Hefei, Jinan, Kunming, Lanzhou, Nanchang, Nanjing, Nanning, Ningbo, Qingdao, Shanghai, Shenyang, Shenzhen, Shijiazhuang, Suzhou, Taiyuan, Tianjin, Wuhan, Xi'an, Xiamen and Zhengzhou. For the details of the project, please refer to Wu *et al.* (2011).

recreational services; environmental protection; public transportation; and government efficacy. A total of 29 measurements were adopted to assess one of the four major dimensions, Citizens Satisfaction With Public Services Quality, in their home city.

This chapter aims to explores the influence of interviewee's demographic variables including gender, age, education attainment, income, and the length of residence and city level socioeconomic variables on citizens' overall satisfaction with public service quality by employing a two-level analysis. Therefore, the first sub-index of the aforementioned index, Citizen Satisfaction with Public Services Quality or subjectively measured public service quality, will be taken as the *dependent variable* of the study. Meanwhile, the fourth sub-index of the assess index, General Public Service Provision, are measured by ten city-level objective indicators in accordance with the ten subjective indictors included in the Citizen Satisfaction. The ten objective indicators include 34 measurements collected from official statistical yearbooks (hard data) and most of the 34 measurements are public spending on respective public services. It is reasonable to include this hard-data dimension as an independent variable to purify the effects of individual demographic and city-level variables on the Citizen Satisfaction.

9.2. Literature Review

Saich (2008) conducted a nationwide survey in China between 2003 and 2005 to study how citizens evaluated government performance in providing public goods and services. Saich found that family planning, water and electricity supply, road and bridge construction, oversight of religious worship, traffic management, and management of middle and elementary schools received the highest ratings of citizens. By contrast, combating corruption, job creation, unemployment insurance, tax management, medical insurance, and hardship family relief received the lowest approval. However, Saich's purposive stratified survey covered eight cities, seven towns, and eight villages.[2]

Li (2008) studies how and why the government in Hubei Province designed and implemented institutional reforms which sought to improve the incentives of rural service providers to provide more and better public services in the countryside. Tsai (2007) explains variations in the

---

[2]The eight cities included: Beijing, Shanghai, Guangzhou, Wuhan, Chengdu, Shenyang, Xi'an and Nantong.

government provision of public goods in rural China, arguing that the existence of encompassing and embedding community solidarity groups is the key. Tsai's study is mainly based on fieldwork covering over 300 villages in four provinces.

While Li (2008) and Tsai (2007) provide important insights of the major factors affecting the quality and quantity of public service provision, they only cover rural China. Although Saich (2008) studies urban China, his research merely includes eight cities.

Additionally, a couple of survey studies on political culture, government performance evaluation, or/and satisfaction and confidence with government have been conducted by other scholars in China studies since 1990s (Shi, 2000; Nathan and Shi, 1993; Nathan and Shi, 1996). Most of these study employed respondent's demographic variables (such as age, gender, education attainment, income, etc.) as predictors of their respective dependent variables. For example, Zhong, Chen and Scheb (1998) argued that education attainment was a significant predictor of citizens' evaluation of government performance, income could significantly explain citizens' satisfaction with government, and age was significantly associated with citizens' confidence with government.

Although most of the existing studies use national level survey data, none of them differentiate the effects of individual-level variables from that of organization-level (say, province- or city-level) variables as applicable statistical tools were not available for analyzing nested data at the time when the authors conducted their research. With the HLM7.0 software, the current study seeks to fill in this academic gap by exploring the effects of individual level variables as well as that of organizational level variables.

This chapter enquires: Do different demographic and socioeconomic groups (citizen-level variables) differ in their satisfaction with the public service quality? In addition to citizen-level variables, do city-level variables play any role in the citizen's level of satisfaction with the public service quality? Moreover, to what extent do citizen- and city-level variables explain the variance of citizens' satisfaction with public service quality?

9.3. Data

A questionnaire was designed in order to investigate citizens' evaluation of the quality of ten major public services within their cities through face-to-face interviews. The survey was conducted in spring and summer

2010 by NCPA with the collaboration of the School of Public Affairs at Xiamen University in China. Research teams in each sample city were required to randomly choose about 1,000 interviewees in commercial and residential districts, colleges, transportation hubs, public libraries, social security centers, and administrative service centers. A total of 31,335 questionnaires were collected, making the Lien Program has a largest sample size among studies on public services quality in China. Respondents were asked how they evaluated the quality of ten public services within their cities. These measurements were presented in a five-point Likert-format, with response options ranging from completely satisfied (5 points) to completely dissatisfied (1 point). Respondents were also able to state that they "don't know" the answer.

However, this study has 16,942 valid samples after deleting samples with the "don't know" answer or missing value. (For each city's valid return questionnaires, please refer to Appendix 1). Table 9.1 shows the socioeconomic characteristics of our respondents. In addition to the dependent variable, Citizen Satisfaction With Public Service Quality (labelled as PSQ hereafter), the study has five citizen-level independent variables including age, gender, education attainment, household monthly income, and the length of residence in home city.

As mentioned above, PSQ is a dimension or a sub-index, actually, including 29 subjective measurements in the questionnaire and the table shows it ranges from −25.25 to 20.94. The mean of PSQ is zero as the original survey data was standardized to Z-scores. Gender is a dummy variable where male was coded 1. Table 9.1 shows that 53% of 16942 samples are male. All of the rest four variables are ordinal data; the coding and frequency analysis were displayed in the first two columns of the table. The questionnaire was exclusively designed for evaluation purpose; this explains why some other possible or potential predictors were not included and why the aforementioned four variables were collected as ordinal, rather than interval variables. Yet in this study the four variables were taken as interval variables when HLM regressions were run because of following concerns. Firstly, the range of each age group is 10, which means the difference between every two neighboring age groups has been largely equalized. The same can be said to the household monthly income as the range of each income group is CNY 2,000, excluding the no-regular-income group. It is logical to view both variables as interval variables, even though this may mathematically not as perfect as surveys having exact age and income of respondents. But, technologically speaking, asking exact age and income

Table 9.1.	Descriptive Statistics, Citizen-Level Variables.

	N	%	Min	Max	Mean	Std. D.
PSQ (Citizen Satisfcation)	16942		−25.25	20.94	0.0000	7.37333
GEN (male = 1)	16942		0	1	0.53	0.499
EDU (Education Attainment)	16942		1	6	4.18	1.202
Primary sch. and lower (= 1)	391	2.31				
Junior middle school (= 2)	1314	7.76				
High middle school (= 3)	3036	17.92				
College (= 4)	4080	24.08				
University (= 5)	6432	37.96				
Above University (= 6)	1689	9.97				
AGE	16942		1	6	2.34	1.220
15–24 (= 1)	4607	27.19				
25–34 (= 2)	6223	36.73				
35–44 (= 3)	3291	19.43				
45–54 (= 4)	1671	9.86				
55–64 (= 5)	825	4.87				
>=65 (= 6)	325	1.92				
INC (Household Monthly Income)	16942		0	6	2.35	1.456
No regular income (= 0)	1371	8.09				
0–1999 (= 1)	3260	19.24				
2000–3999 (= 2)	5781	34.12				
4000–5999 (= 3)	3617	21.35				
6000–7999 (= 4)	1232	7.27				
8000–9999 (= 5)	884	5.22				
>= 10000 (= 6)	797	4.70				
RES (Length of Residence)	16942		1	4	2.91	1.075
<2 years (= 1)	1997	11.79				
2–5 years (= 2)	4658	27.49				
5–10 years (= 3)	3204	18.91				
>10 years (= 4)	7083	41.81				

will decrease the rate of valid respondent. Secondly, according the education system in China, the difference of every two neighboring education groups is either two or three years while primary education requires five- or six-year formal schooling. It is fine to take education attainment as an interval variable. Thirdly, for the length of residence, the range of each category is increasing. By taking it as an interval, the study assumes the marginal effect of the variable is decreasing.

As the survey were conducted in 32 Chinese cities, it is logical to enquire the influence of socioeconomic environment on citizens' evaluation of public service quality. Data of the current study could be considered

as citizens nested within cities. In statistics, hierarchical linear modelling (HLM), also known as multi-level analysis, is a more advanced form of simple linear regression and multiple linear regression. Multilevel analysis allows variance in outcome variables to be analysed at multiple hierarchical levels, whereas in simple linear and multiple linear regression all effects are modelled to occur at a single level. Thus, HLM is appropriate for use with nested data. Within HLM, each of the levels in the data structure (for example, citizens within cities as constructed in this study) is formally represented by its own sub-model. Each sub-model represents the structural relations occurring at that level and the residual variability at that level.

By defining citizen-level data as level-1 in HLM, the study also adopts city-level data as level-2 in following HLM analysis. Table 9.2 describes variables at city-level. Excepting the general public service provision or the objectively measured public service quality which was collected by NCPA's research program for the purpose of ranking, the rest variables are collected from an official statistical publication of Chinese government, *China City Statistical Yearbook 2010*.

Table 9.2.   Descriptive Statistics, City-Level Variables.

	N	Min	Max	Mean	Std. D
General Public Service Provision (Hard Data)	32	−21.90	19.91	0.00	8.8633
GDP per capita (CNY)	32	18025	106863	47182.59	22169.5320
Population (10,000)	32	150.86	2808.00	725.15	472.4850
Public Expenditure per capita (CNY)	32	1786.01	82878.05	9185.88	14332.9380
Foreign Direct Investment per capita (USD)	32	19.75	1661.08	286.55	335.6807

Correlations Between City-Level Variables

	Hard Data	GDP	Pop	FIN	FDI
Hard Data	1	0.734**	−0.022	0.217	0.466**
GDP	0.734**	1	−0.157	0.598**	0.807**
Pop.	−0.022	−0.157	1	−0.241	−0.222
FIN	0.217	0.598**	−0.241	1	0.861**
FDI	0.466**	0.807**	−0.222	0.861**	1

**Correlation is significant at the 0.01 level (2-tailed).

The correlation analysis shows that the objectively measured index of public service quality is significantly correlated with GDP per capita, public expenditure per capita, and FDI per capita respectively. It might not proper to include GDP per capita as a predictor when the objectively measured index is taken a control variable, otherwise this will lead to the collinearity problem in regression models. Meanwhile, GDP per capita is also highly correlated with public expenditure per capita as well as FDI per capita. Hence, either public expenditure or FDI could be used as an alternative measurement of economic development in HLM analysis.

9.4. Statistical Analysis

HLM was used to statistically analyze a data structure where citizens (level-1) were nested within cities (level-2). Our specific interest was the relationship between citizen's ratings of public service quality in their own city (level-1 outcome variable) and the two-level predictors (both level-1 and level-2 variables). Model testing proceeded in four phases for the purpose of comparison: intercept-only model or null model, means-as-outcome model, random-regression coefficients model, and the intercepts- and slopes-as-outcomes model.

Table 9.3 details the intercept-only model (Figure 9.2). According to the estimation of variance components, variance within cities is 45.95382 while variance between cities is 7.41655. It is easy to compute that an intra-city correlation coefficient of 0.14. Thus, 14% of the variance in PSQ is between-cities and 86% of the variance in PSQ is at the citizen-level. More importantly, p-value <0.001 indicates that the PSQ difference between the cities is statistically significant and deserves further analysis.

The means-as-outcomes model (Figure 9.3 and Table 9.4) added city-level variables as level-2 predictors. (By running models with different predictors measuring economic development, the study finds FDI is a better predictor than public expenditure.) The statistically significant and positive

Table 9.3.   Estimation of Variance Components, Intercept-only Model.

Random Effect	Standard Deviation	Variance Component	d.f.	χ^2	p-Value
INTRCPT1, u_0	2.72334	7.41655	30	3144.34215	<0.001
level-1, r	6.77892	45.95382			

Level-1 Model

$$PSQ_{ij} = \beta_{0j} + r_{ij}$$

Level-2 Model

$$\beta_{0j} = \gamma_{00} + u_{0j}$$

Mixed Model

$$PSQ_{ij} = \gamma_{00} + u_{0j} + r_{ij}$$

Figure 9.2. Summary of the Intercept-Only Model.

Level-1 Model

$$PSQ_{ij} = \beta_{0j} + r_{ij}$$

Level-2 Model

$$\beta_{0j} = \gamma_{00} + \gamma_{01}{}^*(HDATA_j) + \gamma_{02}{}^*(POP_j) + \gamma_{03}{}^*(FDIP_j) + u_{0j}$$

Mixed Model

$$PSQ_{ij} = \gamma_{00} + \gamma_{01}{}^*HDATA_j + \gamma_{02}{}^*POP_j + \gamma_{03}{}^*FDIP_j + u_{0j} + r_{ij}$$

Figure 9.3. Summary of the Means-as-Outcome Model.

Table 9.4. Estimation of Fixed Effects (With Robust Standard Errors).

Fixed Effect	Coefficient	Standard Error	t-Ratio	Approx. $d.f.$	p-Value
For INTRCPT1, β_0					
INTRCPT2, γ_{00}	−0.190791	0.362943	−0.526	27	0.603
HDATA, γ_{01}	0.094622	0.037788	2.504	27	0.019
POP, γ_{02}	0.000306	0.000502	0.610	27	0.547
FDIP, γ_{03}	0.004040	0.000632	6.393	27	<0.001

Estimation of Variance Components

Random Effect	Standard Deviation	Variance Component	$d.f.$	χ^2	p-Value
INTRCPT1, u_0	2.14512	4.60155	27	1692.51062	<0.001
level-1, r	6.77892	45.95378			

regression coefficient relation between the foreign direct investment per capita of city (FDIP) and PSQ tells us that cities having more foreign direct investment per capita (relative to cities that had less FDI) are more likely to have higher public service quality. Meanwhile, the significantly positive coefficient of objectively measured public service quality echoes people's common sense that the better public service quality measured by objective indicators will increase citizen's satisfaction with PSQ. However, the rest city-level predictor, population, has no significant direct influence on PSQ. By comparing the means-as-outcome model with the intercept-only model, they study finds that variance explained based on the level-2 predictors $(7.41655 - 4.60155 = 2.81500)$ accounts 38% of the between-city variance (7.41655) in PSQ.

The random-coefficient model (Figure 9.4) just includes all level-1 predictors. HLM coefficients (Table 9.5) show that citizen age (AGE) and family monthly income (INC) are significantly and positively related to PSQ within cities: elder citizens are more likely to have a better evaluation

Level-1 Model

$$PSQ_{ij} = \beta_{0j} + \beta_{1j}{}^*(GEN_{ij}) + \beta_{2j}{}^*(EDU_{ij}) + \beta_{3j}{}^*(AGE_{ij})$$
$$+ \beta_{4j}{}^*(INC_{ij}) + \beta_{5j}{}^*(RES_{ij}) + r_{ij}$$

Level-2 Model

$$\beta_{0j} = \gamma_{00} + u_{0j}$$
$$\beta_{1j} = \gamma_{10} + u_{1j}$$
$$\beta_{2j} = \gamma_{20} + u_{2j}$$
$$\beta_{3j} = \gamma_{30} + u_{3j}$$
$$\beta_{4j} = \gamma_{40} + u_{4j}$$
$$\beta_{5j} = \gamma_{50} + u_{5j}$$

Mixed Model

$$PSQ_{ij} = \gamma_{00} + \gamma_{10}{}^*GEN_{ij} + \gamma_{20}{}^*EDU_{ij} + \gamma_{30}{}^*AGE_{ij} + \gamma_{40}{}^*INC_{ij}$$
$$+ \gamma_{50}{}^*RES_{ij} + u_{0j} + u_{1j}{}^*GEN_{ij} + u_{2j}{}^*EDU_{ij} + u_{3j}{}^*AGE_{ij}$$
$$+ u_{4j}{}^*INC_{ij} + u_{5j}{}^*RES_{ij} + r_{ij}$$

Figure 9.4.   Summary of the Random-Coefficient Model.

Table 9.5. Estimation of Fixed Effects.

Fixed Effect	Coefficient	Standard Error	t-Ratio	Approx. $d.f.$	p-Value
For INTRCPT1, β_0					
INTRCPT2, γ_{00}	-0.189732	0.492059	-0.386	30	0.703
For GEN slope, β_1					
INTRCPT2, γ_{10}	-0.168724	0.145108	-1.163	30	0.254
For EDU slope, β_2					
INTRCPT2, γ_{20}	-0.047141	0.107669	-0.438	30	0.665
For AGE slope, β_3					
INTRCPT2, γ_{30}	0.213030	0.104539	2.038	30	0.050
For INC slope, β_4					
INTRCPT2, γ_{40}	0.140334	0.075578	1.857	30	0.073
For RES slope, β_5					
INTRCPT2, γ_{50}	-0.347768	0.130179	-2.671	30	0.012

Estimation of Variance Components

Random Effect	Standard Deviation	Variance Component	$d.f.$	χ^2	p-Value
INTRCPT1, u_0	2.72389	7.41958	30	3252.28974	<0.001
GEN slope, u_1	0.55780	0.31114	30	58.56388	0.002
EDU slope, u_2	0.52826	0.27906	30	146.71084	<0.001
AGE slope, u_3	0.50710	0.25715	30	118.97624	<0.001
INC slope, u_4	0.35247	0.12424	30	102.49170	<0.001
RES slope, u_5	0.65175	0.42478	30	177.56979	<0.001
level-1, r	6.66552	44.42921			

of PSQ in their home city. Meanwhile, richer citizens are more likely to be satisfied with PSQ. However, the length of residence (RES) have a significantly negative effects implying that the longer a person living in a city, the less his/her satisfaction with city's PSQ. Gender and education attainment cannot significantly explain the different satisfaction with PSQ within cities. Comparing the random-coefficients regression model with the null model, the reduction in variance based on the level-1 predictors is $(45.95382 - 44.42921 = 1.52461)$, explaining 3.32% of the variance in citizen-level PSQ.

Finally, the intercepts- and slopes-as-outcomes model, which includes both level-1 and level-2 predictors in the model simultaneously, was tested and the results were displayed in Figure 9.5 and Table 9.6.

Level-1 Model

$$PSQ_{ij} = \beta_{0j} + \beta_{1j}{}^*(GEN_{ij}) + \beta_{2j}{}^*(EDU_{ij}) + \beta_{3j}{}^*(AGE_{ij})$$
$$+ \beta_{4j}{}^*(INC_{ij}) + \beta_{5j}{}^*(RES_{ij}) + r_{ij}$$

Level-2 Model

$$\beta_{0j} = \gamma_{00} + \gamma_{01}{}^*(HDATA_j) + \gamma_{02}{}^*(FDIP_j) + u_{0j}$$
$$\beta_{1j} = \gamma_{10} + \gamma_{11}{}^*(HDATA_j) + \gamma_{12}{}^*(POP_j) + u_{1j}$$
$$\beta_{2j} = \gamma_{20} + \gamma_{21}{}^*(HDATA_j) + \gamma_{22}{}^*(POP_j) + \gamma_{23}{}^*(FDIP_j) + u_{2j}$$
$$\beta_{3j} = \gamma_{30} + \gamma_{31}{}^*(HDATA_j) + \gamma_{32}{}^*(FDIP_j) + u_{3j}$$
$$\beta_{4j} = \gamma_{40} + \gamma_{41}{}^*(HDATA_j) + u_{4j}$$
$$\beta_{5j} = \gamma_{50} + \gamma_{51}{}^*(HDATA_j) + \gamma_{52}{}^*(POP_j) + \gamma_{53}{}^*(FDIP_j) + u_{5j}$$

Mixed Model

$$PSQ_{ij} = \gamma_{00} + \gamma_{01}{}^*HDATA_j + \gamma_{02}{}^*FDIP_j$$
$$+ \gamma_{10}{}^*GEN_{ij} + \gamma_{11}{}^*HDATA_j{}^*GEN_{ij} + \gamma_{12}{}^*POP_j{}^*GEN_{ij}$$
$$+ \gamma_{20}{}^*EDU_{ij} + \gamma_{21}{}^*HDATA_j{}^*EDU_{ij} + \gamma_{22}{}^*POP_j{}^*EDU_{ij}$$
$$+ \gamma_{23}{}^*FDIP_j{}^*EDU_{ij}$$
$$+ \gamma_{30}{}^*AGE_{ij} + \gamma_{31}{}^*HDATA_j{}^*AGE_{ij} + \gamma_{32}{}^*FDIP_j{}^*AGE_{ij}$$
$$+ \gamma_{40}{}^*INC_{ij} + \gamma_{41}{}^*HDATA_j{}^*INC_{ij}$$
$$+ \gamma_{50}{}^*RES_{ij} + \gamma_{51}{}^*HDATA_j{}^*RES_{ij} + \gamma_{52}{}^*POP_j{}^*RES_{ij}$$
$$+ \gamma_{53}{}^*FDIP_j{}^*RES_{ij}$$
$$+ u_{0j} + u_{1j}{}^*GEN_{ij} + u_{2j}{}^*EDU_{ij} + u_{3j}{}^*AGE_{ij}$$
$$+ u_{4j}{}^*INC_{ij} + u_{5j}{}^*RES_{ij} + r_{ij}$$

Figure 9.5. Summary of the Intercepts- and Slopes-as-Outcomes Model.

9.5. Findings and Discussions

As shown in Table 9.6, the coefficients relating citizens' age and house-hold monthly income to PSQ continued to be positive and statistically significant. Meanwhile, the coefficient relating citizens' length of residences to PSQ continued to be significantly negative. Additionally, the model once again shows that citizen's gender and education background do not have significant influences on PSQ. But the insignificant coefficients variables does not necessarily mean that citizen's gender and education background do not matter at all. As we will discuss later on, some cross-level interactions between variables including the aforementioned two variables are statistically significant.

Table 9.6. Estimation of Fixed Effects (With Robust Standard Errors).

Fixed Effect	Coefficient	Standard Error	t-Ratio	Approx. *d.f.*	p-Value
For INTRCPT1, β_0					
INTRCPT2, γ_{00}	-0.190853	0.363746	-0.525	28	0.604
HDATA, γ_{01}	0.095277	0.037957	2.510	28	0.018
FDIP, γ_{02}	0.003913	0.000595	6.581	28	<0.001
For GEN slope, β_1					
INTRCPT2, γ_{10}	-0.164920	0.128587	-1.283	28	0.210
HDATA, γ_{11}	0.029740	0.020355	1.461	28	0.155
POP, γ_{12}	-0.000533	0.000214	-2.491	28	0.019
For EDU slope, β_2					
INTRCPT2, γ_{20}	-0.049725	0.087111	-0.571	27	0.573
HDATA, γ_{21}	0.018525	0.009196	2.014	27	0.054
POP, γ_{22}	0.000352	0.000135	2.603	27	0.015
FDIP, γ_{23}	0.000681	0.000180	3.791	27	<0.001
For AGE slope, β_3					
INTRCPT2, γ_{30}	0.210303	0.092275	2.279	28	0.030
HDATA, γ_{31}	-0.030989	0.011989	-2.585	28	0.015
FDIP, γ_{32}	0.000506	0.000377	1.340	28	0.191
For INC slope, β_4					
INTRCPT2, γ_{40}	0.139875	0.071094	1.967	29	0.059
HDATA, γ_{41}	-0.016998	0.009624	-1.766	29	0.088
For RES slope, β_5					
INTRCPT2, γ_{50}	-0.340794	0.110286	-3.090	27	0.005
HDATA, γ_{51}	0.040492	0.018717	2.163	27	0.040
POP, γ_{52}	-0.000430	0.000133	-3.240	27	0.003
FDIP, γ_{53}	-0.000499	0.000482	-1.036	27	0.309

Estimation of Variance Components

Random Effect	Standard Deviation	Variance Component	*d.f.*	χ^2	p-Value
INTRCPT1, u_0	2.11029	4.45334	28	1756.88957	<0.001
GEN slope, u_1	0.49771	0.24771	28	48.56129	0.009
EDU slope, u_2	0.43943	0.19310	27	104.46069	<0.001
AGE slope, u_3	0.46150	0.21298	28	98.53384	<0.001
INC slope, u_4	0.33591	0.11284	29	91.82805	<0.001
RES slope, u_5	0.59027	0.34842	27	137.77533	<0.001
level-1, r	6.66553	44.42931			

However, the coefficients relating city's objectively measured public service quality (HDATA) and FDI per capita (FDIP) to PSQ continued to be positive and statistically significant when others variables are controlled, indicating better economic situation of city will lead to a better PSQ. This

is consistent with people's common sense that a better economic situation will enable city government to deliver quality public services. Even though FDI per capita is highly correlated with GDP per capita, the implication of FDI per capita is more than economic development. To some extent, it also reflects the openness of city's economy. Hence, this finding may implies that a city with more FDI will push local governments to improve in delivering public services. Meanwhile, the significant influence of the objectively measured public service quality (HDATA), a city-level variable, on PSQ is consistent with people's expectation, indicating that a better public service quality measured by objective indicators somewhat guarantee a high level of citizen's satisfaction with the city's public service.

As the main strength of HLM is to estimate the effects of the cross-level inactions between variables on the dependent variable, the following paragraphs will discuss the impacts of the cross-level interactions on citizens' satisfaction with PSQ.

9.5.1. *Gender*

Even though gender and the interaction between gender and objectively measured public service quality (HDATA) have insignificant effects on the dependent variable, it is hard to say that Gender does not affect citizens' evaluating the public service quality. The significantly negative coefficient of the interactions between gender and population not only reveals that male citizen's satisfaction with PSQ is significantly different from female's, but also reveals that the degree of the difference is negatively correlated with city's population size. This means that the difference of the satisfaction with PSQ between male and female in a city with smaller population size is greater than that in a city with larger population size. But it is necessary to note that males always have a lower satisfaction with PSQ than females, others being equal.

9.5.2. *Education attainment*

As the model reveals, the cross-level interaction between objectively measured public service quality and citizen's education background has significantly positive influence on PSQ, implying the marginal effect of education attainment is increasing when a city has a better record of the objectively measured public service quality. Similarly, Table 9.6 also shows that the cross-level interaction between citizen's education and FDI per capita has a significantly positive effect on PSQ, indicating that

the marginally positive influence of citizen's education on PSQ not only depends on city's objectively measured public service quality, but also depends on the economic development of city or the openness of city's economy. Therefore, the impact of citizens' education attainment will be more sensitive in a city with high scores in objective predictors. The city-level predictors really changed the effect of the citizen-level predictors.

9.5.3. *Age*

Even though age has a significantly positive coefficient on PSQ, the coefficient of the cross-level interaction between age and objectively measured public service quality is significantly negative, indicating that the marginal influence of age on citizens' satisfaction is negatively correlated with objectively measured public service quality, meaning that the marginal effect of age on PSQ will be significantly decreasing when the objective measured public service quality of city is increasing. In different cities, age affects PSQ in different ways. Moreover, the effect of age is more sensitive in a city with lower objectively measured public service.

Meanwhile, the empirical analysis also reveals that the effect of the interaction between age and economic development is statistically insignificant.

9.5.4. *Household monthly income*

Even though household monthly income (INC) has a significant positive coefficient on PSQ, the coefficient of the cross-level interaction between the income and the objectively measured public service quality has a significantly negative impact on PSQ, revealing that the marginal influence of family income on citizens' satisfaction with PSQ is somewhat negatively associated with the objective indicators of public services.

9.5.5. *The length of residence*

As mentioned above, the length of residence (RES) has a significantly negative influence on citizen's satisfaction with PSQ, meaning permanent residents are more likely to have lower satisfaction with PSQ. But the influences of the cross-level interactions between the length of residence and other city-level predictors are very complex.

Firstly, the interaction between the length of residence and objectively measured public service quality is statistically significant which means

the marginal influence of the length of residence on PSQ is affected by objectively measured public service quality. Government's efforts on enhance objective indictors of public service quality will affirm residents with longer duration in the city to have a higher satisfaction with PSQ, further proofing the convergence between objectively measured public services quality and subjectively perceived PSQ.

Secondly, the interaction between the length of residence and city's population size has a significant and negative effect on PSQ, explicating the marginal effect of the length of residence will be relatively weaker in a city with a larger population.

However, the coefficient of the interaction between the length of residence and a city-level variable, FDI, is insignificant. But the aforementioned two points are sufficient to support that the length of residence, as a citizen-level variable, affects citizen's attitude to PSQ differently in different cities.

The HLM analyses show that respondents' education attainment, age, household monthly income and the duration of residing in the city are important factors affecting their evaluation of public service quality. Moreover, the HLM models reveal that city-level variables also significantly influence citizens' evaluation of public service quality. But more importantly, the marginal effects of citizen-level variables on PSQ are significantly correlated to city-level variables, implying the citizen-level variables will affect PSQ differently in the 32 cities, in accordance with the city-level variables.

9.6. Conclusion

Based on the "Lien Public Service Excellence Index for Chinese Cities" developed by NCPA and the surveys of citizens' evaluation of public service quality in 32 Chinese cities conducted in 2010, this study examines how citizens across urban China evaluate public service quality in their home cities.

The study makes a couple of contributions. It is the first time to use such large-scale survey data on public service quality in Chinese cities, which substantially complements the data weaknesses of previous studies. Moreover, the study is innovative not only because it enquires the determinants of demographic factors on citizens' satisfaction with public service quality, but also it estimates the effects of city-level variables on the satisfaction.

The HLM analyses highlight that the marginal effects of the demographic and socioeconomic variables including age, gender, household monthly income, education attainment and the length of duration on citizens' evaluation of public service quality are significantly correlated with city's economic development and/or objectively measured public service quality of city. Citizens, with similar demographic characteristics, in different cities will evaluate the public service quality in different ways. This actually implies that enquiries of citizen-level demographic and socioeconomic variables on public service quality in China deserve to be examined with local socioeconomic conditions. Thus, the current study laid down a foundation for further research on modeling citizens' behaviors in evaluating public service quality in China.

As the survey data analyzed in this study is collected exclusively for the purpose of ranking public service quality among the 32 Chinese cities, some citizen-level predictors identified by previous studies are not included. Due to the large-scale sample size of the survey, some interval variables were collected as ordinal variables. While the HLM analyses in this study included them as interval variables. These are weaknesses of the current study. Actually there remains much to be done in deepening our understanding of public service provision in China.

References

Li, LC (2008). State and market in public service provision: Opportunities and traps for institutional change in rural China. *Pacific Review*, 21(3), 257–278.

Nathan, A and T Shi (1993). Cultural prerequisites for democracy in China: Some findings from a survey. *Daedalus*, 122(2), 95–123.

Nathan, A and T Shi (1996). Left and right with Chinese characteristics: Issues and alignments in Deng Xiaoping's China. *World Politics*, 48(4), 522–550.

Saich, T (2008). *Providing Public Goods in Transitional China*. New York: Palgrave Macmillan.

Shi, T (2000). Cultural values and democracy in Mainland China. *China Quarterly*, 162, 540–59.

Tsai, L (2007). *Accountability Without Democracy: Solidarity Groups and Public Goods Provision in Rural China*. New York: Cambridge University Press.

Yang, D (2006). Economic transformation and its political discontents in China: Authoritarianism, unequal growth, and the dilemmas of political development. *Annual Review of Political Science*, 9, 143–164.

Zhong, Y, J Chen and J Scheb II (1998). Mass political culture in Beijing: Findings from two public opinion surveys. *Asian Survey*, 38(8).

Appendix 1: Number of Valid Return Questionnaires

City	N	%
1	840	5.0
2	584	3.4
3	516	3.0
4	563	3.3
5	575	3.4
6	690	4.1
7	625	3.7
8	660	3.9
9	360	2.1
10	571	3.4
12	596	3.5
13	522	3.1
14	497	2.9
15	526	3.1
16	747	4.4
17	585	3.5
18	612	3.6
19	666	3.9
20	241	1.4
21	408	2.4
22	468	2.8
23	611	3.6
24	414	2.4
25	745	4.4
26	473	2.8
27	472	2.8
28	515	3.0
29	408	2.4
30	405	2.4
31	579	3.4
32	468	2.8
Total	16942	100.0

Chapter 10

Public Satisfaction Survey and Its Analysis on Chinese Cities Public Education Service — An Empirical Study Based on 2010 Lien Chinese Cities Public Service Quality Evaluation Survey Data

Wang Jun[*] and Wu Wei[†]

In 1980s, the "New Public Management" (NPM) reform was initiated in Western countries. It aimed at getting rid of financial difficulties and improving public administration efficiency. Principles of the NPM are "customer oriented," "focus on results and performance," and "let the public participate in evaluation of government performance." The NPM emphasizes on citizens' role as recipients of public services and makes citizens' satisfaction as the orientation of public services delivery, in turn evaluates government performance from the public's perspective and based on the public's value. With the spread of the NPM reform, many countries started to develop and apply methods and models for evaluating public satisfaction of the government performance and their public services. Since the American developed the American Customer Satisfaction Index (ACSI), practices of government performance evaluation have been widely used and become an important tool for countries' public sector performance evaluation.[1] While in China, there is still shortage of large sample size studies on public satisfaction evaluation with public services. The 2010 Lien Chinese Cities' Public Services Quality Index and Survey project

---

[*]Research Associate, Nanyang Centre for Public Administration, Nanyang Technological University.

[†]Associate Professor, Director of Nanyang Centre for Public Administration, Nanyang Technological University.

[1]Some widely used models are UKCSI from the UK, DK modeling from Germany, SCSB model approach in Sweden, KCSI model in South Korea, MCSI in Malaysia.

sponsored by Lien Foundation was thus initiated by Nanyang Centre for
Public Administration of Nanyang Technological University (NTU), and
it provides large sample survey data for public satisfaction evaluation.
Analyzing data of the three sub-areas of public education service, namely
school facilities, education quality and education equity, this report aims at
investigating the major factors influencing public education satisfaction,
and especially exploring whether and to what extent the cities' fiscal
expenditures impact on the public satisfaction on public education.

10.1. Literature Review: What Factors Impact on Public Education Service?

Some English studies attribute difficulties in public education development
to the lack of financial investment, but this is shortage of justification by
empirical studies. Raymond (1968) conducted an empirical study and used
multiple regression analysis to conclude that the determinant of the quality
of primary and secondary school education is teachers' salaries. Hanushek
(1986) argued that the root causes that impact the quality of school
education are not the investment in education, class size, and a monthly
evaluation of schools and teachers, but teachers' technical skills. Downs
(1992) pointed out that the education financial reform, equalization of per
student education spending and the relative increase in fiscal expenditures
on education did not get a corresponding increase in the poverty-stricken
areas' educational development performance, that is, the education financial
reform and input has no direct impact on the quality of education. Thus,
the difference of economic and social development, education development
characteristics and different stage of education development determine that
relevant studies in western countries' have limited reference effect for China.

Chinese studies on public education satisfaction can be divided into
two categories. The first one mainly aims at public education satisfaction
survey, most of which are organized by relevant government institutions
or non-governmental organizations. These studies examined the current
situation of Chinese public education and the public satisfaction with it by
designing survey questionnaire and conducting survey. For example, since
2006, the 21st Century Education Research Institute publishes "Annual
Chinese Cities Citizen Education Satisfaction Report"; between 2009 and
2010, *Xiaokang Magazine* office issued the "China Education *Xiaokang*
Index" by the Chinese well-off research center; and in 2008, *Oriental
Outlook* by the Xinhua News Agency published Chinese Happiest City

Survey results using data from the online poll and questionnaire survey to the citizens. Besides, some city education institutions conducted citizens' education satisfaction survey. For instance, in May 2002, Tianjin Academy of Education Sciences conducted Tianjin citizen's satisfaction with public education survey; between 2008 and 2009, Shanghai city government surveyed the public satisfaction with Shanghai's basic education and reported their results. In brief, the above mentioned studies usually develop reports with comprehensive survey results and have repercussions on society, and some can be referred to public policymaking. However, they only report direct results and preliminary analysis of the survey data, which should have been further examined and analyzed.

The other category of researches are usually conducted by academia with designed index and survey questionnaire. These studies investigate students and parents' satisfaction with the city public education, which can provide more in-depth findings from professional perspective. For example, Zhang (2003) surveyed with open-ended questionnaire in two selected elementary schools in Songjiang district in Shanghai. Respondents of this study are consists of parents and students and they feedbacked on teacher's quality, environment and facilities, school management, student performance and student pressure. Gao and Hu (2006) conducted survey in 8 districts in Beijing city and found out that family income has no significant impact on parents' satisfaction, but parents' education does. Wang (2008) reported citizen satisfaction with primary and secondary schools in 5 Chinese cities and found that the school fees and admission policies are major reasons that led to dissatisfaction. Meanwhile, public opinion expression and appeal institutions are ineffective. The poor usually have limited access to good public education services and the disadvantaged groups have multi-dimension weaknesses in obtaining good public services. Li, Wei and Du (2010) examined 2234 parents' satisfaction with public teachers in Beijing. They concluded that the better the school education quality, the higher the public satisfaction with teachers, and a higher education level has a relative lower satisfaction.

To sum up, the previous studies mainly focus on factors related directly to education itself, such as school facilities, teaching level and education quality. Influencing factors beyond education were only extended to family income and parents' education. While we expect to examine factors on more dimensions, for example the city level factors, that impact on public education satisfaction. And we find that established conclusions in this regard are rare. In addition, there is also lack of empirical studies on

government spending for public education. Prior studies on fiscal spending on education by Huang (2009) and Xu (2010) concluded that fiscal education expenditures can help to increase knowledge and human capital stock of the society, and can improve resources utilization efficiency, which in turn demonstrates that expenditures on education plays an important role in economic growth. This also confirms that increase of government spending on public education to 4% of GDP is indispensable and urgent. In this study, we aim to explore what factors on city level influence public satisfaction with public education and try to explain whether and how Chinese government spending impact on public education satisfaction by empirical study, which is a complement to the existing studies.

10.2. Index of Public Education Satisfaction and Data Description

There are 3 indicators in the public education service area of the 2010 Lien Chinese Cities Public Service Quality Index,[2] namely school facilities, education quality and education equity. We report the top 10 cities of public education satisfaction and apply multiple regression method to explore determinants of citizens' satisfaction with public education service.

2010 Lien Chinese Cities Public Service Quality Survey was conducted from April to July in 2010, and its data were from citizen questionnaires and business questionnaires. In this chapter, we use citizens' public education satisfaction data. And the total score of public education satisfaction is the sum of standardized scores of the three fore mentioned indicators. The designed questions measure the respondent's satisfaction with public education using a five-point Likert scale, where 1 means "very dissatisfied," 2 means "dissatisfied," 3 means "moderate," 4 means "satisfied," and 5 means "very satisfied." The survey used convenience sampling and we trained the surveyors to interview citizens in business districts, residential areas, campus, transportation hubs, city libraries, social security centers and public service centers, etc. in selected 32 Chinese cities. Finally we received 31,335 valid citizen questionnaires in 32 cities. Table 10.1 reports

---

[2]The 2010 Lien Chinese Cities Public Service Quality Index includes 10 public service areas, which are constructed by 29 indicators. The 10 public service areas surveyed are public education, employment, public health, housing and social security, public safety, infrastructure, culture and entertainment, environment protection, public transportation, and government efficiency.

Table 10.1.   Respondents' Demographical Characteristics.

Variables	Samples Size (N)	Percentage (%)
Gender		
Male	16,343	52.16
Female	14,992	47.84
Education		
Secondary school or below	3,648	11.6
High school and Vocational technique school	6,594	21
Bachelor degree or above	21,093	67.3
Age		
25 or below	9,796	31.3
25–34	10,573	33.7
35–44	5,529	17.6
45–54	2,942	9.4
55–64	1,672	5.3
65 or above	823	2.6
Family monthly income (RMB)		
Below 2,000	6,543	20.9
2,000–3,999	10,272	32.8
4,000–5,999	6,152	19.6
6,000–7,999	2,199	7
8,000–9,999	1,544	4.9
Above 10,000	1,424	4.5
No fixed income	3,201	10.2

respondents' demographical characteristics. 2010 Lien project conducted a large sample size survey and got first-hand data of citizen satisfaction, which is rare in previous studies and in turn fills in the blank. The database becomes a good resource for academic study and policy-making. And we will continue this project for time series comparative studies.

10.3. Findings of Public Education Satisfaction

In the statistical analysis process, we use simple arithmetic average, multiple regression standardized coefficient and principal component analysis (factor analysis) in weighting the indicators, but the ranking results are not sensitive to different weighting methods. We can see from Table 10.2 that the 3 indicators in public education service are highly correlated. Therefore, we use equal weighting method to calculate the indicators' scores and rank the targeted cities' school facilities, education quality and education equity.

Table 10.2. Pearson Correlation Coefficient of Public Education Satisfaction and Its 3 Indicators (Double Tailed).

$N = 32$

	Public Education Satisfaction score	School Facilities Score	Education Quality Score	Education Quality Score
Public Education Satisfaction score	1	0.959**	0.974**	0.880**
School facilities score	0.959**	1	0.944**	0.733**
Education quality score	0.974**	0.944**	1	0.794**
Education quality score	0.880**	0.733**	0.794**	1

**. $P < 0.01$

10.3.1. *Overall ranking of Chinese cities' public education satisfaction*

In overall ranking of public education satisfaction, three cities with higher scores ranked in the first tier. The cities and their scores are Shenzhen (6.83), Ningbo (5.91), and Suzhou (5.20), in which Shenzhen has the best public evaluation with its public education and certainly topping the list in 32 cities. Xiamen (3.27), Hangzhou (2.70), Beijing (2.59), Nanjing (2.22), Changchun (1.66), Dalian (1.63), and Qingdao (0.83) obtained a relative good evaluation from the public and are the second tier of all 32 cities. And the above mentioned cities are the top ten of overall public education satisfaction. Given education resources and investment, cities like Beijing, Shanghai, and Guangzhou have more educational resources and inputs, but their public satisfaction with education are not as high as expected. From the geographical perspective, cities with better evaluation are mainly from more developed eastern coastal region, while central region has a relative low satisfaction. And the less developed western region got the lowest scores with public education. It can be seen that satisfaction is highly correlated with city's social and economic development.

10.3.2. *Public satisfaction with school facilities*

Shenzhen scored high (2.92) in school facilities, which is nearly double the score of the second ranked city Ningbo (1.49). And Xiamen (1.37), Hangzhou (1.31), Suzhou (1.24), Beijing (1.11), Nanjing (0.77), Shanghai (0.63), Dalian (0.48), and Tianjin (0.21) also entered the top ten. We can see that citizens of these cities are quite satisfied with the city's primary and

secondary educational facilities. From the angle of geography and social eco-nomic development, the top ten cities basically located in developed area, which reflects a similar trend with the overall public education satisfaction. Seeing from the standardized score, the gap between eastern and western-central region is large, which indicates that sub-developed region has a long way to go in public education development. The school facilities indicator is of importance to reflect government's attitude and investment in public education. Citizens' satisfaction evaluation with public school facilities will be helpful and worthy of reference for government policy making.

10.3.3. *Public satisfaction with education quality*

Public education quality is a multi-dimensional and comprehensive indi-cator, and we do not define what it is and let the respondent to evaluate according to their understanding. The satisfaction with education quality in 32 cities is overall low. And the top two cities Shenzhen and Ningbo only scored 2.10 and 1.95 respectively. Beijing (1.42), Suzhou (1.28), Nanjing (1.14), Xiamen (1.14), Changchun (0.86), Hangzhou (0.85), Dalian (0.82), and Shanghai (0.45) all entered top ten, which get better evaluation than the rest. Economically less developed western and central region lowest the rank. We will discuss factors impact on education quality in part 4 of this chapter.

10.3.4. *Public satisfaction with education equity*

Suzhou tops the list in citizens' perceived education equity and its score is 2.68. Ningbo and Shenzhen ranks the second and third and score 2.46 and 1.80 respectively. These three cities get a far better evaluation in education equity compared with others. The other top ten are Changchun (0.81), Xiamen (0.76), Qingdao (0.71), Hangzhou (0.53), Harbin (0.46), Zhengzhou (0.34), and Dalian (0.33). We can see that first tier cities like Beijing, Shanghai and Guangzhou are absent from the top 10. Economically less developed cities in western and central region still rank low in the list. But compared with the other two indicators, education equity has a low degree of correlation with economic development and the cities' ranking changes. We find that a couple of cities with low scores in prior two indicators get good evaluation of education equity, which shows that the situation of school facilities and education quality are not necessarily correlated positively with education equity. It also indicates that the public satisfaction survey can reflect the effect of education inputs and outputs on different dimensions.

10.4. Multiple Regression Analysis on Influencing Factors of Public Education Satisfaction

In this chapter, we take "population," "teacher-student ratio of primary school," "teacher-student ratio of secondary school," "high school gross enrollment rate" and "college gross enrollment rate" as the control variables, where the population indicates the city size, the other four variables stand for the development level of city's public education. In addition, we use "fiscal education spending per capita," "fiscal education spending level" which is the ratio of fiscal education spending to public finance expenditure of a city, "ratio of public finance expenditure to GDP," and "GDP per capita" as independent variables, which are supposed to be the major factors influence the public education satisfaction. As shown in Equation 1, we try to explore how these factors impact on public education satisfaction.

Equation 1: $Y = \beta_1 + \beta_2 X_1 + \beta_3 X_2 + \beta_4 X_3 + \beta_5 X_4 + \beta_6 X_5 + \beta_7 X_6 + \beta_8 X_7 + \beta_9 X_8 + \beta_{10} X_9 + \mu$

Where Y = "public education satisfaction"
X_1 = "population (ten thousands)";
X_2 = "teacher-student ratio of primary school";
X_3 = "teacher-student ratio of secondary school";
X_4 = "high school gross enrolment rate";
X_5 = "college gross enrolment rate";
X_6 = "fiscal education spending per capita";
X_7 = "fiscal education spending level";
X_8 = "ratio of public finance expenditure to GDP";
X_9 = "GDP per capita".

In Equation 1, data of X_1, X_2, X_3, X_6, X_7, X_8, and X_9 are from "2010 Chinese City Statistical Yearbook"; data of X_4 and X_5 are from "2009 government statistical yearbook." Table 10.3 are the descriptive statistics for variables, in addition, Table 10.4 shows correlations between the dependent, independent, and control variables, which can remove the multi-collinearity in multi-regression analysis.

Two regression models are established to explain the factors determining public education satisfaction. They are model 1 and model 2, and the corresponding results are reported in Table 10.5.

Seeing model 1 analysis results, our study has the following important findings: (1) the control variable "population" is positively significant in

Table 10.3.   Descriptive Statistics for Variables.

	N	Minimum	Maximum	Mean	Sd. Deviation
Public Education Satisfaction	32	−4.63	6.83	0.0000	2.81811
Population (ten thousands)	32	158.24	3275.61	757.5806	541.73184
Teacher-student ratio of primary school	32	0.0470	0.0843	0.060091	0.0099890
Teacher-student ratio of secondary school	32	0.0555	0.0962	0.071513	0.0103309
High school gross enrolment rate	32	0.4490	1.2944	0.892997	0.1566739
College gross enrolment rate	32	0.1180	0.8380	0.462297	0.1883050
Fiscal education spending per capita (yuan)	32	458.26	5554.83	1163.6378	994.03726
Fiscal education spending level	32	11.61	25.43	15.7724	3.06329
Ratio of public finance expenditure to GDP	32	7.76	20.19	12.0469	3.43116
GDP per capita (yuan)	32	21945	122565	51340.28	23457.060

influencing the "public education satisfaction," which indicates that the larger the city size, the higher the public education satisfaction. This finding coincides with our experience and China's actual conditions that large cities like Beijing, Shanghai, Guangzhou, Shenzhen and Tianjin, usually occupy more public education resources and are capable to provide better public education services, thus have a relative high public education satisfaction. More importantly, (2) we find that "fiscal education spending per capita" is positively impact on "public education satisfaction" and its statistical significance level is at level 1%, which means that increase of "fiscal education spending per capita" will improve citizens' satisfaction with public education. At the meanwhile, (3) two variables, the "fiscal education spending level" and the "ratio of public finance expenditure to GDP" negatively effect on the "public education satisfaction," and the latter presents a statistical significance level at 5%. This finding demonstrates that with control of the "fiscal education spending per capita," the higher the "fiscal education spending level," the lower the public education satisfaction. Similarly, the larger the proportion of public finance expenditure to GDP, the lower the public education satisfaction. This seemingly illogical result actually

Table 10.4. Correlations between the Dependent, Independent, and Control Variables.

	Public Education Satisfaction	Population (Ten Thousands)	Teacher-Student Ratio of Secondary School	Teacher-Student Ratio of Primary School	High School Gross Enrolment Rate	College Gross Enrolment Rate	Fiscal Education Spending Per Capita	Fiscal Education Spending Level (Yuan)	GDP Per Capita (Yuan)
Public Education Satisfaction	1								
Population (ten thousands)	0.022	1							
Teacher-student ratio of secondary school	0.368*	−0.053	1						
Teacher-student ratio of primary school	0.078	0.225	0.589**	1					
High school gross enrolment rate	0.266	−0.232	0.170	−0.236	1				
College gross enrolment rate	0.343	−0.066	0.496**	0.046	0.555**	1			
Fiscal education spending per capita (yuan)	0.651**	−0.096	0.334	−0.043	0.132	0.314	1		
Fiscal education spending level	−0.278	−0.117	−0.042	0.180	−0.194	−0.276	−0.233	1	
GDP per capita (yuan)	0.750**	−0.132	0.540**	0.026	0.506**	0.570**	0.636**	−0.383**	1

$*p < 0.05$; $**p < 0.01$.

Table 10.5.   Results of Multiple Regression Analysis for Public Education Satisfaction.

Independent Variables	Dependent variable: Public Education Satisfaction	
	Model 1	Model 2
(Constant)	−2.699	−3.625
	(4.860)	(4.671)
Population (ten thousands)	0.001*	0.001
	(0.001)	(0.001)
Teacher-student ratio of primary school	9.887	29.639
	(56.718)	(55.290)
Teacher-student ratio of secondary school	36.676	−23.405
	(59.701)	(66.165)
High school gross enrolment rate	2.965	0.366
	(3.086)	(3.286)
College gross enrolment rate	−0.443	−0.854
	(2.828)	(2.711)
Fiscal education spending per capita (yuan)	**0.002*****	**0.001***
	(0.000)	**(0.001)**
Fiscal education spending level	**−0.157[3]**	**−0.025**
	(0.135)	**(0.148)**
Ratio of public finance expenditure to GDP	**−0.324****	**−0.118**
	(0.135)	**(0.172)**
GDP per capita (yuan)		**6.707E-5***
		(0.000)
R	0.777	0.809
R^2	0.604	0.654
N	32	32

***$p < 0.001$, **$p < 0.05$, *$p < 0.10$.

reflects a deep correlation between educational finance and public education satisfaction. In fact, with holding "fiscal education spending per capita" as a constant, the larger the two rates are, namely the "fiscal education spending level" and the "ratio of public finance expenditure to GDP," the worse the urban public finances and its economic performance. In other

---

[3] Although "financial education spending level" is not significant in impact on "public education satisfaction" (Sig. = 0.256) in model 1 analysis results, there are only 32 selected cities but 8 independent variables in model 1, which may be the reason why the significance level is low. In other words, if the selected cities number increased, "financial education spending level" will be highly likely to be a significant variable in influence the public education satisfaction.

words, with holding "fiscal education spending per capita," the city needs to spend a larger proportion of its public finance expenditure on education, which does not mean that the city government attaches importance to public education, but indicates the city's bad public finances situation. Therefore, it is reasonable to see in above analysis that a higher fiscal education spending level and a higher ratio of public finance expenditure to GDP lead to a bad public education satisfaction. We add "GDP per capita" variable in model 2 to further test this logic and see its impact on public education satisfaction. (4) As shown in model 2, "GDP per capita" effects positively on public education satisfaction. And with its involving, "fiscal education spending level" and "ratio of public finance expenditure to GDP" play a less important role in influencing public education satisfaction, where their statistical significance level in the multiple regression analysis are lowered to insignificant level. This analysis results indicates that "GDP per capita," i.e., the city economic development has a strong explanatory power in explaining public education satisfaction. That is, economic development is more determinant in effecting on public education satisfaction.

10.5. Conclusion

This study investigates and reports Chinese cities' public education satisfaction with using 2010 Lien Chinese Cities Public Service Quality index and data. In terms of public evaluation of overall public education satisfaction, school facilities, and education quality, cities locate in eastern coastal developed region outplay their counterparts in less developed western and central region, which indicate a high correlation between economic development level and public education service, while public evaluation on "education equity" shows a weak correlation between "equity" and "economic performance."

Based on the 2010 Lien project data, we examine whether and how the city fiscal education expenditure determines public education satisfaction with using quantitative analysis. We find that "fiscal education expenditure per capita" significantly effects on public education satisfaction, at the meanwhile, "fiscal education spending level" and "ratio of public finance expenditure to GDP" play a negatively significant role in influencing public education satisfaction. As above mentioned, holding "educational expenditures" and other variables as constant, a low public education satisfaction with a high "fiscal education spending level" and a high "ratio of financial expenditures to GDP" indicates the city's bad public finances and

economic development. In addition, "GDP per capita" is a fundamental determinant of public education satisfaction, which justifies the public satisfaction ranking results.

As 2010 Lien Chinese Cities Public Service Quality Survey does not focus on public education service evaluation, variables can be used in our study is limited. As an exploratory study, we expect to contribute to current empirical studies regarding public education satisfaction. And with working for Lien Project, we aim at collecting data on more dimensions and do further systemic investigations and explanation.

References

Downes, TA (1992). Evaluating the impact of school finance reform on the provision of public education: The California case. *National Tax Journal*, 45, 405–419.

Gao, B and YM Hu (2006). An empirical study of students and parents' satisfaction with primary and secondary education. *Journal of Nei Monggol Normal University*, 19, 73–76.

Hanushek, EA (1986). The economics of schooling: production and efficiency in public schools. *Journal of Economic Literature*, 24, 1141–1177.

Huang, JL and L Li (2009). Analysis on public expenditures on education and social productivity growth effect. *Science and Technology Management Research*, 9, 152–154.

Jimenez, E (1986). The public subsidization of education and health in developing countries: A review of equity and efficiency. *World Bank Research Observer*, 1, 111–129.

Li, Q, XM Wei and L Du (2010). A survey of citizens' satisfaction with Beijing city primary and secondary school teachers. *Teacher Education Research*, 22(4), 47–52.

Raymond, R (1968). Determinants of the quality of primary and secondary public education in West Virginia. *The Journal of Human Resources III*, 3, 450–470.

Wang, R (2008). Building schools to people's satisfaction: A citizens survey on primary and secondary schools' education satisfaction. *Peking University Education Review*, 6(4), 38–46.

Xu, J (2010). A empirical study on public education expenditures on economic growth. *Journal of Lanzhou Jiaotong University*, 2, 37–39.

Zhang, ZS (2003). A study on parents' satisfaction with primary school. *Shang Education Research*, 3, 8–11.

Index